# MANAGERIAL ACCOUNTING

PHILIP E. FESS, CPA, PhD
Professor of Accountancy
University of Illinois, Champaign-Urbana

CARL S. WARREN, CPA, PhD
Professor of Accounting
University of Georgia, Athens

*Published by*

A60 **SOUTH-WESTERN PUBLISHING CO.**

CINCINNATI    WEST CHICAGO, IL    DALLAS    PELHAM MANOR, NY    PALO ALTO, CA

# Preface

MANAGERIAL ACCOUNTING presents fundamental accounting concepts that are useful to management in planning and controlling operations in a logical, concise, and clear manner. Thus, the text permits instructors to focus on clarifying issues and solidifying the student's understanding of managerial accounting.

To provide a sense of direction for the study of the text material, learning objectives are utilized. To this end, the objectives of the text are presented first, and then each chapter begins with a listing of the objectives for that chapter. The objectives thus serve as stimuli for the student's study and learning.

The text is organized into 18 chapters. The nature of managerial accounting is discussed early in the text and serves as the foundation for the introduction, in subsequent chapters, of accounting principles that are especially useful to management in conducting operations. As the principles are presented in subsequent chapters, they are integrated with the principles of the management process to enable the student to understand accounting as it affects managerial decision making.

Chapter 1 is an introductory chapter in which the nature of managerial accounting is presented and contrasted with financial accounting. The management process is also described and related to the ways in which accounting can be used by management in planning and controlling operations.

Chapters 2 and 3 describe and illustrate accounting systems for manufacturing operations, with emphasis on job order cost systems and process cost systems. The basic principles of a general accounting system for manufacturing operations are presented in Appendix D.

Chapters 4 and 5 present the concepts of budgeting and standard cost systems in a clear style, with extensive illustrations of these concepts.

Chapters 6–10 focus on analyses for management's use in decision making, including presentations of absorption costing, variable costing, cost-volume-profit analysis, differential analysis, capital investment analysis, and the impact of income taxes on management decisions.

Chapters 11 and 12 describe and illustrate responsibility accounting for cost, profit, and investment centers. Transfer pricing is also discussed.

Chapters 13 and 14 present quantitative techniques that are especially useful to management in controlling inventory, estimating costs, and coping with uncertainty. The basic concepts are presented in a format that is easy to understand and that focuses on management's use of these concepts in decision making.

Chapters 15–17 stress financial analyses for management use, including financial statement analysis, reporting changes in price levels, and the statement of changes in financial position.

Chapter 18 describes and illustrates managerial aids useful to management of nonprofit organizations.

Five self-examination questions are provided at the end of each chapter. After studying the chapter, the students can answer these questions and compare their answers to those appearing in Appendix C. In this manner, students can assess their understanding of the material presented in each chapter. It should be noted that Appendix C presents an explanation of both the correct and incorrect answers for each question and thus increases understanding and enhances learning.

The questions, exercises, problems, and mini-cases presented at the end of the chapters provide a wide choice of subject matter and range of difficulty for assignment material. They have been carefully written to be both practical and comprehensive. The mini-cases are designed to stimulate student interest by presenting situations with which students may easily identify. Each case emphasizes important chapter concepts. An additional series of problems is provided in Appendix B. The working papers correlating with the problems and mini-cases are designed to relieve students of the burden of repetitive details, so that attention may be more effectively directed to the mastery of the underlying concepts. A list of check figures for the problems is included in Appendix G for use by the student in checking the basic accuracy of a significant portion of the problems.

A glossary of technical terms and common business and accounting expressions is included in Appendix A. The terms included in the glossary are printed in color the first time they are presented in the text. In Appendix D, general accounting for manufacturing operations is presented for those who wish to review the general accounting system while they study the job order and process cost systems of accounting for manufacturing operations. Appendix E is provided for those who wish to use the work sheet in preparing the statement of changes in financial position. In Appendix F, a complete set of financial statements from the annual reports of two companies, and selected statements for other companies are reproduced.

A study guide with solutions, transparencies of solutions to exercises and problems, examination problems, true-false questions, multiple-choice questions, and a computerized testing program are also available.

Philip E. Fess
Carl S. Warren

# Contents

# 1

CHAPTER

# Nature of
# Managerial Accounting

**CHAPTER OBJECTIVES**

*Describe the nature of accounting.*

*Describe the differences between financial accounting
and managerial accounting.*

*Describe the management process and the basic
structure of managerial accounting.*

# PART 1

# Basic Structure of
# Managerial Accounting

# 1

## CHAPTER

Accounting[1] is often called "the language of business." In fulfilling this role, the accounting system communicates economic information about an organization to many different users for use in making informed judgments and decisions. For example, investors in a business enterprise use accounting information about the firm's financial status and its future prospects to make decisions regarding their investments. Creditors seek information useful in appraising the financial soundness of a business organization and assessing the risks involved before making loans or granting credit. Government agencies require economic information for purposes of taxation and regulation. Employees and their union representatives use economic information to evaluate the stability and the profitability of the organization that employs them.

The individuals most dependent upon and most involved with accounting are those charged with the responsibility for directing the operations of enterprises. They are often referred to collectively as management. The types of accounting data needed by management and the use of these data by management in directing operations are the focus of this text.

## FINANCIAL ACCOUNTING AND MANAGERIAL ACCOUNTING

Although economic information can be classified in many ways, accountants often divide accounting information into two types: financial and managerial. A brief discussion of each of these is useful in understanding the nature of the information needed by management.

Financial accounting is concerned with the recording of transactions for a business enterprise or other economic unit and with the periodic preparation of various statements from such records. In performing these functions, financial accountants use generally accepted accounting principles (GAAP). The financial statements, which report the results of past financial activities, are intended primarily for the use of persons who are "outside" or external to the enterprise, such as shareholders, creditors, governmental agencies, and the general public. However, these statements are also useful to management in directing the operations of the enterprise. For example, in planning future operations, management often begins by evaluating the results of relevant past activities as reported in the basic financial statements.

Managerial accounting employs both historical and estimated data, which management uses in conducting daily operations and in planning future operations. For example, in directing day-to-day operations, management relies upon accounting to provide information concerning the amount owed to each creditor, the amount owed by each customer, and the date each amount is due. The treasurer uses these data and other data in the management of cash. Accounting data may be used by top management in determining the selling price of a new product. Production managers, by comparing past performances with planned objectives, can take steps to accelerate favorable trends and reduce those trends that are unfavorable.

---

[1]A glossary of terms appears in Appendix A. The terms included in the glossary are printed in color the first time they appear in the text.

As indicated in the following diagram, managerial accounting overlaps financial accounting to the extent that management uses the financial statements in directing current operations and planning future operations. However, managerial accounting extends beyond financial accounting by providing additional information and reports for management's use. In providing this additional information, the accountant is *not* governed by generally accepted accounting principles. Since these data are used only by management, the accountant provides the data in the format that is most useful for management. The principle of "usefulness," then, is dominant in guiding the accountant in preparing management reports. The nature of managerial accounting reports and the concepts underlying their preparation are discussed in the following paragraphs.

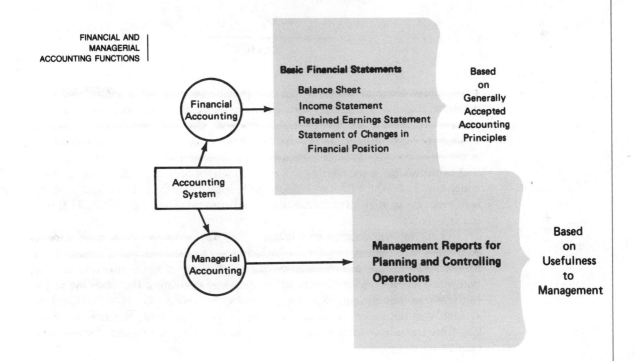

FINANCIAL AND MANAGERIAL ACCOUNTING FUNCTIONS

Financial Accounting

Accounting System

Managerial Accounting

**Basic Financial Statements**

Balance Sheet

Income Statement

Retained Earnings Statement

Statement of Changes in Financial Position

Based on Generally Accepted Accounting Principles

**Management Reports for Planning and Controlling Operations**

Based on Usefulness to Management

**CHARACTERISTICS OF MANAGERIAL ACCOUNTING REPORTS**

The managerial accountant can be viewed as the observer and reporter of the business's operations. In carrying out this reporting function, the usefulness of the accountant's reports for management depends on the characteristics presented in the diagram on page 4.

**Relevance**

Relevance means that the economic information reported must be pertinent to the specific action being considered by management. In applying this concept, the accountant must be familiar with the operations of the firm and the needs of

CHARACTERISTICS OF
USEFUL MANAGERIAL
ACCOUNTING REPORTS

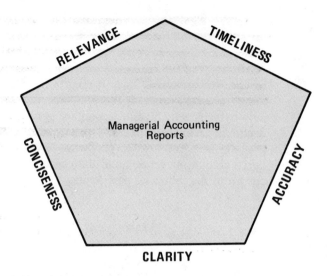

management in order to select what is important from the masses of data that are available. Especially in this modern age of the information explosion, this selection process can be difficult. To accomplish this task, the accountant must determine the needs of management for the decision at hand, examine the available data, and select only the relevant data for reporting to management. To illustrate, assume that management is considering the replacement of fully depreciated equipment, which cost $100,000, with new equipment costing $150,000. It is the $150,000 that is relevant for an analysis of financing the replacement. The original cost, $100,000, is irrelevant.

In applying the concept of relevance, it is important to recognize that some accounting information may have a high degree of relevance for one use but may have little or no relevance for another use. For example, in the previous illustration, the $100,000 was irrelevant for purposes of evaluating the financing of the replacement equipment. For tax purposes, however, the $100,000 (and its accumulated depreciation) would be relevant for determining the amount of the gain from the sale or trade-in of the old equipment and the amount of the income tax due on any gain.

Timeliness |
Timeliness refers to the need for accounting reports to contain the most up-to-date information. In many cases, outdated data can lead to unwise decisions. For example, if prior years' costs are relied upon in setting the selling price of a product, the resulting selling price may not be sufficient to cover the current year's costs and to provide a satisfactory profit.

In some cases, the timeliness concept may require the accountant to prepare reports on a prearranged schedule, such as daily, weekly, or monthly. For example, daily reports of cash receipts and disbursements assist management in effectively managing the use of cash on a day-to-day basis. On the other hand, weekly reports of the cost of products manufactured may be satisfactory to assist management in the control of costs. In other cases, reports are prepared on an irregular basis or only when needed. For example, if management is evaluating a proposed advertising promotion for the month of May, a report of current costs and other current relevant data for this specific proposal would be needed in sufficient time for management to make and implement the decision.

**Accuracy** | Accuracy refers to the need for the report to be correct within the constraints of the use of the report and the inherent inaccuracies in the measurement process. If the report is not accurate, management's decision may not be prudent. For example, if an inaccurate report on a customer's past payment practices is presented to management, an unwise decision in granting credit may be made.

As previously indicated, the concept of accuracy must be applied within the constraint of the use to be made of the report. In other words, there are occasions when accuracy should be sacrificed for less precise data that are more useful to management. For example, in planning production, estimates (forecasts) of future sales may be more useful than more accurate data from past sales. In addition, it should be noted that there are inherent inaccuracies in accounting data that are based on estimates and approximations. For example, in determining the unit cost of a product manufactured, an estimate of depreciation expense on factory equipment used in the manufacturing process must be made. Without this estimate, the cost of the product would be of limited usefulness in establishing the product selling price.

**Clarity** | Clarity refers to the need for reports to be clear and understandable in both format and content. Reports that are clear and understandable will enable management to focus on significant factors in planning and controlling operations. For example, for management's use in controlling the costs of manufacturing a product, a report that compares actual costs with expected costs and clearly indicates the differences enables management to give its attention to significant differences and to take any necessary corrective action.

**Conciseness** | Conciseness refers to the requirement that the report should be brief and to the point. Although the report must be complete and include all relevant information, the inclusion of unnecessary information wastes management's time and makes it more difficult for management to focus on the significant factors related to a decision. For example, reports prepared for the top level of management should usually be broad in scope and present summaries of data rather than small details.

**Cost-Benefit Balance** | The characteristics of managerial accounting reports provide general guidelines for the preparation of reports to meet the various needs of management. In applying these guidelines, consideration must be given to the specific needs of each manager, and the reports should be tailored to meet these needs. In preparing reports, costs are incurred, and a primary consideration is that the value of the management reports must at least equal the cost of producing them. This overriding cost-benefit evaluation must be considered, no matter how informational a report may be. A report should not be prepared if its cost exceeds the benefits derived by users.

**THE MANAGEMENT PROCESS**

Managerial accountants supply accounting information to assist management in the basic functions of planning and control. Planning is the process of setting goals for the use of an organization's resources and of developing plans to achieve these goals. Accountants provide information to enable management to plan effectively. For example, accountants provide information to assist management in setting product selling prices. In this context, projections indicating the anticipated results of alternate selling prices can be useful to management in deciding among alternatives.

Control is the process of directing operations to achieve the organization's goals and plans. For example, accounting reports comparing the actual costs with the planned costs of producing products provide management with the basis for making decisions to control costs.

A common ingredient of both planning and control is decision making, and accountants provide information useful to management in making decisions. For example, decisions need to be made in selecting from among alternate proposed plans. Decisions also need to be made to keep actual costs within the bounds of proposed costs. The relationship between managerial accounting, the management process, and decision making is shown in the following diagram:

MANAGERIAL ACCOUNTING AND THE BASIC FUNCTIONS OF MANAGEMENT

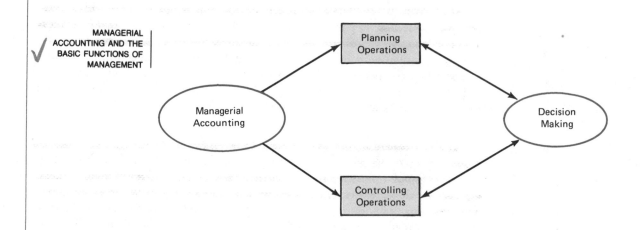

As indicated in the diagram, decisions must be made by management in planning and controlling operations. As the results of these decisions evolve and are reviewed, additional decisions may be necessary to revise plans and modify steps taken to control operations. For example, if accounting information indicates that actual performance is below planned performance, the plans may be revised or the controls modified in an attempt to improve performance. Thus, the interrelationships of the planning and control functions of management may be viewed as an endless loop, with the managerial accountant providing input for the use of management in carrying out both functions.

The accounting system of a particular firm must be responsive to the needs of management for both the planning and control functions. To meet the needs of management, the management accountant applies various concepts of usefulness (discussed in preceding paragraphs) in extracting data from the accounting system for reporting to management.

The accounting system must also be responsive to the needs of those external to the firm. As discussed in preceding paragraphs, generally accepted accounting principles guide the accountant in extracting data from the accounting system for external reporting. The relationship of the basic concepts of management to both financial accounting and managerial accounting is summarized in the following diagram:

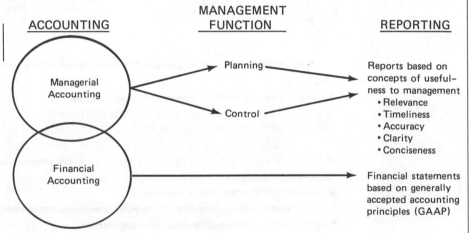

RELATIONSHIP OF ACCOUNTING TO THE MANAGEMENT FUNCTIONS AND REPORTING

**ORGANIZATION OF THE MANAGERIAL ACCOUNTING FUNCTION**

Business enterprises may be divided into departments or similar units, so that the activities of the business are more manageable. The responsibilities of specific departments can be indicated in an organization chart. The simplified organization chart on page 8 is typical for a manufacturing firm.

The individual reporting units can be viewed as having either (1) line or (2) staff responsibilities. A line department is one directly involved in the basic objectives of the organization. In the illustration, the vice-president of production and the managers of plants A, B, and C occupy line positions because they are responsible for an activity that directly contributes to earnings. A staff department is one that provides services and assistance to the operating and other units in the organization. The vice-president of personnel in the illustration occupies a staff position because that person's function is to assist line managers and others in staffing their departments.

ORGANIZATION
CHART FOR A
MANUFACTURING FIRM

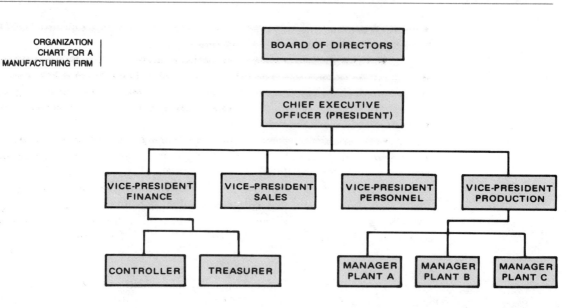

In most business organizations, the chief managerial accountant is called the controller. The controller, who may report to the vice-president of finance, has a staff relationship with others in the organization, providing advice and assistance to management but assuming no responsibility for the operations of the business. The controller's function might be compared to that of an airplane's navigator. The navigator, with special skills and training, assists the pilot, but the pilot is responsible for flying the airplane. Likewise, the controller, with special accounting training and skills, advises management, but management is responsible for planning and controlling operations.

The controller's staff often consists of several accountants, each of whom is responsible for a specialized accounting function. The following organization chart is typical for an accounting department that reports to the controller:

ORGANIZATION CHART—
        CONTROLLER'S
        DEPARTMENT

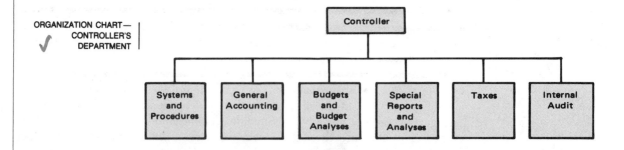

The most important functions of an accounting department are systems and procedures, general accounting, budgets and budget analyses, special reports and analyses, taxes, and internal audit. These functions are briefly described in the following paragraphs.

**Systems and procedures** is concerned with the design and implementation of procedures for the accumulation and reporting of accounting data to all interested users. In performing this function, the accountant must evaluate the usefulness of various types of data processing equipment for the firm. The systems accountant must also devise appropriate "checks and balances" to safeguard business assets and provide for an information flow that will be efficient and helpful to management. The accounting system must provide financial and managerial accounting data, as discussed in preceding paragraphs.

**General accounting** is primarily concerned with the recording of transactions and the periodic preparation of the basic financial statements. Of particular importance to this area is the gathering of data in conformity with the generally accepted accounting principles for preparing the basic financial statements.

**Budgets and budget analyses** focuses on the plan for financial operations for future periods and, through records and summaries, focuses on the comparison of actual operations with these plans. This function provides much of the information for planning and controlling operations.

**Special reports and analyses** is concerned with data that will be useful to management in analyzing current problems and considering alternate courses for future operations. Much of the analysis focuses on providing data related to specific problems that confront management and identifying alternative courses of action related to proposed new projects. Often the accountants who perform this function prepare special reports according to the requirements of regulatory agencies.

**Taxes** encompasses the preparation of tax returns and the consideration of the tax consequences of proposed business transactions or alternate courses of action. Accountants in this area must be familiar with the tax statutes affecting their business and must also keep up-to-date on administrative regulations and court decisions on tax cases.

**Internal audit** is a staff of company employees whose principal responsibility is to determine to what extent, if any, the various operating units are deviating from the policies and procedures prescribed by management.

Regardless of the makeup of the controller's department, the main responsibility of the department is to assist managers in carrying out their responsibilities. Since managerial accountants work closely with management, it is not surprising that many managerial accountants are promoted to top management positions.

**PROFESSION OF
MANAGERIAL
ACCOUNTING**

In general, financial accounting has received more attention than managerial accounting. In recent years, however, managerial accounting has gained recognition through the efforts of the **National Association of Accountants (NAA)**, which is the largest organization of managerial accountants in the world.

In 1972, the National Association of Accountants established a program to recognize managerial accounting as a profession. The specific objectives of the program, which leads to the **Certificate in Management Accounting (CMA)**, were stated by the NAA as follows:

1. To establish management accounting as a recognized profession by identifying the role of the management accountant and the underlying body of knowledge, and by outlining a course of study by which such knowledge can be acquired.
2. To foster higher educational standards in the field of management accounting.
3. To establish an objective measure of an individual's knowledge and competence in the field of management accounting.

The requirements for the CMA designation include the baccalaureate degree or equivalent, two years of experience in management accounting, and successful completion of a 2½-day examination. Participation in a program of continuing professional education is also required for renewal of the certificate.

The CMA program is administered by the Institute of Management Accounting. Since its inception, the program has increased in stature. The CMA certificate now serves as evidence of professional competence in managerial accounting, just as the CPA certificate is evidence of professional competence in public accounting. Unlike the CPA certificate, however, the CMA certificate does not convey to the holder any special rights.

---

**Discussion Questions**

1. Is the information classified as financial accounting useful to management? Discuss.

2. In preparing the basic financial statements, must generally accepted accounting principles be used? Discuss.

3. In preparing reports for the use of management, must the managerial accountant use generally accepted accounting principles? Discuss.

4. Contrast financial accounting information with managerial accounting information in terms of those who use the information.

5. What is the dominant principle that guides the managerial accountant in preparing management reports?

6. Alexander Company is contemplating the expansion of its operations through the purchase of the assets of Zimmer Lumber Company. Included among the assets of Zimmer Lumber Company is lumber purchased for $275,000 and having a current replacement cost of $310,000. Which cost ($275,000 or $310,000) is relevant for the decision to be made by Alexander Company? Briefly explain the reason for your answer.

7. A bank loan officer is evaluating a request for a loan that is to be secured by a mortgage on the borrower's property. The property cost $450,000 twenty years ago and has a current market value of $600,000. Which figure, $450,000 or $600,000, is relevant for the loan officer's use in evaluating the request for the loan? Discuss.

8. What is meant by cost-benefit balance as it relates to the preparation of management reports?

9. Briefly describe the two basic functions of management.

10. (a) Differentiate between a department with line responsibility and a department with staff responsibility. (b) In an organization that has a sales department and a personnel department, among others, which of the two departments has (1) a line responsibility and (2) a staff responsibility?

11. (a) What is the role of the controller in a business organization? (b) Does the controller have a line or a staff responsibility?

12. What is the principal responsibility of the staff of internal auditors?

13. What do the initials CMA signify?

14. Describe the role that the National Association of Accountants has played in recent years in promoting increased recognition of managerial accountants.

15. Briefly discuss the requirements for the CMA designation.

# 2
CHAPTER

# Manufacturing Operations and Job Order Cost Systems

**CHAPTER OBJECTIVES**

*Identify and illustrate concepts and procedures used in accounting for manufacturing operations.*

*Describe the basic characteristics of cost accounting systems.*

*Identify alternative cost accounting systems for manufacturing operations.*

*Describe and illustrate a job order cost accounting system.*

# PART 2

## Accounting Systems for Manufacturing Operations

# 2

**CHAPTER**

Managerial accounting has evolved over many centuries in response to the changing needs of management in planning and controlling operations. Perhaps the most significant change began with the Industrial Revolution, which occurred in England from the mid-eighteenth to the mid-nineteenth centuries. The revolution brought a change from the handicraft method of producing marketable goods to the factory system. With the use of machinery to make many identical products came the need to determine and control the cost of a large volume of machine-made products instead of a relatively small number of individually handcrafted products.

As manufacturing enterprises became larger and more complex and as competition among manufacturers increased, the "scientific management concept" evolved. This concept emphasized a systematic approach to the solution of management problems. Paralleling this trend was the development of more sophisticated managerial accounting concepts to supply management with analytical techniques for measuring the efficiency of current operations and in planning for future operations. This trend was accelerated in the twentieth century by the advent of the electronic computer with its capacity for manipulating large masses of data and its ability to determine the potential effect of alternative courses of action.

In this and later chapters, attention is directed to accounting concepts for manufacturing enterprises. Although the concepts are presented in the context of a manufacturing enterprise, many of them apply equally to service and merchandising enterprises.

## MANUFAC-
## TURING
## OPERATIONS

Manufacturers employ labor and use machinery to change materials into finished products. In thus changing the form of goods, their activities differ from those of merchandisers. The furniture manufacturer, for example, changes lumber and other materials into furniture. The furniture dealer in turn purchases the finished goods from the manufacturer and sells them without additional processing.

Some functions of manufacturing companies, such as selling, administration, and financing, are like those of merchandising organizations. The accounting procedures for these functions are the same for both types of enterprises.

Accounting procedures for manufacturing businesses must also provide for the accumulation of the accounting data identified with the production processes. Additional ledger accounts are needed and internal controls must be established over the manufacturing operations. Periodic reports to management and other interested parties must include data that will be useful in measuring the efficiency of manufacturing operations and in guiding future operations.

The cost of merchandise acquired for resale to customers is a composite of invoice prices and various additions and deductions to cover such items as delivery charges, allowances, and cash discounts. The merchandise is sold rather than consumed, and the amount sold is called the **cost of merchandise sold.** The cost of manufacturing a product includes not only the cost of tangible materials but also the many costs incurred in changing the materials into a finished product ready for sale. The cost of the manufactured product sold is called the cost of goods sold.

**Cost of
Manufactured
Products**

Unlike a merchandising enterprise, which maintains one inventory account, manufacturing businesses maintain three inventory accounts for (1) goods in the state in which they are to be sold, (2) goods in the process of manufacture, and (3) goods in the state in which they were acquired. These inventories are called respectively finished goods, work in process, and materials. The balances in the inventory accounts may be presented in the balance sheet in the following manner:

Inventories:
Finished goods................................. $300,000
Work in process...............................    55,000
Materials .....................................   123,000 $478,000

The finished goods inventory and work in process inventory are composed of three separate categories of manufacturing costs: direct materials, direct labor, and factory overhead. Direct materials represent the delivered cost of the materials that enter directly into the finished product. Direct labor represents the wages of the factory workers who change the materials into a finished product. Factory overhead includes all of the remaining costs of operating the factory, such as wages for factory supervision, supplies used in the factory but not entering directly into the finished product, and taxes, insurance, depreciation, and maintenance related to factory plant and equipment.

The direct materials, direct labor, and factory overhead costs incurred in the process of manufacturing are reported on the balance sheet as work in process inventory until the goods are completed. After the goods are completed, they are reported as finished goods inventory on the balance sheet. The goods that have been sold are reported on the income statement as cost of goods sold. The relationship between the costs incurred in the manufacturing process, inventories, and the cost of goods sold is illustrated in the top portion of the diagram on page 15. The relationship between purchases of merchandise, merchandise inventory, and the cost of merchandise sold is illustrated in the bottom portion of the diagram.

**Accounting
Systems**

Two basic accounting systems are commonly used by manufacturers: general accounting systems and cost accounting systems. A general accounting system is essentially an extension to manufacturing operations of the common system for merchandising enterprises which use periodic inventory procedures.[1] A cost accounting system uses perpetual inventory procedures and provides more detailed information concerning costs of production.

In the remainder of this chapter, the basic concepts of cost accounting systems for manufacturing operations are described, followed by a discussion and illustration of one of the two main types of cost accounting systems. The other main type of cost accounting system is illustrated in Chapter 3.

---

[1]The basic principles of a general accounting system are presented in Appendix D.

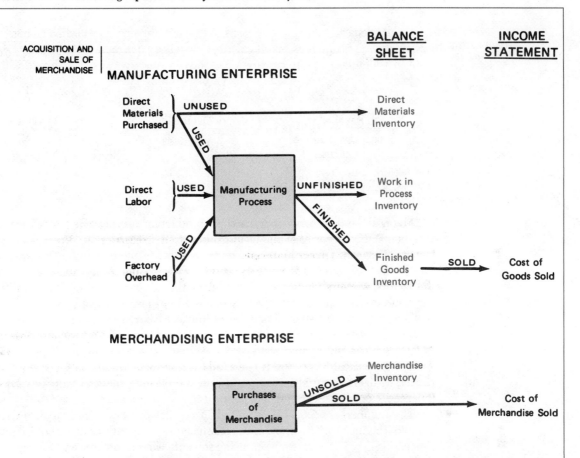

ACQUISITION AND
SALE OF
MERCHANDISE

BALANCE
SHEET

INCOME
STATEMENT

MANUFACTURING ENTERPRISE

Direct Materials Purchased — UNUSED → Direct Materials Inventory

USED

Direct Labor — USED → Manufacturing Process — UNFINISHED → Work in Process Inventory

FINISHED

Factory Overhead — USED

→ Finished Goods Inventory — SOLD → Cost of Goods Sold

MERCHANDISING ENTERPRISE

Purchases of Merchandise — UNSOLD → Merchandise Inventory

SOLD → Cost of Merchandise Sold

**COST
ACCOUNTING
SYSTEM FOR
MANUFAC-
TURING
OPERATIONS**

Through the use of perpetual inventory procedures, a cost accounting system achieves greater accuracy in the determination of costs than is possible with a general accounting system that uses periodic inventory procedures. Cost accounting procedures also permit far more effective control by supplying data on the costs incurred by each factory department and the unit cost of manufacturing each type of product. Such procedures provide not only data useful to management in minimizing costs but also other valuable information about production methods to use, quantities to produce, product lines to promote, and sales prices to charge.

**Perpetual
Inventory
Procedures**

Perpetual inventory controlling accounts and subsidiary ledgers are maintained for materials, work in process, and finished goods in cost accounting systems. Each of these accounts is debited for all additions and is credited for all deductions. The balance of each account thus represents the inventory on hand.

All expenditures incidental to manufacturing move through the work in process account, the finished goods account, and eventually into the cost of goods sold account. The flow of costs through the perpetual inventory accounts and into the cost of goods sold account is illustrated as follows:

FLOW OF COSTS
THROUGH
PERPETUAL
INVENTORY
ACCOUNTS

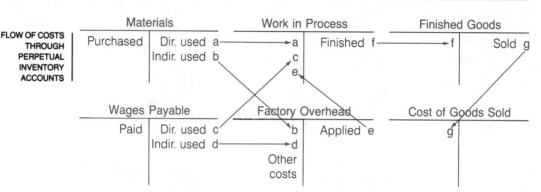

Materials and factory labor used in production are classified as direct and indirect. The materials and the factory labor used directly in the process of manufacturing are debited to Work in Process (**a** and **c** in the diagram). The materials and the factory labor used that do not enter directly into the finished product are debited to Factory Overhead (**b** and **d** in the diagram). Examples of indirect materials are oils and greases, abrasives and polishes, cleaning supplies, gloves, drilling soap, and brushes. Examples of indirect labor are salaries of supervisors, inspectors, material handlers, security guards, and janitors. The proper amount of factory overhead costs are transferred to Work in Process (**e** in the diagram). The costs of the goods finished are transferred from Work in Process to Finished Goods (**f** in the diagram). When the goods are sold, their costs are transferred from Finished Goods to Cost of Goods Sold (**g** in the diagram).

The number of accounts presented in the flowchart was limited in order to simplify the illustration. In practice, manufacturing operations may require many processing departments, each requiring separate work in process and factory overhead accounts.

**Types of Cost Accounting Systems**

There are two main types of cost systems for manufacturing operations — job order cost and process cost. Each of the two systems is widely used, and a manufacturer may use a job order cost system for some of its products and a process cost system for others.

A job order cost system provides for a separate record of the cost of each particular quantity of product that passes through the factory. It is best suited to industries that manufacture goods to fill special orders from customers and to industries that produce different lines of products for stock. It is also appropriate when standard products are manufactured in batches rather than on a continuous basis. In a job order cost system, a summary such as the following would show the cost incurred in completing a job.

**Job 565**
**1,000 Units of Product X200**

| | |
|---|---:|
| Direct materials used...................... | $2,380 |
| Direct labor used ....................... | 4,400 |
| Factory overhead applied................. | 3,080 |
| Total cost ........................... | $9,860 |
| Unit cost ($9,860 ÷ 1,000)................ | $ 9.86 |

Under a process cost system, the costs are accumulated for each of the departments or processes within the factory. A process system is best used by manufacturers of like units of product that are not distinguishable from each other during a continuous production process.

**JOB ORDER COST SYSTEMS**

The basic concepts of job order cost systems are illustrated in this chapter, while process cost systems are discussed in Chapter 3. To simplify the illustration, a nondepartmentalized operation is assumed. In factories with departmentalized operations, costs are accumulated in factory overhead and work in process accounts maintained for each department. The discussion focuses attention on the source documents that serve as the basis for the entries in the job order cost system and to the managerial uses of cost accounting in planning and controlling business operations.

**Materials**

Procedures used in the procurement and issuance of materials differ considerably among manufacturers and even among departments of a particular manufacturer. The discussion that follows is confined to the basic principles, however, and will disregard relatively minor variations and details.

Some time in advance of the date that production of a certain commodity is to begin, the department responsible for scheduling informs the purchasing department, by means of purchase requisitions, of the materials that will be needed. The purchasing department then issues the necessary purchase orders to suppliers. After the goods have been received and inspected, the receiving department personnel prepare a receiving report, showing the quantity received and its condition. Quantities, unit costs, and total costs of the goods billed, as reported on the supplier's invoice, are then compared with the purchase order and the receiving report to make sure that the amounts billed agree with the materials ordered and received. After such verifications, the invoice is recorded in the voucher register or purchases journal as a debit to Materials and a credit to Accounts Payable.

The account Materials in the general ledger is a controlling account. A separate account for each type of material is maintained in a subsidiary ledger called the materials ledger. Details as to quantity and cost of materials received are recorded in the materials ledger on the basis of the receiving reports or purchase invoices. A typical form of materials ledger account is illustrated as follows:

**MATERIALS LEDGER ACCOUNT**

MATERIAL NO. 23                                                ORDER POINT 1,000

| | RECEIVED | | | ISSUED | | | BALANCE | | |
|---|---|---|---|---|---|---|---|---|---|
| REC. REPORT NO. | QUAN-TITY | AMOUNT | MAT. REQ. NO. | QUAN-TITY | AMOUNT | DATE | QUAN-TITY | AMOUNT | UNIT PRICE |
| | | | | | | Jan. 1 | 1,200 | 600.00 | .50 |
| | | | 672 | 500 | 250.00 | 4 | 700 | 350.00 | .50 |
| 196 | 3,000 | 1,620.00 | | | | 8 | 700 | 350.00 | .50 |
| | | | | | | | 3,000 | 1,620.00 | .54 |
| | | | 704 | 800 | 404.00 | 18 | 2,900 | 1,566.00 | .54 |

The accounts in the materials ledger may also be used as an aid in maintaining proper inventory quantities of stock items. Frequent comparisons of quantity balances with predetermined order points enable management to avoid costly idle time caused by lack of materials. The subsidiary ledger form may also include columns for recording quantities ordered and dates of the purchase orders.

Materials are transferred from the storeroom to the factory in response to materials requisitions, which may be issued by the manufacturing department concerned or by a central scheduling department. Storeroom personnel record the issuances on the materials requisition by inserting the physical quantity data. Transfer of responsibility for the materials is evidenced by the signature or initials of the storeroom and factory personnel concerned. The requisition is then routed to the materials ledger clerk, who inserts unit prices and amounts. A typical materials requisition is illustrated as follows:

MATERIALS
REQUISITION

| MATERIALS REQUISITION | | | | |
|---|---|---|---|---|
| Job No. 62 | | Requisition No. 704 | | |
| Authorized by R. A. Sanders | | Date January 18, 19-- | | |
| Description | Quantity Authorized | Quantity Issued | Unit Price | Amount |
| Material No. 23 | 800 | 700<br>100 | $.50<br>.54 | $350<br>54 |
| Total issued | | | | $404 |
| Issued by M. K. | | Received by J. B. | | |

The completed requisition serves as the basis for posting quantities and dollar data to the materials ledger accounts. In the illustration, the first-in, first-out pricing method was used. A summary of the materials requisitions completed during the month serves as the basis for transferring the cost of materials from the controlling account in the general ledger to the controlling accounts for work in process and factory overhead. The flow of materials into production is illustrated by the following entry:

| | | |
|---|---|---|
| Work in Process | 13,000 | |
| Factory Overhead | 840 | |
| Materials | | 13,840 |

The perpetual inventory system for materials has three important advantages: (1) it provides for prompt and accurate charging of materials to jobs and factory overhead, (2) it permits the work of inventory-taking to be spread out rather than concentrated at the end of a fiscal period, and (3) it aids in the disclosure of inventory shortages or other irregularities. As physical quantities of the various materials are determined, the actual inventories are compared with the balances of the respective subsidiary ledger accounts. The causes of significant differences between the two should be determined and the responsibility for the differences assigned to specific individuals. Remedial action can then be taken.

**Factory Labor**

Unlike materials, factory labor is not tangible, nor is it acquired and stored in advance of its use. Hence, there is no perpetual inventory account for labor. The two main objectives in accounting for labor are (1) determination of the correct amount to be paid each employee for each payroll period, and (2) appropriate allocation of labor costs to factory overhead and individual job orders.

The amount of time spent by an employee in the factory is usually recorded on clock cards, which are also called in-and-out cards. The amount of time spent by each employee and the labor cost incurred for each individual job, or for factory overhead, are recorded on time tickets. A typical time ticket form is illustrated as follows:

**TIME TICKET**

### Time Ticket

Employee Name  Gail Berry      No.  4521

Employee No.  240      Date  January 18, 19--

Description of work  Finishing      Job No.  62

| Time Started | Time Stopped | Hours Worked | Hourly Rate | Cost |
|---|---|---|---|---|
| 10:00 | 12:00 | 2 | $6.50 | $13.00 |
| 1:00 | 2:00 | 1 | 6.50 | 6.50 |
| Total cost | | | | $19.50 |
| Approved by  T. D. | | | | |

The times reported on an employee's time tickets are compared with the related clock cards as an internal check on the accuracy of payroll disbursements.

A summary of the time tickets at the end of each month serves as the basis for recording the direct and indirect labor costs incurred. The flow of labor costs into production is illustrated by the following entry:

| | | |
|---|---|---|
| Work in Process | 10,000 | |
| Factory Overhead | 2,200 | |
| Wages Payable | | 12,200 |

**Factory Overhead**

Factory overhead includes all manufacturing costs, except direct materials and direct labor. Examples of factory overhead costs, in addition to indirect materials and indirect labor, are depreciation, electricity, fuel, insurance, and property taxes. It is customary to have a factory overhead controlling account in the general ledger. Details of the various types of cost are accumulated in a subsidiary ledger.

Debits to Factory Overhead come from various sources. For example, the cost of indirect materials is obtained from the summary of the materials requisitions, the cost of indirect labor is obtained from the summary of the time tickets, costs of electricity and water may be posted from the voucher register (or purchases journal), and the cost of depreciation and expired insurance may be recorded as adjustments at the end of the accounting period.

Although factory overhead cannot be specifically identified with particular jobs, it is as much a part of manufacturing costs as direct materials and labor. As the use of machines and automation has increased, factory overhead has represented an ever larger part of total costs. Many items of factory overhead cost are incurred for the entire factory and cannot be directly related to the finished product. The problem is further complicated because some items of factory overhead cost are relatively fixed in amount while others tend to vary according to changes in productivity.

To wait until the end of an accounting period to allocate factory overhead to the various jobs would be quite acceptable from the standpoint of accuracy but highly unsatisfactory in terms of timeliness. If the cost system is to be of maximum usefulness, it is imperative that cost data be available as each job is completed, even though there is a sacrifice in accuracy. It is only through timely reporting that management can make whatever adjustments seem necessary in pricing and manufacturing methods to achieve the best possible combination of revenue and cost on future jobs. Therefore, in order that job costs may be available currently, it is customary to apply factory overhead to production by using a predetermined factory overhead rate.

### Predetermined Factory Overhead Rate

The factory overhead rate is determined by relating the estimated amount of factory overhead for the forthcoming year to some common activity base, one that will equitably apply the factory overhead costs to the goods manufactured. The common bases include direct labor costs, direct labor hours, and machine hours. For example, if it is estimated that the total factory overhead costs for the year will be $100,000 and that the total direct labor cost will be $125,000, an overhead rate of 80% ($100,000 ÷ $125,000) will be applied to the direct labor cost incurred during the year.

As factory overhead costs are incurred, they are debited to the factory overhead account. The factory overhead costs applied to production are periodically credited to the factory overhead account and debited to the work in process account. The application of factory overhead costs to production (80% of direct labor cost of $10,000) is illustrated by the following entry:

| | | |
|---|---|---|
| Work in Process.................................... | 8,000 | |
| Factory Overhead ................................. | | 8,000 |

Inevitably, factory overhead costs applied and actual factory overhead costs incurred during a particular period will differ. If the amount applied exceeds the actual costs, the factory overhead account will have a credit balance and the overhead is said to be **overapplied** or **overabsorbed**. If the amount applied is less than the actual costs, the account will have a debit balance and the overhead is said to be **underapplied** or **underabsorbed**. Both cases are illustrated in the following account:

ACCOUNT  **FACTORY OVERHEAD**                                  ACCOUNT NO.

| Date | | Item | Debit | Credit | Balance | |
|---|---|---|---|---|---|---|
| | | | | | Debit | Credit |
| May | 1 | Balance | | | | 200 |
| | 31 | Costs incurred | 8,320 | | | |
| | 31 | Cost applied | | 8,000 | 120 | |

Underapplied Balance————
Overapplied Balance————

### Disposition of Factory Overhead Balance

The balance in the factory overhead account is carried forward from month to month until the end of the year. The amount of the balance is reported on interim balance sheets as a deferred item.

The nature of the balance in the factory overhead account (underapplied or overapplied), as well as the amount, will change during the year. If there is a decided trend in either direction and the amount is substantial, the reason should be determined. If the variation is caused by alterations in manufacturing methods or by substantial changes in production goals, it may be advisable to revise the factory overhead rate. The accumulation of a large underapplied balance is more serious than a trend in the opposite direction and may indicate inefficiencies in production methods, excessive expenditures, or a combination of factors.

Despite any corrective actions that may be taken to avoid an underapplication or overapplication of factory overhead, the account will usually have a balance at the end of the fiscal year. Since the balance represents the underapplied or over-applied factory overhead applicable to the operations of the year just ended, it is not proper to report it in the year-end balance sheet as a deferred item.

There are two main alternatives for disposing of the balance of factory overhead at the end of the year: (1) by allocation of the balance among work in process, finished goods, and cost of goods sold accounts on the basis of the total amounts of applied factory overhead included in those accounts at the end of the year, or (2) by transfer of the balance to the cost of goods sold account. Theoretically, only the first alternative is sound because it represents a correction of the estimated overhead rate and brings the accounts into agreement with the costs actually incurred. On the other hand, much time and expense may be required to make the allocation and to revise the unit costs of the work in process and finished goods inventories. Furthermore, in most manufacturing enterprises, a very large part of the total manufacturing costs for the year passes through the work in process and the finished goods accounts into the cost of goods sold account before the end of the year. Therefore, unless the total amount of the underapplied or overapplied balance is great, it is satisfactory to transfer it to Cost of Goods Sold.

**Work in Process** | Costs incurred for the various jobs are debited to Work in Process. The job costs described in the preceding sections may be summarized as follows:

Direct materials, $13,000 — Work in Process debited and Materials credited; data obtained from summary of materials requisitions.

Direct labor, $10,000 — Work in Process debited and Wages Payable credited; data obtained from summary of time tickets.

Factory overhead, $8,000 — Work in Process debited and Factory Overhead credited; data obtained by applying overhead rate to direct labor cost (80% of $10,000).

The work in process account to which these costs were charged is illustrated as follows:

| ACCOUNT **WORK IN PROCESS** | | | | ACCOUNT NO. | |
|---|---|---|---|---|---|
| Date | Item | Debit | Credit | Balance | |
| | | | | Debit | Credit |
| May 1 | Balance | | | 3,000 | |
| 31 | Direct materials | 13,000 | | 16,000 | |
| 31 | Direct labor | 10,000 | | 26,000 | |
| 31 | Factory overhead | 8,000 | | 34,000 | |
| 31 | Jobs completed | | 31,920 | 2,080 | |

The work in process account is a controlling account that contains summary information only. The details concerning the costs incurred on each job order are accumulated in a subsidiary ledger known as the cost ledger. Each account in the cost ledger, called a job cost sheet, has spaces for recording all direct materials and direct labor chargeable to the job and for the application of factory overhead at the predetermined rate. Postings to the job cost sheets are made from materials requisitions and time tickets or from summaries of these documents.

The four cost sheets in the subsidiary ledger for the work in process account illustrated are summarized as follows:

## COST LEDGER

| Job 71 (Summary) | |
|---|---|
| Balance.................... | 3,000 |
| Direct materials ........... | 2,000 |
| Direct labor................ | 2,400 |
| Factory overhead .......... | 1,920 |
| | 9,320 |

| Job 73 (Summary) | |
|---|---|
| Direct materials ........... | 6,000 |
| Direct labor................ | 4,000 |
| Factory overhead ......... | 3,200 |
| | 13,200 |

| Job 72 (Summary) | |
|---|---|
| Direct materials ........... | 4,000 |
| Direct labor................ | 3,000 |
| Factory overhead ......... | 2,400 |
| | 9,400 |

| Job 74 (Summary) | |
|---|---|
| Direct materials ........... | 1,000 |
| Direct labor................ | 600 |
| Factory overhead ......... | 480 |
| | *2,080* |

The relationship between the work in process controlling account on page 22 and the subsidiary cost ledger may be observed in the following tabulation:

| Work in Process (Controlling) | | Cost Ledger (Subsidiary) | |
|---|---|---|---|
| Beginning balance.......... | $ 3,000⟷ | Beginning balance Job 71.................. | $ 3,000 |
| | | Direct materials | |
| | | Job 71.................. | $ 2,000 |
| Direct materials ........... | $13,000⟷ | Job 72.................. | 4,000 |
| | | Job 73.................. | 6,000 |
| | | Job 74.................. | 1,000 |
| | | | $13,000 |
| | | Direct labor | |
| | | Job 71.................. | $ 2,400 |
| Direct labor............... | $10,000⟷ | Job 72.................. | 3,000 |
| | | Job 73.................. | 4,000 |
| | | Job 74.................. | 600 |
| | | | $10,000 |

Factory overhead . . . . . . . . .   $ 8,000 ⟷ ⎰ Factory overhead
 

| | |
|---|---|
| Factory overhead | |
| Job 71 . . . . . . . . . . . . . . . . | $ 1,920 |
| Job 72 . . . . . . . . . . . . . . . . | 2,400 |
| Job 73 . . . . . . . . . . . . . . . . | 3,200 |
| Job 74 . . . . . . . . . . . . . . . . | 480 |
| | $ 8,000 |

Jobs completed . . . . . . . . . . .   $31,920 ⟷

| | |
|---|---|
| Jobs completed | |
| Job 71 . . . . . . . . . . . . . . . . | $ 9,320 |
| Job 72 . . . . . . . . . . . . . . . . | 9,400 |
| Job 73 . . . . . . . . . . . . . . . . | 13,200 |
| | $31,920 |

Ending balance . . . . . . . . . . .   $ 2,080 ⟷

| | |
|---|---|
| Ending balance | |
| Job 74 . . . . . . . . . . . . . . . . | $ 2,080 |

The data in the cost ledger were presented in summary form for illustrative purposes. A job cost sheet for Job 72, providing for the current accumulation of cost elements entering into the job order and for a summary when the job is completed, is as follows:

JOB COST SHEET

Job No.  72       Date _____ May 7, 19-- _____

Item  5,000 Type C Containers       Date wanted _____ May 23, 19-- _____

For  Stock       Date completed _____ May 21, 19-- _____

| Direct Materials | | Direct Labor | | | | Summary | |
|---|---|---|---|---|---|---|---|
| Mat. Req. No. | Amount | Time Summary No. | Amount | Time Summary No. | Amount | Item | Amount |
| 834 | 800.00 | 2202 | 83.60 | 2248 | 122.50 | Direct | |
| 838 | 1,000.00 | 2204 | 208.40 | 2250 | 187.30 | materials | 4,000.00 |
| 841 | 1,400.00 | 2205 | 167.00 | 2253 | 155.40 | Direct labor | 3,000.00 |
| 864 | 800.00 | 2210 | 229.00 | | 3,000.00 | Factory | |
| | 4,000.00 | 2211 | 198.30 | | | overhead | |
| | | 2213 | 107.20 | | | (80% of | |
| | | 2216 | 110.00 | | | direct | |
| | | 2222 | 277.60 | | | labor cost) | 2,400.00 |
| | | 2224 | 217.40 | | | Total cost | 9,400.00 |
| | | 2225 | 106.30 | | | | |
| | | 2231 | 153.20 | | | No. of units | |
| | | 2234 | 245.20 | | | finished | 5,000 |
| | | 2237 | 170.00 | | | Cost per unit | 1.88 |
| | | 2242 | 261.60 | | | | |

When Job 72 was completed, the direct materials costs and the direct labor costs were totaled and entered in the Summary column. Factory overhead was added at the predetermined rate of 80% of the direct labor cost, and the total cost of the job was determined. The total cost of the job, $9,400, divided by the number of units produced, 5,000, yielded a unit cost of $1.88 for the Type C Containers produced.

Upon the completion of Job 72, the job cost sheet was removed from the cost ledger and filed for future reference. At the end of the accounting period, the sum of the total costs on all cost sheets completed during the period is determined and the following entry is made:

```
Finished Goods......................................    31,920
    Work in Process ..................................              31,920
```

✓   The remaining balance in the work in process account represents the total cost charged to the uncompleted job cost sheets.

**Finished Goods and Cost of Goods Sold**

The finished goods account is a controlling account. The related subsidiary ledger, which has an account for each kind of commodity produced, is called the finished goods ledger or **stock ledger**. Each account in the subsidiary finished goods ledger provides columns for recording the quantity and the cost of goods manufactured, the quantity and the cost of goods shipped, and the quantity, the total cost, and the unit cost of goods on hand. An account in the finished goods ledger is illustrated as follows:

**FINISHED GOODS LEDGER ACCOUNT**

ITEM: TYPE C CONTAINER

| JOB ORDER NO. | QUAN- TITY | AMOUNT | SHIP. ORDER NO. | QUAN- TITY | AMOUNT | DATE | QUAN- TITY | AMOUNT | UNIT COST |
|---|---|---|---|---|---|---|---|---|---|
| | MANUFACTURED | | | SHIPPED | | | BALANCE | | |
| | | | | | | May 1 | 2,000 | 3,920.00 | 1.96 |
| | | | 643 | 2,000 | 3,920.00 | 8 | — | — | — |
| 72 | 5,000 | 9,400.00 | | | | 21 | 5,000 | 9,400.00 | 1.88 |
| | | | 646 | 2,000 | 3,760.00 | 23 | 3,000 | 5,640.00 | 1.88 |

Just as there are various methods of pricing materials entering into production, there are various methods of determining the cost of the finished goods sold. In the illustration, the first-in, first-out method is used. The quantities shipped are posted to the finished goods ledger from a copy of the shipping order or other memorandum. The finished goods ledger clerk then records on the copy of the shipping order the unit cost and the total amount of the commodity sold. A summary of the cost data on these shipping orders becomes the basis for the following entry:

| | | |
|---|---|---|
| Cost of Goods Sold ................................. | 30,168 | |
| Finished Goods................................... | | 30,168 |

✓ If goods are returned by a buyer and are put back in stock, it is necessary to debit Finished Goods and credit Cost of Goods Sold for the cost.

Sales | For each sale of finished goods, it is necessary to maintain a record of both the cost price and the selling price of the goods sold. As previously stated, the cost data may be recorded on the shipping orders. The sales journal may be expanded by the addition of a column for recording the total cost of the goods billed. At the end of the month, the total of the column is posted as a debit to Cost of Goods Sold and a credit to Finished Goods. The total of the sales price column is posted as a debit to Accounts Receivable and a credit to Sales.

ILLUSTRATION
OF JOB
ORDER COST
ACCOUNTING | To illustrate further the procedures described in the preceding sections, assume that the Spencer Co. uses a job order cost accounting system. The trial balance of the general ledger on January 1, the first day of the fiscal year, is as follows:

Spencer Co.
Trial Balance
January 1, 19--

| | | |
|---|---|---|
| Cash ......................................... | 85,000 | |
| Accounts Receivable.............................. | 73,000 | |
| Finished Goods................................. | 40,000 | |
| Work in Process ............................... | 20,000 | |
| Materials...................................... | 30,000 | |
| Prepaid Expenses ............................... | 2,000 | |
| Plant Assets................................... | 850,000 | |
| Accumulated Depreciation—Plant Assets .............. | | 473,000 |
| Accounts Payable............................... | | 70,000 |
| Wages Payable................................. | | 15,000 |
| Common Stock ................................. | | 500,000 |
| Retained Earnings .............................. | | 42,000 |
| | 1,100,000 | 1,100,000 |

A summary of the transactions and the adjustments for January, followed in each case by the related entry in general journal form, is presented below and on pages 28 and 29. In practice, the transactions would be recorded daily in various journals.

(a) *Materials purchased and prepaid expenses incurred.*
Summary of receiving reports:

| | |
|---|---|
| Material A | $ 29,000 |
| Material B | 17,000 |
| Material C | 12,000 |
| Material D | 4,000 |
| Total | $ 62,000 |

*Entry:* 

| | | |
|---|---|---|
| Materials | 62,000 | |
| Prepaid Expenses | 1,000 | |
| Accounts Payable | | 63,000 |

(b) *Materials requisitioned for use.*
Summary of requisitions:

**By Use**

| | | |
|---|---|---|
| Job 1001 | $12,000 | |
| Job 1002 | 26,000 | |
| Job 1003 | 22,000 | $ 60,000 |
| Factory Overhead | | 3,000 |
| Total | | $ 63,000 |

**By Types**

| | | |
|---|---|---|
| Material A | $27,000 | |
| Material B | 18,000 | |
| Material C | 15,000 | |
| Material D | 3,000 | |
| Total | | $ 63,000 |

*Entry:* 

| | | |
|---|---|---|
| Work in Process | 60,000 | |
| Factory Overhead | 3,000 | |
| Materials | | 63,000 |

(c)  *Factory labor used.*

Summary of time tickets:

| | | |
|---|---:|---:|
| Job 1001 . . . . . . . . . . . . . . . . | $ 60,000 | |
| Job 1002 . . . . . . . . . . . . . . . . | 30,000 | |
| Job 1003 . . . . . . . . . . . . . . . . | 10,000 | $100,000 |
| Factory Overhead . . . . . . . . . | | 20,000 |
| Total . . . . . . . . . . . . . . . . . . . | | $120,000 |

*Entry:* Work in Process . . . . . . . . . . . . . . . . . . . . . . . . . . .  100,000
       Factory Overhead . . . . . . . . . . . . . . . . . . . . . . . . . . .  20,000
          Wages Payable . . . . . . . . . . . . . . . . . . . . . . . . . . .            120,000

(d)  *Other costs incurred.*

*Entry:* Factory Overhead . . . . . . . . . . . . . . . . . . . . . . . . . . .  56,000
       Selling Expenses . . . . . . . . . . . . . . . . . . . . . . . . . . . .  25,000
       General Expenses . . . . . . . . . . . . . . . . . . . . . . . . . . .  10,000
          Accounts Payable . . . . . . . . . . . . . . . . . . . . . . . . . .            91,000

(e)  *Expiration of prepaid expenses.*

*Entry:* Factory Overhead . . . . . . . . . . . . . . . . . . . . . . . . . . .  1,000
       Selling Expenses . . . . . . . . . . . . . . . . . . . . . . . . . . . .  100
       General Expenses . . . . . . . . . . . . . . . . . . . . . . . . . . .  100
          Prepaid Expenses . . . . . . . . . . . . . . . . . . . . . . . . . .            1,200

(f)  *Depreciation.*

*Entry:* Factory Overhead . . . . . . . . . . . . . . . . . . . . . . . . . . .  7,000
       Selling Expenses . . . . . . . . . . . . . . . . . . . . . . . . . . . .  200
       General Expenses . . . . . . . . . . . . . . . . . . . . . . . . . . .  100
          Accumulated Depreciation — Plant Assets . . . . .            7,300

(g)  *Application of factory overhead costs to jobs.* The predetermined rate was **90%** of direct labor cost.

Summary of factory overhead applied:

| | | |
|---|---:|---:|
| Job 1001 (90% of $60,000) . . . . . . . . . . | $ 54,000 |
| Job 1002 (90% of $30,000) . . . . . . . . . . | 27,000 |
| Job 1003 (90% of $10,000) . . . . . . . . . . | 9,000 |
| Total . . . . . . . . . . . . . . . . . . . . . . . . | $ 90,000 |

*Entry:* Work in Process . . . . . . . . . . . . . . . . . . . . . . . . . . .  90,000
       Factory Overhead . . . . . . . . . . . . . . . . . . . . . . . . . . .            90,000

*(h) Jobs completed.*

Summary of completed job cost sheets:

| | |
|---|---:|
| Job 1001............................ | $146,000 |
| Job 1002......................... | 83,000 |
| Total ............................. | $229,000 |

*Entry:* Finished Goods............................... 229,000
Work in Process............................             229,000

*(i) Sales and cost of goods sold.*

Summary of sales invoices and shipping orders:

| | Sales Price | Cost Price |
|---|---:|---:|
| Product X .............. | $ 19,600 | $ 15,000 |
| Product Y .............. | 165,100 | 125,000 |
| Product Z ............. | 105,300 | 80,000 |
| Total .................. | $290,000 | $220,000 |

*Entry:* Accounts Receivable......................... 290,000
Sales .......................................         290,000

*Entry:* Cost of Goods Sold .......................... 220,000
Finished Goods..............................         220,000

*(j) Cash received.*

*Entry:* Cash ....................................... 300,000
Accounts Receivable .......................         300,000

*(k) Cash disbursed.*

*Entry:* Accounts Payable............................ 190,000
Wages Payable ............................. 125,000
Cash.......................................         315,000

The flow of costs through the manufacturing accounts, together with summary details of the subsidiary ledgers, is illustrated on page 30. Entries in the accounts are identified by letters to facilitate comparisons with the foregoing summary journal entries.

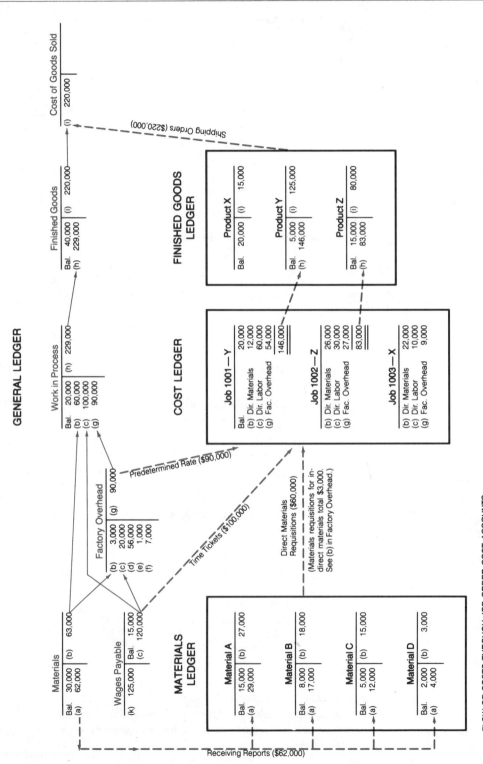

FLOW OF COSTS THROUGH JOB ORDER COST ACCOUNTS

The trial balance taken from the general ledger of the Spencer Co. on January 31 is as follows:

Spencer Co.
Trial Balance
January 31, 19--

| | | |
|---|---:|---:|
| Cash | 70,000 | |
| Accounts Receivable | 63,000 | |
| Finished Goods | 49,000 | |
| Work in Process | 41,000 | |
| Materials | 29,000 | |
| Prepaid Expenses | 1,800 | |
| Plant Assets | 850,000 | |
| Accumulated Depreciation — Plant Assets | | 480,300 |
| Accounts Payable | | 34,000 |
| Wages Payable | | 10,000 |
| Common Stock | | 500,000 |
| Retained Earnings | | 42,000 |
| Sales | | 290,000 |
| Cost of Goods Sold | 220,000 | |
| Factory Overhead | | 3,000 |
| Selling Expenses | 25,300 | |
| General Expenses | 10,200 | |
| | 1,359,300 | 1,359,300 |

The balances of the three inventory accounts — Materials, Work in Process, and Finished Goods — represent the respective ending inventories on January 31. A comparison of the balances of the general ledger controlling accounts with their respective subsidiary ledgers is as follows:

<table>
<tr><td></td><td colspan="2" align="center">Controlling Accounts</td><td colspan="2" align="center">Subsidiary Ledgers</td></tr>
<tr><td rowspan="4" valign="top">CONTROLLING AND<br>SUBSIDIARY<br>ACCOUNTS<br>COMPARED</td><td>Account</td><td>Balance</td><td>Account</td><td>Balance</td></tr>
</table>

| Controlling Account | Balance | | Subsidiary Account | Balance | Total |
|---|---|---|---|---|---|
| Materials | $29,000 | ⟷ | Material A | $17,000 | |
| | | | Material B | 7,000 | |
| | | | Material C | 2,000 | |
| | | | Material D | 3,000 | $29,000 |
| Work in Process | $41,000 | ⟷ | Job 1003 | | $41,000 |
| Finished Goods | $49,000 | ⟷ | Product X | $ 5,000 | |
| | | | Product Y | 26,000 | |
| | | | Product Z | 18,000 | $49,000 |

To simplify the illustration, only one work in process account and one factory overhead account have been used. Usually, a manufacturing business has several processing departments, each requiring separate work in process and factory overhead accounts. In the illustration, one predetermined rate was used in applying the factory overhead to jobs. In a factory with several processing departments, a single factory overhead rate may not provide accurate product costs and effective cost control. A single rate for the entire factory cannot take into consideration such factors as differences among departments in the nature of their operations and in amounts of factory overhead incurred. In such cases, each factory department should have a separate factory overhead rate. For example, in a factory with twenty distinct operating departments, one department might have an overhead rate of 110% of direct labor cost, another a rate of $4 per direct labor hour, and another a rate of $3.50 per machine hour.

The following financial statements are based on the data for Spencer Co. It should be noted that the overapplied factory overhead on January 31 is reported on the balance sheet as a deferred item.

| Spencer Co. Income Statement For Month Ended January 31, 19-- | | |
|---|---|---|
| Sales.......................................... | | $290,000 |
| Cost of goods sold............................... | | 220,000 |
| Gross profit..................................... | | $ 70,000 |
| Operating expenses: | | |
| Selling expenses ............................. | $25,300 | |
| General expenses ............................ | 10,200 | |
| Total operating expenses..................... | | 35,500 |
| Income from operations .......................... | | $ 34,500 |

| Spencer Co. Retained Earnings Statement For Month Ended January 31, 19-- | |
|---|---|
| Retained earnings, January 1, 19-- .......................... | $42,000 |
| Income for the month ........................................ | 34,500 |
| Retained earnings, January 31, 19-- ......................... | $76,500 |

**Spencer Co.**
**Balance Sheet**
**January 31, 19--**

## Assets

Current assets:

| | | |
|---|---:|---:|
| Cash................................ | | $ 70,000 |
| Accounts receivable................ | | 63,000 |

Inventories:

| | | | |
|---|---:|---:|---:|
| Finished goods................... | $49,000 | | |
| Work in process.................. | 41,000 | | |
| Materials ........................ | 29,000 | 119,000 | |
| Prepaid expenses ................... | | 1,800 | |
| Total current assets............... | | | $253,800 |

Plant assets:

| | | | |
|---|---:|---:|---:|
| Plant assets........................ | | $850,000 | |
| Less accumulated depreciation .... | | 480,300 | 369,700 |
| Total assets......................... | | | $623,500 |

## Liabilities

Current liabilities:

| | | | |
|---|---:|---:|---:|
| Accounts payable.................. | $34,000 | | |
| Wages payable .................... | 10,000 | | |
| Total current liabilities............. | | $ 44,000 | |

Deferred credits:

| | | | |
|---|---:|---:|---:|
| Factory overhead................... | | 3,000 | |
| Total liabilities....................... | | | $ 47,000 |

## Stockholders' Equity

| | | | |
|---|---:|---:|---:|
| Common stock....................... | | $500,000 | |
| Retained earnings ................... | | 76,500 | |
| Total stockholders' equity............. | | | 576,500 |
| Total liabilities and stockholders' equity . | | | $623,500 |

**Self-Examination Questions**
*(Answers in Appendix C.)*

1. An example of a factory overhead cost is:
   A. gloves for factory workers
   B. salaries for factory plant supervisors
   C. salaries for material handlers
   D. all of the above

2. For which of the following would the job order cost system be appropriate?
   A. Antique furniture repair shop
   B. Rubber manufacturer
   C. Coal manufacturer
   D. All of the above

3. Materials are transferred from the storeroom to the factory in response to:
   A. purchase requisitions
   B. purchase orders
   C. receiving reports
   D. materials requisitions

4. If the factory overhead account has a credit balance, factory overhead is said to be:
   A. underapplied
   B. overapplied
   C. underabsorbed
   D. none of the above

5. The details concerning the costs incurred on each job order are accumulated in a subsidiary ledger known as a:
   A. cost ledger
   B. job cost sheet
   C. stock ledger
   D. none of the above

---

**Discussion Questions**

1. Name the three inventory accounts for a manufacturing business and describe what each balance represents at the end of an accounting period.

2. Name and describe the three categories of manufacturing costs included in the cost of finished goods and the cost of work in process.

3. (a) Name the two principal types of cost accounting systems. (b) Which system provides for a separate record of each particular quantity of product that passes through the factory? (c) Which system accumulates the costs for each department or process within the factory?

4. Distinguish between the purchase requisition and the purchase order used in the procurement of materials.

5. Briefly discuss how the purchase order, purchase invoice,and receiving report can be used to assist in controlling cash disbursements for materials acquired.

6. What document is the source for (a) debiting the accounts in the materials ledger, and (b) crediting the accounts in the materials ledger?

7. Briefly discuss how the accounts in the materials ledger can be used as an aid in maintaining appropriate inventory quantities of stock items.

8. How does use of the materials requisition help control the issuance of materials for the storeroom?

9. Discuss the major advantages of a perpetual inventory system over a periodic system for materials.

10. (a) Differentiate between the clock card and the time ticket. (b) Why should the total time reported on an employee's time tickets for a payroll period be compared with the time reported on the employee's clock cards for the same period?

11. Discuss how the predetermined factory overhead rate can be used in job order cost accounting to assist management in pricing jobs.

12. (a) How is a predetermined factory overhead rate determined? (b) Name three common bases used in determining the rate.

13. (a) What is (1) overapplied factory overhead and (2) underapplied factory overhead? (b) If the factory overhead account has a debit balance, was factory overhead underapplied or overapplied? (c) If the factory overhead account has a credit balance at the end of the first month of the fiscal year, where will the amount of this balance be reported on the interim balance sheet?

14. At the end of a fiscal year, there was a relatively minor balance in the factory overhead account. What is the simplest satisfactory procedure for the disposition of the balance in the account?

15. What name is given to the individual accounts in the cost ledger?

16. What document serves as the basis for posting to (a) the direct materials section of the job cost sheet, and (b) the direct labor section of the job cost sheet?

17. Describe the source of the data for debiting Work in Process for (a) direct materials, (b) direct labor, and (c) factory overhead.

18. What account is the controlling account for (a) the materials ledger, (b) the cost ledger, and (c) the finished goods ledger or stock ledger?

**Exercises**

**Exercise 2-1.** The balance of Material F on February 1 and the receipts and issuances during February are as follows:

Balance, February 1, 120 units at $20.00
Received during February:
Feb. 8, 300 units at $21.00
Feb. 15, 240 units at $21.30
Feb. 22, 180 units at $21.60
Issued during February:
Feb. 10, 180 units for Job 231
Feb. 18, 150 units for Job 258
Feb. 27, 210 units for Job 261

Determine the cost of each of the three issuances under a perpetual system, using (a) the first-in, first-out method and (b) the last-in, first-out method.

**Exercise 2-2.** The issuances of materials for the current month are as follows:

| Requisition No. | Material | Job No. | Amount |
|---|---|---|---|
| 365 | W-8 | 714 | $3,640 |
| 366 | D-2 | 706 | 1,876 |
| 367 | N-06 | General factory use | 480 |
| 368 | I-16 | 720 | 2,320 |
| 369 | Q-4 | 707 | 3,564 |

Present the general journal entry to record the issuances of materials.

**Exercise 2-3.** A summary of the time tickets for the current month follows:

| Job. No. | Amount | Job No. | Amount |
|---|---|---|---|
| 901 | $1,120 | Indirect labor | $1,280 |
| 902 | 3,020 | 904 | 3,120 |
| 903 | 1,850 | 905 | 2,310 |

Present the general journal entry to record the factory labor costs.

**Exercise 2-4.** Wong Company applies factory overhead to jobs on the basis of machine hours in Department 10 and on the basis of direct labor dollars in Department 11. Estimated factory overhead costs, direct labor costs, and machine hours for the year, and actual factory overhead costs, direct labor costs, and machine hours for August are as follows. Departmental accounts are maintained for work in process and factory overhead.

|  | Department 10 | Department 11 |
|---|---|---|
| Estimated factory overhead cost for year.............. | $57,600 | $153,120 |
| Estimated direct labor costs for year.................. |  | $264,000 |
| Estimated machine hours for year .................... | 12,000 hours |  |
| Actual factory overhead costs for August ............. | $ 6,820 | $ 12,820 |
| Actual direct labor costs for August ................. |  | $ 22,500 |
| Actual machine hours for August..................... | 1,350 hours |  |

(a) Determine the factory overhead rate for Department 10. (b) Determine the factory overhead rate for Department 11. (c) Prepare the general journal entry to apply factory overhead to production for August. (d) Determine the balances of the departmental factory overhead accounts as of August 31 and indicate whether the amounts represent overapplied or underapplied factory overhead.

**Exercise 2-5.** The following account appears in the ledger after only part of the postings have been completed for April:

### Work in Process

| Balance, April 1 | 12,250 |
| Direct Materials | 30,820 |
| Direct Labor | 48,180 |
| Factory Overhead | 26,400 |

Jobs finished during April are summarized as follows:

| Job 602.................. | $18,140 | Job 611 ................. | $29,100 |
| Job 608.................. | 32,400 | Job 618 ................. | 18,660 |

(a) Prepare the general journal entry to record the jobs completed and (b) determine the cost of the unfinished jobs at April 30.

**Exercise 2-6.** Chien Enterprises Inc. began manufacturing operations on October 1. Jobs 101 and 102 were completed during the month, and all costs applicable to them were recorded on the related cost sheets. Jobs 103 and 104 are still in process at the end of the month, and all applicable costs except factory overhead have been recorded on the related cost sheets. In addition to the materials and labor charged directly to the jobs, $1,050 of indirect materials and $1,890 of indirect labor were used during the month. The cost sheets for the four jobs entering production during the month are as follows, in summary form:

| Job 101 | | Job 102 | |
| --- | --- | --- | --- |
| Direct materials........... | 8,750 | Direct materials.......... | 15,680 |
| Direct labor.............. | 7,000 | Direct labor.............. | 11,200 |
| Factory overhead......... | 3,500 | Factory overhead........ | 5,600 |
| Total.................. | 19,250 | Total................. | 32,480 |

| Job 103 | | Job 104 | |
| --- | --- | --- | --- |
| Direct materials........... | 11,900 | Direct materials.......... | 3,080 |
| Direct labor.............. | 9,800 | Direct labor.............. | 4,340 |
| Factory overhead......... | | Factory overhead........ | |

Prepare an entry, in general journal form, to record each of the following operations for the month (one entry for each operation):
(a) Direct and indirect materials used.
(b) Direct and indirect labor used.
(c) Factory overhead applied (a single overhead rate is used, based on direct labor cost).
(d) Completion of Jobs 101 and 102.

**Problems**
*(Problems in Appendix B: 2-1B, 2-2B, 2-4B, 2-5B.)*

**Problem 2-1A.** Chatham Printing Company uses a job order cost system. The following data summarize the operations related to production for March, the first month of operations:
(a) Materials purchased on account, $69,850.
(b) Materials requisitioned and factory labor used:

| | Materials | Factory Labor |
| --- | --- | --- |
| Job 101............................... | $ 9,900 | $5,940 |
| Job 102............................... | 6,490 | 4,400 |
| Job 103............................... | 8,700 | 3,190 |
| Job 104............................... | 13,090 | 8,360 |
| Job 105............................... | 7,150 | 4,180 |
| Job 106............................... | 4,180 | 1,870 |
| For general factory use ................. | 1,490 | 1,100 |

(c) Factory overhead costs incurred on account, $13,250.
(d) Depreciation of machinery and equipment, $4,850.
(e) The factory overhead rate is 80% of direct labor cost.
(f) Jobs completed: 101, 102, 104, and 105.
(g) Jobs 101, 102, and 104 were shipped and customers were billed for $30,800, $19,450, and $38,300 respectively.

Instructions:
(1) Prepare entries in general journal form to record the foregoing summarized operations.

(2) Open T accounts for Work in Process and Finished Goods and post the appropriate entries, using the identifying letters as dates. Insert memorandum account balances as of the end of the month.
(3) Prepare a schedule of unfinished jobs to support the balance in the work in process account.
(4) Prepare a schedule of completed jobs on hand to support the balance in the finished goods account.

*(If the working papers correlating with the textbook are not used, omit Problem 2-2A.)*

√Problem 2-2A. Graco Furniture Company repairs, refinishes, and reupholsters furniture. A job order cost system was installed recently to facilitate (1) the determination of price quotations to prospective customers, (2) the determination of actual costs incurred on each job, and (3) cost reductions.

In response to a prospective customer's request for a price quotation on a job, the estimated cost data are inserted on an unnumbered job cost sheet. If the offer is accepted, a number is assigned to the job and the costs incurred are recorded in the usual manner on the job cost sheet. After the job is completed, reasons for the variances between the estimated and actual costs are noted on the sheet. The data are then available to management in evaluating the efficiency of operations and in preparing quotations on future jobs.

On May 5, an estimate of $510 for reupholstering a couch was given to Jean Ladd. The estimate was based upon the following data:

| | |
|---|---:|
| Estimated direct materials: | |
| 14 meters at $12 per meter.............................. | $168 |
| Estimated direct labor: | |
| 10 hours at $15 per hour.................................. | 150 |
| Estimated factory overhead (60% of direct labor cost).......... | 90 |
| Total estimated costs ...................................... | $408 |
| Markup (25% of production costs) ......................... | 102 |
| Total estimate.......................................... | $510 |

On May 9, the couch was picked up from the residence of Jean Ladd, 1460 Madison Drive, Clearwater, with a commitment to return it on May 20.

The job was completed on May 18. The related materials requisitions and time tickets are summarized as follows:

| Materials Requisition No. | Description | Amount |
|---|---|---|
| 1215 | 10 meters at $12 | $120 |
| 1219 | 5 meters at $12 | 60 |

| Time Ticket No. | Description | Amount |
|---|---|---|
| 3140 | 4 hours at $15 | $ 60 |
| 3146 | 8 hours at $15 | 120 |

Instructions:
(1) Complete that portion of the job order cost sheet that would be completed when the estimate is given to the customer.

(2) Assign number 84-5-6 to the job, record the costs incurred, and complete the job order cost sheet. In commenting upon the variances between actual costs and estimated costs, assume that 1 meter of materials was spoiled, the factory overhead rate has been proved to be satisfactory, and an inexperienced employee performed the work.

**Problem 2-3A.** The trial balance of Y. M. McInnis Inc., at the beginning of the current fiscal year, is as follows:

Y. M. McInnis Inc.
Trial Balance
October 1, 19--

| | | |
|---|---:|---:|
| Cash | 38,610 | |
| Accounts Receivable | 58,550 | |
| Finished Goods | 55,380 | |
| Work in Process | 20,300 | |
| Materials | 26,840 | |
| Prepaid Expenses | 13,240 | |
| Plant Assets | 485,200 | |
| Accumulated Depreciation — Plant Assets | | 274,640 |
| Accounts Payable | | 19,800 |
| Wages Payable | | — |
| Common Stock | | 300,000 |
| Retained Earnings | | 103,680 |
| Sales | | — |
| Cost of Goods Sold | — | |
| Factory Overhead | — | |
| Selling Expenses | — | |
| General Expenses | — | |
| | 698,120 | 698,120 |

Transactions completed during October and adjustments required on October 31 are summarized as follows:

(a) Materials purchased on account. . . . . . . . . . . . . .           $ 22,900

(b) Materials requisitioned for factory use:

| | | |
|---|---:|---:|
| Direct | $ 21,500 | |
| Indirect | 270 | 21,770 |

(c) Factory labor costs incurred:

| | | |
|---|---:|---:|
| Direct | $ 10,800 | |
| Indirect | 1,520 | 12,320 |

(d) Other costs and expenses incurred on account:

| | | |
|---|---:|---:|
| Factory overhead | $ 5,610 | |
| Selling expenses | 5,480 | |
| General expenses | 4,000 | 15,090 |

(e) Cash disbursed:

| | | |
|---|---:|---:|
| Accounts payable | $ 41,000 | |
| Wages payable | 11,080 | 52,080 |

(f) Depreciation charged:
    Factory equipment........................              $3,600
    Office equipment .........................                 300

(g) Prepaid expenses expired:
    Chargeable to factory ....................   $   540
    Chargeable to selling expenses ............     120
    Chargeable to general expenses ...........     115         775

(h) Applied factory overhead at a predeter-
    mined rate:
    110% of direct labor cost.

(i) Total cost of jobs completed ................            43,000

(j) Sales, all on account:
    Selling price.............................            56,000
    Cost price ..............................            38,600

(k) Cash received on account...................            57,000

Instructions:

(1) Open T accounts and record the initial balances indicated in the October 1 trial balance, identifying each as "Bal."
(2) Record the transactions directly in the accounts, using the identifying letters in place of dates.
(3) Prepare an income statement for the month ended October 31, 19--.
(4) Prepare a retained earnings statement for the month ended October 31, 19--.
(5) Prepare a balance sheet as of October 31, 19--.

**Problem 2-4A.** The trial balance of the general ledger of Lafayette Corporation as of March 31, the end of the first month of the current fiscal year, is as follows:

Lafayette Corporation
Trial Balance
March 31, 19--

| | | |
|---|---:|---:|
| Cash ......................................... | 109,680 | |
| Accounts Receivable................................ | 222,360 | |
| Finished Goods..................................... | 212,760 | |
| Work in Process .................................... | 73,680 | |
| Materials.......................................... | 88,560 | |
| Plant Assets....................................... | 949,200 | |
| Accumulated Depreciation—Plant Assets .............. | | 423,480 |
| Accounts Payable.................................... | | 159,560 |
| Wages Payable...................................... | | 18,000 |
| Capital Stock....................................... | | 720,000 |
| Retained Earnings ................................... | | 300,780 |
| Sales............................................. | | 318,480 |
| Cost of Goods Sold ................................. | 236,160 | |
| Factory Overhead................................... | 1,100 | |
| Selling and General Expenses........................ | 46,800 | |
| | 1,940,300 | 1,940,300 |

As of the same date, balances in the accounts of selected subsidiary ledgers are as follows:

Finished goods ledger:
    Commodity A, 2,640 units, $23,760; Commodity B, 6,000 units, $132,000;
    Commodity C, 3,000 units, $57,000.
Cost ledger:
    Job 318, $73,680.
Materials ledger:
    Material X, $48,480; Material Y, $37,920; Material Z, $2,160.

The transactions completed during April are summarized as follows:

(a) Materials were purchased on account as follows:

| | |
|---|---:|
| Material X | $66,000 |
| Material Y | 46,200 |
| Material Z | 1,800 |

(b) Materials were requisitioned from stores as follows:

| | |
|---|---:|
| Job 318, Material X, $25,440; Material Y, $20,160. | $45,600 |
| Job 319, Material X, $32,400; Material Y, $28,560 | 60,960 |
| Job 320, Material X, $16,560; Material Y, $6,720. | 23,280 |
| For general factory use, Material Z | 1,920 |

(c) Time tickets for the month were chargeable as follows:

| | | | |
|---|---:|---|---:|
| Job 318 | $23,520 | Job 320 | $19,680 |
| Job 319 | 20,160 | Indirect labor | 7,200 |

(d) Factory payroll checks for $77,280 were issued.
(e) Various factory overhead charges of $26,850 were incurred on account.
(f) Depreciation of $10,800 on factory plant and equipment was recorded.
(g) Factory overhead was applied to jobs at 75% of direct labor cost.
(h) Jobs completed during the month were as follows: Job 318 produced 6,720 units of Commodity B; Job 319 produced 4,800 units of Commodity C.
(i) Selling and general expenses of $45,840 were incurred on account.
(j) Payments on account were $171,600.
(k) Total sales on account were $295,080. The goods sold were as follows (use first-in, first-out method): 1,200 units of Commodity A; 6,480 units of Commodity B; 3,600 units of Commodity C.
(l) Cash of $301,200 was received on accounts receivable.

Instructions:

(1) Open T accounts for the general ledger, the finished goods ledger, the cost ledger, and the materials ledger. Record directly in these accounts the balances as of March 31, identifying them as "Bal." Record the quantities as well as the dollar amounts in the finished goods ledger.
(2) Prepare entries in general journal form to record the April transactions. After recording each transaction, post to the T accounts, using the identifying letters as dates. When posting to the finished goods ledger, record quantities as well as dollar amounts.
(3) Prepare a trial balance.
(4) Prepare schedules of the account balances in the finished goods ledger, the cost ledger, and the materials ledger.
(5) Prepare an income statement for the two months ended April 30.

**Problem 2-5A.** Following are selected accounts for Fabco Products. For the purposes of this problem, some of the debits and credits have been omitted.

### Accounts Receivable

| May | 1 | Balance | 59,500 | May 31 | Collections | 127,300 |
|-----|---|---------|--------|--------|-------------|---------|
|     | 31 | Sales  | (A)    |        |             |         |

### Materials

| May | 1 | Balance | 14,350 | May 31 | Requisitions | (B) |
|-----|---|---------|--------|--------|--------------|-----|
|     | 31 | Purchases | 21,070 |      |              |     |

### Work In Process

| May | 1 | Balance | 26,250 | May 31 | Goods finished | (E) |
|-----|---|---------|--------|--------|----------------|-----|
|     | 31 | Direct materials | (C) | | | |
|     | 31 | Direct labor | 28,000 | | | |
|     | 31 | Factory overhead | (D) | | | |

### Finished Goods

| May | 1 | Balance | 48,650 | May 31 | Cost of goods sold | (G) |
|-----|---|---------|--------|--------|--------------------|-----|
|     | 31 | Goods finished | (F) | | | |

### Factory Overhead

| May | 1 | Balance | 140 | May 31 | Applied (75% of | |
|-----|---|---------|-----|--------|------------------|---|
|     | 1–31 | Costs incurred | 22,100 | | direct labor cost) | (H) |

### Cost of Goods Sold

| May 31 | (I) |
|--------|-----|

### Sales

| | May 31 | (J) |
|--|--------|-----|

Selected balances at May 31:

| | |
|--|--|
| Accounts receivable . . . . . . . . . . . . . . . . . . . . . . | $65,000 |
| Finished goods . . . . . . . . . . . . . . . . . . . . . . . . . . | 30,100 |
| Work in process . . . . . . . . . . . . . . . . . . . . . . . . . | 22,260 |
| Materials . . . . . . . . . . . . . . . . . . . . . . . . . . . . . . | 11,760 |

Materials requisitions for May included $700 of materials issued for general factory use. All sales are made on account, terms n/30.

Instructions:

(1) Determine the amounts represented by the letters (A) through (J), presenting your computations.

(2) Determine the amount of factory overhead overapplied or underapplied as of May 31.

**Mini-Case**

As an assistant cost accountant for Hanratty Industries, you have been assigned to review the activity base for the predetermined factory overhead rate. The president, G. H. Hanratty, has expressed concern that the over- or underapplied overhead has fluctuated excessively over the years.

An analysis of the company's operations and use of the current overhead base (direct materials usage) have narrowed the possible alternative overhead bases to direct labor cost and machine hours. For the past five years, the following data have been gathered:

|  | 1984 | 1983 | 1982 | 1981 | 1980 |
|---|---|---|---|---|---|
| Actual overhead...... | $ 580,000 | $ 540,000 | $ 640,000 | $ 490,000 | $ 450,000 |
| Applied overhead .... | 575,000 | 565,000 | 600,000 | 500,000 | 440,000 |
| (Over)underapplied overhead........ | $ 5,000 | $ (25,000) | $ 40,000 | $ (10,000) | $ 10,000 |
| Direct labor cost ..... | $1,800,000 | $1,400,000 | $2,100,000 | $1,150,000 | $1,050,000 |
| Machine hours ....... | 363,500 | 340,000 | 402,000 | 302,000 | 280,000 |

Instructions:

(1) Calculate a predetermined factory overhead rate for each alternative base, assuming that the rates would have been determined by relating the amount of factory overhead for the past five years to the base.

(2) For each of the past five years, determine the over- or underapplied overhead, based on the two predetermined overhead rates developed in (1).

(3) Which predetermined overhead rate would you recommend? Discuss the basis for your recommendation.

# 3

# Process Cost Systems

**CHAPTER OBJECTIVES**

*Distinguish process cost accounting systems from job order cost accounting systems.*

*Describe and illustrate a process cost accounting system, including the preparation of a cost of production report.*

3

**CHAPTER**

**PROCESS COST
AND JOB
ORDER COST
SYSTEMS
DISTINGUISHED**

In many industries, job orders as described in Chapter 2 are not suitable for scheduling production and accumulating the manufacturing costs. Companies manufacturing cement, flour, or paint, for example, do so on a continuous basis. The principal product is a homogeneous mass rather than a collection of distinct units. No useful purpose would be served by maintaining job orders for particular amounts of a product as the material passes through the several stages of production.

Many of the methods, procedures, and managerial applications presented in the preceding chapter in the discussion of job order cost systems apply equally to process cost systems. For example, perpetual inventory accounts with subsidiary ledgers for materials, work in process, and finished goods are requisites of both systems. In job order cost accounting, however, the costs of direct materials, direct labor, and factory overhead are charged directly to job orders. In process cost accounting, the costs are charged to processing departments, and the cost of a finished unit is determined by dividing the total cost incurred in each process by the number of units produced. Since all goods produced in a department are identical units, it is not necessary to classify production into job orders.

In factories with departmentalized operations, costs are accumulated in factory overhead and work in process accounts maintained for each department. If there is only one processing department in a factory, the cost accounting procedures are simple. The manufacturing cost elements are charged to the single work in process account, and the unit cost of the finished product is determined by dividing the total cost by the number of units produced.

When the manufacturing procedure requires a sequence of different processes, the output of Process 1 becomes the direct materials of Process 2, the output of Process 2 becomes the direct materials of Process 3, and so on until the finished product emerges. Additional direct materials requisitioned from stores may also be introduced during subsequent processes.

A work in process account for a departmentalized factory is illustrated as follows. In this illustration, the total cost of $96,000 is divided by the output, 10,000 units, to obtain a unit cost of $9.60.

Work in Process — Assembly Department

| Direct materials | 32,000 | To Sanding Dept., 10,000 units | 96,000 |
|---|---|---|---|
| Direct labor | 40,000 | Cost per unit: | |
| Factory overhead | 24,000 | $96,000 ÷ 10,000 = $9.60 | |
| | 96,000 | | 96,000 |

**SERVICE
DEPARTMENTS
AND PROCESS
COSTS**

In a factory with several processes, there may be one or more service departments that do not process the materials directly. Examples of service departments are the factory office, the power plant, and the maintenance and repair shop. These departments perform services for the benefit of other production departments.

The costs that they incur, therefore, are part of the total manufacturing costs and must be charged to the processing departments.

The services performed by a service department give rise to internal transactions with the processing departments benefited. These internal transactions are recorded periodically in order to charge the factory overhead accounts of the processing departments with their share of the costs incurred by the service departments. The period usually chosen is a month, although a different period of time may be used. To illustrate, assume that the Power Department produced 500 000 kilowatt-hours during the month at a total cost of $30,000, or 6¢ per kilowatt-hour ($30,000 ÷ 500 000). The factory overhead accounts for the departments that used the power are accordingly charged for power at the 6¢ rate. Assuming that during the month the Assembly Department used 200 000 kwh and the Sanding Department used 300 000 kwh, the accounts affected by the interdepartmental transfer of cost would appear as follows:

SERVICE DEPARTMENT COSTS CHARGED TO PROCESSING DEPARTMENTS

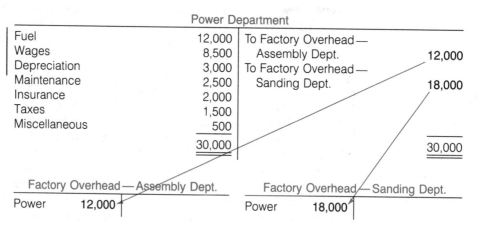

| Power Department | | | |
|---|---|---|---|
| Fuel | 12,000 | To Factory Overhead— Assembly Dept. | 12,000 |
| Wages | 8,500 | | |
| Depreciation | 3,000 | To Factory Overhead— Sanding Dept. | 18,000 |
| Maintenance | 2,500 | | |
| Insurance | 2,000 | | |
| Taxes | 1,500 | | |
| Miscellaneous | 500 | | |
| | 30,000 | | 30,000 |

| Factory Overhead—Assembly Dept. | | Factory Overhead—Sanding Dept. | |
|---|---|---|---|
| Power 12,000 | | Power 18,000 | |

Some service departments render services to other service departments. For example, the power department may supply electric current to light the factory office and to operate data processing equipment. At the same time, the factory office provides general supervision for the power department, maintains its payroll records, buys its fuel, and so on. In such cases, the costs of the department rendering the greatest service to other service departments may be distributed first, despite the fact that it receives benefits from other service departments.

**PROCESSING COSTS**

The accumulated costs transferred from preceding departments and the costs of direct materials and direct labor incurred in each processing department are debited to the related work in process account. Each work in process account is also debited for the factory overhead applied. The costs incurred are summarized periodically, usually at the end of the month. The costs related to the output of each department during the month are then transferred to the next processing department or to Finished Goods, as the case may be. This flow of costs through a work in process account is illustrated as follows:

| Work in Process — Sanding Department | | | | |
|---|---|---|---|---|
| 10,000 units at $9.60 | | | To Polishing Dept., 10,000 units | 160,000 |
| from Assembly Dept. | | 96,000 | Cost per unit: | |
| Direct labor | 36,800 | | $160,000 ÷ 10,000 = $16 | |
| Factory overhead | 27,200 | 64,000 | | |
| | | 160,000 | | 160,000 |

The three debits in the preceding account may be grouped into two separate categories: (1) direct materials or partially processed materials received from another department, which in this case is composed of 10,000 units received from the Assembly Department, with a total cost of $96,000, and (2) direct labor and factory overhead applied in the Sanding Department, which in this case totaled $64,000. This second group of costs is called the processing cost.

Again referring to the illustration, all of the 10,000 units were completely processed in the Sanding Department and were passed on to the Polishing Department. The $16 unit cost of the product transferred to the Polishing Department is made up of Assembly Department cost of $9.60 ($96,000 ÷ 10,000 units) and processing cost of $6.40 ($64,000 ÷ 10,000 units) incurred in the Sanding Department.

**INVENTORIES OF PARTIALLY PROCESSED MATERIALS**

In the preceding illustration, all materials entering a process were completely processed at the end of the accounting period. In such a case, the determination of unit costs is quite simple. The total of costs transferred from other departments, direct materials, direct labor, and factory overhead charged to a department, is divided by the number of units completed and passed on to the next department or to finished goods. Often, however, some partially processed materials remain in various stages of production in a department at the end of a period. In this case, the costs in work in process must be allocated between the units that have been completed and transferred to the next process or to finished goods and those that are only partially completed and remain within the department.

To allocate direct materials and transferred costs between the output completed and transferred to the next process and inventory of goods within the department, it is necessary to determine the manner in which materials are placed in production. For some products, all materials must be on hand before any work begins. For other products, materials may be added to production in about the same proportion as processing costs are incurred. In still other situations, materials may enter the process at relatively few points, which may or may not be evenly spaced throughout the process.

To allocate processing costs between the output completed and transferred to the next process and the inventory of goods within the process, it is necessary to determine (1) the number of *equivalent units* of production during the period and (2) the *processing cost per equivalent unit* for the same period. The equivalent units of production are the number of units that could have been manufactured from start to finish during the period. To illustrate, assume that there is no inventory of goods in process in a certain processing department at the beginning of the period, that 1,000 units of materials enter the process during the period, and that at the end of the period all of the units are 75% completed. The equivalent production in the processing department for the period would be 750 units (75% of 1,000). Assuming further that the processing costs incurred during the period totaled $15,000, the processing cost per equivalent unit would be $20 ($15,000 ÷ 750).

Usually there is an inventory of partially processed units in the department at the beginning of the period. These units are normally completed during the period and transferred to the next department along with units started and completed in the current period. Other units started in the period are only partially processed and thus make up the ending inventory. To illustrate the computation of equivalent units under such circumstances, the following data are assumed for the Polishing Department:

| | |
|---|---|
| Inventory within Polishing Department on March 1........ | 600 units, ⅓ completed |
| Completed in Polishing Department and transferred to finished goods during March ....................... | 9,800 units, completed |
| Inventory within Polishing Department on March 31 ...... | 800 units, ⅖ completed |

The equivalent units of production are determined as follows:

<table>
<tr><td rowspan="4">DETERMINATION OF EQUIVALENT UNITS OF PRODUCTION</td></tr>
</table>

| | | |
|---|---|---|
| To process units in inventory on March 1.......... 600 units × ⅔........ | | 400 |
| To process units started and completed in March .. 9,800 units − 600 units | | 9,200 |
| To process units in inventory on March 31........ 800 units × ⅖........ | | 320 |
| Equivalent units of production in March............................... | | 9,920 |

The 9,920 equivalent units of production represent the number of units that would have been produced if there had been no inventories within the process either at the beginning or at the end of the period.

Continuing with the illustration, the next step is to allocate the costs incurred in the Polishing Department between the units completed during March and those remaining in process at the end of the month. If materials (including transferred costs) were used and processing costs were incurred uniformly throughout the month, the total costs of the process would be divided by 9,920 units to obtain the unit cost. On the other hand, if all materials were introduced at the beginning of the process, the full materials cost per unit must be assigned to the uncompleted units. The processing costs would then be allocated to the finished and the uncompleted units on the basis of equivalent units of production. Entries in the following account are based on the latter assumption:

ACCOUNT   WORK IN PROCESS—POLISHING DEPARTMENT     ACCOUNT NO.

| Date | | Item | Debit | Credit | Balance Debit | Balance Credit |
|---|---|---|---|---|---|---|
| Mar. | 1 | Bal., 600 units, ⅓ completed | | | 10,200 | |
| | 31 | Sanding Dept., 10,000 units at $16 | 160,000 | | 170,200 | |
| | 31 | Direct labor | 26,640 | | 196,840 | |
| | 31 | Factory overhead | 18,000 | | 214,840 | |
| | 31 | Goods finished, 9,800 units | | 200,600 | | |
| | 31 | Bal., 800 units, ⅖ completed | | | 14,240 | |

The processing costs incurred in the Polishing Department during March total $44,640 ($26,640 + $18,000). The equivalent units of production for March, determined above, is 9,920. The processing cost per equivalent unit is therefore $4.50 ($44,640 ÷ 9,920). Of the $214,840 debited to the Polishing Department, $200,600 was transferred to Finished Goods and $14,240 remained in the account as work in process inventory. The computation of the allocations to finished goods and to inventory is as follows:

ALLOCATION OF DEPARTMENTAL CHARGES TO FINISHED GOODS AND INVENTORY

### Goods Finished During March

| | |
|---|---|
| 600 units: Inventory on March 1, ⅓ completed............... | $ 10,200 |
| Processing cost in March: | |
| 600 × ⅔, or 400 units at $4.50................. | 1,800 |
| Total........................................ | $ 12,000 |
| (Unit cost: $12,000 ÷ 600 = $20) | |
| 9,200 units: Materials cost in March, at $16 per unit........... | $147,200 |
| Processing cost in March: | |
| 9,200 at $4.50 per unit........................ | 41,400 |
| Total........................................ | 188,600 |
| (Unit cost: $188,600 ÷ 9,200 = $20.50) | |
| 9,800 units: Goods finished during March.................... | $200,600 |

### Polishing Department Inventory on March 31

| | |
|---|---|
| 800 units: Materials cost in March, at $16 per unit........... | $ 12,800 |
| Processing cost in March: | |
| 800 × ⅖, or 320 at $4.50..................... | 1,440 |
| 800 units: Polishing Department inventory on March 31....... | $ 14,240 |

COST OF PRODUCTION REPORT

A report prepared periodically for each processing department summarizes (1) the units for which the department is accountable and the disposition of these units and (2) the costs charged to the department and the allocation of these costs. This report, termed the cost of production report, may be used as the source of the computation of unit production costs and the allocation of the processing costs in the general ledger to the finished and the uncompleted units. More importantly, the report is used to control costs. Each department head is held responsible for the units entering production and the costs incurred in the department. Any differences in unit product costs from one month to another are studied carefully and the causes of significant differences are determined.

The cost of production report based on the data presented in the preceding section for the Polishing Department is shown on page 50.

JOINT PRODUCTS AND BY-PRODUCTS

In some manufacturing processes, more than one product is produced. In processing cattle, for example, the meat packer produces dressed beef, hides, and other products. In processing logs, the lumber mill produces several grades of lumber in addition to scraps and sawdust. When the output of a manufacturing process consists of two or more different products, the products are either joint products or by-products.

COST OF
PRODUCTION
REPORT

*or*

*process cost
summary*

**Haworth Manufacturing Company**
**Cost of Production Report—Polishing Department**
**For the Month Ended March 31, 19--**

Quantities:
  Charged to production:
    In process, March 1 ............................ 600
    Received from Sanding Department ............... 10,000
    Total units to be accounted for ............... 10,600

  Units accounted for:
    Transferred to finished goods .................. 9,800
    In process, March 31 ........................... 800
    Total units accounted for ...................... 10,600

Costs:
  Charged to production:
    In process, March 1 ........................... $ 10,200

    March costs:
      Direct materials from Sanding Department ($16 per
        unit) ..................................... 160,000

      Processing costs:
        Direct labor .......................... $ 26,640
        Factory overhead ...................... 18,000
        Total processing costs ($4.50 per unit) ...... 44,640
    Total costs to be accounted for ................ $214,840

Costs allocated as follows:
  Transferred to finished goods:
    600 units at $20 .............................. $ 12,000
    9,200 units at $20.50 ......................... 188,600
    Total cost of finished goods .................. $200,600

  In process, March 31:
    Direct materials (800 units at $16) ........... $ 12,800
    Processing costs (800 units × ⅖ × $4.50) ...... 1,440
    Total cost of inventory in process, March 31 ... 14,240
  Total costs accounted for ...................... $214,840

Computations:
  Equivalent units of production:
    To process units in inventory on March 1:
      600 units × ⅔ ............................ 400
    To process units started and completed in March:
      9,800 units − 600 units ................... 9,200
    To process units in inventory on March 31:
      800 units × ⅖ ............................ 320
    Equivalent units of production ................ 9,920
  Unit processing cost:
    $44,640 ÷ 9,920 ............................... $ 4.50

When two or more goods of significant value are produced from a single principal direct material, the products are termed joint products. Similarly, the costs incurred in the manufacture of joint products are called joint costs. Common examples of joint products are gasoline, naphtha, kerosene, paraffin, benzine, and other related goods, all of which come from the processing of crude oil.

If one of the products resulting from a process has little value in relation to the main product or joint products, it is known as a by-product. The emergence of a by-product is only incidental to the manufacture of the main product or joint products. By-products may be leftover materials, such as sawdust and scraps of wood in a lumber mill, or they may be separated from the material at the beginning of production, as in the case of cottonseed from raw cotton.

**Accounting for Joint Products**

In management decisions concerning the production and sale of joint products, only the relationship of the total revenue to be derived from the entire group to their total production cost is relevant. Nothing is to be gained from an allocation of joint costs to each product because one product cannot be produced without the others. A decision to produce a joint product is in effect a decision to produce all of the products.

Since joint products come from the processing of a common parent material, the assignment of cost to each separate product cannot be based on actual expenditures. It is impossible to determine the amount of cost incurred in the manufacture of each separate product. However, for purposes of inventory valuation, it is necessary to allocate joint costs among the joint products.

One method of allocation commonly used is the market (sales) value method. Its main feature is the assignment of costs to the different products according to their relative sales values. To illustrate, assume that 10,000 units of Product X and 50,000 units of Product Y were produced at a total cost of $63,000. The sales values of the two products and the allocation of the joint costs are as follows:

**ALLOCATION OF JOINT COSTS**

| Joint Costs | Joint Product | Units Produced | Sales Value per Unit | Total Sales Value |
|---|---|---|---|---|
| $63,000 | {X | 10,000 | $3.00 | $30,000 |
| | {Y | 50,000 | 1.20 | 60,000 |
| Total sales value | | | | $90,000 |

Allocation of joint costs:

X: $\frac{30,000}{90,000} \times \$63,000$ .................................... $21,000

Y: $\frac{60,000}{90,000} \times \$63,000$ .................................... 42,000

Unit cost:

X: $21,000 ÷ 10,000 units ................................. $2.10

Y: $42,000 ÷ 50,000 units ................................. .84

**Accounting for By-Products**

The amount of manufacturing cost usually assigned to a by-product is the sales value of the by-product reduced by any additional costs necessary to complete and sell it. The amount of cost thus determined is removed from the proper work in process account and transferred to a finished goods inventory account. To illustrate, assume that for a certain period the costs accumulated in Department 4 total

$24,400, and that during the same period of time 1,000 units of by-product B, having an estimated value of $200, emerge from the processing in Department 4. Finished Goods—Product B would be debited for $200 and Work in Process—Department 4 would be credited for the same amount, as illustrated in the following accounts:

| Work in Process—Department 4 | | Finished Goods—Product B | |
|---|---|---|---|
| 24,400 | 200 ─────────→ | 200 | |

The accounting for the manufacturing costs remaining in the work in process account and for sale of the by-product would follow the usual procedures.

ILLUSTRATION OF PROCESS COST ACCOUNTING

To illustrate further the basic procedures of the process costing system, assume that Conway Company manufactures Product A. The manufacturing activity begins in Department 1, where all materials enter production. The materials remain in Department 1 for a relatively short time, and there is usually no inventory of work in process in that department at the end of the accounting period. From Department 1, the materials are transferred to Department 2. In Department 2, there are usually inventories at the end of the accounting period. Separate factory overhead accounts are maintained for Departments 1 and 2. Factory overhead is applied at 80% and 50% of direct labor cost for Departments 1 and 2 respectively. There are two service departments, Maintenance and Power.

The trial balance of the general ledger on January 1, the first day of the fiscal year, is as follows:

### Conway Company
### Trial Balance
### January 1, 19--

| | | |
|---|---|---|
| Cash | 39,400 | |
| Accounts Receivable | 45,000 | |
| Finished Goods—Product A (1,000 units at $36.50) | 36,500 | |
| Work in Process—Department 2 (800 units, ½ completed) | 24,600 | |
| Materials | 32,000 | |
| Prepaid Expenses | 6,150 | |
| Plant Assets | 510,000 | |
| Accumulated Depreciation—Plant Assets | | 295,000 |
| Accounts Payable | | 51,180 |
| Wages Payable | | 3,400 |
| Common Stock | | 250,000 |
| Retained Earnings | | 94,070 |
| | 693,650 | 693,650 |

To reduce the illustrative entries to a manageable number and to avoid repetition, the transactions and the adjustments for January are stated as summaries. In practice, the transactions would be recorded from day to day in various journals. The descriptions of the transactions, followed in each case by the entry in general journal form, are as follows:

*(a) Materials purchased and prepaid expenses incurred.*

| *Entry:* Materials. . . . . . . . . . . . . . . . . . . . . . . . . . . . . . . . | 80,500 | |
|---|---|---|
| Prepaid Expenses . . . . . . . . . . . . . . . . . . . . . . . . | 3,300 | |
| Accounts Payable . . . . . . . . . . . . . . . . . . . . . . | | 83,800 |

*(b) Materials requisitioned for use.*

| *Entry:* Maintenance Department. . . . . . . . . . . . . . . . . . . | 1,200 | |
|---|---|---|
| Power Department. . . . . . . . . . . . . . . . . . . . . . . . | 6,000 | |
| Factory Overhead — Department 1 . . . . . . . . . . | 3,720 | |
| Factory Overhead — Department 2 . . . . . . . . . . | 2,700 | |
| Work in Process — Department 1 . . . . . . . . . . . . | 58,500 | |
| Materials. . . . . . . . . . . . . . . . . . . . . . . . . . . . . . | | 72,120 |

*(c) Factory labor used.*

| *Entry:* Maintenance Department. . . . . . . . . . . . . . . . . . . | 3,600 | |
|---|---|---|
| Power Department. . . . . . . . . . . . . . . . . . . . . . . . | 4,500 | |
| Factory Overhead — Department 1 . . . . . . . . . . | 2,850 | |
| Factory Overhead — Department 2 . . . . . . . . . . | 2,100 | |
| Work in Process — Department 1 . . . . . . . . . . . . | 24,900 | |
| Work in Process — Department 2 . . . . . . . . . . . . | 37,800 | |
| Wages Payable. . . . . . . . . . . . . . . . . . . . . . . . | | 75,750 |

*(d) Other costs incurred.*

| *Entry:* Maintenance Department. . . . . . . . . . . . . . . . . . . | 600 | |
|---|---|---|
| Power Department. . . . . . . . . . . . . . . . . . . . . . . . | 900 | |
| Factory Overhead — Department 1 . . . . . . . . . . | 1,800 | |
| Factory Overhead — Department 2 . . . . . . . . . . | 1,200 | |
| Selling Expenses . . . . . . . . . . . . . . . . . . . . . . . | 15,000 | |
| General Expenses . . . . . . . . . . . . . . . . . . . . . . | 13,500 | |
| Accounts Payable . . . . . . . . . . . . . . . . . . . . . . | | 33,000 |

*(e) Expiration of prepaid expenses.*

| *Entry:* Maintenance Department. . . . . . . . . . . . . . . . . . . | 300 | |
|---|---|---|
| Power Department. . . . . . . . . . . . . . . . . . . . . . . . | 750 | |
| Factory Overhead — Department 1 . . . . . . . . . . | 1,350 | |
| Factory Overhead — Department 2 . . . . . . . . . . | 1,050 | |
| Selling Expenses . . . . . . . . . . . . . . . . . . . . . . . | 900 | |
| General Expenses . . . . . . . . . . . . . . . . . . . . . . | 600 | |
| Prepaid Expenses . . . . . . . . . . . . . . . . . . . . . . | | 4,950 |

*(f) Depreciation.*

| *Entry:* Maintenance Department. . . . . . . . . . . . . . . . . . . | 300 | |
|---|---|---|
| Power Department. . . . . . . . . . . . . . . . . . . . . . . . | 1,050 | |
| Factory Overhead — Department 1 . . . . . . . . . . | 1,800 | |
| Factory Overhead — Department 2 . . . . . . . . . . | 2,700 | |
| Selling Expenses . . . . . . . . . . . . . . . . . . . . . . . | 600 | |
| General Expenses . . . . . . . . . . . . . . . . . . . . . . | 300 | |
| Accumulated Depreciation — Plant Assets . . . | | 6,750 |

*(g) Distribution of Maintenance Department costs.*

*Entry:* Power Department......................... 300
Factory Overhead — Department 1 .......... 2,700
Factory Overhead — Department 2 .......... 3,000
    Maintenance Department................. 6,000

*(h) Distribution of Power Department costs.*

*Entry:* Factory Overhead — Department 1 .......... 5,400
Factory Overhead — Department 2 .......... 8,100
    Power Department....................... 13,500

*(i) Application of factory overhead costs to work in process.*
The predetermined rates were 80% and 50% of direct labor cost for Departments 1 and 2 respectively. See transaction (c) for the monthly direct labor costs.

*Entry:* Work in Process — Department 1 ............. 19,920
Work in Process — Department 2 ............. 18,900
    Factory Overhead — Department 1 ......... 19,920
    Factory Overhead — Department 2 ......... 18,900

*(j) Transfer of production costs from Department 1 to Department 2.*
4,100 units were fully processed, and there is no work in process in Department 1 at the beginning or at the end of the month.

Total costs charged to Department 1:
Direct materials .............................. $ 58,500
Direct labor.................................. 24,900
Factory overhead ............................ 19,920
  Total costs.................................. $103,320

Unit cost of product transferred to Department 2:
$103,320 ÷ 4,100 ........................... $ 25.20

*Entry:* Work in Process — Department 2 ............. 103,320
    Work in Process — Department 1 .......... 103,320

*(k) Transfer of production costs from Department 2 to Finished Goods.*
4,000 units were completed, and the remaining 900 units were ⅔ completed at the end of the month.

Equivalent units of production:
To process units in inventory on January 1:
  800 × ½................................... 400
To process units started and completed in January:
  4,000 − 800.............................. 3,200
To process units in inventory on January 31:
  900 × ⅔................................... 600
Equivalent units of production in January ......... 4,200

Processing costs:

| | |
|---|---:|
| Direct labor (c)................................ | $ 37,800 |
| Factory overhead (i).......................... | 18,900 |
| Total processing costs........................ | $ 56,700 |

Unit processing costs:

| | |
|---|---:|
| $56,700 ÷ 4,200............................. | $    13.50 |

Allocation of costs of Department 2:

Units started in December, completed in January:

| | | |
|---|---:|---:|
| Inventory on January 1, 800 units ½ completed .. | $ 24,600 | |
| Processing costs in January, 400 at $13.50 .... | 5,400 | |
| Total ($30,000 ÷ 800 = $37.50 unit cost) .... | | $ 30,000 |

Units started and completed in January:

| | | |
|---|---:|---:|
| From Department 1, 3,200 units at $25.20 ..... | $ 80,640 | |
| Processing costs, 3,200 at $13.50............. | 43,200 | |
| Total ($123,840 ÷ 3,200 = $38.70 unit cost) ... | | 123,840 |
| Total transferred to Product A............... | | $153,840 |

Units started in January, ⅔ completed:

| | | |
|---|---:|---:|
| From Department 1, 900 units at $25.20 ....... | $ 22,680 | |
| Processing costs, 600 at $13.50 ............. | 8,100 | |
| Total work in process—Department 2 ....... | | 30,780 |
| Total costs charged to Department 2 ........... | | $184,620 |

| | | |
|---|---:|---:|
| *Entry:* Finished Goods—Product A................. | 153,840 | |
| Work in Process—Department 2........... | | 153,840 |

(*l*) *Cost of goods sold.*

Product A, 3,800 units:

| | |
|---|---:|
| 1,000 units at $36.50......................... | $ 36,500 |
| 800 units at $37.50......................... | 30,000 |
| 2,000 units at $38.70......................... | 77,400 |
| Total cost of goods sold ...................... | $143,900 |

| | | |
|---|---:|---:|
| *Entry:* Cost of Goods Sold........................ | 143,900 | |
| Finished Goods—Product A.............. | | 143,900 |

(*m*) *Sales.*

| | | |
|---|---:|---:|
| *Entry:* Accounts Receivable....................... | 210,500 | |
| Sales.................................... | | 210,500 |

(*n*) *Cash received.*

| | | |
|---|---:|---:|
| *Entry:* Cash...................................... | 200,000 | |
| Accounts Receivable.................... | | 200,000 |

*(o) Cash disbursed.*

*Entry:* Accounts Payable ......................... 120,000
    Wages Payable............................ 72,500
        Cash.................................... 192,500

A chart of the flow of costs from the service and processing department accounts into the finished goods accounts and then to the cost of goods sold account is as follows. Entries in the accounts are identified by letters to aid the comparison with the summary journal entries.

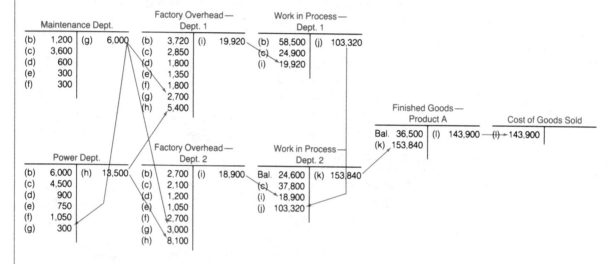

FLOW OF COSTS THROUGH PROCESS COST ACCOUNTS

**Cost of Production Reports**

The cost of production reports for Departments 1 and 2 are as follows:

Conway Company
Cost of Production Report — Department 1
For Month Ended January 31, 19--

Quantities:
    Units charged to production and to be accounted for........... 4,100
    Units accounted for and transferred to Department 2 ........... 4,100

Costs:
    Costs charged to production in January:
        Direct materials....................................... $ 58,500
        Direct labor ......................................... 24,900
        Factory overhead ..................................... 19,920
    Total costs to be accounted for............................ $103,320

    Total costs accounted for and transferred to Department 2 (4,100
        units × $25.20)...................................... $103,320

<br>

**Conway Company**
**Cost of Production Report — Department 2**
**For Month Ended January 31, 19--**

**Quantities:**
Charged to production:
   In process, January 1 .......................... 800
   Received from Department 1 .................. 4,100

Total units to be accounted for ................. 4,900

Units accounted for:
   Transferred to finished goods ................. 4,000
   In process, January 31 ........................ 900

Total units accounted for ..................... 4,900

**Costs:**
Charged to production:
   In process, January 1 ......................... $ 24,600

January costs:
   Direct materials from Department 1 ($25.20 per
   unit) ..................................... 103,320

Processing costs:
   Direct labor ........................... $37,800
   Factory overhead ....................... 18,900
     Total processing costs ($13.50 per unit)..... 56,700

Total costs to be accounted for................. $184,620

Costs allocated as follows:
Transferred to finished goods:
   800 units at $37.50.......................... $ 30,000
   3,200 units at $38.70....................... 123,840
    Total cost of finished goods................. $153,840

In process, January 31:
   Direct materials (900 units at $25.20) ......... $ 22,680
   Processing costs (900 units × 2/3 × $13.50) ... 8,100
    Total cost of inventory in process, January 31.. 30,780

Total costs accounted for..................... $184,620

Computations:
Equivalent units of production:
To process units in inventory on January 1:
   800 units × 1/2 ........................... 400
To process units started and completed in
January:
   4,000 units − 800 units.................... 3,200
To process units in inventory on January 31:
   900 units × 2/3 .......................... 600

Equivalent units of production............... 4,200

Unit processing cost:
$56,700 ÷ 4,200............................. $13.50

**Financial Statements**   The financial statements for process cost systems are similar to those for job order cost systems. To illustrate, the trial balance and the condensed financial statements for Conway Company are presented as follows. Note that the net underapplied factory overhead of $1,650 ($1,950 − $300) on January 31 is reported on the balance sheet as a deferred item.

**Conway Company**
**Trial Balance**
**January 31, 19--**

| | | |
|---|---:|---:|
| Cash. . . . . . . . . . . . . . . . . . . . . . . . . . . . . . . . . . . . . . . . . . . . . . . . | 46,900 | |
| Accounts Receivable . . . . . . . . . . . . . . . . . . . . . . . . . . . . . . . . . | 55,500 | |
| Finished Goods—Product A (1,200 units at $38.70). . . . . . . . . . | 46,440 | |
| Work in Process—Department 2 (900 units, ⅔ completed) . . . . . | 30,780 | |
| Materials . . . . . . . . . . . . . . . . . . . . . . . . . . . . . . . . . . . . . . . . . . . | 40,380 | |
| Prepaid Expenses . . . . . . . . . . . . . . . . . . . . . . . . . . . . . . . . . . . . | 4,500 | |
| Plant Assets . . . . . . . . . . . . . . . . . . . . . . . . . . . . . . . . . . . . . . . . | 510,000 | |
| Accumulated Depreciation—Plant Assets. . . . . . . . . . . . . . . . . . | | 301,750 |
| Accounts Payable . . . . . . . . . . . . . . . . . . . . . . . . . . . . . . . . . . . . | | 47,980 |
| Wages Payable . . . . . . . . . . . . . . . . . . . . . . . . . . . . . . . . . . . . . . | | 6,650 |
| Common Stock. . . . . . . . . . . . . . . . . . . . . . . . . . . . . . . . . . . . . . . | | 250,000 |
| Retained Earnings . . . . . . . . . . . . . . . . . . . . . . . . . . . . . . . . . . . . | | 94,070 |
| Sales. . . . . . . . . . . . . . . . . . . . . . . . . . . . . . . . . . . . . . . . . . . . . . . | | 210,500 |
| Cost of Goods Sold. . . . . . . . . . . . . . . . . . . . . . . . . . . . . . . . . . . | 143,900 | |
| Factory Overhead—Department 1 . . . . . . . . . . . . . . . . . . . . . . . . | | 300 |
| Factory Overhead—Department 2 . . . . . . . . . . . . . . . . . . . . . . . . | 1,950 | |
| Selling Expenses . . . . . . . . . . . . . . . . . . . . . . . . . . . . . . . . . . . . . | 16,500 | |
| General Expenses . . . . . . . . . . . . . . . . . . . . . . . . . . . . . . . . . . . . | 14,400 | |
| | 911,250 | 911,250 |

**Conway Company**
**Income Statement**
**For Month Ended January 31, 19--**

| | | |
|---|---:|---:|
| Sales. . . . . . . . . . . . . . . . . . . . . . . . . . . . . . . . . . . . . . . . . . . . . | | $210,500 |
| Cost of goods sold. . . . . . . . . . . . . . . . . . . . . . . . . . . . . . . . . . | | 143,900 |
| Gross profit . . . . . . . . . . . . . . . . . . . . . . . . . . . . . . . . . . . . . . . | | $ 66,600 |
| Operating expenses: | | |
|    Selling expenses. . . . . . . . . . . . . . . . . . . . . . . . . . . . . . . . | $ 16,500 | |
|    General expenses . . . . . . . . . . . . . . . . . . . . . . . . . . . . . . . | 14,400 | |
|      Total operating expenses . . . . . . . . . . . . . . . . . . . . . | | 30,900 |
| Income from operations . . . . . . . . . . . . . . . . . . . . . . . . . . . . . | | $ 35,700 |

```
                    Conway Company
                Retained Earnings Statement
              For Month Ended January 31, 19--
```

| | |
|---|---:|
| Retained earnings, January 1, 19--.............................. | $ 94,070 |
| Income for the month......................................... | 35,700 |
| Retained earnings, January 31, 19--.......................... | $129,770 |

```
                    Conway Company
                     Balance Sheet
                    January 31, 19--
```

### Assets

Current assets:

| | | | |
|---|---:|---:|---:|
| Cash ................................ | | $ 46,900 | |
| Accounts receivable ............... | | 55,500 | |
| Inventories: | | | |
| Finished goods................... | $ 46,440 | | |
| Work in process ................. | 30,780 | | |
| Materials........................ | 40,380 | 117,600 | |
| Prepaid expenses................... | | 4,500 | |
| Total current assets .............. | | | $224,500 |
| Plant assets: | | | |
| Plant assets ....................... | | $510,000 | |
| Less accumulated depreciation .... | | 301,750 | 208,250 |
| Deferred debits: | | | |
| Factory overhead underapplied ...... | | | 1,650 |
| Total assets .......................... | | | $434,400 |

### Liabilities

Current liabilities:

| | | | |
|---|---:|---:|---:|
| Accounts payable.................. | | $ 47,980 | |
| Wages payable.................... | | 6,650 | |
| Total liabilities ....................... | | | $ 54,630 |

### Stockholders' Equity

| | | | |
|---|---:|---:|---:|
| Common stock ...................... | | $250,000 | |
| Retained earnings ................. | | 129,770 | |
| Total stockholders' equity............ | | | 379,770 |
| Total liabilities and stockholders' equity .. | | | $434,400 |

**Self-Examination Questions**
*(Answers in Appendix C.)*

1. For which of the following businesses would the process cost system be most appropriate?
   A. Custom furniture manufacturer
   B. Commercial building contractor
   C. Crude oil refinery
   D. None of the above

2. The group of manufacturing costs referred to as *processing costs* includes:
   A. direct materials and direct labor
   B. direct materials and factory overhead
   C. direct labor and factory overhead
   D. none of the above

3. Information relating to production in Department A for May is as follows:

   | | |
   |---|---:|
   | May 1 Balance, 1,000 units, ¾ completed | $22,150 |
   | 31 Direct materials, 5,000 units | 75,000 |
   | 31 Direct labor | 32,500 |
   | 31 Factory overhead | 16,250 |

   If 500 units were ¼ completed at May 31 and 5,500 units were completed during May, what was the number of equivalent units of production for May?
   A. 4,500
   B. 4,875
   C. 5,500
   D. None of the above

4. Based on the data presented in Question 3, what is the unit processing cost?
   A. $10
   B. $15
   C. $25
   D. None of the above

5. If one of the products resulting from a process has little value in relation to the principal products, it is known as a:
   A. joint product
   B. by-product
   C. direct material
   D. none of the above

**Discussion Questions**

1. Which type of cost system, process or job order, would be best suited for each of the following: (a) washing machine manufacturer, (b) oil refinery, (c) furniture upholsterer, (d) building contractor, (e) paint manufacturer? Give reasons for your answers.

2. In job order cost accounting, the three elements of manufacturing cost are charged directly to job orders. Why is it not necessary to charge manufacturing costs in process cost accounting to job orders?

3. (a) How does a service department differ from a processing department? (b) Give two examples of a service department.

4. Parnell Company maintains a cafeteria for its employees at a cost of $1,400 per month. On what basis would the company most likely allocate the cost of the cafeteria among the production departments?

5. What two groups of manufacturing costs are referred to as processing costs?

6. In the manufacture of 5,000 units of a product, direct materials cost incurred was $15,000, direct labor cost incurred was $8,000, and factory overhead applied was $4,000. (a) What is the total processing cost? (b) What is the processing cost per unit? (c) What is the total manufacturing cost? (d) What is the manufacturing cost per unit?

7. What is meant by the term "equivalent units"?

8. If Department 1 had no work in process at the beginning of the period, 6,000 units were completed during the period, and 2,000 units were 25% completed at the end of the period, what was the number of equivalent units of production for the period?

9. The following information concerns production in Department 14 for January. All direct materials are placed in process at the beginning of production. Determine the number of units in work in process inventory at the end of the month.

### WORK IN PROCESS—DEPARTMENT 14

| Date | | Item | Debit | Credit | Balance Debit | Balance Credit |
|---|---|---|---|---|---|---|
| Jan. | 1 | Bal., 4,000 units, ¾ completed | | | 6,750 | |
| | 31 | Direct materials, 15,000 units | 7,200 | | | |
| | 31 | Direct labor | 16,800 | | | |
| | 31 | Factory overhead | 4,400 | | | |
| | 31 | Goods finished, 13,500 units | | 28,110 | | |
| | 31 | Bal.,____ units, ½ completed | | | 7,040 | |

10. For No. 9., determine the equivalent units of production for January.

11. What data are summarized in the two principal sections of the cost of production report?

12. What is the most important purpose of the cost of production report?

13. Distinguish between a joint product and a by-product.

14. Department 25 produces two products. How should the costs be allocated (a) if the products are joint products and (b) if one of the products is a by-product?

15. Factory employees in Department 1 of Cargile Co. are paid widely varying wage rates. In such circumstances, would direct labor hours or direct labor cost be the more equitable base for applying factory overhead to the production of the department? Explain.

16. In a factory with several processing departments, a separate factory overhead rate may be determined for each department. Why is a single factory overhead rate often inadequate in such circumstances?

**Exercises**     **Exercise 3-1.** Wright & Wright Co. manufactures two products. The entire output of Department 1 is transferred to Department 2. Part of the fully processed goods from Department 2 are sold as Product A and the remainder of the goods are transferred to

Department 3 for further processing into Product B. The service department, Factory Office, provides services for each of the processing departments.

Prepare a chart of the flow of costs from the service and processing department accounts into the finished goods accounts and then into the cost of goods sold account. The relevant accounts are as follows:

| | |
|---|---|
| Cost of Goods Sold | Finished Goods — Product A |
| Factory Office | Finished Goods — Product B |
| Factory Overhead — Department 1 | Work in Process — Department 1 |
| Factory Overhead — Department 2 | Work in Process — Department 2 |
| Factory Overhead — Department 3 | Work in Process — Department 3 |

**Exercise 3-2.** The Maintenance and Repair Department provides services to processing Departments X, Y, and Z. During June of the current year, the total cost incurred by the Maintenance and Repair Department was $72,000. During June, it was estimated that 36% of the services were provided to Department X, 54% to Department Y, and 10% to Department Z.

Prepare a general journal entry to record the allocation of the Maintenance and Repair Department cost for June to the processing departments.

**Exercise 3-3.** Upchurch Company manufactures a single product by a continuous process, involving five production departments. The records indicate that $80,500 of direct materials were issued to and $98,000 of direct labor incurred by Department 1 in the manufacture of the product; the factory overhead rate is 40% of direct labor cost; work in process in the department at the beginning of the period totaled $45,150; and work in process at the end of the period totaled $48,650.

Prepare general journal entries to record (a) the flow of costs into Department 1 during the period for (1) direct materials, (2) direct labor, and (3) factory overhead; (b) the transfer of production costs to Department 2.

**Exercise 3-4.** The chief cost accountant for Pratt Electronics estimates total factory overhead cost for Department 10 for the year at $96,000 and total direct labor costs at $128,000. During August, actual direct labor cost totaled $16,000 and factory overhead cost incurred totaled $11,500. (a) What is the predetermined factory overhead rate based on direct labor cost? (b) Prepare the entry to apply factory overhead to production for August. (c) What is the August 31 balance of the account Factory Overhead — Department 10? (d) Does the balance in (c) represent overapplied or underapplied factory overhead?

**Exercise 3-5.** The charges to Work in Process — Department 1 for a period, together with information concerning production, are as follows. All direct materials are placed in process at the beginning of production.

**Work in Process — Department 1**

| | | | |
|---|---|---|---|
| 1,200 units, 80% completed | 25,920 | To Dept. 2, 4,200 units | 102,258 |
| Direct materials, 3,000 at $12 | 36,000 | | |
| Direct labor | 25,200 | | |
| Factory overhead | 15,138 | | |

Determine the following, presenting your computations: (a) equivalent units of production, (b) processing cost per equivalent unit of production, (c) total and unit cost of product started in prior period and completed in the current period, and (d) total and unit cost of product started and completed in the current period.

**Exercise 3-6.** Prepare a cost of production report for the Polishing Department of McNair Company for July of the current fiscal year, using the following data:

| | |
|---|---|
| Inventory, July 1, 5,400 units, 60% completed | $131,760 |
| Materials from the Sanding Department, 15,000 units | 324,000 |
| Direct labor for July | 52,200 |
| Factory overhead for July | 28,980 |
| Goods finished during July (includes units in process, July 1), 16,400 units | —— |
| Inventory, July 31, 4,000 units, 40% completed | —— |

**Exercise 3-7.** The charges to Work in Process—Department 6, together with units of product completed during the period, are indicated in the following account:

**Work in Process—Department 6**

| | | |
|---|---|---|
| From Department 5 | 172,700 | By-product N, 2,000 units |
| Direct labor | 62,800 | Joint product R, 12,800 units |
| Factory overhead | 30,900 | Joint product S, 6,000 units |

There is no inventory of goods in process at either the beginning or the end of the period. The value of N is $2 a unit; R sells at $15 a unit and S sells at $48 a unit.

Allocate the costs to the three products and determine the unit cost of each, presenting your computations.

**Problems**
*(Problems in Appendix B: 3-1B, 3-4B, 3-6B.)*

**Problem 3-1A.** Ferguson Company manufactures Product W. Material C is placed in process in Department 1 where it is ground and partially refined. The output of Department 1 is transferred to Department 2, where Material D is added at the beginning of the process and the refining is completed. On May 1, Ferguson Company had the following inventories:

| | |
|---|---|
| Finished goods (5,000 units) | $121,000 |
| Work in process—Department 1 | —— |
| Work in process—Department 2 (1,000 units, ¾ completed) | 20,100 |
| Materials | 27,100 |

Departmental accounts are maintained for factory overhead and there is one service department, Factory Office. Manufacturing operations for May are summarized as follows:

(a) Materials purchased on account............................. $48,950

(b) Materials requisitioned for use:

| | |
|---|---|
| Material C............................................. | $26,510 |
| Material D............................................. | 22,000 |
| Indirect materials — Department 1........................... | 1,760 |
| Indirect materials — Department 2........................... | 1,265 |

(c) Labor used:

| | |
|---|---|
| Direct labor — Department 1................................ | $55,000 |
| Direct labor — Department 2................................ | 39,250 |
| Indirect labor — Department 1 ............................. | 2,090 |
| Indirect labor — Department 2 ............................. | 1,980 |
| Factory Office ......................................... | 1,870 |

(d) Miscellaneous costs incurred on account:

| | |
|---|---|
| Department 1........................................... | $7,350 |
| Department 2........................................... | 5,170 |
| Factory Office ......................................... | 2,140 |

(e) Expiration of prepaid expenses:

| | |
|---|---|
| Department 1........................................... | $1,045 |
| Department 2........................................... | 715 |
| Factory Office ......................................... | 300 |

(f) Depreciation charged on plant assets:

| | |
|---|---|
| Department 1........................................... | $14,680 |
| Department 2........................................... | 12,520 |
| Factory Office ......................................... | 950 |

(g) Distribution of Factory Office costs:

| | |
|---|---|
| Department 1.....................75% of total Factory Office costs |
| Department 2.....................25% of total Factory Office costs |

(h) Application of factory overhead costs:

| | |
|---|---|
| Department 1................................55% of direct labor cost |
| Department 2................................60% of direct labor cost |

(i) Production costs transferred from Department 1 to Department 2:
8,800 units were fully processed and there was no inventory of work in process in Department 1 at May 31.

(j) Production costs transferred from Department 2 to finished goods:
8,000 units, including the inventory at May 1, were fully processed. 1,800 units were ⅓ completed at May 31.

(k) Cost of goods sold during May:
9,500 units (use the first-in, first-out method in crediting the finished goods account).

Instructions:

(1) Prepare entries in general journal form to record the foregoing operations. Identify each entry by letter.

(2) Compute the May 31 work in process inventory for Department 2.

**Problem 3-2A.**    The data related to production during May of the current year for Department 2 of Ferguson Company are presented in Problem 3-1A.

Instructions:

Prepare a cost of production report for Department 2 for May.

**Problem 3-3A.** The trial balance of Mathews Inc. at July 31, the end of the first month of the current fiscal year, is as follows:

Mathews Inc.
Trial Balance
July 31, 19--

| | | |
|---|---:|---:|
| Cash | 78,180 | |
| Marketable Securities | 60,000 | |
| Accounts Receivable | 210,600 | |
| Finished Goods — Product P1 | 85,800 | |
| Finished Goods — Product P2 | 142,200 | |
| Work in Process — Department 1 | 18,180 | |
| Work in Process — Department 2 | 31,620 | |
| Work in Process — Department 3 | 28,800 | |
| Materials | 57,000 | |
| Prepaid Expenses | 15,000 | |
| Plant Assets | 930,220 | |
| Accumulated Depreciation — Plant Assets | | 491,410 |
| Accounts Payable | | 119,400 |
| Wages Payable | | 17,640 |
| Common Stock | | 600,000 |
| Retained Earnings | | 378,630 |
| Sales | | 528,600 |
| Cost of Goods Sold | 377,700 | |
| Factory Overhead — Department 1 | 660 | |
| Factory Overhead — Department 2 | | 270 |
| Factory Overhead — Department 3 | 750 | |
| Selling Expenses | 59,520 | |
| General Expenses | 39,720 | |
| | 2,135,950 | 2,135,950 |

Instructions:

(1) Prepare an income statement.
(2) Prepare a retained earnings statement.
(3) Prepare a balance sheet.

**Problem 3-4A.** Townsend Company manufactures Product H by a series of three processes, all materials being introduced in Department 1. From Department 1, the materials pass through Departments 2 and 3, emerging as finished Product H. All inventories are priced at cost by the first-in, first-out method.

The balances in the accounts Work in Process — Department 3 and Finished Goods were as follows on October 1:

| | |
|---|---:|
| Work in Process — Department 3 (3,500 units, ½ completed) | $106,050 |
| Finished Goods (6,000 units at $36.20 a unit) | 217,200 |

The following costs were charged to Work in Process—Department 3 during October:

| | |
|---|---|
| Direct materials transferred from Department 2: 18,500 units at $24 a unit. . . . . . . . . . . . . . . . . . . . . . . . . . . . . . . . . . . . . . . . . . . . . . . . | $444,000 |
| Direct labor . . . . . . . . . . . . . . . . . . . . . . . . . . . . . . . . . . . . . . . . . . . . . . . . . | 116,300 |
| Factory overhead . . . . . . . . . . . . . . . . . . . . . . . . . . . . . . . . . . . . . . . . . . . | 70,000 |

During October, 17,500 units of H were completed and 18,600 units were sold. Inventories on October 31 were as follows:

Work in Process—Department 3: 4,500 units, ⅓ completed
Finished Goods: 4,900 units

Instructions:

(1) Determine the following, presenting computations in good order:
    (a) Equivalent units of production for Department 3 during October.
    (b) Unit processing cost for Department 3 for October.
    (c) Total and unit cost of Product H started in a prior period and finished in October.
    (d) Total and unit cost of Product H started and finished in October.
    (e) Total cost of goods transferred to finished goods.
    (f) Work in process inventory for Department 3, October 31.
    (g) Cost of goods sold (indicate number of units and unit costs).
    (h) Finished goods inventory, October 31.
(2) Prepare a cost of production report for Department 3 for October.

**Problem 3-5A.** Sikes Products manufactures joint products M and N. Materials are placed in production in Department 1, and after processing, are transferred to Department 2, where more materials are added. The finished products emerge from Department 2. There are two service departments: Factory Office, and Maintenance and Repair.

There were no inventories of work in process at the beginning or at the end of December. Finished goods inventories at December 1 were as follows:

| | |
|---|---|
| Product M, 4,900 units . . . . . . . . . . . . . . . . | $56,350 |
| Product N, 940 units . . . . . . . . . . . . . . . . . | 18,330 |

Transactions related to manufacturing operations for December are summarized as follows:

(a) Materials purchased on account, $70,000.
(b) Materials requisitioned for use: Department 1, $32,550 ($28,350 entered directly into the products); Department 2, $22,210 ($18,290 entered directly into the products); Maintenance and Repair, $2,660.
(c) Labor costs incurred: Department 1, $23,520 ($21,000 entered directly into the products); Department 2, $25,340 ($22,400 entered directly into the products); Factory Office, $3,850; Maintenance and Repair, $9,170.
(d) Miscellaneous costs and expenses incurred on account: Department 1, $3,570; Department 2, $3,150; Factory Office, $1,400; and Maintenance and Repair, $2,170.
(e) Depreciation charged on plant assets: Department 1, $4,900; Department 2, $3,360; Factory Office, $700; and Maintenance and Repair, $980.

(f) Expiration of various prepaid expenses: Department 1, $280; Department 2, $245; Factory Office, $350; and Maintenance and Repair, $490.

(g) Factory office costs allocated on the basis of hours worked: Department 1, 2,240 hours; Department 2, 2,800 hours; Maintenance and Repair, 560 hours.

(h) Maintenance and repair costs allocated on the basis of services rendered: Department 1, 45%; Department 2, 55%.

(i) Factory overhead applied to production at the predetermined rates: 120% and 115% of direct labor cost for Departments 1 and 2 respectively.

(j) Output of Department 1: 5,460 units.

(k) Output of Department 2: 7,050 units of Product M and 2,820 units of Product N. Unit selling price is $16.80 for Product M and $28 for Product N.

(l) Sales on account: 7,750 units of Product M at $16.80 and 2,660 units of Product N at $28. Credits to the finished goods accounts are to be priced in accordance with the first-in, first-out method.

Instructions:

Present entries in general journal form to record the transactions, identifying each by letter. Include as an explanation for entry (k) the computations for the allocation of the production costs for Department 2 to the joint products, and as an explanation for entry (l) the number of units and the unit costs for each product sold.

**Problem 3-6A.** A process cost system is used to record the costs of manufacturing Product A24C, which requires a series of four processes. The inventory of Work in Process—Department 4 on April 1 and debits to the account during April were as follows:

| | |
|---|---|
| Balance, 1,600 units, ¼ completed ..................... | $ 6,520 |
| From Department 3, 9,200 units ....................... | 25,760 |
| Direct labor ......................................... | 38,500 |
| Factory overhead .................................... | 9,625 |

During April, the 1,600 units in process on April 1 were completed, and of the 9,200 units entering the department, all were completed except 2,200 units, which were ¼ completed.

Charges to Work in Process—Department 4 for May were made as follows:

| | |
|---|---|
| From Department 3, 8,250 units ....................... | $23,925 |
| Direct labor ......................................... | 41,724 |
| Factory overhead .................................... | 10,431 |

During May, the units in process at the beginning of the month were completed, and of the 8,250 units entering the department, all were completed except 1,500 units, which were ½ completed.

Instructions:

(1) Set up an account for Work in Process—Department 4. Enter the balance as of April 1 and record the debits and the credits in the account for April. Present computations for the determination of (a) equivalent units of production, (b) unit processing cost, (c) cost of goods finished, differentiating between units started in the prior period and units started and finished in April, and (d) work in process inventory.

(2) Record the transactions for May in the account. Present the computations listed in instruction (1).

(3) Determine the difference in unit cost between the product started and completed in April and the product started and completed in May. Determine also the amount of the difference attributable collectively to operations in Departments 1 through 3 and the amount attributable to operations in Department 4.

**Mini-Case**

Rivera Inc. manufactures product A68 by a series of four processes. All materials are placed in production in the Die Casting Department and, after processing, are transferred to the Tooling, Assembly, and Polishing Departments, emerging as finished product A68.

On April 1, the balance in the account Work in Process—Polishing was $336,600, determined as follows:

| | |
|---|---:|
| Direct materials: 12,000 units ........................... | $203,400 |
| Direct labor: 12,000 units, ¾ completed................... | 107,550 |
| Factory overhead: 12,000 units, ¾ completed ............. | 25,650 |
| Total........................................... | $336,600 |

The following costs were charged to Work in Process—Polishing during April:

| | |
|---|---:|
| Direct materials transferred from Assembly Department: | |
|    136,000 units ....................................... | $2,380,000 |
| Direct labor....................................... | 1,648,200 |
| Factory overhead..................................... | 361,800 |

During April, 138,000 units of A68 were completed and transferred to Finished Goods. On April 30, the inventory in the Polishing Department consisted of 10,000 units, one-half completed.

As a new cost accountant for Rivera Inc., you have just received a phone call from George Herschman, the superintendent of the Polishing Department. He was extremely upset with the cost of production report, which he says does not balance. In addition, he commented:

"I give up! These reports are a waste of time. My department has always been the best department in the plant, so why should I bother with these reports? Just what purpose do they serve?"

The report to which Herschman referred is on page 69.

Instructions:

(1) Based upon the data for April, prepare a revised cost of production report for the Polishing Department.

(2) Assume that for March, the unit direct materials cost was $16.95 and the unit processing cost was $14.80. Determine the change in the direct materials unit cost and unit processing cost for April.

(3) Based upon (2), what are some possible explanations for the changing unit costs?

(4) Describe how you would explain to Herschman that cost of production reports are useful.

RIVERA INC.
Cost of Production Report—Polishing Department
For Month Ended April 30, 19--

**Quantities:**
Charged to production:
In process, April 1 .................................... 9,000
Received from Assembly Department .................. 136,000
Total units to be accounted for ........................ 145,000

Units accounted for:
Transferred to finished goods ........................ 138,000
In process, April 30 .................................... 5,000
Total units accounted for ............................. 143,000

**Costs:**
Charged to production:
In process, April 1 .................................... $ 336,600

April costs:
Direct materials from Assembly Department ($15.70 per
unit) .......................................... 2,380,000

Processing costs:
Direct labor ............................ $1,648,200
Factory overhead ....................... 361,800
Total processing costs ($13.40 per unit) .............. 2,010,000
Total costs to be accounted for ......................... $4,726,600

Costs allocated as follows:
Transferred to finished goods:
138,000 units at $29.10 ($15.70 + $13.40) ........... $4,015,800

In process, April 30:
Materials (5,000 units × $15.70) ......... $ 78,500
Processing costs (5,000 units × $13.40) ... 67,000
Total cost of inventory in process ......... 145,500
Total costs accounted for ............................. $4,161,300

**Computations:**
Equivalent units of production:
To process units in inventory on April 1:
12,000 units × ¾ .................................... 9,000
To process units started and completed in April ........ 136,000
To process units in inventory on April 30:
10,000 units × ½ ................................. 5,000
Equivalent units of production ...................... 150,000

Unit processing cost:
$2,010,000 ÷ 150,000 ............................. $ 13.40

# 4

# Budgeting

**CHAPTER OBJECTIVES**

*Describe the nature and objectives of budgeting and the budget process.*

*Identify the components of the master budget and illustrate the preparation of a master budget for a small manufacturing enterprise.*

*Describe and illustrate budget performance reports and flexible budgets.*

# PART 3 Planning and Control

## 4

**CHAPTER**

Various uses of accounting data by management have been described in earlier chapters. For example, the role of cost accounting in planning production and controlling costs has been discussed and illustrated. This chapter and Chapter 5 are devoted to budgeting and standard costs, two additional accounting devices that assist management in planning and controlling the operations of the business.

**NATURE OF BUDGETS**

A budget is a formal written statement of management's plans for the future, expressed in financial terms. A budget charts the course of future action. Thus, it aids management in fulfilling its planning function in the same manner that the architect's blueprints aid the builder and the navigator's flight plan aids the pilot.

A budget, like a blueprint and a flight plan, should contain sound, attainable objectives. If the budget is to contain such objectives, planning must be based on careful study, investigation, and research. Reliance by management on data thus obtained lessens the role of guesses and intuition in managing a business enterprise.

To be effective, managerial planning must be accompanied by control. The control feature of budgeting lies in periodic comparisons of planned objectives and actual performance. Management can then take corrective action in areas where significant differences between the budget and actual performance are reported. The role of accounting is to aid management in the investigation phase of budget preparation, to translate management's plans into financial terms, and to prepare budget performance reports and related analyses.

Although budgets are commonly associated with profit-making enterprises, they play an important role in operating most instrumentalities of government, ranging from rural school districts and small villages to gigantic agencies of the federal government. They are also an important part of the operations of churches, hospitals, and other nonprofit institutions. In this chapter, the principles of budgeting are discussed in the context of profit-making enterprises. The application of the basic principles to nonprofit organizations is presented in Chapter 18.

**BUDGET PERIOD**

Budgets of operating activities usually include the fiscal year of an enterprise. A year is short enough to make possible fairly dependable estimates of future operations, and yet long enough to make it possible to view the future in a reasonably broad context. However, to achieve effective control, the annual budgets must be subdivided into shorter time periods, such as quarters of the year, months, or weeks. It is also necessary to review the budgets from time to time and make any changes that become necessary as a result of unforeseen changes in general business conditions, in the particular industry, or in the individual enterprise.

A frequent variant of fiscal-year budgeting, sometimes called continuous budgeting, provides for maintenance of a twelve-month projection into the future. At the end of each time interval used, the twelve-month budget is revised by removing the data for the period just ended and adding the newly estimated budget data for the same period next year.

**BUDGETING PROCEDURES**    The details of budgeting systems are affected by the type and degree of complexity of a particular company, the amount of its revenues, the relative importance of its various divisions, and many other factors. Budget procedures used by a large manufacturer of automobiles would obviously differ in many ways from a system designed for a small manufacturer of paper products. The differences between a system designed for factory operations of any type and a financial enterprise such as a bank would be even more marked.

The development of budgets for a following fiscal year usually begins several months prior to the end of the current year. The responsibility for their development is ordinarily assigned to a committee made up of the budget director and such high-level executives as the controller, treasurer, production manager, and sales manager. The process is started by requesting estimates of sales, production, and other operating data from the various administrative units concerned. It is important that all levels of management and all departments participate in the preparation and submission of budget estimates. The involvement of all supervisory personnel fosters cooperation both within and among departments and also heightens awareness of each department's importance in the overall processes of the company. All levels of management are thus encouraged to set goals and to control operations in a manner that strengthens the possibilities of achieving the goals.

The process of developing budget estimates differs among enterprises. One method is to require all levels of management to start from zero and estimate sales, production, and other operating data as though operations were being started for the first time. Although this concept, called zero-base budgeting, has received wide attention in regard to budgeting for governmental units, it is equally useful to commercial enterprises. Another method of developing estimates is for each level of management to modify last year's budgeted amounts in light of last year's operating results and expected changes for the coming year.

The various estimates received by the budget committee are revised, reviewed, coordinated, cross-referenced, and finally put together to form the master budget. The estimates submitted should not be substantially revised by the committee without first giving the originators an opportunity to defend their proposals. After agreement has been reached and the master budget has been adopted by the budget committee, copies of the pertinent sections are distributed to the proper personnel in the chain of accountability. Periodic reports comparing actual results with the budget should likewise be distributed to all supervisory personnel.

As a framework for describing and illustrating budgeting, a small manufacturing enterprise will be assumed. The major parts of its master budget are as follows:

**COMPONENTS OF MASTER BUDGET**

✔ Budgeted income statement
   Sales budget
   Cost of goods sold budget
     Production budget
     Direct materials purchases budget
     Direct labor cost budget
     Factory overhead cost budget
   Operating expenses budget

✔ Budgeted balance sheet
   Capital expenditures budget
   Cash budget

**Sales Budget**

The first budget to be prepared is usually the sales budget. An estimate of the dollar volume of sales revenue serves as the foundation upon which the other budgets are based. Sales volume will have a significant effect on all of the factors entering into the determination of operating income.

The sales budget ordinarily indicates (1) the quantity of forecasted sales for each product and (2) the expected unit selling price of each product. These data are often classified by areas and/or sales representatives.

In forecasting the quantity of each product expected to be sold, the starting point is generally past sales volumes. These amounts are revised for various factors expected to affect future sales, such as a backlog of unfilled sales orders, planned advertising and promotion, expected industry and general economic conditions, productive capacity, projected pricing policy, and market research study findings. Statistical analysis can be used in this process to evaluate the effect of these factors on past sales volume. Such analysis can provide a mathematical association between past sales and the several variables expected to affect future sales.

Once the forecast of sales volume is completed, the anticipated sales revenue is then determined by multiplying the volume of forecasted sales by the expected unit sales price, as shown in the following sales budget:

**SALES BUDGET**

Bowers Company
Sales Budget
For Year Ending December 31, 19--

| Product and Area | Unit Sales Volume | Unit Selling Price | Total Sales |
|---|---|---|---|
| Product X: | | | |
| Area A | 208,000 | $ 9.90 | $2,059,200 |
| Area B | 162,000 | 9.90 | 1,603,800 |
| Area C | 158,000 | 9.90 | 1,564,200 |
| Total | 528,000 | | $5,227,200 |
| Product Y: | | | |
| Area A | 111,600 | $16.50 | $1,841,400 |
| Area B | 78,800 | 16.50 | 1,300,200 |
| Area C | 89,600 | 16.50 | 1,478,400 |
| Total | 280,000 | | $4,620,000 |
| Total revenue from sales | | | $9,847,200 |

Frequent comparisons of actual sales with the budgeted volume, by product, area, and/or sales representative, will show differences between the two. Management is then able to investigate the probable cause of the significant differences and attempt corrective action.

**Production Budget**

The number of units of each commodity expected to be manufactured to meet budgeted sales and inventory requirements is set forth in the production budget. The budgeted volume of production is based on the sum of (1) the expected sales volume and (2) the desired year-end inventory, less (3) the inventory expected to be available at the beginning of the year. A production budget is illustrated as follows:

PRODUCTION
BUDGET

Bowers Company
Production Budget
For Year Ending December 31, 19--

|  | Units | |
| --- | --- | --- |
|  | Product X | Product Y |
| Sales........................................ | 528,000 | 280,000 |
| Plus desired ending inventory, December 31, 19--........ | 80,000 | 60,000 |
| Total..................................... | 608,000 | 340,000 |
| Less estimated beginning inventory, January 1, 19--...... | 88,000 | 48,000 |
| Total production..................................... | 520,000 | 292,000 |

 The production needs must be carefully coordinated with the sales budget to assure that production and sales are kept in balance during the period. Ideally, manufacturing operations should be maintained at capacity, and inventories should be neither excessive nor insufficient to fill sales orders.

**Direct Materials Purchases Budget**    The production needs shown by the production budget, combined with data on direct materials needed, provide the data for the direct materials purchases budget. The quantities of direct materials purchases necessary to meet production needs is based on the sum of (1) the materials expected to be needed to meet production requirements and (2) the desired year-end inventory, less (3) the inventory expected to be available at the beginning of the year. The quantities of direct materials required are then multiplied by the expected unit purchase price to determine the total cost of direct materials purchases.

In the following direct materials purchases budget, materials A and C are required for Product X, and materials A, B, and C are required for Product Y.

DIRECT MATERIALS
PURCHASES
BUDGET

Bowers Company
Direct Materials Purchases Budget
For Year Ending December 31, 19--

|  | Direct Materials | | |
| --- | --- | --- | --- |
|  | A | B | C |
| Units required for production: |  |  |  |
| Product X.................................... | 390,000 | —— | 520,000 |
| Product Y.................................... | 146,000 | 292,000 | 294,200 |
| Plus desired ending inventory, Dec. 31, 19--......... | 80,000 | 40,000 | 120,000 |
| Total...................................... | 616,000 | 332,000 | 934,200 |
| Less estimated beginning inventory, Jan. 1, 19--..... | 103,000 | 44,000 | 114,200 |
| Total units to be purchased.................... | 513,000 | 288,000 | 820,000 |
| Unit price..................................... | $ .60 | $ 1.70 | $ 1.00 |
| Total direct materials purchases ................. | $307,800 | $489,600 | $820,000 |

The timing of the direct materials purchases requires close coordination between the purchasing and production departments so that inventory levels can be maintained within reasonable limits.

**Direct Labor Cost Budget**  The needs indicated by the production budget provide the starting point for the preparation of the direct labor cost budget. The direct labor hours necessary to meet production needs are multiplied by the estimated hourly rate to yield the total direct labor cost. The manufacturing operations for both Products X and Y are performed in Departments 1 and 2. A direct labor cost budget is illustrated as follows:

 DIRECT LABOR COST BUDGET

**Bowers Company**
**Direct Labor Cost Budget**
**For Year Ending December 31, 19--**

|  | Department 1 | Department 2 |
| --- | --- | --- |
| Hours required for production: | | |
| Product X | 75,000 | 104,000 |
| Product Y | 46,800 | 116,800 |
| Total | 121,800 | 220,800 |
| Hourly rate | $10 | $8 |
| Total direct labor cost | $1,218,000 | $1,766,400 |

The direct labor requirements must be carefully coordinated with available labor time to assure that sufficient labor will be available to meet production needs. Efficient manufacturing operations minimize idle time and labor shortages.

**Factory Overhead Cost Budget**  The factory overhead costs estimated to be necessary to meet production needs are presented in the factory overhead cost budget. For use as a part of the master budget, the factory overhead cost budget usually presents the total estimated cost for each item of factory overhead. A factory overhead cost budget is illustrated as follows:

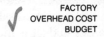 FACTORY OVERHEAD COST BUDGET

**Bowers Company**
**Factory Overhead Cost Budget**
**For Year Ending December 31, 19--**

| | |
| --- | --- |
| Indirect factory wages | $ 732,800 |
| Supervisory salaries | 360,000 |
| Power and light | 306,000 |
| Depreciation of plant and equipment | 288,000 |
| Indirect materials | 182,800 |
| Maintenance | 140,280 |
| Insurance and property taxes | 79,200 |
| Total factory overhead cost | $2,089,080 |

Supplemental schedules are often prepared to present the factory overhead cost for each individual department. Such schedules enable department supervisors to direct attention to those costs for which each is solely responsible. They also aid the production manager in evaluating performance in each department.

**Cost of Goods Sold Budget**

The budget for the cost of goods sold is prepared by combining the relevant estimates of quantities and costs in the budget for (1) direct materials purchases, (2) direct labor costs, and (3) factory overhead costs, with the addition of data on estimated inventories. A cost of goods sold budget is illustrated as follows:

**✓ COST OF GOODS SOLD BUDGET**

### Bowers Company
### Cost of Goods Sold Budget
### For Year Ending December 31, 19--

| | | | |
|---|---|---|---|
| Finished goods inventory, January 1, 19-- . . . . . . . | | | $1,125,600 |
| Work in process inventory, January 1, 19-- . . . . . . | | $ 184,400 | |
| Direct materials: | | | |
|   Direct materials inventory, January 1, 19-- . . . . . | $ 250,800 | | |
|   Direct materials purchases . . . . . . . . . . . . . . . . | 1,617,400 | | |
|   Cost of direct materials available for use . . . . . . | $1,868,200 | | |
|   Less direct materials inventory, Dec. 31, 19-- . . | 236,000 | | |
|     Cost of direct materials placed in production . | $1,632,200 | | |
| Direct labor . . . . . . . . . . . . . . . . . . . . . . . . . . . . . | 2,984,400 | | |
| Factory overhead . . . . . . . . . . . . . . . . . . . . . . . . . | 2,089,080 | | |
| Total manufacturing costs . . . . . . . . . . . . . . . . . . | | 6,705,680 | |
| Total work in process during period . . . . . . . . . . . | | $6,890,080 | |
| Less work in process inventory, Dec. 31, 19-- . . . . | | 220,000 | |
| Cost of goods manufactured . . . . . . . . . . . . . . . . . | | | 6,670,080 |
| Cost of finished goods available for sale . . . . . . . . | | | $7,795,680 |
| Less finished goods inventory, December 31, 19-- | | | 1,195,000 |
| Cost of goods sold . . . . . . . . . . . . . . . . . . . . . . . . | | | $6,600,680 |

**Operating Expenses Budget**

Based on past experiences, which are adjusted for future expectations, the estimated selling and general expenses are set forth in the operating expenses budget. For use as part of the master budget, the operating expenses budget ordinarily presents the expenses by nature or type of expenditure, such as sales salaries, rent, insurance, and advertising. An operating expenses budget is illustrated on page 77.

Detailed supplemental schedules based on departmental responsibility are often prepared for major items in the operating expenses budget. The advertising expense schedule, for example, should include such details as the advertising media to be used (newspaper, direct mail, television), quantities (column inches, number of pieces, minutes), cost per unit, frequency of use, and sectional totals. A realistic budget is prepared through careful attention to details, and effective control is achieved through assignment of responsibility to departmental supervisors.

**Bowers Company
Operating Expenses Budget
For Year Ending December 31, 19--**

Selling expenses:
  Sales salaries expense ............................... $595,000
  Advertising expense .................................. 360,000
  Travel expense........................................ 115,000
  Telephone expense—selling ........................... 95,000
  Miscellaneous selling expense ........................ 25,000
    Total selling expenses ............................................. $1,190,000

General expenses:
  Officers' salaries expense ........................... $360,000
  Office salaries expense .............................. 105,000
  Heating and lighting expense......................... 75,000
  Taxes expense........................................ 60,000
  Depreciation expense—office equipment ............... 27,000
  Telephone expense—general .......................... 18,000
  Insurance expense ................................... 17,500
  Office supplies expense.............................. 7,500
  Miscellaneous general expense ....................... 25,000
    Total general expenses ............................................. 695,000
Total operating expenses................................. $1,885,000

**Budgeted Income
Statement**

A budgeted income statement can usually be prepared from the estimated data presented in the budgets for sales, cost of goods sold, and operating expenses, with the addition of data on other income, other expense, and income tax. A budgeted income statement is illustrated as follows:

**Bowers Company
Budgeted Income Statement
For Year Ending December 31, 19--**

Revenue from sales........................................ $9,847,200
Cost of goods sold ....................................... 6,600,680
Gross profit.............................................. $3,246,520
Operating expenses:
  Selling expenses .................................... $1,190,000
  General expenses .................................... 695,000
    Total operating expenses................................ 1,885,000
Income from operations ................................... $1,361,520
Other income:
  Interest income...................................... $  98,000
Other expense:
  Interest expense..................................... 90,000    8,000
Income before income tax................................. $1,369,520
Income tax............................................... 610,000
Net income .............................................. $  759,520

The budgeted income statement brings together in condensed form the projection of all profit-making phases of operations and enables management to weigh the effects of the individual budgets on the profit plan for the year. If the budgeted net income in relationship to sales or to stockholders' equity is disappointingly low, additional review of all factors involved should be undertaken in an attempt to improve the plans.

**Capital Expenditures Budget**

The capital expenditures budget summarizes future plans for acquisition of plant facilities and equipment.[1] Substantial expenditures may be needed to replace machinery and other plant assets as they wear out, become obsolete, or for other reasons fall below minimum standards of efficiency. In addition, an expansion of plant facilities may be planned to keep pace with increasing demand for a company's product or to provide for additions to the product line.

The useful life of many plant assets extends over relatively long periods of time, and the amount of the expenditures for such assets usually changes a great deal from year to year. The customary practice, therefore, is to project the plans for a number of years into the future in preparing the capital expenditures budget. A five-year capital expenditures budget is illustrated as follows:

CAPITAL EXPENDITURES BUDGET

Bowers Company
Capital Expenditures Budget
For Five Years Ending December 31, 1990

| Item | 1986 | 1987 | 1988 | 1989 | 1990 |
|---|---|---|---|---|---|
| Machinery—Department 1... | $400,000 | | | $280,000 | $360,000 |
| Machinery—Department 2... | 180,000 | $260,000 | $560,000 | 200,000 | |
| Office equipment.......... | | 90,000 | | | 60,000 |
| Total................. | $580,000 | $350,000 | $560,000 | $480,000 | $420,000 |

The various proposals recognized in the capital expenditures budget must be considered in preparing certain operating budgets. For example, the expected amount of depreciation on new equipment to be acquired in the current year must be taken into consideration when the budgets for factory overhead and operating expenses are prepared. The manner in which the proposed expenditures are to be financed will also affect the cash budget.

**Cash Budget**

The cash budget presents the expected inflow and outflow of cash for a day, week, month, or longer period. Receipts are classified by source and disbursements by purpose. The expected cash balance at the end of the period is then compared with the amount established as the minimum balance and the difference is the anticipated excess or deficiency for the period.

---

[1]The methods of evaluating alternate capital expenditure proposals are discussed in Chapter 9.

The minimum cash balance represents a safety buffer for mistakes in cash planning and for emergencies. However, the amount stated as the minimum balance need not remain fixed. It should perhaps be larger during periods of "peak" business activity than during the "slow" season. In addition, for effective cash management, much of the minimum cash balance can often be deposited in interest-bearing accounts.

The interrelationship of the cash budget with other budgets may be seen from the following illustration. Data from the sales budget, the various budgets for manufacturing costs and operating expenses, and the capital expenditures budget affect the cash budget. Consideration must also be given to dividend policies, plans for equity or long-term debt financing, and other projected plans that will affect cash.

CASH BUDGET

**Bowers Company**
**Cash Budget**
**For Three Months Ending March 31, 19--**

|  | January | February | March |
|---|---|---|---|
| Estimated cash receipts from: |  |  |  |
| Cash sales . . . . . . . . . . . . . . . . . . . . . . . . . . . . . . | $168,000 | $185,000 | $115,000 |
| Collections of accounts receivable . . . . . . . . . . . | 699,000 | 712,800 | 572,000 |
| Other sources (issuance of securities, interest, etc.). . . . . . . . . . . . . . . . . . . . . . . . . . . . . . . . . | — | — | 27,000 |
| Total cash receipts . . . . . . . . . . . . . . . . . . . . . . | $867,000 | $897,800 | $714,000 |
| Estimated cash disbursements for: |  |  |  |
| Manufacturing costs . . . . . . . . . . . . . . . . . . . . . . . | $541,200 | $557,000 | $536,000 |
| Operating expenses . . . . . . . . . . . . . . . . . . . . . . . | 150,200 | 151,200 | 140,800 |
| Capital expenditures. . . . . . . . . . . . . . . . . . . . . . . | — | 144,000 | 80,000 |
| Other purposes (notes, income tax, etc.). . . . . . . | 47,000 | 20,000 | 160,000 |
| Total cash disbursements . . . . . . . . . . . . . . . . | $738,400 | $872,200 | $916,800 |
| Cash increase (decrease) . . . . . . . . . . . . . . . . . . . | $128,600 | $ 25,600 | $(202,800) |
| Cash balance at beginning of month . . . . . . . . . . . | 280,000 | 408,600 | 434,200 |
| Cash balance at end of month. . . . . . . . . . . . . . . . | $408,600 | $434,200 | $231,400 |
| Minimum cash balance . . . . . . . . . . . . . . . . . . . . . . | 300,000 | 300,000 | 300,000 |
| Excess (deficiency). . . . . . . . . . . . . . . . . . . . . . . . | $108,600 | $134,200 | $ (68,600) |

In some cases, it is useful to present supplemental schedules to indicate the details of some of the amounts in the cash budget. For example, the following schedule illustrates the determination of the estimated cash receipts arising from collections of accounts receivable. For the illustration, it is assumed that the accounts receivable balance was $295,800 on January 1, and sales for each of the three months ending March 31 are $840,000, $925,000, and $575,000, respectively. Bowers Company expects to sell 20% of its merchandise for cash. Of the sales on account, 60% are expected to be collected in the month of the sale and the remainder in the following month.

Bowers Company
Schedule of Collections of Accounts Receivable
For Three Months Ending March 31, 19--

|  | January | February | March |
|---|---|---|---|
| January 1 balance ............................. | $295,800 |  |  |
| January sales on account (80% × $840,000): |  |  |  |
| Collected in January (60% × $672,000) ....... | 403,200 |  |  |
| Collected in February (40% × $672,000) ...... |  | $268,800 |  |
| February sales on account (80% × $925,000): |  |  |  |
| Collected in February (60% × $740,000) ...... |  | 444,000 |  |
| Collected in March (40% × $740,000)......... |  |  | $296,000 |
| March sales on account (80% × $575,000): |  |  |  |
| Collected in March (60% × $460,000)......... |  |  | 276,000 |
| Totals........................................ | $699,000 | $712,800 | $572,000 |

The importance of accurate cash budgeting can scarcely be overemphasized. An unanticipated lack of cash can result in loss of discounts, unfavorable borrowing terms on loans, and damage to the credit rating. On the other hand, an excess amount of idle cash also shows poor management. When the budget shows periods of excess cash, such funds can be used to reduce loans or purchase investments in readily marketable income-producing securities. Reference to the Bowers Company cash budget shows excess cash during January and February and a deficiency during March.

## Budgeted Balance Sheet

The budgeted balance sheet presents estimated details of financial condition at the end of a budget period, assuming that all budgeted operating and financing plans are fulfilled. A budgeted balance sheet is illustrated on page 81.

The budgeted balance sheet may reveal weaknesses in financial position, such as an abnormally large amount of current liabilities in relation to current assets, or excessive long-term debt in relation to stockholders' equity. If such conditions are indicated, the relevant factors should be given further study, so that the proper corrective action may be taken.

## BUDGET PERFORMANCE REPORTS

A budget performance report comparing actual results with the budgeted figures should be prepared periodically for each budget. This "feedback" enables management to investigate significant differences to determine their cause and to seek means of preventing their recurrence. If corrective action cannot be taken because of changed conditions that have occurred since the budget was prepared, future budget figures should be revised accordingly. A budget performance report is illustrated on page 82.

The amounts reported in the "Budget" column were obtained from supplemental schedules accompanying the master budget. The amounts in the "Actual" column are the costs actually incurred. The last two columns show the amounts by which actual costs exceeded or were below budgeted figures. As shown in the

**Bowers Company**
**Budgeted Balance Sheet**
**December 31, 19--**

## Assets

| | | | |
|---|---|---|---|
| Current assets: | | | |
| Cash........................ | | $ 360,000 | |
| Accounts receivable............. | | 214,000 | |
| Marketable securities............ | | 650,000 | |
| Inventories: | | | |
| Finished goods ............... | $1,195,000 | | |
| Work in process............... | 220,000 | | |
| Materials..................... | 236,000 | 1,651,000 | |
| Prepaid expenses............... | | 37,500 | |
| Total current assets ........... | | | $2,912,500 |

| | Cost | Accumulated Depreciation | Book Value |
|---|---|---|---|
| Plant assets: | | | |
| Land........................ | $ 275,000 | — | $ 275,000 |
| Buildings..................... | 3,100,000 | $1,950,000 | 1,150,000 |
| Machinery..................... | 950,000 | 380,000 | 570,000 |
| Office equipment............... | 180,000 | 75,000 | 105,000 |
| Total plant assets ............. | $4,505,000 | $2,405,000 | 2,100,000 |
| Total assets .................... | | | $5,012,500 |

## Liabilities

| | | | |
|---|---|---|---|
| Current liabilities: | | | |
| Accounts payable............... | | $ 580,000 | |
| Accrued liabilities ............... | | 175,000 | |
| Total current liabilities........... | | $ 755,000 | |
| Long-term liabilities: | | | |
| Mortgage note payable........... | | 900,000 | |
| Total liabilities.................... | | | $1,655,000 |

## Stockholders' Equity

| | | | |
|---|---|---|---|
| Common stock............................. | | $2,000,000 | |
| Retained earnings........................... | | 1,357,500 | |
| Total stockholders' equity ..................... | | | 3,357,500 |
| Total liabilities and stockholders' equity.......... | | | $5,012,500 |

illustration, there were differences between the actual and budgeted amounts for some of the items of overhead cost. The cause of the significant difference in indirect materials cost should be investigated, and an attempt to find means of corrective action should be made. For example, if the difference in indirect materials cost were found to be caused by a marketwide increase in the price of materials used, a corrective action may not be possible. On the other hand, if the difference resulted from the inefficient use of materials in the production process, it may be possible to eliminate the inefficiency and effect a savings in future indirect materials costs.

**BUDGET PERFORMANCE REPORT** ✓

Bowers Company
Budget Performance Report—Factory Overhead Cost, Department 1
For Month Ended June 30, 19--

| | Budget | Actual | Over | Under |
|---|---|---|---|---|
| Indirect factory wages.................... | $30,200 | $30,400 | $200 | |
| Supervisory salaries...................... | 15,000 | 15,000 | | |
| Power and light.......................... | 12,800 | 12,750 | | $ 50 |
| Depreciation of plant and equipment....... | 12,000 | 12,000 | | |
| Indirect materials ...................... | 7,600 | 8,250 | 650 | |
| Maintenance ............................ | 5,800 | 5,700 | | 100 |
| Insurance and property taxes ............ | 3,300 | 3,300 | | |
| | $86,700 | $87,400 | $850 | $150 |

## FLEXIBLE BUDGETS

In the discussion of budget systems, it has been assumed that the amount of sales and the level of manufacturing activity achieved during a period approximated the goals established in the budgets. When substantial changes in expectations occur during a budget period, the budgets should be revised to give effect to such changes. Otherwise, they will be of questionable value as incentives and instruments for controlling costs and expenses.

The effect of changes in volume of activity can be "built in" to the system by what are termed flexible budgets. Particularly useful in estimating and controlling factory overhead costs and operating expenses, a flexible budget is in reality a series of budgets for varying rates of activity. To illustrate, assume that because of extreme variations in demand and other uncontrollable factors, the output of a particular manufacturing enterprise fluctuates widely from month to month. In such circumstances, the total factory overhead costs incurred during periods of high activity are certain to be greater than during periods of low activity. It is equally certain, however, that fluctuations in total factory overhead costs will not be exactly proportionate to the volume of production. For example, if $100,000 of factory overhead costs are usually incurred during a month in which production totals 10,000 units, the factory overhead for a month in which only 5,000 units are produced would unquestionably be more than $50,000.

Items of factory cost and operating expense that tend to remain constant in amount regardless of changes in volume of activity may be said to be fixed. Real estate taxes, property insurance, and depreciation expense on buildings are examples of fixed costs. The amounts incurred are substantially independent of the level of operations. Costs and expenses which tend to fluctuate in amount according to changes in volume of activity are called variable. Supplies and indirect materials used and sales commissions are examples of variable costs and expenses. The degree of variability is not the same for all variable items; few, if any, vary in exact proportion to sales or production. The terms **semivariable** or **semifixed** are sometimes applied to items that have both fixed and variable characteristics to a significant degree. An example is electric power, for which there is often an initial flat fee and a rate for additional usage. For example, the charge for electricity used might be $700 for the first 10 000 kwh consumed during a month and $.05 per kwh used above 10 000.

Although there are many approaches to the preparation of a flexible budget, the first step is to identify the fixed and variable components of the various factory overhead and operating expenses being budgeted. The costs and expenses can then be presented in variable and fixed categories. For example, in the following flexible budget for factory overhead cost for one department and one product, "electric power" is broken down into its fixed and variable cost components for three different levels of production. The fixed portion is $10,000 for all levels of production. The variable portion is $30,000 for 10,000 units of product, $27,000 ($30,000 × 9,000/10,000) for 9,000 units of product, and $24,000 ($30,000 × 8,000/10,000) for 8,000 units of product.

FLEXIBLE BUDGET
FOR FACTORY
OVERHEAD COST

**Collins Manufacturing Company**
**Monthly Factory Overhead Cost Budget**

| | 8,000 | 9,000 | 10,000 |
|---|---|---|---|
| Units of product | | | |
| Variable cost: | | | |
| Indirect factory wages | $ 32,000 | $ 36,000 | $ 40,000 |
| Electric power | 24,000 | 27,000 | 30,000 |
| Indirect materials | 12,000 | 13,500 | 15,000 |
| Total variable cost | $ 68,000 | $ 76,500 | $ 85,000 |
| Fixed cost: | | | |
| Supervisory salaries | $ 40,000 | $ 40,000 | $ 40,000 |
| Depreciation of plant and equipment | 25,000 | 25,000 | 25,000 |
| Property taxes | 15,000 | 15,000 | 15,000 |
| Insurance | 12,000 | 12,000 | 12,000 |
| Electric power | 10,000 | 10,000 | 10,000 |
| Total fixed cost | $102,000 | $102,000 | $102,000 |
| Total factory overhead cost | $170,000 | $178,500 | $187,000 |

In practice, the number of production levels and the interval between levels in a flexible budget will vary with the range of production volume. For example, instead of budgeting for 8,000, 9,000, and 10,000 units of product, it might be necessary to provide for levels, at intervals of 500, from 6,000 to 12,000 units. Alternative bases, such as hours of departmental operation or direct labor hours, may also be used in measuring the volume of activity.

In preparing budget performance reports, the actual results would be compared with the flexible budget figures for the level of operations achieved. For example, if Collins Manufacturing Company manufactured 10,000 units during a month, the budget figures reported in the budget performance report would be those appearing in the "10,000 units" column of Collins' flexible budget.

## AUTOMATED BUDGETING PROCEDURES

Many firms use computers in the budgeting process. Computers can not only speed up the budgeting process, but they can also reduce the cost of budget preparation when large quantities of data need to be processed. Computers are especially useful in preparing flexible budgets and in continuous budgeting. Budget performance reports can also be prepared on a timely basis by the use of the computer.

By using computerized simulation models, which are mathematical statements of the relationships among various operating activities, management can determine the impact of various operating alternatives on the master budget. For example, if management wishes to evaluate the impact of a proposed change in direct labor wage rates, the computer can quickly provide a revised master budget that reflects the new rates. If management wishes to evaluate a proposal to add a new product line, the computer can quickly update current budgeted data and indicate the effect of the proposal on the master budget.

## BUDGETING AND HUMAN BEHAVIOR

The budgeting process sets the overall goals of the business as well as the specific goals for individual units. Significant human behavior problems can develop if these goals are viewed as unrealistic or unachievable by management personnel. In such a case, management may become discouraged as well as uncommitted to the achievement of the goals. As a result, the budget becomes worthless as a tool for planning and controlling operations. On the other hand, goals set within a range that management considers attainable are likely to inspire management's efforts to achieve the goals. Therefore, it is important that all levels of management be involved in establishing the goals which they will be expected to achieve. In such an environment, the budget is a planning tool that will favorably affect human behavior and increase the possibility of achieving the goals.

Human behavior problems can also arise when the budgeted and actual results are compared and reported. These problems can be minimized if budget performance reports are used exclusively to evaluate operating performance and to initiate corrective action when performance can be improved. However, if budget performance reports are also used to evaluate management performance, management may concentrate more on defending its performance than on using the budgeting system to plan and control operations.

There is little doubt that budgets and budget performance reports can have a significant influence on management behavior. Behavioral factors have received increased attention by management accountants and behavioral scientists in recent years, and many behavioral issues are the subject of ongoing research.

## Self-Examination Questions
*(Answers in Appendix C.)*

1. Budgeting of operating activities to provide at all times for maintenance of a twelve-month projection into the future is called:
   A. fixed budgeting
   B. variable budgeting
   C. continuous budgeting
   D. none of the above

2. The budget that summarizes future plans for acquisition of plant facilities and equipment is the:
   A. cash budget                     C. capital expenditures budget
   B. sales budget                   D. none of the above

3. A report comparing actual results with the budget figures is called a:
   A. budget report                  C. flexible budget report
   B. budget performance report      D. none of the above

4. Costs that tend to remain constant in amount, regardless of variations in volume of activity, are called:
   A. fixed costs                      C. semifixed costs
   B. variable costs                  D. semivariable costs

5. The system that "builds in" the effect of fluctuations in volume of activity into the various budgets is termed:
   A. budget performance reporting      C. flexible budgeting
   B. continuous budgeting            D. none of the above

---

**Discussion Questions**

1. What is a budget?

2. (a) Name the two basic functions of management in which accounting is involved. (b) How does a budget aid management in the discharge of these basic functions?

3. What is meant by *continuous budgeting*?

4. Why should all levels of management and all departments participate in the preparation and submission of budget estimates?

5. Which budgetary concept requires all levels of management to start from zero and estimate sales, production, and other operating data as though the operations were being initiated for the first time?

6. Why should the production requirements as set forth in the production budget be carefully coordinated with the sales budget?

7. Why should the timing of direct materials purchases be closely coordinated with the production budget?

8. What is a capital expenditures budget?

9. (a) Discuss the purpose of the cash budget. (b) If the cash budget for the first quarter of the fiscal year indicates excess cash at the end of each of the first two months, how might the excess cash be used?

10. What is a budget performance report?

11. What is a flexible budget?

12. Distinguish between (a) fixed costs and (b) variable costs.

13. Which of the following costs incurred by a manufacturing enterprise tend to be fixed and which tend to be variable: (a) rent on factory building, (b) cost of raw materials entering into finished product, (c) depreciation on factory building, (d) real estate taxes on factory building, (e) salary of factory superintendent, (f) direct labor, (g) factory supplies?

14. What is a semivariable (or semifixed) cost?

15. Haas Corporation uses flexible budgets. For each of the following variable operating expenses, indicate whether there has been a saving or an excess of expenses, assuming that actual sales were $400,000.

| Expense Item | Actual Amount | Budget Allowance Based on Sales |
|---|---|---|
| Factory supplies expense | $ 7,850 | 2% |
| Uncollectible accounts expense | 17,840 | 4% |

16. Briefly discuss the type of human behavior problem that might arise if goals used in developing budgets are unrealistic or unachievable.

**Exercises**

**Exercise 4-1.** Kipling Company manufactures two models of heating pads, HP-1 and HP-2. Based on the following production and sales data for April of the current year, prepare (a) a sales budget and (b) a production budget.

|  | HP-1 | HP-2 |
|---|---|---|
| Estimated inventory (units), April 1 | 30,000 | 13,800 |
| Desired inventory (units), April 30 | 36,000 | 12,000 |
| Expected sales volume (units): | | |
| Area 20 | 21,000 | 5,400 |
| Area 30 | 10,800 | 2,400 |
| Unit sales price | $9.60 | $13.20 |

**Exercise 4-2.** James Company was organized on April 1 of the current year. Projected sales for each of the first three months of operations are as follows:

| | |
|---|---|
| April | $200,000 |
| May | 250,000 |
| June | 350,000 |

The company expects to sell 30% of its merchandise for cash. Of sales on account, 40% are expected to be collected in the month of sale, 50% in the month following sale, and the remainder in the following month. Prepare a schedule indicating cash collections of accounts receivable for April, May, and June.

**Exercise 4-3.** Burton Company was organized on June 30 of the current year. Projected operating expenses for each of the first three months of operations are as follows:

| | |
|---|---|
| July | $ 75,000 |
| August | 90,000 |
| September | 111,000 |

Depreciation, insurance, and property taxes represent $15,000 of estimated monthly operating expenses. Insurance was paid on June 30, and property taxes will be paid in December. Two thirds of the remainder of the operating expenses are expected to be paid in the month in which they are incurred, with the balance to be paid in the following month. Prepare a schedule indicating cash disbursements for operating expenses for July, August, and September.

**Exercise 4-4.** Humphreys Company uses flexible budgets. Prepare a flexible operating expenses budget for February of the current year for sales volumes of $400,000, $500,000, and $600,000, based on the following data:

| | |
|---|---|
| Sales commissions ...................... | 9% of sales |
| Advertising expense .................... | $20,000 for $400,000 of sales |
| | $24,000 for $500,000 of sales |
| | $28,000 for $600,000 of sales |
| Miscellaneous selling expense ............. | $2,000 plus 1% of sales |
| Office salaries expense ................. | $18,600 |
| Office supplies expense.................. | 1½% of sales |
| Miscellaneous general expense ........... | $850 plus 1% of sales |

**Exercise 4-5.** The operating expenses incurred during February of the current year by Humphreys Company were as follows:

| | |
|---|---|
| Sales commissions..................... | $46,500 |
| Advertising expense ................... | 22,000 |
| Miscellaneous selling expense .......... | 7,200 |
| Office salaries expense................. | 18,600 |
| Office supplies expense ............... | 8,100 |
| Miscellaneous general expense ......... | 5,600 |

Assuming that the total sales for February were $500,000, prepare a budget performance report for operating expenses on the basis of the data presented above and in Exercise 4-4.

**Exercise 4-6.** Arness Company prepared the following factory overhead cost budget for Department F for September of the current year, during which it expected to manufacture 12,000 units:

| | | |
|---|---|---|
| Variable cost: | | |
| Indirect factory wages ............................... | $10,000 | |
| Power and light ..................................... | 8,500 | |
| Indirect materials.................................... | 3,000 | |
| Total variable cost................................. | | $21,500 |
| Fixed cost: | | |
| Supervisory salaries ................................. | $ 8,250 | |
| Depreciation of plant and equipment .................... | 4,100 | |
| Insurance and property taxes.......................... | 3,250 | |
| Total fixed cost .................................... | | 15,600 |
| Total factory overhead cost.............................. | | $37,100 |

Assuming that the estimated costs in September are applicable to October operations, prepare a flexible factory overhead cost budget for October for 11,400, 12,000, and 12,600 units of product.

**Exercise 4-7.** During October, Arness Company manufactured 11,400 units, and the factory overhead costs incurred were: indirect factory wages, $9,690; power and light, $8,180; indirect materials, $2,675; supervisory salaries, $8,250; depreciation of plant and equipment, $4,100; and insurance and property taxes, $3,250.

Prepare a budget performance report for October. To be useful for cost control, the budgeted amounts should be based on the data for 11,400 units, as revealed in Exercise 4-6.

**Problems**
*(Problems in Appendix B: 4-1B, 4-3B, 4-4B.)*

**Problem 4-1A.** T. I. C. Inc. prepared the following factory overhead cost budget for October of the current year for 9,000 units of product:

T. I. C. Inc.
Factory Overhead Cost Budget
For Month Ending October 31, 19--

| | | |
|---|---:|---:|
| Variable cost: | | |
|    Indirect factory wages | $14,175 | |
|    Indirect materials | 10,125 | |
|    Power and light | 9,000 | |
|      Total variable cost | | $33,300 |
| Fixed cost: | | |
|    Supervisory salaries | $11,500 | |
|    Indirect factory wages | 4,100 | |
|    Depreciation of plant and equipment | 3,800 | |
|    Insurance | 2,250 | |
|    Power and light | 2,000 | |
|    Property taxes | 1,350 | |
|      Total fixed cost | | 25,000 |
| Total factory overhead cost | | $58,300 |

The following factory overhead costs were incurred in producing 8,000 units:

| | |
|---|---:|
| Indirect factory wages | $16,500 |
| Supervisory salaries | 11,500 |
| Power and light | 10,600 |
| Indirect materials | 9,450 |
| Depreciation of plant and equipment | 3,800 |
| Insurance | 2,250 |
| Property taxes | 1,350 |
|    Total factory overhead cost incurred | $55,450 |

Instructions:
  (1) Prepare a flexible factory overhead cost budget for October, indicating capacities of 8,000, 9,000, 10,000, and 11,000 units of product.
  (2) Prepare a budget performance report for October.

**Problem 4-2A.** The budget director of Feinberg Company requests estimates of sales, production, and other operating data from the various administrative units every month. Selected information concerning sales and production for March of the current year are summarized as follows:

(a) Estimated sales for March by sales territory:
   East:
     Product P1 . . . . . . . . . . . . . . . . . . . . . . . . 10,000 units at $75 per unit
     Product P2 . . . . . . . . . . . . . . . . . . . . . . . . 12,000 units at $88 per unit
   Midwest:
     Product P1 . . . . . . . . . . . . . . . . . . . . . . . . 8,000 units at $75 per unit
     Product P2 . . . . . . . . . . . . . . . . . . . . . . . . 11,500 units at $88 per unit
   West:
     Product P1 . . . . . . . . . . . . . . . . . . . . . . . . 14,000 units at $75 per unit
     Product P2 . . . . . . . . . . . . . . . . . . . . . . . . 18,000 units at $88 per unit

(b) Estimated inventories at March 1:
   Direct materials:
     Material E:  10,600 lbs.
     Material F:   9,200 lbs.
     Material G:   4,800 lbs.
     Material H:  11,500 lbs.
   Finished products:
     Product P1:   4,000 units
     Product P2:   7,100 units

(c) Desired inventories at March 31:
   Direct materials:
     Material E:  12,000 lbs.
     Material F:   8,000 lbs.
     Material G:   5,000 lbs.
     Material H:  10,000 lbs.
   Finished products:
     Product P1:   5,000 units
     Product P2:   6,000 units

(d) Direct materials used in production:
   In manufacture of Product P1:
     Material E:  3.0 lbs. per unit of product
     Material F:  1.6 lbs. per unit of product
     Material G:  2.2 lbs. per unit of product
   In manufacture of Product P2:
     Material E:  1.5 lbs. per unit of product
     Material F:  1.0 lbs. per unit of product
     Material H:  3.0 lbs. per unit of product

(e) Anticipated purchase price for direct materials:
     Material E:  $ .45 per lb.
     Material F:  $1.80 per lb.
     Material G:  $ .80 per lb.
     Material H:  $ .75 per lb.

(f)  Direct labor requirements:
   Product P1:
      Department 10:   1.0 hour at $12 per hour
      Department 20:   1.5 hours at $15 per hour
   Product P2:
      Department 10:   2.0 hours at $12 per hour
      Department 30:   1.5 hours at $18 per hour

Instructions:
   (1)  Prepare a sales budget for March.
   (2)  Prepare a production budget for March.
   (3)  Prepare a direct materials purchases budget for March.
   (4)  Prepare a direct labor cost budget for March.

**Problem 4-3A.** Trane Company prepared the following sales budget for the current year:

Trane Company
Sales Budget
For Year Ending December 31, 1985

| Product and Area | Unit Sales Volume | Unit Selling Price | Total Sales |
|---|---|---|---|
| Product A: | | | |
| East | 28,000 | $22.50 | $   630,000 |
| Central | 18,000 | 22.50 | 405,000 |
| West | 25,000 | 22.50 | 562,500 |
| Total | 71,000 | | $1,597,500 |
| Product B: | | | |
| East | 42,000 | 10.00 | $   420,000 |
| Central | 30,000 | 10.00 | 300,000 |
| West | 45,000 | 10.00 | 450,000 |
| Total | 117,000 | | $1,170,000 |
| Total revenue from sales | | | $2,767,500 |

At the end of September, 1985, the following unit sales data were reported for the first nine months of the year:

| | Unit Sales | |
|---|---|---|
| | Product A | Product B |
| East | 23,100 | 34,650 |
| Central | 13,500 | 20,250 |
| West | 21,565 | 33,750 |

For the year ending December 31, 1986, unit sales are expected to follow the patterns established during the first nine months of the year ending December 31, 1985. The unit selling price for Product A is not expected to change, and the unit selling price for Product B is expected to be increased to $10.50, effective January 1, 1986.

Instructions:

(1) Compute the increase or decrease of actual *unit* sales for the nine months ended September 30, 1985, over expectations for this nine-month period. Since sales have historically occurred evenly throughout the year, budgeted sales for the first nine months of a year would be 75% of the year's budgeted sales. Comparison of this amount with actual sales will indicate the percentage increase or decrease of actual sales for the nine months over budgeted sales for the nine months. (Round percent changes to the nearest whole percent.) Place your answers in a columnar table with the following format:

| | Unit Budgeted Sales | | Actual Sales | Increase (Decrease) | |
|---|---|---|---|---|---|
| | Year | Nine Months | for Nine Months | Amount | Percent |
| **Product A** | | | | | |
| East | | | | | |
| Central | | | | | |
| West | | | | | |
| **Product B** | | | | | |
| East | | | | | |
| Central | | | | | |
| West | | | | | |

(2) Assuming that the trend of sales indicated in (1) is to continue in 1986, compute the unit sales volume to be used for preparing the sales budget for the year ending December 31, 1986. Place your answers in a columnar table with the following format:

| | 1985 Budgeted Units | Percentage Increase (Decrease) | 1986 Budgeted Units |
|---|---|---|---|
| **Product A** | | | |
| East | | | |
| Central | | | |
| West | | | |
| **Product B** | | | |
| East | | | |
| Central | | | |
| West | | | |

(3) Prepare a sales budget for the year ending December 31, 1986.

**Problem 4-4A.** The treasurer of Epstein Company instructs you to prepare a monthly cash budget for the next three months. You are presented with the following budget information:

| | August | September | October |
|---|---|---|---|
| Sales | $480,000 | $450,000 | $510,000 |
| Manufacturing costs | 284,000 | 230,000 | 288,000 |
| Operating expenses | 162,000 | 150,000 | 176,000 |
| Capital expenditures | —— | 200,000 | —— |

The company expects to sell about 30% of its merchandise for cash. Of sales on account, 80% are expected to be collected in full in the month following the sale and the remainder the following month. Depreciation, insurance, and property taxes represent $12,000 of the estimated monthly manufacturing costs and $4,000 of the probable monthly operating expenses. Insurance and property taxes are paid in June and December respectively. Of the remainder of the manufacturing costs and operating expenses, 60% are expected to be paid in the month in which they are incurred and the balance in the following month.

Current assets as of August 1 are composed of cash of $58,500, marketable securities of $50,000, and accounts receivable of $474,500 ($383,500 from July sales and $91,000 from June sales). Current liabilities as of August 1 are composed of an $80,000, 15%, 120-day note payable due September 15, $82,500 of accounts payable incurred in July for manufacturing costs, and accrued liabilities of $48,200 incurred in July for operating expenses.

It is expected that $1,800 in dividends will be received in August. An estimated income tax payment of $26,000 will be made in October. Epstein Company's regular semiannual dividend of $15,000 is expected to be declared in September and paid in October. Management desires to maintain a minimum cash balance of $50,000.

Instructions:

(1) Prepare a monthly cash budget for August, September, and October.
(2) On the basis of the cash budget prepared in (1), what recommendation should be made to the treasurer?

**Problem 4-5A.** As a preliminary to requesting budget estimates of sales, costs, and expenses for the fiscal year beginning January 1, 1984, the following tentative trial balance as of December 31 of the preceding year is prepared by the accounting department of Bromley Company:

| | | |
|---|---:|---:|
| Cash.......................................................... | 58,000 | |
| Accounts Receivable ................................... | 56,000 | |
| Finished Goods ......................................... | 102,200 | |
| Work in Process......................................... | 59,200 | |
| Materials .................................................. | 34,800 | |
| Prepaid Expenses ...................................... | 6,800 | |
| Plant and Equipment.................................... | 540,000 | |
| Accumulated Depreciation — Plant and Equipment.......... | | 216,000 |
| Accounts Payable ....................................... | | 66,000 |
| Notes Payable ........................................... | | 40,000 |
| Common Stock, $10 par................................. | | 100,000 |
| Retained Earnings ...................................... | | 435,000 |
| | 857,000 | 857,000 |

Factory output and sales for 1984 are expected to total 40,000 units of product, which are to be sold at $18 per unit. The quantities and costs of the inventories (lifo method) at December 31, 1984, are expected to remain unchanged from the balances at the beginning of the year.

Budget estimates of manufacturing costs and operating expenses for the year are summarized as follows:

|  | Estimated Costs and Expenses | |
|---|---|---|
|  | Fixed (Total for Year) | Variable (Per Unit Sold) |
| Cost of goods manufactured and sold: | | |
| Direct materials | —— | $2.30 |
| Direct labor | —— | 5.60 |
| Factory overhead: | | |
| Depreciation of plant and equipment | $28,800 | —— |
| Other factory overhead | 19,200 | 1.70 |
| Selling expenses: | | |
| Sales salaries and commissions | 40,000 | .90 |
| Advertising | 20,500 | —— |
| Miscellaneous selling expense | 1,500 | .10 |
| General expenses: | | |
| Office and officers salaries | 50,000 | .40 |
| Supplies | 3,400 | .10 |
| Miscellaneous general expense | 2,600 | .05 |

Balances of accounts receivable, prepaid expenses, and accounts payable at the end of the year are expected to differ from the beginning balances by only inconsequential amounts.

For purposes of this problem, assume that federal income tax of $24,000 on 1984 taxable income will be paid during 1984. Regular quarterly cash dividends of $.20 a share are expected to be declared and paid in March, June, September, and December. It is anticipated that plant and equipment will be purchased for $125,000 cash in September.

Instructions:

(1) Prepare a budgeted income statement for 1984.
(2) Prepare a budgeted balance sheet as of December 31, 1984.

**Mini-Case**

Your father is president and chief operating officer of Thomas Manufacturing Company and has hired you as a summer intern to assist the controller. The controller has asked you to visit with the production supervisor of the Sanding Department and evaluate the supervisor's concerns with the budgeting process. After this evaluation, you are to meet with the controller to discuss suggestions for improving the budgeting process.

This morning, you met with the supervisor, who expressed dissatisfaction with the budgets and budget performance reports prepared for the factory overhead costs for the Sanding Department. Specifically, June's budget performance report was mentioned as an example. The supervisor indicated that this report is not useful in evaluating the efficiency of the department, because most of the overages for the individual factory overhead items are not caused by inefficiencies, but by variations in the volume of activity between actual and budget. Although you were not provided with a copy of the budget for June, the supervisor indicated that it is standard practice for the plant manager to prepare a budget based on the production of 10,000 units. Actual production varies widely, however, with approximately 11,000 to 12,000 units being produced each month for the past several months. You are provided with the following budget performance report for June of the current year, when actual production was 11,000 units. All of the overages relate to variable costs, and the other costs are fixed.

Thomas Manufacturing Company
Budget Performance Report — Factory Overhead Cost, Sanding Department
For Month Ended June 30, 19--

|  | Budget | Actual | Over | Under |
|---|---|---|---|---|
| Indirect factory wages ................. | $10,000 | $10,900 | $ 900 | |
| Electric power ....................... | 8,000 | 8,950 | 950 | |
| Supervisory salaries................... | 7,500 | 7,500 | | |
| Depreciation of plant assets............ | 5,250 | 5,250 | | |
| Indirect materials .................... | 5,000 | 5,400 | 400 | |
| Insurance and property taxes........... | 3,000 | 3,000 | | |
| | $38,750 | $41,000 | $2,250 | |

In your discussion, you learned that the department supervisor has little faith in the budgeting process. The supervisor views the budgets as worthless and the budget performance reports as a waste of time, because they require an explanation of the budget overages, which, for the most part, are not departmentally controlled.

Instructions:

Prepare a list of suggestions for improving the budgeting process. Include any reports that you might find useful when you meet with the controller to discuss your suggestions.

# 5

# Standard Cost Systems

**CHAPTER OBJECTIVES**

*Describe the nature of standard costs.*

*Describe the use of standard costs in planning and controlling operations.*

*Illustrate the use of variance analysis in controlling operations.*

# 5

## CHAPTER

The preceding chapter focused on the use of budgets as an aid to management in planning and controlling the operations of a business. This chapter will focus on standard cost systems and variance analysis, which can also be used by management in planning and controlling operations.

## THE NATURE AND OBJECTIVES OF STANDARDS

Standards are used to measure and evaluate performance in many areas of life. For example, colleges and universities set standards for graduation, such as a C average. They may establish a B+ average for graduation with honors. Golfers use par as a standard in evaluating their play on the golf course. In each of these cases, the predetermined standard is used to measure and evaluate an individual's performance. In a like manner, business enterprises may use carefully predetermined standards to evaluate and control operations.

Service, merchandising, and manufacturing enterprises can all use standards. For example, an automobile repair garage may use a *standard* amount of time, as expressed in service manuals, as the basis for computing the labor charges for automobile repairs and measuring the performance of the mechanic. The driver of a truck delivering merchandise may be expected to make a *standard* number of deliveries each day. The widest use of standards is by manufacturing enterprises, which establish standard costs for the three categories of manufacturing costs: direct materials, direct labor, and factory overhead.

Accounting systems that use standards for each element of manufacturing cost entering into the finished product are sometimes called standard cost systems. Such systems enable management to determine how much a product should cost (standard), how much it does cost (actual), and the causes of any difference (variance) between the two. Standard costs thus serve as a device for measuring efficiency. If the actual costs are compared with the standard costs, unfavorable conditions can be determined and corrective actions taken. Thus, management has a device for controlling costs and motivating employees to become more cost conscious.

Standard costs may be used in either the process cost or the job order cost systems. Both of these systems, as discussed in Chapters 2 and 3, can provide management with timely data on manufacturing costs and may aid in cost control and profit maximization. For more effective control, standard costs should be used for each department or cost center in the factory. It is possible, however, to use standard costs in some departments and actual costs in others.

## Setting Standards

The starting point in setting standards is often a review of past operations. In this review, management and the management accountant rely on their knowledge and judgment of past processes and costs to estimate the costs to produce a unit of product. However, standards should not be merely an extension of past costs. Inefficiencies may be reflected in past costs, and these inefficiencies should be considered in determining what the costs should be (standards). In addition, changes in technology, machinery, production methods, and economic conditions must be considered.

The setting of standards is both an art and a science. Although the standard-setting process varies among enterprises, it often requires the joint efforts of accountants, engineers, personnel administrators, and other management personnel. The management accountant plays an important role by expressing the results of judgments and studies in terms of dollars and subsequently reporting how actual results compare with these standards. Engineers contribute to the standard-setting process by studying the requirements of the product and the production process. For example, direct materials requirements can be determined by studying such factors as the materials specifications for the product and the normal spoilage in production. Time and motion studies may be used to determine the length of time required for each of the various manufacturing operations. Engineering studies may also be used to determine standards for some of the elements of factory overhead, such as the amount of power needed to operate machinery.

**Types of Standards**

Implicit in the use of standards is the concept of an acceptable level of production efficiency. One of the major objectives in selecting this performance level is to motivate workers to expend the efforts necessary to achieve the most efficient operations.

Standards that are too high, that is, standards that are unrealistic, may have a negative impact on performance because workers may become frustrated with their inability to meet the standards and, therefore, may not be motivated to do their best. Such standards represent levels of performance that can be achieved only under perfect operating conditions, such as no idle time, no machine breakdowns, and no materials spoilage. Such standards, often called theoretical standards or **ideal standards**, are not widely used.

Standards that are too low might not motivate employees to perform at their best because the standard level of performance can be reached too easily. As a result, productivity may be lower than that which could be achieved.

Most companies use currently attainable standards (sometimes called **normal standards**), which represent levels of operation that can be attained with reasonable effort. Such currently attainable standards allow for reasonable production problems and errors, such as normal materials spoilage and machinery downtime for maintenance. When reasonable standards are used, employees often become cost conscious and expend their best efforts to achieve the best possible results at the lowest possible cost. Also, if employees are given bonuses for exceeding normal standards, the standards may be even more effective in motivating employees to perform at their best.

**VARIANCES FROM STANDARDS**

One of the primary purposes of a standard cost system is to facilitate control over costs by comparing actual costs with standard costs. Control is achieved by the action of management in investigating significant deviations of performance from standards and taking corrective action. Differences between the standard costs of a department or product and the actual costs incurred are termed variances. If the actual cost incurred is less than the standard cost, the variance is favorable. If the actual cost exceeds the standard cost, the variance is unfavorable. When actual costs are compared with standard costs, only the "exceptions" or variances are reported to the person responsible for cost control. This reporting by the "principle of exceptions" enables the one responsible for cost control to concentrate on the cause and correction of the variances.

When manufacturing operations are automated, standard cost data can be integrated with the computer that directs operations. Variances can then be detected and reported automatically by the computer system, and adjustments can be made to operations in progress.

The total variance for a certain period is usually made up of several variances, some of which may be favorable and some unfavorable. There may be variances from standards in direct materials costs, in direct labor costs, and in factory overhead costs. Illustrations and analyses of these variances for Ballard Company, a manufacturing enterprise, are presented in the following paragraphs. For illustrative purposes, it is assumed that only one type of direct material is used, that there is a single processing department, and that Product X is the only commodity manufactured by the enterprise. The standard costs for direct materials, direct labor, and factory overhead for a unit of Product X are as follows:

| | |
|---|---|
| Direct materials: | |
| 2 pounds at $1 per pound | $ 2.00 |
| Direct labor: | |
| .4 hour at $16 per hour | 6.40 |
| Factory overhead: | |
| .4 hour at $8.40 per hour | 3.36 |
| Total per unit | $11.76 |

**Direct Materials Cost Variance**

Two major factors enter into the determination of standards for direct materials cost: (1) the quantity (usage) standard and (2) the price standard. If the actual quantity of direct materials used in producing a commodity differs from the standard quantity, there is a quantity variance. If the actual unit price of the materials differs from the standard price, there is a price variance. To illustrate, assume that the standard direct materials cost of producing 10,000 units of Product X and the direct materials cost actually incurred during June were as follows:

Actual:     20,600 pounds at $1.04 . . . . . . . . $21,424
Standard:  20,000 pounds at $1.00 . . . . . . . .  20,000

The unfavorable variance of $1,424 resulted in part from an excess usage of 600 pounds of direct materials and in part from an excess cost of $.04 per pound. The analysis of the materials cost variance is as follows:

✓ **DIRECT MATERIALS COST VARIANCE**

| | | |
|---|---|---|
| Quantity variance: | | |
| Actual quantity | 20,600 pounds | |
| Standard quantity | 20,000 pounds | |
| Variance—unfavorable | 600 pounds × standard price, $1 | $ 600 |
| Price variance: | | |
| Actual price | $1.04 per pound | |
| Standard price | 1.00 per pound | |
| Variance—unfavorable | $ .04 per pound × actual quantity, 20,600 | 824 |
| Total direct materials cost variance—unfavorable | | $1,424 |

### Direct Materials Quantity Variance

The direct materials quantity variance is the difference between the actual quantity used and the standard quantity, multiplied by the standard price per unit. If the standard quantity exceeds the actual quantity used, the variance is favorable. If the actual quantity of materials used exceeds the standard quantity, the variance is unfavorable, as shown for Ballard Company in the following illustration:

**DIRECT MATERIALS QUANTITY VARIANCE**

$$\text{Direct Materials Quantity Variance} = \frac{\text{Actual Quantity Used} -}{\text{Standard Quantity}} \times \frac{\text{Standard Price}}{\text{per Unit}}$$

Quantity variance = (20,600 pounds − 20,000 pounds) × $1.00 per pound
Quantity variance = 600 pounds × $1.00 per pound
Quantity variance = $600 unfavorable

### Direct Materials Price Variance

The direct materials price variance is the difference between the actual price per unit and the standard price per unit, multiplied by the actual quantity used. If the standard price per unit exceeds the actual price per unit, the variance is favorable. If the actual price per unit exceeds the standard price per unit, the variance is unfavorable, as shown for Ballard Company in the following illustration:

**DIRECT MATERIALS PRICE VARIANCE**

$$\text{Direct Materials Price Variance} = \frac{\text{Actual Price per Unit} -}{\text{Standard Price}} \times \frac{\text{Actual Quantity}}{\text{Used}}$$

Price variance = ($1.04 per pound − $1.00 per pound) × 20,600 pounds
Price variance = $.04 per pound × 20,600 pounds
Price variance = $824 unfavorable

### Reporting Direct Materials Cost Variance

The physical quantity and the dollar amount of the quantity variance should be reported to the factory superintendent and other personnel responsible for production. If excessive amounts of direct materials were used because of the malfunction of equipment or some other failure within the production department, those responsible should correct the situation. However, an unfavorable direct materials quantity variance is not necessarily the result of inefficiency within the production department. If the excess usage of 600 pounds of materials in the example above had been caused by inferior materials, the purchasing department should be held responsible.

The unit price and the total amount of the materials price variance should be reported to the purchasing department, which may or may not be able to control this variance. If materials of the same quality could have been purchased from another supplier at the standard price, the variance was controllable. On the other hand, if the variance resulted from a marketwide price increase, the variance was not subject to control.

**Direct Labor Cost Variance**

As in the case of direct materials, two major factors enter into the determination of standards for direct labor cost: (1) the time (usage or efficiency) standard, and (2) the rate (price or wage) standard. If the actual direct labor hours spent producing a product differ from the standard hours, there is a time variance. If the wage rate paid differs from the standard rate, there is a ~~rate variance~~. The standard cost and the actual cost of direct labor in the production of 10,000 units of Product X during June are assumed to be as follows:

> Actual:    3,950 hours at $16.40......... $64,780
> Standard:  4,000 hours at   16.00.........  64,000

The unfavorable direct labor variance of $780 is made up of a favorable time variance and an unfavorable rate variance, determined as follows:

**✓ DIRECT LABOR COST VARIANCE**

Time variance:
Actual time ............. 3,950 hours
Standard time........... 4,000 hours

    Variance—favorable....    50 hours × standard rate, $16.......... $  800

Rate variance:
Actual rate.............. $16.40 per hour
Standard rate ........... 16.00 per hour

    Variance—unfavorable.. $  .40 per hour × actual time, 3,950 hours ..  1,580

Total direct labor cost variance—unfavorable ........................... $  780

## Direct Labor Time Variance

The direct labor time variance is the difference between the actual hours worked and the standard hours, multiplied by the standard rate per hour. If the actual hours worked exceed the standard hours, the variance is ~~unfavorable~~. If the actual hours worked are less than the standard hours, the variance is ~~favorable~~, as shown for Ballard Company in the following illustration:

**✓ DIRECT LABOR TIME VARIANCE**

$$\frac{\text{Direct Labor}}{\text{Time Variance}} = \frac{\text{Actual Hours Worked} -}{\text{Standard Hours}} \times \frac{\text{Standard Rate}}{\text{per Hour}}$$

Time variance = (3,950 hours − 4,000 hours) × $16 per hour
Time variance = −50 hours                      × $16 per hour
Time variance = $800 favorable

In the illustration, when the standard hours (4,000) are subtracted from the actual hours worked (3,950), the difference is "−50 hours." The minus sign indicates that the variance of 50 hours, or $800 (50 hours × $16), is favorable.

## Direct Labor Rate Variance

The ~~direct labor rate variance~~ is the difference between the actual rate per hour and the standard rate per hour, multiplied by the actual hours worked. If the standard rate per hour exceeds the actual rate per hour, the variance is ~~favorable~~. If the actual rate per hour exceeds the standard rate per hour, the variance is ~~unfavorable~~, as shown for Ballard Company in the following illustration:

**✓ DIRECT LABOR RATE VARIANCE**

$$\frac{\text{Direct Labor}}{\text{Rate Variance}} = \frac{\text{Actual Rate per Hour} -}{\text{Standard Rate}} \times \frac{\text{Actual Hours}}{\text{Worked}}$$

Rate variance = ($16.40 per hour − $16.00 per hour) × 3,950 hours
Rate variance = $.40 per hour                        × 3,950 hours
Rate variance = $1,580 unfavorable

### Reporting Direct Labor Cost Variance

The control of direct labor cost is often in the hands of production supervisors. To aid them, daily or weekly reports analyzing the cause of any direct labor variance may be prepared. A comparison of standard direct labor hours and actual direct labor hours will provide the basis for an investigation into the efficiency of direct labor (time variance). A comparison of the rates paid for direct labor with the standard rates highlights the efficiency of the supervisors or the personnel department in selecting the proper grade of direct labor for production (rate variance).

**Factory Overhead Cost Variance**

Some of the difficulties encountered in allocating factory overhead costs among products manufactured have been considered in Chapter 2. These difficulties stem from the great variety of costs that are included in factory overhead and their nature as indirect costs. For the same reasons, the procedures used in determining standards and variances for factory overhead cost are more complex than those used for direct materials cost and direct labor cost.

A flexible budget is used to establish the standard factory overhead rate and to aid in determining subsequent variations from standard. The standard rate is determined by dividing the standard factory overhead costs by the standard amount of productive activity, generally expressed in direct labor hours, direct labor cost, or machine hours. A flexible budget showing the standard factory overhead rate for a month is as follows:

**FACTORY OVERHEAD COST BUDGET INDICATING STANDARD FACTORY OVERHEAD RATE**

| Ballard Company Factory Overhead Cost Budget For Month Ending June 30, 19-- | | | | |
|---|---|---|---|---|
| Percent of productive capacity.............. | 80% | 90% | 100% | 110% |
| Direct labor hours ........................ | 4,000 | 4,500 | 5,000 | 5,500 |
| **Budgeted factory overhead:** | | | | |
| Variable cost: | | | | |
| Indirect factory wages ................ | $12,800 | $14,400 | $16,000 | $17,600 |
| Power and light ..................... | 5,600 | 6,300 | 7,000 | 7,700 |
| Indirect materials..................... | 3,200 | 3,600 | 4,000 | 4,400 |
| Maintenance......................... | 2,400 | 2,700 | 3,000 | 3,300 |
| Total variable cost.................. | $24,000 | $27,000 | $30,000 | $33,000 |
| Fixed cost: | | | | |
| Supervisory salaries .................. | $ 5,500 | $ 5,500 | $ 5,500 | $ 5,500 |
| Depreciation of plant and equipment ... | 4,500 | 4,500 | 4,500 | 4,500 |
| Insurance and property taxes.......... | 2,000 | 2,000 | 2,000 | 2,000 |
| Total fixed cost..................... | $12,000 | $12,000 | $12,000 | $12,000 |
| Total factory overhead cost............. | $36,000 | $39,000 | $42,000 | $45,000 |
| Factory overhead rate per direct labor hour ($42,000 ÷ 5,000).... | | $8.40 | | |

The standard factory overhead cost rate is determined on the basis of the projected factory overhead costs at 100% of productive capacity, where this level of capacity represents the general expectation of business activity under normal operating conditions. In the illustration, the standard factory overhead rate is $8.40 per direct labor hour. This rate can be subdivided into $6 per hour for variable factory overhead ($30,000 ÷ 5,000 hours) and $2.40 per hour for fixed factory overhead ($12,000 ÷ 5,000 hours).

Variances from standard for factory overhead cost result (1) from operating at a level above or below 100% of capacity and (2) from incurring a total amount of factory overhead cost greater or less than the amount budgeted for the level of operations achieved. The first factor results in the volume variance, which is a measure of the penalty of operating at less than 100% of productive capacity or the benefit from operating at a level above 100% of productive capacity. The second factor results in the controllable variance, which is the difference between the actual amount of factory overhead incurred and the amount of factory overhead budgeted for the level of production achieved during the period. To illustrate, assume that the actual cost and standard cost of factory overhead for Ballard Company's production of 10,000 units of Product X during June were as follows:

Actual:  Variable factory overhead...... $24,600
         Fixed factory overhead ........ 12,000  $36,600
Standard: 4,000 hours at $8.40 .........         33,600

The unfavorable factory overhead cost variance of $3,000 is made up of a volume variance and a controllable variance, determined as follows:

**FACTORY OVERHEAD COST VARIANCE**

Volume variance:
Productive capacity of 100%........................... 5,000 hours
Standard for amount produced......................... 4,000 hours
Productive capacity not used ......................... 1,000 hours
Standard fixed factory overhead cost rate.............. × $2.40
    Variance—unfavorable....................................... $2,400
Controllable variance:
Actual factory overhead cost incurred .................. $36,600
Budgeted factory overhead for standard product produced.. 36,000
    Variance—unfavorable........................................ 600
Total factory overhead cost variance—unfavorable .................... $3,000

## Factory Overhead Volume Variance

The factory overhead volume variance is the difference between the productive capacity at 100% and the standard productive capacity, multiplied by the standard fixed factory overhead rate. If the standard capacity for the amount produced exceeds the productive capacity at 100%, the variance is favorable. If the productive capacity at 100% exceeds the standard capacity for the amount

The foregoing brief introduction to analysis of factory overhead cost variance suggests the many difficulties that may be encountered in actual practice. The rapid increase of automation in factory operations has been accompanied by increased attention to factory overhead costs. The use of predetermined standards and the analysis of variances from such standards provides management with the best possible means of establishing responsibility and controlling factory overhead costs.

**STANDARDS IN THE ACCOUNTS**

Although standard costs can be used solely as a statistical device apart from the ledger, it is generally considered preferable to incorporate them in the accounts. One approach, when this plan is used, is to identify the variances in the accounts at the time the manufacturing costs are recorded in the accounts. To illustrate, assume that Marin Corporation purchased, on account, 10,000 pounds of direct materials at $1 per pound, when the standard price was $.95 per pound. The entry, in general journal form, to record the purchase and the unfavorable direct materials price variance is as follows:

| | | |
|---|---:|---:|
| Materials . . . . . . . . . . . . . . . . . . . . . . . . . . . . . . . . . . . . . . . . . . . . . . . . | 9,500 | |
| Direct Materials Price Variance . . . . . . . . . . . . . . . . . . . . . . . | 500 | |
| Accounts Payable . . . . . . . . . . . . . . . . . . . . . . . . . . . . . . . . . . . . | | 10,000 |

The materials account is debited for the 10,000 pounds at the standard price of $.95 per pound. The unfavorable direct materials price variance is $500 [($1.00 actual price per pound − $.95 standard price per pound) × 10,000 pounds purchased] and is recorded by a debit to Direct Materials Price Variance. Accounts Payable is credited for the actual amount owed, $10,000 (10,000 pounds at $1 per pound). If the variance had been favorable, Direct Materials Price Variance would have been credited for the amount of the variance.

The accounts affected by the purchase of direct materials would appear as follows:

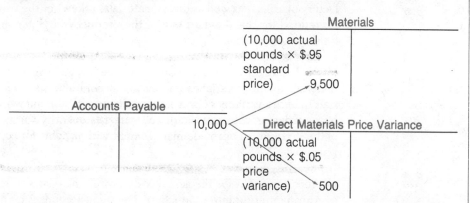

Variances in other manufacturing costs are recorded in a manner similar to the direct materials price variance. For example, if Marin Corporation used 4,900 pounds of direct materials to produce a product with a standard of 5,000 pounds, the entry to record the variance and the materials used would be as follows:

| | | | |
|---|---|---:|---:|
| ✓ | Work in Process. . . . . . . . . . . . . . . . . . . . . . . . . . . . . . . . . . . . . . . . . | 4,750 | |
| | Materials . . . . . . . . . . . . . . . . . . . . . . . . . . . . . . . . . . . . . . . . . . . . | | 4,655 |
| | Direct Materials Quantity Variance . . . . . . . . . . . . . . . . . . . . | | 95 |

The work in process account is debited for the standard price of the standard amount of direct materials required, $4,750 (5,000 pounds × $.95). Materials is credited for the actual amount of materials used at the standard price, $4,655 (4,900 pounds × $.95). The favorable direct materials quantity variance of $95 [(5,000 standard pounds − 4,900 actual pounds) × $.95 standard price per pound] is credited to Direct Materials Quantity Variance. If the variance had been unfavorable, Direct Materials Quantity Variance would have been debited for the amount of the variance.

The accounts affected by the use of direct materials would appear as follows:

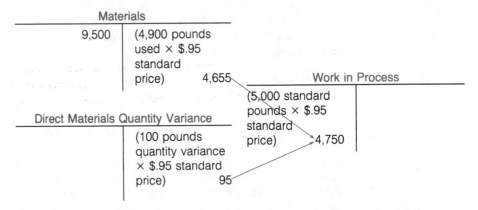

For Marin Corporation, the entries for direct labor, factory overhead, and other variances are recorded in a manner similar to the entries for direct materials. The work in process account is debited for the standard costs of direct labor and factory overhead as well as direct materials. Likewise, the work in process account is credited for the standard cost of the product completed and transferred to the finished goods account.

In a given period, it is possible to have both favorable and unfavorable variances. For example, if a favorable variance has been recorded, such as the direct materials quantity variance for Marin Corporation, and unfavorable direct materials quantity variances occur later in the period, the unfavorable variances would be recorded as debits in the direct materials quantity variance account. Analyses of this account may provide management with insights for controlling direct materials usage.

Another means of incorporating standards in the accounts is to debit the work in process account for the actual cost of direct materials, direct labor, and factory overhead entering into production. The same account is credited for the standard cost of the product completed and transferred to the finished goods account. The balance remaining in the work in process account is then made up of the ending inventory of work in process and the variances of actual cost from standard cost. In the following accounts for Ballard Company, there is assumed to be no ending inventory of work in process:

### Work in Process

| | | | |
|---|---|---|---|
| Direct materials (actual) | 21,424 | To finished goods (standard) | 117,600 |
| Direct labor (actual) | 64,780 | | |
| Factory overhead (actual) | 36,600 | | |
| *5,204* | 122,804 | | |

### Finished Goods

| | |
|---|---|
| From work in process (standard) | 117,600 |

The balance in the work in process account is the sum of the variances between the standard and actual costs. In the illustration, the debit balance of $5,204 indicates a net unfavorable variance. If the balance had been a credit, it would have indicated a net favorable variance.

**REPORTING VARIANCES ON THE INCOME STATEMENT**

Variances from standard costs are usually not reported to stockholders and others outside of management. If standards are recorded in the accounts, however, it is customary to disclose the variances on income statements prepared for management. An interim monthly income statement prepared for Ballard Company's internal use is illustrated as follows:

VARIANCES FROM STANDARDS IN INCOME STATEMENT

**Ballard Company**
**Income Statement**
**For Month Ended June 30, 19--**

| | Favorable | Unfavorable | |
|---|---|---|---|
| Sales........................................ | | | $185,400 |
| Cost of goods sold—at standard........ | | | 113,500 |
| Gross profit—at standard .............. | | | $ 71,900 |
| Less variances from standard cost: | | | |
| Direct materials quantity.............. | | $ 600 | |
| Direct materials price................. | | 824 | |
| Direct labor time..................... | $800 | | |
| Direct labor rate ..................... | | 1,580 | |
| Factory overhead volume............. | | 2,400 | |
| Factory overhead controllable........ | ___ | 600 | 5,204 |
| Gross profit .......................... | | | $ 66,696 |
| Operating expenses: | | | |
| Selling expenses..................... | | $22,500 | |
| General expenses ................... | | 19,225 | 41,725 |
| Income from operations .............. | | | $ 24,971 |

At the end of the fiscal year, the variances from standard are usually transferred to the cost of goods sold account. However, if the variances are significant or if many of the products manufactured are still on hand, the variances should be allocated to the work in process, finished goods, and cost of goods sold accounts. The result of such an allocation is to convert these account balances from standard cost to actual cost.

**REVISION OF STANDARDS**

Standard costs should be continuously reviewed, and when they no longer represent the conditions that were present when the standards were set, they should be changed. Standards should not be revised merely because of variances, but because they no longer reflect the conditions that they were intended to measure. For example, the direct labor cost standard would not be revised simply because workers were unable to meet properly determined standards. On the other hand, standards should be revised when prices, product designs, labor rates, manufacturing methods, or other circumstances change to such an extent that the current standards no longer represent a useful measure of performance.

**STANDARDS FOR NONMANUFAC-TURING EXPENSES**

The use of standards for nonmanufacturing expenses is not as common as the use of standards for manufacturing costs. This difference in the use of standards is due in part to the fact that nonmanufacturing expenses are, in many cases, not nearly as large as the manufacturing costs. Another major reason is that while many manufacturing operations are repetitive and thus subject to the determination of a per unit cost of output, many nonmanufacturing expenses do not lend themselves to such measurement. In many cases, for example, the costs associated with an assembly line can be measured and related to a uniform product unit. On the other hand, the expenses associated with the work of the office manager are not easily related to any unit of output.

When nonmanufacturing activities are repetitive and generate a somewhat homogeneous product, the concept of standards can be applied. In these cases, the process of estimating and using standards can be similar to that described for a manufactured product. For example, standards can be applied to the work of office personnel who process sales orders, and a standard unit expense for processing a sales order could be determined. The variance between the actual cost of processing a sales order with the standard expense can then be evaluated by management and corrective action taken.

In practice, standards are not widely used for nonmanufacturing expenses. Instead, these expenses are generally controlled by the use of budgets and budget performance reports, as discussed in Chapter 4. However, the use of standards appears to be gaining in acceptance as more attention is being given to the non-manufacturing expenses by the managerial accountant.

---

**Self-Examination Questions**
*(Answers in Appendix C.)*

1. The actual and standard direct materials costs for producing a specified quantity of product are as follows:

| | | |
|---|---|---|
| Actual: | 51,000 pounds at $5.05 ....... | $257,550 |
| Standard: | 50,000 pounds at $5.00 ....... | 250,000 |

The direct materials price variance is:

A. $2,500 unfavorable      C. $7,550 unfavorable
B. $2,550 unfavorable      D. none of the above

2. The actual and standard direct labor costs for producing a specified quantity of product are as follows:

| | | |
|---|---|---|
| Actual: | 990 hours at $10.90 ......... | $10,791 |
| Standard: | 1,000 hours at $11.00 .......... | 11,000 |

The direct labor cost time variance is:

A. $99 favorable      C. $110 favorable
B. $99 unfavorable      D. $110 unfavorable

3. The actual and standard factory overhead costs for producing a specified quantity of product are as follows:

| | | | |
|---|---|---|---|
| Actual: | Variable factory overhead ....$72,500 | | |
| | Fixed factory overhead....... 40,000 | $112,500 | |
| Standard: | 19,000 hours at $6 | | |
| | ($4 variable and $2 fixed) .... | | 114,000 |

If 1,000 hours of productive capacity were unused, the factory overhead volume variance would be:

A. $1,500 favorable      C. $4,000 unfavorable
B. $2,000 unfavorable      D. none of the above

4. Based on the data in Question 3, the factory overhead controllable variance would be:

A. $3,500 favorable      C. $1,500 favorable
B. $3,500 unfavorable      D. none of the above

5. Variances from standard costs are reported on interim income statements as:

A. selling expenses      C. other expenses
B. general expenses      D. none of the above

**Discussion Questions**

1. What are the basic objectives in the use of standard costs?

2. (a) Describe theoretical (ideal) standards and discuss the possible impact of theoretical standards on worker performance. (b) Describe currently attainable (normal) standards and discuss the possible impact of currently attainable standards on worker performance.

3. How can standards be used by management to achieve control over costs?

4. As the term is used in reference to standard costs, what is a *variance*?

5. What is meant by reporting by the "principle of exceptions" as the term is used in reference to cost control?

6. (a) What are the two variances between actual cost and standard cost for direct materials? (b) Discuss some possible causes of these variances.

7. (a) What are the two variances between actual cost and standard cost for direct labor? (b) Who generally has control over the direct labor cost?

8. (a) Describe the two variances between actual costs and standard costs for factory overhead. (b) What is a factory overhead cost variance report?

9. If variances are recorded in the accounts at the time the manufacturing costs are incurred, what does a credit balance in Direct Materials Price Variance represent?

10. If variances are recorded in the accounts at the time the manufacturing costs are incurred, what does a debit balance in Direct Materials Quantity Variance represent?

11. If standards are recorded in the accounts and Work in Process is debited for the actual manufacturing costs and credited for the standard cost of products produced, what does the balance in Work in Process represent?

12. Are variances from standard costs usually reported in financial statements issued to stockholders and others outside the firm?

13. Assuming that the variances from standards are not significant at the end of the period, to what account are they transferred?

14. How often should standards be revised?

15. Are standards for nonmanufacturing expenses as widely used as standards for manufacturing costs?

**Exercises**

**Exercise 5-1.** The following data relate to the direct materials cost for the production of 50,000 units of product:

Actual: 101,000 pounds at $2.95 .......................... $297,950
Standard: 100,000 pounds at 3.00 .......................... 300,000

Determine the quantity variance, price variance, and total direct materials cost variance. _& explain_

**Exercise 5-2.** The following data relating to direct materials cost for June of the current year are taken from the records of D. J. Drury Company:

Quantity of direct materials used ..................... 28 000 kilograms
Unit cost of direct materials......................... $2 per kilogram
Units of finished product manufactured ............... 10,100 units
Standard direct materials per unit of finished product... 2.5 kilograms
Direct materials quantity variance—unfavorable ....... $5,720
Direct materials price variance—favorable ........... $2,240

Determine the standard direct materials cost per unit of finished product, assuming that there was no inventory of work in process at either the beginning or the end of the month. Present your computations.

**Exercise 5-3.** The following data relate to direct labor cost for the production of 40,000 units of product:

Actual:     39,500 hours at $15.50 . . . . . . . . $612,250
Standard:  40,000 hours at  15.00 . . . . . . . .  600,000

Determine the time variance, rate variance, and total direct labor cost variance. ✓ explain.

**Exercise 5-4.** The following data relate to factory overhead cost for the production of 80,000 units of product:

Actual:     Variable factory overhead. . . $177,500
             Fixed factory overhead . . . . .  150,000  $327,500
Standard:  40,000 hours at $7.50. . . . . . .      300,000

If productive capacity of 100% was 50,000 hours and the factory overhead costs budgeted at the level of 40,000 standard hours was $330,000, determine the volume variance, controllable variance, and total factory overhead cost variance. The fixed factory overhead rate was $3 per hour.

**Exercise 5-5.** Mann Company prepared the following factory overhead cost budget for Department X for September of the current year, when the company expected to operate at 9,600 direct labor hours:

Variable cost:
  Indirect factory wages . . . . . . . . . . . . . . . . . . . . . . . . . . . . . $10,000
  Power and light . . . . . . . . . . . . . . . . . . . . . . . . . . . . . . . . . . . 8,800
  Indirect materials. . . . . . . . . . . . . . . . . . . . . . . . . . . . . . . . . . 3,000

    Total variable cost. . . . . . . . . . . . . . . . . . . . . . . . . . . . .   $21,800
Fixed cost:
  Supervisory salaries . . . . . . . . . . . . . . . . . . . . . . . . . . . . . . . $ 8,250
  Depreciation of plant and equipment . . . . . . . . . . . . . . . . 4,100
  Insurance and property taxes. . . . . . . . . . . . . . . . . . . . . . 3,000

    Total fixed cost . . . . . . . . . . . . . . . . . . . . . . . . . . . . . . 15,350
Total factory overhead cost. . . . . . . . . . . . . . . . . . . . . . . . $37,150

Mann Company has decided to install a standard cost system and has determined that productive capacity is 12,000 direct labor hours. Prepare a flexible budget indicating production levels of 9,600, 10,800, and 12,000 direct labor hours and showing the standard factory overhead rate.

**Exercise 5-6.** Black Manufacturing Company incorporates standards in the accounts and identifies variances at the time the manufacturing costs are incurred. Prepare entries to record the following transactions:
  (a) Purchased 500 units of direct material X at $12.25 per unit. The standard price is $12.50 per unit.
  (b) Used 255 units of direct material X in the process of manufacturing 125 units of finished product. Two units of material X are required, at standard, to produce a finished unit.

**Problems**
*(Problems in
Appendix B: 5-1B,
5-3B, 5-5B.)*

**Problem 5-1A.** Standard costs and actual costs for direct materials, direct labor, and factory overhead incurred for the manufacture of 3,000 units of product were as follows:

|  | Standard Costs | Actual Costs |
|---|---|---|
| Direct materials | 3,000 pounds at $20 | 2,900 pounds at $21.50 |
| Direct labor | 4,500 hours at $12 | 4,800 hours at $12.50 |
| Factory overhead | Rates per direct labor hour, based on 100% of capacity of 5,000 labor hours: | |
|  | Variable cost, $4.20 | $20,500 variable cost |
|  | Fixed cost, $2.80 | $14,000 fixed cost |

Instructions:

Determine (a) the quantity variance, price variance, and total direct materials cost variance; (b) the time variance, rate variance, and total direct labor cost variance; and (c) the volume variance, controllable variance, and total factory overhead cost variance.

**Problem 5-2A.** Wade Company prepared the following factory overhead cost budget for Department I for June of the current year. The company expected to operate the department at 100% of capacity of 20,000 direct labor hours.

| | | |
|---|---|---|
| Variable cost: | | |
| Indirect factory wages | $18,000 | |
| Power and light | 15,300 | |
| Indirect materials | 5,400 | |
| Total variable cost | | $38,700 |
| Fixed cost: | | |
| Supervisory salaries | $14,850 | |
| Depreciation of plant and equipment | 7,300 | |
| Insurance and property taxes | 5,850 | |
| Total fixed cost | | 28,000 |
| Total factory overhead cost | | $66,700 |

During June, the department operated at 15,000 direct labor hours, and the factory overhead costs incurred were: indirect factory wages, $13,600; power and light, $11,200; indirect materials, $4,250; supervisory salaries, $14,850; depreciation of plant and equipment, $7,300; and insurance and property taxes, $5,850.

Instructions:

Prepare a standard factory overhead variance report for June. To be useful for cost control, the budgeted amounts should be based on 15,000 direct labor hours.

**Problem 5-3A.** Grant Company prepared the following factory overhead cost budget for the Sanding Department for April of the current year:

Grant Company
Factory Overhead Cost Budget—Sanding Department
For Month Ending April 30, 19--

| | | |
|---|---:|---:|
| Direct labor hours: | | |
| Productive capacity of 100%........................ | | 18,000 |
| Hours budgeted.................................... | | 15,300 |
| Variable cost: | | |
| Indirect factory wages............................. | $20,060 | |
| Indirect materials ................................. | 14,280 | |
| Power and light.................................... | 5,440 | |
| Total variable cost ............................. | | $39,780 |
| Fixed cost: | | |
| Supervisory salaries............................... | $18,300 | |
| Indirect factory wages............................. | 12,100 | |
| Depreciation of plant and equipment................. | 8,100 | |
| Insurance......................................... | 6,800 | |
| Power and light.................................... | 5,450 | |
| Property taxes..................................... | 3,250 | |
| Total fixed cost .................................... | | 54,000 |
| Total factory overhead cost ......................... | | $93,780 |

During April, the Sanding Department was operated for 15,300 direct labor hours and the following factory overhead costs were incurred:

| | |
|---|---:|
| Indirect factory wages................................ | $32,600 |
| Supervisory salaries.................................. | 18,300 |
| Indirect materials ................................... | 13,950 |
| Power and light....................................... | 11,200 |
| Depreciation of plant and equipment................... | 8,100 |
| Insurance............................................ | 6,800 |
| Property taxes........................................ | 3,250 |
| Total factory overhead cost incurred ................. | $94,200 |

Instructions:

(1) Prepare a flexible budget for April, indicating capacities of 13,500, 15,300, 18,000, and 21,600 direct labor hours and the determination of a standard factory overhead rate per direct labor hour.
(2) Prepare a standard factory overhead cost variance report for April.

**Problem 5-4A.** The following data were taken from the records of Briscoe Company for July of the current year:

| | |
|---|---:|
| Cost of goods sold (at standard)............................. | $277,770 |
| Direct materials quantity variance—favorable ................. | 1,860 |
| Direct materials price variance—favorable.................... | 2,550 |
| Direct labor time variance—favorable ........................ | 690 |
| Direct labor rate variance—unfavorable ...................... | 2,535 |
| Factory overhead volume variance—unfavorable .............. | 3,000 |
| Factory overhead controllable variance—favorable ............ | 1,140 |
| General expenses ........................................... | 16,290 |

Sales. . . . . . . . . . . . . . . . . . . . . . . . . . . . . . . . . . . . . . . . . . . . . . . . $362,700
Selling expenses . . . . . . . . . . . . . . . . . . . . . . . . . . . . . . . . . . .     29,970

Instructions:

Prepare an income statement for presentation to management.

**Problem 5-5A.** Delwood Inc. maintains perpetual inventory accounts for materials, work in process, and finished goods and uses a standard cost system based on the following data:

| | Standard Cost per Unit |
|---|---|
| Direct materials: 2 kilograms at $3.50 per kg. . . . . . . . . . . | $ 7 |
| Direct labor: 4 hours at $17.50 per hr . . . . . . . . . . . . . . . . | 70 |
| Factory overhead: $1.50 per direct labor hour. . . . . . . . . . | 6 |
| Total. . . . . . . . . . . . . . . . . . . . . . . . . . . . . . . . . . . . . . . . . | $83 |

There was no inventory of work in process at the beginning or end of October, the first month of the current fiscal year. The transactions relating to production completed during October are summarized as follows:

(a) Materials purchased on account, $62,480.
(b) Direct materials used, $55,025. This represented 15 500 kilograms at $3.55 per kilogram.
(c) Direct labor paid, $560,700. This represented 31,500 hours at $17.80 per hour. There were no accruals at either the beginning or the end of the period.
(d) Factory overhead incurred during the month was composed of depreciation on plant and equipment, $18,650; indirect labor, $14,300; insurance, $8,000; and miscellaneous factory costs, $9,550. The indirect labor and miscellaneous factory costs were paid during the period, and the insurance represents an expiration of prepaid insurance. Of the total factory overhead of $50,500, fixed costs amounted to $27,200 and variable costs were $23,300.
(e) Goods finished during the period, 8,000 units.

Instructions:

(1) Prepare entries in general journal form to record the transactions, assuming that the work in process account is debited for actual production costs and credited with standard costs for goods finished.
(2) Prepare a T account for Work in Process and post to the account, using the identifying letters as dates.
(3) Prepare schedules of variances for direct materials cost, direct labor cost, and factory overhead cost. Productive capacity for the plant is 34,000 direct labor hours.
(4) Total the amount of the standard cost variances and compare this total with the balance of the work in process account.

**Mini-Case**

Daughtrey Company operates a plant in Mountain View, Missouri, where you have been assigned as the new cost analyst. To familiarize yourself with your new responsibilities, you have gathered the following cost variance data for October. During October, 30,600 units of product were manufactured.

## Factory Overhead Cost Variance Report

Productive capacity for the month (100%) . . . . . . . . . . . . . . . . . . . . . . . . 18,000 hours
Standard for amount produced during month . . . . . . . . . . . . . . . . . . . . . 15,300 hours

| | Budget | Actual | Variances Favorable | Variances Unfavorable |
|---|---|---|---|---|
| **Variable cost:** | | | | |
| Indirect factory wages . . . . . . . . . . . . | $ 22,185 | $ 22,600 | | $ 415 |
| Power and light . . . . . . . . . . . . . . . . . . | 42,840 | 42,590 | $250 | |
| Indirect materials. . . . . . . . . . . . . . . . . | 7,650 | 8,000 | | 350 |
| Maintenance. . . . . . . . . . . . . . . . . . . . . | 5,355 | 5,500 | | 145 |
| Total variable cost. . . . . . . . . . . . . . | $ 78,030 | $ 78,690 | | |
| **Fixed cost:** | | | | |
| Supervisory salaries . . . . . . . . . . . . . . | $ 32,500 | $ 32,500 | | |
| Depreciation of plant and equipment . . | 8,500 | 8,500 | | |
| Insurance and property taxes . . . . . . . | 2,200 | 2,200 | | |
| Total fixed cost . . . . . . . . . . . . . . . . | $ 43,200 | $ 43,200 | | |
| Total factory overhead cost. . . . . . . . . . | $121,230 | $121,890 | | |
| Total controllable variances. . . . . . . . . . . . . . . . . . . . . . . . . . . . . . | | | $250 | $ 910 |

Net controllable variance — unfavorable . . . . . . . . . . . . . . . . . . . . . . . . . . $ 660
Volume variance — unfavorable:
  Idle hours at the standard rate for
    fixed factory overhead — 2,700 × $2.40. . . . . . . . . . . . . . . . . . . . . . . 6,480
Total factory overhead cost variance — unfavorable . . . . . . . . . . . . . . . $7,140

## Direct Materials Cost Variance

Quantity variance:
  Actual quantity . . . . . . . . . . . . . 48,300 pounds
  Standard quantity. . . . . . . . . . . 45,900 pounds
    Variance — unfavorable. . . .   2,400 pounds × standard price, $1.40 . . . . $ 3,360
Price variance:
  Actual price . . . . . . . . . . . . . . . $1.60 per pound
  Standard price . . . . . . . . . . . . .   1.40 per pound
    Variance — unfavorable. . . .   $ .20 per pound × actual quantity, 48,300 . . 9,660
Total direct materials cost variance — unfavorable . . . . . . . . . . . . . . . . . . . . $13,020

## Direct Labor Cost Variance

Time variance:
  Actual time. . . . . . . . . . . . . . . . 15,450 hours
  Standard time . . . . . . . . . . . . . . 15,300 hours
    Variance — unfavorable. . . .   150 hours × standard rate, $16 . . . . . . . . $ 2,400
Rate variance:
  Standard rate . . . . . . . . . . . . . . $16.00 per hour
  Actual rate . . . . . . . . . . . . . . . .   15.60 per hour
    Variance — favorable. . . . . .   $ .40 per hour × actual hours, 15,450 . . . . 6,180
Total direct labor cost variance — favorable . . . . . . . . . . . . . . . . . . . . . . . . . $ 3,780

After your review of the October cost variance data, you arranged a meeting with the factory superintendent to discuss manufacturing operations. During this meeting, the factory superintendent made the following comment:

"Why do you have to compute a factory overhead volume variance? I don't have any control over the level of operations. I can only control costs for the level of production at which I am told to operate. Why not just eliminate the volume variance from the factory overhead cost variance report?"

You next discussed the direct materials variance analyses with the purchasing department manager, who made the following comment:

"The materials price variance is computed incorrectly. The computations should be actual price minus standard price times the standard quantity of materials for the amount produced. By multiplying the difference in the actual and standard price by the actual quantity of materials used, my department is being penalized for the inefficiencies of the production department."

During November, the standard costs were not changed, productive capacity was 18,000 hours, and the following data were taken from the records for the production of 24,000 units of product:

| | |
|---|---|
| Quantity of direct materials used ........................ | 37,900 pounds |
| Cost of direct materials............................... | $ 1.62 per pound |
| Quantity of direct labor used .......................... | 12,260 hours |
| Cost of direct labor .................................. | $15.70 per hour |
| Factory overhead costs: | |
| Power and light..................................... | $33,520 |
| Supervisory salaries ............................... | 32,500 |
| Indirect factory wages.............................. | 18,100 |
| Depreciation of plant and equipment ................. | 8,500 |
| Indirect materials .................................. | 6,940 |
| Maintenance ....................................... | 4,250 |
| Insurance and property taxes ....................... | 2,200 |

Instructions:

(1) Prepare a factory overhead cost variance report for November.
(2) Determine (a) the quantity variance, price variance, and total direct materials cost variance, and (b) the time variance, rate variance, and total direct labor cost variance for November.
(3) Based upon the cost variances for October and November, what areas of operations would you investigate and why?
(4) How would you respond to the comments of the factory superintendent?
(5) How would you respond to the comments of the manager of the purchasing department?

# 6

# Profit Reporting for Management Analysis

## CHAPTER OBJECTIVES

*Describe and illustrate gross profit analysis.*

*Describe and illustrate absorption and variable costing concepts.*

*Describe and illustrate managerial uses of variable costing.*

# PART 4

## Analyses for Decision Making

# 6

**CHAPTER**

The basic accounting systems used by manufacturers to provide accounting information useful to management in planning and controlling operations were described and illustrated in previous chapters. Also presented were budgetary control concepts and standard costs and their use by management. In this chapter, various analyses useful to management in establishing profit goals and developing plans for achieving these goals are presented. Specifically, management's use of gross profit analysis and variable costing is described and illustrated. Gross profit analysis is useful in planning profits because it highlights the effects of changes in sales quantities, unit costs, and unit sales prices on profit. Variable costing is an aid in cost control, product pricing, production planning, and sales analysis.

**GROSS PROFIT ANALYSIS**

Gross profit is often considered the most significant intermediate figure in the income statement. It is common to determine its percentage relationship to sales and to make comparisons with prior periods. However, the mere knowledge of the percentages and the degree and direction of change from prior periods is insufficient. Management needs information about the causes. The procedure used in developing such information is termed gross profit analysis.

Since gross profit is the excess of sales over the cost of goods sold, a change in the amount of gross profit can be caused by (1) an increase or decrease in the amount of sales and (2) an increase or decrease in the amount of cost of goods sold. An increase or decrease in either element may in turn be due to (1) a change in the number of units sold and (2) a change in the unit price. The effect of these two factors on either sales or cost of goods sold may be stated as follows:

1. **Quantity factor.** The effect of a change in the number of units sold, assuming no change in unit price.
2. **Price factor.** The effect of a change in unit price on the number of units sold.

The following data are to be used as the basis for illustrating gross profit analysis. For the sake of simplicity, a single commodity is assumed. The amount of detail entering into the analysis would be greater if a number of different commodities were sold, but the basic principles would not be affected.

|  | 1985 | 1984 | Increase Decrease* |
|---|---|---|---|
| Sales | $900,000 | $800,000 | $100,000 |
| Cost of goods sold | 650,000 | 570,000 | 80,000 |
| Gross profit | $250,000 | $230,000 | $ 20,000 |
| Number of units sold | 125,000 | 100,000 | 25,000 |
| Unit sales price | $7.20 | $8.00 | $.80* |
| Unit cost price | $5.20 | $5.70 | $.50* |

The following analysis of these data shows that the favorable increase in the number of units sold was partially offset by a decrease in unit selling price. Also, the increase in the cost of goods sold due to increased quantity was partially offset by a decrease in unit cost.

GROSS PROFIT
ANALYSIS REPORT

### Analysis of Increase in Gross Profit
### For Year Ended December 31, 1985

Increase in amount of sales attributed to:
Quantity factor:

| | | | |
|---|---|---|---|
| Increase in number of units sold in 1985 ... | 25,000 | | |
| Unit sales price in 1984................... | × | $8 | $200,000 |

Price factor:

| | | | |
|---|---|---|---|
| Decrease in unit sales price in 1985 ....... | $.80 | | |
| Number of units sold in 1985............. | ×125,000 | 100,000 | |

| | | |
|---|---|---|
| Net increase in amount of sales ............ | | $100,000 |

Increase in amount of cost of goods sold attributed to:
Quantity factor:

| | | | |
|---|---|---|---|
| Increase in number of units sold in 1985 ... | 25,000 | | |
| Unit cost price in 1984 .................. | × $5.70 | $142,500 | |

Price factor:

| | | | |
|---|---|---|---|
| Decrease in unit cost price in 1985 ........ | $.50 | | |
| Number of units sold in 1985............. | ×125,000 | 62,500 | |

| | | |
|---|---|---|
| Net increase in amount of cost of goods sold . | | 80,000 |
| Increase in gross profit ...................... | | $ 20,000 |

The data presented in the report may be useful both in evaluating past performance and in planning for the future. The importance of the cost reduction of $.50 a unit is quite clear. If the unit cost had not changed from the preceding year, the net increase in the amount of sales ($100,000) would have been more than offset by the increase in the cost of goods sold ($142,500), causing a decrease of $42,500 in gross profit. The $20,000 increase in gross profit actually attained was made possible, therefore, by the ability of management to reduce the unit cost of the commodity.

The means by which the $.50 reduction in the unit cost of the commodity was accomplished is also significant. If it was due to the spreading of fixed factory overhead costs over the larger number of units produced, the decision to reduce the sales price in order to achieve a larger volume was probably wise. On the other hand, if the $.50 reduction in unit cost was due to operating efficiencies entirely unrelated to the increased production, the $.80 reduction in the unit sales price was unwise. The accuracy of the conclusion can be demonstrated by comparing actual results with hypothetical results. The hypothetical results are based on (1) a sales volume that did not change from the 1984 level and (2) a unit cost reduction to $5.20 due to operating efficiencies. The following analysis shows the possible loss of an opportunity to have realized an additional gross profit of $30,000 ($280,000 − $250,000).

|                         | Actual   |          | Hypothetical |          |
|-------------------------|----------|----------|--------------|----------|
| Number of units sold    | 125,000  |          | 100,000      |          |
| Unit sales price        | $7.20    |          | $8.00        |          |
| Sales                   |          | $900,000 |              | $800,000 |
| Unit cost price         | $5.20    |          | $5.20        |          |
| Cost of goods sold      |          | 650,000  |              | 520,000  |
| Gross profit            |          | $250,000 |              | $280,000 |

If the reduction in unit cost had been achieved by a combination of spreading the fixed factory overhead over more production units and achieving operating efficiencies related to the increased production, the approximate effects of each could be determined by additional analyses. The methods used in gross profit analysis may also be extended, with some changes, to the analysis of changes in selling and general expenses.

**ABSORPTION COSTING AND VARIABLE COSTING**

In the preceding illustration of gross profit analysis, the importance of the cost of goods sold in determining income was emphasized. In determining the cost of goods sold, two alternate costing concepts can be used. These two costing concepts are absorption costing and variable costing.

The cost of manufactured products consists of direct materials, direct labor, and factory overhead. All such costs become a part of the finished goods inventory and remain there as an asset until the goods are sold. This conventional treatment of manufacturing costs is sometimes called absorption costing because all costs are "absorbed" into finished goods. Although the concept is necessary in determining historical costs and taxable income, another costing concept may be more useful to management in making decisions.

In variable costing, which is also termed direct costing, the cost of goods manufactured is composed only of variable costs — those manufacturing costs that increase or decrease as the volume of production rises or falls. These costs are the direct materials, direct labor, and only those factory overhead costs which vary with the rate of production. The remaining factory overhead costs, which are the fixed or nonvariable items, are related to the productive capacity of the manufacturing plant and are not affected by changes in the quantity of product manufactured. Accordingly, the fixed factory overhead does not become a part of the cost of goods manufactured, but is considered an expense of the period.

The distinction between absorption costing and variable costing is illustrated in the diagram on page 121. Note that the difference between the two costing concepts is in the treatment of the fixed manufacturing costs, which consist of the fixed factory overhead costs.

**Variable Costing and the Income Statement**

The arrangement of data in the variable costing income statement differs considerably from the format of the conventional income statement. Variable costs and expenses are presented separately from fixed costs and expenses, with significant

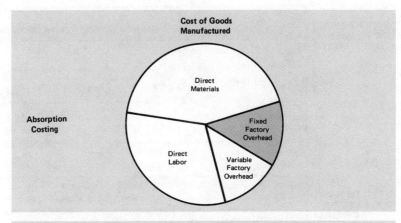

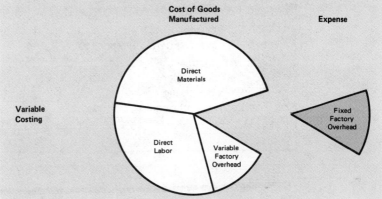

summarizing amounts inserted at intermediate points. As a basis for illustrating the differences between the two forms, assume that 15,000 units were manufactured and sold at a unit price of $50 and the costs and expenses were as follows:

|  | Total Cost or Expense | Number of Units | Unit Cost |
|---|---|---|---|
| Manufacturing costs: | | | |
|   Variable | $375,000 | 15,000 | $25 |
|   Fixed | 150,000 | 15,000 | 10 |
|     Total | $525,000 | | $35 |
| Selling and general expenses: | | | |
|   Variable | $ 75,000 | | |
|   Fixed | 50,000 | | |
|     Total | $125,000 | | |

The two income statements prepared from this information are as follows. The computations in parentheses are shown as an aid to understanding.

ABSORPTION
COSTING INCOME
STATEMENT

| Absorption Costing Income Statement | |
| --- | --- |
| Sales (15,000 × $50) .................................................... | $750,000 |
| Cost of goods sold (15,000 × $35) ............................. | 525,000 |
| Gross profit ............................................................. | $225,000 |
| Selling and general expenses ($75,000 + $50,000) ............. | 125,000 |
| Income from operations ................................ | $100,000 |

VARIABLE
COSTING INCOME
STATEMENT

| Variable Costing Income Statement | | |
| --- | --- | --- |
| Sales (15,000 × $50) ................................... | | $750,000 |
| Variable cost of goods sold (15,000 × $25) ........... | | 375,000 |
| Manufacturing margin ................................. | | $375,000 |
| Variable selling and general expenses ............... | | 75,000 |
| Contribution margin ................................... | | $300,000 |
| Fixed costs and expenses: | | |
|    Fixed manufacturing costs ..................... | $150,000 | |
|    Fixed selling and general expenses ............... | 50,000 | 200,000 |
| Income from operations ............................ | | $100,000 |

The absorption costing income statement does not distinguish between variable and fixed costs and expenses. All manufacturing costs are included in the cost of goods sold. The deduction of the cost of goods sold from sales yields the intermediate amount, gross profit. Deduction of selling and general expenses then yields income from operations.

In contrast, the variable costing income statement includes only the variable manufacturing costs in the cost of goods sold. Deduction of the cost of goods sold from sales yields an intermediate amount, termed manufacturing margin. Deduction of the variable selling and general expenses yields the contribution margin, or **marginal income.** The fixed costs and expenses are then deducted from the contribution margin to yield income from operations.

### Units Manufactured Equal Units Sold

In the preceding illustration, 15,000 units were manufactured and sold. Both the absorption and the variable costing income statements reported the same income from operations of $100,000. Assuming no other changes, this equality of income will always be the case when the number of units manufactured and the number of units sold are equal. Only when the number of units manufactured and the number of units sold are not equal, which creates a change in the quantity of finished goods in inventory, will the income from operations differ under the two concepts.

## Units Manufactured Exceed Units Sold

For any period in which the number of units manufactured exceeds the number of units sold, the operating income reported under the absorption costing concept will be larger than the operating income reported under the variable costing concept. To illustrate, assume that in the preceding example only 12,000 units of the 15,000 units manufactured were sold. The two income statements that result are as follows. Computations are inserted parenthetically as an aid to understanding.

ABSORPTION
COSTING INCOME
STATEMENT

| Absorption Costing Income Statement | | |
|---|---:|---:|
| Sales (12,000 × $50) ............................... | | $600,000 |
| Cost of goods sold: | | |
| Cost of goods manufactured (15,000 × $35) ........ | $525,000 | |
| Less ending inventory (3,000 × $35) .............. | 105,000 | |
| Cost of goods sold .......................... | | 420,000 |
| Gross profit........................................ | | $180,000 |
| Selling and general expenses ($60,000 + $50,000) .... | | 110,000 |
| Income from operations .............................. | | $ 70,000 |

VARIABLE
COSTING INCOME
STATEMENT

| Variable Costing Income Statement | | |
|---|---:|---:|
| Sales (12,000 × $50) ............................... | | $600,000 |
| Variable cost of goods sold: | | |
| Variable cost of goods manufactured | | |
| (15,000 × $25)................................... | $375,000 | |
| Less ending inventory (3,000 × $25) .............. | 75,000 | |
| Variable cost of goods sold...................... | | 300,000 |
| Manufacturing margin................................ | | $300,000 |
| Variable selling and general expenses .............. | | 60,000 |
| Contribution margin................................. | | $240,000 |
| Fixed costs and expenses: | | |
| Fixed manufacturing costs........................ | $150,000 | |
| Fixed selling and general expenses .............. | 50,000 | 200,000 |
| Income from operations .............................. | | $ 40,000 |

The $30,000 difference in the amount of income from operations ($70,000 − $40,000) is due to the different treatment of the fixed manufacturing costs. The entire amount of the $150,000 of fixed manufacturing costs is included as an expense of the period in the variable costing statement. The ending inventory in the absorption costing statement includes $30,000 (3,000 × $10) of fixed manufacturing costs. This $30,000, by being included in inventory on hand, is thus excluded from current cost of goods sold and instead is deferred to another period.

### Units Manufactured Less Than Units Sold

For any period in which the number of units manufactured is less than the number of units sold, the operating income reported under the absorption costing concept will be less than the operating income reported under the variable costing concept. To illustrate, assume that 5,000 units of inventory were on hand at the beginning of a period, 10,000 units were manufactured during the period, and 15,000 units were sold (10,000 units manufactured during the period plus the 5,000 units on hand at the beginning of the period) at $50 per unit. The manufacturing costs and selling and general expenses are as follows:

|  | Total Cost or Expense | Number of Units | Unit Cost |
|---|---|---|---|
| **Beginning inventory:** | | | |
| Manufacturing costs: | | | |
| Variable | $125,000 | 5,000 | $25 |
| Fixed | 50,000 | 5,000 | 10 |
| Total | $175,000 | | $35 |
| **Current period:** | | | |
| Manufacturing costs: | | | |
| Variable | $250,000 | 10,000 | $25 |
| Fixed | 150,000 | 10,000 | 15 |
| Total | $400,000 | | $40 |
| **Selling and general expenses:** | | | |
| Variable | $ 75,000 | | |
| Fixed | 50,000 | | |
| Total | $125,000 | | |

The two income statements prepared from this information are as follows. Computations are inserted parenthetically as an aid to understanding.

ABSORPTION COSTING INCOME STATEMENT

| Absorption Costing Income Statement | | |
|---|---|---|
| Sales (15,000 × $50) | | $750,000 |
| Cost of goods sold: | | |
| Beginning inventory (5,000 × $35) | $175,000 | |
| Cost of goods manufactured (10,000 × $40) | 400,000 | |
| Cost of goods sold | | 575,000 |
| Gross profit | | $175,000 |
| Selling and general expenses ($75,000 + $50,000) | | 125,000 |
| Income from operations | | $ 50,000 |

| Variable Costing Income Statement | | |
|---|---|---|
| Sales (15,000 × $50). . . . . . . . . . . . . . . . . . . . . . . . . . . . . . . . . . | | $750,000 |
| Variable cost of goods sold: | | |
| Beginning inventory (5,000 × $25) . . . . . . . . . . . . . . . . | $125,000 | |
| Variable cost of goods manufactured | | |
| (10,000 × $25). . . . . . . . . . . . . . . . . . . . . . . . . . . . . . . | 250,000 | |
| Variable cost of goods sold. . . . . . . . . . . . . . . . . . . . . | | 375,000 |
| Manufacturing margin. . . . . . . . . . . . . . . . . . . . . . . . . . . . . . | | $375,000 |
| Variable selling and general expenses. . . . . . . . . . . . . . . | | 75,000 |
| Contribution margin. . . . . . . . . . . . . . . . . . . . . . . . . . . . . . . | | $300,000 |
| Fixed costs and expenses: | | |
| Fixed manufacturing costs. . . . . . . . . . . . . . . . . . . . . . . | $150,000 | |
| Fixed selling and general expenses . . . . . . . . . . . . . . | 50,000 | 200,000 |
| Income from operations . . . . . . . . . . . . . . . . . . . . . . . . . . . | | $100,000 |

The $50,000 difference ($100,000 − $50,000) in the amount of income from operations is attributable to the different treatment of the fixed manufacturing costs. The beginning inventory in the absorption costing income statement includes $50,000 (5,000 units × $10) of fixed manufacturing costs incurred in the preceding period. By being included in the beginning inventory, this $50,000 is included in the cost of goods sold for the current period. This $50,000 was included as an expense in a variable costing income statement of a prior period, however. Therefore, none of it is included as an expense in the current period variable costing income statement.

**Comparison of Income Reported Under the Two Concepts**

The examples presented in the preceding sections illustrated the effects of the absorption costing and variable costing concepts on income from operations when the level of inventory changes during a period. These effects may be summarized as follows:

Units manufactured:

| | |
|---|---|
| Equal units sold. . . . . . . . . . . . . . . . . . . . . . | Absorption costing income equals variable costing income. |
| Exceed units sold . . . . . . . . . . . . . . . . . . . . | Absorption costing income is greater than variable costing income. |
| Less than units sold . . . . . . . . . . . . . . . . . | Absorption costing income is less than variable costing income. |

**Income Analysis Under Absorption Costing**

As was illustrated in the preceding examples, changes in the quantity of the finished goods inventory, caused by differences in the levels of sales and production, directly affect the amount of income from operations reported under absorption costing. Management should therefore be aware of the possible effects of changing inventory levels on operating income reported under absorption costing in analyzing and evaluating operations. To illustrate, assume that the following two proposed production levels are being evaluated by the management of Brownstein Manufacturing Company:

### Proposal 1: 20,000 Units To Be Manufactured

|  | Total Cost or Expense | Number of Units | Unit Cost |
|---|---|---|---|
| Manufacturing costs: |  |  |  |
|   Variable ........................ | $ 700,000 | 20,000 | $35 |
|   Fixed........................... | 400,000 | 20,000 | 20 |
|     Total ...................... | $1,100,000 |  | $55 |
| Selling and general expenses: |  |  |  |
|   Variable ........................ | $ 100,000 |  |  |
|   Fixed........................... | 100,000 |  |  |
|     Total ...................... | $ 200,000 |  |  |

### Proposal 2: 25,000 Units To Be Manufactured

|  | Total Cost or Expense | Number of Units | Unit Cost |
|---|---|---|---|
| Manufacturing costs: |  |  |  |
|   Variable ........................ | $ 875,000 | 25,000 | $35 |
|   Fixed........................... | 400,000 | 25,000 | 16 |
|     Total ...................... | $1,275,000 |  | $51 |
| Selling and general expenses: |  |  |  |
|   Variable ........................ | $ 100,000 |  |  |
|   Fixed........................... | 100,000 |  |  |
|     Total ...................... | $ 200,000 |  |  |

Brownstein Manufacturing Company has no beginning inventory, and sales are estimated to be 20,000 units at $75 per unit, regardless of production levels. If the company manufactures 20,000 units, which is an amount equal to the estimated sales, income from operations under absorption costing would be $200,000. However, the reported income from operations could be increased by $80,000 by manufacturing 25,000 units and adding 5,000 units to the finished goods inventory. The absorption costing income statements illustrating this effect are at the top of page 127.

The increase in operating income of $80,000 would be caused by the allocation of the fixed manufacturing costs of $400,000 over a greater number of units of production. Specifically, an increase in production from 20,000 units to 25,000 units meant that the fixed manufacturing costs per unit decreased from $20 ($400,000 ÷ 20,000 units) to $16 ($400,000 ÷ 25,000 units). Thus, the cost of goods sold when 25,000 units are manufactured would be $4 per unit less, or $80,000 less in total (20,000 units sold times $4). Since the cost of goods sold is less, operating income is $80,000 more when 25,000 units are manufactured rather than 20,000 units.

Under the variable costing concept, income from operations would have been $200,000, regardless of the amount by which units manufactured exceeded sales, because no fixed manufacturing costs are allocated to the units manufactured. To illustrate, the variable costing income statements at the bottom of page 127 are presented for Brownstein for the production of 20,000 units, 25,000 units, and 30,000 units. In each case, the income from operations is $200,000.

ABSORPTION
COSTING INCOME
STATEMENTS

| Absorption Costing Income Statements | 20,000 Units Manufactured | 25,000 Units Manufactured |
|---|---|---|
| Sales (20,000 units × $75) ...................... | $1,500,000 | $1,500,000 |
| Cost of goods sold: | | |
| Cost of goods manufactured: | | |
| (20,000 units × $55)......................... | $1,100,000 | |
| (25,000 units × $51)......................... | | $1,275,000 |
| Less ending inventory: | | |
| (5,000 units × $51)......................... | | 255,000 |
| Cost of goods sold ...................... | $1,100,000 | $1,020,000 |
| Gross profit...................................... | $ 400,000 | $ 480,000 |
| Selling and general expenses | | |
| ($100,000 + $100,000)...................... | 200,000 | 200,000 |
| Income from operations ......................... | $ 200,000 | $ 280,000 |

VARIABLE COSTING
INCOME
STATEMENTS

| Variable Costing Income Statements | 20,000 Units Manufactured | 25,000 Units Manufactured | 30,000 Units Manufactured |
|---|---|---|---|
| Sales (20,000 units × $75) .......... | $1,500,000 | $1,500,000 | $1,500,000 |
| Variable cost of goods sold: | | | |
| Variable cost of goods manufactured: | | | |
| (20,000 units × $35)............. | $ 700,000 | | |
| (25,000 units × $35)............. | | $ 875,000 | |
| (30,000 units × $35)............. | | | $1,050,000 |
| Less ending inventory: | | | |
| (0 units × $35).................. | 0 | | |
| (5,000 units × $35)............. | | 175,000 | |
| (10,000 units × $35)............ | | | 350,000 |
| Variable cost of goods sold...... | $ 700,000 | $ 700,000 | $ 700,000 |
| Manufacturing margin................ | $ 800,000 | $ 800,000 | $ 800,000 |
| Variable selling and general | | | |
| expenses......................... | 100,000 | 100,000 | 100,000 |
| Contribution margin................. | $ 700,000 | $ 700,000 | $ 700,000 |
| Fixed costs and expenses: | | | |
| Fixed manufacturing costs......... | $ 400,000 | $ 400,000 | $ 400,000 |
| Fixed selling and general expenses | 100,000 | 100,000 | 100,000 |
| Total fixed costs and expenses .... | $ 500,000 | $ 500,000 | $ 500,000 |
| Income from operations ............. | $ 200,000 | $ 200,000 | $ 200,000 |

As illustrated, if absorption costing is used, management should be careful in analyzing income from operations when large changes in inventory levels occur. Otherwise, increases or decreases in income from operations due to changes in inventory levels could be misinterpreted to be the result of operating efficiencies or inefficiencies.

**MANAGEMENT'S USE OF VARIABLE COSTING AND ABSORPTION COSTING**

Both variable costing and absorption costing serve useful purposes for management. However, there are limitations to the use of both concepts in certain circumstances. Therefore, management accountants must carefully analyze each situation in evaluating whether variable costing reports or absorption costing reports would be more useful. In many situations, the preparation of reports under both concepts will provide useful insights. Such reports and their advantages and disadvantages are discussed in the following paragraphs.

**Cost Control**

All costs are controllable by someone within a business enterprise, but they are not all controllable at the same level of management. For example, plant supervisors, as members of operating management, are responsible for controlling the use of direct materials in their departments. They have no control, however, of the amount of insurance coverage or premium costs related to the buildings housing their departments. For a specific level of management, **controllable costs** are costs that it controls directly, and **uncontrollable costs** are costs that another level of management controls. This distinction, as applied to specific levels of management, is useful in fixing the responsibility for incurrence of costs and then for reporting the cost data to those responsible for cost control.

Variable manufacturing costs are controlled at the operating level because the amount of such costs varies with changes in the volume of production. By including only variable manufacturing costs in the cost of the product, variable costing provides a product cost figure that can be controlled by operating management. The fixed factory overhead costs are ordinarily the responsibility of a higher level of management. When the fixed factory overhead costs are reported as a separate item in the variable costing income statement, they are easier to identify and control than when they are spread among units of product as they are under absorption costing.

As is the case with the fixed and variable manufacturing costs, the control of the variable and fixed operating expenses is usually the responsibility of different levels of management. Under variable costing, the variable selling and general expenses are reported in a separate category from the fixed selling and general expenses. Because they are reported in this manner, both types of operating expenses are easier to identify and control than is the case under absorption costing, where they are not reported separately.

**Product Pricing**

Many factors enter into the determination of the selling price of a product. The cost of making the product is clearly significant. Microeconomic theory deduces, from a set of restrictive assumptions, that income is maximized by expanding output to the volume where the revenue realized by the sale of the final unit (marginal revenue) equals the cost of that unit (marginal cost). Although the degree of exactness assumed in economic theory is rarely attainable, the concepts of marginal revenue and marginal cost are useful in setting selling prices.

In the short run, an enterprise is committed to the existing capacity of its manufacturing facilities. The pricing decision should be based upon making the best use of such capacity. The fixed costs and expenses cannot be avoided, but the variable costs and expenses can be eliminated if the company does not manufacture the product. The selling price of a product, therefore, should at least be equal to the variable costs and expenses of making and selling it. Any price above this minimum selling price contributes an amount toward covering fixed costs and expenses and providing operating income. Variable costing procedures yield data that emphasize these relationships.

In the long run, plant capacity can be increased or decreased. If an enterprise is to continue in business, the selling prices of its products must cover all costs and expenses and provide a reasonable operating income. Hence, in establishing pricing policies for the long run, information provided by absorption costing procedures is needed.

There are no simple solutions to most pricing problems. Consideration must be given to many factors of varying importance. Accounting can contribute by preparing analyses of various pricing plans for both the short run and the long run. Concepts of product pricing are further discussed in Chapter 8.

**Production Planning**

Production planning also has both short-run and long-run implications. In the short run, production is limited to existing capacity, and operating decisions must be made quickly before opportunities are lost. For example, a company manufacturing products with a seasonal demand may have an opportunity to obtain an off-season order that will not interfere with its production schedule nor reduce the sales of its other products. The relevant factors for such a short-run decision are the revenues and the variable costs and expenses. If the revenues from the special order will provide a contribution margin, the order should be accepted because it will increase the company's operating income. For long-run planning, management must also consider the fixed costs and expenses.

**Sales Analysis**

The primary objective of the marketing and sales functions is to offer the company's products for sale at prices that will result in an adequate amount of income relative to the total assets employed. To evaluate these functions properly, management needs information concerning the profitability of various types of products and sales mixes, sales territories, and salespersons. Variable costing can make a significant contribution to management decision making in such areas.

### Sales Mix Analysis

Sales mix, sometimes referred to as product mix, is generally defined as the relative distribution of sales among the various products manufactured. Some products are more profitable than others, and management should concentrate its sales efforts on those that will provide the maximum total operating income.

Sales mix studies are based on assumptions, such as the ability to sell one product in place of another and the ability to convert production facilities to accommodate the manufacture of one product instead of another. Proposed changes in the sales mix often affect only small segments of a company's total operations. In such cases, changes in sales mix may be possible within the limits of existing capacity, and the presentation of cost and revenue data in the variable costing form is useful in achieving the most profitable sales mix.

Two very important factors that should be determined for each product are (1) the production facilities needed for its manufacture and (2) the amount of contribution margin to be gained from its manufacture. If two or more products require equal use of limited production facilities, then management should concentrate its sales and production efforts on the product or products with the highest contribution margin per unit. The following report, which focuses on product contribution margins, is an example of the type of data needed for an evaluation of sales mix. The enterprise, which manufactures two products and is operating at full capacity, is considering whether to change the emphasis of its advertising and other promotional efforts.

CONTRIBUTION MARGIN STATEMENT—UNIT OF PRODUCT

Contribution Margin by Unit of Product
April 15, 19--

|  | Product A | Product B |
|---|---|---|
| Sales price | $6.00 | $8.50 |
| Variable cost of goods sold | 3.50 | 5.50 |
| Manufacturing margin | $2.50 | $3.00 |
| Variable selling and general expenses | 1.00 | 1.00 |
| Contribution margin | $1.50 | $2.00 |

The statement indicates that Product B yields a greater amount of contribution margin per unit than Product A. Therefore, Product B provides the larger contribution to the recovery of fixed costs and expenses and realization of operating income. If the amount of production facilities used for each product is assumed to be equal, it would be desirable to increase the sales of Product B.

If two or more products require unequal use of production resources, management should concentrate its sales and production efforts on that product or products with the highest contribution margin per unit of resource. For example, assume that in the above illustration, to manufacture Product B requires twice the machine hours required for Product A. Specifically, Product B requires 2 machine hours per unit, while Product A requires only 1 machine hour per unit. Under this assumption, the contribution margin per unit of resource (machine hours) is $1.50 ($1.50 contribution margin ÷ 1 machine hour) for Product A and $1 ($2 contribution margin ÷ 2 machine hours) for Product B. Under such circumstances, a change in sales mix designed to increase sales of Product A would be desirable.

To illustrate, if 2,000 additional units of Product A (requiring 2,000 machine hours) could be sold in place of 1,000 units of Product B (also requiring 2,000 machine hours), the total company contribution margin would increase by $1,000, as follows:

| | |
|---|---|
| Additional contribution margin from sale of additional 2,000 units of Product A ($1.50 × 2,000 units) | $3,000 |
| Less contribution margin from forgoing production and sale of 1,000 units of Product B ($2 × 1,000 units) | 2,000 |
| Increase in total contribution margin | $1,000 |

## Sales Territory Analysis

An income statement presenting the contribution margin by sales territories is often useful to management in appraising past performance and in directing future sales efforts. The following income statement is prepared in such a format, in abbreviated form:

CONTRIBUTION
MARGIN
STATEMENT—
SALES
TERRITORIES

**Contribution Margin Statement by Sales Territory**
**For Month Ended July 31, 19--**

|  | Territory A | Territory B | Total |
|---|---|---|---|
| Sales | $315,000 | $502,500 | $817,500 |
| Less variable costs and expenses | 189,000 | 251,250 | 440,250 |
| Contribution margin | $126,000 | $251,250 | $377,250 |
| Less fixed costs and expenses | | | 242,750 |
| Income from operations | | | $134,500 |

In addition to the contribution margin, the contribution margin ratio (contribution margin divided by sales) for each territory is useful in evaluating sales territories and directing operations toward more profitable activities. For Territory A, the contribution margin ratio is 40% ($126,000 ÷ $315,000), and for Territory B the ratio is 50% ($251,250 ÷ $502,500). Consequently, more profitability could be achieved by efforts to increase the sales of Territory B relative to Territory A.

## Salespersons' Analysis

A report to management for use in evaluating the sales performance of each salesperson could include total sales, gross profit, gross profit percentage, total selling expenses, and contribution to company profit. Such a report is illustrated as follows:

SALESPERSONS'
ANALYSIS

**Salespersons' Analysis**
**For Six Months Ended June 30, 19--**

| Sales-person | Total Sales | Gross Profit | Gross Profit Percentage | Total Selling Expenses | Contribution to Company Profit |
|---|---|---|---|---|---|
| A | $300,000 | $120,000 | 40% | $24,000 | $ 96,000 |
| B | 250,000 | 75,000 | 30 | 22,500 | 52,500 |
| C | 500,000 | 125,000 | 25 | 35,000 | 90,000 |
| D | 180,000 | 72,000 | 40 | 18,000 | 54,000 |
| E | 460,000 | 197,800 | 43 | 27,600 | 170,200 |
| F | 320,000 | 112,000 | 35 | 22,400 | 89,600 |

The preceding report illustrates that the total sales figure is not the only consideration in evaluating a salesperson. For example, although salesperson C has the highest total sales, C's sales are not contributing as much to overall company profits as are the sales of A and E, primarily because C's sales have the lowest gross profit percentage. Of the six salespersons, E is generating the highest dollar contribution to company profit, but E is selling the most profitable mix of products, as measured by a gross profit percentage of 43%.

Other factors should also be considered in evaluating the performance of salespersons. For example, sales growth rates, years of experience, and actual performance compared to budgeted performance may be more important than total sales.

**Self-Examination Questions**
*(Answers in Appendix C.)*

1. If sales totaled $800,000 for the current year (80,000 units at $10 each) and $765,000 for the preceding year (85,000 units at $9 each), the effect of the quantity factor on the change in sales is:
   - A. a $50,000 increase
   - B. a $35,000 decrease
   - C. a $45,000 decrease
   - D. none of the above.

2. The concept that considers the cost of products manufactured to be composed only of those manufacturing costs that vary with the rate of production is known as:
   - A. absorption costing
   - B. variable costing
   - C. replacement cost
   - D. none of the above

3. In an income statement prepared under the variable costing concept, the deduction of the variable cost of goods sold from sales yields an intermediate amount referred to as:
   - A. gross profit
   - B. contribution margin
   - C. manufacturing margin
   - D. none of the above

4. Sales were $750,000, variable cost of goods sold was $400,000, variable selling and general expenses were $90,000, and fixed costs and expenses were $200,000. The contribution margin was:
   - A. $60,000
   - B. $260,000
   - C. $350,000
   - D. none of the above

5. During a year in which the number of units manufactured exceeded the number of units sold, the operating income reported under the absorption costing concept would be:
   - A. larger than the operating income reported under the variable costing concept
   - B. smaller than the operating income reported under the variable costing concept
   - C. the same as the operating income reported under the variable costing concept
   - D. none of the above

**Discussion Questions**

1. Discuss the two factors affecting both sales and cost of goods sold to which a change in gross profit can be attributed.

2. The analysis of increase in gross profit for a company includes the effect that an increase in the quantity of goods sold has had on the cost of goods sold. How is this figure determined?

3. What types of costs are customarily included in the cost of manufactured products under (a) the *absorption costing* concept and (b) the *variable costing* concept?

4. Which type of manufacturing cost (direct materials, direct labor, variable factory overhead, fixed factory overhead) is included in the cost of goods manufactured under the absorption costing concept but is excluded from the cost of goods manufactured under the variable costing concept?

5. At the end of the first year of operations, 1,000 units remained in finished goods inventory. The unit manufacturing costs during the year were as follows:

    Direct materials....................................... $5.00
    Direct labor ........................................... 3.50
    Fixed factory overhead ............................... 1.50
    Variable factory overhead............................. 1.00

    What would be the cost of the finished goods inventory reported on the balance sheet under (a) the absorption costing concept and (b) the variable costing concept?

6. Which of the following costs would be included in the cost of a manufactured product according to the variable costing concept? (a) property taxes on factory building, (b) salary of factory supervisor, (c) direct labor, (d) rent on factory building, (e) depreciation on factory equipment, (f) direct materials, and (g) electricity purchased to operate factory equipment.

7. In the variable costing income statement, how are the fixed manufacturing costs reported and how are the fixed selling and general expenses reported?

8. In the following equations, based on the variable costing income statement, identify the items designated by **X**:
    (a) Net sales − **X** = manufacturing margin
    (b) Manufacturing margin − **X** = contribution margin
    (c) Contribution margin − **X** = income from operations

9. If the quantity of ending inventory is smaller than that of beginning inventory, will the amount of income from operations determined by absorption costing be greater than or less than the amount determined by variable costing? Explain.

10. Since all costs of operating a business are controllable, what is the significance of the term *uncontrollable cost*?

11. Discuss how financial data prepared on the basis of variable costing can assist management in the development of short-run pricing policies.

12. What term is used to refer to the relative distribution of sales among the various products manufactured?

13. A company, operating at full capacity, manufactures two products, with Product A requiring twice the production facilities as Product B. The contribution margin is $30 per unit for Product A and $12 per unit for Product B. How much would the total contribution margin be increased or decreased for the coming year if the sales of Product A could be increased by 500 units by changing the emphasis of promotional efforts?

**Exercises**

**Exercise 6-1.** From the following data for Gossage Company, prepare an analysis of the decrease in gross profit for the year ended December 31, 1985:

|  | 1985 | | 1984 | |
|---|---|---|---|---|
| Sales................. | 40,000 units @ $18 | $720,000 | 48,000 units @ $16.80 | $806,400 |
| Cost of goods sold....... | 40,000 units @ $12 | 480,000 | 48,000 units @ $11.20 | 537,600 |
| Gross profit............ | | $240,000 | | $268,800 |

**Exercise 6-2.** Borg Company began operations on October 1 and operated at 100% of capacity during the first month. The following data summarize the results for October:

| | | |
|---|---|---|
| Sales (6,000 units)................................. | | $90,000 |
| Production costs (8,000 units): | | |
| Direct materials ................................ | $20,000 | |
| Direct labor..................................... | 36,000 | |
| Variable factory overhead ........................ | 6,000 | |
| Fixed factory overhead........................... | 10,000 | 72,000 |
| | | |
| Selling and general expenses: | | |
| Variable selling and general expenses.............. | $ 8,400 | |
| Fixed selling and general expenses ................ | 4,800 | 13,200 |

(a) Prepare an income statement in accordance with the absorption costing concept. (b) Prepare an income statement in accordance with the variable costing concept. (c) What is the reason for the difference in the amount of operating income reported in (a) and (b)?

**Exercise 6-3.** On December 31, the end of the first year of operations, Hart Company manufactured 24,000 units and sold 20,000 units. The following income statement was prepared, based on the variable costing concept:

Hart Company
Income Statement
For Year Ended December 31, 19--

| | | |
|---|---|---|
| Sales......................................... | | $400,000 |
| Variable cost of goods sold: | | |
| Variable cost of goods manufactured............... | $240,000 | |
| Less ending inventory............................ | 40,000 | |
| Variable cost of goods sold..................... | | 200,000 |
| Manufacturing margin............................ | | $200,000 |
| Variable selling and general expenses............... | | 60,000 |
| Contribution margin................................ | | $140,000 |
| Fixed costs and expenses: | | |
| Fixed manufacturing costs......................... | $ 72,000 | |
| Fixed selling and general expenses ............... | 28,000 | 100,000 |
| Income from operations ........................... | | $ 40,000 |

Determine the unit cost of goods manufactured, based on (a) the variable costing concept and (b) the absorption costing concept.

**Exercise 6-4.** On January 31, the end of the first month of operations, Pablo Company prepared the following income statement, based on the absorption costing concept:

Pablo Company
Income Statement
For Month Ended January 31, 19--

| | | |
|---|---:|---:|
| Sales (1,000 units)..................................... | | $95,000 |
| Cost of goods sold: | | |
|   Cost of goods manufactured........................ | $84,000 | |
|   Less ending inventory (200 units) ................... | 14,000 | |
|     Cost of goods sold ............................ | | 70,000 |
| Gross profit........................................ | | $25,000 |
| Selling and general expenses....................... | | 17,500 |
| Income from operations ............................ | | $ 7,500 |

If the fixed manufacturing costs were $24,000 and the variable selling and general expenses were $4,750, prepare an income statement in accordance with the variable costing concept.

**Exercise 6-5.** On July 31, the end of the first month of operations, Stein Company prepared the following income statement, based on the variable costing concept:

Stein Company
Income Statement
For Month Ended July 31, 19--

| | | |
|---|---:|---:|
| Sales (10,000 units)............................... | | $120,000 |
| Variable cost of goods sold: | | |
|   Variable cost of goods manufactured.............. | $104,000 | |
|   Less ending inventory (3,000 units)................ | 24,000 | |
|     Variable cost of goods sold...................... | | 80,000 |
| Manufacturing margin............................... | | $ 40,000 |
| Variable selling and general expenses............... | | 7,500 |
| Contribution margin................................ | | $ 32,500 |
| Fixed costs and expenses: | | |
|   Fixed manufacturing costs........................ | $ 19,500 | |
|   Fixed selling and general expenses ............... | 10,000 | 29,500 |
| Income from operations ............................ | | $ 3,000 |

Prepare an income statement in accordance with the absorption costing concept.

**Exercise 6-6.** Prior to the first month of operations ending June 30, Ryan Company estimated the following operating results:

| | |
|---|---:|
| Sales (500 × $75)..................................... | $37,500 |
| Manufacturing costs (500 units): | |
|   Direct materials .................................... | 15,000 |
|   Direct labor....................................... | 3,500 |
|   Variable factory overhead .......................... | 1,500 |
|   Fixed factory overhead.............................. | 7,500 |
| Fixed selling and general expenses .................... | 5,000 |
| Variable selling and general expenses.................. | 2,500 |

The company is evaluating a proposal to manufacture 750 units instead of 500 units.

(a) Assuming no change in sales, unit variable manufacturing costs, and total fixed factory overhead and selling and general expenses, prepare an estimated income statement, comparing operating results if 500 and 750 units are manufactured, in the (1) absorption costing format and (2) variable costing format. (b) What is the reason for the difference in income from operations reported for the two levels of production by the absorption costing income statement?

**Exercise 6-7.** Carter Company manufactures Products X and Y and is operating at full capacity. To manufacture Product X requires twice the number of machine hours as required for Product Y. Market research indicates that 500 additional units of Product X could be sold. The contribution margin by unit of product is as follows:

|  | Product X | Product Y |
|---|---|---|
| Sales price | $50 | $30 |
| Variable cost of goods sold | 25 | 15 |
| Manufacturing margin | $25 | $15 |
| Variable selling and general expenses | 15 | 9 |
| Contribution margin | $10 | $ 6 |

Prepare a tabulation indicating the increase or decrease in total contribution margin if 500 additional units of Product X are produced and sold.

**Problems**
*(Problems in Appendix B: 6-1B, 6-2B, 6-3B.)*

**Problem 6-1A.** Gibbons Company manufactures only one product. In 1984, the plant operated at full capacity. At a meeting of the board of directors on December 18, 1984, it was decided to raise the price of this product from $32, which had prevailed last year, to $35, effective January 1, 1985. Although the cost price was expected to rise about $1.50 per unit in 1985 because of a direct materials and direct labor wage increase, the increase in selling price was expected to cover this increase and also add to operating income. The comparative income statement for 1984 and 1985 is as follows:

|  | 1985 | | 1984 | |
|---|---|---|---|---|
| Sales | | $420,000 | | $480,000 |
| Cost of goods sold: variable | $150,000 | | $165,000 | |
| fixed | 120,000 | 270,000 | 120,000 | 285,000 |
| Gross profit | | $150,000 | | $195,000 |
| Operating expenses: variable | $ 43,200 | | $52,500 | |
| fixed | 75,000 | 118,200 | 75,000 | 127,500 |
| Operating income | | $ 31,800 | | $ 67,500 |

Instructions:

(1) Prepare a gross profit analysis report for the year 1985.
(2) At a meeting of the board of directors on March 2, 1986, the president, after reading the gross profit analysis report, made the following comment:
   "It looks as if the increase in unit cost price was $3.50 and not the anticipated $1.50. The failure of operating management to keep these costs within the bounds of those in 1984, except for the anticipated $1.50 increase in

direct materials and direct labor cost, was a major factor in the decrease in gross profit."

Do you agree with this analysis of the increase in unit cost price? Explain.

**Problem 6-2A.** During the first month of operations ended January 31, Dixon Company manufactured 120,000 units, of which 100,000 were sold. Operating data for the month are summarized as follows:

| | | |
|---|---|---|
| Sales......................................... | | $900,000 |
| Manufacturing costs: | | |
| Direct materials .............................. | $360,000 | |
| Direct labor................................. | 240,000 | |
| Variable factory overhead .................... | 120,000 | |
| Fixed factory overhead....................... | 90,000 | 810,000 |
| | | |
| Selling and general expenses: | | |
| Variable .................................... | $ 90,000 | |
| Fixed....................................... | 60,000 | 150,000 |

Instructions:

(1) Prepare an income statement based on the absorption costing concept.
(2) Prepare an income statement based on the variable costing concept.
(3) Explain the reason for the difference in the amount of operating income reported in (1) and (2).

**Problem 6-3A.** The demand for Product D, one of numerous products manufactured by UGA Inc., has dropped sharply because of recent competition from a similar product. The company's chemists are currently completing tests of various new formulas, and it is anticipated that the manufacture of a superior product can be started on October 1, one month hence. No changes will be needed in the present production facilities to manufacture the new product because only the mixture of the various materials will be changed.

The controller has been asked by the president of the company for advice on whether to continue production during September or to suspend the manufacture of Product D until October 1. The controller has assembled the following pertinent data:

UGA Inc.
Estimated Income Statement—Product D
For Month Ending August 31, 19--

| | |
|---|---|
| Sales (50,000 units)......................... | $375,000 |
| Cost of goods sold ......................... | 294,000 |
| Gross profit................................ | $ 81,000 |
| Selling and general expenses................. | 95,000 |
| Loss from operations........................ | $ 14,000 |

The estimated production costs and selling and general expenses, based on a production of 50,000 units, are as follows:

| | |
|---|---|
| Direct materials .................................... | $2.30 per unit |
| Direct labor...................................... | 1.60 per unit |
| Variable factory overhead .......................... | .70 per unit |
| Variable selling and general expenses............... | 1.15 per unit |

Fixed factory overhead............................. $64,000 for August
Fixed selling and general expenses ................ $37,500 for August

Sales for September are expected to drop about 40% below those of the preceding month. No significant changes are anticipated in the production costs or operating expenses. No extra costs will be incurred in discontinuing operations in the portion of the plant associated with Product D. The inventory of Product D at the beginning and end of September is expected to be inconsequential.

Instructions:

(1) Prepare an estimated income statement in absorption costing form for September for Product D, assuming that production continues during the month.
(2) Prepare an estimated income statement in variable costing form for September for Product D, assuming that production continues during the month.
(3) State the estimated operating loss arising from the activities associated with Product D for September if production is temporarily suspended.
(4) Prepare a brief statement of the advice the controller should give.

**Problem 6-4A.** Chung Company employs seven salespersons to sell and distribute its product throughout the state. Data extracted from reports received from the salespersons during the current year ended December 31 are as follows:

| Salesperson | Total Sales | Cost of Goods Sold | Total Selling Expenses |
|---|---|---|---|
| A | $400,000 | $248,000 | $ 94,000 |
| B | 350,000 | 210,000 | 76,000 |
| C | 320,000 | 185,600 | 75,000 |
| D | 600,000 | 390,000 | 145,000 |
| E | 450,000 | 274,500 | 117,000 |
| F | 370,000 | 218,300 | 79,000 |
| G | 250,000 | 150,000 | 52,500 |

Instructions:

(1) Prepare a report for the year, indicating total sales, gross profit, gross profit percentage, total selling expenses, and contribution to company profit by salesperson.
(2) Which salesperson contributed the highest dollar amount to company profit during the year?
(3) Briefly list factors other than contribution to company profit that should be considered in evaluating the performance of salespersons.

**Problem 6-5A.** R. A. Frazier Company manufactures three styles of folding chairs, X, Y, and Z. The income statement has consistently indicated a net loss for Style Z, and management is considering three proposals: (1) continue Style Z, (2) discontinue Style Z and reduce total output accordingly, or (3) discontinue Style Z and conduct an advertising campaign to expand the sales of Style Y so that the entire plant capacity can continue to be used.

If Proposal 2 is selected and Style Z is discontinued and production curtailed, the annual fixed production costs and fixed operating expenses could be reduced by $14,500 and $8,000 respectively. If Proposal 3 is selected, it is anticipated that an additional annual expenditure of $20,000 for advertising Style Y would yield an increase of 35% in its sales volume, and that the increased production of Style Y would utilize the plant facilities released by the discontinuance of Style Z.

The sales, costs, and expenses have been relatively stable over the past few years and they are expected to remain so for the foreseeable future. The income statement for the past year ended December 31 is:

| | Style | | | |
| --- | --- | --- | --- | --- |
| | X | Y | Z | Total |
| Sales.................................. | $400,000 | $432,000 | $126,000 | $958,000 |
| Cost of goods sold: | | | | |
|   Variable costs........................ | $220,000 | $246,000 | $ 88,200 | $554,200 |
|   Fixed costs ......................... | 80,000 | 84,000 | 28,000 | 192,000 |
|   Total cost of goods sold.............. | $300,000 | $330,000 | $116,200 | $746,200 |
| Gross profit........................... | $100,000 | $102,000 | $ 9,800 | $211,800 |
| Less operating expenses: | | | | |
|   Variable expenses.................... | $ 40,000 | $ 43,200 | $ 12,600 | $ 95,800 |
|   Fixed expenses ..................... | 24,000 | 24,000 | 10,500 | 58,500 |
|   Total operating expenses.............. | $ 64,000 | $ 67,200 | $ 23,100 | $154,300 |
| Income from operations ................. | $ 36,000 | $ 34,800 | $(13,300) | $ 57,500 |

Instructions:

(1) Prepare an income statement for the past year in the variable costing format. Use the following headings:

| | Style | | |
| --- | --- | --- | --- |
| X | Y | Z | Total |

Data for each style should be reported through contribution margin. The fixed costs and expenses should be deducted from the total contribution margin, as reported in the "total" column, to determine income from operations.

(2) Based on the income statement prepared in (1) and the other data presented above, determine the amount by which total annual operating income would be reduced below its present level if Proposal 2 is accepted.

(3) Prepare an income statement in the variable costing format, indicating the projected annual operating income if Proposal 3 is accepted. Use the following headings:

| | Style | |
| --- | --- | --- |
| X | Y | Total |

Data for each style should be reported through contribution margin. The fixed costs and expenses should be deducted from the total contribution margin as reported in the "total" column. For purposes of this problem, the additional expenditure of $20,000 for advertising can be added to the fixed operating expenses.

(4) By how much would total annual income increase above its present level if Proposal 3 is accepted? Explain.

---

**Mini-Case**

Caswell Company is a family-owned business in which you own 20% of the common stock and your brothers and sisters own the remaining shares. The employment contract of Caswell's new president, Ray Hackett, stipulates a base salary of $50,000 per year plus 10% of income from operations in excess of $4,000,000.

Caswell uses the absorption costing method of reporting income from operations, which has averaged approximately $4,000,000 for the past several years.

Estimated sales for 1985, Hackett's first year as president of Caswell Company, is estimated at 100,000 units at a selling price of $200 per unit. To maximize the use of Caswell's productive capacity, Hackett has decided to manufacture 120,000 units rather than 100,000 units of estimated sales. The beginning inventory at January 1, 1985, is insignificant in amount, and the manufacturing costs and selling and general expenses for the production of 100,000 and 120,000 units are as follows:

### 100,000 Units To Be Manufactured

| | Total Cost or Expense | Number of Units | Unit Cost |
|---|---|---|---|
| Manufacturing costs: | | | |
| Variable ....................... | $ 9,000,000 | 100,000 | $ 90 |
| Fixed......................... | 3,000,000 | 100,000 | 30 |
| Total ...................... | $12,000,000 | | $120 |
| | | | |
| Selling and general expenses: | | | |
| Variable ..................... | $ 3,000,000 | | |
| Fixed......................... | 1,000,000 | | |
| Total ...................... | $ 4,000,000 | | |

### 120,000 Units To Be Manufactured

| | Total Cost or Expense | Number of Units | Unit Cost |
|---|---|---|---|
| Manufacturing costs: | | | |
| Variable ....................... | $10,800,000 | 120,000 | $ 90 |
| Fixed......................... | 3,000,000 | 120,000 | 25 |
| Total ...................... | $13,800,000 | | $115 |
| Selling and general expenses: | | | |
| Variable ..................... | $ 3,000,000 | | |
| Fixed......................... | 1,000,000 | | |
| Total ...................... | $ 4,000,000 | | |

Instructions:

(1) Prepare absorption costing income statements for the year ending December 31, 1985, based upon sales of 100,000 units and the manufacture of (a) 100,000 units and (b) 120,000 units.

(2) Explain the difference in the income from operations reported in (1).

(3) Compute Hackett's total salary for 1985, based on sales of 100,000 units and the manufacture of (a) 100,000 units and (b) 120,000 units.

(4) In addition to maximizing the use of Caswell Company's productive capacity, why might Hackett wish to manufacture 120,000 units rather than 100,000 units?

(5) Can you suggest an alternative way in which Hackett's salary could be determined, using a base salary of $50,000 and 10% of income from operations in excess of $4,000,000, so that the salary could not be increased by simply manufacturing more units?

# 7

CHAPTER

# Cost-Volume-Profit Analysis

**CHAPTER OBJECTIVES**

*Describe the use of analyses of cost-volume-profit relationships in planning operations.*

*Describe and illustrate the mathematical approach to cost-volume-profit analysis.*

*Describe and illustrate the graphic approach to cost-volume-profit analysis.*

*Describe and illustrate special cost-volume-profit relationships.*

# 7

## CHAPTER

In Chapter 6, three forms of profit analysis—gross profit analysis, absorption costing, and variable costing—were discussed. Cost-volume-profit analysis, described in this chapter, is the systematic examination of the interrelationships between selling prices, volume of sales and production, costs, expenses, and profits. Cost-volume-profit analysis is another tool for management's use in making decisions affecting the profitability of the business.

## COST-VOLUME-PROFIT RELATIONSHIPS

The examination of cost-volume-profit relationships is a complex matter, since these relationships are often affected by forces entirely or partially beyond management's control. For example, the determination of the selling price of a product is often affected by not only the costs of production, but also by uncontrollable factors in the marketplace. On the other hand, the cost of producing the product is affected by such controllable factors as the efficiency of operations and the volume of production.

Accounting can play an important role in cost-volume-profit analysis by providing management with information on the relative profitability of its various products, the probable effects of changes in selling price, and other variables. Such information can help management improve the relationship between these variables. For example, an analysis of sales and cost data can be helpful in determining the level of sales volume necessary for the business to earn a satisfactory profit.

Costs represent one of the most significant factors in cost-volume-profit analysis. For this purpose, all operating costs and expenses must be subdivided into two categories: (1) fixed and (2) variable. In this chapter, the term "cost" is often used as a convenience to represent both "costs" and "expenses."

## Variable Costs

Variable costs are costs that change, in total, as the volume of activity changes. For example, assume that Product Q requires $5 of direct materials per unit. The total direct materials cost of manufacturing 10,000 units is $50,000; 20,000 units require direct materials of $100,000; and so on. Note that the unit cost of the direct materials ($5) remains constant with changes in volume. These variable cost relationships are shown in the graphs at the top of page 143.

Direct labor, as well as direct materials, is a variable cost. Similarly, items such as supplies, electricity, indirect materials, and sales commissions are additional examples of variable costs and expenses.

## Fixed Costs

Fixed costs remain constant, in total, as the volume of activity changes. For example, straight-line depreciation of $200,000 on factory buildings and equipment will not change, regardless of whether 10,000 units or 20,000 units of product are manufactured. Although fixed costs do not vary in total with changes in volume of activity, the unit cost will change with changes in activity. If volume increases, the unit cost will decrease, and if volume decreases, the unit cost will increase. For

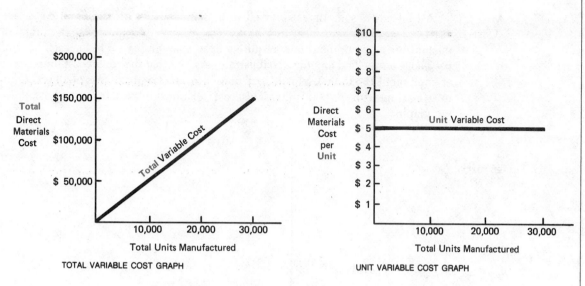

TOTAL VARIABLE COST GRAPH                    UNIT VARIABLE COST GRAPH

example, the unit cost of straight-line depreciation of $200,000 for 10,000 units is $20, and for 20,000 units of product, the unit cost is $10. These fixed cost relationships are shown in the following graphs:

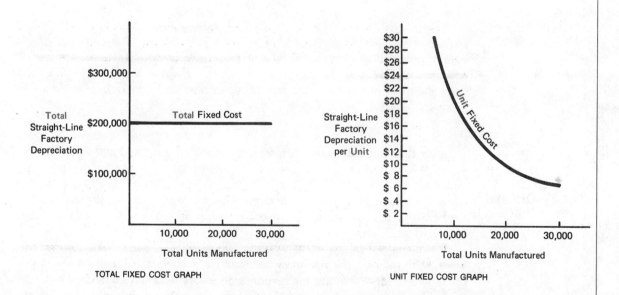

TOTAL FIXED COST GRAPH                       UNIT FIXED COST GRAPH

Examples of additional fixed costs include real estate taxes, property insurance, rent, and office salaries. Although such costs do not vary in total with changes in volume of activity, they may change because of other factors. For example, changes in property tax rates or property insurance rates will change the total property tax cost or the total property insurance cost.

**Mixed Costs**

Mixed costs, sometimes referred to as **semivariable** or **semifixed** costs, are ~~costs that have both variable and fixed characteristics. For example,~~ the rental of manufacturing equipment may require a fixed charge plus a rate for each hour of use above a specified amount. To illustrate, assume that the rental cost for an item of equipment is $15,000, plus $1 per unit of production in excess of 10,000 units to a maximum of 30,000 units. This cost relationship is shown in the following graph:

**MIXED COST GRAPH**

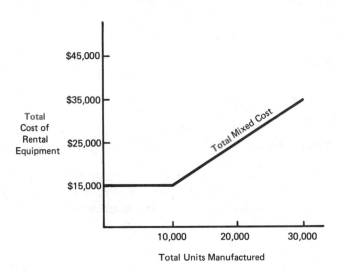

For purposes of analysis, mixed costs ~~can generally be separated into variable and fixed components~~. In the remainder of this chapter, the variable and fixed components of mixed costs are used in describing and illustrating cost-volume-profit analysis.

**MATHEMATICAL APPROACH TO COST-VOLUME-PROFIT ANALYSIS**

After the costs and expenses have been classified into fixed and variable components, the effect on profit of these costs and expenses, along with revenues and volume, can be expressed in the form of cost-volume-profit analysis. Although accountants have proposed various approaches for cost-volume-profit analysis, the mathematical approach is one of two common approaches described and illustrated in this chapter.

~~The mathematical approach to cost-volume-profit analysis generally uses equations~~ (1) to indicate the revenues necessary to achieve the break-even point in operations or (2) to indicate the revenues necessary to achieve a desired or target profit. These two equations and their use by management in profit planning are described and illustrated in the paragraphs that follow.

**Break-Even Point**

The point in the operations of an enterprise at which revenues and expired costs are exactly equal is called the ~~break-even point~~. At this level of operations, an enterprise will neither realize an operating income nor incur an operating loss.

Break-even analysis can be applied to past periods, but it is most useful when applied to future periods as a guide to business planning, particularly if either an expansion or a curtailment of operations is expected. In such cases, it is concerned with future prospects and future operations and hence relies upon estimates. The reliability of the analysis is greatly influenced by the accuracy of the estimates.

The break-even point can be computed by means of a mathematical formula which indicates the relationship between revenue, costs, and capacity. The data required are (1) total estimated fixed costs for a future period, such as a year, and (2) the total estimated variable costs for the same period, stated as a percent of net sales. To illustrate, assume that fixed costs are estimated at $90,000 and that variable costs are expected to be 60% of sales. The break-even point is $225,000 of sales, computed as follows:

Break-Even Sales (in $) = Fixed Costs (in $) + Variable Costs (as % of Break-Even Sales)

$$S = \$90,000 + 60\%S$$
$$40\%S = \$90,000$$
$$S = \$225,000$$

The validity of the preceding computation is shown in the following income statement:

| | | |
|---|---:|---:|
| Sales | | $225,000 |
| Expenses: | | |
| Variable costs ($225,000 × 60%) | $135,000 | |
| Fixed costs | 90,000 | 225,000 |
| Operating profit | | –0– |

The break-even point can be expressed either in terms of total sales dollars, as in the preceding illustration, or in terms of units of sales. For example, in the preceding illustration, if the unit selling price is $25, the break-even point can be expressed as either $225,000 of sales or 9,000 units ($225,000 ÷ $25).

The break-even point can be affected by changes in the fixed costs, unit variable costs, and unit selling price. The effect of each of these factors on the break-even point is briefly described in the following paragraphs.

## Effect of Changes in Fixed Costs

Although fixed costs do not change in total with changes in volume of activity, they may change because of other factors, such as changes in property tax rates and salary increases given to factory supervisors. Increases in fixed costs will raise the break-even point. Similarly, decreases in fixed costs will lower the break-even point.

To illustrate, assume that Bishop Co. is evaluating a proposal to budget an additional $100,000 for advertising. Fixed costs (before the additional expenditure of $100,000 is considered) are estimated at $600,000, and variable costs are estimated at 75% of sales. The break-even point (before the additional expenditure is considered) is $2,400,000, computed as follows:

Break-Even Sales (in $) = Fixed Costs (in $) + Variable Costs (as % of Break-Even Sales)
$$S = \$600,000 + 75\%S$$
$$25\%S = \$600,000$$
$$S = \$2,400,000$$

If advertising expense is increased by $100,000, the break-even point is raised to $2,800,000, computed as follows:

Break-Even Sales (in $) = Fixed Costs (in $) + Variable Costs (as % of Break-Even Sales)
$$S = \$700,000 + 75\%S$$
$$25\%S = \$700,000$$
$$S = \$2,800,000$$

The increased fixed cost of $100,000 increases the break-even point by $400,000 of sales, since 75 cents of each sales dollar must cover variable costs. Hence, $4 of additional sales are needed for each $1 increase in fixed costs if the break-even point for Bishop Co. is to remain unchanged.

### Effect of Changes in Variable Costs

Although unit variable costs do not change with changes in volume of activity, they may change because of other factors, such as changes in the price of direct materials and salary increases given to factory workers providing direct labor. Increases in unit variable costs will raise the break-even point. Similarly, decreases in unit variable costs will lower the break-even point.

To illustrate, assume that Park Co. is evaluating a proposal to pay an additional 2% sales commission to its sales representatives as an incentive to increase sales. Fixed costs are estimated at $84,000, and variable costs are estimated at 58% of sales (before the additional 2% commission is considered). The break-even point (before the additional commission is considered) is $200,000, computed as follows:

Break-Even Sales (in $) = Fixed Costs (in $) + Variable Costs (as % of Break-Even Sales)
$$S = \$84,000 + 58\%S$$
$$42\%S = \$84,000$$
$$S = \$200,000$$

If the sales commission proposal is adopted, the break-even point is raised to $210,000, computed as follows:

Break-Even Sales (in $) = Fixed Costs (in $) + Variable Costs (as % of Break-Even Sales)
$$S = \$84,000 + 60\%S$$
$$40\%S = \$84,000$$
$$S = \$210,000$$

The additional 2% sales commission (a variable cost) increases the break-even point by $10,000 of sales. If the proposal is adopted, 2% less of each sales dollar is available to cover the fixed costs of $84,000.

### Effect of Changing Unit Selling Price

Increases in the unit selling price will lower the break-even point, while decreases in the unit selling price will raise the break-even point. To illustrate the effect of changing the unit selling price, assume that Graham Co. is evaluating a proposal to increase the unit selling price of its product from its current price of $50 to $60 and has accumulated the following relevant data:

|  | Current | Proposed |
|---|---|---|
| Unit selling price | $50 | $60 |
| Unit variable cost | $30 | $30 |
| Variable costs (as % of break-even sales): | | |
| $30 unit variable cost ÷ $50 unit selling price | 60% | |
| $30 unit variable cost ÷ $60 unit selling price | | 50% |
| Total fixed costs | $600,000 | $600,000 |

The break-even point based on the current selling price is $1,500,000, computed as follows:

Break-Even Sales (in $) = Fixed Costs (in $) + Variable Costs (as % of Break-Even Sales)
$$S = \$600,000 + 60\%S$$
$$40\%S = \$600,000$$
$$S = \$1,500,000$$

If the selling price is increased by $10 per unit, the break-even point is decreased to $1,200,000, computed as follows:

Break-Even Sales (in $) = Fixed Costs (in $) + Variable Costs (as % of Break-Even Sales)
$$S = \$600,000 + 50\%S$$
$$50\%S = \$600,000$$
$$S = \$1,200,000$$

The increase in selling price of $10 per unit decreases the break-even point by $300,000 (from $1,500,000 to $1,200,000). In terms of units of sales, the decrease is from 30,000 units ($1,500,000 ÷ $50) to 20,000 units ($1,200,000 ÷ $60).

**Desired Profit**  At the break-even point, sales and costs are exactly equal. However, business enterprises do not use the break-even point as their goal for future operations. Rather, they seek to achieve the largest possible volume of sales above the break-even point. By modifying the break-even equation, the sales volume required to earn a desired amount of profit may be estimated. For this purpose, a factor for desired profit is added to the standard break-even formula. To illustrate, assume that fixed costs are estimated at $200,000, variable costs are estimated at 60% of sales, and the desired profit is $100,000. The sales volume is $750,000, computed as follows:

Sales (in $) = Fixed Costs (in $) + Variable Costs (as % of Sales) + Desired Profit
$$S = \$200,000 + 60\%S + \$100,000$$
$$40\%S = \$300,000$$
$$S = \$750,000$$

The validity of the preceding computation is shown in the following income statement:

| Sales ................................................. | | $750,000 |
| Expenses: | | |
| Variable costs ($750,000 × 60%) .................. | $450,000 | |
| Fixed costs.................................... | 200,000 | 650,000 |
| Operating profit................................. | | $100,000 |

**GRAPHIC APPROACH TO COST-VOLUME-PROFIT ANALYSIS**

Cost-volume-profit analysis can be presented graphically as well as in equation form. ~~Many managers prefer the graphic format because the operating profit or loss for any given level of capacity can be readily determined, without the necessity of solving an equation.~~ The following paragraphs describe ~~two graphic approaches~~ which managers find useful.

**Cost-Volume-Profit (Break-Even) Chart**

A ~~cost-volume-profit chart~~, ~~sometimes called a break-even chart~~, is used to assist management in understanding the relationships between costs, sales, and operating profit or loss. To illustrate the cost-volume-profit chart, assume that fixed costs are estimated at $90,000, and variable costs are estimated as 60% of sales. The maximum sales at 100% of capacity is $400,000. The following cost-volume-profit chart is based on the foregoing data:

**COST-VOLUME-PROFIT CHART**

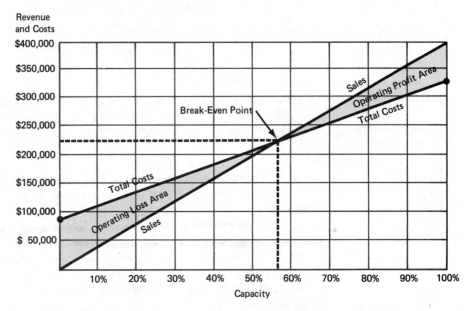

~~The cost-volume-profit chart is constructed in the following manner.~~

1. Percentages of capacity of the enterprise are spread along the horizontal axis, and dollar amounts representing operating data are spread along the vertical axis. The outside limits of the chart represent 100% of capacity and the maximum sales potential at that level of capacity.
2. A diagonal line representing sales is drawn from the lower left corner to the upper right corner.

3. A point representing fixed costs is plotted on the vertical axis at the left, and a point representing total costs at maximum capacity is plotted at the right edge of the chart. A diagonal line representing total costs at various percentages of capacity is then drawn connecting these two points.
4. Horizontal and vertical lines are drawn at the point of intersection of the sales and cost lines, which is the break-even point, and the areas representing operating profit and operating loss are identified.

In the illustration, the total costs at maximum capacity are $330,000 (fixed costs of $90,000 plus variable costs of $240,000, which is 60% of $400,000). The dotted line drawn from the point of intersection to the vertical axis identifies the break-even sales amount of $225,000. The dotted line drawn from the point of intersection to the horizontal axis identifies the break-even point in terms of capacity of approximately 56%. Operating profits will be earned when sales levels are to the right of the break-even point (operating profit area), and operating losses will be incurred when sales levels are to the left of the break-even point (operating loss area).

Changes in the unit selling price, total fixed costs, and unit variable costs can also be analyzed using a cost-volume-profit chart. To illustrate, using the preceding example, assume that a proposal to reduce fixed costs by $42,000 is to be evaluated. In this situation, the total fixed costs would be $48,000 ($90,000 − $42,000), and the total costs at maximum capacity would amount to $288,000 ($48,000 of fixed costs plus variable costs of $240,000). The preceding cost-volume-profit chart is revised by plotting the total fixed cost and total cost points and drawing a line between the two points, indicating the proposed total cost line. The following revised chart indicates that the break-even point would decrease to $120,000 of sales (30% of capacity).

**REVISED COST-VOLUME-PROFIT CHART**

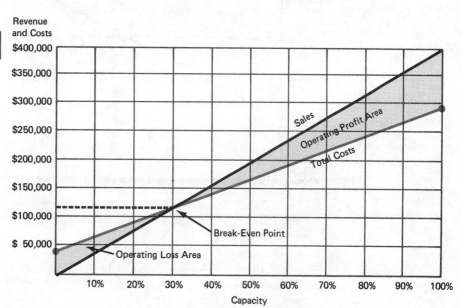

2  Profit-Volume
   Chart

Another graphic approach to cost-volume-profit analysis, called the profit-volume chart, focuses on profitability rather than on sales revenues and costs, as was the case for the cost-volume-profit chart. On the profit-volume chart, only the difference between total sales revenues and total costs is plotted, which enables management to determine the operating profit (or loss) for various levels of operations.

To illustrate the profit-volume chart, assume that fixed costs are estimated at $50,000, variable costs are estimated at 75% of sales, and the maximum capacity is $500,000 of sales. The maximum operating loss is equal to the fixed costs of $50,000, and the maximum operating profit at 100% of capacity is $75,000, computed as follows:

| | | |
|---|---:|---:|
| Sales .............................................. | | $500,000 |
| Expenses: | | |
|     Variable costs ($500,000 × 75%) ................. | $375,000 | |
|     Fixed costs ...................................... | 50,000 | 425,000 |
| Operating profit ................................... | | $ 75,000 |

The following profit-volume chart is based on the foregoing data:

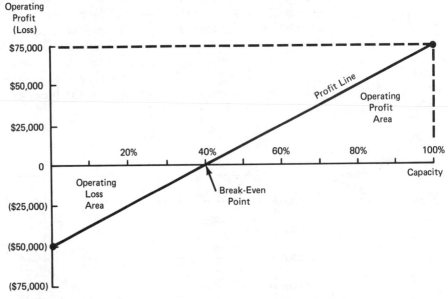

The profit-volume chart is constructed in the following manner:

1. Percentages of capacity of the enterprise are spread along the horizontal axis, and dollar amounts representing operating profits and losses are spread along the vertical axis.
2. A point representing the maximum operating loss is plotted on the vertical axis at the left. This loss is equal to the total fixed costs at 0% of capacity.
3. A point representing the maximum operating profit at 100% of capacity is plotted on the right.

4. A diagonal profit line is drawn connecting the maximum operating loss point with the maximum operating profit point.
5. The profit line intersects the horizontal axis at the break-even point expressed as a percentage of capacity, and the areas representing operating profit and operating loss are identified.

In the illustration, the break-even point is 40% of productive capacity, which can be converted to $200,000 of total sales (maximum capacity of $500,000 × 40%). Operating profit will be earned when sales levels are to the right of the break-even point (operating profit area), and operating losses will be incurred when sales levels are to the left of the break-even point (operating loss area). For example, at 60% of productive capacity, an operating profit of $25,000 will be earned, as indicated in the following profit-volume chart:

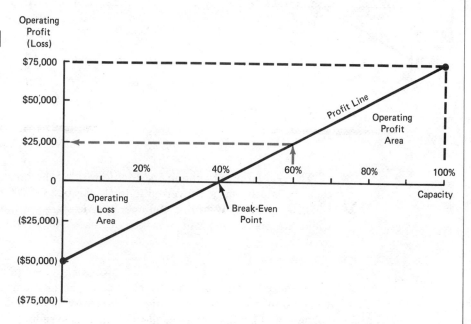

The effect of changes in the unit selling price, total fixed costs, and unit variable costs on profit can be analyzed using a profit-volume chart. To illustrate, using the preceding example, assume that the effect on profit of an increase of $25,000 in fixed costs is to be evaluated. In this case, the total fixed costs would be $75,000 ($50,000 + $25,000), and the maximum operating loss at 0% of capacity would be $75,000. The maximum operating profit at 100% of capacity would be $50,000, computed as follows:

| | | |
|---|---:|---:|
| Sales . . . . . . . . . . . . . . . . . . . . . . . . . . . . . . . . . . . . . . . . . . . . . | | $500,000 |
| Expenses: | | |
|    Variable costs ($500,000 × 75%) . . . . . . . . . . . . . . . . . | $375,000 | |
|    Fixed costs . . . . . . . . . . . . . . . . . . . . . . . . . . . . . . . . . . . . | 75,000 | 450,000 |
| Operating profit . . . . . . . . . . . . . . . . . . . . . . . . . . . . . . . . . . . | | $ 50,000 |

A revised profit-volume chart is constructed by plotting the maximum operating loss and maximum operating profit points and drawing a line between the two points, indicating the revised profit line. The original and the revised profit-volume charts are as follows:

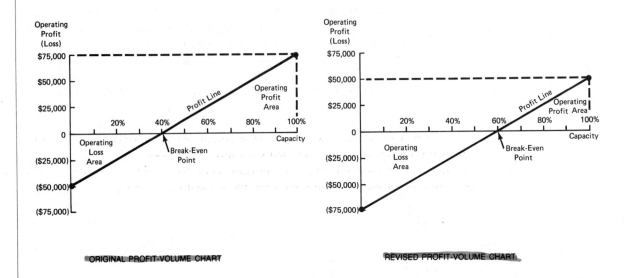

ORIGINAL PROFIT-VOLUME CHART                                    REVISED PROFIT-VOLUME CHART

The revised profit-volume chart indicates that the break-even point is 60% of capacity, which can be converted to total sales of $300,000 (maximum capacity of $500,000 × 60%). Note that the operating loss area of the chart has increased, while the operating profit area has decreased under the proposed change in fixed costs.

**USE OF COMPUTERS IN COST-VOLUME-PROFIT ANALYSIS**

In the preceding paragraphs, the use of the mathematical approach to cost-volume-profit analysis and the use of the cost-volume-profit chart and the profit-volume chart for analyzing the effect of changes in selling price, costs, and volume on profits have been demonstrated. Both the mathematical and graphic approaches are becoming increasingly popular and easy to use when managers have access to a computer terminal or a microcomputer. With the wide variety of computer software that is available, managers can vary assumptions regarding selling prices, costs, and volume and can instantaneously analyze the effects of the assumptions on the break-even point and profit.

**SALES MIX CONSIDER-ATIONS**

In many businesses, more than one product is sold at varying selling prices. In addition, the products often have different unit variable costs, and each product makes a different contribution to profits. Thus, the total business profit, as well as the break-even point, depends upon the proportions in which the products are sold.

Sales mix is the relative distribution of sales among the various products sold by an enterprise. For example, assume that the sales for Cascade Company during the past year, a typical year for the company, are as follows:

| Product | Units Sold | Sales Mix |
|---------|-----------|-----------|
| A | 8,000 | 80% |
| B | 2,000 | 20 |
| | 10,000 | 100% |

The sales mix for products A and B can be expressed as a relative percentage, as shown above, or as the ratio of 80:20.

**Sales Mix and the Break-Even Point**

The break-even point for an enterprise selling two or more products must be calculated on the basis of a specified sales mix. If the sales mix is assumed to be constant, the break-even point and the sales necessary to achieve desired levels of operating profit can be computed using the standard calculations.

To illustrate the computation of the break-even point for Cascade Company, assume that fixed costs are $200,000. In addition, assume that the unit selling prices, unit variable costs, and sales mix for products A and B are as follows:

| Product | Selling Price per Unit | Variable Cost per Unit | Sales Mix |
|---------|-----------------------|------------------------|-----------|
| A | $ 90 | $70 | 80% |
| B | 140 | 95 | 20 |

To compute the break-even point when several products are sold, it is useful to think of the individual products as components of one overall enterprise product. For Cascade Company, assume that this overall enterprise product is arbitrarily labeled E. The unit selling price of E can be thought of as equal to the total of the unit selling prices of the individual products A and B, multiplied by their respective sales mix percentages. Likewise, the unit variable cost of E can be thought of as equal to the total of the unit variable costs of products A and B, multiplied by the sales mix percentages. These computations are as follows:

Unit selling price of E:  ($90 × .8) + ($140 × .2) = $100
Unit variable cost of E:  ($70 × .8) + ($95 × .2) = $75

The variable costs for enterprise product E are therefore expected to be 75% of sales ($75 ÷ $100). The break-even point can be determined in the normal manner, using the equation, as follows:

Break-Even Sales (in $) = Fixed Costs (in $) + Variable Costs (as % of Break-Even Sales)
S = $200,000 + 75%S
25%S = $200,000
S = $800,000

The break-even point of $800,000 of sales of enterprise product E is equivalent to 8,000 total sales units ($800,000 ÷ $100). Since the sales mix for products A and B is 80% and 20% respectively, the break-even quantity of A is 6,400 (8,000 × 80%) and B is 1,600 (8,000 × 20%) units.

The validity of the preceding analysis can be verified by preparing the following income statement:

Cascade Company
Income Statement
For Year Ended December 31, 19--

|  | Product A | Product B | Total |
|---|---|---|---|
| Sales: |  |  |  |
| 6,400 units × $90 | $576,000 |  | $576,000 |
| 1,600 units × $140 |  | $224,000 | 224,000 |
| Total sales | $576,000 | $224,000 | $800,000 |
| Variable costs: |  |  |  |
| 6,400 units × $70 | $448,000 |  | $448,000 |
| 1,600 units × $95 |  | $152,000 | 152,000 |
| Total variable costs | $448,000 | $152,000 | $600,000 |
| Fixed costs |  |  | 200,000 |
| Total costs |  |  | $800,000 |
| Operating profit |  |  | –0– |

The effects of changes in the sales mix on the break-even point can be determined by repeating the preceding analysis, assuming a different sales mix.

**Sales Mix and Desired Profit**

The sales volume needed to earn an amount of profit when an enterprise sells two or more products can be computed using an approach similar to that described in the previous section. For example, the total sales necessary for Cascade Company to earn an operating profit of $40,000, with the original sales mix of 80% and 20% (where fixed costs were $200,000 and variable costs were 75% of sales), can be computed by use of the concept of an overall enterprise product E and solving the following equation:

Sales (in $) = Fixed Costs (in $) + Variable Costs (as a % of Sales) + Desired Profit
$$S = \$200,000 + 75\%S + \$40,000$$
$$25\%S = \$240,000$$
$$S = \$960,000$$

Sales of $960,000 of enterprise product E is equivalent to 9,600 total sales units ($960,000 ÷ $100). Since the sales mix for products A and B is 80% and 20% respectively, the quantity of A to be sold is 7,680 (9,600 × 80%) and B is 1,920 (9,600 × 20%) units. The validity of this approach can be verified by preparing the following income statement:

Cascade Company
Income Statement
For Year Ended December 31, 19--

| | Product A | Product B | Total |
|---|---|---|---|
| Sales: | | | |
| 7,680 units × $90 ........................ | $691,200 | | $691,200 |
| 1,920 units × $140 ........................ | | $268,800 | 268,800 |
| Total sales........................ | $691,200 | $268,800 | $960,000 |
| Variable costs: | | | |
| 7,680 units × $70 ........................ | $537,600 | | $537,600 |
| 1,920 units × $95 ........................ | | $182,400 | 182,400 |
| Total variable costs........................ | $537,600 | $182,400 | $720,000 |
| Fixed costs ........................ | | | 200,000 |
| Total costs........................ | | | $920,000 |
| Operating profit ........................ | | | $ 40,000 |

## SPECIAL COST-VOLUME-PROFIT RELATIONSHIPS

Additional relationships can be developed from the information presented in both the mathematical and graphic approaches to cost-volume-profit analysis. Two of these relationships that are especially useful to management in decision making are discussed in the following paragraphs.

### Margin of Safety

The difference between the current sales revenue and the sales at the break-even point is called the margin of safety. It represents the possible decrease in sales revenue that may occur before an operating loss results, and it may be stated either in terms of dollars or as a percentage of sales. For example, if the volume of sales is $250,000 and sales at the break-even point amount to $200,000, the margin of safety is $50,000 or 20%, as shown by the following computation:

$$\text{Margin of Safety} = \frac{\text{Sales} - \text{Sales at Break-Even Point}}{\text{Sales}}$$

$$\text{Margin of Safety} = \frac{\$250,000 - \$200,000}{\$250,000} = 20\%$$

The margin of safety is useful in evaluating past operations and as a guide to business planning. For example, if the margin of safety is low, management should carefully study forecasts of future sales because even a small decline in sales revenue will result in an operating loss.

### Contribution Margin Ratio

Another relationship between cost, volume, and profits that is especially useful in business planning because it gives an insight into the profit potential of a firm is the contribution margin ratio, sometimes called the profit-volume ratio. This ratio indicates the percentage of each sales dollar available to cover the fixed expenses and to provide operating income. For example, if the volume of sales is $250,000 and variable expenses amount to $175,000, the contribution margin ratio is 30%, as shown by the following computation:

$$\text{Contribution Margin Ratio} = \frac{\text{Sales} - \text{Variable Expenses}}{\text{Sales}}$$

$$\text{Contribution Margin Ratio} = \frac{\$250,000 - \$175,000}{\$250,000} = 30\%$$

The contribution margin ratio permits the quick determination of the effect on operating income of an increase or a decrease in sales volume. To illustrate, assume that the management of a firm with a contribution margin ratio of 30% is studying the effect on operating income of adding $25,000 in sales orders. Multiplying the ratio (30%) by the change in sales volume ($25,000) indicates an increase in operating income of $7,500 if the additional orders are obtained. In using the analysis in such a case, factors other than sales volume, such as the amount of fixed expenses, the percentage of variable expenses to sales, and the unit sales price, are assumed to remain constant. If these factors are not constant, the effect of any change in these factors must be considered in applying the analysis.

The contribution margin ratio is also useful in setting business policy. For example, if the contribution margin ratio of a firm is large and production is at a level below 100% capacity, a comparatively large increase in operating income can be expected from an increase in sales volume. On the other hand, a comparatively large decrease in operating income can be expected from a decline in sales volume. A firm in such a position might decide to devote more effort to additional sales promotion because of the large change in operating income that will result from changes in sales volume. On the other hand, a firm with a small contribution margin ratio will probably want to give more attention to reducing costs and expenses before concentrating large efforts on additional sales promotion.

**LIMITATIONS OF COST-VOLUME-PROFIT ANALYSIS**

The reliability of cost-volume-profit analysis depends upon the validity of several assumptions. One major assumption is that there is no change in inventory quantities during the year; that is, the quantity of units in the beginning inventory equals the quantity of units in the ending inventory. When changes in inventory quantities occur, the computations for cost-volume-profit analysis become more complex.

For cost-volume-profit analysis, a relevant range of activity is assumed, within which all costs can be classified as either fixed or variable. Within the relevant range, which is usually a range of activity within which the company is likely to operate, the unit variable costs and the total fixed costs will not change. For example, within the relevant range of activity, factory supervisory salaries are fixed. For cost-volume-profit analysis, it is assumed that a significant change in activity that would cause these salaries to change, such as adding a night shift that would double production, will not occur.

These assumptions simplify cost-volume-profit relationships, and since substantial ~~variations in~~ the ~~assumptions~~ are often ~~uncommon in practice, cost-volume-profit analysis can be used quite effectively in decision making~~. Under conditions of substantial variations from the assumptions, the analysis of the cost-volume-profit relationships must be used cautiously.

**Self-Examination Questions**
*(Answers in Appendix C.)*

1. For cost-volume-profit analysis, costs must be classified as either fixed or variable. Variable costs:
   A. change in total as the volume of activity changes
   B. do not change in total as the volume of activity changes
   C. change on a per unit basis as the volume of activity changes
   D. none of the above

2. If variable costs are 40% of sales and fixed costs are $240,000, what is the break-even point?
   A. $200,000      C. $400,000
   B. $240,000      D. None of the above

3. Based on the data presented in Question 2, how much sales would be required to realize operating profit of $30,000?
   A. $400,000      C. $600,000
   B. $450,000      D. None of the above

4. If sales are $500,000, variable costs are $200,000, and fixed costs are $240,000, what is the margin of safety?
   A. 20%      C. 60%
   B. 40%      D. None of the above

5. Based on the data presented in Question 4, what is the contribution margin ratio?
   A. 40%      C. 88%
   B. 48%      D. None of the above

**Discussion Questions**

1. How do changes in volume of activity affect total (a) variable costs and (b) fixed costs?

2. If total fixed costs are $150,000, what is the unit fixed cost if production is (a) 50,000 units and (b) 60,000 units?

3. (a) What are mixed costs? (b) If a leased copying machine costs $200 per month plus 3¢ per copy and 5,000 copies were made during June, what was the total cost for June?

4. (a) What is the break-even point? (b) What equation can be used to determine the break-even point?

5. If fixed costs are $420,000 and variable costs are 70% of sales, what is the break-even point?

6. If sales are $1,000,000, variable costs are $400,000, and fixed costs are $480,000, what is the break-even point?

7. If the property tax rates are increased, what effect will this change in fixed costs have on the break-even point?

8. If the unit cost of direct materials is decreased, what effect will this change have on the break-even point?

9. If fixed costs are $630,000 and variable costs are 70% of sales, what sales are required to realize operating profit of $150,000?

10. What is the advantage of presenting cost-volume-profit analysis in the chart form over the equation form?

11. Name the following chart and identify the items represented by the letters a through f.

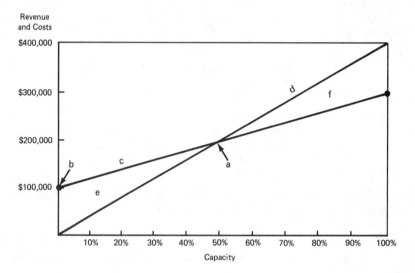

12. Name the following chart and identify the items represented by the letters a through f.

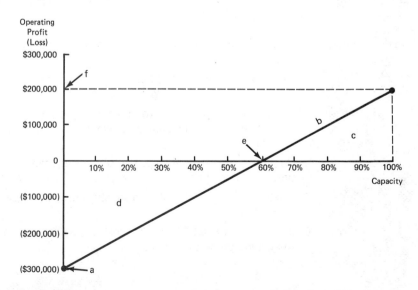

13. Both McBride Company and Sherwood Company had the same sales, total costs, and operating profit for the current fiscal year, yet McBride Company had a lower break-even point than Sherwood Company. Explain the reason for this difference in break-even points.

14. (a) What is meant by "sales mix"? (b) For conventional break-even analysis, is the sales mix assumed to be constant?

15. (a) What is meant by the term "margin of safety"? (b) If sales are $750,000, net income $60,000, and sales at the break-even point $480,000, what is the margin of safety?

16. What ratio indicates the percentage of each sales dollar that is available to cover fixed costs and to provide a profit?

17. (a) If sales are $350,000 and variable costs are $210,000, what is the contribution margin ratio? (b) What is the contribution margin ratio if variable costs are 55% of sales?

18. An examination of the accounting records of Valentine Company disclosed a high contribution margin ratio and production at a level below maximum capacity. Based on this information, suggest a likely means of improving operating profit. Explain.

---

**Exercises**

**Exercise 7-1.** For the current year ending June 30, Overman Company expects fixed costs and expenses of $360,000 and variable costs and expenses equal to 55% of sales.

   (a)   Compute the anticipated break-even point.
   (b)   Compute the sales required to realize operating profit of $90,000.

**Exercise 7-2.** For the past year, Vega Company had fixed costs of $600,000 and variable costs equal to 40% of sales. All revenues and costs are expected to remain constant for the coming year, except that property taxes are expected to increase by $30,000 during the year.

   (a)   Compute the break-even point for the past year.
   (b)   Compute the anticipated break-even point for the coming year.

**Exercise 7-3.** For the current year ending December 31, Rossi Company expects fixed costs of $900,000 and variable costs equal to 50% of sales. For the coming year, a new wage contract will increase variable costs to 55% of sales.

   (a)   Compute the break-even point for the current year.
   (b)   Compute the anticipated break-even point for the coming year, assuming that all revenues and costs are to remain constant, with the exception of the costs represented by the new wage contract.

**Exercise 7-4.** Currently the unit selling price is $300, unit variable cost is $195, and total fixed costs are $700,000. A proposal is being evaluated to increase the unit selling price to $325.

   (a)   Compute the current break-even point.
   (b)   Compute the anticipated break-even point, assuming that the unit selling price is increased and all costs remain constant.

Exercise 7-5. For the coming year, Rosebud Inc. anticipates fixed costs of $100,000, variable costs equal to 75% of sales, and maximum capacity of $800,000 of sales.

    (a)  What is the maximum possible operating loss?
    (b)  Compute the maximum possible operating profit.
    (c)  Construct a profit-volume chart.
    (d)  Determine the break-even point as a percentage of capacity by using the profit-volume chart constructed in (c).

Exercise 7-6. (a) If Pridemore Company, with a break-even point at $600,000 of sales has actual sales of $750,000, what is the margin of safety expressed (1) in dollars and (2) as a percentage of sales? (b) If the margin of safety for Strauss Company was 36%, fixed costs were $180,000, and variable costs were 55% of sales, what was the amount of actual sales?

Exercise 7-7. (a) If Torino Company budgets sales of $800,000, fixed costs and expenses of $224,000, and variable costs and expenses of $512,000, what is the anticipated contribution margin ratio? (b) If the contribution margin ratio for Underwood Company is 40%, sales were $2,400,000, and fixed costs and expenses were $670,000, what was the operating profit?

Exercise 7-8. For the past year, Zeller Company had sales of $650,000, a margin of safety of 20%, and a contribution margin ratio of 45%. Compute:

    (a)  The break-even point.
    (b)  The variable costs and expenses.
    (c)  The fixed costs and expenses.
    (d)  The operating profit.

Exercise 7-9. For 1984, a company had sales of $2,400,000, fixed costs of $600,000, and a contribution margin ratio of 30%. During 1985, the variable costs were 70% of sales, the fixed costs did not change from the previous year, and the margin of safety was 20%.

    (a)  What was the operating profit for 1984?
    (b)  What was the break-even point for 1985?
    (c)  What was the amount of sales for 1985?
    (d)  What was the operating profit for 1985?

**Problems**
*(Problems in Appendix B: 7-1B, 7-2B, 7-3B, 7-5B.)*

Problem 7-1A. For the coming year, Margo Company anticipates fixed costs of $240,000 and variable costs equal to 60% of sales.

Instructions:

    (1)  Compute the anticipated break-even point.
    (2)  Compute the sales required to realize operating profit of $80,000.
    (3)  Construct a cost-volume-profit chart, assuming sales of $1,000,000 at full capacity.
    (4)  Determine the probable operating profit if sales total $750,000.

Problem 7-2A. Elton Company operated at 75% of capacity last year, when sales were $3,000,000. Fixed costs were $1,000,000, and variable costs were 50% of sales.

Elton Company is considering a proposal to spend an additional $250,000 on billboard advertising during the current year in an attempt to increase sales and utilize additional capacity.

Instructions:

(1)  Construct a cost-volume-profit chart indicating the break-even point for last year.
(2)  Using the cost-volume-profit chart prepared in (1), determine (a) the operating profit for last year and (b) the maximum operating profit that could have been realized during the year.
(3)  Construct a cost-volume-profit chart indicating the break-even point for the current year, assuming that a noncancelable contract is signed for the additional billboard advertising. No changes are expected in unit selling price or other costs.
(4)  Using the cost-volume-profit chart prepared in (3), determine (a) the operating profit if sales total $3,000,000 and (b) the maximum operating profit that could be realized during the year.

**Problem 7-3A.** Last year, Nagle Company had sales of $800,000, fixed costs of $200,000, and variable costs of $480,000. Nagle Company is considering a proposal to spend $50,000 to hire a public relations firm, hoping that the company's image can be improved and sales increased. Maximum operating capacity is $1,000,000 of sales.

Instructions:

(1)  Construct a profit-volume chart for last year.
(2)  Using the profit-volume chart prepared in (1), determine for last year (a) the break-even point, (b) the operating profit, and (c) the maximum operating profit that could have been realized.
(3)  Construct a profit-volume chart for the current year, assuming that the additional $50,000 expenditure is made and there is no change in unit selling price or other costs.
(4)  Using the profit-volume chart prepared in (3), determine (a) the break-even point, (b) the operating profit if sales total $800,000, and (c) the maximum operating profit that could be realized.

**Problem 7-4A.** The expected sales of products X and Y for Baker Company for the current year, which is typical of recent years, are as follows:

| Product | Selling Price per Unit | Variable Cost per Unit | Sales Mix |
|---------|------------------------|------------------------|-----------|
| X | $100 | $ 80 | 60% |
| Y | 150 | 120 | 40 |

The estimated fixed costs for the current year are $180,000.

Instructions:

(1)  Determine the estimated sales revenues necessary to reach the break-even point for the current year.
(2)  Based on the break-even point in (1), determine the unit sales of both X and Y for the current year.
(3)  Determine the estimated sales revenues necessary for Baker Company to realize an operating profit of $60,000 for the current year.
(4)  Based on the sales revenues determined in (3), determine the unit sales of both X and Y for the current year.

**Problem 7-5A.** Blier Company expects to maintain the same inventories at the end of 1985 as at the beginning of the year. The total of all production costs for the year is therefore assumed to be equal to the cost of goods sold. With this in mind, the various department heads were asked to submit estimates of the expenses for their departments during 1985. A summary report of these estimates is as follows:

|  | Estimated Fixed Expense | Estimated Variable Expense (per unit sold) |
|---|---|---|
| Production costs: |  |  |
| Direct materials | — | $7.50 |
| Direct labor | — | 5.70 |
| Factory overhead | $284,000 | 1.80 |
| Selling expenses: |  |  |
| Sales salaries and commissions | 104,000 | .90 |
| Advertising | 63,000 | — |
| Travel | 30,900 | — |
| Miscellaneous selling expense | 16,300 | .30 |
| General expenses: |  |  |
| Office and officers' salaries | 135,100 | — |
| Supplies | 16,900 | .15 |
| Miscellaneous general expense | 9,800 | .15 |
|  | $660,000 | $16.50 |

It is expected that 80,000 units will be sold at a selling price of $27.50 a unit. Capacity output is 100,000 units.

Instructions:

(1) Determine the break-even point (a) in dollars of sales, (b) in units, and (c) in terms of capacity.
(2) Prepare an estimated income statement for 1985.
(3) Construct a cost-volume-profit chart, indicating the break-even point in dollars of sales.
(4) What is the expected margin of safety?
(5) What is the expected contribution margin ratio?

**Problem 7-6A.** Portnoy Company operated at full capacity during 1984. Its income statement for 1984 is as follows:

| | | |
|---|---|---|
| Sales | | $3,300,000 |
| Cost of goods sold | | 1,872,000 |
| Gross profit | | $1,428,000 |
| Operating expenses: | | |
| Selling expenses | $648,000 | |
| General expenses | 180,000 | |
| Total operating expenses | | 828,000 |
| Operating profit | | $ 600,000 |

An analysis of costs and expenses reveals the following division of costs and expenses between fixed and variable:

|                      | Fixed | Variable |
|----------------------|-------|----------|
| Cost of goods sold.......  | 25%   | 75%      |
| Selling expenses.........  | 20%   | 80%      |
| General expenses .......   | 68%   | 32%      |

Management is considering a plant expansion program that will permit an increase of $700,000 in yearly sales. The expansion will increase fixed costs and expenses by $120,000, but will not affect the relationship between sales and variable costs and expenses.

Instructions:

(1) Determine for present capacity (a) the total fixed costs and expenses and (b) the total variable costs and expenses.
(2) Determine the percentage of total variable costs and expenses to sales.
(3) Compute the break-even point under present conditions.
(4) Compute the break-even point under the proposed program.
(5) Determine the amount of sales that would be necessary under the proposed program to realize the $600,000 of operating profit that was earned in 1984.
(6) Determine the maximum operating profit possible with the expanded plant.
(7) If the proposal is accepted and sales remain at the 1984 level, what will the operating profit be for 1985?
(8) Based upon the data given, would you recommend accepting the proposal? Explain.

**Mini-Case**

Hardman Company manufactures product P, which sold for $20 per unit in 1984. For the past several years, sales and net income have been declining. On sales of $540,000 in 1984, the company operated near the break-even point and used only 60% of its productive capacity. John Hardman, your father-in-law, is considering several proposals to reverse the trend of declining sales and net income, to more fully use production facilities, and to increase profits. One proposal under consideration is to reduce the unit selling price to $19.20.

Your father-in-law has asked you to aid him in assessing the proposal to reduce the sales price by $.80. For this purpose, he provided the following summary of the estimated fixed and variable costs and expenses for 1985, which are unchanged from 1984:

Variable costs and expenses:

| | |
|---|---|
| Production costs .................... | $8.60 per unit |
| Selling expenses .................... | 2.00 per unit |
| General expenses ................... | 1.40 per unit |

Fixed costs and expenses:

| | |
|---|---|
| Production costs..................... | $100,000 |
| Selling expenses ..................... | 40,000 |
| General expenses ................... | 60,000 |

Instructions:
  (1) Determine the break-even point for 1985 in dollars, assuming (a) no change in sales price and (b) the proposed sales price.
  (2) How much additional sales are necessary for Hardman Company to break even in 1985 under the proposal?
  (3) Determine the net income for 1985, assuming (a) no change in sales price and volume from 1984 and (b) the new sales price and no change in volume from 1984.
  (4) Determine the maximum net income for 1985, assuming the proposed sales price.
  (5) Briefly list factors that you would discuss with your father-in-law in evaluating the proposal.

# 8

# Differential Analysis and Product Pricing

## CHAPTER OBJECTIVES

*Describe and illustrate differential analysis.*

*Describe and illustrate a practical approach to product pricing.*

*Describe and illustrate economic theory underlying product pricing.*

# 8

## CHAPTER

A primary objective of accounting is to provide management with analyses and reports that will be useful in resolving current problems and planning for the future. The types of analyses and reports depend on the nature of the decisions to be made. However, all decisions require careful consideration of the consequences of alternative courses of action. This chapter discusses differential analysis, which provides management with data on the differences in total revenues and costs associated with alternative actions.

This chapter also describes and illustrates a practical approach frequently used by managers in setting product prices. In addition, the relationship of economic theory to the more practical approaches to product pricing is briefly discussed.

## DIFFERENTIAL ANALYSIS

Planning for future operations is chiefly decision making. For some decisions, revenue and cost information drawn from the general ledger and other basic accounting records is very useful. For example, historical cost data in the absorption costing format are helpful in planning production for the long run. Historical cost data in the variable costing format are useful in planning production for the short run. However, the revenue and cost data needed to evaluate courses of future operations or to choose among competing alternatives are often not available in the basic accounting records.

The relevant revenue and cost data in the analysis of future possibilities are the differences between the alternatives under consideration. The amounts of such differences are called **differentials** and the area of accounting concerned with the effect of alternative courses of action on revenues and costs is called differential analysis.

Differential revenue is the amount of increase or decrease in revenue expected from a particular course of action as compared with an alternative. To illustrate, assume that certain equipment is being used to manufacture a product that provides revenue of $150,000. If the equipment could be used to make another product that would provide revenue of $175,000, the differential revenue from the alternative would be $25,000.

Differential cost is the amount of increase or decrease in cost that is expected from a particular course of action as compared with an alternative. For example, if an increase in advertising expenditures from $100,000 to $150,000 is being considered, the differential cost of the action would be $50,000.

Differential analysis can aid management in making decisions on a variety of alternatives, including (1) whether equipment should be leased or sold, (2) whether to discontinue an unprofitable segment, (3) whether to manufacture or purchase a needed part, (4) whether to replace usable plant assets, (5) whether to process further or sell an intermediate product, and (6) whether to accept additional business at a special price. The following discussion relates to the use of differential analysis in analyzing these alternatives.

## Lease or Sell

The main advantage of differential analysis is its selection of relevant revenues and costs related to alternative courses of action. Differential analysis reports emphasize the significant factors bearing on the decision, help to clarify the issues, and save the time of the reader. To illustrate, assume that an enterprise is considering the disposal of an item of equipment that is no longer needed in the business.

Its original cost is $200,000 and accumulated depreciation to date totals $120,000. A tentative offer has been received to lease the machine for a number of years for a total of $160,000, after which the machine would be sold as scrap for a small amount. The repair, insurance, and property tax expenses during the period of the lease are estimated at $35,000. Alternatively, the equipment can be sold through a broker for $100,000 less a 6% commission. The decision to be made is whether the equipment should be leased or sold. The report of the analysis is as follows:

<table>
<tr><td rowspan="14" style="vertical-align: top;">DIFFERENTIAL ANALYSIS REPORT—LEASE OR SELL</td><td colspan="3" style="text-align: center;">Proposal to Lease or Sell Equipment<br>June 22, 19--</td></tr>
<tr><td>Differential revenue from alternatives:</td><td></td><td></td></tr>
<tr><td>  Revenue from lease...............................</td><td>$160,000</td><td></td></tr>
<tr><td>  Revenue from sale................................</td><td>100,000</td><td></td></tr>
<tr><td>    Differential revenue from lease.......................</td><td></td><td>$60,000</td></tr>
<tr><td>Differential cost of alternatives:</td><td></td><td></td></tr>
<tr><td>  Repair, insurance, and property tax expenses ............</td><td>$ 35,000</td><td></td></tr>
<tr><td>  Commission expense on sale.........................</td><td>6,000</td><td></td></tr>
<tr><td>    Differential cost of lease.............................</td><td></td><td>29,000</td></tr>
<tr><td>Net advantage of lease alternative.......................</td><td></td><td>$31,000</td></tr>
</table>

It should be noted that it was not necessary to consider the $80,000 book value ($200,000 − $120,000) of the equipment. The $80,000 is a sunk cost; that is, it is a cost that will not be affected by later decisions. In the illustration, the expenditure to acquire the equipment had already been made, and the choice is now between leasing or selling the equipment. The relevant factors to be considered are the differential revenues and differential costs associated with the lease or sell decision. The undepreciated cost of the equipment is irrelevant. The validity of the foregoing report can be shown by the following conventional analysis:

| | | | |
|---|---|---|---|
| Lease alternative: | | | |
|   Revenue from lease.............................. | | $160,000 | |
|   Depreciation expense.......................... | $80,000 | | |
|   Repair, insurance, and property tax expenses ..... | 35,000 | 115,000 | |
|     Net gain..................................... | | | $45,000 |
| Sell alternative: | | | |
|   Sale price ...................................... | | $100,000 | |
|   Book value of equipment....................... | $80,000 | | |
|   Commission expense .......................... | 6,000 | 86,000 | |
|     Net gain..................................... | | | 14,000 |
| Net advantage of lease alternative.................... | | | $31,000 |

**Discontinuance of an Unprofitable Segment**

When a department, branch, territory, or other segment of an enterprise has been operating at a loss, management should consider eliminating the unprofitable segment. It might be natural to assume (sometimes mistakenly) that the total operating income of the enterprise would be increased if the operating loss could be eliminated. Discontinuance of the unprofitable segment will usually eliminate all of the related variable costs and expenses. However, if the segment represents a relatively small part of the enterprise, the fixed costs and expenses (depreciation, insurance, property taxes, etc.) will not be reduced by its discontinuance. It is entirely possible in this situation for the total operating income of a company to be reduced rather than increased by eliminating an unprofitable segment. As a basis for illustrating this type of situation, the following income statement is presented for the year just ended, which was a normal year. For purposes of the illustration, it is assumed that discontinuance of Product A, on which losses are incurred annually, will have no effect on total fixed costs and expenses.

**Condensed Income Statement**
**For Year Ended August 31, 19--**

|  | Product | | | |
|---|---|---|---|---|
|  | A | B | C | Total |
| Sales.......................... | $100,000 | $400,000 | $500,000 | $1,000,000 |
| Cost of goods sold: |  |  |  |  |
|   Variable costs.................... | $ 60,000 | $200,000 | $220,000 | $ 480,000 |
|   Fixed costs ..................... | 20,000 | 80,000 | 120,000 | 220,000 |
|     Total cost of goods sold........ | $ 80,000 | $280,000 | $340,000 | $ 700,000 |
| Gross profit...................... | $ 20,000 | $120,000 | $160,000 | $ 300,000 |
| Operating expenses: |  |  |  |  |
|   Variable expenses................ | $ 25,000 | $ 60,000 | $ 95,000 | $ 180,000 |
|   Fixed expenses ................. | 6,000 | 20,000 | 25,000 | 51,000 |
|     Total operating expenses........ | $ 31,000 | $ 80,000 | $120,000 | $ 231,000 |
| Income (loss) from operations ....... | $ (11,000) | $ 40,000 | $ 40,000 | $ 69,000 |

Data on the estimated differential revenue and differential cost related to discontinuing Product A, on which an operating loss of $11,000 was incurred during the past year, may be assembled in a report such as the following. This report emphasizes the significant factors bearing on the decision.

**Proposal to Discontinue Product A**
**September 29, 19--**

DIFFERENTIAL
ANALYSIS
REPORT—
DISCONTINUANCE
OF UNPROFITABLE
SEGMENT

| | | |
|---|---|---|
| Differential revenue from annual sales of product: |  |  |
|   Revenue from sales ................................ |  | $100,000 |
| Differential cost of annual sales of product: |  |  |
|   Variable cost of goods sold ......................... | $60,000 |  |
|   Variable operating expenses ........................ | 25,000 | 85,000 |
|   Annual differential income from sales of Product A........ |  | $ 15,000 |

Instead of an increase in annual operating income to $80,000 (Product B, $40,000; Product C, $40,000) that might seem to be indicated by the income statement, the discontinuance of Product A would reduce operating income to an estimated $54,000 ($69,000 − $15,000). The validity of this conclusion can be shown by the following conventional analysis:

**Proposal to Discontinue Product A**
**September 29, 19--**

| | Current Operations | | | Discontinuance of Product A |
| --- | --- | --- | --- | --- |
| | Product A | Products B and C | Total | |
| Sales........................ | $100,000 | $900,000 | $1,000,000 | $900,000 |
| Cost of goods sold: | | | | |
| Variable costs................ | $ 60,000 | $420,000 | $ 480,000 | $420,000 |
| Fixed costs .................. | 20,000 | 200,000 | 220,000 | 220,000 |
| Total cost of goods sold...... | $ 80,000 | $620,000 | $ 700,000 | $640,000 |
| Gross profit.................... | $ 20,000 | $280,000 | $ 300,000 | $260,000 |
| Operating expenses: | | | | |
| Variable expenses............. | $ 25,000 | $155,000 | $ 180,000 | $155,000 |
| Fixed expenses .............. | 6,000 | 45,000 | 51,000 | 51,000 |
| Total operating expenses..... | $ 31,000 | $200,000 | $ 231,000 | $206,000 |
| Income (loss) from operations..... | $ (11,000) | $ 80,000 | $ 69,000 | $ 54,000 |

For purposes of the illustration, it was assumed that the discontinuance of Product A would not cause any significant reduction in the volume of fixed costs and expenses. If plant capacity made available by discontinuance of a losing operation can be used in some other manner or if plant capacity can be reduced, with a resulting reduction in fixed costs and expenses, additional analysis would be needed.

In decisions involving the elimination of an unprofitable segment, management must also consider such other factors as its effect on employees and customers. If a segment of the business is discontinued, some employees may have to be laid off and others may have to be relocated and retrained. Also important is the possible decline in sales of the more profitable products to customers who were attracted to the firm by the discontinued product.

**Make or Buy**

The assembly of many parts is often a substantial element in manufacturing operations. Many of the large factory complexes of automobile manufacturers are specifically called assembly plants. Some of the parts of the finished automobile, such as the motor, are produced by the automobile manufacturer, while other parts, such as tires, are often purchased from other manufacturers. Even in manufacturing the motors, such items as spark plugs and nuts and bolts may be acquired from suppliers in their finished state. When parts or components are purchased, management has usually evaluated the question of "make or buy" and has concluded that a savings in cost results from buying the part rather than manufacturing it. However, "make or buy" options are likely to arise anew when a manufacturer has excess productive capacity in the form of unused equipment, space, and labor.

As a basis for illustrating such alternatives, assume that a manufacturer has been purchasing a component, Part X, for $5 a unit. The factory is currently operating at 80% of capacity, and no significant increase in production is anticipated in the near future. The cost of manufacturing Part X, determined by absorption costing methods, is estimated at $1 for direct materials, $2 for direct labor, and $3 for factory overhead (at the predetermined rate of 150% of direct labor cost), or a total of $6. The decision based on a simple comparison of a "make" price of $6 with a "buy" price of $5 is obvious. However, to the extent that unused capacity could be used in manufacturing the part, there would be no increase in the total amount of fixed factory overhead costs. Hence, only the variable factory overhead costs need to be considered. Variable factory overhead costs such as power and maintenance are determined to amount to approximately 65% of the direct labor cost of $2, or $1.30. The cost factors to be considered are summarized in the following report:

DIFFERENTIAL ANALYSIS REPORT—MAKE OR BUY

### Proposal to Manufacture Part X
### February 15, 19--

| | | |
|---|---:|---:|
| Purchase price of part...................................... | | $5.00 |
| Differential cost to manufacture part: | | |
|     Direct materials...................................... | $1.00 | |
|     Direct labor ......................................... | 2.00 | |
|     Variable factory overhead............................. | 1.30 | 4.30 |
| Cost reduction from manufacturing Part X.................. | | $ .70 |

Other possible effects of a change in policy should also be considered, such as the possibility that a future increase in volume of production would require the use of the currently idle capacity of 20%. The possible effect of the alternatives on employees and on future business relations with the supplier of the part, who may be providing other essential components, are additional factors that might need study.

Equipment Replacement

The usefulness of plant assets may be impaired long before they are considered to be "worn out." Equipment may no longer be ideally adequate for the purpose for which it is used, but on the other hand it may not have reached the point of complete inadequacy. Similarly, the point in time when equipment becomes obsolete may be difficult to determine. Decisions to replace usable plant assets should be based on studies of relevant costs rather than on whims or subjective opinions. The costs to be considered are the alternative future costs of retention as opposed to replacement. The book values of the plant assets being replaced are sunk costs and are irrelevant.

To illustrate some of the factors involved in replacement decisions, assume that an enterprise is considering the disposal of several identical machines having a total book value of $100,000 and an estimated remaining life of five years. The old machines can be sold for $25,000. They can be replaced by a single high-speed machine at a cost of $250,000, with an estimated useful life of five years and no residual value. Analysis of the specifications of the new machine and of accompanying changes in manufacturing methods indicate an estimated annual reduction in variable manufacturing costs from $225,000 to $150,000. No other changes in the manufacturing costs or the operating expenses are expected. The basic data to be considered are summarized in the following report:

**Proposal to Replace Equipment**
**November 28, 19--**

DIFFERENTIAL
ANALYSIS
REPORT—
EQUIPMENT
REPLACEMENT

| | | |
|---|---:|---:|
| Annual variable costs — present equipment.............. | $225,000 | |
| Annual variable costs — new equipment................. | 150,000 | |
| Annual differential decrease in cost..................... | $ 75,000 | |
| Number of years applicable........................... | × 5 | |
| Total differential decrease in cost....................... | $375,000 | |
| Proceeds from sale of present equipment ............... | 25,000 | $400,000 |
| Cost of new equipment................................ | | 250,000 |
| Net differential decrease in cost, 5-year total............. | | $150,000 |
| Annual differential decrease in cost — new equipment..... | | $ 30,000 |

Complicating features could be added to the foregoing illustration, such as a disparity between the remaining useful life of the old equipment and the estimated life of the new equipment, or possible improvement in the product due to the new machine, with a resulting increase in selling price or volume of sales. Another factor that should be considered is the importance of alternative uses for the cash outlay needed to obtain the new equipment. The amount of income that would result from the best available alternative to the proposed use of cash or its equivalent is sometimes called opportunity cost. If, for example, it is assumed that the cash outlay of $250,000 for the new equipment, less the $25,000 proceeds from the sale of the present equipment, could be used to yield a 10% return, the opportunity cost of the proposal would amount to 10% of $225,000, or $22,500.

The term "opportunity cost" introduces a new concept of "cost." In reality, it is not a cost in any usual sense of the word. Instead, it represents the forgoing of possible income associated with a lost opportunity. Although opportunity cost computations do not appear as a part of historical accounting data, they are unquestionably useful in analyses involving choices between alternative courses of action.

Process
or Sell

When a product is manufactured, it progresses through various stages of production. Often, a product can be sold at an intermediate stage of production, or it can be processed further and then sold. In deciding whether to sell a product at an intermediate stage or to process it further, the differential revenues that would be provided and the differential costs that would be incurred from further processing must be considered. Since the costs of producing the intermediate product do not change, regardless of whether the intermediate product is sold or processed further, these costs are not differential costs and are not considered.

To illustrate, assume that an enterprise produces Product Y in batches of 4,000 gallons by processing standard quantities of 4,000 gallons of direct materials, which cost $1.20 per gallon. Product Y can be sold without further processing for $2 per gallon. It is possible for the enterprise to process Product Y further to yield Product Z, which can be sold for $5 per gallon. Product Z will require additional processing costs of $5,760 per batch, and 20% of the gallons of Product Y will evaporate during production. The differential revenues and costs to be considered in deciding whether to process Product Y to produce Product Z are summarized in the following report:

**Proposal To Process Product Y Further**
**October 1, 19--**

DIFFERENTIAL ANALYSIS
REPORT—PROCESS
OR SELL

| | | |
|---|---:|---:|
| Differential revenue from further processing per batch: | | |
| Revenue from sale of Product Z [(4,000 gallons − 800 gallons | | |
| evaporation) × $5] | $16,000 | |
| Revenue from sale of Product Y (4,000 gallons × $2) | 8,000 | |
| Differential revenue | | $8,000 |
| Differential cost per batch: | | |
| Additional cost of producing Product Z | | 5,760 |
| Net advantage of further processing Product Y per batch | | $2,240 |

The net advantage of further processing Product Y into Product Z is $2,240 per batch. Note that the initial cost of producing the intermediate Product Y, $4,800 (4,000 gallons × $1.20), is not considered in deciding whether to process Product Y further. This initial cost will be incurred regardless of whether Product Z is produced.

**Acceptance of Business at a Special Price**

In determining whether to accept additional business at a special price, management must consider the differential revenue that would be provided and the differential cost that would be incurred. If the company is operating at full capacity, the additional production will increase both fixed and variable production costs. But if the normal production of the company is below full capacity, additional business may be undertaken without increasing fixed production costs. In the latter case, the variable costs will be the differential cost of the additional production. Variable costs are the only costs to be considered in making a decision to accept or reject the order. If the operating expenses are likely to increase, these differentials must also be considered.

To illustrate, assume that the usual monthly production of an enterprise is 10,000 units of a certain commodity. At this level of operation, which is well below capacity, the manufacturing cost is $20 per unit, composed of variable costs of $12.50 and fixed costs of $7.50. The normal selling price of the product in the domestic market is $30. The manufacturer receives an offer from an exporter for 5,000 units of the product at $18 each. Production can be spread over a three-month period without interfering with normal production or incurring overtime costs. Pricing policies in the domestic market will not be affected. Comparison of a sales price of $18 with the present unit cost of $20 would indicate that this offer should be rejected. However, if attention is limited to the differential cost, which in this case is composed of the variable costs and expenses, the conclusion is quite different. The essentials of the analysis are presented in the following brief report:

DIFFERENTIAL<br>ANALYSIS<br>REPORT—SALE AT<br>REDUCED PRICE

|                                                                                          |          |
|------------------------------------------------------------------------------------------|----------|
| Proposal to Sell to Exporter<br>March 10, 19-- |          |
| Differential revenue from acceptance of offer:<br>Revenue from sale of 5,000 additional units at $18 . . . . . . . . . . . . . . . . . . . | $90,000 |
| Differential cost of acceptance of offer:<br>Variable costs and expenses of 5,000 additional units at $12.50 . . . . . . . . | 62,500 |
| Gain from acceptance of offer . . . . . . . . . . . . . . . . . . . . . . . . . . . . . . . . . . . . . . . . | $27,500 |

Proposals to sell an increased output in the domestic market at a reduction from the normal price may require additional considerations of a difficult nature. It would clearly be unwise to increase sales volume in one territory by means of a price reduction if sales volume would thereby be jeopardized in other areas. Manufacturers must also exercise care to avoid violations of the Robinson-Patman Act, which prohibits price discrimination within the United States unless the difference in price can be justified by a difference in the cost of serving different customers.

**SETTING<br>NORMAL<br>PRODUCT<br>PRICES**

Differential analysis, as illustrated, is useful to management in setting product selling prices for special short-run decisions, such as whether to accept business at a price lower than the normal price. In such situations, the short-run price is set high enough to cover all variable costs and expenses plus provide an excess to cover some of the fixed costs and perhaps provide for profit. Such a pricing plan will improve profits in the short run. In the long run, however, the normal selling price must be set high enough to cover all costs and expenses (both fixed and variable) and provide a reasonable amount for profit. Otherwise, the long-run survival of the firm may be jeopardized.

The normal selling price can be viewed as the target selling price which must be achieved in the long run, but which may be deviated from in the short run because of such factors as competition and general market conditions. A practical approach to setting the normal price is the cost-plus approach. Using this approach, managers determine product prices by adding to a "cost" amount a plus, called a markup, so that all costs plus a profit are covered in the price.

Three cost concepts commonly used in applying the cost-plus approach are (1) total cost, (2) product cost, and (3) variable cost. Each of these cost concepts is described and illustrated in the following paragraphs.

Total Cost<br>Concept

Using the total cost concept of determining the product price, all costs of manufacturing a product plus the selling and general expenses are included in the cost amount to which the markup is added. Since all costs and expenses are included in the cost amount, the dollar amount of the markup equals the desired profit.

The first step in applying the total cost concept is to determine the total cost of manufacturing the product. Under the absorption costing system of accounting for manufacturing operations, the costs of direct materials, direct labor, and factory overhead should be available from the accounting records. The next step is to add the estimated selling and general expenses to the total cost of manufacturing the product. The cost amount per unit is then computed by dividing the total costs and expenses by the total units expected to be produced and sold.

After the cost amount per unit has been determined, the dollar amount of the markup is determined. For this purpose, the markup is expressed as a percentage of cost. This percentage is then multiplied by the cost amount per unit. The dollar amount of the markup is then added to the cost amount per unit to arrive at the selling price.

The markup percentage for the total cost concept is determined by applying the following formula:

$$\text{Markup Percentage} = \frac{\text{Desired Profit}}{\text{Total Costs and Expenses}}$$

The numerator of the markup percentage formula includes only the desired profit, since all costs and expenses will be covered by the cost amount to which the markup will be added. The denominator of the formula includes the total costs and expenses, which are covered by the cost amount.

To illustrate the use of the total cost concept, assume that the costs and expenses for Product N of Moyer Co. are as follows:

| | |
|---|---|
| Variable costs and expenses: | |
|     Direct materials.................. | $ 3.00 per unit |
|     Direct labor .................... | 10.00 |
|     Factory overhead ............... | 1.50 |
|     Selling and general expenses ..... | 1.50 |
|         Total........................ | $16.00 per unit |
| Fixed costs and expenses: | |
|     Factory overhead ............... | $50,000 |
|     Selling and general expenses ..... | 20,000 |

Moyer Co. desires a profit equal to a 20% rate of return on assets, $800,000 of assets are devoted to producing Product N, and 100,000 units are expected to be produced and sold. The cost amount for Product N is **$1,670,000**, or **$16.70** per unit, computed as follows:

| | | |
|---|---|---|
| Variable costs and expenses ($16.00 × 100,000 units)...... | | $1,600,000 |
| Fixed costs and expenses: | | |
|     Factory overhead .................................... | $50,000 | |
|     Selling and general expenses ........................ | 20,000 | 70,000 |
| Total costs and expenses ................................ | | $1,670,000 |
| Cost amount per unit ($1,670,000 ÷ 100,000 units) ......... | | $16.70 |

The desired profit is $160,000 (20% × $800,000), and the markup percentage for Product N is **9.6%**, computed as follows:

$$\text{Markup Percentage} = \frac{\text{Desired Profit}}{\text{Total Costs and Expenses}}$$

$$\text{Markup Percentage} = \frac{\$160,000}{\$1,670,000}$$

$$\text{Markup Percentage} = 9.6\%$$

Based on the cost amount per unit and the markup percentage for Product N, Moyer Co. would price Product N at **$18.30** per unit, as shown in the following computation:

| | |
|---|---:|
| Cost amount per unit......... | $16.70 |
| Markup ($16.70 × 9.6%) ..... | 1.60 |
| Selling price................ | $18.30 |

The ability of the selling price of $18.30 to generate the desired profit of $160,000 is shown in the following condensed income statement for Moyer Co.:

**Moyer Co.**
**Income Statement**
**For Year Ended December 31, 19--**

| | | |
|---|---:|---:|
| Sales (100,000 units × $18.30) ...................... | | $1,830,000 |
| Expenses: | | |
| Variable (100,000 units × $16.00)................. | $1,600,000 | |
| Fixed ($50,000 + $20,000) ........................ | 70,000 | 1,670,000 |
| Income from operations ............................ | | $ 160,000 |

The total cost concept of applying the cost-plus approach to product pricing is frequently used by contractors who sell products to government agencies. In many cases, government contractors are required by law to be reimbursed for their products on a total-cost-plus-profit basis.

**Product Cost Concept**    Using the product cost concept of determining the product price, only the costs of manufacturing the product, termed the product cost, are included in the cost amount to which the markup is added. Selling expenses, general expenses, and profit are covered in the markup. The markup percentage is determined by applying the following formula:

$$\text{Markup Percentage} = \frac{\text{Desired Profit} + \text{Total Selling and General Expenses}}{\text{Total Manufacturing Costs}}$$

The numerator of the markup percentage formula includes the desired profit plus the total selling and general expenses. Selling and general expenses must be covered by the markup, since they are not covered by the cost amount to which the markup will be added. The denominator of the formula includes the costs of direct materials, direct labor, and factory overhead, which are covered by the cost amount.

To illustrate the use of the product cost concept, assume the same data that were used in the preceding illustration. The cost amount for Moyer Co.'s Product N is $1,500,000, or $15 per unit, computed as follows:

| | | |
|---|---|---|
| Direct materials ($3 × 100,000 units) | | $ 300,000 |
| Direct labor ($10 × 100,000 units) | | 1,000,000 |
| Factory overhead: | | |
| Variable ($1.50 × 100,000 units) | $150,000 | |
| Fixed | 50,000 | 200,000 |
| Total manufacturing costs | | $1,500,000 |
| Cost amount per unit ($1,500,000 ÷ 100,000 units) | | $15 |

The desired profit is $160,000 (20% × $800,000), and the total selling and general expenses are $170,000 [(100,000 units × $1.50 per unit) + $20,000]. The markup percentage for Product N is 22%, computed as follows:

$$\text{Markup Percentage} = \frac{\text{Desired Profit + Total Selling and General Expenses}}{\text{Total Manufacturing Costs}}$$

$$\text{Markup Percentage} = \frac{\$160,000 + \$170,000}{\$1,500,000}$$

$$\text{Markup Percentage} = \frac{\$330,000}{\$1,500,000}$$

$$\text{Markup Percentage} = 22\%$$

Based on the cost amount per unit and the markup percentage for Product N, Moyer Co. would price Product N at $18.30 per unit, as shown in the following computation:

| | |
|---|---|
| Cost amount per unit | $15.00 |
| Markup ($15 × 22%) | 3.30 |
| Selling price | $18.30 |

**Variable Cost Concept**

Using the variable cost concept of determining the product price, only variable costs and expenses are included in the cost amount to which the markup is added. All variable manufacturing costs, as well as variable selling and general expenses, are included in the cost amount. Fixed manufacturing costs, fixed selling and general expenses, and profit are covered in the markup.

The markup percentage for the variable cost concept is determined by applying the following formula:

$$\text{Markup Percentage} = \frac{\substack{\text{Desired Profit + Total Fixed Manufacturing Costs +} \\ \text{Total Fixed Selling and General Expenses}}}{\text{Total Variable Costs and Expenses}}$$

The numerator of the markup percentage formula includes the desired profit plus the total fixed manufacturing costs and the total fixed selling and general expenses. Fixed manufacturing costs and fixed selling and general expenses must be covered by the markup, since they are not covered by the cost amount to which the markup will be added. The denominator of the formula includes the total variable costs and expenses, which are covered by the cost amount.

To illustrate the use of the variable cost concept, assume the same data that were used in the two preceding illustrations. The cost amount for Product N is **$1,600,000**, or **$16.00** per unit, computed as follows:

| | |
|---|---:|
| Variable costs and expenses: | |
| Direct materials ($3 × 100,000 units) ................ | $ 300,000 |
| Direct labor ($10 × 100,000 units).................... | 1,000,000 |
| Factory overhead ($1.50 × 100,000 units) ............ | 150,000 |
| Selling and general expenses ($1.50 × 100,000 units).. | 150,000 |
| Total variable costs and expenses ..................... | $1,600,000 |
| Cost amount per unit ($1,600,000 ÷ 100,000 units)....... | $16.00 |

The desired profit is $160,000 (20% × $800,000), the total fixed manufacturing costs are $50,000, and the total fixed selling and general expenses are $20,000. The markup percentage for Product N is **14.4%**, computed as follows:

$$\text{Markup Percentage} = \frac{\substack{\text{Desired Profit + Total Fixed Manufacturing Costs +} \\ \text{Total Fixed Selling and General Expenses}}}{\text{Total Variable Costs and Expenses}}$$

$$\text{Markup Percentage} = \frac{\$160,000 + \$50,000 + \$20,000}{\$1,600,000}$$

$$\text{Markup Percentage} = \frac{\$230,000}{\$1,600,000}$$

$$\text{Markup Percentage} = 14.4\%$$

Based on the cost amount per unit and the markup percentage for Product N, Moyer Co. would price Product N at **$18.30** per unit, as shown in the following computation:

| | |
|---|---:|
| Cost amount per unit........................... | $16.00 |
| Markup ($16.00 × 14.4%)........................ | 2.30 |
| Selling price................................... | $18.30 |

The variable cost concept emphasizes the distinction between variable and fixed costs and expenses in product pricing. This distinction is similar to the distinction between absorption and variable costing described in Chapter 6.

Choosing a Cost-Plus Approach Cost Concept | The three cost concepts commonly used in applying the cost-plus approach to product pricing are summarized as follows:

| Cost Concept | Covered in Cost Amount | Covered in Markup |
| --- | --- | --- |
| Total cost | Total costs and expenses | Desired profit |
| Product cost | Total manufacturing costs | Desired profit + Total selling and general expenses |
| Variable cost | Total variable costs and expenses | Desired profit + Total fixed manufacturing costs + Total fixed selling and general expenses |

As demonstrated in the Moyer Co. illustration, all three cost concepts will yield the same selling price ($18.30) when the concepts are properly applied. Which of the three cost concepts should be used by management depends on such factors as the cost of gathering the data and the decision needs of management. For example, the data for the product cost concept can be easily gathered by a company using an absorption cost accounting system.

To reduce the costs of gathering data, standard costs rather than actual costs may be used with any of the three cost concepts. However, caution should be exercised by management when using standard costs in applying the cost-plus approach. As discussed in Chapter 5, the standards should be based on normal (attainable) operating levels and not theoretical (ideal) levels of performance. In product pricing, the use of standards based on ideal or maximum capacity operating levels might lead to the establishment of product prices which are too low, since the costs of such factors as normal spoilage or normal periods of idle time would not be covered in the price. As a result, the desired profit would be reduced by these costs and expenses.

ECONOMIC THEORY OF PRODUCT PRICING | As discussed in the preceding paragraphs, the cost-plus approach is frequently used as a general guideline for setting normal product prices. However, other factors may influence the pricing decision. In considering these factors, which include the prices of competing products and the general economic conditions of the marketplace, a knowledge of the economic theory underlying product pricing is useful to the managerial accountant. Although the study of price theory is generally considered a separate discipline in the area of microeconomics, the following paragraphs present an overview of the economic models for explaining pricing behavior.

**Maximization of Profits**

In microeconomic theory, management's primary objective is assumed to be the maximization of profits. Profits will be maximized at the point at which the difference between total revenues and total costs and expenses is the greatest amount. Consequently, microeconomic theory focuses on the behavior of total revenues as price and sales volume vary and the behavior of total costs and expenses as production varies.

**Revenues**

Generally, it is not possible to sell an unlimited number of units of product at the same price. At some point, price reductions will be necessary in order to sell more units. Total revenue may increase as the price is reduced, but there comes a point when further price decreases will reduce total revenue. To illustrate, the following revenue schedule shows the effect on revenue when each $1 reduction in the unit selling price increases by 1 unit the number of units sold:

### Revenue Schedule

| Price | Units Sold | Total Revenue | Marginal Revenue |
|-------|-----------|---------------|------------------|
| $11   | 1         | $11           | $11              |
| 10    | 2         | 20            | 9                |
| 9     | 3         | 27            | 7                |
| 8     | 4         | 32            | 5                |
| 7     | 5         | 35            | 3                |
| 6     | 6         | 36            | 1                |
| 5     | 7         | 35            | −1               |

In the revenue schedule illustrated, a price reduction from $11 to $10 increases total revenue by $9 (from $11 to $20). This increase (or decrease) in total revenue realized from the sale of an additional unit of product is called the **marginal revenue**. With each successive price reduction from $11 to $6, the total revenue increase is less. Finally, a price reduction from $6 to $5 decreases total revenue by $1.

**Costs**

As production and sales increase, the total cost increases. The amount by which total cost increases, however, varies as more and more production and sales are squeezed from limited facilities. Economists assume that as the total number of units produced and sold increases from a relatively low level, the total cost increases but in decreasing amounts. This assumption is based on efficiencies created by **economies of scale**. Economies of scale generally imply that, for a given amount of facilities, it is more efficient to produce and sell large quantities than small quantities. At some point, however, the total cost will begin to increase by increasing amounts because of inefficiencies created by such factors as employees getting in each other's way and machine breakdowns caused by heavy use. The increase in total cost from producing and selling an additional unit of product is known as **marginal cost**. To illustrate, the following cost schedule shows the effect on cost when one additional unit is produced and sold:

Cost Schedule

| Units Produced and Sold | Total Cost | Marginal Cost |
|---|---|---|
| 1 | $ 9 | $9 |
| 2 | 17 | 8 |
| 3 | 24 | 7 |
| 4 | 30 | 6 |
| 5 | 37 | 7 |
| 6 | 45 | 8 |
| 7 | 54 | 9 |

In the cost schedule, the cost of producing 1 unit is $9, and for each additional unit the total cost per unit increases by $8, $7, $6, $7, $8, and $9 respectively. The marginal cost of producing and selling the second unit is $8, which is the difference between the total cost of producing and selling 2 units ($17) and the total cost of 1 unit ($9). As production and sales increase from 1 unit to 4 units, the marginal cost decreases from $9 to $6. After the production and sale of 4 units, however, the marginal cost increases from $6 for the fourth unit to $7 for producing and selling the fifth unit.

**Product Price Determination**

A price-cost combination that maximizes the total profit of an enterprise can be determined by plotting the marginal revenues and marginal costs on a price graph. To illustrate, the marginal revenues and marginal costs for the preceding illustration are plotted on the graph on page 181.

A price graph is constructed in the following manner:

1. The horizontal axis is drawn to represent units of production and sales.
2. The vertical axis is drawn to represent dollars for marginal revenues and marginal costs.
3. The marginal revenue for each unit of sales is plotted on the graph by first locating the number of units of sales along the horizontal axis and then proceeding upward until the proper amount of marginal revenue is indicated on the vertical axis.
4. The marginal revenue line is drawn on the price graph by connecting the marginal revenue points.
5. The marginal cost for each unit of production is plotted on the graph by first locating the number of units of production along the horizontal axis and then proceeding upward until the proper amount of marginal cost is indicated on the vertical axis.
6. The marginal cost line is drawn on the price graph by connecting the marginal cost points.

The point at which the marginal revenue line intersects the marginal cost line on the price graph indicates a level of sales and production at which profits are maximized. In other words, there is no other level of production and sales that

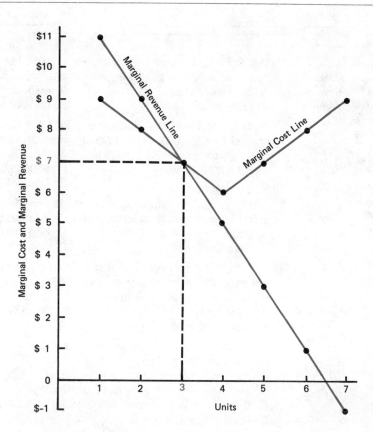

will provide a larger amount of profit. For example, at higher levels of production and sales, the change in total cost is greater than the change in total revenue. Therefore, less profit would be achieved by manufacturing and selling more units.

In the illustration, the marginal revenue line intersects the marginal cost line at 3 units of sales and production. At this point, marginal revenue and marginal cost equal $7. To sell 3 units, the revenue schedule on page 179 indicates that the price should be set at $9 per unit. A price of $9 per unit will provide total revenue of $27, and the cost schedule on page 180 indicates that the total cost will be $24. Thus, profit will be $3, as follows:

| | |
|---|---|
| Total revenue (3 units × $9) . . . . . . . . | $27 |
| Total cost (from cost schedule) . . . . . | 24 |
| Profit. . . . . . . . . . . . . . . . . . . . . . . . . . . . | $ 3 |

The more theoretical economic approach is not often used for product pricing because the data required by the economic approach are often unavailable. For example, it is difficult to predict the amount that customers will purchase over a range of prices without actually offering the product for sale at those prices. Therefore, since total cost data can be estimated reliably from accounting records, the cost-plus approach to product pricing is frequently used.

1. The amount of increase or decrease in cost that is expected from a particular course of action as compared with an alternative is referred to as:
   A. differential cost                     C. sunk cost
   B. replacement cost                      D. none of the above

2. Victor Company is considering the disposal of equipment that was originally purchased for $200,000 and has accumulated depreciation to date of $150,000. The same equipment would cost $310,000 to replace. What is the sunk cost?
   A. $50,000                               C. $200,000
   B. $150,000                              D. None of the above

3. The amount of income that would result from the best available alternative to a proposed use of cash or its equivalent is referred to as:
   A. actual cost                           C. opportunity cost
   B. historical cost                       D. none of the above

4. For which cost concept used in applying the cost-plus approach to product pricing are fixed manufacturing costs, fixed selling and general expenses, and desired profit allowed for in the determination of markup?
   A. Total cost                            C. Variable cost
   B. Product cost                          D. None of the above

5. According to microeconomic theory, profits of a business enterprise will be maximized at the point where:
   A. marginal revenue equals marginal cost
   B. the change in total revenue is greater than the change in total cost
   C. the change in total cost is greater than the change in total revenue
   D. none of the above

**Discussion
Questions**

1. What term is applied to the type of analysis that emphasizes the difference between the revenues and costs for proposed alternative courses of action?

2. Explain the meaning of (a) *differential revenue* and (b) *differential cost*.

3. Norton Lumber Company incurs a cost of $60 per thousand board feet in processing a certain "rough-cut" lumber which it sells for $115 per thousand board feet. An alternative is to produce a "finished-cut" at a total processing cost of $82 per thousand board feet, which can be sold for $150 per thousand board feet. What is the amount of (a) the differential revenue and (b) the differential cost associated with the alternative?

4. (a) What is meant by *sunk costs*? (b) A company is contemplating replacing an old piece of machinery which cost $210,000 and has $180,000 accumulated depreciation to date. A new machine costs $300,000. What is the sunk cost in this situation?

5. The condensed income statement for Yancey Company for the current year is as follows:

| | Product | | | |
|---|---|---|---|---|
| | M | N | O | Total |
| Sales............................... | $60,000 | $380,000 | $340,000 | $780,000 |
| Less variable costs and expenses......... | 44,400 | 260,000 | 233,400 | 537,800 |
| Contribution margin...................... | $15,600 | $120,000 | $106,600 | $242,200 |
| Less fixed costs and expenses ........... | 20,000 | 80,000 | 76,000 | 176,000 |
| Income (loss) from operations ............ | $(4,400) | $ 40,000 | $ 30,600 | $ 66,200 |

Management decided to discontinue the manufacture and sale of Product M. Assuming that the discontinuance will have no effect on the total fixed costs and expenses or on the sales of Products N and O, has management made the correct decision? Explain.

6. (a) What is meant by *opportunity cost*? (b) Draper Company is currently earning 12% on $100,000 invested in marketable securities. It proposes to use the $100,000 to acquire plant facilities to manufacture a new product that is expected to add $20,000 annually to net income. What is the opportunity cost involved in the decision to manufacture the new product?

7. In the long run, the normal selling price must be set high enough to cover what factors?

8. What are three cost concepts commonly used in applying the cost-plus approach to product pricing?

9. In using the product cost concept of applying the cost-plus approach to product pricing, what factors are included in the markup?

10. The variable cost concept used in applying the cost-plus approach to product pricing includes what costs in the cost amount to which the markup is added?

11. In determining the markup percentage for the variable cost concept of applying the cost-plus approach, what is included in the denominator?

12. Why might the use of ideal standards in applying the cost-plus approach to product pricing lead to setting product prices which are too low?

13. Although the cost-plus approach to product pricing may be used by management as a general guideline, what are some examples of other factors that managers should also consider in setting product prices?

14. In microeconomic theory, what is assumed to be management's primary objective for a business enterprise?

15. Why is it generally not possible to sell an unlimited number of units of product at the same price?

16. As the terms are used in microeconomic theory, what is meant by (a) marginal revenue and (b) marginal cost?

17. If the total revenue for selling 3 units of Product Y is $20 and the total revenue for selling 4 units is $25, what is the marginal revenue associated with selling the fourth unit?

18. What does the concept of economies of scale generally imply?

19. For a given amount of facilities, why will the total costs and expenses begin to increase by increasing amounts at some point?

20. What point on the price graph indicates a maximum level of profit?

21. Why is the more theoretical economic approach to product pricing not used as often as the cost-plus approach?

**Exercises**

**Exercise 8-1.** DeLorenzo Company expects to operate at 80% of productive capacity during July. The total manufacturing costs for July for the production of 12,500 grinders are budgeted as follows:

| | |
|---|---:|
| Direct materials...................................... | $ 56,250 |
| Direct labor .......................................... | 156,250 |
| Variable factory overhead............................ | 75,000 |
| Fixed factory overhead ............................... | 31,250 |
| Total manufacturing costs............................ | $318,750 |

The company has an opportunity to submit a bid for 3,000 grinders to be delivered by July 31 to a government agency. If the contract is obtained, it is anticipated that the additional activity will not interfere with normal production during July or increase the selling or general expenses. (a) What is the unit cost below which DeLorenzo Company should not go in bidding on the government contract? (b) Is a unit cost figure based on absorption costing or one based on variable costing more useful in arriving at a bid on this contract? Explain.

**Exercise 8-2.** Farley Company has a plant capacity of 50,000 units and current production is 35,000 units. Monthly fixed costs and expenses are $140,000 and variable costs and expenses are $12.50 per unit. The present selling price is $18 per unit. On February 3, the company received an offer from Wong Yu Company for 5,000 units of the product at $15 each. The Wong Yu Company will market the units in a foreign country under its own brand name. The additional business is not expected to affect the regular selling price or quantity of sales of Farley Company. (a) Prepare a differential analysis report for the proposed sale to Wong Yu Company. (b) Briefly explain the reason why the acceptance of this additional business will increase operating income. (c) What is the minimum price per unit that would produce a contribution margin?

**Exercise 8-3.** A condensed income statement by product line for McCaffrey Co. indicated the following for Product X for the past year:

| | |
|---|---:|
| Sales ................................................. | $160,000 |
| Cost of goods sold.................................... | 108,000 |
| Gross profit .......................................... | $ 52,000 |
| Operating expenses.................................... | 72,000 |
| Loss from operations.................................. | $(20,000) |

It is estimated that 15% of the cost of goods sold represents fixed factory overhead costs and that 20% of operating expenses is fixed. Since Product X is only one of many products, the fixed costs and expenses will not be materially affected if the product is discontinued. (a) Prepare a differential analysis report, dated January 2 of the current year, for the proposed discontinuance of Product X. (b) Should Product X be retained? Explain.

**Exercise 8-4.** Quigley Company has been purchasing carrying cases for its portable typewriters at a delivered cost of $18.75 per unit. The company, which is currently operating below full capacity, charges factory overhead to production at the rate of 60% of direct labor cost. The direct materials and direct labor costs per unit to produce comparable carrying cases are expected to be $5 and $12 respectively. If Quigley Company manufactures the carrying cases, fixed factory overhead costs will not increase and variable factory overhead costs associated with the cases are expected to be 20% of direct labor costs. (a) Prepare a differential analysis report, dated March 6 of the current year, for the make or buy decision. (b) On the basis of the data presented, would it be advisable to make or to continue buying the carrying cases? Explain.

**Exercise 8-5.** Rowe Company produces a commodity by applying a machine and direct labor to the direct material. The original cost of the machine is $180,000, the accumulated depreciation is $108,000, its remaining useful life is 8 years, and its salvage value is negligible. On January 18, a proposal was made to replace the present manufacturing procedure with a fully automatic machine that will cost $340,000. The automatic machine has an estimated useful life of 8 years and no significant salvage value. For use in evaluating the proposal, the accountant accumulated the following annual data on present and proposed operations:

|  | Present Operations | Proposed Operations |
|---|---|---|
| Sales | $440,000 | $440,000 |
| Direct materials | 184,800 | 184,800 |
| Direct labor | 79,200 | —— |
| Power and maintenance | 13,600 | 31,500 |
| Taxes, insurance, etc. | 8,800 | 12,800 |
| Selling and general expenses | 35,200 | 35,200 |

(a) Prepare a differential analysis report for the proposal to replace the machine. Include in the analysis both the net differential decrease in costs and expenses anticipated over the 8 years and the annual differential decrease in costs and expenses anticipated. (b) Based only on the data presented, should the proposal be accepted? (c) What are some of the other factors that should be considered before a final decision is made?

**Exercise 8-6.** Glasner Company uses the total cost concept of applying the cost-plus approach to product pricing. The costs and expenses of producing and selling 50,000 units of Product M are as follows:

Variable costs and expenses:
| | |
|---|---|
| Direct materials | $1.60 per unit |
| Direct labor | 3.00 |
| Factory overhead | 1.00 |
| Selling and general expenses | .40 |
| Total | $6.00 per unit |

Fixed costs and expenses:
| | |
|---|---|
| Factory overhead | $70,000 |
| Selling and general expenses | 30,000 |

Glasner Company desires a profit equal to a 20% rate of return on invested assets of $450,000. (a) Determine the amount of desired profit from the production and sale of Product M. (b) Determine the total costs and expenses and the cost amount per unit for the production and sale of 50,000 units of Product M. (c) Determine the markup percentage for Product M. (d) Determine the selling price of Product M.

**Exercise 8-7.** Based on the data presented in Exercise 8-6, assume that Glasner Company uses the product cost concept of applying the cost-plus approach to product pricing. (a) Determine the total manufacturing costs and the cost amount per unit for the production and sale of 50,000 units of Product M. (b) Determine the markup percentage for Product M. (c) Determine the selling price of Product M.

**Exercise 8-8.** Based on the data presented in Exercise 8-6, assume that Glasner Company uses the variable cost concept of applying the cost-plus approach to product pricing. (a) Determine the cost amount per unit for the production and sale of 50,000 units of Product M. (b) Determine the markup percentage for Product M. (c) Determine the selling price of Product M. Round to the nearest cent.

**Exercise 8-9.** For the following revenue schedule and cost schedule for Product Y, (a) construct a price graph, (b) determine the level of sales and production at which the marginal cost and marginal revenue lines intersect, (c) determine the unit sales price at the level of sales determined in (b), and (d) determine the maximum profit for Product Y at the level of sales determined in (b).

### Revenue Schedule

| Price | Units Sold | Total Revenue | Marginal Revenue |
|---|---|---|---|
| $9 | 1 | $ 9 | $9 |
| 8 | 2 | 16 | 7 |
| 7 | 3 | 21 | 5 |
| 6 | 4 | 24 | 3 |
| 5 | 5 | 25 | 1 |
| 4 | 6 | 24 | −1 |

### Cost Schedule

| Units Produced and Sold | Total Cost | Marginal Cost |
|---|---|---|
| 1 | $ 6 | $6 |
| 2 | 11 | 5 |
| 3 | 15 | 4 |
| 4 | 18 | 3 |
| 5 | 22 | 4 |
| 6 | 27 | 5 |

**Problems**
*(Problems in Appendix B: 8-1B, 8-2B, 8-5B, 8-6B.)*

**Problem 8-1A.** On April 1, Muller Company is considering leasing a building and purchasing the necessary equipment to operate a public warehouse. The project would be financed by selling $500,000 of 10% U.S. Treasury bonds that mature in 15 years. The bonds were purchased at face value and are currently selling at face value. The following data have been assembled:

| | |
|---|---|
| Cost of equipment. . . . . . . . . . . . . . . . . . . . . . . . . . . . . . . . . . . . . . . . . . . . . . . . . | $500,000 |
| Life of equipment . . . . . . . . . . . . . . . . . . . . . . . . . . . . . . . . . . . . . . . . . . . . . . . . | 15 years |
| Estimated residual value of equipment . . . . . . . . . . . . . . . . . . . . . . . . . . . . | $ 80,000 |
| Yearly costs to operate the warehouse, in addition to depreciation of equipment. . . . . . . . . . . . . . . . . . . . . . . . . . . . . . . . . . . . . . . . . . . . . . . . . . | $ 48,500 |
| Yearly expected revenues—first 5 years . . . . . . . . . . . . . . . . . . . . . . . . | $120,000 |
| Yearly expected revenues—next 10 years. . . . . . . . . . . . . . . . . . . . . . . | $150,000 |

Instructions:

(1) Prepare a differential analysis report presenting the differential revenue and the differential cost associated with the proposed operation of the warehouse for the 15 years as compared with present conditions.

(2) Based on the results disclosed by the differential analysis, should the proposal be accepted?

(3) If the proposal is accepted, what is the total estimated income from operation of the warehouse for the 15 years?

**Problem 8-2A.** Packard Company is considering the replacement of a machine that has been used in its factory for three years. Relevant data associated with the operations of the old machine and the new machine, neither of which has any residual value, are as follows:

### Old Machine

| | |
|---|---|
| Cost of machine, 8-year life. . . . . . . . . . . . . . . . . . . . . . . . . . . . . . . . . . . . . . . . . . . | $270,000 |
| Annual depreciation . . . . . . . . . . . . . . . . . . . . . . . . . . . . . . . . . . . . . . . . . . . . . . . . | 33,750 |
| Annual manufacturing costs, exclusive of depreciation. . . . . . . . . . . . . . . . . . | 425,000 |
| Related annual operating expenses . . . . . . . . . . . . . . . . . . . . . . . . . . . . . . . . . . | 280,000 |
| Associated annual revenue . . . . . . . . . . . . . . . . . . . . . . . . . . . . . . . . . . . . . . . . . | 940,000 |
| Estimated selling price of old machine. . . . . . . . . . . . . . . . . . . . . . . . . . . . . . | 190,000 |

### New Machine

| | |
|---|---|
| Cost of machine, 5-year life. . . . . . . . . . . . . . . . . . . . . . . . . . . . . . . . . . . . . . . . . | $525,000 |
| Annual depreciation . . . . . . . . . . . . . . . . . . . . . . . . . . . . . . . . . . . . . . . . . . . . . . . . | 105,000 |
| Estimated annual manufacturing costs, exclusive of depreciation . . . . . . . . . | 325,000 |

Annual operating expenses and revenue are not expected to be affected by purchase of the new machine.

Instructions:

(1) Prepare a differential analysis report as of January 4 of the current year, comparing operations utilizing the new machine with operations using the present equipment. The analysis should indicate the total differential decrease or increase in costs that would result over the 5-year period if the new machine is acquired.

(2) List other factors that should be considered before a final decision is reached.

**Problem 8-3A.** Edens Company is planning a one-month campaign for August to promote sales of one of its two products. A total of $120,000 has been budgeted for advertising, contests, redeemable coupons, and other promotional activities. The following data have been assembled for their possible usefulness in deciding which of the products to select for the campaign:

|                                        | Product A | Product B |
|----------------------------------------|-----------|-----------|
| Unit selling price                     | $100      | $120      |
| Unit production costs:                 |           |           |
|   Direct materials           | $28       | $36       |
|   Direct labor               | 20        | 28        |
|   Variable factory overhead  | 16        | 16        |
|   Fixed factory overhead     | 12        | 12        |
|   Total unit production costs | $ 76     | $ 92      |
| Unit variable operating expenses       | 10        | 10        |
| Unit fixed operating expenses          | 6         | 6         |
|   Total unit costs and expenses | $ 92   | $108      |
| Operating income per unit              | $ 8       | $ 12      |

No increase in facilities would be necessary to produce and sell the increased output. It is anticipated that 18,000 additional units of Product A or 12,500 additional units of Product B could be sold without changing the unit selling price of either product.

Instructions:

(1) Prepare a differential analysis report as of July 6 of the current year, presenting the additional revenue and additional costs and expenses anticipated from the promotion of Product A and Product B.

(2) The sales manager had tentatively decided to promote Product B, estimating that operating income would be increased by $30,000 ($12 operating income per unit for 12,500 units, less promotion expenses of $120,000). It was also believed that the selection of Product A would increase operating income by only $24,000 ($8 operating income per unit for 18,000 units, less promotion expenses of $120,000). State briefly your reasons for supporting or opposing the tentative decision.

**Problem 8-4A.** The management of Kesner Company is considering whether to process further Product H into Product Q. Product Q can be sold for $40 per pound and Product H can be sold without further processing for $6 per pound. Product H is produced in batches of 200 pounds by processing 300 pounds of raw material, which costs $2 per pound. Product Q will require additional processing costs of $5 per pound of Product H, and 4 pounds of Product H will produce 1 pound of Product Q.

Instructions:

(1) Prepare a differential analysis report as of November 15, presenting the differential revenue and differential cost per batch associated with the further processing of Product H to produce Product Q.

(2) Briefly report your recommendations.

**Problem 8-5A.** Ingersoll Refining Inc. refines Product C in batches of 80,000 gallons, which it sells for $.28 per gallon. The associated unit costs and expenses are currently as follows:

| | |
|---|---|
| Direct materials | $.144 per gallon |
| Direct labor | .040 |
| Variable factory overhead | .020 |
| Fixed factory overhead | .012 |

Sales commissions . . . . . . . . . . . . . . . . . . . . . . . .    $.028 per gallon
Fixed selling and general expenses . . . . . . . . . . .    .008

The company is presently considering a proposal to put Product C through several additional processes to yield Products C and D. Although the company had determined such further processing to be unwise, new processing methods have now been developed. Existing facilities can be used for the additional processing, but since the factory is operating at full 8-hour-day capacity, the processing would have to be performed at night. Additional costs of processing would be $3,200 per batch and there would be an evaporation loss of 15%, with 60% of the processed material evolving as Product C and 25% as Product D. The selling price of Product D is $.80 per gallon. Sales commissions are a uniform percentage based on the sales price.

Instructions:

(1) Prepare a differential analysis report as of March 14, presenting the differential revenue and the differential cost per batch associated with the processing to produce Products C and D, compared with processing to produce Product C only.

(2) Briefly report your recommendations.

**Problem 8-6A.** Conklin Company recently began production of a new product, W, which required the investment of $2,000,000 in assets. The costs and expenses of producing and selling 100,000 units of Product W are estimated as follows:

Variable costs and expenses:
    Direct materials . . . . . . . . . . . . . . . . . . . .    $ 2.40 per unit
    Direct labor. . . . . . . . . . . . . . . . . . . . . . .    6.50
    Factory overhead . . . . . . . . . . . . . . . . . .    .90
    Selling and general expenses . . . . . . .    .20
        Total . . . . . . . . . . . . . . . . . . . . . . . . . .    $10.00 per unit

Fixed costs and expenses:
    Factory overhead . . . . . . . . . . . . . . . . . .    $ 60,000
    Selling and general expenses . . . . . . .    140,000

Conklin Company is currently considering the establishment of a selling price for Product W. The President of Conklin Company has decided to use the cost-plus approach to product pricing and has indicated that Product W must earn an 18% rate of return on invested assets.

Instructions:

(1) Determine the amount of desired profit from the production and sale of Product W.

(2) Assuming that the total cost concept is used, determine (a) the cost amount per unit, (b) the markup percentage, and (c) the selling price of Product W.

(3) Assuming that the product cost concept is used, determine (a) the cost amount per unit, (b) the markup percentage, and (c) the selling price of Product W.

(4) Assuming that the variable cost concept is used, determine (a) the cost amount per unit, (b) the markup percentage, and (c) the selling price of Product W.

(5) Comment on any additional considerations that could influence the establishment of the selling price for Product W.

**Mini-Case**

Your father operates a family-owned automotive dealership. Recently, the city government has requested bids on the purchase of 20 sedans for use by the city police department. Although the city prefers to purchase from local dealerships, state law requires the acceptance of the lowest bid. The past several contracts for automotive purchases have been granted to dealerships from surrounding communities.

The following data were taken from the dealership records for the normal sale of the automobile for which current bids have been requested:

| | |
|---|---|
| Retail list price of sedan | $12,100 |
| Cost allocated to normal sale: | |
|   Dealer cost from manufacturer | 8,470 |
|   Fixed overhead | 1,200 |
|   Shipping charges from manufacturer | 500 |
|   Preparation charges | 100 |
|   Sales commission based on selling price | 5% |

Your father has asked you to help him in arriving at a "winning" bid price for this contract. In the past, your father has always bid $250 above the total cost (including fixed overhead). No sales commissions will be paid if the bid is accepted, and your father has indicated that the bid price must contribute at least $250 per car to the profits of the dealership.

Instructions:
(1) Do you think that your father has used good bidding procedures for prior contracts? Explain.
(2) What should be the bid price, based upon your father's profit objectives?
(3) Explain why the bid price determined in (2) would not be an acceptable price for normal customers.

# 9

# Capital Investment Analysis

## CHAPTER OBJECTIVES

*Describe and illustrate methods used for evaluating capital investment proposals.*

*Describe and illustrate the capital rationing process.*

*Describe the basic concepts for planning and controlling capital investment expenditures.*

# 9

## CHAPTER

With the accelerated growth of American industry, increasing attention has been given to long-term investment decisions involving property, plant, and equipment. The process by which management plans, evaluates, and controls such investments is called capital investment analysis, or **capital budgeting**. This chapter describes analyses useful for making capital investment decisions, which may involve thousands, millions, or even billions of dollars. Capital investment expenditures normally involve a long-term commitment of funds and thus affect operations for many years. These expenditures must earn a reasonable rate of return, so that the enterprise can meet its obligations to creditors and provide dividends to stockholders. Because capital investment decisions are some of the most important decisions that management makes, the systems and procedures for evaluating, planning, and controlling capital investments must be carefully developed and implemented.

A capital investment program should include a plan for encouraging employees at all levels of an enterprise to submit proposals for capital investments. The plan should provide for communicating to the employees the long-range goals of the enterprise, so that useful proposals are submitted. In addition, the plan may provide for rewarding employees whose proposals are implemented. All reasonable proposals should be given serious consideration, and the effects of the economic implications expected from these proposals should be identified.

The essentials of the most commonly used methods of evaluating capital investment proposals are described in the following sections. The similarities and differences between the methods, as well as the uses of each method, are emphasized. Finally, considerations complicating capital investment analyses, the process of allocating available investment funds among competing proposals (capital rationing), and planning and controlling capital expenditures are briefly discussed.

## METHODS OF EVALUATING CAPITAL INVESTMENT PROPOSALS

The methods of evaluating capital investment proposals can be grouped into two general categories that can be referred to as (1) methods that ignore present value and (2) present value methods. The characteristic that distinguishes one category from the other is the way in which the concept of the time value of money is treated. Both the time value of money and the concept of present value are discussed in more detail later in the chapter. Because cash on hand can be invested to earn more cash, while cash to be received in the future cannot, money has a time value. However, the methods that ignore present value do not give consideration to the fact that cash on hand is more valuable than cash to be received in the future. The two methods in this category are (1) the average rate of return method and (2) the cash payback method.

By converting dollars to be received in the future into current dollars, using the concept of present value, the present value methods take into consideration the fact that money has a time value. The two common present value methods used in evaluating capital investment proposals are (1) the discounted cash flow method and (2) the discounted internal rate of return method.

Each of the four methods of analyzing capital investment proposals has both advantages and limitations. Often management will use some combination of the four methods in evaluating the various economic aspects of capital investment proposals.

Methods That
Ignore Present
Value

The average rate of return and the cash payback methods of evaluating capital investment proposals are simple to use and are especially useful in screening proposals. Management often establishes a minimum standard, and proposals not meeting this minimum standard are dropped from further consideration. When several alternative proposals meet the minimum standard, management will often rank the proposals from the most desirable to the least desirable.

The methods that ignore present value are also useful in evaluating capital investment proposals that have relatively short useful lives. In such situations, management generally focuses its attention on the amount of income to be earned from the investment and the total net cash flows to be received from the investment.

### Average Rate of Return Method

The expected average rate of return, sometimes referred to as the **accounting rate of return,** is a measure of the expected profitability of an investment in plant assets. The amount of income expected to be earned from the investment is stated as an annual average over the number of years the asset is to be used. The amount of the investment may be considered to be the original cost of the plant asset, or recognition may be given to the effect of depreciation on the amount of the investment. According to the latter view, the investment gradually declines from the original cost to the estimated residual value at the end of its useful life. If straight-line depreciation and no residual value are assumed, the average investment would be equal to one half of the original expenditure.

To illustrate, assume that management is considering the purchase of a certain machine at a cost of $500,000. The machine is expected to have a useful life of 4 years, with no residual value, and its use during the 4 years is expected to yield total income of $200,000. The estimated average annual income is therefore $50,000 ($200,000 ÷ 4), and the average investment is $250,000 [($500,000 + $0 residual value) ÷ 2]. Accordingly, the expected average rate of return on the average investment is 20%, computed as follows:

$$\text{Average Rate of Return} = \frac{\text{Estimated Average Annual Income}}{\text{Average Investment}}$$

$$\text{Average Rate of Return} = \frac{\$200,000 \div 4}{(\$500,000 + \$0) \div 2}$$

$$\text{Average Rate of Return} = 20\%$$

The expected average rate of return of 20% should be compared with the rate established by management as the minimum reward for the risks involved in the investment. The attractiveness of the proposed purchase of additional equipment is indicated by the difference between the expected rate and the minimum desired rate.

When several alternative capital investment proposals are being considered, the proposals can be ranked by their average rates of return. The higher the average rate of return, the more desirable the proposal. For example, assume that management is considering the following alternative capital investment proposals and has computed the indicated average rates of return:

|  | Proposal A | Proposal B |
|---|---|---|
| Estimated average annual income.................. | $ 30,000 | $ 36,000 |
| Average investment.............................. | $120,000 | $180,000 |
| Average rate of return: |  |  |
| $30,000 ÷ $120,000........................... | 25% |  |
| $36,000 ÷ $180,000........................... |  | 20% |

If only the average rate of return is considered, Proposal A would be preferred over Proposal B, based on its average rate of return of 25%.

The primary advantages of the average rate of return method are its ease of computation and the fact that it emphasizes the amount of income earned over the entire life of the proposal. Its main disadvantages are its lack of consideration of the expected cash flows from the proposal and the timing of these cash flows. These cash flows are important because cash coming from an investment can be reinvested in other income-producing activities. Therefore, the more funds and the sooner the funds become available, the more income that can be generated from their reinvestment.

### Cash Payback Method

The expected period of time that will pass between the date of a capital investment and the complete recovery in cash (or equivalent) of the amount invested is called the cash payback period. To simplify the analysis, the revenues and the out-of-pocket operating expenses expected to be associated with the operation of the plant assets are assumed to be entirely in the form of cash. The excess of the cash flowing in from revenue over the cash flowing out for expenses is termed net cash flow. The time required for the net cash flow to equal the initial outlay for the plant asset is the payback period.

For purposes of illustration, assume that the proposed investment in a plant asset with an 8-year life is $200,000 and that the annual net cash flow is expected to be $40,000. The estimated cash payback period for the investment is 5 years, computed as follows:

$$\frac{\$200,000}{\$40,000} = \text{5-year cash payback period}$$

In the preceding illustration, the annual net cash flows were equal ($40,000 per year). If these annual net cash flows are not equal, the cash payback period is determined by summing the annual net cash flows until the cumulative sum equals the amount of the proposed investment. To illustrate, assume that for a proposed investment, the cumulative net cash flow at the end of the fourth year equals the amount of the investment, $400,000. Therefore, the payback period is 4 years. The annual net cash flows and cumulative net cash flows over the proposal's 6-year life are as follows:

| Year | Net Cash Flow | Cumulative Net Cash Flow |
|------|---------------|--------------------------|
| 1 | $ 60,000 | $ 60,000 |
| 2 | 80,000 | 140,000 |
| 3 | 105,000 | 245,000 |
| 4 | 155,000 | 400,000 |
| 5 | 140,000 | 540,000 |
| 6 | 90,000 | 630,000 |

The cash payback method is widely used in evaluating proposals for expansion and for investment in new projects. A relatively short payback period is desirable, because the sooner the cash is recovered the sooner it becomes available for reinvestment in other projects. In addition, there is likely to be less possibility of loss from changes in economic conditions, obsolescence, and other unavoidable risks when the commitment is short-term. The cash payback concept is also of interest to bankers and other creditors who may be dependent upon net cash flow for the repayment of claims associated with the initial capital investment. The sooner the cash is recovered, the sooner the debt or other liabilities can be paid. Thus, the cash payback method would be especially useful to managers whose primary concern is liquidity.

One of the primary disadvantages of the cash payback method as a basis for decisions is its failure to take into consideration the expected profitability of a proposal. A project with a very short payback period, coupled with relatively poor profitability, would be less desirable than one with a longer payback period but with satisfactory profitability. Another disadvantage of the cash payback method is that the cash flows occurring after the payback period are ignored. A 5-year project with a 3-year payback period and two additional years of substantial cash flows is more desirable than a 5-year project with a 3-year payback period that has lower cash flows in the last two years.

## Present Value Methods

An investment in plant and equipment may be viewed as the acquisition of a series of future net cash flows composed of two elements: (1) recovery of the initial investment and (2) income. The period of time over which these net cash flows will be received may be an important factor in determining the value of an investment.

The concept of present values is that any specified amount of cash to be received at some date in the future is not the equivalent of the same amount of cash held at an earlier date. A sum of cash to be received in the future is not as valuable as the same sum on hand today, because cash on hand today can be invested to earn income. For example, $100 on hand today would be more valuable than $100 to be received a year from today. In other words, if cash can be invested to earn 10% per year, the $100 on hand today will accumulate to $110 ($100 plus $10 earnings) by one year from today. The $100 on hand today can be referred to as the present value amount that is equivalent to $110 to be received a year from today.

### Discounted Cash Flow Method

The discounted cash flow method, sometimes referred to as the net present value method, uses present value concepts to compute the present value of the cash flows expected from a proposal. To illustrate, if the rate of earnings is 12% and the cash to be received in one year is $1,000, the present value amount is $892.86 ($1,000 ÷ 1.12). If the cash is to be received one year later (two years in all), with the earnings compounded at the end of the first year, the present value amount would be $797.20 ($892.86 ÷ 1.12).

Instead of determining the present value of future cash flows by a series of divisions in the manner just illustrated, it is customary to find the present value of 1 from a table of present values and to multiply it by the amount of the future cash flow. Reference to the following partial table indicates that the present value of 1 to be received two years hence, with earnings at the rate of 12% a year, is .797. Multiplication of .797 by $1,000 yields $797, which is the same amount that was determined in the preceding paragraph by two successive divisions. The small difference is due to rounding the present value factors in the table to three decimal places.

PRESENT VALUE OF 1 AT COMPOUND INTEREST

| Year | 6% | 10% | 12% | 15% | 20% |
|------|------|------|------|------|------|
| 1 | .943 | .909 | .893 | .870 | .833 |
| 2 | .890 | .826 | .797 | .756 | .694 |
| 3 | .840 | .751 | .712 | .658 | .579 |
| 4 | .792 | .683 | .636 | .572 | .482 |
| 5 | .747 | .621 | .567 | .497 | .402 |
| 6 | .705 | .564 | .507 | .432 | .335 |
| 7 | .665 | .513 | .452 | .376 | .279 |
| 8 | .627 | .467 | .404 | .327 | .233 |
| 9 | .592 | .424 | .361 | .284 | .194 |
| 10 | .558 | .386 | .322 | .247 | .162 |

The particular rate of return selected in discounted cash flow analysis is affected by the nature of the business enterprise and its relative profitability, the purpose of the capital investment, the cost of securing funds for the investment, the minimum desired rate of return, and other related factors. If the present value of the net cash flow expected from a proposed investment, at the selected rate, equals or exceeds the amount of the investment, the proposal is desirable. For purposes of illustration, assume a proposal for the acquisition of $200,000 of equipment with an expected useful life of 5 years and a minimum desired rate of return of 10%. The anticipated net cash flow for each of the 5 years and the analysis of the proposal are as follows. The calculation shows that the proposal is expected to recover the investment and provide more than the minimum rate of return.

DISCOUNTED CASH FLOW ANALYSIS

| Year | Present Value of 1 at 10% | Net Cash Flow | Present Value of Net Cash Flow |
|------|------|------|------|
| 1 | .909 | $ 70,000 | $ 63,630 |
| 2 | .826 | 60,000 | 49,560 |
| 3 | .751 | 50,000 | 37,550 |
| 4 | .683 | 40,000 | 27,320 |
| 5 | .621 | 40,000 | 24,840 |
| Total | | $260,000 | $202,900 |

Amount to be invested. . . . . . . . . . . . . . . . . . . . . . . . . . . . . . . . . . . . 200,000

Excess of present value over amount to be invested . . . . . . . . $ 2,900

When several alternative investment proposals of the same amount are being considered, the one with the largest excess of present value over the amount to be invested is the most desirable. If the alternative proposals involve different amounts of investment, it is useful to prepare a relative ranking of the proposals by using a present value index. The present value index for the previous illustration is computed by dividing the total present value of the net cash flow by the amount to be invested, as follows:

$$\text{Present Value Index} = \frac{\text{Total Present Value of Net Cash Flow}}{\text{Amount To Be Invested}}$$

$$\text{Present Value Index} = \frac{\$202,900}{\$200,000}$$

$$\text{Present Value Index} = 1.01$$

To illustrate the ranking of proposals by use of the present value index, assume that the total present values of the net cash flow and the amounts to be invested for three alternative proposals are as follows:

|  | Proposal A | Proposal B | Proposal C |
|---|---|---|---|
| Total present value of net cash flow..... | $107,000 | $86,400 | $93,600 |
| Amount to be invested................. | 100,000 | 80,000 | 90,000 |
| Excess of present value over amount to be invested........................ | $ 7,000 | $ 6,400 | $ 3,600 |

The present value index for each proposal is as follows:

|  | Present Value Index |
|---|---|
| Proposal A .................................. | 1.07 ($107,000 ÷ $100,000) |
| Proposal B .................................. | 1.08 ($ 86,400 ÷ $ 80,000) |
| Proposal C .................................. | 1.04 ($ 93,600 ÷ $ 90,000) |

The present value indexes indicate that although Proposal A has the largest excess of present value over the amount to be invested, it is not as attractive as Proposal B in terms of the amount of present value per dollar invested. It should be noted, however, that Proposal B requires an investment of only $80,000, while Proposal A requires an investment of $100,000. The possible use of the $20,000 if B is selected should be considered before a final decision is made.

The primary advantage of the discounted cash flow method is that it gives consideration to the time value of money. A disadvantage of the method is that the computations are more complex than those for the methods that ignore present value. In addition, this method assumes that the cash received from the proposal during its useful life will be reinvested at the rate of return used to compute the present value of the proposal. Because of changing economic conditions, this assumption may not always be reasonable.

### Discounted Internal Rate of Return Method

The discounted internal rate of return method, sometimes called the **internal rate of return** or **time-adjusted rate of return method**, uses present value concepts to compute the rate of return from the net cash flows expected from capital investment proposals. Thus, it is similar to the discounted cash flow method, in that it focuses on the present value of the net cash flows. However, the discounted internal rate of return method starts with the net cash flows and, in a sense, works backwards to determine the discounted rate of return expected from the proposal. The discounted cash flow method requires management to specify a minimum rate of return, which is then used to determine the excess (deficiency) of the present value of the net cash flow over the investment.

To illustrate the use of the discounted internal rate of return method, assume that management is evaluating a proposal to acquire equipment costing $33,530, which is expected to provide annual net cash flows of $10,000 per year for 5 years. If a rate of return of 12% is assumed, the present value of the net cash flows can be computed using the present value of 1 table on page 196, as follows:

| Year | Present Value of 1 at 12% | Net Cash Flow | Present Value of Net Cash Flow |
|---|---|---|---|
| 1 | .893 | $10,000 | $ 8,930 |
| 2 | .797 | 10,000 | 7,970 |
| 3 | .712 | 10,000 | 7,120 |
| 4 | .636 | 10,000 | 6,360 |
| 5 | .567 | 10,000 | 5,670 |
| Total | | $50,000 | $36,050 |

Since the present value of the net cash flow based on a 12% rate of return, $36,050, is greater than the $33,530 to be invested, 12% is obviously not the discounted internal rate of return. The following analysis indicates that 15% is the rate of return that equates the $33,530 cost of the investment with the present value of the net cash flows.

| Year | Present Value of 1 at 15% | Net Cash Flow | Present Value of Net Cash Flow |
|---|---|---|---|
| 1 | .870 | $10,000 | $ 8,700 |
| 2 | .756 | 10,000 | 7,560 |
| 3 | .658 | 10,000 | 6,580 |
| 4 | .572 | 10,000 | 5,720 |
| 5 | .497 | 10,000 | 4,970 |
| Total | | $50,000 | $33,530 |

In the illustration, the discounted internal rate of return was determined by trial and error. A rate of 12% was assumed before the discounted internal rate of return of 15% was identified. Such procedures are tedious and time consuming. When equal annual net cash flows are expected from a proposal, as in the illustration, the computations can be simplified by using a table of the present value of an annuity.[1]

A series of equal cash flows at fixed intervals is termed an ~~annuity~~. The ~~present value of an annuity~~ is the sum of the present values of each cash flow. From another point of view, the present value of an annuity is the amount of cash that would be needed today to yield a series of equal cash flows at fixed intervals in the future. For example, reference to the following table of the present value of an annuity of 1 shows that the present value of cash flows at the end of each of five years, with a discounted internal rate of return of 15% per year, is 3.353. Multiplication of $10,000 by 3.353 yields the same amount ($33,530) that was determined in the preceding illustration by five successive multiplications.

PRESENT VALUE
OF AN ANNUITY OF
1 AT COMPOUND
INTEREST

| Year | 6% | 10% | 12% | 15% | 20% |
|------|-------|-------|-------|-------|-------|
| 1 | .943 | .909 | .893 | .870 | .833 |
| 2 | 1.833 | 1.736 | 1.690 | 1.626 | 1.528 |
| 3 | 2.673 | 2.487 | 2.402 | 2.283 | 2.106 |
| 4 | 3.465 | 3.170 | 3.037 | 2.855 | 2.589 |
| 5 | 4.212 | 3.791 | 3.605 | 3.353 | 2.991 |
| 6 | 4.917 | 4.355 | 4.111 | 3.785 | 3.326 |
| 7 | 5.582 | 4.868 | 4.564 | 4.160 | 3.605 |
| 8 | 6.210 | 5.335 | 4.968 | 4.487 | 3.837 |
| 9 | 6.802 | 5.759 | 5.328 | 4.772 | 4.031 |
| 10 | 7.360 | 6.145 | 5.650 | 5.019 | 4.192 |

The procedures for using the present value of an annuity of 1 table to determine the discounted internal rate of return are as follows:

1. A present value factor for an annuity of 1 is determined by dividing the amount to be invested by the annual net cash flow, as expressed in the following formula:

$$\text{Present Value Factor for an Annuity of 1} = \frac{\text{Amount To Be Invested}}{\text{Annual Net Cash Flow}}$$

2. The present value factor determined in (1) is located in the present value of an annuity of 1 table by first locating the number of years of expected useful life of the investment in the Year column and then proceeding horizontally across the table until the present value factor determined in (1) is found.

3. The discounted internal rate of return is then identified by the heading of the column in which the present value factor in (2) is located.

---

[1]In the illustration, equal annual net cash flows are assumed, so that attention can be focused on the basic concepts. If the annual net cash flows are not equal, the procedures are more complex, but the basic concepts are not affected. In such cases, computers can be used to perform the computations.

To illustrate the use of the present value of an annuity of 1 table, assume that management is considering a proposal to acquire equipment costing $97,360, which is expected to provide equal annual net cash flows of $20,000 for 7 years. The present value factor for an annuity of 1 is 4.868, computed as follows:

$$\text{Present Value Factor for an Annuity of 1} = \frac{\text{Amount To Be Invested}}{\text{Annual Net Cash Flow}}$$

$$\text{Present Value Factor for an Annuity of 1} = \frac{\$97,360}{\$20,000}$$

$$\text{Present Value Factor for an Annuity of 1} = 4.868$$

For a period of 7 years, the following table for the present value of an annuity of 1 indicates that the factor 4.868 is associated with a percentage of 10%. Thus, 10% is the discounted internal rate of return for this proposal.

PRESENT VALUE
OF AN ANNUITY OF
1 AT COMPOUND
INTEREST

| Year | 6% | 10% | 12% |
|------|-------|-------|-------|
| 1 | .943 | .909 | .893 |
| 2 | 1.833 | 1.736 | 1.690 |
| 3 | 2.673 | 2.487 | 2.402 |
| 4 | 3.465 | 3.170 | 3.037 |
| 5 | 4.212 | 3.791 | 3.605 |
| 6 | 4.917 | 4.355 | 4.111 |
| 7 | 5.582 → | 4.868 | 4.564 |
| 8 | 6.210 | 5.335 | 4.968 |
| 9 | 6.802 | 5.759 | 5.328 |
| 10 | 7.360 | 6.145 | 5.650 |

If the minimum acceptable rate of return for similar proposals is 10% or less, then the proposed equipment acquisition should be considered desirable. When several proposals are under consideration, management often ranks the proposals by their discounted internal rates of return, and the proposal with the highest rate is considered the most attractive.

The primary advantage of the discounted internal rate of return method is that the present values of the net cash flows over the entire useful life of the proposal are considered. An additional advantage of the method is that by determining a rate of return for each proposal, all proposals are automatically placed on a common basis for comparison, without the need to compute a present value index as was the case for the discounted cash flow method. The primary disadvantage of the discounted internal rate of return method is that the computations are somewhat more complex than for some of the other methods. In addition, like the discounted cash flow method, this method assumes that the cash received from a proposal during its useful life will be reinvested at the discounted internal rate of return. Because of changing economic conditions, this assumption may not always be reasonable.

FACTORS THAT
COMPLICATE
CAPITAL
INVESTMENT
ANALYSIS

In the preceding paragraphs, the basic concepts for four widely used methods of evaluating capital investment proposals were discussed. In practice, additional factors may have an impact on the outcome of a capital investment decision. Some of the most important of these factors, which are described in the following paragraphs, are the federal income tax, the unequal lives of alternative proposals, the leasing alternative, uncertainty, and changes in price levels.

Income
Tax

In many cases, the impact of the federal income tax on capital investment decisions can be very significant. Two provisions of the Internal Revenue Code (IRC) which should be considered in capital investment analysis are the investment tax credit and depreciation.[2]

The investment tax credit, which reduces the amount of income tax by the amount of the credit, was enacted in 1962 to encourage businesses to purchase equipment and thereby stimulate the economy. Since its original enactment, the IRC has been changed often in attempts to fine tune the economy. In general, the credit is granted for purchases of certain new or used tangible personal property with a useful life of at least 3 years that is used in the taxpayer's trade or business. The maximum credit is 10% of the cost of property with a life of 5 years or more and 6% for property with a life of three to five years. In determining depreciation, the cost of the asset is generally reduced by one half of the amount of the credit. The basic reduction can be avoided if the taxpayer elects to take a smaller investment credit (8% for property with a life of five years or more, 4% for property with a life of three to five years). Also, the maximum amount of the credit in any year is limited if the potential credit is more than $25,000.

For determining depreciation, or the "cost recovery deduction," which is the expensing of the cost of plant assets over their useful lives, the IRC specifies the use of the Accelerated Cost Recovery System (ACRS). ACRS generally provides for three classes for most business property (3-year, 5-year, and 18-year classes) and provides for depreciation that approximates the use of the 150 percent declining-balance method. The 3-year class includes automobiles and special tools, while most machinery and equipment is included in the 5-year class, and buildings fall into the 18-year class.

ACRS simplifies depreciation accounting by eliminating the need to estimate useful life and salvage value and to decide on a depreciation method. Although a short-run tax saving can usually be realized by using the regular ACRS cost recovery allowance, a taxpayer may elect to use a straight-line deduction based on the property classes prescribed under ACRS. The accelerated write-off of depreciable assets provided by ACRS does not, however, effect a long-run net saving in income tax. The tax reduction of the early years of use is offset by higher taxes as the annual cost recovery allowance diminishes.[3]

---

[2]Other income tax considerations relevant for managerial decision making are discussed in Chapter 10.
[3]Taxpayers may also choose to deduct, as a current expense, a limited amount of the cost of plant asset acquisitions that qualify for the investment tax credit. Amounts expended under this provision are not available for computing the investment tax credit or the cost recovery allowance. To simplify the discussions and illustrations in this chapter, it is assumed that this current expense deduction is not applicable to the capital investment analysis being illustrated.

To illustrate the potential impact of the investment tax credit and ACRS depreciation on capital investment decisions, assume that Sierra Company is using the discounted cash flow method[4] in evaluating a proposal. The cost of the investment acquired in year 1 is $180,000, with an expected useful life of 3 years, no residual value, and a minimum desired rate of return of 12%. If Sierra Company elects the straight-line method of depreciation, the IRC requires one half of a full year's depreciation to be taken in the first year and one half of a full year's depreciation to be taken in the fourth year. Thus, Sierra Company would deduct the following depreciation amounts during the 3-year life of the asset:

| | Depreciation Expense |
|---|---|
| First year | $30,000 [($180,000 ÷ 3) × 1/2] |
| Second year | $60,000 ($180,000 ÷ 3) |
| Third year | $60,000 ($180,000 ÷ 3) |
| Fourth year | $30,000 [($180,000 ÷ 3) × 1/2] |

During the four years in which depreciation expense is deducted, the investment is expected to yield annual operating income, before depreciation and income taxes, of $85,000, $70,000, $70,000, and $30,000, respectively. To simplify the illustration, all revenues and operating expenses except depreciation represent current period cash flows, and no investment credit applies to the acquisition. If the income tax rate is 46%, the annual net aftertax cash flows from acquisition of the asset are as follows:

| | \multicolumn{4}{c}{Year} | | | |
|---|---|---|---|---|
| | 1 | 2 | 3 | 4 |
| Net cash flow before income taxes | $85,000 | $70,000 | $70,000 | $30,000 |
| Income tax expense* | 25,300 | 4,600 | 4,600 | 0 |
| Net cash flow | $59,700 | $65,400 | $65,400 | $30,000 |

| *Income tax expense: | | | | |
|---|---|---|---|---|
| Operating income before depreciation and income taxes | $85,000 | $70,000 | $70,000 | $30,000 |
| Depreciation expense | 30,000 | 60,000 | 60,000 | 30,000 |
| Income before income taxes | $55,000 | $10,000 | $10,000 | 0 |
| Income tax rate | 46% | 46% | 46% | 46% |
| Income tax expense | $25,300 | $4,600 | $4,600 | 0 |

Based on the preceding data, using the discounted cash flow method with no investment tax credit, an $8,919 deficiency of the present value over the amount to be invested is computed, as follows:

[4]The same general impact of the investment tax credit and depreciation on capital investment decisions would occur, regardless of which of the four capital investment evaluation methods was used. To simplify the discussion in this chapter, only the discounted cash flow method is illustrated.

| Year | Present Value of 1 at 12% | Net Cash Flow | Present Value of Net Cash Flow |
|------|---------------------------|---------------|--------------------------------|
| 1 | .893 | $ 59,700 | $ 53,312 |
| 2 | .797 | 65,400 | 52,124 |
| 3 | .712 | 65,400 | 46,565 |
| 4 | .636 | 30,000 | 19,080 |
| Total | | $220,500 | $171,081 |
| Amount to be invested . . . . . . . . . . . . . . . . . . . . . . . . . . . . . . . . | | | 180,000 |
| Deficiency of present value over amount to be invested . . . . | | | $   8,919 |

Because the discounted cash flow method indicates that there is a deficiency of the present value over the amount to be invested, the decision would be to reject the proposal. However, if the investment tax credit had been available, the present value of the acquisition changes significantly and might lead to a different decision. To illustrate, assume that Sierra Company could take the 6% maximum credit allowable for plant assets with a useful life of 3 years, or $10,800 ($180,000 × 6%). When the maximum investment tax credit is taken, the IRC requires that, for depreciation purposes, the cost of the asset be reduced by one half of the credit. Thus, only $174,600 [$180,000 − (1/2 × $10,800)] of the cost will be available for depreciation purposes. Using the straight-line method, with one half of a full year's depreciation taken in the first and fourth years, the depreciation for Sierra Company will be as follows:

|  | Depreciation Expense |
|--|----------------------|
| First year . . . . . . . . . . . . . . . . . . . | $29,100 [($174,600 ÷ 3) × 1/2] |
| Second year . . . . . . . . . . . . . . . | $58,200 ($174,600 ÷ 3) |
| Third year . . . . . . . . . . . . . . . . . | $58,200 ($174,600 ÷ 3) |
| Fourth year . . . . . . . . . . . . . . . . | $29,100 [($174,600 ÷ 3) × 1/2] |

The annual aftertax net cash flows from the acquisition, including the effect of the investment tax credit, are as follows:

|  | Year 1 | Year 2 | Year 3 | Year 4 |
|--|--------|--------|--------|--------|
| Net cash flow before income taxes . . . . | $85,000 | $70,000 | $70,000 | $30,000 |
| Income tax expense* . . . . . . . . . . . . . . . | 14,914 | 5,428 | 5,428 | 414 |
| Net cash flow . . . . . . . . . . . . . . . . . . . . . | $70,086 | $64,572 | $64,572 | $29,586 |
| *Income tax expense: | | | | |
| Operating income before depreciation and income taxes . . . . . . . . | $85,000 | $70,000 | $70,000 | $30,000 |
| Depreciation expense . . . . . . . . . . . . | 29,100 | 58,200 | 58,200 | 29,100 |
| Income before income taxes . . . . . . . | $55,900 | $11,800 | $11,800 | $    900 |
| Income tax rate . . . . . . . . . . . . . . . . . . | 46% | 46% | 46% | 46% |
| Income tax expense before investment tax credit . . . . . . . . . . . . . . . . . | $25,714 | $ 5,428 | $ 5,428 | $    414 |
| Investment tax credit . . . . . . . . . . . . . | 10,800 | 0 | 0 | 0 |
| Income tax expense . . . . . . . . . . . . | $14,914 | $ 5,428 | $ 5,428 | $    414 |

Based on the preceding data, using the discounted cash flow method, a $1,157 deficiency of the present value over the amount to be invested is computed, as follows:

| Year | Present Value of 1 at 12% | Net Cash Flow | Present Value of Net Cash Flow |
|------|---------------------------|---------------|-------------------------------|
| 1 | .893 | $ 70,086 | $ 62,587 |
| 2 | .797 | 64,572 | 51,464 |
| 3 | .712 | 64,572 | 45,975 |
| 4 | .636 | 29,586 | 18,817 |
| Total | | $228,816 | $178,843 |

Amount to be invested . . . . . . . . . . . . . . . . . . . . . . . . . . . . . . . . . . . . . . .   180,000

Deficiency of present value over amount to be invested . . . . . . . . . .   $   1,157

Although the deficiency of the present value over the amount to be invested, $1,157, is less than that computed in the preceding illustration where the investment tax credit was not taken, the decision would still be to reject the proposal. However, if the effects of ACRS depreciation as well as the investment tax credit on income tax expense are considered, the evaluation of the proposal changes even more. To illustrate, assume that Sierra Company can take the maximum investment tax credit of $10,800. The amount available for depreciation will be $174,600 [$180,000 − (1/2 × $10,800)]. Sierra Company is permitted to deduct depreciation over a 3-year period beginning with the year the asset is acquired, using the following ACRS percentages:

| | ACRS Percentage Deduction Allowed for Depreciation |
|---|---|
| First year . . . . . . . . . . . . . . . . . . . . . . | 25% |
| Second year . . . . . . . . . . . . . . . . . . . | 38% |
| Third year . . . . . . . . . . . . . . . . . . . . . | 37% |

Using ACRS, the depreciation for Sierra Company will be as follows:

| | Depreciation Expense |
|---|---|
| First year . . . . . . . . . . . . . . . . . . . . . . | $43,650 ($174,600 × 25%) |
| Second year . . . . . . . . . . . . . . . . . . . | $66,348 ($174,600 × 38%) |
| Third year . . . . . . . . . . . . . . . . . . . . . | $64,602 ($174,600 × 37%) |

The annual aftertax net cash flows from the acquisition of the plant asset, including the effect of ACRS depreciation and the investment tax credit, are as follows:

| | Year | | | |
|---|---|---|---|---|
| | 1 | 2 | 3 | 4 |
| Net cash flow before income taxes.... | $85,000 | $70,000 | $70,000 | $30,000 |
| Income tax expense* ............... | 8,221 | 1,680 | 2,483 | 13,800 |
| Net cash flow...................... | $76,779 | $68,320 | $67,517 | $16,200 |

| *Income tax expense: | | | | |
|---|---|---|---|---|
| Operating income before depre- | | | | |
| ciation and income taxes ........ | $85,000 | $70,000 | $70,000 | $30,000 |
| Depreciation expense ............ | 43,650 | 66,348 | 64,602 | 0 |
| Income before income taxes ....... | $41,350 | $ 3,652 | $ 5,398 | $30,000 |
| Income tax rate .................. | 46% | 46% | 46% | 46% |
| Income tax expense before invest- | | | | |
| ment tax credit.................. | $19,021 | $ 1,680 | $ 2,483 | $13,800 |
| Investment tax credit ............. | 10,800 | 0 | 0 | 0 |
| Income tax expense.............. | $ 8,221 | $ 1,680 | $ 2,483 | $13,800 |

Based on the preceding data, using the discounted cash flow method, a $1,390 excess of the present value over the amount to be invested is computed, as follows:

| Year | Present Value of 1 at 12% | Net Cash Flow | Present Value of Net Cash Flow |
|---|---|---|---|
| 1 | .893 | $ 76,779 | $ 68,564 |
| 2 | .797 | 68,320 | 54,451 |
| 3 | .712 | 67,517 | 48,072 |
| 4 | .636 | 16,200 | 10,303 |
| Total | | $228,816 | $181,390 |

Amount to be invested ....................................... 180,000

Excess of present value over amount to be invested ............. $ 1,390

The specific dollar effects of tax considerations on the evaluation of capital investment proposals will depend on the deductions and credits allowed by the Internal Revenue Code at the time the capital investment decision is to be made. In this illustration, the discounted cash flow analysis indicates an excess of the present value over the amount to be invested, and the decision would be to invest in the asset.

**Unequal Proposal Lives**

In the preceding sections, the discussion of the methods of analyzing capital investment proposals was based on the assumption that alternate proposals had the same useful lives. In practice, however, alternate proposals may have unequal lives. In such cases, the proposals must be made comparable. One widely used method is to adjust the lives of projects with the longest lives to a time period that is equal to the life of the project with the shortest life. In this manner, the useful lives of all proposals are made equal. To illustrate, assume that the discounted cash flow method is being used to compare the following two proposals, each of which has an initial investment of $100,000:

| | Net Cash Flows | |
|---|---|---|
| Year | Proposal X | Proposal Y |
| 1 | $30,000 | $30,000 |
| 2 | 30,000 | 30,000 |
| 3 | 25,000 | 30,000 |
| 4 | 20,000 | 30,000 |
| 5 | 15,000 | 30,000 |
| 6 | 15,000 | — |
| 7 | 10,000 | — |
| 8 | 10,000 | — |

If the desired rate of return is 10%, the proposals have an excess of present value over the amount to be invested, as follows:

| | Proposal X | | |
|---|---|---|---|
| Year | Present Value of 1 at 10% | Net Cash Flow | Present Value of Net Cash Flow |
| 1 | .909 | $ 30,000 | $ 27,270 |
| 2 | .826 | 30,000 | 24,780 |
| 3 | .751 | 25,000 | 18,775 |
| 4 | .683 | 20,000 | 13,660 |
| 5 | .621 | 15,000 | 9,315 |
| 6 | .564 | 15,000 | 8,460 |
| 7 | .513 | 10,000 | 5,130 |
| 8 | .467 | 10,000 | 4,670 |
| Total | | $155,000 | $112,060 |

Amount to be invested . . . . . . . . . . . . . . . . . . . . . . . . . . .     100,000

Excess of present value over amount to be invested . . . . .     $ 12,060

| | Proposal Y | | |
|---|---|---|---|
| Year | Present Value of 1 at 10% | Net Cash Flow | Present Value of Net Cash Flow |
| 1 | .909 | $ 30,000 | $ 27,270 |
| 2 | .826 | 30,000 | 24,780 |
| 3 | .751 | 30,000 | 22,530 |
| 4 | .683 | 30,000 | 20,490 |
| 5 | .621 | 30,000 | 18,630 |
| Total | | $150,000 | $113,700 |

Amount to be invested . . . . . . . . . . . . . . . . . . . . . . . . . . .     100,000

Excess of present value over amount to be invested . . . . .     $ 13,700

The two proposals cannot be compared by focusing on the amount of the excess of the present value over the amount to be invested, because Proposal Y has a life of 5 years while Proposal X has a life of 8 years. Proposal X can be adjusted to a 5-year life by assuming that it is to be terminated at the end of 5 years and the asset sold. This assumption requires that the residual value be estimated at the end of 5 years and that this value be considered a cash flow at that date. Both proposals will then cover 5 years, and the results of the discounted cash flow analysis can be used to compare the relative attractiveness of the two proposals. For example, assume that Proposal X has an estimated residual value at the end of year 5 of $40,000. For Proposal X, the excess of the present value over the amount to be invested is $18,640 for a 5-year life, as follows:

|  | Proposal X | | |
|---|---|---|---|
| Year | Present Value of 1 at 10% | Net Cash Flow | Present Value of Net Cash Flow |
| 1 | .909 | $ 30,000 | $ 27,270 |
| 2 | .826 | 30,000 | 24,780 |
| 3 | .751 | 25,000 | 18,775 |
| 4 | .683 | 20,000 | 13,660 |
| 5 | .621 | 15,000 | 9,315 |
| 5 (Residual value) | .621 | 40,000 | 24,840 |
| Total | | $160,000 | $118,640 |
| Amount to be invested . . . . . . . . . . . . . . . . . . . . . . . . . . . . . | | | 100,000 |
| Excess of present value over amount to be invested . . . . . | | | $ 18,640 |

Since the present value over the amount to be invested for Proposal X exceeds that for Proposal Y by $4,940 ($18,640 − $13,700), Proposal X may be viewed as the more attractive of the two proposals.

**Lease Versus Capital Investment**

Leasing of plant assets has become common in many industries in recent years. Leasing allows an enterprise to acquire the use of plant assets without the necessity of using large amounts of cash to purchase them. In addition, if management believes that a plant asset has a high degree of risk of becoming obsolete before the end of its useful life, then leasing rather than purchasing the asset may be more attractive. By leasing the asset, management reduces the risk of suffering a loss due to obsolescence. Finally, the Internal Revenue Code provisions which allow the lessor (the owner of the asset) to pass tax deductions and tax credits on to the lessee (the party leasing the asset) have increased the popularity of leasing in recent years. For example, a company that leases for its use a $200,000 plant asset with a life of 8 years for $50,000 per year is permitted to deduct annual lease payments of $50,000 as well as take an investment tax credit of $20,000 ($200,000 × 10%) for the first year of use.

In many cases, before a final decision is made, management should consider the possibility of leasing assets instead of purchasing them. Ordinarily, leasing assets is more costly than purchasing because the lessor must include in the rental price the costs associated with owning the assets as well as a profit. Nevertheless, using the methods of evaluating capital investment proposals, management should consider whether or not the profitability and cash flows from the lease alternative with its risks compares favorably to the profitability and cash flows from the purchase alternative with its risks.

**Uncertainty**

All capital investment analyses rely on factors that are uncertain; that is, the accuracy of the estimates involved, including estimates of expected revenues, expenses, and cash flows, are uncertain. Although the estimates are subject to varying degrees of risk or uncertainty, the long-term nature of capital investments suggests that many of the estimates are likely to involve considerable uncertainty. Errors in one or more of the estimates could lead to unwise decisions.

Because of the importance of capital investment decisions, management should be aware of the potential impact of uncertainty on their decisions. Some techniques that can be used to assist management in evaluating the effects of uncertainties on capital investment proposals are presented in Chapter 14.

**Changes in Price Levels**

The past three decades have been characterized by increasing price levels.[5] Such periods are described as periods of inflation. In recent years, the rates of inflation have fluctuated widely, making the estimation of future revenues, expenses, and cash flows more difficult. Therefore, management should consider the expected future price levels and their likely effect on the estimates used in capital investment analyses. Fluctuations in the price levels assumed could significantly affect the analyses.

**CAPITAL RATIONING**

Capital rationing refers to the process by which management allocates available investment funds among competing capital investment proposals. Generally, management will use various combinations of the evaluation methods described in this chapter in developing an effective approach to capital rationing.

In capital rationing, an initial screening of alternative proposals is usually performed by establishing minimum standards for the cash payback and the average rate of return methods. The proposals that survive this initial screening are subjected to the more rigorous discounted cash flow and discounted internal rate of return methods of analysis. The proposals that survive this final screening are evaluated in terms of nonfinancial factors, such as employee morale. For example, the acquisition of new, more efficient equipment which eliminates several jobs could lower employee morale to a level that could decrease overall plant productivity.

The final step in the capital rationing process is a ranking of the proposals and a comparison of proposals with the funds available to determine which proposals will be funded. The unfunded proposals are reconsidered if funds subsequently become available. The following flowchart portrays the capital rationing decision process:

---

[5]The subject of price-level changes is discussed in Chapter 16.

CAPITAL RATIONING
DECISION PROCESS

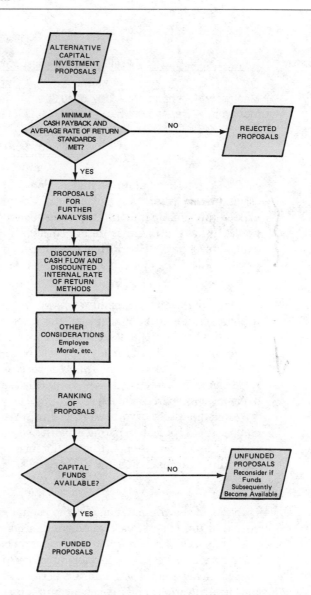

Capital
Expenditures
Budget

Once capital investment expenditures for a period have been approved, a capital expenditures budget should be prepared and procedures should be established for controlling the expenditures. After the assets are placed in service, the actual results of operations should be compared to the initial projected results to determine whether the capital expenditures are meeting management's expectations.

The capital expenditures budget facilitates the planning of operations and the financing of capital expenditures. A capital expenditures budget, which is integrated with the master budget as discussed in Chapter 4, summarizes acquisition decisions for a period typically ranging from one to five years. The following capital expenditures budget was prepared for Sealy Company:

CAPITAL
EXPENDITURES
BUDGET

| Sealy Company Capital Expenditures Budget For Five Years Ending December 31, 1989 | | | | | |
|---|---|---|---|---|---|
| Item | 1985 | 1986 | 1987 | 1988 | 1989 |
| Machinery—Department A... | $240,000 | — | — | $168,000 | $216,000 |
| Machinery—Department B... | 108,000 | $156,000 | $336,000 | 120,000 | — |
| Delivery equipment......... | — | 54,000 | — | — | 36,000 |
| Total................... | $348,000 | $210,000 | $336,000 | $288,000 | $252,000 |

The capital expenditures budget does not authorize the acquisition of plant assets. Rather, it serves as a planning device to determine the effects of the capital expenditures on operations after management has evaluated the alternative proposals, using the methods described in this chapter. Final authority for capital expenditures must come from the proper level of management. In some corporations, large capital expenditures must be approved by the board of directors.

## Control of Capital Expenditures

Once the capital expenditures have been approved, control must be established over the costs of acquiring the assets, including the costs of installation and testing before the assets are placed in service. Throughout this period of acquiring the assets and readying them for use, actual costs should be compared to planned (budgeted) costs. Timely reports should be prepared, so that management can take corrective actions as quickly as possible and thereby minimize cost overruns and operating delays.

After the assets have been placed in service, attention should be focused on comparisons of actual operating expenses with budgeted operating expenses. Such comparisons provide opportunities for management to follow up on successful expenditures or to terminate or otherwise attempt to salvage failing expenditures.

## USE OF COMPUTERS IN CAPITAL INVESTMENT ANALYSIS

Some of the computations for the capital investment evaluation methods discussed in this chapter can become rather complex. By use of the computer, the calculations can be performed easily and quickly. The most important use of the computer, however, is in developing various models which indicate the effect of changes in key factors on the results of capital investment proposals. For example, the effect of various potential changes in future price levels on a proposal could be simulated and the results presented to management for its use in decision making.

---

**Self-Examination Questions**
*(Answers in Appendix C.)*

1. Methods of evaluating capital investment proposals that ignore present value include:
   A. average rate of return
   B. cash payback
   C. both A and B
   D. neither A nor B

2. Management is considering a $100,000 investment in a project with a 5-year life and no residual value. If the total income from the project is expected to be $60,000

and recognition is given to the effect of straight-line depreciation on the investment, the average rate of return is:

A. 12%  C. 60%
B. 24%  D. none of the above

3. As used in the analysis of proposed capital investments, the expected period of time that will elapse between the date of a capital investment and the complete recovery of the amount of cash invested is called:

A. the average rate of return period  C. the discounted cash flow period
B. the cash payback period  D. none of the above

4. Which method of analyzing capital investment proposals determines the total present value of the cash flows expected from the investment and compares this value with the amount to be invested?

A. Average rate of return  C. Discounted cash flow
B. Cash payback  D. Discounted internal rate of return

5. The process by which management allocates available investment funds among competing capital investment proposals is referred to as:

A. capital rationing  C. leasing
B. capital expenditure budgeting  D. none of the above

---

**Discussion Questions**

1. Which two methods of capital investment analysis ignore present value?

2. Which two methods of capital investment analysis can be described as present value methods?

3. What is the "time value of money" concept?

4. (a) How is the average rate of return computed for capital investment analysis, assuming that consideration is given to the effect of straight-line depreciation on the amount of the investment? (b) If the amount of a 6-year investment is $150,000, the straight-line method of depreciation is used, there is no residual value, and the total income expected from the investment is $135,000, what is the average rate of return?

5. What are the principal objections to the use of the average rate of return method in evaluating capital investment proposals?

6. (a) As used in analyses of proposed capital investments, what is the cash payback period? (b) Discuss the principal limitations of the cash payback method for evaluating capital investment proposals.

7. What is the present value of $5,500 to be received one year from today, assuming an earnings rate of 10%?

8. Which method of evaluating capital investment proposals reduces their expected future net cash flows to present values and compares the total present values to the amount of the investment?

9. A discounted cash flow analysis used to evaluate a proposed equipment acquisition indicated a $5,000 excess of present value over the amount to be invested. What is the meaning of the $5,000 as it relates to the desirability of the proposal?

10. How is the present value index for a proposal determined?

11. What are the major disadvantages of the use of the discounted cash flow method of analyzing capital investment proposals?

12. What is an annuity?

13. What are the major disadvantages of the use of the discounted internal rate of return method of analyzing capital investment proposals?

14. What two provisions of the Internal Revenue Code are especially important for consideration in analyzing capital investment proposals?

15. What method can be used to place two capital investment proposals with unequal useful lives on a comparable basis?

16. What are the major advantages of leasing a plant asset rather than purchasing it?

17. What is capital rationing?

**Exercises**

**Exercise 9-1.** The following data are accumulated by Baxter Company in evaluating two competing capital investment proposals:

|  | Proposal X | Proposal Y |
|---|---|---|
| Amount of investment......................... | $300,000 | $400,000 |
| Useful life..................................... | 4 years | 6 years |
| Estimated residual value ...................... | 0 | 0 |
| Estimated total income....................... | $ 90,000 | $156,000 |

Determine the expected average rate of return for each proposal, giving effect to straight-line depreciation on each investment.

**Exercise 9-2.** Horten Company is evaluating two capital investment proposals, each requiring an investment of $100,000 and each with a 6-year life and expected total net cash flows of $150,000. Proposal 1 is expected to provide equal annual net cash flows of $25,000, and Proposal 2 is expected to have the following unequal annual net cash flows:

| | |
|---|---|
| Year 1 .............. | $20,000 |
| Year 2 .............. | 30,000 |
| Year 3 .............. | 50,000 |
| Year 4 .............. | 25,000 |
| Year 5 .............. | 15,000 |
| Year 6 .............. | 10,000 |

Determine the cash payback period for both proposals.

**Exercise 9-3.** The following data are accumulated by Jackson Company in evaluating the purchase of $100,000 of equipment having a 4-year useful life:

| | Net Income | Net Cash Flow |
|---|---|---|
| Year 1.................. | $15,000 | $40,000 |
| Year 2.................. | 15,000 | 40,000 |
| Year 3.................. | 5,000 | 30,000 |
| Year 4.................. | 5,000 | 30,000 |

(a) Assuming that the desired rate of return is 15%, determine the excess (deficiency) of present value over the amount to be invested for the proposal. Use the table of the present value of 1 appearing in this chapter. (b) Would management be likely to look with favor on the proposal? Explain.

**Exercise 9-4.** Berliner Company has computed the excess of present value over the amount to be invested for capital expenditure proposals G and H, using the discounted cash flow method. Relevant data related to the computation are as follows:

|  | Proposal G | Proposal H |
|---|---|---|
| Total present value of net cash flow | $520,000 | $824,000 |
| Amount to be invested | 500,000 | 800,000 |
| Excess of present value over amount to be invested | 20,000 | 24,000 |

Determine the present value index for each proposal.

**Exercise 9-5.** Walsh Company is considering the acquisition of machinery at a cost of $200,000. The machinery has an estimated life of 4 years and no residual value. It is expected to provide yearly income of $30,000 and yearly net cash flows of $80,000. The company's minimum desired rate of return for discounted cash flow analysis is 15%. Compute the following:
(a) The average rate of return, giving effect to straight-line depreciation on the investment.
(b) The cash payback period.
(c) The excess (deficiency) of present value over the amount to be invested, as determined by the discounted cash flow method. Use the table of the present value of 1 appearing in this chapter.

**Exercise 9-6.** The discounted internal rate of return method is used by Herr Company in analyzing a capital expenditure proposal that involves an investment of $500,000 and annual net cash flows of $138,700 for each of the 5 years of useful life. (a) Determine a "present value factor for an annuity of 1" which can be used in determining the discounted internal rate of return. (b) Using the factor determined in (a) and the present value of an annuity of 1 table appearing in this chapter, determine the discounted internal rate of return for the proposal.

**Exercise 9-7.** Vance and Vance Inc. is evaluating a proposed expenditure of $151,850 on a 4-year project whose estimated net cash flows are $50,000 for each of the four years.
(a) Compute the excess (deficiency) of present value over the amount to be invested, using the discounted cash flow method and an assumed rate of return of 10%. (b) Based on the analysis prepared in (a), is the rate of return (1) more than 10%, (2) 10%, or (3) less than 10%? Explain. (c) Determine the discounted internal rate of return by computing a "present value factor for an annuity of 1" and using the table of the present value of an annuity of 1 presented in the text.

**Problems**
*(Problems in Appendix B: 9-1B, 9-2B, 9-3B 9-4B.)*

**Problem 9-1A.** The capital investments budget committee is considering two projects. The estimated operating income and net cash flows from each project are as follows:

|  | Project A | | Project B | |
| --- | --- | --- | --- | --- |
| Year | Operating Income | Net Cash Flow | Operating Income | Net Cash Flow |
| 1 | $12,000 | $ 40,000 | $10,800 | $ 24,000 |
| 2 | 9,000 | 30,000 | 10,800 | 24,000 |
| 3 | 6,000 | 20,000 | 7,200 | 36,000 |
| 4 | 6,000 | 20,000 | 3,600 | 24,000 |
| 5 | 3,000 | 6,000 | 3,600 | 8,000 |
| Total | $36,000 | $116,000 | $36,000 | $116,000 |

Each project requires an investment of $80,000, with no residual value expected. The committee has selected a rate of 12% for purposes of the discounted cash flow analysis.

Instructions:

(1) Compute the following:
    (a) The average rate of return for each project, giving effect to straight-line depreciation on the investment.
    (b) The excess (deficiency) of present value over the amount to be invested, as determined by the discounted cash flow method for each project. Use the present value of 1 table appearing in this chapter.
(2) Prepare a brief report for the budget committee, advising it on the relative merits of the two projects.

**Problem 9-2A.** Jefferson Company is considering two projects. The estimated net cash flows from each project are as follows:

| Year | Project P | Project Q |
| --- | --- | --- |
| 1 | $250,000 | $ 50,000 |
| 2 | 150,000 | 150,000 |
| 3 | 100,000 | 300,000 |
| 4 | 100,000 | 150,000 |
| 5 | 100,000 | 50,000 |
| Total | $700,000 | $700,000 |

Each project requires an investment of $500,000, with no residual value expected. A rate of 15% has been selected for the discounted cash flow analysis.

Instructions:

(1) Compute the following for each project:
    (a) Cash payback period.
    (b) The excess (deficiency) of present value over the amount to be invested, as determined by the discounted cash flow method. Use the present value of 1 table appearing in this chapter.
(2) Prepare a brief report advising management on the relative merits of each of the two projects.

**Problem 9-3A.** Murphy Company wishes to evaluate three capital investment proposals by using the discounted cash flow method. Relevant data related to the proposals are summarized as follows:

| | Proposal X | Proposal Y | Proposal Z |
|---|---|---|---|
| Amount to be invested.............. | $200,000 | $200,000 | $300,000 |
| Annual net cash flows: | | | |
| Year 1 ........................ | 90,000 | 120,000 | 150,000 |
| Year 2 ........................ | 80,000 | 90,000 | 140,000 |
| Year 3 ........................ | 60,000 | 60,000 | 120,000 |

Instructions:

(1) Assuming that the desired rate of return is 15%, prepare a discounted cash flow analysis for each proposal. Use the present value of 1 table appearing in this chapter.
(2) Determine a present value index for each proposal.
(3) Which proposal offers the largest amount of present value per dollar of investment? Explain.

**Problem 9-4A.** Management is considering two capital investment proposals. The estimated net cash flows from each proposal are as follows:

| Year | Proposal I | Proposal II |
|---|---|---|
| 1 | $120,000 | $40,000 |
| 2 | 120,000 | 40,000 |
| 3 | 120,000 | 40,000 |
| 4 | 120,000 | 40,000 |

Proposal I requires an investment of $364,400 while Proposal II requires an investment of $114,200. No residual value is expected from either proposal.

Instructions:

(1) Compute the following for each proposal:
  (a) The excess (deficiency) of present value over the amount to be invested, as determined by the discounted cash flow method. Use a rate of 10% and the present value of 1 table appearing in this chapter.
  (b) A present value index.
(2) Determine the discounted internal rate of return for each proposal by (a) computing a "present value factor for an annuity of 1" and (b) using the present value of an annuity of 1 table appearing in this chapter.
(3) What advantage does the discounted internal rate of return method have over the discounted cash flow method in comparing proposals?

**Problem 9-5A.** Using the discounted cash flow method, the accountant for Collins Company prepared the following analysis of a project expected to be undertaken during Year 1:

| Year | Present Value of 1 at 15% | Net Cash Flow | Present Value of Net Cash Flow |
|---|---|---|---|
| 1 | .870 | $ 80,000 | $ 69,600 |
| 2 | .756 | 115,000 | 86,940 |
| 3 | .658 | 130,000 | 85,540 |
| 4 | .572 | 100,000 | 57,200 |
| Total | | $425,000 | $299,280 |

| | |
|---|---|
| Amount to be invested..................................... | 300,000 |
| Deficiency of present value over amount to be invested ........ | $    720 |

A review of the analysis and related items disclosed the following:

(a) The straight-line method was used for computing depreciation, with one half of a year's depreciation taken in the first year and the fourth year.

(b) Operating income (and net cash flow) before depreciation and taxes is expected to be $110,000, $130,000, $160,000, and $150,000 for the first through fourth years, respectively.

(c) The income tax rate is 50%.

(d) Although the project qualifies for a 6% investment tax credit, the credit was not considered in the analysis.

Instructions:

(1) Assuming the use of the straight-line depreciation method with a 3-year life, no residual value, and no investment credit, compute the following:

(a) Amount of depreciation expense for each of the four years covered by the project.

(b) Income tax expense for each of the four years covered by the project.

(c) Net cash flow for each of the four years covered by the project. (Note: The net cash flows calculated should agree with those included in the analysis presented in the first paragraph of this problem.)

(2) Compute the following:

(a) Investment tax credit available for the project.

(b) Depreciation expense for each of the four years covered by the project, assuming that the investment tax credit is taken and the 3-year-class ACRS depreciation rates appearing in this chapter are used.

(c) Income tax expense for each of the four years, based on the use of ACRS depreciation and the investment tax credit.

(d) Net cash flow for each of the four years covered by the project, based on the income tax expense computed in (c).

(e) The excess (deficiency) of present value over the amount to be invested, based on the net cash flows determined in (d) and as determined by the discounted cash flow method. Use the present value of 1 table appearing in this chapter and round computations to the nearest dollar.

(3) Should the project be accepted? Explain.

**Problem 9-6A.** The investment committee of Tyler Company is evaluating two projects. The projects have different useful lives, but each requires an investment of $100,000. The estimated net cash flows from each project are as follows:

| | Net Cash Flows | |
|---|---|---|
| Year | Project Y | Project Z |
| 1 | $40,000 | $30,000 |
| 2 | 40,000 | 30,000 |
| 3 | 40,000 | 30,000 |
| 4 | 40,000 | 30,000 |
| 5 | 0 | 30,000 |
| 6 | 0 | 30,000 |

The committee has selected a rate of 15% for purposes of discounted cash flow analysis. It also estimates that the residual value at the end of each project's useful life is $0, but at the end of the fourth year, Project Z's residual value would be $60,000.

Instructions:

(1) For each project, compute the excess (deficiency) of present value over the amount to be invested, as determined by the discounted cash flow method. Use the present value of 1 table appearing in this chapter. (Ignore the unequal lives of the projects.)

(2) For each project, compute the excess (deficiency) of present value over the amount to be invested, as determined by the discounted cash flow method, assuming that Project Z is adjusted to a four-year life for purposes of analysis. Use the present value of 1 table appearing in this chapter.

(3) In reporting to the investment committee, what advice would you give on the relative merits of the two projects?

---

**Mini-Case**

Your father is considering an investment of $200,000 in either Project A or Project B. In discussing the two projects with an advisor, it was decided that, for the risk involved, a return of 15% on the cash investment would be required. For this purpose, your father estimated the following economic factors for the projects:

|  | Project A | Project B |
|---|---|---|
| Useful life | 4 years | 4 years |
| Residual value | –0– | –0– |
| Net income: |  |  |
| Year 1 | $40,000 | $10,000 |
| 2 | 20,000 | 20,000 |
| 3 | 10,000 | 20,000 |
| 4 | 6,000 | 30,000 |
| Net cash flows: |  |  |
| Year 1 | $90,000 | $60,000 |
| 2 | 70,000 | 70,000 |
| 3 | 60,000 | 70,000 |
| 4 | 56,000 | 80,000 |

Although the average rate of return exceeded 15% on both projects, your father has tentatively decided to invest in Project B because the rate was higher for Project B. Although he doesn't fully understand the importance of cash flow, he has heard others talk about its importance in evaluating investments. In this respect, he noted that the total net cash flow from Project B is $280,000, which exceeds that from Project A by $4,000.

Instructions:

(1) Determine the average rate of return for both projects.

(2) How would you explain the importance of net cash flows in the analysis of investment projects? Include a specific example to demonstrate the importance of net cash flows and their timing to these two projects.

# 10

CHAPTER

# Income Taxes and Their Impact on Management Decisions

## CHAPTER OBJECTIVES

*Describe the federal income tax system and the basic components and computations for determining federal income taxes.*

*Describe and illustrate the importance of income taxes in management decision making.*

# 10

**CHAPTER**

The federal government and more than three fourths of the states levy an income tax. In addition, some of the states permit municipalities or other political subdivisions to levy income taxes. For most businesses, the amount of income tax is a significant cost of operations, and it is often one of the most important factors influencing a business decision.

Since the federal income tax regulations are quite complex, many businesses engage professional tax specialists to assist in minimizing taxes and in reviewing the tax effects of major business proposals. Nevertheless, it is important for management and the managerial accountant to be aware of the possible tax consequences of business decisions and to recognize areas in which tax factors may play an important part. If management and the managerial accountant understand the general concepts, the tax specialist can be consulted about the details and the specifics of the tax.

For many reasons, Congress frequently changes the tax laws. For example, the laws may be changed to increase revenues, encourage employment, stimulate economic growth, or help control inflation. Although the current law should be examined before decisions are made, the following discussion should be useful in demonstrating the essential characteristics of the tax system and its effect on business decisions. For demonstration purposes, the explanations and illustrations are brief and relatively free of the many complexities encountered in actual practice.

**FEDERAL INCOME TAX SYSTEM**

The income tax is not imposed upon business units as such, but upon taxable entities. The principal taxable entities are individuals, corporations, estates, and trusts. Business enterprises organized as sole proprietorships are not taxable entities. The revenues and expenses of such business enterprises are reported in the individual tax returns of the owners. Partnerships are not taxable entities but are required to report in an informational return the details of their revenues, expenses, and allocations to partners. The partners then report on their individual tax returns the amount of net income and other special items allocated to them on the partnership return.

Corporations engaged in business for profit are generally treated as distinct taxable entities. However, it is possible for two or more corporations with common ownership to join in filing a consolidated return. The federal tax laws also permit a nonpublic corporation that conforms to specified requirements to elect to be treated in a manner similar to a partnership. The effect of the election is to tax the shareholders on their distributive shares of the net income instead of taxing the corporation.

**INCOME TAX RATES**

The federal tax regulations generally provide for a graduated series of tax rates; that is, successively higher rates are applied to successively higher segments of taxable income. Because of this progression of rates, the income tax is sometimes termed a **progressive tax**. This characteristic is illustrated by both the corporate tax rates and the rates for a married couple filing a joint return, as follows:

CORPORATE
INCOME
TAX RATES

| Taxable Income | Tax Rate |
|---|---|
| $0          – $25,000 ......... | 15% |
| Over $25,000 – $50,000 ......... | 18% |
| Over $50,000 – $75,000 ......... | 30% |
| Over $75,000 – $100,000 ........ | 40% |
| Over $100,000 ................... | 46% |

TAX RATE
SCHEDULE FOR
MARRIED PERSONS
FILING JOINTLY

| If taxable income is: | | | | The tax is: | |
|---|---|---|---|---|---|
| Not over $3,400 .... | | | | –0– | |
| Over— | But not over— | | | | of the amount over— |
| $  3,400 | $  5,500 | ....... | | 11% | $  3,400 |
| 5,500 | 7,600 | $   231 | + | 12% | 5,500 |
| 7,600 | 11,900 | 483 | + | 14% | 7,600 |
| 11,900 | 16,000 | 1,085 | + | 16% | 11,900 |
| 16,000 | 20,200 | 1,741 | + | 18% | 16,000 |
| 20,200 | 24,600 | 2,497 | + | 22% | 20,200 |
| 24,600 | 29,900 | 3,465 | + | 25% | 24,600 |
| 29,900 | 35,200 | 4,790 | + | 28% | 29,900 |
| 35,200 | 45,800 | 6,274 | + | 33% | 35,200 |
| 45,800 | 60,000 | 9,772 | + | 38% | 45,800 |
| 60,000 | 85,600 | 15,168 | + | 42% | 60,000 |
| 85,600 | 109,400 | 25,920 | + | 45% | 85,600 |
| 109,400 | 162,400 | 36,630 | + | 49% | 109,400 |
| 162,400 | ....... | 62,600 | + | 50% | 162,400 |

The highest rate applied to the income of any particular taxpayer is sometimes called the taxpayer's marginal tax rate. For a corporate taxpayer with taxable income of $80,000, the marginal tax rate is 40%. For this corporation, the last dollar of income was taxed at the 40% rate and any additional income, up to $100,000, would be taxed at 40%. Likewise, if a corporation's taxable income exceeds $100,000, the marginal tax rate is 46%.

The use of the marginal tax rate, which is the rate of tax on the increase in income, enables management to consider the impact of income tax on proposed courses of action. For example, a corporation with a marginal tax rate of 46% would gain 54% from any increase in income, after tax. If a proposed course of action is expected to result in incremental income of $100,000 before tax, the income after tax will be $54,000 ($100,000 × 54%).

The same analysis would be applied to the evaluation of the tax effect of a potential expense or loss. For example, if a corporation with a marginal tax rate of 46% is considering the expenditure of $10,000, it would view the aftertax cost as being $5,400 ($10,000 less the tax savings of $4,600).

ILLUSTRATIONS
OF IMPACT OF
INCOME TAXES
ON DECISION
MAKING

The importance of income tax on various business decisions has been mentioned in previous chapters. For example, the impact of the income tax on capital investment proposals and equipment replacement proposals has been discussed. The remainder of this chapter is devoted to illustrations of the importance of income tax considerations on management decision making, including various legal means of minimizing federal income tax.

Form of Business
Organization

One of the most important considerations in selecting the form of organization to use in operating a business enterprise is the impact of the federal income tax. If a business is a sole proprietorship, income must be reported on the owner's personal income tax return. In a partnership, each individual partner is taxed on the distributive share of the business income in much the same manner as a sole proprietor. If the business is incorporated, the corporation must pay an income tax on its earnings. When the remaining earnings are distributed in the form of dividends, they are taxed to the owners (shareholders).

The double taxation feature of the corporation form might seem to outweigh any possible advantages of using it for a family enterprise or other nonpublic business. This is not necessarily the case, however. For most business enterprises, there are likely to be both advantages and disadvantages in the corporate form. Among the many factors that need to be considered are the following: (1) amount of net income, (2) changes in net income from year to year, (3) disposition of aftertax income (withdrawn from the enterprise or used for expansion), (4) method of financing, (5) number of owners and shares of ownership, and (6) the owners' income from other sources. The type of analysis needed to appraise the relative merits of alternative forms of organization is described in the following paragraphs.

For purposes of illustration, assume that a taxpayer and spouse are engaged in a business partnership and are considering incorporation. The business, in which personal services and capital investment are material income-producing factors, has been yielding income of $77,000 before income tax. The other investments and allowable tax deductions result in a net addition of $16,000 to the income of the taxpayers, making a total taxable income of $93,000 ($77,000 + $16,000). The partners' business withdrawals of $50,000 a year would be treated as salary expense if the enterprise were incorporated. The federal income tax consequences under the partnership and corporate forms of organization are as follows:

### Organized as a Partnership

| | |
|---|---:|
| **Tax on individuals:** | |
| Business income | $77,000 |
| Other items | 16,000 |
| Taxable income | $93,000 |
| Income tax liability: | |
| On $85,600 | $25,920 |
| On $7,400 at 45% | 3,330 |
| Total income tax—partnership form | $29,250 |

### Organized as a Corporation

Tax on corporation:
Taxable income ($77,000 − $50,000 salary expense) . . . . .   $27,000

Income tax liability:
On $25,000 at 15%. . . . . . . . . . . . . . . . . . . . . . . . . . . . . . . .   $ 3,750
On $2,000 at 18%. . . . . . . . . . . . . . . . . . . . . . . . . . . . . . . .       360      $ 4,110

Tax on individuals:
Salary. . . . . . . . . . . . . . . . . . . . . . . . . . . . . . . . . . . . . . . . . .   $50,000
Other items. . . . . . . . . . . . . . . . . . . . . . . . . . . . . . . . . . . . . .    16,000
Taxable income. . . . . . . . . . . . . . . . . . . . . . . . . . . . . . . . . . .   $66,000

Income tax liability:
On $60,000. . . . . . . . . . . . . . . . . . . . . . . . . . . . . . . . . . . . . .   $15,168
On $6,000 at 42%. . . . . . . . . . . . . . . . . . . . . . . . . . . . . . . .     2,520      17,688
Total income tax—corporation form . . . . . . . . . . . . . . . . . . . . .                  $21,798

Comparison of the two tax liabilities indicates an annual tax savings of $7,452 ($29,250 − $21,798) by using the corporate form. However, the possible distribution of the corporation's net income as dividends was not taken into consideration. If the corporation's aftertax income of $22,890 ($27,000 − $4,110) were paid as dividends to the owners, their taxable income would total $88,890 ($66,000 + $22,890) instead of $66,000.[1] This would result in a personal income tax of $31,510.50, computed as follows:

### Organized as a Corporation—Aftertax Income Distributed as Dividend

Tax on corporation (as previously computed). . . . . . .   $ 4,110.00
Tax on individuals:
Salary. . . . . . . . . . . . . . . . . . . . . . . . . . . . . . . . . . . . . . . . . .   $50,000.00
Other items. . . . . . . . . . . . . . . . . . . . . . . . . . . . . . . . . . . . .    16,000.00
Dividends . . . . . . . . . . . . . . . . . . . . . . . . . . . . . . . . . . . . . .    22,890.00
Taxable income. . . . . . . . . . . . . . . . . . . . . . . . . . . . .   $88,890.00

Income tax liability:
On $85,600. . . . . . . . . . . . . . . . . . . . . . . . . . . . . . . . . .   $25,920.00
On $3,290 at 45%. . . . . . . . . . . . . . . . . . . . . . . . . .     1,480.50      27,400.50
Total tax . . . . . . . . . . . . . . . . . . . . . . . . . . . . . . . . . . . . .                  $31,510.50

If the corporation's aftertax income is distributed as dividends, the total income tax would be $31,510.50, or $2,260.50 more than the total income tax under the partnership form ($31,510.50 − $29,250). In other words, the resulting increase of $9,712.50 ($27,400.50 − $17,688) in the personal income tax would convert the expected $7,452 advantage of the corporate form to a $2,260.50 disadvantage.

---

[1]For the sake of simplicity, this example is based on the assumption that the dividend exclusion available to individual taxpayers does not apply.

Another factor to consider in the analysis is the possibility that earnings accumulated by a corporation may be subject to an accumulated earnings tax. Ordinarily, accumulations up to $250,000 are exempt from this tax. Additional accumulations are subject to the accumulated earnings tax unless it can be proved that they are not in excess of the reasonable needs of the business. The tax rate is 27.5% of the first $100,000 of accumulated taxable income and 38.5% of the excess over $100,000. If additional accumulations are beyond the reasonable needs of the business and the corporation meets certain requirements of the tax laws, the shareholders might then elect partnership treatment and thus avoid the double tax on corporate earnings. Additional information about the intentions of the owners and prospects for the future would be needed to explore additional ramifications of the problem.

Earnings accumulated by the corporation in the foregoing example might at some future time become available to the stockholders through sale of their stock. They would thus be converted into long-term capital gains, which are generally taxable at lower rates than ordinary income. (Capital gains are discussed in a later section.)

The purpose of the above discussion was to indicate that the best form of organization from the standpoint of the federal income tax can be determined only by a detailed analysis of the particular situation. Generalizations are likely to be of little benefit and may even be misleading. The impact of state and local taxes also varies according to the form of business organization, and the importance of such nontax factors as limited liability and transferability of ownership should be considered.

## Choice Between Accounting Principles

There are many cases in which an enterprise may choose from among two or more optional accounting principles in determining the amount of income tax. The particular principle chosen may have a great effect on the amount of income tax, not only in the year in which the choice is made but also in later years. Examples of such cases, described in the following paragraphs, are cash versus accrual methods of accounting, alternate methods of determining cost of inventory, accelerated cost recovery method of determining depreciation, installment method of recognizing sales revenue, and completed-contract method of recognizing income from long-term construction projects.

### Accounting Methods

In general, taxpayers have the option of using either the cash method or the accrual method of accounting. Under the cash method, revenues are not considered to be earned until payment is received. Similarly, expenses are recorded only at the time of cash payment. Generally, however, it is not permissible to treat the entire cost of long-lived assets as an expense of the period in which the cash payment is made. Deductions for depreciation on equipment and buildings used for business purposes may be claimed in the same manner as under the accrual basis, regardless of when payment is made. Similarly, when advance payments for insurance premiums or rentals on business property exceed a period of one year, the total cost must be prorated over the life of the contract.

For businesses in which production or trading in merchandise is an important factor, purchases and sales must be accounted for on the accrual basis. Thus, revenues from sales must be reported in the year in which the goods are sold, regardless of when the cash is received. Similarly, the cost of goods purchased or manufactured must be reported in the year in which the liabilities are incurred, regardless of when payment is made. The usual adjustments must also be made for the beginning and ending inventories in order to determine the cost of goods sold and the gross profit.

Business organizations that regularly have taxable incomes so that they have a marginal tax rate at the highest tax rate are unlikely to be greatly affected by their choice of the cash or accrual method of accounting. For example, corporations that regularly have taxable income in excess of $100,000, and thus have a marginal tax rate of 46%, are unlikely to be greatly affected by the choice of accounting method. On the other hand, a small corporation whose taxable income tends to fluctuate above and below $100,000 from year to year may be better able to control the fluctuation if the cash method is used. For example, near the end of a taxable year in which taxable income is likely to exceed $100,000, some of the excess which will be subject to the tax rate of 46% may be shifted to the following year when the marginal rate may be less than 46%. It may be possible to postpone the receipt of gross income by delayed billings for services, or expenses may be increased by payment of outstanding bills before the end of the year. The timing of expenditures and payments for such expenses as redecorating, repairs, and advertising may also be readily subject to control.

### Inventory Methods

Basically the tax law permits the enterprise to choose its method of determining the cost of inventory. Two widely used methods are fifo (first-in, first-out) and lifo (last-in, first-out). The more traditional method is fifo, while the more widely used method is lifo. The method chosen may have a significant effect on income and the tax on income in periods of changing price levels.

Under fifo, the first goods purchased during a year are assumed to be the first goods sold. During a period of rising prices, the first goods purchased are the least costly. If the least costly goods are sold, they are charged against revenue, and the most costly goods are included in inventory. Under lifo, however, the last goods purchased during a year are assumed to be the first goods sold. During a period of rising prices, the last goods purchased are the most costly. If the most costly goods are sold, they are charged against revenue, and the least costly goods are included in inventory. Thus, in periods of rising prices, lifo results in a higher cost of goods sold, lower income, and lower taxes than fifo.

To illustrate the effect of fifo and lifo on the cost of goods sold and gross profit (and consequently net income and income taxes) in a period of rising prices, assume the following activity for a year for a firm that sells one product:

Sales, 1,000 units at $200 . . . . . . . . . . . . . . . . . . . . . . . . . . . . . . . . . . . . . $200,000
Beginning inventory, 500 units at $150 . . . . . . . . . . . . . . . . . . . . . . .      75,000
Purchases, 1,000 units at $160 . . . . . . . . . . . . . . . . . . . . . . . . . . . . .     160,000
Ending inventory, 500 units . . . . . . . . . . . . . . . . . . . . . . . . . . . . . . . .        —

The effect of using fifo and lifo on the year's gross profit is as follows:

|                                   | Fifo      | Lifo      |
|-----------------------------------|-----------|-----------|
| Sales .........................   | $200,000  | $200,000  |
| Cost of goods sold:               |           |           |
|   Beginning inventory ........... | $ 75,000 | $ 75,000 |
|   Purchases................... | 160,000 | 160,000 |
| Goods available for sale ....... | $235,000 | $235,000 |
| Ending inventory:                 |           |           |
|    500 units at $160........... | 80,000 | |
|    500 units at $150........... | | 75,000 |
| Cost of goods sold ........... | 155,000 | 160,000 |
| Gross profit................... | $ 45,000 | $ 40,000 |

Under fifo, the 1,000 units sold include the 500 in beginning inventory at
$150, or $75,000, plus 500 of those purchased at $160, or $80,000, for a total of
$155,000. Under lifo, the 1,000 units sold would be the 1,000 purchased at $160,
or $160,000. Thus, using lifo results in a $5,000 higher cost of goods sold (and lower
gross profit). From another view, the $5,000 difference in gross profit can be
viewed as the difference in the ending inventory amounts ($80,000 − $75,000).

The income tax effect of using fifo versus lifo during periods of declining prices
would be the reverse of that illustrated. During periods of declining prices, gross
profit (and net income and income taxes) under lifo would exceed that of fifo.

In times of inflation, which has been the long-term trend in the United States
since World War II, the use of lifo not only results in a lower annual income tax,
but it also permits the taxpayer to retain more funds, by lowering tax payments,
to replace goods sold with higher-priced goods. Clearly, this advantage is one of
the most important reasons for lifo's popularity.

### Depreciation

In the preceding chapter, the effect of using the Accelerated Cost Recovery
System (ACRS) in evaluating capital investment proposals was discussed and illustrated. ACRS can also be used to determine the annual depreciation expense
deduction for tax purposes to realize a short-run saving in taxes. The accelerated
write-off of depreciable assets provided by ACRS does not, however, effect a
long-run net savings in income tax. The accelerated tax deductions provided by the
use of ACRS in the early years of an asset's life are offset by lower deductions in
the later years.

ACRS provides for depreciation that approximates the use of the 150%-
declining-balance method and permits the use of asset lives that are often much
shorter than actual useful lives. ACRS generally provides for three classes of useful
life for most business property (3-year, 5-year, and 18-year classes). The 3-year
class includes automobiles, light-duty trucks, and some special tools. Most machinery and equipment is included in the 5-year class, while buildings fall in the
18-year class. Tables are available that indicate the annual percentages to be used
in determining depreciation for each class. In using these percentages, salvage
value is ignored, and a full year's percentage is allowed for the year of acquisition.
The following schedule indicates the ACRS depreciation rates for the 3-year and
5-year classes:

| | Year | 3-Year-Class Assets | 5-Year-Class Assets |
|---|---|---|---|
| ACRS DEPRECIATION RATE SCHEDULE | 1 | 25% | 15% |
| | 2 | 38 | 22 |
| | 3 | 37 | 21 |
| | 4 | | 21 |
| | 5 | | 21 |
| | | 100% | 100% |

To illustrate the effect of the use of ACRS on income taxes, assume that $90,000 of special tools that qualify as ACRS 3-year-class assets are acquired in the middle of year 1. The tools have a 3-year life for tax purposes and no residual value, and the straight-line method of depreciation is used for book purposes. Although the straight-line method could be elected for tax purposes (in which case only one-half year's depreciation would be available for the year of acquisition and disposal), it is advantageous to use the ACRS rates, as illustrated by the following tabulation:

| | Year 1 | Year 2 | Year 3 | Year 4 |
|---|---|---|---|---|
| **ACRS depreciation:** | | | | |
| Year 1: $90,000 × 25%............ | $22,500 | | | |
| Year 2: $90,000 × 38%............ | | $34,200 | | |
| Year 3: $90,000 × 37%............ | | | $33,300 | |
| Year 4: ......................... | | | | —— |
| **Straight-line depreciation:** | | | | |
| Year 1: ($90,000 ÷ 3) × 1/2........ | 15,000 | | | |
| Year 2: $90,000 ÷ 3 ............. | | 30,000 | | |
| Year 3: $90,000 ÷ 3 ............. | | | 30,000 | |
| Year 4: ($90,000 ÷ 3) × 1/2........ | | | | $15,000 |
| Excess (deficiency) of ACRS over straight-line....................... | $ 7,500 | $ 4,200 | $ 3,300 | ($15,000) |

Although the depreciation deduction is the same over the four-year period, $15,000 ($7,500 + $4,200 + $3,300) more depreciation is allowable under ACRS during the first 3 years. During the last year, $15,000 more depreciation would be available under the straight-line method. The ability to delay cash payments for income taxes means that the taxpayer can retain funds longer, and these funds can be invested to earn income, used to reduce debt and thus save on interest costs, or used for some other purpose.

The possibility of adverse changes in tax rates in future years is a factor that must be considered in evaluating the use of ACRS. However, the additional funds made available in the early years of the life of an asset are usually considered to be advantageous enough to justify the use of ACRS for income tax purposes.

**Installment Method**

Although the point of sale method is used for recognizing income from most sales, the installment method of determining income from merchandise sold on the installment plan is widely used for income tax purposes. To illustrate the savings that may result from the use of the installment method for tax purposes, assume that a company with a marginal tax rate of 46% added a new product line during the year. The installment method may be used to report income from the new line. The data on the first year of sales are as follows (for purposes of illustration, the gross profit for this product is assumed to be taxable income):

| | |
|---|---|
| Installment sales | $500,000 |
| Cost of installment sales | 350,000 |
| Gross profit on installment sales (30% of sales) | $150,000 |
| Collection of installment sales: | |
| First year | $200,000 |
| Second year | 200,000 |
| Third year | 100,000 |

Using the point of sale method of reporting income, the tax for the first year would be $69,000 ($150,000 gross profit × 46%). Using the installment sales method of reporting income, the tax would still be $69,000, but it would be spread over the three years during which the collections were made, as follows:

| | Year 1 | Year 2 | Year 3 | Total Tax |
|---|---|---|---|---|
| **Point of sale method:** | | | | |
| Gross profit | $150,000 | — | — | |
| Marginal tax rate | × 46% | — | — | |
| Income tax | $ 69,000 | — | — | $69,000 |
| **Installment method:** | | | | |
| Gross profit (collections × rate of gross profit): | | | | |
| $200,000 × 30% | $ 60,000 | | | |
| 200,000 × 30% | | $60,000 | | |
| 100,000 × 30% | | | $30,000 | |
| Marginal tax rate | × 46% | × 46% | × 46% | |
| Income tax | $ 27,600 | $27,600 | $13,800 | $69,000 |

Only $27,600 of tax would be due at the end of the first year if the installment method is used. At the end of the second year, no additional tax would be payable if the point of sale method is used, but $27,600 would be payable if the installment method is used. Likewise, the remaining tax of $13,800 would be payable at the end of the third year if the installment method is used. Although the same amount of tax is payable under both methods, management postpones payment of a portion of the total tax by using the installment method. As explained in preceding sections, cash payments that can be delayed are more valuable than cash payments due currently, since money saved can be invested, or interest on borrowing can be reduced.

## Long-Term Construction Contracts

Companies engaged in large construction projects may devote several years to the completion of a particular contract. In such cases, the company can use either the percentage-of-completion method or the completed-contract method for reporting income. Under the percentage-of-completion method, income on a contract is recognized over the life of the contract. Under the completed-contract method, income is recognized when the project is completed. In either case, the total amount of income for a contract would be the same.

As illustrated in the preceding section, it is advantageous to employ the method that enables the company to postpone the payment of as much of the tax as possible. Therefore, regardless of the method used in preparing the published financial statements, the completed-contract method should be used for reporting income taxes. To illustrate, assume that a taxpayer had a project that took three years to complete, the contract price was $3,000,000, and the construction activities for the three years were as follows:

| Year | Costs Incurred | Percent Completed |
|------|----------------|-------------------|
| 1    | $  525,000     | 20%               |
| 2    | 1,075,000      | 40                |
| 3    | 1,100,000      | 40                |

The taxable income reported for each of the three years under the percentage-of-completion and completed-contract methods would be as follows:

|  | Years | | | |
|---|---|---|---|---|
|  | 1 | 2 | 3 | Total |
| **Percentage-of-completion method:** | | | | |
| Year 1: | | | | |
| Revenue (20% × $3,000,000) .. | $600,000 | | | |
| Costs . . . . . . . . . . . . . . . . . . . . . . | 525,000 | | | |
| Year 2: | | | | |
| Revenue (40% × $3,000,000) .. | | $1,200,000 | | |
| Costs . . . . . . . . . . . . . . . . . . . . . . | | 1,075,000 | | |
| Year 3: | | | | |
| Revenue (40% × $3,000,000). . . | | | $1,200,000 | |
| Costs . . . . . . . . . . . . . . . . . . . . . . | | | 1,100,000 | |
| Taxable income . . . . . . . . . . . . . . . | $ 75,000 | $ 125,000 | $ 100,000 | $300,000 |
| **Completed-contract method:** | | | | |
| Year 3: | | | | |
| Revenue . . . . . . . . . . . . . . . . . . . . | | | $3,000,000 | |
| Costs ($525,000 + $1,075,000 + $1,100,000). . . . . . . . . . . . . . . | | | 2,700,000 | |
| Taxable income . . . . . . . . . . . . . . . | | | $ 300,000 | $300,000 |

The taxable income from the project over the three years is $300,000. However, none of the income is reported as taxable income until the project is completed under the completed-contract method. A portion of the $300,000— $75,000, $125,000, and $100,000—would be reported in each of the three years, respectively, using the percentage-of-completion method. As explained in the preceding section, the delay of cash payments means that the company can retain funds longer, and these funds can be invested to earn income or can be used to reduce debt and thus save on interest costs.

**Capital Gains and Losses**

Gains and losses resulting from individuals selling or exchanging certain types of assets, called **capital assets,** are given special treatment for income tax purposes. Capital assets most commonly owned by taxpayers are stocks and bonds. Under certain conditions, land, buildings, and equipment used in business may also be treated as capital assets.

The gains and losses from the sale or exchange of capital assets are classified as **short-term** or **long-term,** based on the length of time the assets are held (owned). The holding period for short-term gains and losses is six months or less. For long-term gains and losses, the holding period is more than six months.

The aggregate of all short-term gains and losses during a taxable year is called a **net short-term capital gain** (or **loss**) and the aggregate of all long-term gains and losses is similarly identified as a **net long-term capital gain** (or **loss**). The net short-term and net long-term results are then combined to form the **net capital gain** (or **loss**).

For both individuals and corporations, capital gains and losses are accorded special treatment. Although there are some differences in the treatment of capital gains and losses between individuals and corporations, the significance of this special treatment for management decision making is illustrated in the following paragraphs.

## Capital Gains

In general, net short-term capital gains are taxed at ordinary rates. Net long-term capital gains are given preferential treatment, with the result that they are often subject to lower rates than those applicable to ordinary income. For a corporation, for example, the maximum tax rate on long-term capital gains is 28%. Thus, for a corporation with a marginal tax rate of 46%, it would be advantageous to convert as much ordinary income as possible to long-term capital gain. To illustrate, assume that a company with a marginal tax rate of 46% is the lessor of a patent (capital asset) which has a zero tax basis. The annual rental income is $100,000, and the total rental income over the patent's remaining life of four years is $400,000. If an offer of $350,000 for the patent is received, it appears that the proposal should be rejected, because the sales price ($350,000) is less than the total income from rentals ($400,000). However, since the gain on the sale of the patent is subject to a maximum tax of 28% and the income from the rental is taxed at 46%, the aftertax income is higher with the sale alternative, shown as follows:

**Sale alternative:**

| | | |
|---|---|---|
| Sales price (gain) .............................. | $350,000 | |
| Tax, long-term capital gain rate of 28% ........... | 98,000 | |
| Net after tax .................................... | | $252,000 |

**Lease alternative:**

| | | |
|---|---|---|
| Revenue from lease ........................... | $400,000 | |
| Tax, marginal rate of 46% ..................... | 184,000 | |
| Net after tax .................................... | | 216,000 |
| Net advantage of sale alternative ................... | | $ 36,000 |

Although this analysis focuses only on the tax impact of the decision, other factors may also have an effect. One such factor that should be considered is the differential revenue from investing the funds generated by the alternatives.

### Capital Losses

Capital losses are deducted from capital gains. If this deduction results in a net capital loss, corporate taxpayers are not permitted to deduct the loss against ordinary income. Corporations may carry back net capital losses to the three preceding years to offset capital gains, and if the total losses are not absorbed, the losses may be carried forward for five years. Thus, if a capital loss is about to expire and therefore be lost as a tax deduction, the corporation should consider selling some capital assets at a gain (to offset the losses) if such assets are available.

### Timing of Capital Gains and Losses

The timing of capital gains and losses can usually be controlled because the taxpayer can select the time to sell the capital assets. Delaying a sale by only one day can result in a substantial tax savings. To illustrate, assume that the only sale of a capital asset during the year is the sale of listed stocks that had been held for exactly six months, realizing a gain of $40,000. The gain would be classified as a short-term capital gain and taxed as ordinary income. Assuming that the marginal tax rate is 46%, the tax on the $40,000 gain would be $18,400. Alternatively, if the securities had been held for at least one additional day, the $40,000 gain (assuming no change in selling price) would have qualified as a long-term capital gain, which is subject to a maximum tax of $11,200 (28% of $40,000). Thus, if the sale had occurred at least one day later, there would have been a tax savings of $7,200 ($18,400-$11,200).

When a taxpayer owns various lots of an identical security that were acquired at different dates and at different prices, it may be possible to choose between realizing a gain and realizing a loss, and perhaps to a limited extent to govern the amount realized. For example, a taxpayer who has realized gains from the sale of securities may wish to offset them, in whole or in part, by losses from the sales of other securities. To illustrate, assume that a taxpayer who owns three 100-share lots of common stock in the same corporation, purchased at $40, $48, and $60 a share respectively, plans to sell 100 shares at the current market price of $52.

Depending upon which of the three 100-share lots is sold, the taxpayer will realize a gain of $1,200, a gain of $400, or a loss of $800. If the identity of the particular lot sold cannot be determined, the first-in, first-out cost flow assumption must be used. The use of average cost is not permitted.

Use of
Corporate Debt

If a corporation is in need of relatively permanent funds, it generally considers borrowing money on a long-term basis or issuing stock. Since interest on debt is a deductible expense in determining taxable income and dividends paid on stock are not, this impact on income tax is one of the important factors to consider in evaluating the two methods of financing. To illustrate, assume that a corporation with a marginal tax rate of 46% is considering issuing (1) $1,000,000 of 10% bonds or (2) $1,000,000 of 10% cumulative preferred stock. If the bonds are issued, the deduction of the yearly $100,000 of interest in determining taxable income results in an annual net borrowing cost of $54,000 ($100,000 less tax savings of 46% of $100,000). If the preferred stock is issued, the dividends are not deductible in determining taxable income and the net annual outlay for this method of financing is $100,000. Thus, issuing bonds instead of preferred stock reduced the annual financing expenditures by $46,000 ($100,000 − $54,000).

Another aspect of evaluating a proposal to use debt instead of stock for financing corporate operations is the impact of the tax on the earnings per share. To illustrate, assume that the corporation is considering the issuance of $1,000,000 of 10% bonds or $1,000,000 of 10% cumulative preferred stock, has 100,000 shares of common stock outstanding, and the income after tax but before interest and preferred dividends is expected to be $400,000 annually. Although there are other factors to consider, the issuance of bonds appears to be more favorable, based on the results of the following calculation of the expected earnings per share on common stock under each possibility:

| | Preferred Stock | Bonds |
|---|---|---|
| Income after tax, before interest and preferred dividends.. | $400,000 | $400,000 |
| Preferred dividends .................................. | 100,000 | |
| Interest less tax savings [$100,000 − (46% of $100,000)].. | | 54,000 |
| Remainder—identified with common stock .............. | $300,000 | $346,000 |
| Shares of common stock............................... | 100,000 | 100,000 |
| Earnings per share on common stock .................. | $3.00 | $3.46 |

Corporate debt can sometimes be used to convert an apparently uneconomical investment into a profitable investment. For example, a corporation with a marginal tax rate of 46% has an opportunity to invest $100,000 in preferred stock yielding 10%. However, it will need to borrow the $100,000 at 15% to make the investment. Although this investment appears to be unattractive, it provides an annual net profit when the effect of income taxes is considered.

When a corporation borrows money, the interest expense is deductible in determining taxable income. The aftertax cost of borrowing is therefore less than the interest expense. Also, when a corporation owns shares of another domestic corporation and receives dividends on the stock, 85% of the dividends received are generally allowed as a special deduction. Thus, only 15% of such dividends are taxable. As shown in the following calculation, the result of a $100,000 investment in preferred stock, financed by debt, is an annual net profit of $1,210:

| | | |
|---|---|---|
| Dividend income ($100,000 × 10%) | | $10,000 |
| Tax on dividend income: | | |
| Dividend | $10,000 | |
| Dividend exclusion | 8,500 | |
| Taxable amount | $ 1,500 | |
| Tax rate | × 46% | |
| Tax | | 690 |
| Net dividend income after tax | | $ 9,310 |
| Interest expense ($100,000 × 15%) | | $15,000 |
| Tax savings on interest: | | |
| Interest deduction | $15,000 | |
| Tax rate | × 46% | 6,900 |
| Net interest expense after tax | | $ 8,100 |
| Net dividend income after tax | | $ 9,310 |
| Net interest expense after tax | | 8,100 |
| Net profit | | $ 1,210 |

**Nontaxable Investment Income**　　Interest on bonds issued by a state or political subdivision is exempt from the federal income tax. Such investments are especially attractive to taxpayers with a high marginal tax rate. To illustrate, the following table compares the income after tax on a $100,000 investment in a 10% industrial bond and a $100,000 investment in a 6% municipal bond for a corporation with a marginal tax rate of 46%.

| | Taxable 10% Industrial Bond | Nontaxable 6% Municipal Bond |
|---|---|---|
| Income | $10,000 | $6,000 |
| Tax (46% of $10,000) | 4,600 | — |
| Income after tax | $ 5,400 | $6,000 |

Although the interest rate on the municipal bond (6%) is less than the rate on the industrial bond (10%), the aftertax income is larger from the investment in the municipal bond.

**Operating Losses**　　The net operating loss of a corporation may be used to offset taxable income by being carried back to each of the three preceding years. If the loss is not fully absorbed in those three years, in which case past taxes paid would be refunded, the unused portion may be carried forward to each of the fifteen following years.

In addition, this net operating loss carryforward can often be transferred to a successor corporation. Thus, a net operating loss can play an important role in decisions involving the acquisition of one corporation by another. To illustrate, assume that A Corporation with a marginal tax rate of 46%, a profitable past, and a profitable future anticipated is considering the acquisition of Z Company, which has a $1,000,000 operating loss carryforward. Although the operating loss carryforward may be somewhat limited in such cases, one of the factors to be evaluated by A Corporation is the value of the deductibility of the $1,000,000 in computing income tax, should Z Corporation be acquired. For A Corporation, the operating loss carryforward might save $460,000 in future taxes ($1,000,000 × 46%). As with many aspects of the federal income tax, the rules governing the use of the net operating loss are quite complex and should be consulted before a decision is made.

|  |  |
|---|---|
| Investment Tax Credit | As discussed in Chapter 9, the investment tax credit is granted for purchases of certain new or used tangible personal property that has a useful life of at least three years and is used in the taxpayer's trade or business. Since the investment credit is a deduction from the amount of the income tax, it has the effect of lowering the purchase price of the property. Obviously, this lowered price is the relevant cost for evaluating proposed property acquisitions. |

The maximum credit is 10% of the cost of property with a life of five years or more and 6% for property with a life of between three and five years. In determining depreciation, the cost of the asset is generally reduced by one half of the amount of the credit. This basic reduction can be avoided if the taxpayer elects to take a smaller investment credit (8% for property with a life of five years or more, 4% for property with a life of between three and five years). Also, the maximum amount of the credit in any year is limited if the potential credit is more than $25,000. Management should therefore consider both the amount of the investment credit and the allowable depreciation in evaluating the best mix of the two in maximizing the return from investments.

|  |  |
|---|---|
| Trade Versus Sale of Property | In many cases, especially when ACRS is used for determining depreciation, property that is being replaced has a fair market value that exceeds its book value. If this property is sold, the gain is subject to income tax. On the other hand, if the property is to be replaced with similar property, a trade of the old property for the new property can delay the payment of the tax associated with the gain. |

Neither gains nor losses are recognized for income tax purposes when one asset is exchanged for an asset of similar use and cash is paid. Since the trade-in allowance granted by the seller is frequently greater or less than the book value of the asset traded, an unrecognized gain or loss results. To illustrate, assume that old equipment with a book value of $1,000 is to be traded for new equipment with a fair market price of $20,000, and a trade-in allowance of $5,000 is granted for the old equipment. Cash of $15,000 ($20,000 − $5,000) would be paid, and the transaction would result in an unrecognized gain of $4,000 (trade-in allowance of $5,000 less book value of $1,000). The unrecognized gain reduces the basis of the equipment acquired to $16,000 ($20,000 fair market value − $4,000 gain) for tax purposes. The unrecognized gain also decreases the total amount of depreciation allowed for income tax purposes during the life of the equipment. Thus, the same amount of income will be subject to income tax over the life of the property.

From the standpoint of delaying the payment of income tax, it is advantageous to trade property that has a fair market value above book value, rather than sell the old property and purchase the new property. In the previous illustration, if the old equipment is sold for $5,000, a gain of $4,000 would be reported for tax purposes. By trading the equipment, there is no tax on the $4,000 gain at the date of the trade. Instead, the tax will be postponed to future periods, when the depreciation allowed on the new equipment will be reduced by the amount of the gain, or from $20,000 to $16,000.

As in all cases, the amount of the income tax is but one factor to consider in evaluating a proposal. If the equipment in the illustration is sold rather than traded, the amount of tax on the gain, whether the gain is subject to special capital gains treatment, the value of effectively postponing the payment of the tax, the marginal tax rates at the date of the sale or exchange transaction, and the marginal tax rates expected in the future should also be considered.

Contributions of Property Rather Than Cash

Donations to charitable, educational, and other qualifying institutions are generally deductible, up to specified maximum limits, in determining income tax. Donations of property, such as marketable securities, can be more advantageous than donations of cash, if the value of the property has risen since acquisition. The increase in the value of the donated property is not taxed, but the deduction allowed from taxable income is equal to the fair market value of the property. To illustrate, assume that a corporation with a marginal tax rate of 46% wishes to donate $50,000 to a charity, and that it has a capital asset with a cost of $20,000 and a current fair market value of $50,000. If a $50,000 cash gift is given, the net cost to the corporation would be $27,000 ($50,000 donation less tax savings of 46% of $50,000). If the capital asset is sold, an income tax of $8,400 would need to be paid on the gain (classified as long-term), computed as follows:

| | |
|---|---:|
| Sales price | $50,000 |
| Less cost | 20,000 |
| Gain on sale | $30,000 |
| Tax rate for long-term capital gain | × 28% |
| Tax | $ 8,400 |

If the capital asset is sold, only $41,600 ($50,000 − $8,400) is available, after tax, for the contribution. Thus, to make a $50,000 donation, an additional $8,400 would need to be contributed. If the capital asset were donated, the taxpayer would still receive the $50,000 charitable contribution and the charity could sell it for $50,000 without paying an income tax. By donating the property, the taxpayer can save $8,400 without loss of value to the charity.

1. Business enterprises that are treated as taxable entities for federal income tax purposes include:
   A. sole proprietorships    C. corporations
   B. partnerships    D. all of the above
2. The highest tax rate applied to the income of any particular taxpayer is called the:
   A. normal tax rate    C. maximum tax rate
   B. marginal tax rate    D. none of the above
3. In periods of rising prices, the use of lifo (last-in, first-out) instead of fifo (first-in, first-out) for inventory costing results in a:
   A. higher cost of goods sold    C. lower income tax
   B. lower net income    D. all of the above
4. A taxpayer may postpone payment of a portion of the income tax by:
   A. using the installment method rather than the point of sale method for reporting sales
   B. using the completed-contract method of reporting income on long-term construction projects rather than the percentage-of-completion method
   C. both A and B
   D. neither A nor B
5. The maximum tax rate on long-term capital gains for a corporation is:
   A. 20%    C. 46%
   B. 28%    D. 50%

**Discussion
Questions**

1. (a) What are the principal taxable entities subject to the federal income tax? (b) How is the income of sole proprietorships and partnerships taxed?
2. (a) What is a progressive tax? (b) Is the federal income tax a progressive tax?
3. (a) What is meant by the term marginal tax rate? (b) If a corporation has a marginal tax rate of 46%, how much tax would be paid if a proposal were to provide $200,000 of taxable income?
4. What is meant by the statement that the income of corporations is subject to double taxation?
5. Is it possible that earnings accumulated by a corporation may be subject to an accumulated earnings tax? Explain.
6. If the cash method of accounting is used for federal income taxes, is it permissible to deduct payments for the acquisition of long-lived assets as expenses? Explain.
7. Which inventory method (lifo or fifo) would result in the lower income tax during a period of rising prices? Explain.
8. Is the Accelerated Cost Recovery System (ACRS) for determining depreciation an accelerated method of determining depreciation? Explain.
9. For income tax purposes, is it advisable to use the installment method of determining income from merchandise sold on the installment plan? Explain.

10. For income tax purposes, is it advantageous to use the percentage-of-completion method for reporting income on long-term construction projects? Explain.

11. What criterion distinguishes long-term capital gains or losses from short-term capital gains or losses?

12. Are long-term gains from the sale of capital assets taxed at normal tax rates? Discuss.

13. If a net capital loss results from deducting capital losses from capital gains, can the net loss be used by a corporation to reduce ordinary income? Discuss.

14. During the current year, a taxpayer purchased 100 shares of X stock on January 30 at $40 and 100 shares of X stock on August 1 at $50. If 100 shares are sold on December 10 at $60, what is the amount of the gain on the sale for tax purposes?

15. When a corporation owns shares of another domestic corporation and receives dividends on the stock, what percentage of the dividends received is generally taxable?

16. A taxpayer with a marginal tax rate of 40% is considering an investment in a 6%, tax-exempt municipal bond. What rate would need to be earned on a taxable bond to yield the same aftertax return as would be earned on the municipal bond investment?

17. A corporation has a net operating loss of $100,000 for the current year. How can the loss be used to offset taxable income?

18. A taxpayer who has a marginal tax rate of 40% is entitled to an investment tax credit of $25,000. How much will income taxes be reduced by the credit?

19. A taxpayer donates an investment in A stock to a charity. If the cost of the stock is $5,000 and its fair market value at the date of the donation is $7,000, what deduction from taxable income is allowed the taxpayer for the donation?

---

**Exercises**

**Exercise 10-1.** On April 1 of the current year, Frank Baker began Liquigreen Lawn Service. On December 1, Baker estimated that net income for the current year ending December 31 would be $10,000 by the accrual method, and for the following year it would be $50,000. Liquigreen has no inventory and bills all customers on terms net 30.

    (a) Can Liquigreen Lawn Service use either the cash method or the accrual method for reporting income for tax purposes? Explain.

    (b) Assuming that all of Baker's income is from Liquigreen Lawn Service and the cash method is used, would it be advisable for tax purposes for Baker to consider transferring some net income from the following year to the current year? Explain.

    (c) Determine the maximum amount of income that should be considered for transfer from the following year to the current year. Explain your answer.

    (d) Assuming the use of the cash method, suggest ways in which net income can be transferred from the following year to the current year.

**Exercise 10-2.** On January 10 of the current year, Linda Marie Fell opened the Old Fashioned Ice Cream Parlor. During the year, ice cream was purchased at three different prices, as follows:

|  | Price per Gallon |
|---|---|
| January 10–May 1 . . . . . . . . . . . . . . . . . . . . . | $1.50 |
| May 2–August 20 . . . . . . . . . . . . . . . . . . . . | 1.55 |
| August 21–December 31 . . . . . . . . . . . . . . . | 1.65 |

Sales averaged 400 gallons of ice cream per month, and 150 gallons were on hand at December 31.

(a) Assuming the use of the fifo (first-in, first-out) inventory method, determine the cost of the inventory balance at December 31.

(b) Assuming the use of the lifo (last-in, first-out) inventory method, determine the cost of the inventory balance at December 31.

(c) Which inventory method, fifo or lifo, will result in the lower net income, and by how much will the income be lower?

**Exercise 10-3.** Cosell Company acquired machinery with a 5-year life and no residual value for $80,000 on July 1, 1985. The machinery qualifies as a 5-year-class asset under ACRS. Determine the excess (or deficiency) of ACRS depreciation over straight-line depreciation for each of the years 1985–1990, applying the ACRS depreciation rate schedule presented in this chapter.

**Exercise 10-4.** Fox Corporation, which has never incurred a capital gain or loss, owns 1,000 shares of A Company stock purchased for $100,000 and 500 shares of B Company stock purchased for $250,000. Both stocks qualify as long-term capital assets and can be sold for $300,000 and $50,000, respectively. The Corporation expects to need $250,000 near the end of the current year but foresees no immediate need for additional cash. The long-term capital gains tax rate is 28%, and the Corporation's marginal tax rate is 46%.

(a) If the A Company stock were sold in the current year, determine the amount of tax that would be owed on the sale.

(b) If all of the stocks were sold before the end of the current year, determine the amount of tax that would be owed on the sales.

(c) Discuss why Fox Corporation should consider selling both stocks in the current year, even though only $250,000 is expected to be needed in the current year.

**Exercise 10-5.** During the current year, three corporations realized the following income:

|  | Ordinary Income | Long-Term Capital Gain |
|---|---|---|
| Corporation A . . . . . . . . . . . . . . . . . . . . . . . | $ 10,000 | $10,000 |
| Corporation B . . . . . . . . . . . . . . . . . . . . . . . | 20,000 | 30,000 |
| Corporation C . . . . . . . . . . . . . . . . . . . . . . . | 100,000 | 50,000 |

Using the tax rates indicated in the chapter, determine the amount of income tax owed by each corporation.

**Exercise 10-6.** A and B are considering the form of organization for their new business. Each will invest $300,000, will devote only part-time to the business, and will receive no salary. Income before tax is expected to be relatively constant at about $150,000 per year. The owners have 50% marginal income tax rates and are expected to make annual withdrawals (or receive dividends) equal to all of the net income (after tax, if applicable) from the business. (a) Determine the amount of cash that will be available to each owner, after taxes, if the business is organized as (1) a partnership (in which income is shared equally among the partners), (2) a corporation. (b) List some of the other factors that should be considered in evaluating the decision.

**Exercise 10-7.** Adams Company and Zimmer Company are investigating the acquisition of X Corporation, which has a $25,000 net operating loss carryforward that can be used by both companies. If Adams Company and Zimmer Company have marginal tax rates of 46% and 30% respectively, determine the value of X Corporation's net operating loss carryforward to (a) Adams Company and (b) Zimmer Company.

**Exercise 10-8.** Grant Company has 1,000 shares of ICD common stock, which it acquired 10 years ago at $50 per share. The current market price of the stock is $100, Grant Company's marginal tax rate is 46%, and the long-term capital gains maximum tax rate is 28%. (a) Determine the amount of proceeds available to the University of Illinois if (1) the stock is donated to the university and then sold, or (2) the stock is sold by Grant Company, the associated income tax paid, and the proceeds donated to the university. (b) Determine the tax benefits for Grant Company from the deduction of the charitable donation if it (1) donates the stock to the university or (2) sells the stock and donates the aftertax proceeds to the university.

---

**Problems**
*(Problems in Appendix B: 10-3B, 10-4B, 10-5B.)*

**Problem 10-1A.** Three married individuals, A, B, and C, are engaged in related types of businesses as sole proprietors, but plan to combine their enterprises to form Allen Co. They have discussed the relative merits of the partnership and the corporation forms of organization, exclusive of the effect of the federal income tax. You are engaged to assemble and analyze the relevant data and to determine the immediate income tax consequences to each of them of the two forms of organization. The consolidation is planned to take effect as of January 1, the beginning of the company's fiscal year.

The combined annual net income of the three separate enterprises has typically totaled $150,000. It is anticipated that economies of operation and other advantages of the consolidation will have the immediate effect of increasing annual net income by $30,000, making a total of $180,000 before deducting owners' salaries totaling $90,000.

Each of the owners is to be assigned managerial duties as a partner or, alternatively, be designated an officer of the corporation. In either event, each is to be paid an annual salary, which is to be treated as an operating expense of the enterprise. In addition, they plan to distribute $27,000 of earnings annually, which are to be allocated among them in accordance with their original investments (the income-sharing ratio). It is anticipated that the remaining earnings will be retained for use in expanding operations. The agreed capital investments, salaries, and distributions of earnings are to be as follows:

|  | A | B | C | Total |
|---|---|---|---|---|
| Capital investment | $150,000 | $200,000 | $150,000 | $500,000 |
| Salary | 27,000 | 36,000 | 27,000 | 90,000 |
| Distribution of earnings | 8,100 | 10,800 | 8,100 | 27,000 |

Dividends are fully taxable, and each owner files a joint return for the calendar year, prepared in accordance with the cash method. For each individual, the estimated taxable income from sources other than Allen Co. is as follows:

|   |   |
|---|---|
| A ..................... | $23,000 |
| B ..................... | 9,000 |
| C ..................... | 24,000 |

Instructions:

(1) Present the following reports of estimated results of the first year of operations, assuming that Allen Co. is to be organized as a partnership: (a) estimated capital statement of the partners of Allen Co. and (b) statement of estimated federal income tax of A, B, and C, applying the appropriate schedule of tax rates presented in this chapter.

(2) Present the following reports of estimated results of the first year of operations, based on the assumption that Allen Co. is to be organized as a corporation: (a) statement of estimated federal income tax of Allen Co., applying the corporation tax rates presented in this chapter; (b) estimated statement of stockholders' equity of each of the stockholders in Allen Co., allocating each increase and decrease in the manner employed in (1a) above; and (c) estimated federal income tax of A, B, and C, applying the appropriate schedule of tax rates presented in this chapter.

(3) Present a report comparing the estimated federal income tax effects of the two methods of organization on each of the three individuals. For purposes of this report, the income tax on the corporation should be allocated among the individuals as in (2b).

**Problem 10-2A.** Nancy Young, DDS, opened her dental office after graduation from dental school in early January of the current year. On December 30, the accounting records indicated the following for the current year to date:

|   | Total | Cash Received | Cash Paid |
|---|---|---|---|
| Fees earned............................. | $92,000 | $79,000 | — |
| Lease of dental office and equipment ....... | 24,000 | — | $22,000 |
| Dental assistant salary.................... | 18,000 | — | 16,500 |
| Dental supplies, utilities, etc. .............. | 9,000 | — | 7,400 |

Instructions:

(1) Determine the amount of net income Young would report from her dental practice for the current year under the (a) cash method and (b) accrual method.
(2) List the advantages of using the cash method rather than the accrual method in accounting for Young's dental practice.
(3) What is the principal advantage of using the accrual method rather than the cash method in accounting for Young's dental practice?

**Problem 10-3A.** Acme Limousine Sales sold 25 limousines for $22,500 each during the first year of operations. Data related to purchases during the year are as follows:

|   | Quantity | Unit Cost |
|---|---|---|
| January 3............... | 5 | $20,000 |
| April 10 ............... | 4 | 20,100 |
| June 30 ............... | 7 | 20,250 |
| August 22 ............. | 10 | 20,300 |
| November 5 ........... | 5 | 20,500 |

Sales of limousines are the company's only source of income, and operating expenses for the current year are $19,750.

Instructions:

(1) Determine the net income for the current year, using the fifo (first-in, first-out) inventory method.
(2) Determine the net income for the current year, using the lifo (last-in, first-out) inventory method.
(3) Which method of inventory costing, fifo or lifo, would you recommend for tax purposes? Discuss.

**Problem 10-4A.** Day Company began construction on three contracts during 1984. The contract prices and construction activities for 1984, 1985, and 1986 were as follows:

| | | 1984 | | 1985 | | 1986 | |
|---|---|---|---|---|---|---|---|
| Contract | Contract Price | Costs Incurred | Percent Completed | Costs Incurred | Percent Completed | Costs Incurred | Percent Completed |
| 1 | $ 5,000,000 | $1,780,000 | 40% | $1,550,000 | 35% | $1,062,400 | 25% |
| 2 | 10,000,000 | 2,550,000 | 30 | 2,625,000 | 30 | 2,695,000 | 30 |
| 3 | 3,600,000 | 1,495,500 | 50 | 1,555,500 | 50 | — | — |

Instructions:

(1) Determine the amount of income to be recognized in 1984, 1985, and 1986 by using (a) the percentage-of-completion method and (b) the completed-contract method. Present computations in good order.
(2) Would the total amount of income to be recognized by using the percentage-of-completion method for each contract be the same as the total amount recognized by using the completed-contract method?
(3) What is the principal advantage for tax purposes of using the completed-contract method of recognizing income from long-term contracts?

**Problem 10-5A.** The board of directors of Highland Inc. is planning an expansion of plant facilities expected to cost $2,000,000. The board is undecided about the method of financing this expansion and is considering two plans:

Plan 1. Issue 20,000 shares of $100, 8% cumulative preferred stock at par.
Plan 2. Issue $2,000,000 of 20-year, 12% bonds at face amount.

The condensed balance sheet of the corporation at the end of the most recent fiscal year is as follows:

Highland Inc.
Balance Sheet
December 31, 19--

| Assets | | Liabilities and Capital | |
|---|---|---|---|
| Current assets . . . . . . . . . . . . . | $1,400,000 | Current liabilities . . . . . . . . . . . | $1,140,000 |
| Plant assets. . . . . . . . . . . . . . . | 4,600,000 | Common stock, $25 par . . . . . | 2,500,000 |
| | | Premium on common stock. . . | 1,000,000 |
| | | Retained earnings . . . . . . . . . . | 1,360,000 |
| Total assets. . . . . . . . . . . . . . . | $6,000,000 | Total liabilities and capital. . . . | $6,000,000 |

Net income has remained relatively constant over the past several years. As a result of the expansion program, yearly income after tax but before bond interest and related income tax is expected to increase to $450,000.

Instructions:

(1) Prepare a tabulation indicating the net annual outlay (dividends and interest after tax) for financing under each plan. (Use the income tax rates indicated in the chapter.)

(2) Prepare a tabulation indicating the expected earnings per share on common stock under each plan.

(3) List factors other than the net cost of financing and earnings per share that the board should consider in evaluating the two plans.

**Mini-Case**

Your father recently signed a contract for the purchase of a vacation cottage on a nearby mountain lake. A $15,000 down payment is required by December 11, 1985. To raise the $15,000, your father is considering selling 150 of the 200 shares of CBC common stock that he acquired on July 19, 1985, at a total cost of $18,000.

Your father has asked your advice as to whether he should sell the stock or borrow the $15,000 for a maximum of 60 days at the current short-term interest rate of 12%. The stock is currently selling at $101 per share, and brokerage fees are expected to be $150 if the 150 shares are sold.

Instructions:

(1) If your father is in the 50% marginal tax bracket and 60% of long-term capital gains are exempt from taxable income, how much tax would be due if the stock is sold on December 11, 1985?

(2) What would you suggest that your father consider concerning the selling of the stock? Discuss. Assume that any interest paid is deductible in determining taxable income.

# 11

# Responsibility Accounting for Cost and Profit Centers

**CHAPTER OBJECTIVES**

*Describe the nature of decentralized operations and the special accounting needs of the management of such operations.*

*Describe and illustrate responsibility accounting for cost centers.*

*Describe and illustrate responsibility accounting for profit centers.*

# PART 5 Accounting for Decentralized Operations

# 11

**CHAPTER**

In a small business, virtually all plans and decisions can be made by one individual. As a business grows or its operations become more diverse, it becomes difficult, if not impossible, for one individual to perform these functions. For example, the responsibility for planning and controlling operations is clear in a one-person real estate agency. If the agency expands by opening an office in a distant city, some of the authority and responsibility for planning and decision making in a given area of operations might be delegated to others. In other words, if centralized operations become unwieldy as a business grows, the need to delegate responsibility for portions of operations arises. This separation of a business into more manageable units is termed decentralization. In a decentralized business, an important function of the managerial accountant is to assist individual managers in evaluating and controlling their areas of responsibility.

A term frequently applied to the process of measuring and reporting operating data by areas of responsibility is responsibility accounting. Some of the concepts useful in responsibility accounting were presented in preceding chapters. For example, in discussing budgetary control of operations, the use of the master budget, budgets for various departments, and budget performance reports in controlling operations by areas of responsibility were discussed. In this chapter, the concept of responsibility accounting as it relates to two types of decentralized operations is described and illustrated. A third type of decentralization is discussed in Chapter 12.

## CHARAC-TERISTICS OF DECEN-TRALIZED OPERATIONS

A completely centralized business organization is one in which all major planning and operating decisions are made by the top echelon of management. For example, a one-person, owner-manager-operated business is centralized because all plans and decisions are made by one person. In a small owner-manager-operated business, centralization may be desirable, since the owner-manager's close supervision ensures that the business will be operated in conformity with the manager's wishes and desires.

In a decentralized business organization, responsibility for planning and controlling operations is delegated among managers. These managers have the authority to make decisions without first seeking the approval of higher management. The level of decentralization varies significantly, and there is no one best level of decentralization for all businesses. In some companies, for example, plant managers have authority over all plant operations, including plant asset acquisitions and retirements. In other companies, a plant manager may only have authority for scheduling production and for controlling the costs of direct materials, direct labor, and factory overhead. The proper level of decentralization for a company depends on the advantages and disadvantages of decentralization as they apply to a company's specific, unique circumstances.

### Advantages of Decentralization

As a business grows, it becomes more difficult for top management to maintain close daily contact with all operations. Hence, a top management that delegates authority in such circumstances has a better chance of sound decisions being made, and the managers closest to the operations may anticipate and react to operating information more quickly. In addition, as a company diversifies into a wide range of products and services, it becomes more difficult for top management to maintain operating expertise in all product lines and services. In such cases, decentralization allows managers to concentrate on acquiring expertise in their areas of responsibility. For example, in a company that maintains diversified operations in oil refining, banking, and the manufacture of office equipment, individual managers could become "expert" in the area of their responsibility.

The delegation of responsibility for day-to-day operations from top management to middle management frees top management to concentrate more on strategic planning. Strategic planning is the process of establishing long-term goals for an enterprise and developing plans to achieve these goals. For example, a goal to expand an enterprise's product line into new markets and a plan to finance this expansion through the issuance of long-term debt rather than additional common stock are examples of strategic planning decisions. As the business environment becomes more complex and as companies grow, strategic planning assumes an increasingly important role in the long-run success of a company.

Decentralized decision making provides excellent training for managers, which may be a factor in enabling a company to retain quality managers. Since the art of management can best be acquired through experience, the delegation of responsibility enables managers to acquire and develop managerial expertise early in their careers. Also, the operating personnel may be more creative in suggesting operating improvements, since personnel in a decentralized company tend to identify closely with the operations for which they are responsible.

The delegation of responsibility also serves as a positive reinforcement for managers, in that they may view such delegation as an indication of top management's confidence in their abilities. Thus, manager morale tends to increase because managers feel that they have more control over factors affecting their careers and their performance evaluation.

**Disadvantages of Decentralization**

The primary disadvantage of decentralized operations is that decisions made by one manager may affect other managers in such a way that the profitability of the entire company may suffer. For example, two managers competing in a common product market may engage in price cutting to win customers. However, the overall company profits are less than the profits that could have been if the price cutting had not occurred.

Other potential disadvantages of decentralized operations may be the duplication of various assets and costs in the operating divisions. For example, each manager of a product line might have a separate sales force and administrative office staff, but centralization of these personnel could save money. Likewise, the costs of gathering and processing operating information in a decentralized operation might be greater than if such information were gathered and processed centrally.

**TYPES OF DE-CENTRALIZED OPERATIONS**

Decentralized operations can be classified by the scope of responsibility assigned and the decision making authority given to individual managers. The three common types of decentralized operations are referred to as cost centers, profit centers, and investment centers. Each of these types of decentralized operations is briefly described in the following paragraphs. Responsibility accounting for cost centers and profit centers is then discussed and illustrated in the remainder of this chapter, while responsibility accounting for investment centers is discussed in Chapter 12.

Cost
Centers

In a cost center, the responsibility for the control of costs incurred and the authority to make decisions that affect these costs is the responsibility of the department or division manager. For example, the marketing manager has responsibility for the costs of the Marketing Department, and the supervisor of the Power Department has responsibility for the costs incurred in providing power. The department manager does not make decisions concerning sales of the cost center's output, nor does the department manager have control over the plant assets available to the cost center.

Cost centers are the most widely used type of decentralization, because the organization and operation of most businesses allow for an easy identification of areas where managers can be assigned responsibility for and authority over costs. Cost centers may vary in size from a small department with a few employees to an entire plant. In addition, cost centers may exist within other cost centers. For example, a manager of a manufacturing plant organized as a cost center may treat individual departments within the plant as separate cost centers, with the department managers reporting directly to the plant manager.

Profit
Centers

In a profit center, the manager has the responsibility and the authority to make decisions that affect both costs and revenues (and thus profits) for the department or division. For example, a retail department store might decentralize its operations by product line. The manager of each product line would have responsibility for the cost of merchandise and decisions regarding revenues, such as the determination of sales prices. The manager of a profit center does not make decisions concerning the plant assets available to the center. For example, the manager of the Sporting Goods Department does not make the decision to expand the available floor space for that department.

Profit centers are widely used in businesses in which individual departments or divisions sell products or services to those outside the company. A partial organization chart for a department store decentralized by retail departments as profit centers is shown at the top of page 246.

Occasionally, profit centers are established when the center's product or service is consumed entirely within the company. For example, a Repairs and Maintenance Department of a manufacturing plant could be treated as a profit center if its manager were allowed to bill other departments, such as the various production departments, for services rendered. Likewise, the Data Processing Department of a company might bill each of the company's administrative and operating units for computing services.

In a sense, a profit center may be viewed as a business within a business. While the primary concern of a cost center manager is the control of costs, the profit center manager is concerned with both revenues and costs.

PARTIAL ORGANIZATION
CHART FOR
DEPARTMENT STORE
WITH PROFIT CENTERS

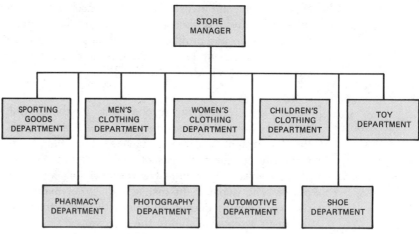

## Investment Centers

In an **investment center,** the manager has the responsibility and the authority to make decisions that affect not only costs and revenues, but also the plant assets available to the center. The plant manager sets selling prices of products and establishes controls over costs. In addition, the plant manager could, within general constraints established by top management, expand production facilities through equipment acquisitions and retirements.

The manager of an investment center has more authority and responsibility than the manager of either a cost center or a profit center. The manager of an investment center occupies a position similar to that of a chief operating officer or president of a separate company. As such, an investment center manager is evaluated in much the same way as a manager of a separate company is evaluated.

Investment centers are widely used in highly diversified companies. A partial organization chart for a diversified company with divisions organized as investment centers is as follows:

PARTIAL ORGANIZATION
CHART FOR DIVERSIFIED
COMPANY WITH
INVESTMENT CENTERS

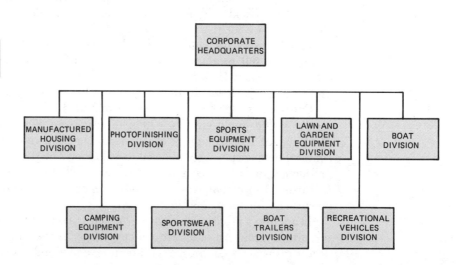

RESPONSIBILITY
ACCOUNTING
FOR COST
CENTERS

Since managers of cost centers have responsibility for and authority to make decisions regarding costs, responsibility accounting for cost centers focuses on costs. The primary accounting tools appropriate for controlling and reporting costs are budgets and standard costs. Since budgets and standard costs were described and illustrated in Chapters 4 and 5, they will not be discussed in detail in this chapter. Instead, responsibility accounting for a cost center which uses budgeting to assist in the control of costs will be illustrated. The basic concepts of responsibility accounting, as illustrated, are equally applicable to cost centers that use standard cost systems to aid in cost control.

For purposes of illustration, assume that the responsibility for the manufacturing operations of an enterprise is as represented in the following organization chart:

ORGANIZATION
CHART DEPICTING
MANAGEMENT
RESPONSIBILITY
FOR PRODUCTION

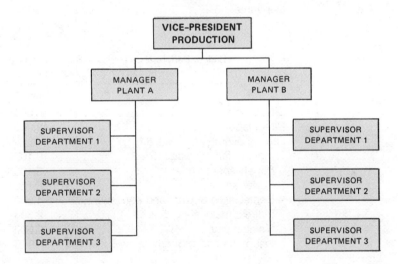

Also assume that there are three levels of cost centers within the organizational structure. At the operating level, each department is a cost center, with the department supervisors responsible for controlling costs within their departments. At the next level of the organization, each plant is a cost center, with each plant manager responsible for controlling plant administrative costs as well as supervising the control of costs in the plant departments. Finally, at the top level, the office of the vice-president of production is a cost center with responsibility for controlling the administrative costs of the office as well as supervising the control of costs in each plant.

Management reports aid each level of management in carrying out its assigned responsibilities for the control of costs. To illustrate, the following budget performance reports are part of a responsibility accounting system for the enterprise:

Budget Performance Report—Vice-President, Production
For Month Ended October 31, 19--

|  | Budget | Actual | Over | Under |
|---|---|---|---|---|
| Administration........................ | $ 19,500 | $ 19,700 | $ 200 | |
| Plant A ............................. | 467,475 | 470,330 | 2,855 | |
| Plant B ............................ | 395,225 | 394,300 | | $925 |
| | $882,200 | $884,330 | $3,055 | $925 |

Budget Performance Report—Manager, Plant A
For Month Ended October 31, 19--

|  | Budget | Actual | Over | Under |
|---|---|---|---|---|
| Administration........................ | $ 17,500 | $ 17,350 | | $150 |
| Department 1 ........................ | 109,725 | 111,280 | $1,555 | |
| Department 2 ........................ | 190,500 | 192,600 | 2,100 | |
| Department 3 ........................ | 149,750 | 149,100 | | 650 |
| | $467,475 | $470,330 | $3,655 | $800 |

Budget Performance Report—Supervisor, Department 1-Plant A
For Month Ended October 31, 19--

|  | Budget | Actual | Over | Under |
|---|---|---|---|---|
| Direct materials...................... | $ 30,000 | $ 31,700 | $1,700 | |
| Direct labor ........................ | 48,000 | 47,750 | | $250 |
| Factory overhead: | | | | |
|   Indirect factory wages.............. | 10,100 | 10,250 | 150 | |
|   Supervisory salaries................ | 6,400 | 6,400 | | |
|   Power and light.................... | 5,750 | 5,690 | | 60 |
|   Depreciation of plant and equipment... | 4,000 | 4,000 | | |
|   Indirect materials ................. | 2,500 | 2,525 | 25 | |
|   Maintenance ...................... | 2,000 | 1,990 | | 10 |
|   Insurance and property taxes ....... | 975 | 975 | | |
| | $109,725 | $111,280 | $1,875 | $320 |

The amount of detail presented in the budget performance report depends upon the level of management to which the report is directed. The reports prepared for the department supervisors present details of the budgeted and actual manufacturing costs for their departments. Each supervisor can then concentrate on the individual items that resulted in significant variations. In the illustration, the budget performance report for Department 1-Plant A indicates a significant variation between the budget and actual amounts for direct materials. It is clear that supplemental reports providing detailed data on the causes of the variation would aid the supervisor in taking corrective action. One such report, a scrap report, is illustrated as follows. This report indicates the cause of a significant part of the variation.

SCRAP
REPORT

| Material No. | Units Spoiled | Unit Cost | Dollar Loss | Remarks |
|---|---|---|---|---|
| A392 | 50 | $3.10 | $ 155.00 | Machine malfunction |
| C417 | 76 | .80 | 60.80 | Inexperienced employee |
| G118 | 5 | 1.10 | 5.50 | |
| J510 | 120 | 8.25 | 990.00 | Substandard materials |
| K277 | 2 | 1.50 | 3.00 | |
| P719 | 7 | 2.10 | 14.70 | |
| V112 | 22 | 4.25 | 93.50 | Machine malfunction |
| | | | $1,322.50 | |

Direct Materials Scrap Report—Department 1-Plant A
For Month Ended October 31, 19--

The scrap report is one example of the type of supplemental report that can be provided to department supervisors. Other examples would include reports on direct labor rate variance, direct labor usage variance, and cost of idle time.

The budget performance reports for the plant managers contain summarized data on the budgeted and actual costs for the departments under their jurisdiction. These reports enable them to identify the department supervisors responsible for significant variances. The report for the vice-president in charge of production summarizes the data by plant so that the persons responsible for plant operations can be held accountable for significant variations from predetermined objectives.

RESPONSIBILITY ACCOUNTING FOR PROFIT CENTERS

Since managers of profit centers have responsibility for and authority to make decisions regarding costs and revenues, responsibility accounting reports for profit centers are normally in the form of income statements. These income statements for individual profit centers report costs and revenues by departments through either gross profit or operating income. Alternatively, profit center income statements may include a breakdown of revenues and expenses by responsibility for their incurrence, and may identify contributions made by each department to overall company profit.

Since profit centers are widely used by merchandising enterprises, such as department stores, a merchandising enterprise is used as the basis for the following discussion and illustration of responsibility accounting for profit centers. Although the degree to which profit centers are used by a merchandising enterprise varies, profit centers are typically established for each major retail department. The enterprise in the illustrations, Garrison Company, has established Departments A and B as profit centers.

Gross Profit by Departments

To compute gross profit by departments, it is necessary to determine by departments each element entering into gross profit. An income statement showing gross profit by departments for Garrison Company appears on page 250. For illustrative purposes, the operating expenses are shown in condensed form. Usually they would be listed in detail.

**Garrison Company**
**Income Statement**
**For Year Ended December 31, 19--**

| | Department A | | | Department B | | | Total | | |
|---|---:|---:|---:|---:|---:|---:|---:|---:|---:|
| Revenue from sales: | | | | | | | | | |
| Sales | | $630,000 | | | $270,000 | | | $900,000 | |
| Less sales returns and allowances | | 15,300 | | | 7,100 | | | 22,400 | |
| Net sales | | | $614,700 | | | $262,900 | | | $877,600 |
| Cost of merchandise sold: | | | | | | | | | |
| Merchandise inventory, January 1, 19-- | | $ 80,150 | | | $ 61,750 | | | $141,900 | |
| Purchases | $334,550 | | | $200,350 | | | $534,900 | | |
| Less purchases discount | 6,200 | | | 2,400 | | | 8,600 | | |
| | | 328,350 | | | 197,950 | | | 526,300 | |
| Merchandise available for sale | | $408,500 | | | $259,700 | | | $668,200 | |
| Less merchandise inventory, December 31, 19-- | | 85,150 | | | 78,950 | | | 164,100 | |
| Cost of merchandise sold | | | 323,350 | | | 180,750 | | | 504,100 |
| Gross profit | | | $291,350 | | | $ 82,150 | | | $373,500 |
| Operating expenses: | | | | | | | | | |
| Selling expenses | | | | | | | | $113,000 | |
| General expenses | | | | | | | | 110,200 | |
| Total operating expenses | | | | | | | | | 223,200 |
| Income from operations | | | | | | | | | $150,300 |
| Other expense: | | | | | | | | | |
| Interest expense | | | | | | | | | 2,500 |
| Income before income tax | | | | | | | | | $147,800 |
| Income tax | | | | | | | | | 64,444 |
| Net income | | | | | | | | | $ 83,356 |

INCOME STATEMENT DEPARTMENTALIZED THROUGH GROSS PROFIT

For a merchandising enterprise, the gross profit is one of the most significant figures in the income statement. Since the sales and the cost of merchandise sold are both controlled by departmental management, the reporting of gross profit by departments is useful in cost analysis and control. In addition, such reports aid management in directing its efforts toward obtaining a mix of sales that will maximize profits. For example, after studying the reports, management may decide to change sales or purchases policies to achieve a higher gross profit for each department. Caution must be exercised in the use of such reports to insure that proposed changes affecting gross profit do not have an adverse effect on net income. A change that increases gross profit could result in an even greater increase in operating expenses and thereby decrease net income.

**Operating Income by Departments**

Departmental reporting may be extended to operating income. In such cases, each department must be assigned not only the related revenues and the cost of merchandise sold (as in the preceding illustration), but also that part of operating expenses incurred for its benefit. Some of these expenses may be easily identified with the department benefited. For example, if each salesperson is restricted to a certain sales department, the sales salaries may be assigned to the proper departmental salary accounts each time the payroll is prepared. On the other hand, the salaries of company officers, executives, and office personnel are not identifiable with specific sales departments and must therefore be allocated if an equitable and reasonable basis for allocation exists.

When operating expenses are allocated, they should be apportioned to the respective departments as nearly as possible in accordance with the cost of services rendered to them. Determining the amount of an expense chargeable to each department is not always a simple matter. In the first place, it requires the exercise of judgment; and accountants of equal ability may well differ in their opinions as to the proper basis for the apportionment of operating expenses. Second, the cost of collecting data for use in making an apportionment must be kept within reasonable bounds. Consequently, information that is readily available and is substantially reliable may be used instead of more accurate information that would be more costly to collect.

To illustrate the apportionment of operating expenses, assume that Garrison Company extends its departmental reporting through income from operations. The company's operating expenses for the calendar year and the methods used in apportioning them are presented in the paragraphs that follow.

**Sales Salaries Expense** is apportioned to the two departments according to the distributions shown in the payroll records. Of the $84,900 total in the account, $54,000 is chargeable to Department A and $30,900 is chargeable to Department B.

**Advertising Expense,** covering billboard advertising and newspaper advertising, is apportioned according to the amount of advertising incurred for each department. The billboard advertising totaling $5,000 emphasizes the name and the location of the company. This expense is allocated on the basis of sales, the assumption being that this basis represents a fair allocation of billboard advertising to each department. Analysis of the newspaper space costing $14,000 indicates that 65% of the space was devoted to Department A and 35% to Department B. The computations of the apportionment of the total advertising expense are as follows:

|  | Total | Department A | Department B |
|---|---|---|---|
| Sales — dollars | $900,000 | $630,000 | $270,000 |
| Sales — percent | 100% | 70% | 30% |
| Billboard advertising | $ 5,000 | $ 3,500 | $ 1,500 |
| Newspaper space — percent | 100% | 65% | 35% |
| Newspaper advertising | 14,000 | 9,100 | 4,900 |
| Advertising expense | $19,000 | $12,600 | $ 6,400 |

**Depreciation Expense — Store Equipment** is apportioned according to the average cost of the equipment in each of the two departments. The computations for the apportionment of the depreciation expense are as follows:

|  | Total | Department A | Department B |
|---|---|---|---|
| Cost of store equipment: |  |  |  |
| January 1 | $28,300 | $16,400 | $11,900 |
| December 31 | 31,700 | 19,600 | 12,100 |
| Total | $60,000 | $36,000 | $24,000 |
| Average | $30,000 | $18,000 | $12,000 |
| Percent | 100% | 60% | 40% |
| Depreciation expense | $ 4,400 | $ 2,640 | $ 1,760 |

**Officers' Salaries Expense** and **Office Salaries Expense** are apportioned on the basis of the relative amount of time devoted to each department by the officers and by the office personnel. Obviously, this can be only an approximation. The number of sales transactions may have some bearing on the matter, as may billing and collection procedures and other factors such as promotional campaigns that might vary from period to period. Of the total officers' salaries of $52,000 and office salaries of $17,600, it is estimated that 60%, or $31,200 and $10,560 respectively, is chargeable to Department A and that 40%, or $20,800 and $7,040 respectively, is chargeable to Department B.

**Rent Expense** and **Heating and Lighting Expense** are usually apportioned on the basis of the floor space devoted to each department. In apportioning rent expense for a multistory building, differences in the value of the various floors and locations may be taken into account. For example, the space near the main entrance of a department store is more valuable than the same amount of floor space located far from the elevator on the sixth floor. For Garrison Company, rent expense is apportioned on the basis of floor space used because there is no significant difference in the value of the floor areas used by each department. In allocating heating and lighting expense, it is assumed that the number of lights, their wattage, and the extent of use are uniform throughout the sales departments. If there are major variations and the total lighting expense is material, further analysis and separate apportionment may be advisable. The rent expense and the heating and lighting expense are apportioned as follows:

| | Total | Department A | Department B |
|---|---|---|---|
| Floor space, square feet | 160,000 | 104,000 | 56,000 |
| Percent | 100% | 65% | 35% |
| Rent expense | $15,400 | $10,010 | $ 5,390 |
| Heating and lighting expense | $ 5,100 | $ 3,315 | $ 1,785 |

**Property Tax Expense** and **Insurance Expense** are related primarily to the cost of the merchandise inventory and the store equipment. Although the cost of these assets may differ from their assessed value for tax purposes and their value for insurance purposes, the cost is most readily available and is considered to be satisfactory as a basis for apportioning these expenses. The computations of the apportionment of the personal property tax expense and the insurance expense are as follows:

| | Total | Department A | Department B |
|---|---|---|---|
| Merchandise inventory: | | | |
| January 1 | $141,900 | $ 80,150 | $ 61,750 |
| December 31 | 164,100 | 85,150 | 78,950 |
| Total | $306,000 | $165,300 | $140,700 |
| Average | $153,000 | $ 82,650 | $ 70,350 |
| Average cost of store equipment (computed previously) | 30,000 | 18,000 | 12,000 |
| Total | $183,000 | $100,650 | $ 82,350 |
| Percent | 100% | 55% | 45% |
| Property tax expense | $ 6,800 | $ 3,740 | $ 3,060 |
| Insurance expense | $ 3,900 | $ 2,145 | $ 1,755 |

**Uncollectible Accounts Expense, Miscellaneous Selling Expense,** and **Miscellaneous General Expense** are apportioned on the basis of sales. Although the uncollectible accounts expense may be apportioned on the basis of an analysis of accounts receivable written off, it is assumed that the expense is closely related to sales. The miscellaneous selling and general expenses are apportioned on the basis of sales, which are assumed to be a reasonable measure of the benefit to each department. The computation of the apportionment is as follows:

| | Total | Department A | Department B |
|---|---|---|---|
| Sales | $900,000 | $630,000 | $270,000 |
| Percent | 100% | 70% | 30% |
| Uncollectible accounts expense | $ 4,600 | $ 3,220 | $ 1,380 |
| Miscellaneous selling expense | $ 4,700 | $ 3,290 | $ 1,410 |
| Miscellaneous general expense | $ 4,800 | $ 3,360 | $ 1,440 |

An income statement presenting income from operations by departments for Garrison Company appears on the following page. The amounts for sales and cost of merchandise sold are presented in condensed form. Details could be reported, if desired, in the manner illustrated on page 250.

Garrison Company
Income Statement
For Year Ended December 31, 19--

| | Department A | | Department B | | Total | |
|---|---|---|---|---|---|---|
| Net sales | | $614,700 | | $262,900 | | $877,600 |
| Cost of merchandise sold | | 323,350 | | 180,750 | | 504,100 |
| Gross profit | | $291,350 | | $ 82,150 | | $373,500 |
| Operating expenses: | | | | | | |
| Selling expenses: | | | | | | |
|   Sales salaries expense | $ 54,000 | | $ 30,900 | | $ 84,900 | |
|   Advertising expense | 12,600 | | 6,400 | | 19,000 | |
|   Depreciation expense—store equipment | 2,640 | | 1,760 | | 4,400 | |
|   Miscellaneous selling expense | 3,290 | | 1,410 | | 4,700 | |
|   Total selling expenses | | $ 72,530 | | $ 40,470 | | $113,000 |
| General expenses: | | | | | | |
|   Officers' salaries expense | $ 31,200 | | $ 20,800 | | $ 52,000 | |
|   Office salaries expense | 10,560 | | 7,040 | | 17,600 | |
|   Rent expense | 10,010 | | 5,390 | | 15,400 | |
|   Property tax expense | 3,740 | | 3,060 | | 6,800 | |
|   Heating and lighting expense | 3,315 | | 1,785 | | 5,100 | |
|   Uncollectible accounts expense | 3,220 | | 1,380 | | 4,600 | |
|   Insurance expense | 2,145 | | 1,755 | | 3,900 | |
|   Miscellaneous general expense | 3,360 | | 1,440 | | 4,800 | |
|   Total general expenses | | 67,550 | | 42,650 | | 110,200 |
| Total operating expenses | | 140,080 | | 83,120 | | 223,200 |
| Income (loss) from operations | | $151,270 | | $ (970) | | $150,300 |
| Other expense: | | | | | | |
|   Interest expense | | | | | | 2,500 |
| Income before income tax | | | | | | $147,800 |
| Income tax | | | | | | 64,444 |
| Net income | | | | | | $ 83,356 |

INCOME STATEMENT DEPARTMENTALIZED THROUGH INCOME FROM OPERATIONS

Departmental
Margin

Not all accountants agree as to the merits of the type of responsibility accounting reports for profit centers (departments) discussed in the preceding section. In relying on income statements departmentalized through income from operations, caution should be used, since the use of arbitrary bases in allocating operating expenses is likely to yield incorrect amounts of departmental operating income. In addition, the reporting of operating income by departments may be misleading, since the departments are not independent operating units. The departments are segments of a business enterprise, and no single department of a business can earn an income independently. For these reasons, income statements of segmented businesses may follow a somewhat different format than the one illustrated on page 254. The alternative format emphasizes the contribution of each department to overall company net income and to covering the overall operating expenses incurred on behalf of the business. Income statements prepared in this alternative format are said to follow the departmental margin or contribution margin approach to responsibility accounting.

Prior to the preparation of an income statement in the departmental margin format, it is necessary to differentiate between operating expenses that are direct and those that are indirect. The two categories may be described in general terms as follows:

Direct expense — Operating expenses directly traceable to or incurred for the sole benefit of a specific department and usually subject to the control of the department manager.
Indirect expense — Operating expenses incurred for the entire enterprise as a unit and hence not subject to the control of individual department managers.

The details of departmental sales and the cost of merchandise sold are presented on the income statement in the usual manner. The direct expenses of each department are then deducted from the related departmental gross profit, yielding balances which are identified as **departmental margin**. The remaining expenses, including the indirect operating expenses, are not departmentalized. They are reported singly below the total departmental margin.

An income statement in the departmental margin format for the Garrison Company is presented on the following page. The basic revenue, cost, and expense data for the period are identical with those reported in the earlier illustration. The expenses identified as "direct" are sales salaries, property tax, uncollectible accounts, insurance, depreciation, and the newspaper advertising portion of advertising. The billboard portion of advertising, which is for the benefit of the business as a whole, as well as officers' and office salaries, and the remaining operating expenses, are identified as "indirect." Although a $970 net loss from operations is reported for Department B on page 254, a departmental margin of $38,395 is reported for the same department on the statement on page 256.

With departmental margin income statements, the manager of each department can be held responsible for operating expenses traceable to the department. A reduction in the direct expenses of a department will have a favorable effect on that department's contribution to the net income of the enterprise.

The departmental margin income statement may also be useful to management in making plans for future operations. For example, this type of analysis can be

**Garrison Company**
**Income Statement**
**For Year Ended December 31, 19--**

| | Department A | | Department B | | Total | |
|---|---|---|---|---|---|---|
| Net sales . . . . . . . . . . | . . . . . . . . | $614,700 | . . . . . . . . | $262,900 | . . . . . . . . | $877,600 |
| Cost of merchandise sold . . . . . . . . . . . . . | . . . . . . . . | 323,350 | . . . . . . . . | 180,750 | . . . . . . . . | 504,100 |
| Gross profit . . . . . . . . . | . . . . . . . . | $291,350 | . . . . . . . . | $ 82,150 | . . . . . . . . | $373,500 |
| Direct departmental expenses: | | | | | | |
| Sales salaries expense . . . . . . . . . . | $54,000 | . . . . . . . . | $30,900 | . . . . . . . . | $84,900 | . . . . . . . . |
| Advertising expense . . | 9,100 | . . . . . . . . | 4,900 | . . . . . . . . | 14,000 | . . . . . . . . |
| Property tax expense . . . . . . . . . . . | 3,740 | . . . . . . . . | 3,060 | . . . . . . . . | 6,800 | . . . . . . . . |
| Uncollectible accounts expense . . . . . . . . . . | 3,220 | . . . . . . . . | 1,380 | . . . . . . . . | 4,600 | . . . . . . . . |
| Depreciation expense — store equipment . . . . . . . . | 2,640 | . . . . . . . . | 1,760 | . . . . . . . . | 4,400 | . . . . . . . . |
| Insurance expense . . | 2,145 | . . . . . . . . | 1,755 | . . . . . . . . | 3,900 | . . . . . . . . |
| Total direct departmental expenses . . | . . . . . . . . | 74,845 | . . . . . . . . | 43,755 | . . . . . . . . | 118,600 |
| Departmental margin . . | . . . . . . . . | $216,505 | . . . . . . . . | $ 38,395 | . . . . . . . . | $254,900 |
| Indirect expenses: | | | | | | |
| Officers' salaries expense . . . . . . . . . . . . | | | | | $52,000 | . . . . . . . . |
| Office salaries expense . . . . . . . . . . . . | | | | | 17,600 | . . . . . . . . |
| Rent expense . . . . . . . | | | | | 15,400 | . . . . . . . . |
| Heating and lighting expense . . . . . . . . . . | | | | | 5,100 | . . . . . . . . |
| Advertising expense . . | | | | | 5,000 | . . . . . . . . |
| Miscellaneous selling expense . . . . . . . . . . | | | | | 4,700 | . . . . . . . . |
| Miscellaneous general expense . . . . . . . . . . | | | | | 4,800 | . . . . . . . . |
| Total indirect expenses . . . . . . . . . . . | | | | | . . . . . . . . | 104,600 |
| Income from operations . . . . . . . . . . . . . | | | | | . . . . . . . . | $150,300 |
| Other expense: Interest expense . . . . . | | | | | . . . . . . . . | 2,500 |
| Income before income tax . . . . . . . . . . . . | | | | | . . . . . . . . | $147,800 |
| Income tax . . . . . . . . . . | | | | | . . . . . . . . | 64,444 |
| Net income . . . . . . . . . . | . . . . . . . . | . . . . . . . . | . . . . . . . . | . . . . . . . . | . . . . . . . . | $ 83,356 |

used when the discontinuance of a certain operation or department is being considered. If a specific department yields a departmental margin, it generally should be retained, even though the allocation of the indirect operating expenses would result in a net loss for that department. This observation is based upon the assumption that the department in question represents a relatively small segment of the enterprise. Its termination, therefore, would not cause any significant reduction in the amount of indirect expenses.

To illustrate the application of the departmental margin approach to long-range planning, assume that a business occupies a rented three-story building. If the enterprise is divided into twenty departments, each occupying about the same amount of space, termination of the least profitable department would probably not cause any reduction in rent or other occupancy expenses. The space vacated would probably be absorbed by the remaining nineteen departments. On the other hand, if the enterprise were divided into three departments, each occupying approximately equal areas, the discontinuance of one could result in vacating an entire floor and significantly reducing occupancy expenses. When the departmental margin analysis is applied to problems of this type, consideration should be given to proposals for the use of the vacated space.

To further illustrate the departmental margin approach, assume that an enterprise with six departments has earned $70,000 before income tax during the past year, which is fairly typical of recent operations. Assume also that recent income statements, in which all operating expenses are allocated, indicate that Department F has been incurring losses, the net loss having amounted to $5,000 for the past year. Departmental margin analysis shows that, in spite of the losses, Department F should not be discontinued unless there is enough assurance that a proportionate increase in the gross profit of other departments or a decrease in indirect expenses can be effected. The following analysis, which is considerably condensed, shows a possible reduction of $10,000 in net income (the amount of the departmental margin for Department F) if Department F is discontinued.

|  | Proposal to Discontinue Department F January 25, 19-- | | | |
|---|---|---|---|---|
|  | Current Operations | | | Discontinuance of Department F |
|  | Department F | Departments A–E | Total | |
| Sales............................ | $100,000 | $900,000 | $1,000,000 | $900,000 |
| Cost of merchandise sold ...... | 70,000 | 540,000 | 610,000 | 540,000 |
| Gross profit................... | $ 30,000 | $360,000 | $ 390,000 | $360,000 |
| Direct departmental expenses ... | 20,000 | 210,000 | 230,000 | 210,000 |
| Departmental margin .......... | $ 10,000 | $150,000 | $ 160,000 | $150,000 |
| Indirect expenses ............. |  |  | 90,000 | 90,000 |
| Income before income tax...... |  |  | $ 70,000 | $ 60,000 |

DEPARTMENTAL ANALYSIS— DISCONTINUANCE OF UNPROFITABLE DEPARTMENT

In addition to departmental margin analysis, there are other factors that may need to be considered. For example, there may be problems regarding the displacement of sales personnel. Or customers attracted by the least profitable department may make large purchases in other departments, so that discontinuance of that department may adversely affect the sales of other departments.

The foregoing discussion of departmental income statements has suggested various ways in which income data may be made useful to management in making important policy decisions. Note that the format selected for the presentation of income data to management must be that which will be most useful for evaluating, controlling, and planning departmental operations.

**Self-Examination Questions**
*(Answers in Appendix C.)*

1. When the manager has the responsibility for and authority to make decisions that affect costs and revenues, but no responsibility for or authority over assets invested in the department, the department is referred to as:
   A. a cost center
   B. a profit center
   C. an investment center
   D. none of the above

2. Which of the following would be the most appropriate basis for allocating rent expense for use in arriving at operating income by departments?
   A. Departmental sales
   B. Physical space occupied
   C. Cost of inventory
   D. Time devoted to departments

3. The term used to describe the excess of departmental gross profit over direct departmental expenses is:
   A. income from operations
   B. net income
   C. departmental margin
   D. none of the above

4. On an income statement departmentalized through departmental margin, sales commissions expense would be reported as:
   A. a direct expense
   B. an indirect expense
   C. an other expense
   D. none of the above

5. On an income statement departmentalized through departmental margin, office salaries would be reported as:
   A. a direct expense
   B. an indirect expense
   C. an other expense
   D. none of the above

**Discussion Questions**

1. What is responsibility accounting?

2. What is a decentralized business organization?

3. Name three common types of responsibility centers for decentralized operations.

4. Differentiate between a cost center and a profit center.

5. Differentiate between a profit center and an investment center.

6. In what major respect would budget performance reports prepared for the use of plant managers of a manufacturing enterprise with cost centers differ from those prepared for the use of the various department supervisors who report to the plant managers?

7. The newly appointed manager of the Appliance Department in a department store is studying the income statements presenting gross profit by departments in an attempt to adjust operations to achieve the highest possible gross profit for the department. (a) Suggest ways in which an income statement departmentalized through gross profit can be used in achieving this goal. (b) Suggest reasons why caution must be exercised in using such statements.

8. Describe the underlying principle of apportionment of operating expenses to departments for income statements departmentalized through income from operations.

9. For each of the following types of expenses, select the allocation basis listed that is most appropriate for use in arriving at operating income by departments.

| Expense: | Basis of allocation: |
|---|---|
| (a) Property tax expense | (1) Cost of inventory and equipment |
| (b) Sales salaries | (2) Departmental sales |
| (c) Rent expense | (3) Time devoted to departments |
| (d) Advertising expense | (4) Physical space occupied |

10. Describe an appropriate basis for apportioning Officers' Salaries Expense among departments for purposes of the income statement departmentalized through income from operations.

11. Differentiate between a direct and an indirect operating expense.

12. Indicate whether each of the following operating expenses incurred by a department store is a direct or an indirect expense:
(a) Uncollectible accounts expense   (d) Insurance expense
(b) General manager's salary          (e) Sales commissions
(c) Depreciation of store equipment   (f) Heating and lighting expense

13. What term is applied to the dollar amount representing the excess of departmental gross profit over direct departmental expenses?

14. Recent income statements departmentalized through income from operations report operating losses for Department 19, a relatively minor segment of the business. Management studies indicate that discontinuance of Department 19 would not affect sales of other departments or the volume of indirect expenses. Under what circumstances would the discontinuance of Department 19 result in a decrease of net income of the enterprise?

15. A portion of an income statement in condensed form, departmentalized through departmental margin for the year just ended, is as follows:

|  | Department E |
|---|---|
| Net sales | $112,300 |
| Cost of merchandise sold | 89,840 |
| Gross profit | $ 22,460 |
| Direct expenses | 31,500 |
| Departmental margin | $ (9,040) |

It is believed that the discontinuance of Department E would not affect the sales of the other departments nor reduce the indirect expenses of the enterprise. Based on this information, what would have been the effect on the income from operations of the enterprise if Department E had been discontinued prior to the year just ended?

**Exercises**

**Exercise 11-1.** The budget for Department A of Plant 2 for the current month ended June 30 is as follows:

| | |
|---|---:|
| Direct materials | $ 95,000 |
| Direct labor | 120,000 |
| Power and light | 42,500 |
| Supervisory salaries | 30,000 |
| Indirect materials | 27,500 |
| Indirect factory wages | 20,000 |
| Depreciation of plant and equipment | 17,750 |
| Maintenance | 15,250 |
| Insurance and property taxes | 10,000 |

During June, the costs incurred in Department A of Plant 2 were: direct materials, $95,400; direct labor, $120,600; power and light, $43,000; supervisory salaries, $30,000; indirect materials, $27,200; indirect factory wages, $20,000; depreciation of plant and equipment, $17,750; maintenance, $19,750; insurance and property taxes, $10,000. (a) Prepare a budget performance report for the supervisor of Department A, Plant 2, for the month of June. (b) For what significant variations might the supervisor be expected to request supplemental reports?

**Exercise 11-2.** The chief accountant of Emerson Company prepares weekly reports of idleness of direct labor employees. These reports for the plant manager classify the idle time by departments. Idle time data for the week ended March 20 of the current year are as follows:

| Department | Standard Hours | Productive Hours |
|:---:|:---:|:---:|
| 1 | 4,200 | 3,990 |
| 2 | 2,800 | 2,800 |
| 3 | 6,100 | 5,978 |
| 4 | 1,900 | 1,786 |

The hourly direct labor rates are $18.60, $14.00, $16.50, and $15.50 respectively for Departments 1 through 4. The idleness was caused by a machine breakdown in Department 1, a materials shortage in Department 3, and a lack of sales orders in Department 4. Prepare an idle time report, classified by departments, for the week ended March 20. Use the following columnar headings for the report:

| | Production | | | Idle Time | | |
|---|---|---|---|---|---|---|
| Dept. | Standard Hours | Actual Hours | Percentage of Standard | Hours | Cost of Idle Time | Remarks |

**Exercise 11-3.** C. J. Lubin Company occupies a two-story building. The departments and the floor space occupied by each are as follows:

Receiving and Storage........ basement ......... 4,000 sq. ft.
Department 1 ............... basement ......... 6,000 sq. ft.
Department 2 ............... first floor .......... 3,200 sq. ft.
Department 3 ............... first floor .......... 8,000 sq. ft.
Department 4 ............... first floor .......... 4,800 sq. ft.
Department 5 ............... second floor ...... 9,800 sq. ft.
Department 6 ............... second floor ...... 4,200 sq. ft.

The building is leased at an annual rental of $80,000, allocated to the floors as follows: basement, 25%; first floor, 40%; second floor, 35%. Determine the amount of rent to be apportioned to each department.

**Exercise 11-4.** Mulford Company apportions depreciation expense on equipment on the basis of the average cost of the equipment, and apportions property tax expense on the basis of the combined total of average cost of the equipment and average cost of the merchandise inventories. Depreciation expense on equipment amounted to $110,000 and property tax expense amounted to $26,000 for the year. Determine the apportionment of the depreciation expense and the property tax expense, based on the following data:

| Departments | Average Cost | |
| --- | --- | --- |
| | Equipment | Inventories |
| Service: | | |
| R | $  120,000 | |
| M | 60,000 | |
| Sales: | | |
| 100 | 240,000 | $160,000 |
| 200 | 420,000 | 360,000 |
| 300 | 360,000 | 280,000 |
| Total | $1,200,000 | $800,000 |

**Exercise 11-5.** The following data were summarized from the accounting records for Hart Company for the current year ended December 31:

Cost of merchandise sold:
   Department 1 ..................................... $208,500
   Department 2 ..................................... 296,250

Direct expenses:
   Department 1 ..................................... 110,000
   Department 2 ..................................... 149,000
Income tax...................................... 48,000
Indirect expenses .............................. 95,500
Interest Income................................. 20,000

Net sales:
   Department 1 ..................................... 410,500
   Department 2 ..................................... 582,750

Prepare an income statement departmentalized through departmental margin.

**Exercise 11-6.** A portion of an income statement in condensed form, departmentalized through loss from operations for the year just ended, is as follows:

|  | Department 5 |
|---|---|
| Net sales | $226,600 |
| Cost of merchandise sold | 179,700 |
| Gross profit | $ 46,900 |
| Operating expenses | 63,000 |
| Loss from operations | $(16,100) |

The operating expenses of Dept. 5 include $30,000 for indirect expenses. It is believed that the discontinuance of Department 5 would not affect the sales of the other departments nor reduce the indirect expenses of the enterprise. Based on this information, determine the increase or decrease in income from operations of the enterprise if Department 5 had been discontinued prior to the year just ended.

**Problems**
*(Problems in Appendix B: 11-1B, 11-2B, 11-3B, 11-4B.)*

*(If the working papers correlating with the textbook are not used, omit Problem 11-1A.)*

**Problem 11-1A.** The organization chart for manufacturing operations for Carlos Inc. is presented in the working papers. Also presented are the budget performance reports for the three departments in Plant 3 and a partially completed budget performance report prepared for the vice-president in charge of production.

In response to an inquiry into the cause of the direct labor variance in the Plating Shop-Plant 3, the following data were accumulated:

| Job No. | Budgeted Hours | Actual Hours | Hourly Rate |
|---|---|---|---|
| 940 | 110 | 116 | $14.00 |
| 942 | 120 | 124 | 14.50 |
| 944 | 80 | 78 | 14.00 |
| 945 | 100 | 112 | 15.00 |
| 950 | 128 | 120 | 15.50 |
| 951 | 90 | 95 | 14.80 |
| 952 | 130 | 130 | 15.00 |
| 958 | 105 | 115 | 14.60 |

The significant variations from budgeted hours were attributed to machine breakdown on Jobs 940 and 942, to an inexperienced operator on Job 951, and to the fact that Jobs 945 and 958 were of types that were being done for the first time. Experienced operators were assigned to Jobs 944 and 950.

Instructions:

(1) Prepare a direct labor time variance report for the Plating Shop-Plant 3.
(2) Prepare a budget performance report for the use of the manager of Plant 3, detailing the relevant data from the three departments in the plant. Assume that the budgeted and actual administration expenses for the plant were $11,340 and $11,520, respectively.
(3) Complete the budget performance report for the vice-president in charge of production.

**Problem 11-2A.** Howington Co. operates two sales departments: Department A for sporting goods and Department B for camping equipment. The following trial balance was prepared at the end of the current fiscal year, after all adjustments, including the adjustments for merchandise inventory, were recorded and posted.

Howington Co.
Trial Balance
November 30, 19--

| | | |
|---|---:|---:|
| Cash | 48,150 | |
| Accounts Receivable | 83,200 | |
| Merchandise Inventory—Department A | 55,400 | |
| Merchandise Inventory—Department B | 35,300 | |
| Prepaid Insurance | 1,875 | |
| Store Supplies | 1,700 | |
| Store Equipment | 104,100 | |
| Accumulated Depreciation—Store Equipment | | 27,760 |
| Accounts Payable | | 71,680 |
| Income Tax Payable | | 900 |
| Common Stock | | 100,000 |
| Retained Earnings | | 127,045 |
| Cash Dividends | 20,000 | |
| Income Summary | 99,300 | 90,700 |
| Sales—Department A | | 338,000 |
| Sales—Department B | | 182,000 |
| Sales Returns and Allowances—Department A | 3,120 | |
| Sales Returns and Allowances—Department B | 2,240 | |
| Purchases—Department A | 164,500 | |
| Purchases—Department B | 114,800 | |
| Sales Salaries Expense | 86,000 | |
| Advertising Expense | 13,750 | |
| Depreciation Expense—Store Equipment | 6,940 | |
| Store Supplies Expense | 4,540 | |
| Miscellaneous Selling Expense | 3,640 | |
| Office Salaries Expense | 44,200 | |
| Rent Expense | 14,400 | |
| Heating and Lighting Expense | 11,300 | |
| Property Tax Expense | 6,400 | |
| Insurance Expense | 3,750 | |
| Uncollectible Accounts Expense | 3,200 | |
| Miscellaneous General Expense | 1,280 | |
| Interest Expense | 1,400 | |
| Income Tax | 3,600 | |
| | 938,085 | 938,085 |

Merchandise inventories at the beginning of the year were as follows: Department A, $66,000; Department B, $33,300.

The bases to be used in apportioning expenses, together with other essential information, are as follows:

Sales salaries expense—payroll records: Department A, $67,080; Department B, $18,920.

Advertising expense—usage: Department A, $8,250; Department B, $5,500.

Depreciation expense—average cost of equipment. Balances at beginning of year: Department A, $48,600; Department B, $27,300. Balances at end of year: Department A, $59,400; Department B, $44,700.

Store supplies expense—requisitions: Department A, $2,260; Department B, $2,280.

Office salaries expense—Department A, 55%; Department B, 45%.

Rent expense and heating and lighting expense—floor space: Department A, 6,960 sq. ft.; Department B, 5,040 sq. ft.

Property tax expense and insurance expense—average cost of equipment plus average cost of merchandise inventory.

Uncollectible accounts expense, miscellaneous selling expense, and miscellaneous general expense—volume of gross sales.

Instructions:

Prepare an income statement departmentalized through income from operations.

**Problem 11-3A.** M. R. Pierson Company is considering discontinuance of one of its twelve departments. If operations in Department 8 are discontinued, it is estimated that the indirect operating expenses and the level of operations in the other departments will not be affected.

Data from the income statement for the past year ended August 31, which is considered to be a typical year, are as follows:

|  | Department 8 | | Other Departments | |
|---|---|---|---|---|
| Sales. . . . . . . . . . . . . . . . . . . . . . . . . . . . . . . . . | | $68,000 | | $981,000 |
| Cost of merchandise sold . . . . . . . . . . . . . . . | | 44,200 | | 588,600 |
| Gross profit . . . . . . . . . . . . . . . . . . . . . . . . . . . | | $23,800 | | $392,400 |
| Operating expenses: | | | | |
| Direct expenses. . . . . . . . . . . . . . . . . . . . . . | $18,400 | | $208,000 | |
| Indirect expenses . . . . . . . . . . . . . . . . . . . | 9,500 | 27,900 | 114,000 | 322,000 |
| Income (loss) before income tax . . . . . . . . . | | $ (4,100) | | $ 70,400 |

Instructions

(1) Prepare an estimated income statement for the current year ending August 31, assuming the discontinuance of Department 8.

(2) On the basis of the data presented, would it be advisable to retain Department 8?

**Problem 11-4A.** Mitchell's Department Store has 18 departments. Those with the least sales volume are Department 16 and Department 17, which were established about a year ago on a trial basis. The board of directors feels that it is now time to consider the retention or the termination of these two departments. The following adjusted trial balance as of May 31, the end of the first month of the current fiscal year, is severely condensed. May is considered to be a typical month. The income tax accrual has no bearing on the decision and is excluded from consideration.

### Mitchell's Department Store
### Trial Balance
### May 31, 19--

| | | |
|---|---:|---:|
| Current Assets | 333,200 | |
| Plant Assets | 642,700 | |
| Accumulated Depreciation—Plant Assets | | 252,810 |
| Current Liabilities | | 190,920 |
| Common Stock | | 100,000 |
| Retained Earnings | | 291,860 |
| Cash Dividends | 15,000 | |
| Sales—Department 16 | | 31,900 |
| Sales—Department 17 | | 24,200 |
| Sales—Other Departments | | 861,500 |
| Cost of Merchandise Sold—Department 16 | 22,330 | |
| Cost of Merchandise Sold—Department 17 | 15,730 | |
| Cost of Merchandise Sold—Other Departments | 516,900 | |
| Direct Expenses—Department 16 | 11,450 | |
| Direct Expenses—Department 17 | 4,820 | |
| Direct Expenses—Other Departments | 126,760 | |
| Indirect Expenses | 58,300 | |
| Interest Expense | 6,000 | |
| | 1,753,190 | 1,753,190 |

Instructions:

(1) Prepare an income statement for May, departmentalized through departmental margin.

(2) State your recommendations concerning the retention of Departments 16 and 17, giving reasons.

**Problem 11-5A.** The bases to be used in apportioning expenses, together with other essential data for the Northwest Corporation, are as follows:

Sales salaries and commissions expense—basic salary plus 6% of sales. Basic salaries for Department A, $54,600; Department B, $26,520.

Advertising expense for brochures distributed within each department advertising specific products—usage: Department A, $12,745; Department B, $6,090.

Depreciation expense—average cost of store equipment: Department A, $78,300; Department B, $56,700.

Insurance expense—average cost of store equipment plus average cost of merchandise inventory. Average cost of merchandise inventory was $58,100 for Department A and $26,900 for Department B.

Uncollectible accounts expense—⅜% of sales. Departmental managers are responsible for the granting of credit on the sales made by their respective departments.

The following data are obtained from the ledger on April 30, the end of the current fiscal year:

| | | |
|---|---:|---:|
| Sales—Department A | | 740,000 |
| Sales—Department B | | 296,000 |
| Cost of Merchandise Sold—Department A | 495,800 | |
| Cost of Merchandise Sold—Department B | 192,400 | |

| | |
|---|---:|
| Sales Salaries and Commissions Expense............ | 143,280 |
| Advertising Expense................................. | 18,835 |
| Depreciation Expense—Store Equipment............ | 12,500 |
| Miscellaneous Selling Expense...................... | 2,020 |
| Administrative Salaries Expense..................... | 43,850 |
| Rent Expense...................................... | 24,000 |
| Utilities Expense................................... | 14,620 |
| Insurance Expense................................. | 6,500 |
| Uncollectible Accounts Expense.................... | 3,885 |
| Miscellaneous General Expense..................... | 710 |
| Interest Income.................................... | 4,400 |
| Income Tax........................................ | 17,750 |

Instructions:

(1) Prepare an income statement departmentalized through departmental margin.
(2) Determine the rate of gross profit for each department.
(3) Determine the rate of departmental margin to sales for each department.

**Mini-Case**

Assume that you recently started to work in your family-owned hardware store as an assistant store manager. Your father, the store manager and major stockholder, is considering the elimination of the Garden Supply Department, which has been incurring net losses for several years. Condensed revenue and expense data for the most recent year ended December 31, are presented on the following page. These data are typical of recent years. Bases used in allocating operating expenses among departments are as follows:

| Expense | Basis |
|---|---|
| Sales commissions expense | Actual: 8% of net sales |
| Advertising expense | Actual: all advertising consists of brochures distributed by the various departments advertising specific products |
| Depreciation expense | Average cost of store equipment used |
| Miscellaneous selling expense | Amount of net sales |
| Administrative salaries expense | Each of the 10 departments apportioned an equal share |
| Rent expense | Floor space occupied |
| Utilities expense | Floor space occupied |
| Insurance and property tax expense | Average cost of equipment used plus average cost of inventory |
| Miscellaneous general expense | Amount of net sales |

Since the Garden Supply Department is under your supervision, your father has asked your opinion as to whether the Garden Supply Department should be eliminated.

Instructions:

Prepare a brief statement of your recommendation to your father, supported by such schedule(s) as you think will be helpful to him in reaching a decision.

**Trout Hardware**
**Income Statement**
**For Year Ended December 31, 19--**

| | Garden Supply Department | Other Departments | Total |
|---|---|---|---|
| Net sales | $17,000 | $199,200 | $216,200 |
| Cost of merchandise sold | 12,400 | 125,000 | 137,400 |
| Gross profit | $ 4,600 | $ 74,200 | $ 78,800 |
| Operating expenses: | | | |
| Selling expenses: | | | |
| Sales commissions expense | $1,360 | $15,936 | $17,296 |
| Advertising expense | 510 | 6,000 | 6,510 |
| Depreciation expense—store equipment | 400 | 4,700 | 5,100 |
| Miscellaneous selling expense | 255 | 2,988 | 3,243 |
| Total selling expenses | $2,525 | $29,624 | $32,149 |
| General expenses: | | | |
| Administrative salaries expense | $1,730 | $15,570 | $17,300 |
| Rent expense | 568 | 4,544 | 5,112 |
| Utilities expense | 511 | 4,090 | 4,601 |
| Insurance and property tax expense | 350 | 3,340 | 3,690 |
| Miscellaneous general expense | 153 | 1,793 | 1,946 |
| Total general expenses | 3,312 | 29,337 | 32,649 |
| Total operating expenses | 5,837 | 58,961 | 64,798 |
| Income (loss) from operations | $ (1,237) | $ 15,239 | $ 14,002 |
| Other expense: | | | |
| Interest expense | | | 1,200 |
| Income before income tax | | | $ 12,802 |
| Income tax | | | 1,920 |
| Net income | | | $ 10,882 |

# 12

CHAPTER

# Responsibility Accounting for Investment Centers; Transfer Pricing

**CHAPTER OBJECTIVES**

*Describe and illustrate responsibility accounting for investment centers.*

*Describe and illustrate transfer pricing for decentralized operations.*

# 12

**CHAPTER**

Businesses that are separated into two or more manageable units in which divisional managers have authority and responsibility for operations are said to be decentralized. Three types of decentralized operations—cost centers, profit centers, and investment centers—were described in Chapter 11. The role of the managerial accountant in providing useful reports to assist individual managers in evaluating and controlling cost centers and profit centers was also described.

This chapter completes the discussion of decentralized business operations by focusing on responsibility accounting and reporting for investment centers. In addition, the pricing of products or services that are transferred between decentralized segments of a company is discussed.

**RESPONSIBILITY ACCOUNTING FOR INVESTMENT CENTERS**

Since investment center managers have responsibility for revenues and expenses, operating income is an essential part of investment center reporting. In addition, because the investment center manager also has responsibility for the assets invested in the center, two additional measures of performance are often used. These additional measures are the rate of return on investment and residual income. Each of these measures of investment center performance will be described and illustrated for Harrison Company, a diversified company with three operating divisions, as shown in the following organization chart:

**PARTIAL ORGANIZATION CHART FOR A DECENTRALIZED COMPANY WITH INVESTMENT CENTERS**

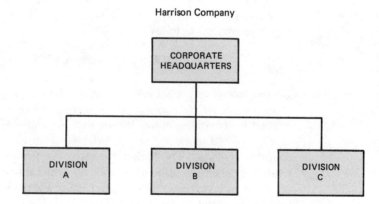

Harrison Company

**Operating Income**

Because investment centers are evaluated as if they were separate companies, traditional financial statements are normally prepared for each center. For purposes of assessing profitability, operating income is the focal point of analysis. Since the determination of operating income for decentralized operations was described and illustrated in Chapter 11, only condensed divisional income statements will be used for illustrative purposes. The condensed divisional income statements for Harrison Company are on page 270.

Based on the amount of divisional operating income, Division B is the most profitable of Harrison Company's divisions, with income from operations of $84,000. Divisions A and C are less profitable, with Division C reporting $5,000 more operating income than Division A.

Although operating income is a useful measure of investment center profitability, it does not reflect the amount of investment in assets committed to each

| Harrison Company Divisional Income Statements For Year Ended December 31, 19-- | Division A | Division B | Division C |
|---|---|---|---|
| Sales | $560,000 | $672,000 | $750,000 |
| Cost of goods sold | 336,000 | 470,400 | 562,500 |
| Gross profit | $224,000 | $201,600 | $187,500 |
| Operating expenses | 154,000 | 117,600 | 112,500 |
| Operating income | $ 70,000 | $ 84,000 | $ 75,000 |

center. For example, if the amount of assets invested in Division B is twice that of the other divisions, then Division B is the least profitable of the divisions in terms of the rate of return on investment. Since investment center managers also control the amount of assets invested in their centers, they should be held accountable for the use of invested assets.

**Rate of Return on Investment**

One of the most widely used measures of divisional performance for investment centers is the rate of return on investment (ROI), or rate of return on assets. This rate is computed as follows:

$$\text{Rate of Return on Investment (ROI)} = \frac{\text{Operating Income}}{\text{Invested Assets}}$$

The rate of return on investment is useful because the three factors subject to control by divisional managers (revenues, expenses, and invested assets) are considered in its computation. By measuring profitability relative to the amount of assets invested in each division, the rate of return on investment can be used to compare divisions. The higher the rate of return on investment, the more effectively the division is utilizing its assets in generating income. To illustrate, the rate of return on investment for each division of Harrison Company, based on the book value of invested assets, is as follows:

| | Operating Income | Invested Assets | Rate of Return on Investment |
|---|---|---|---|
| Division A | $70,000 | $350,000 | 20% |
| Division B | 84,000 | 700,000 | 12% |
| Division C | 75,000 | 500,000 | 15% |

Although Division B generated the largest operating income, its rate of return on investment (12%) is the lowest. Hence, relative to the assets invested, Division B is the least profitable division. In comparison, the rates of return on investment of Divisions A and C are 20% and 15% respectively. These differences in the rates of return on investment may be analyzed by restating the expression for the rate of return on investment in expanded form, as follows:

$$\text{Rate of Return on Investment (ROI)} = \frac{\text{Operating Income}}{\text{Sales}} \times \frac{\text{Sales}}{\text{Invested Assets}}$$

In the expanded form, the rate of return on investment is the product of two factors: (1) the ratio of operating income to sales, often termed the profit margin, and (2) the ratio of sales to invested assets, often termed the investment turnover. As shown in the following computation, the use of this expanded expression yields the same rate of return for Division A, 20%, as the previous expression for the rate of return on investment:

$$\text{Rate of Return on Investment (ROI)} = \frac{\text{Operating Income}}{\text{Sales}} \times \frac{\text{Sales}}{\text{Invested Assets}}$$

$$\text{ROI} = \frac{\$70,000}{\$560,000} \times \frac{\$560,000}{\$350,000}$$

$$\text{ROI} = 12.5\% \times 1.6$$

$$\text{ROI} = 20\%$$

The expanded expression for the rate of return on investment is useful in management's evaluation and control of decentralized operations because the profit margin and the investment turnover focus on the underlying operating relationships of each division. The profit margin component focuses on profitability by indicating the rate of profit earned on each sales dollar. When efforts are aimed at increasing a division's profit margin by changing the division's sales mix, for example, the division's rate of return on investment may increase.

The investment turnover component focuses on efficiency in the use of assets and indicates the rate at which sales are being generated for each dollar of invested assets. The more sales per dollar invested, the greater the efficiency in the use of the assets. When efforts are aimed at increasing a division's investment turnover through special sales promotions, for example, the division's rate of return on investment may increase.

The rate of return on investment, using the expanded expression for each division of Harrison Company, is summarized as follows:

| | Rate of Return on Investment (ROI) = | Profit Margin | × Investment Turnover |
|---|---|---|---|
| | ROI $= \dfrac{\text{Operating Income}}{\text{Sales}} \times \dfrac{\text{Sales}}{\text{Invested Assets}}$ | | |
| Division A: | ROI $= \dfrac{\$70,000}{\$560,000}$ | × | $\dfrac{\$560,000}{\$350,000}$ |
| | ROI $=$ 12.5% | × | 1.6 |
| | ROI $=$ 20% | | |
| Division B: | ROI $= \dfrac{\$84,000}{\$672,000}$ | × | $\dfrac{\$672,000}{\$700,000}$ |
| | ROI $=$ 12.5% | × | .96 |
| | ROI $=$ 12% | | |

Division C:     ROI     $= \dfrac{\$75,000}{\$750,000} \times \dfrac{\$750,000}{\$500,000}$

                ROI     $= \qquad 10\% \qquad \times \qquad 1.5$

                ROI     $= \qquad 15\%$

Although Divisions A and B have the same profit margins, Division A's investment turnover is larger than that of Division B (1.6 to .96). Thus, by more efficiently utilizing its invested assets, Division A has a higher rate of return on investment than Division B. Division C has a 10% profit margin and an investment turnover of 1.5, both slightly lower than that of Division A. However, the product of these factors results in a return on investment of 15% for Division C, as compared to 20% for Division A.

To determine possible ways of increasing the rate of return on investment, the profit margin and investment turnover for a division should be analyzed. For example, if Division A is in a highly competitive industry where the profit margin cannot be easily increased, the division manager should concentrate on increasing the investment turnover. To illustrate, assume that sales of Division A could be increased by $56,000 through changes in advertising expenditures. The cost of goods sold is expected to be 60% of sales, and operating expenses will increase to $169,400. If the advertising changes are undertaken, Division A's operating income would increase from $70,000 to $77,000, as shown in the following condensed income statement:

| | |
|---|---|
| Sales ($560,000 + $56,000) ..................... | $616,000 |
| Cost of goods sold ($616,000 × 60%) ........... | 369,600 |
| Gross profit .................................... | $246,400 |
| Operating expenses ........................... | 169,400 |
| Operating income.............................. | $ 77,000 |

The rate of return on investment for Division A, using the expanded expression, is recomputed as follows:

Rate of Return on Investment (ROI) $= \dfrac{\text{Operating Income}}{\text{Sales}} \times \dfrac{\text{Sales}}{\text{Invested Assets}}$

                ROI $= \dfrac{\$77,000}{\$616,000} \times \dfrac{\$616,000}{\$350,000}$

                ROI $= \qquad 12.5\% \qquad \times \qquad 1.76$

                ROI $= \qquad 22\%$

Although Division A's profit margin remains the same (12.5%), the division's investment turnover has increased from 1.6 to 1.76, an increase of 10% (.16 ÷ 1.6). The 10% increase in investment turnover has the effect of also increasing the rate of return on investment by 10% (from 20% to 22%).

The major advantage of the use of the rate of return on investment over operating income as a divisional performance measure is that the amount of divisional investment is directly considered. Thus, divisional performances can be compared, even though the sizes of the divisions may vary significantly.

In addition to its use as a performance measure, the rate of return on investment can assist management in other ways. For example, in considering a decision to expand the operations of Harrison Company, management should consider giving priority to Division A because it earns the highest rate of return on investment. If the current rates of return on investment can be maintained in the future, an investment in Division A will return 20 cents (20%) on each dollar invested, while investments in Divisions B and C will return only 12 cents and 15 cents respectively.

A major disadvantage of the rate of return on investment as a performance measure is that it may lead divisional managers to reject new investment proposals, even though the rate of return on these investments exceeds the minimum considered acceptable by the company. For example, a division might have an overall rate of return on investment of 25%, and the company might have an overall rate of return on investment of 15%. If the division accepts a new investment that would earn a 20% rate of return on investment, the overall rate of return for the division would decrease, but the overall rate of return for the company as a whole would increase. Thus, the division manager might reject the proposal, even though its acceptance would be in the best interests of the company.

**Residual Income**

In the previous illustration for Harrison Company, two measures of evaluating divisional performance were discussed and illustrated. The advantages and disadvantages of both measures were also discussed. An additional measure, residual income, is useful in overcoming some of the disadvantages associated with the operating income and rate of return on investment measures.

Residual income is the excess of divisional operating income over a minimum amount of desired operating income. The minimum amount of desired divisional operating income is set by top management by establishing a minimum rate of return for the invested assets and then multiplying this rate by the amount of divisional assets. To illustrate, assume that the top management of Harrison Company has established 10% as the minimum rate of return on divisional assets. The residual incomes for Divisions A, B, and C are computed as follows:

| RESIDUAL INCOME BY DIVISION | | Division A | Division B | Division C |
|---|---|---|---|---|
| Divisional operating income | | $70,000 | $84,000 | $75,000 |
| Minimum amount of divisional operating income: | | | | |
| $350,000 × 10% | | 35,000 | | |
| $700,000 × 10% | | | 70,000 | |
| $500,000 × 10% | | | | 50,000 |
| Residual income | | $35,000 | $14,000 | $25,000 |

The major advantage of residual income as a performance measure is that it not only gives consideration to a minimum rate of return on investment, but also to the total magnitude of the operating income earned by each division. For example, Division A has more residual income than the other divisions of Harrison Company, even though it has the least operating income. Also, Division C earns $11,000 more residual income than Division B, even though Division B generates more operating income than Division C. The reason for this difference is that Division B has $200,000 more assets than Division C. Hence, Division B's operating income is reduced by $20,000 ($200,000 × 10%) more than Division C's operating income in determining residual income.

The preceding paragraphs have described and illustrated three measures — operating income, rate of return on investment, and residual income — which management can use in evaluating and controlling investment center performance. In practice, most companies use some combination of all these measures.

## TRANSFER PRICING

The use of responsibility accounting and reporting in measuring performance in decentralized companies can be important in motivating managers to achieve common profit goals. However, when decentralized units transfer products or render services to each other, the transfer price — the price to charge for the products or services — becomes an issue. Since transfer prices affect the revenues and expenses of both the receiving unit and the unit providing the product or service, transfer prices affect the performance measures used for evaluating divisional performance.

The objective of transfer pricing is to encourage each divisional manager to transfer goods and services between divisions if overall company income can be increased by doing so. As will be illustrated, however, transfer prices may be misused to the detriment of overall company income.

The following paragraphs describe and illustrate various approaches to establishing transfer prices, the effect of transfer prices on the evaluation of decentralized performance, and their potential impact on overall company income. Three commonly used approaches are (1) the market price approach, (2) the negotiated price approach, and (3) the cost price approach.

Although transfer prices may apply when decentralized units are organized as cost or profit centers, a diversified company (Wilson Company) with two operating divisions (M and N) organized as investment centers will be used for the illustrations in the remainder of this chapter. Condensed income statements for Wilson Company's divisions, with no intracompany transfers and a breakdown of expenses into variable and fixed components, are on page 275.

## Market Price Approach

Under the market price approach, the transfer price is the price at which the product or service transferred could be sold to outside buyers. If an outside market exists for the product or service transferred, then the current market price at which the purchasing division could buy the product or service outside the company would seem to be a reasonable transfer price for intracompany transfers. However, the appropriateness of the market price approach depends on whether the division supplying the product or service is operating at full capacity and can sell all it produces.

To illustrate, assume that materials used by Wilson Company in producing Division N's product are currently purchased from an outside supplier at $20 per unit. The same materials are produced by Division M. If Division M is operating at full capacity of 50,000 units and can sell all it produces to either Division N or

**Wilson Company**
**Divisional Income Statements**
**For Year Ended December 31, 19--**

|  | Division M | Division N | Total |
|---|---|---|---|
| Sales: |  |  |  |
| 50,000 units × $20 per unit......... | $1,000,000 |  | $1,000,000 |
| 20,000 units × $40 per unit........ |  | $800,000 | 800,000 |
|  |  |  | $1,800,000 |
| Expenses: |  |  |  |
| Variable: |  |  |  |
| 50,000 units × $10 per unit....... | $ 500,000 |  | $ 500,000 |
| 20,000 units × $30* per unit...... |  | $600,000 | 600,000 |
| Fixed......................... | 300,000 | 100,000 | 400,000 |
| Total expenses.................. | $ 800,000 | $700,000 | $1,500,000 |
| Operating income................... | $ 200,000 | $100,000 | $ 300,000 |

*$20 of the $30 per unit represents materials costs, and the remaining
$10 per unit represents other expenses incurred within Division N.

to outside buyers, then the use of a transfer price of $20 per unit (the market price) has no effect on the income of Division M or total company income. Division M will earn revenues of $20 per unit on all its production and sales, regardless of who buys its product, and Division N will pay $20 per unit for materials, regardless of whether it purchases the materials from Division M or from an outside supplier. In this situation, the use of the market price as the transfer price is appropriate. The condensed divisional income statements for Wilson Company under such circumstances would be as shown above.

If unused capacity exists in the supplying division, the use of the market price approach may not lead to the maximization of total company income. To illustrate, assume that Division M has unused capacity of 20,000 units and it can continue to sell only 50,000 units to outside buyers. In this situation, the transfer price should be set to motivate the manager of Division N to purchase from Division M if the variable cost per unit of product of Division M is less than the market price. If the variable costs are less than $20 per unit but the transfer price is set equal to the market price of $20, then the manager of Division N is indifferent as to whether materials are purchased from Division M or from outside suppliers, since the cost per unit to Division N would be the same, $20. However, Division N's purchase of 20,000 units of materials from outside suppliers at a cost of $20 per unit would not maximize overall company income, since this market price per unit is greater than the unit variable expenses of Division M, $10. Hence, the intracompany transfer could save the company the difference between the market price per unit and Division M's unit variable expenses. This savings of $10 per unit would add $200,000 (20,000 units × $10) to overall company income.

**Negotiated Price Approach**

In the previous illustration, the manager of Division N should be encouraged to purchase from Division M by establishing a transfer price at an amount less than the market price of $20 per unit. Division N's materials cost per unit would thus decrease, and its operating income would increase. In such situations, the negotiated price approach can be used to establish an appropriate transfer price.

The negotiated price approach allows the managers of decentralized units to agree (negotiate) among themselves as to the proper transfer price. If agreement cannot be reached among the division managers, the company's top management may have to intervene to set the transfer price. To illustrate, assume that Wilson Company's division managers agree to a transfer price of $15 for Division M's product. By purchasing from Division M, Division N would then report $5 per unit less materials cost. At the same time, Division M would increase its sales to a total of 70,000 units (50,000 units to outside buyers and 20,000 units to Division N). The effect of increasing Division M's sales by $300,000 (20,000 units × $15 per unit) is to increase its income by $100,000 ($300,000 sales − $200,000 variable expenses). The effect of reducing Division N's materials cost by $100,000 (20,000 units × $5 per unit) is to increase its income by $100,000. Therefore, Wilson Company's income is increased by $200,000 ($100,000 reported by Division M and $100,000 reported by Division N), as shown in the following condensed income statements:

**Wilson Company**
**Divisional Income Statements**
**For Year Ended December 31, 19--**

|  | Division M | Division N | Total |
|---|---|---|---|
| Sales: |  |  |  |
| 50,000 units × $20 per unit......... | $1,000,000 |  | $1,000,000 |
| 20,000 units × $15 per unit......... | 300,000 |  | 300,000 |
| 20,000 units × $40 per unit......... |  | $800,000 | 800,000 |
|  | $1,300,000 | $800,000 | $2,100,000 |
| Expenses: |  |  |  |
| Variable: |  |  |  |
| 70,000 units × $10 per unit....... | $ 700,000 |  | $ 700,000 |
| 20,000 units × $25* per unit...... |  | $500,000 | 500,000 |
| Fixed............................ | 300,000 | 100,000 | 400,000 |
| Total expenses................. | $1,000,000 | $600,000 | $1,600,000 |
| Operating income.................. | $ 300,000 | $200,000 | $ 500,000 |

*$10 per unit of the $25 is incurred solely within Division N, and $15 per unit represents the transfer price per unit from Division M.

In the Wilson Company illustration, any transfer price less than the market price of $20 but greater than Division M's unit variable expenses of $10 would increase each division's income and would increase overall company income by

$200,000. By establishing a range of $20 to $10 for the negotiated transfer price, each division manager will have an incentive to negotiate the intracompany transfer of the materials. For example, a transfer price of $18 would increase Division M's income by $160,000 (from $200,000 to $360,000) and Division N's income by $40,000 (from $100,000 to $140,000). Overall company income would still be increased by $200,000 (from $300,000 to $500,000), as shown in the following condensed income statements:

**Wilson Company**
**Divisional Income Statements**
**For Year Ended December 31, 19--**

|  | Division M | Division N | Total |
|---|---|---|---|
| Sales: |  |  |  |
| 50,000 units × $20 per unit......... | $1,000,000 |  | $1,000,000 |
| 20,000 units × $18 per unit......... | 360,000 |  | 360,000 |
| 20,000 units × $40 per unit......... |  | $800,000 | 800,000 |
|  | $1,360,000 | $800,000 | $2,160,000 |
| Expenses: |  |  |  |
| Variable: |  |  |  |
| 70,000 units × $10 per unit....... | $ 700,000 |  | $ 700,000 |
| 20,000 units × $28* per unit...... |  | $560,000 | 560,000 |
| Fixed.......................... | 300,000 | 100,000 | 400,000 |
| Total expenses................. | $1,000,000 | $660,000 | $1,660,000 |
| Operating income.................... | $ 360,000 | $140,000 | $ 500,000 |

*$10 per unit of the $28 is incurred solely within Division N, and $18 per unit represents the transfer price per unit from Division M.

**Cost Price Approach**

Under the cost price approach, cost is used as the basis for setting transfer prices. With this approach, a variety of cost concepts may be used. For example, cost may refer to either total product cost per unit or variable product cost per unit. If total product cost per unit is used, direct materials, direct labor, and factory overhead are included in the transfer price. If variable product cost per unit is used, the fixed factory overhead component of total product cost is excluded from the transfer price.

Either actual costs or standard (budgeted) costs may be used in applying the cost price approach. If actual costs are used, inefficiencies of the producing division are transferred to the purchasing division, and thus there is little incentive for the producing division to control costs carefully. For this reason, most companies use standard costs in the cost price approach, so that differences between actual and standard costs are isolated in the producing divisions for cost control purposes.

When division managers have responsibility for only costs incurred in their divisions, the cost price approach to transfer pricing is frequently used. However,

PART FIVE • Accounting for Decentralized Operations

many accountants argue that the cost price approach is inappropriate for decentralized operations organized as profit or investment centers. In profit and investment centers, division managers have responsibility for both revenues and expenses. The use of cost as a transfer price, however, ignores the supplying division manager's responsibility over revenues. When a supplying division's sales are all intracompany transfers, for example, the use of the cost price approach would prevent the supplying division from reporting any operating income. A cost-based transfer price would therefore not motivate the division manager to make intracompany transfers, even though they are in the best interests of the company.

Self-
Examination
Questions
(Answers in
Appendix C.)

1. Managers of what type of decentralized units have authority and responsibility over revenues, expenses, and invested assets?
   A. Profit center                     C. Investment center
   B. Cost center                       D. None of the above

2. Division A of Kern Co. has sales of $350,000, cost of goods sold of $200,000, operating expenses of $30,000, and invested assets of $600,000. What is the rate of return on investment for Division A?
   A. 20%                               C. 40%
   B. 25%                               D. None of the above

3. Which of the following expressions is frequently referred to as the turnover factor in determining the rate of return on investment?
   A. Operating Income ÷ Sales
   B. Operating Income ÷ Invested Assets
   C. Sales ÷ Invested Assets
   D. None of the above

4. Division L of Liddy Co. has a rate of return on investment of 24% and an investment turnover of 1.6. What is the profit margin?
   A. 6%                                C. 24%
   B. 15%                               D. None of the above

5. Which approach to transfer pricing uses the price at which the product or service transferred could be sold to outside buyers as the transfer price?
   A. Cost price approach               C. Market price approach
   B. Negotiated price approach         D. None of the above

Discussion
Questions

1. What are three ways in which decentralized operations may be organized?

2. Name three performance measures useful in evaluating investment centers.

3. What is the major shortcoming of using operating income as a performance measure for investment centers?

4. Describe how the factors under the control of the investment center manager (revenues, expenses, and invested assets) are considered in the computation of the rate of return on investment?

5. Monahan Co. has $200,000 invested in Division N, which earned $54,000 of operating income. What is the rate of return on investment for Division N?

6. If Monahan Co. in Question 5 had sales of $360,000, what is (a) the profit margin and (b) the investment turnover for Division N?

7. What are two ways of expressing the rate of return on investment?

8. In evaluating investment centers, what does multiplying the profit margin by the investment turnover equal?

9. How could a division of a decentralized company organized as investment centers be considered the least profitable, even though it earned the largest amount of operating income?

10. Which component of the rate of return on investment (profit margin factor or investment turnover factor) focuses on efficiency in the use of assets and indicates the rate at which sales are generated for each dollar of invested assets?

11. Division F of Platt Co. has a rate of return on investment of 18%. (a) If Division F increases its investment turnover by 10%, what would be the new rate of return on investment? (b) If Division F also increases its profit margin from 12% to 18%, what would be the new rate of return on investment?

12. How does the use of the rate of return on investment facilitate comparability of divisions of decentralized companies?

13. The rate of return on investment for Gibbon Co.'s three divisions, C, D, and E, are 20%, 24%, and 18%, respectively. In expanding operations, which of Gibbon Co.'s divisions should be given priority? Explain.

14. What term is used to describe the excess of divisional operating income over a minimum amount of desired operating income?

15. Division Q of Choi Co. reported operating income of $150,000, based on invested assets of $500,000. If the minimum rate of return on divisional investments is 18%, what is the residual income for Division Q?

16. What term is used to describe the amount charged for products transferred or services rendered to other decentralized units in a company?

17. What is the objective of transfer pricing?

18. Name three commonly used approaches to establishing transfer prices.

19. What transfer price approach uses the price at which the product or service transferred could be sold to outside buyers as the transfer price?

20. When is the negotiated price approach preferred over the market price approach in setting transfer prices?

21. If division managers cannot agree among themselves on a transfer price when using the negotiated price approach, how is the transfer price established?

22. When using the negotiated price approach to transfer pricing, within what range should the transfer price be established?

**Exercises**        Exercise 12-1. One item is omitted from each of the following condensed divisional income statements of Weldon Company:

| | Division X | Division Y | Division Z |
|---|---|---|---|
| Sales . . . . . . . . . . . . . . . . | $500,000 | (c) | $560,000 |
| Cost of goods sold . . . . . | (a) | 465,000 | 336,000 |
| Gross profit . . . . . . . . . . | $200,000 | $155,000 | (e) |
| Operating expenses . . . | (b) | 43,000 | 64,000 |
| Operating income . . . . . . | $140,000 | (d) | (f) |

(a) Determine the amount of the missing items, identifying them by letter. (b) Based on operating income, which division is the most profitable?

**Exercise 12-2.** The operating income and the amount of invested assets in each division of Weldon Company are as follows:

| | Operating Income | Invested Assets |
|---|---|---|
| Division X . . . . . . . . . . | $140,000 | $700,000 |
| Division Y . . . . . . . . . . | 112,000 | 350,000 |
| Division Z . . . . . . . . . . | 160,000 | 640,000 |

(a) Compute the rate of return on investment for each division. (b) Which division is the most profitable per dollar invested?

**Exercise 12-3.** Based on the data in Exercise 12-2, assume that management has established a minimum rate of return for invested assets of 10%. (a) Determine the residual income for each division. (b) Based on residual income, which of the divisions is the most profitable?

**Exercise 12-4.** One item is omitted from each of the following computations of the rate of return on investment:

| Rate of Return on Investment | = | Profit Margin | × | Investment Turnover |
|---|---|---|---|---|
| (a) | | 12% | | 1.25 |
| 24% | | (b) | | 1.50 |
| 24% | | 15% | | (c) |
| 20% | | (d) | | 2.50 |
| (e) | | 18% | | 2.00 |

Determine the missing items, identifying each by the appropriate letter.

**Exercise 12-5.** The condensed income statement for Division K of Streer Company is as follows:

| | |
|---|---|
| Sales. . . . . . . . . . . . . . . . . . . . . . . | $400,000 |
| Cost of goods sold . . . . . . . . . . | 240,000 |
| Gross profit . . . . . . . . . . . . . . . . . | $160,000 |
| Operating expenses . . . . . . . . . | 114,000 |
| Operating income . . . . . . . . . . . | $ 46,000 |

The manager of Division K is considering ways to increase the rate of return on investment. (a) Using the expanded expression, determine the profit margin, investment turnover, and rate of return on investment of Division K assuming that $250,000 of assets have been invested in Division K. (b) If expenses could be reduced by $10,000 without decreasing sales, what would be the impact on the profit margin, investment turnover, and rate of return on investment for Division K?

**Exercise 12-6.** One or more items is missing from the following tabulation of rate of return on investment and residual income:

| Invested Assets | Operating Income | Rate of Return on Investment | Minimum Rate of Return | Minimum Amount of Operating Income | Residual Income |
|---|---|---|---|---|---|
| (a) | (b) | 16% | 12% | $48,000 | $16,000 |
| $600,000 | (c) | 18% | (d) | (e) | $48,000 |
| $500,000 | $110,000 | (f) | (g) | $70,000 | (h) |
| $300,000 | $ 57,000 | 19% | 15% | (i) | (j) |

Determine the missing items, identifying each item by the appropriate letter.

**Exercise 12-7.** Materials used by Payne Company in producing Division R's product are currently purchased from outside suppliers at a cost of $40 per unit. However, the same materials are available from Division W. Division W has unused capacity and can produce the materials needed by Division R at a variable cost of $25 per unit. (a) If a transfer price of $32 per unit is established and 50,000 units of material are transferred, with no reduction in Division W's current sales, how much would Payne Company's total operating income increase? (b) How much would operating income of Division R increase? (c) How much would the operating income of Division W increase?

**Exercise 12-8.** Based on the Payne Company data in Exercise 12-7, assume that a transfer price of $30 has been established and 50,000 units of materials are transferred, with no reduction in Division W's current sales. (a) How much would Payne Company's total operating income increase? (b) How much would Division R's operating income increase? (c) How much would Division W's operating income increase? (d) If the negotiated price approach is used, what would be the range of acceptable transfer prices?

**Problems**
*(Problems in Appendix B: 12-1B, 12-3B, 12-4B, 12-5B.)*

**Problem 12-1A.** Turnage Company is a diversified company with three operating divisions organized as investment centers. Condensed data taken from the records of the three divisions for the year ended December 31 are as follows:

|  | Division E | Division F | Division G |
|---|---|---|---|
| Sales . . . . . . . . . . . . . . . . | $1,200,000 | $660,000 | $640,000 |
| Cost of goods sold. . . . | 900,000 | 462,000 | 384,000 |
| Operating expenses . . | 204,000 | 118,800 | 176,000 |
| Invested assets. . . . . . . | 800,000 | 600,000 | 400,000 |

The management of Turnage Company is evaluating each division as a basis for planning a future expansion of operations.

Instructions:

(1) Prepare condensed divisional income statements for Divisions E, F, and G.
(2) Using the expanded expression, compute the profit margin, investment turnover, and rate of return on investment for each division.
(3) If available funds permit the expansion of operations of only one division, which of the divisions would you recommend for expansion, based on (1) and (2)?

**Problem 12-2A.** A condensed income statement for Division P of Fairfax Company for the past year is as follows:

**Fairfax Company—Division P**
**Income Statement**
**For Year Ended December 31, 19--**

| | |
|---|---:|
| Sales....................... | $1,500,000 |
| Cost of goods sold ........... | 1,050,000 |
| Gross profit.................. | $ 450,000 |
| Operating expenses .......... | 270,000 |
| Operating income ........... | $ 180,000 |

The president of Fairfax Company is concerned with Division P's low rate of return on invested assets of $1,200,000, and has indicated that the division's rate of return on investment must be increased to at least 18% by the end of the next year if operations are to continue. The division manager is considering the following three proposals:

Proposal 1: Reduce invested assets by discontinuing a product line. This would eliminate sales of $200,000, cost of goods sold of $140,000, and operating expenses of $49,000. Assets of $160,000 would be transferred to other divisions at no gain or loss.

Proposal 2: Purchase new and more efficient machinery and thereby reduce the cost of goods sold by $93,000. Sales would remain unchanged, and the old machinery, which has no remaining book value, would be scrapped at no gain or loss. The new machinery would increase invested assets by $300,000 for the year.

Proposal 3: Transfer equipment with a book value of $200,000 to other divisions at no gain or loss and lease similar equipment. The annual lease payments would exceed the amount of depreciation expense on the old equipment by $6,000. This increase in expense would be included as part of the cost of goods sold. Sales would remain unchanged.

Instructions:

(1) Using the expanded expression, determine the profit margin, investment turnover, and rate of return on investment for Division P for the past year.
(2) Prepare condensed estimated income statements for Division P for each proposal.
(3) Using the expanded expression, determine the profit margin, investment turnover, and rate of return on investment for Division P under each proposal.

(4) Which of the three proposals would meet the required 18% rate of return on investment?

(5) If Division P were in a highly competitive industry where the profit margin and sales could not be increased, how much would invested assets have to be reduced to meet the president's required 18% rate of return on investment?

**Problem 12-3A.** Data for Divisions V, W, X, Y, and Z of McGarity Company are as follows:

| | Sales | Operating Income | Invested Assets | Rate of Return on Investment | Profit Margin | Investment Turnover |
|---|---|---|---|---|---|---|
| Division V ... | $600,000 | (a) | (b) | (c) | 15% | 1.20 |
| Division W... | (d) | $ 63,000 | (e) | (f) | 11.2% | 1.25 |
| Division X ... | $800,000 | $100,000 | (g) | (h) | (i) | 2.00 |
| Division Y ... | $750,000 | (j) | $300,000 | 24% | (k) | (l) |
| Division Z ... | (m) | (n) | $425,000 | 20% | 12.5% | (o) |

Instructions:

(1) Determine the missing items, identifying each by letters (a) through (o).

(2) Determine the residual income for each division, assuming that the minimum rate of return established by management is 10%.

(3) Which division is the most profitable?

**Problem 12-4A.** The vice-president of operations of Parsons Company is evaluating the performance of two divisions organized as investment centers. Division I generates the largest amount of operating income but has the lowest rate of return on investment. Division J has the highest rate of return on investment but generates the smallest operating income. Invested assets and condensed income statement data for the past year for each division are as follows:

| | Division I | Division J |
|---|---|---|
| Sales........................ | $4,500,000 | $4,800,000 |
| Cost of goods sold ........... | 3,075,000 | 3,120,000 |
| Operating expenses .......... | 831,000 | 1,104,000 |
| Invested assets ............. | 3,600,000 | 3,200,000 |

Instructions:

(1) Prepare condensed income statements for the past year for each division.

(2) Using the expanded expression, determine the profit margin, investment turnover, and rate of return on investment for each division.

(3) If management desires a minimum rate of return of 10%, determine the residual income for each division.

(4) Discuss the evaluation of Divisions I and J, using the performance measures determined in (1), (2), and (3).

**Problem 12-5A.** Smathers Company is diversified, with two operating divisions, F and G. Condensed divisional income statements, which involve no intracompany transfers and which include a breakdown of expenses into variable and fixed components, are as follows:

Smathers Company
Divisional Income Statements
For Year Ended December 31, 19--

|  | Division F | Division G | Total |
|---|---|---|---|
| Sales: |  |  |  |
| 120,000 units × $40 per unit..... | $4,800,000 |  | $4,800,000 |
| 40,000 units × $50 per unit...... |  | $2,000,000 | 2,000,000 |
|  |  |  | $6,800,000 |
| Expenses: |  |  |  |
| Variable: |  |  |  |
| 120,000 units × $24 per unit... | $2,880,000 |  | $2,880,000 |
| 40,000 units × $32* per unit... |  | $1,280,000 | 1,280,000 |
| Fixed......................... | 920,000 | 520,000 | 1,440,000 |
| Total expenses............... | $3,800,000 | $1,800,000 | $5,600,000 |
| Operating income ............... | $1,000,000 | $ 200,000 | $1,200,000 |

*$28 of the $32 per unit represents materials costs, and the remaining $4 per unit represents other expenses incurred within Division G.

Division F is operating at two thirds of its capacity of 180,000 units. Materials used in producing Division G's product are currently purchased from outside suppliers at a price of $28 per unit. The materials used by Division G are produced by Division F. Except for the possible transfer of materials between divisions, no changes are expected in sales and expenses.

Instructions:

(1) Would the market price of $28 per unit be an appropriate transfer price for Smathers Company? Explain.
(2) If Division G purchases 40,000 units from Division F and a transfer price of $26 per unit is negotiated between the managers of Divisions F and G, how much would the operating income of each division and total company operating income increase?
(3) Prepare condensed divisional income statements for Smathers Company, based on the data in (2).
(4) If a transfer price of $27 per unit had been negotiated, how much would the operating income of each division and total company income have increased?
(5) (a) What is the range of possible negotiated transfer prices that would be acceptable for Smathers Company?
   (b) If the division managers of F and G cannot agree on a transfer price, what price would you suggest as the transfer price?

**Problem 12-6A.** The vice-president of operations of Vinson Inc. recently resigned, and the president is considering which one of two division managers to promote to the vacated position. Both division managers have been with the company approximately ten years. Operating data for each division for the past three years are as follows:

| | 1985 | 1984 | 1983 |
|---|---|---|---|
| **Division A:** | | | |
| Sales................ | $ 770,000 | $ 650,000 | $ 600,000 |
| Cost of goods sold..... | 462,000 | 390,000 | 360,000 |
| Gross profit .......... | $ 308,000 | $ 260,000 | $ 240,000 |
| Operating expenses.... | 200,200 | 175,500 | 163,200 |
| Operating income...... | $ 107,800 | $ 84,500 | $ 76,800 |
| Invested assets........ | $ 550,000 | $ 500,000 | $ 480,000 |
| Total industry sales .... | $5,500,000 | $5,200,000 | $5,000,000 |
| **Division B:** | | | |
| Sales................ | $ 966,000 | $ 840,000 | $ 750,000 |
| Cost of goods sold..... | 670,000 | 588,000 | 525,000 |
| Gross profit .......... | $ 296,000 | $ 252,000 | $ 225,000 |
| Operating expenses.... | 151,100 | 117,600 | 105,000 |
| Operating income...... | $ 144,900 | $ 134,400 | $ 120,000 |
| Invested assets........ | $ 700,000 | $ 600,000 | $ 500,000 |
| Total industry sales .... | $6,440,000 | $4,800,000 | $3,750,000 |

Instructions:

(1) For each division for each of the three years, use the expanded expression to determine the profit margin, investment turnover, and rate of return on investment.

(2) Assuming that 15% has been established as a minimum rate of return, determine the residual income for each division for each of the three years.

(3) Determine each division's market share (division sales divided by total industry sales) for each of the three years.

(4) Based on (1), (2), and (3), which division manager would you recommend for promotion to vice-president of operations?

(5) What other factors should be considered in the promotion decision?

---

**Mini-Case**

Your father is the president of Hillsman Company, a privately held, diversified company with five separate divisions organized as investment centers. A condensed income statement for the Sporting Goods Division for the past year is as follows:

Hillsman Company—Sporting Goods Division
Income Statement
For Year Ended December 31, 19--

| | |
|---|---|
| Sales............................................ | $32,000,000 |
| Cost of goods sold............................... | 19,200,000 |
| Gross profit ...................................... | $12,800,000 |
| Operating expenses.............................. | 8,800,000 |
| Operating income................................ | $ 4,000,000 |

The manager of the Sporting Goods Division was recently presented with the opportunity to add an additional product line, which would require invested assets of $6,000,000. A projected income statement for the new product line is as follows:

New Product Line
Projected Income Statement
For Year Ended December 31, 19--

| | |
|---|---|
| Sales. | $7,500,000 |
| Cost of goods sold. | 4,500,000 |
| Gross profit | $3,000,000 |
| Operating expenses. | 2,040,000 |
| Operating income. | $ 960,000 |

The Sporting Goods Division currently has $20,000,000 in invested assets, and Hillsman Company's overall rate of return on investment, including all divisions, is 14%. Each division manager is evaluated on the basis of divisional rate of return on investment, and a bonus equal to $5,000 for each percentage point by which the division's rate of return on investment exceeds the company average is awarded each year.

Your father is concerned that the manager of the Sporting Goods Division rejected the addition of the new product line, when all the estimates indicated that the product line would be profitable and would increase overall company income. You have been asked to analyze the possible reasons why the Sporting Goods Division manager rejected the new product line.

Instructions:

(1) Determine the rate of return on investment for the Sporting Goods Division for the past year.
(2) Determine the Sporting Goods Division manager's bonus for the past year.
(3) Determine the estimated rate of return on investment for the new product line.
(4) Why might the manager of the Sporting Goods Division decide to reject the new product line?
(5) Can you suggest an alternative performance measure for motivating division managers to accept new investment opportunities that would increase the overall company income and rate of return on investment?

# 13
CHAPTER

# Quantitative Techniques: Inventory Control and Cost Estimation

**CHAPTER OBJECTIVES**

*Describe the general use of quantitative techniques by management.*

*Describe and illustrate the use of quantitative techniques for inventory control.*

*Describe and illustrate the use of the high-low, scattergraph, and least squares methods in estimating costs.*

*Describe and illustrate the learning effect in estimating costs.*

# PART 6
## Quantitative Techniques for Management Use

# 13

**CHAPTER**

Previous chapters have discussed many ways in which accounting data can be used by management in planning and controlling business operations, including such analyses as cost-volume-profit analysis, differential analysis, and capital investment analysis. These analyses can be performed using rather simple mathematical relationships, since they usually involve a limited number of objectives and variables. By using quantitative techniques which rely on more sophisticated mathematical relationships and statistical methods, management can consider a larger number of objectives and variables in planning and controlling operations.

The use of quantitative techniques often leads to a clarification of management decision alternatives and their expected effects on the business enterprise. For example, the most economical plan for purchasing materials for a single plant may be easily determined, based on the lowest overall cost per unit of materials. However, the most economical plan for purchasing materials for several plants may not be as easily determined, because transportation costs to the various plant locations may be different, and the amount of purchases from any one supplier may be limited. In this latter case, a quantitative technique known as linear programming may be useful in determining the most economical plan for purchasing materials.

The primary disadvantages of quantitative techniques are their complexity and their reliance on mathematical relationships and statistical methods which may be understood by only the most highly trained experts. When computers are used, however, it is less important to understand these complexities, so that quantitative techniques can be used by all levels of management.

In this chapter and in Chapter 14, several of the most common quantitative techniques are explained, and the practical application of each technique is demonstrated. The quantitative techniques described in this chapter focus on inventory control and the estimation of costs, including the estimation of the fixed and variable cost components. Chapter 14 focuses on quantitative techniques useful for decision making under uncertainty.

## INVENTORY CONTROL

For a business enterprise that needs large quantities of inventory to meet sales orders or production requirements, inventory is one of its most important assets. The lack of sufficient inventory can result in lost sales, idle production facilities, production bottlenecks, and additional purchasing costs due to placing special orders or rush orders. On the other hand, excess inventory can result in large storage costs and large spoilage losses, which reduce the profitability of the enterprise. Thus, it is important for a business enterprise to know the ideal quantity to be purchased in a single order and the minimum and maximum quantities to be on hand at any time. Such factors as economies of large-scale buying, storage costs, work interruption due to shortages, and seasonal and cyclical changes in production schedules need to be considered. Two quantitative techniques that are especially useful in inventory control are (1) the economic order quantity formula and (2) linear programming. In addition, the inventory order point and inventory safety stock are also useful in controlling inventory.

Economic Order Quantity

The optimum quantity of inventory to be ordered at one time is termed the **economic order quantity (EOQ).** Important factors to be considered in determining the optimum quantity are the costs involved in processing an order for the materials and the costs involved in storing the materials.

The annual cost of processing orders for a specified material (cost of placing orders, verifying invoices, processing payments, etc.) increases as the number of orders placed increases. On the other hand, the annual cost of storing the materials (taxes, insurance, occupancy of storage space, etc.) decreases as the number of orders placed increases. The economic order quantity is therefore that quantity that will minimize the combined annual costs of ordering and storing materials.

The combined annual cost incurred in ordering and storing materials can be computed under various assumptions as to the number of orders to be placed during a year. To illustrate, assume the following data for an inventoriable material which is used at the same rate during the year:

Units required during the year . . . . . . . .    1,200
Ordering cost, per order placed . . . . . .   $10.00
Storage cost, per unit. . . . . . . . . . . . . . .     .60

If a single order were placed for the entire year's needs, the cost of ordering the 1,200 units would be $10. The average number of units held in inventory during the year would therefore be 600 (1,200 units ÷ 2) and would result in an annual storage cost of $360 (600 units × $.60). The combined order and storage costs for placing only one order during the year would thus be $370 ($10 + $360). If, instead of a single order, two orders were placed during the year, the order cost would be $20 (2 × $10), 600 units would need to be purchased on each order, the average inventory would be 300 units, and the annual storage cost would be $180 (300 units × $.60). Accordingly, the combined order and storage costs for placing two orders during the year would be $200 ($20 + $180). Successive computations will disclose the EOQ when the combined cost reaches its lowest point and starts upward. The following table shows an optimum of 200 units of materials per order, with 6 orders per year, at a combined cost of $120:

TABULATION OF ECONOMIC ORDER QUANTITY

| Number of Orders | Number of Units per Order | Average Units in Inventory | Order and Storage Costs | | |
|---|---|---|---|---|---|
| | | | Order Cost | Storage Cost | Combined Cost |
| 1 | 1,200 | 600 | $10 | $360 | $370 |
| 2 | 600 | 300 | 20 | 180 | 200 |
| 3 | 400 | 200 | 30 | 120 | 150 |
| 4 | 300 | 150 | 40 | 90 | 130 |
| 5 | 240 | 120 | 50 | 72 | 122 |
| 6 | 200 | 100 | 60 | 60 | 120 |
| 7 | 171 | 86 | 70 | 52 | 122 |

The economic order quantity may also be determined by a formula based on differential calculus. The formula and its application to the illustration is as follows:

ECONOMIC ORDER
QUANTITY FORMULA

$$EOQ = \sqrt{\frac{2 \times \text{Annual Units Required} \times \text{Cost per Order Placed}}{\text{Storage Cost per Unit}}}$$

$$EOQ = \sqrt{\frac{2 \times 1,200 \times \$10}{\$.60}}$$

$$EOQ = \sqrt{40,000}$$

$$EOQ = 200 \text{ units}$$

Inventory Order
Point and
Safety Stock

    The inventory order point, usually expressed in units, is the level to which inventory is allowed to fall before an order for additional inventory is placed. The inventory order point depends on the (1) daily usage of inventory that is expected to be consumed in production or sold, (2) time (in days) that it takes to receive an order for inventory, termed the lead time, and (3) safety stock, which is the amount of inventory that is available for use when unforeseen circumstances arise, such as delays in receiving ordered inventory as a result of a national truckers' strike. Once the order point is reached, the most economical quantity should be ordered.

    The inventory order point is computed by using the following formula:

Inventory Order Point = (Daily Usage × Days of Lead Time) + Safety Stock

    To illustrate, assume that Beacon Company, a printing company, estimates daily usage of 3,000 pounds of paper and a lead time of 30 days to receive an order of paper. Beacon Company desires a safety stock of 10,000 pounds. The inventory order point for the paper is 100,000 pounds, computed as follows:

Inventory Order Point = (Daily Usage × Lead Time) + Safety Stock
Inventory Order Point = (3,000 lbs. × 30 days) + 10,000 lbs.
Inventory Order Point = 90,000 lbs. + 10,000 lbs.
Inventory Order Point = 100,000 lbs.

    In this illustration, a safety stock of 10,000 pounds of paper was assumed. This level of safety stock should be established by management after considering many factors, such as the uncertainty in the estimates of daily inventory usage and lead time. If management were 100% certain that estimates of the daily usage and lead time were correct, no safety stock would be required. As the uncertainty in these estimates increases, the amount of safety stock normally increases. In addition, the level of safety stock carried by an enterprise will also depend on the costs of carrying inventory and the costs of being out of inventory when materials are needed for production or sales. If the costs of carrying inventory are low and the costs of being out of inventory are high, then relatively large amounts of safety stock would normally be carried by a business enterprise.

    Quantitative techniques using statistics and probability theory may be useful to managers in establishing order point and safety stock levels. Such techniques are described in advanced managerial texts.

Linear
Programming for
Inventory Control

    Linear programming is a quantitative method that can provide data for solving a variety of business problems in which management's objective is to minimize costs or maximize profits, subject to several limiting factors. Although a thorough discussion of linear programming is appropriate for more advanced courses, the following simplified illustration demonstrates the way in which linear programming can be applied to determine the most economical purchasing plan. In this situation, management's objective is to minimize the total cost of purchasing materials for several branch locations, subject to the availability of materials from suppliers.

Assume that a manufacturing company purchases Part P for use at both its West Branch and East Branch. Part P is available in limited quantities from two suppliers. The total unit cost price varies considerably for parts acquired from the two suppliers mainly because of differences in transportation charges. The relevant data for the decision regarding the most economical purchase arrangement are summarized in the following diagram:

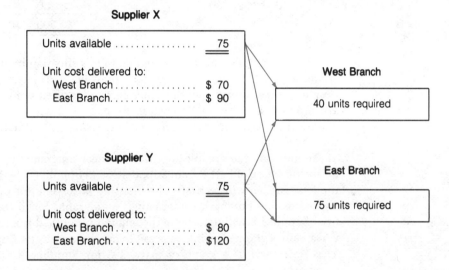

It might appear that the most economical course of action would be to purchase (1) the 40 units required by West Branch from Supplier X at $70 a unit, (2) 35 units for East Branch from Supplier X at $90 a unit, and (3) the remaining 40 units required by East Branch from Supplier Y at $120 a unit. If this course of action were followed, the total cost of the parts needed by the two branches would amount to $10,750, as indicated by the following computation:

|  | Cost of Purchases | | |
|---|---|---|---|
|  | By West Branch | By East Branch | Total |
| From Supplier X: |  |  |  |
| 40 units at $70 ..................... | $2,800 |  | $ 2,800 |
| 35 units at $90 ..................... |  | $3,150 | 3,150 |
| From Supplier Y: |  |  |  |
| 40 units at $120 .................... |  | 4,800 | 4,800 |
| Total ............................. | $2,800 | $7,950 | $10,750 |

Although many different purchasing programs are possible, the most economical course of action would be to purchase (1) the 75 units required by East Branch from Supplier X at $90 a unit and (2) the 40 units required by West Branch from Supplier Y at $80 a unit. If this plan were used, no units would be purchased at the lowest available unit cost, and the total cost of the parts would be $9,950, calculated as follows:

|  | Cost of Purchases | | |
| --- | --- | --- | --- |
|  | By West Branch | By East Branch | Total |
| From Supplier X: | | | |
| 75 units at $90 .................... |  | $6,750 | $6,750 |
| From Supplier Y: | | | |
| 40 units at $80 .................... | $3,200 |  | 3,200 |
| Total ............................. | $3,200 | $6,750 | $9,950 |

Linear programming can be applied to this situation by using either a graphic approach or a mathematical equation approach. This latter approach, called the simplex method, uses algebraic equations and is often used more practically with a computer. Because of its complexity and because it is normally covered in advanced managerial accounting texts, the simplex method is not described in this chapter.

To illustrate the graphic approach to linear programming, the preceding facts for the purchase of Part P from Supplier X and Supplier Y by the West Branch and the East Branch will be used. The first step in solving this problem is to place all of the possible purchasing alternatives on a graph. Since the amount purchased from Supplier X will determine the amount purchased from Supplier Y, and vice versa, only a graph showing all possible purchase plans for Supplier X (or Supplier Y) is necessary. The graph on page 293 for Supplier X is based on the foregoing data.

The linear programming graph is constructed in the following manner:

1. Units for the West Branch are plotted on the horizontal axis, and units for the East Branch are plotted on the vertical axis.
2. A point representing the maximum number of units that could be purchased from Supplier X by the West Branch (75 units) is located on the horizontal axis. A point representing the maximum number of units that could be purchased from Supplier X by the East branch (75 units) is located on the vertical axis.
3. A diagonal line (labeled Line 1) is drawn connecting the points representing the 75 units on the vertical axis with 75 units on the horizontal axis. This line represents the constraint on the maximum number of units (75) that can be purchased from Supplier X by either branch or both branches.
4. The constraint on the number of units that the West Branch would purchase from Supplier X (40) is indicated by a line (labeled Line 2) which is drawn vertically upward from the point of 40 units on the horizontal axis to intersect Line 1.

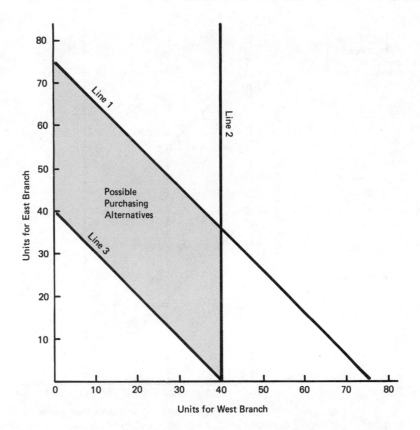

Line 1: Maximum number of units that can be purchased from Supplier X.

Line 2: Maximum number of units that will be purchased by West Branch.

Line 3: Minimum number of units that must be purchased from Supplier X.

5. A line (labeled Line 3) is drawn connecting 40 units on the vertical axis with 40 units on the horizontal axis. This line represents the constraint on minimum purchases from Supplier X (115 units required by the branches less 75 units available from each supplier).

6. The area bounded by the vertical axis and Lines 1, 2, and 3 is shaded. This area represents the set of all possible alternatives for purchases from Supplier X.

To illustrate the interpretation of a linear programming graph, assume that the West Branch purchased no units from Supplier X. The East Branch could then purchase between 40 and 75 units from Supplier X. This purchase alternative is indicated on the following graph between points A and B on the vertical axis. On the other hand, if the West Branch purchased 20 units from Supplier X, the East Branch could purchase between 20 and 55 units from Supplier X. This alternative is indicated on the following graph by the colored dotted line connecting points E and F.

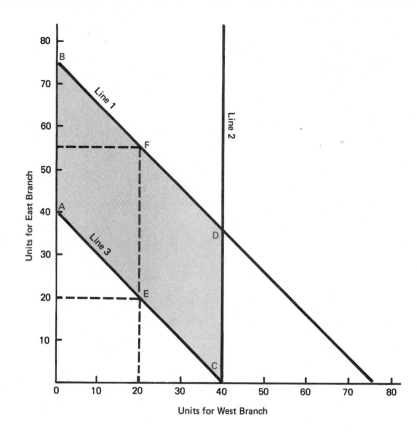

Units for East Branch

Units for West Branch

Although any point in the shaded area of the graph is a possible purchasing plan, managers are interested in selecting the most economical plan. According to the mathematical properties of linear programming, an economical purchase plan is located at one of the four points representing the corners of the shaded area of the graph. These corners are labeled A through D on the graph.

Each of the four corners represents the following purchases from Supplier X by the West Branch and the East Branch:

|  | Purchases by West Branch | Purchases by East Branch |
|---|---|---|
| Corner A: From Supplier X......... | 0 units | 40 units |
| Corner B: From Supplier X......... | 0 | 75 |
| Corner C: From Supplier X......... | 40 | 0 |
| Corner D: From Supplier X......... | 40 | 35 |

Since the amount purchased from Supplier X affects the amount purchased from Supplier Y, the four corners identified above can be rewritten in terms of four separate purchase plans. In other words, if only 40 units are purchased from Supplier X and are shipped to the East Branch (Corner A), then the West Branch must obtain its purchases of 40 units from Supplier Y, and the East Branch must obtain an additional 35 units from Supplier Y to fulfill its total needs of 75 units. The four purchase plans represented by the four corners are as follows:

|  | Purchases by West Branch | Purchases by East Branch |
|---|---|---|
| Plan 1 (Corner A): | | |
| From Supplier X......... | 0 units | 40 units |
| From Supplier Y......... | 40 | 35 |
| Plan 2 (Corner B): | | |
| From Supplier X......... | 0 | 75 |
| From Supplier Y......... | 40 | 0 |
| Plan 3 (Corner C): | | |
| From Supplier X......... | 40 | 0 |
| From Supplier Y......... | 0 | 75 |
| Plan 4 (Corner D): | | |
| From Supplier X......... | 40 | 35 |
| From Supplier Y......... | 0 | 40 |

By computing the total cost of the purchases for the West Branch and the East Branch for each of the purchase plans, the most economical purchase plan can be determined. As described earlier on page 292 and as shown in the following computation, Plan 2 is the most economical of the four purchase plans.

|  | Cost of Purchases | | |
|---|---|---|---|
|  | By West Branch | By East Branch | Total |
| **Plan 1:** | | | |
| From Supplier X: | | | |
| 40 units at $90......... | | $3,600 | $ 3,600 |
| From Supplier Y: | | | |
| 40 units at $80......... | $3,200 | | 3,200 |
| 35 units at $120........ | | 4,200 | 4,200 |
| Total................... | $3,200 | $7,800 | $11,000 |
| **Plan 2:** | | | |
| From Supplier X: | | | |
| 75 units at $90......... | | $6,750 | $ 6,750 |
| From Supplier Y: | | | |
| 40 units at $80......... | $3,200 | | 3,200 |
| Total................... | $3,200 | $6,750 | $ 9,950 |

|  | Cost of Purchases | | |
|  | By West Branch | By East Branch | Total |
|---|---|---|---|
| Plan 3: | | | |
| From Supplier X: | | | |
|   40 units at $70......... | $2,800 | | $ 2,800 |
| From Supplier Y: | | | |
|   75 units at $120........ | | $9,000 | 9,000 |
|    Total................... | $2,800 | $9,000 | $11,800 |
| | | | |
| Plan 4: | | | |
| From Supplier X: | | | |
|   40 units at $70......... | $2,800 | | $ 2,800 |
|   35 units at $90......... | | $3,150 | 3,150 |
| From Supplier Y: | | | |
|   40 units at $120........ | | 4,800 | 4,800 |
|    Total................... | $2,800 | $7,950 | $10,750 |

The preceding illustration of the graphic approach to linear programming required the construction of a graph and the consideration of four alternative purchase plans. Although an economical purchasing plan decision could have been determined by trial and error, such an approach can be time-consuming and costly. The trial and error approach could potentially require consideration of a much larger number of possible purchase plans before the most economical plan is found.

QUANTITATIVE TECHNIQUES FOR ESTIMATING COSTS

Although the costs from past operations are known, it is the estimation of future costs that is important for many analyses useful in decision making. In addition, the separation of estimated total costs into fixed and variable cost components is necessary for many analyses. For example, the use of variable costing for cost control, product pricing, production planning, and sales mix analyses requires the separation of costs into variable and fixed components. Break-even analyses and the computations of the contribution margin and the contribution margin ratio also require the separation of total costs into variable and fixed components.

The following paragraphs describe three methods of cost estimation: the high-low method, the scattergraph method, and the least squares method. Each of these methods provides an estimate of total costs and separates total costs into fixed and variable components.

High-Low Method

The high-low method is used to estimate the total costs as well as the variable and fixed components by using the highest and lowest total costs revealed by past cost patterns. The production levels associated with past cost patterns are usually measured in terms of units of production. For example, the cost of production during January would be measured relative to the total units produced during January.

To estimate the variable cost per unit and the fixed cost, the following steps are used:

1. a. The difference between the total costs at the highest and lowest levels of production is determined.
   b. The difference between the total units produced at the highest and lowest levels of production is determined.
2. Since only the total variable cost will change as the number of units of production changes, the difference in total costs as determined in (1a) is divided by the difference in units produced as determined in (1b) to determine the variable cost per unit.
3. The total variable cost (variable cost per unit × total units produced) at either the highest or the lowest level of production is determined, and the amount is subtracted from the total cost at that level to determine the fixed cost.

To illustrate, assume that Sutton Company has produced Product A and has incurred the following total costs for various production levels during the past 5 months:

|  | Units Produced | Total Costs |
|---|---|---|
| June. . . . . . . . . . . . . . . | 175,000 units | $185,000 |
| July . . . . . . . . . . . . . . | 75,000 | 80,000 |
| August. . . . . . . . . . . . | 200,000 | 210,000 |
| September . . . . . . . . | 325,000 | 320,000 |
| October. . . . . . . . . . | 300,000 | 270,000 |

The total units of production and the total costs at the highest and lowest levels of production and the differences are as follows:

|  | Total Units Produced | Total Costs |
|---|---|---|
| Highest level . . . . . . . . . . | 325,000 units | $320,000 |
| Lowest level. . . . . . . . . . . | 75,000 | 80,000 |
| Differences. . . . . . . . . . . . | 250,000 units | $240,000 |

Since the total fixed cost does not change with changes in volume of production, the $240,000 difference in the total cost represents the change in the total variable cost. Hence, dividing $240,000 by the change in production of 250,000 units provides an estimate of the variable cost per unit. In this illustration, the variable cost per unit is $.96, as shown in the following computation:

$$\text{Variable Cost per Unit} = \frac{\text{Difference in Total Costs}}{\text{Difference in Production}}$$

$$\text{Variable Cost per Unit} = \frac{\$240,000}{250,000 \text{ units}} = \$.96 \text{ per unit}$$

The fixed costs will be the same at both the highest and the lowest levels of production. Thus, the fixed cost of $8,000 can be estimated by subtracting the estimated total variable cost from the total cost at either the highest or the lowest levels of production, as shown in the following computations:

Total Cost = Variable Cost + Fixed Cost

Highest level:

$320,000 = ($.96 × 325,000) + Fixed Cost
$320,000 = $312,000 + Fixed Cost
$   8,000 = Fixed Cost

Lowest level:

$ 80,000 = ($.96 × 75,000) + Fixed Cost
$ 80,000 = $72,000 + Fixed Cost
$   8,000 = Fixed Cost

Since the variable and fixed cost components of the total cost have now been identified, the estimated total cost for any level of production can be determined by using the following equation:

Total Cost = Variable Cost + Fixed Cost
Total Cost = ($.96 × Total Units of Production) + $8,000

For 200,000 units of production, the estimated total cost would be determined as follows:

Total Cost = ($.96 × 200,000 units) + $8,000
Total Cost = $200,000

## Scattergraph Method

The scattergraph method of estimating total costs is based on the use of a graph. A distinguishing characteristic of the scattergraph method relative to the high-low method is that the scattergraph method uses total costs at the levels of past production in the analysis, rather than just the highest and lowest levels. Because the scattergraph method uses all the data available, it tends to be more accurate than the high-low method.

The following cost and production data for Sutton Company, which were used in illustrating the high-low method, are used to illustrate the scattergraph method:

|  | Units Produced | Total Costs |
|---|---|---|
| June | 175,000 | $185,000 |
| July | 75,000 | 80,000 |
| August | 200,000 | 210,000 |
| September | 325,000 | 320,000 |
| October | 300,000 | 270,000 |

The following scattergraph was constructed with these data:

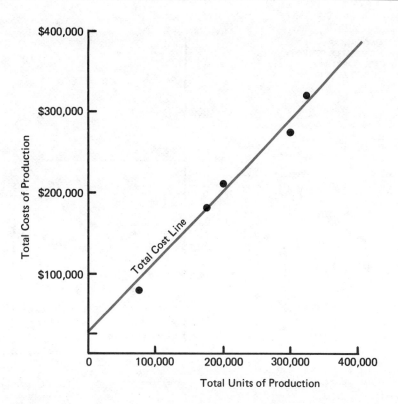

The scattergraph is constructed in the following manner:

1. Levels of total units of production are spread along the horizontal axis. For Sutton Company, it is assumed that a maximum of 400,000 units could be produced.
2. The total costs of production are spread along the vertical axis. For Sutton Company, it is assumed that the total costs of production could not exceed $400,000.
3. The total cost of each past level of production is then plotted on the graph. For example, the total cost of June's 175,000 units of production would be indicated on the graph by a point representing $185,000. The total cost of July's 75,000 units would be indicated by a point representing $80,000.
4. After all the total costs for the past levels of production have been plotted on the graph, a straight line representing the total costs is drawn on the graph. This line is drawn so that the differences between each point and the line are at a minimum in the judgment of the preparer of the graph.

From the following scattergraph for Sutton Company, the estimated total costs for various levels of production and the fixed and variable cost components can be determined. The point at which the total cost line intersects the vertical axis of the scattergraph indicates the estimated fixed cost of production. For Sutton Company, the fixed cost component is approximately $25,000.

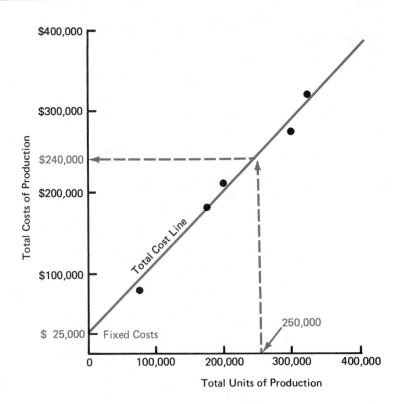

The estimated total cost for any level of production can be determined by locating the total units of production on the horizontal axis and proceeding vertically upward until the total cost line is intersected, then proceeding horizontally to the left until the vertical axis is intersected. On the scattergraph for Sutton Company, the estimated total cost for 250,000 units of production is determined to be approximately $240,000.

The total variable cost for any level of production is the difference between the estimated total cost and the estimated fixed cost. For Sutton Company, the estimated total variable cost for 250,000 units of production is $215,000 ($240,000 − $25,000). The estimated variable cost per unit is $.86 ($215,000 ÷ 250,000 units).

The estimated total fixed cost of $25,000 and the variable cost of $.86 per unit are represented in the following general formula for estimated total cost:

Total Cost = Variable Cost + Fixed Cost
Total Cost = ($.86 × Total Units of Production) + $25,000

For 200,000 units of production, the estimated total cost would be determined as follows:

Total Cost = ($.86 × 200,000 units) + $25,000
Total Cost = $197,000

Least Squares Method

While the scattergraph method requires the judgmental drawing of a total cost line through the plotted total cost points, the least squares method uses statistics to determine the total cost line. Thus, the resulting estimated total cost line is based on more objective statistical criteria.

The least squares method fits a straight line through the plotted total cost, according to the following general formula:

Total Cost = (Variable Cost per Unit × Total Units of Production) + Fixed Cost

The variable cost per unit component of the formula is estimated statistically, using the following computational formula:

$$\text{Variable Cost per Unit} = \frac{n(\Sigma P_i C_i) - (\Sigma P_i)(\Sigma C_i)}{n(\Sigma P_i^2) - (\Sigma P_i)^2}$$

The symbols in the preceding formula are explained as follows:

n   is the number of total cost observations
Σ   is the sum of the numbers
$P_i$   is an observed level of production, in units, at period $i$
$C_i$   is an observation of total cost, in dollars, at period $i$
$P_i^2$   is the square of the value $P_i$; likewise, $(\Sigma P_i)^2$ is the square of the value $(\Sigma P_i)$

The formula can be easily solved through the use of a computational table with columns for $P_i$, $C_i$, $P_i^2$, and $P_i C_i$. To illustrate, the following computational table for the estimation of the variable cost per unit for Sutton Company is prepared, based on the cost and production data that were used in the preceding illustrations. To simplify the computations, the thousands have been deleted from both the cost and production data.

| Total Units Produced $(P_i)$ | Total Costs $(C_i)$ | $P_i^2$ | $P_i C_i$ |
|---|---|---|---|
| 175 | $ 185 | 30,625 | $ 32,375 |
| 75 | 80 | 5,625 | 6,000 |
| 200 | 210 | 40,000 | 42,000 |
| 325 | 320 | 105,625 | 104,000 |
| 300 | 270 | 90,000 | 81,000 |
| 1,075 | $1,065 | 271,875 | $265,375 |
| ↑ | ↑ | ↑ | ↑ |
| $\Sigma P_i$ | $\Sigma C_i$ | $\Sigma P_i^2$ | $\Sigma P_i C_i$ |

Using the values from the table, the computational formula yields the following results:

$$\text{Variable Cost per Unit} = \frac{n(\Sigma P_i C_i) - (\Sigma P_i)(\Sigma C_i)}{n(\Sigma P_i^2) - (\Sigma P_i)^2}$$

$$\text{Variable Cost per Unit} = \frac{5(\$265,375) - (1,075)(\$1,065)}{5(271,875) - (1,075)^2}$$

$$\text{Variable Cost per Unit} = \frac{\$1,326,875 - \$1,144,875}{1,359,375 - 1,155,625}$$

$$\text{Variable Cost per Unit} = \frac{\$182,000}{203,750} = \$.89 \text{ per unit}$$

The fixed cost component of total cost is estimated statistically, using the following computational formula:

$$\text{Fixed Cost} = \overline{C} - (\text{Variable Cost per Unit} \times \overline{P})$$

The symbols are explained as follows:

$\overline{C}$ is the average of the monthly total costs
$\overline{P}$ is the average of the monthly units of production

For Sutton Company, the average total cost is $213,000 ($1,065,000 ÷ 5), and the average units of production is 215,000 units (1,075,000 units ÷ 5). When these values are substituted into the formula, the fixed cost is computed as follows:

Fixed Cost = $213,000 − ($.89 × 215,000 units)
Fixed Cost = $213,000 − $191,350
Fixed Cost = $21,650

The estimated total fixed cost of $21,650 and the variable cost of $.89 per unit are represented in the following general formula for estimated total cost:

Total Cost = Variable Cost + Fixed Cost
Total Cost = ($.89 × Total Units of Production) + $21,650

For 200,000 units of production, the estimated total cost would be determined as follows:

Total Cost = ($.89 × 200,000 units) + $21,650
Total Cost = $199,650

Comparison of
Cost Estimation
Methods

Each of the three methods described provided different estimates of fixed and variable costs, summarized as follows:

|  | Variable Cost per Unit | Total Fixed Costs |
|---|---|---|
| High-low method .............. | $.96 | $ 8,000 |
| Scattergraph method.......... | .86 | 25,000 |
| Least squares method ........ | .89 | 21,650 |

The cost estimation method that should be used in any given situation depends on such considerations as the cost of gathering data for the estimates and the importance of the accuracy of the estimates. Although the high-low method is the easiest and the least costly to apply, it is also normally the least accurate. The least squares method is generally more accurate, but it is more complex and more costly to use.

In this illustration, the high-low method differs significantly in its estimates of variable and fixed costs, $.96 and $8,000, compared to the variable and fixed cost estimates of the scattergraph and least squares method, $.86 and $25,000, and $.89 and $21,650, respectively. These differences result because the high-low method uses only two cost and production observations to estimate costs for all levels of production. If these two observations are not representative of the normal cost and production patterns for all levels of production, then inaccurate variable and fixed cost estimates may be obtained. To illustrate, if the July production and total cost data for Sutton Company are eliminated because they are seasonal and not typical of normal operations, then the high-low method yields representative estimates which are comparable to the estimates provided by the scattergraph and least squares methods, as shown in the following computations. In these computations, the fixed cost is estimated at the highest level of production.

|  | Total Units Produced | Total Costs |
|---|---|---|
| Highest level. . . . . . . . . . . . . . . . . . . . . . . . . . . . . | 325,000 units | $320,000 |
| Lowest level (excluding July data) . . . . . . . . . . | 175,000 | 185,000 |
| Differences . . . . . . . . . . . . . . . . . . . . . . . . . . . . . . | 150,000 units | $135,000 |

$$\text{Variable Cost per Unit} = \frac{\text{Difference in Total Cost}}{\text{Difference in Production}}$$

$$\text{Variable Cost per Unit} = \frac{\$135,000}{150,000 \text{ units}} = \$.90 \text{ per unit}$$

$$\text{Total Cost} = \text{Variable Cost} + \text{Fixed Cost}$$
$$\$320,000 = (\$.90 \times 325,000 \text{ units}) + \text{Fixed Cost}$$
$$\$320,000 = \$292,500 + \text{Fixed Cost}$$
$$\$27,500 = \text{Fixed Cost}$$

Care should also be exercised in using the scattergraph and least squares methods. The scattergraph method depends on the judgment of the individual who draws the total cost line through the points on the graph. Different individuals could fit different lines and thereby arrive at different estimates of the total cost. The least squares method is more objective, but it is difficult to use without a computer. Additional complications of the least squares method are described in more advanced texts.

Regardless of which cost estimation method is used, the estimated total cost should be compared periodically with actual costs. Large differences between estimated total costs and actual costs might indicate that the way in which total costs are estimated should be revised. For example, a change in the manufacturing process will likely require the gathering of total cost and production data related to the new process and the estimation of a new total cost formula, using one of the three methods discussed in this section.

THE LEARNING        Labor costs and thus total costs are affected by how efficiently and effectively
EFFECT IN        employees perform their tasks. In a manufacturing environment, costs will be
ESTIMATING        affected by how rapidly new employees learn their jobs and by how rapidly
COSTS        experienced employees learn new job assignments. For example, as production for
a new product begins or as a new manufacturing process is implemented, workers usually increase their efficiency as more units are produced and as they become more experienced. This learning effect is known as the learning curve phenomenon. When learning occurs, it can have a significant impact on costs and should be considered in estimating costs.

To illustrate, assume that Barker Company manufactures yachts and has added a new yacht to its product line. Past experience indicates that every time a new line of yachts is added, the total time to manufacture each yacht declines by 10% as each of the next 5 yachts is produced. Thus, the second yacht requires 90% of the total time to manufacture the first yacht, the third yacht requires 90% of the time of the second yacht, and so on. However, past experience also indicates that after the sixth yacht is produced, further reductions in time are insignificant.

For Barker Company, it is estimated that the first yacht will require 500 direct labor hours at $20 per hour, and that 10 yachts are scheduled for initial production. The following table illustrates the learning effect on the total direct labor cost per yacht:

| Yacht | Total Direct Labor Hours per Yacht | Direct Labor Cost per Hour | Total Direct Labor Cost per Yacht |
|---|---|---|---|
| 1 | 500 | $20 | $10,000 |
| 2 | 450 | 20 | 9,000 |
| 3 | 405 | 20 | 8,100 |
| 4 | 365 | 20 | 7,300 |
| 5 | 329 | 20 | 6,580 |
| 6 | 296 | 20 | 5,920 |
| 7 | 296 | 20 | 5,920 |
| 8 | 296 | 20 | 5,920 |
| 9 | 296 | 20 | 5,920 |
| 10 | 296 | 20 | 5,920 |

In this table, the total direct labor hours per yacht declined by 10% each time an additional yacht was produced, from a high of 500 hours to a low of 296 hours. The total direct labor cost per yacht declined from a high of $10,000 to a low of $5,920. After the sixth yacht was produced, the employees had learned enough from their experience in building the first 6 yachts that no additional reductions in time could be achieved.

The learning effect for Barker Company in terms of total direct labor hours per yacht is shown in the following graph:

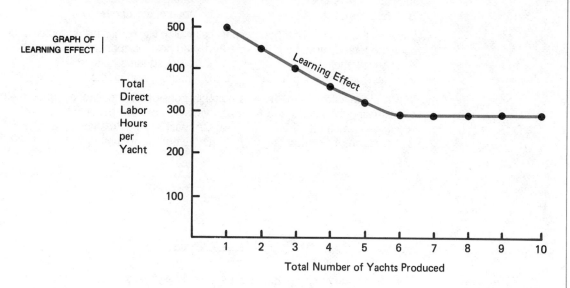

GRAPH OF
LEARNING EFFECT

The learning effect does not occur for all production processes, nor does it affect all production processes in the same way. In the preceding illustration of Barker Company, for example, instead of a 10% learning effect each time an additional yacht was produced, the learning effect could have been 10% for the first 3 yachts and 5% for the following 3 yachts. Generally, the more labor that is used in the production process, the greater the opportunity for the learning effect to occur. As production processes become more automated, less opportunity for learning exists.

The learning effect is important to managers, since it directly affects cost estimation. Estimated costs affect the development of such reports and analyses as budgets, standard costs, and cost-volume-profit analyses.

---

**Self-Examination Questions**
*(Answers in Appendix C.)*

1. A quantitative technique that can be used in solving a variety of business problems in which management's objective is to minimize costs or maximize profits, subject to several limiting factors, is:
   A. economic order quantity
   B. linear programming
   C. least squares method
   D. high-low method

2. In determining the economic order quantity, which, if any, of the following factors are important to consider?
   A. Storage cost per unit
   B. Annual units required
   C. Cost per order placed
   D. All of the above

3. The point at which the total cost line intersects the vertical axis of the scattergraph indicates:
   A. total variable cost
   B. total fixed cost
   C. variable cost per unit
   D. none of the above

4. Which of the following methods of cost estimation uses statistical formulas to determine the total cost and the variable and fixed cost components?
   A. High-low method
   B. Linear programming method
   C. Least squares method
   D. Scattergraph method

5. Which of the following methods is normally considered the least accurate method of estimating total costs and fixed and variable cost components?
   A. High-low method
   B. Scattergraph method
   C. Least squares method
   D. Linear programming

**Discussion Questions**

1. Distinguish quantitative techniques from analyses such as cost-volume-profit analysis and differential analysis.

2. What are the primary disadvantages of quantitative techniques?

3. For a business enterprise that needs large quantities of inventories to meet sales orders or production requirements, what can result from insufficient inventory?

4. What term is used to describe the optimum quantity of inventory to be ordered at one time?

5. Assuming that Product N is used at the same rate throughout the year, 500 units are required during the year, the cost per order placed is $12, and the storage cost per unit is $4.80, what is the economic order quantity for Product N?

6. What quantitative technique is often useful in determining the most economical plan for purchasing materials for several locations?

7. The inventory order point depends on what factors?

8. Assuming that Dooley Co. estimates daily usage of 500 pounds of material A, the lead time to receive an order of material A is 20 days, and a safety stock of 2,000 pounds is desired, what is the inventory order point?

9. If everything else remains the same, as the cost of carrying inventory increases, would the level of safety stock normally carried by a company increase or decrease?

10. What are three methods of cost estimation that are useful to the managerial accountant?

11. In applying the high-low method of cost estimation, how is the total fixed cost estimated?

12. If the variable cost per unit is $1.50 and the total fixed cost is $50,000, what is the estimated total cost for the production of 30,000 units?

13. Describe how the total cost line is drawn on a scattergraph.

14. How is the scattergraph method used to determine the estimated total cost for any level of production?

15. Assuming that the least squares method of cost estimation is used to estimate a variable cost per unit of $2.40, the average of the observed total costs is $200,000, and the average of the observed levels of production is 50,000 units, what is the least squares estimate of the total fixed cost?

16. What might be indicated by large differences between estimated total costs and actual costs?

17. As production for a new product begins or as a new manufacturing process is implemented, workers usually increase their efficiency as they produce more units and acquire more experience. What is this phenomenon called?

18. Why is the learning effect important to managers?

**Exercises**

**Exercise 13-1.** Fernandez Company estimates that 1,680 units of material F will be required during the coming year. Past experience indicates that the storage costs are $.80 per unit and the cost to place an order is $42. Determine the economic order quantity to be purchased.

**Exercise 13-2.** Glaser Company purchases Part Q for use at both its Beloit and Racine branches. Part Q is available in limited quantities from two suppliers. The relevant data for determining an economical purchase plan are as follows:

Units required:
    Beloit Branch..................... 100 units
    Racine Branch ................... 200 units

Supplier M:
    Total units available............... 200 units
    Unit cost delivered to:
        Beloit Branch................... $40 per unit
        Racine Branch ................. $60 per unit

Supplier N:
    Total units available............... 200 units
    Unit cost delivered to:
        Beloit Branch................... $50 per unit
        Racine Branch ................. $75 per unit

The following linear programming graph for units purchased from Supplier M has been constructed, based on the above data:

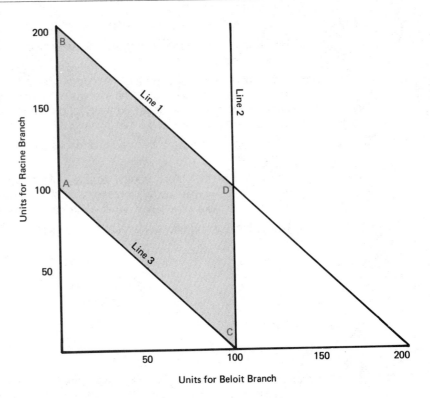

(a) For each of the four corners identified on the above graph by letters A through D, determine the purchases from Supplier M for the Beloit and Racine Branches. Use the same format as shown on page 294.

(b) For each of the four corners in (a), indicate the units purchased from both Suppliers M and N for the Beloit and Racine Branches. Use the same format as shown on page 295 and identify Plan 1 with Corner A, Plan 2 with Corner B, Plan 3 with Corner C, and Plan 4 with Corner D.

(c) Determine the most economical purchase plan by computing the total cost of each purchase plan determined in (b).

**Exercise 13-3.** Auerbach Company has decided to use the high-low method to estimate the total cost and the fixed and variable cost components of the total cost. The data for the highest and lowest levels of production are as follows:

|  | Total Units Produced | Total Costs |
|---|---|---|
| Highest level . . . . . . . . . . . . | 170,000 | $150,000 |
| Lowest level. . . . . . . . . . . . | 80,000 | 96,000 |

(a) Determine the variable cost per unit and the fixed cost for Auerbach Company.
(b) Based on (a), estimate the total cost for 120,000 units of production.

**Exercise 13-4.** A cost accountant for Grimly Company has prepared the following scattergraph as a basis for cost estimation:

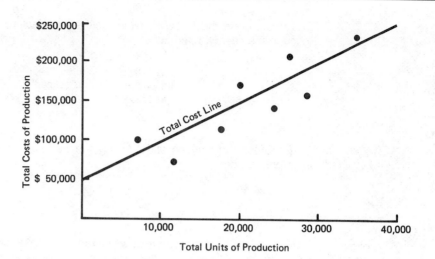

(a) Determine the estimated total fixed cost for Grimly Company.
(b) Determine the estimated total cost for 30,000 units of production.
(c) Compute the estimated variable cost per unit, based on the total cost of producing 30,000 units.

**Exercise 13-5.** The assistant controller for Emerson Company prepared the following table for use in estimating costs:

| Total Units Produced $(P_i)$ | Total Costs $(C_i)$ | $P_i^2$ | $P_iC_i$ |
|---|---|---|---|
| 120 | $100 | 14,400 | $12,000 |
| 150 | 145 | 22,500 | 21,750 |
| 170 | 180 | 28,900 | 30,600 |
| 90 | 90 | 8,100 | 8,100 |
| 70 | 80 | 4,900 | 5,600 |
| 60 | 65 | 3,600 | 3,900 |
| 660 | $660 | 82,400 | $81,950 |

The thousands have been deleted from the table. Thus, 120 units in the table represents 120,000 units of production and $100 represents $100,000.
(a) Determine the estimated variable cost per unit, using the table and the least squares formula on page 301. Round to the nearest cent.
(b) Determine the estimated fixed cost, using the preceding data and the least squares formula on page 302.
(c) Based on (a) and (b), estimate the total cost for 100,000 units of production.

**Exercise 13-6.** Eggers Sails Inc. manufactures sailboats and has added a new model of sailboat to its product line. Past experience indicates that every time a new model of sailboat is added, the total time to manufacture each sailboat declines by 5% as each of the next six sailboats are produced. After the seventh sailboat, no further reduction in time is possible. It is estimated that the first sailboat will require 400 direct labor hours at a cost of $15 per hour.

(a) Complete the following table for the manufacture of the first ten sailboats. Round to the nearest direct labor hour.

| Sailboat | Total Direct Labor Hours per Sailboat | Direct Labor Cost per Hour | Total Direct Labor Cost per Sailboat |
|---|---|---|---|
| 1 | 400 | $15 | $6,000 |

(b) Graph the learning effect for Eggers Sails Inc. in terms of total direct labor hours per sailboat.

**Problems**
*(Problems in Appendix B: 13-1B, 13-3B, 13-4B, 13-6B.)*

**Problem 13-1A.** Lehman Company has recently decided to implement a policy designed to control inventory better. Based on past experience, the following data have been gathered for materials, which are used at a uniform rate throughout the year:

Units required during the year . . . . . . . . . . . . . .   3,600
Ordering cost, per order placed . . . . . . . . . . . .   $30.00
Storage cost, per unit. . . . . . . . . . . . . . . . . . . . .   .15

Instructions:

(1) Complete the following table for "number of orders" of 1 through 6.

| Number of Orders | Number of Units per Order | Average Units in Inventory | Order and Storage Costs | | |
|---|---|---|---|---|---|
| | | | Order Cost | Storage Cost | Combined Cost |
| 1 | 3,600 | 1,800 | $30 | $270.00 | $300.00 |

(2) Determine the economic order quantity, based on the table completed in (1).
(3) Determine the economic order quantity, using the formula on page 290.

**Problem 13-2A.** Based on the data presented in Problem 13-1A, assume that Lehman Company is considering the purchase of new automated storage equipment to facilitate access to materials and to increase storage capacity. In addition, the manager of the purchasing department has requested authorization to purchase five microcomputers to expedite the processing of purchase orders.

Instructions:

(1) Assuming that the new storage equipment will increase the storage cost from $.15 to $.60 per unit, determine the economic order quantity for Lehman Company, using the formula on page 290.
(2) Assuming that the new storage equipment is not purchased and the acquisition of the microcomputer equipment will decrease the cost per order placed from $30 to $7.50, determine the economic order quantity, using the formula on page 290.
(3) Assuming that both the new storage equipment and the microcomputer equipment are purchased, determine the economic order quantity, using the formula on page 290. As indicated in (1) and (2), the purchase of the storage equip-

ment is expected to increase the storage cost per unit from $.15 to $.60, and the microcomputer equipment is expected to decrease the cost per order placed from $30 to $7.50.

(4) Based on the answers to Problem 13-1A and (1), (2), and (3) above, what generalizations can be made concerning how changes in the cost per order placed and the storage cost per unit affect the economic order quantity?

**Problem 13-3A.** Schellenberg Company purchases Part V for use at both its Elgin and Pekin branches. Part V is available in limited quantities from two suppliers. The relevant data are as follows:

Units required:
  Elgin Branch . . . . . . . . . . . . . . . . . . . . . . .  60
  Pekin Branch. . . . . . . . . . . . . . . . . . . . . . .  100

Supplier K:
  Units available. . . . . . . . . . . . . . . . . . . . . .  100
  Unit cost delivered to:
    Elgin Branch . . . . . . . . . . . . . . . . . . . . .  $25
    Pekin Branch. . . . . . . . . . . . . . . . . . . . .  $50

Supplier L:
  Units available. . . . . . . . . . . . . . . . . . . . . .  100
  Unit cost delivered to:
    Elgin Branch . . . . . . . . . . . . . . . . . . . . .  $30
    Pekin Branch. . . . . . . . . . . . . . . . . . . . .  $70

The new manager of the purchasing department of Schellenberg Company has prepared the following purchase plan for the Elgin and Pekin Branches:

|  | Purchases by Elgin Branch | Purchases by Pekin Branch |
|---|---|---|
| From Supplier K . . . . . . . . . | 60 units | 40 units |
| From Supplier L . . . . . . . . . | 0 | 60 |

Instructions:

(1) Construct a linear programming graph for units to be purchased from Supplier K. Plot the units for the Elgin Branch along the horizontal axis.
(2) Identify the four corners at which an economical purchase plan might be identified on the linear programming graph. Label the corners A through D, as shown in the illustration on page 294.
(3) For each corner in (2), indicate purchases from Suppliers K and L for the Elgin and Pekin branches. Identify Plan 1 with Corner A, Plan 2 with Corner B, Plan 3 with Corner C, and Plan 4 with Corner D.
(4) Determine the most economical purchase plan by computing the total cost of purchases for each plan identified in (3).
(5) Was the purchasing department manager's plan the most economical? Explain.

**Problem 13-4A.** The controller for Gillespie Company is preparing some preliminary cost projections for the 1985 budget and has accumulated the following cost and production data for 1984:

| | Units Produced | Total Costs |
|---|---|---|
| January............. | 20,000 | $36,000 |
| February............. | 30,000 | 44,000 |
| March............... | 40,000 | 52,000 |
| April................ | 25,000 | 40,000 |
| May................. | 35,000 | 50,000 |
| June ............... | 42,000 | 54,000 |
| July ................ | 50,000 | 65,000 |
| August ............. | 60,000 | 70,000 |
| September........... | 64,000 | 72,000 |
| October ............ | 70,000 | 75,000 |
| November ........... | 74,000 | 76,500 |
| December ........... | 68,000 | 72,000 |

Instructions:

(1) Estimate the variable cost per unit and the total fixed cost, using the high-low method of cost estimation.
(2) Construct a scattergraph, including the total cost line.
(3) Based on the scattergraph in (2), estimate the variable cost per unit and the total fixed cost at 50,000 units of production.
(4) Why are there differences between the estimates in (1) and (3)?

**Problem 13-5A.** The controller of Vaugh Company recently decided to use quantitative techniques for cost estimation purposes. Cost estimates were prepared using the high-low, scattergraph, and least squares methods, with the following results:

| | Variable Cost per Unit | Total Fixed Costs |
|---|---|---|
| High-low method ............. | $1.00 | $45,000 |
| Scattergraph method.......... | 1.05 | 34,500 |
| Least squares method ........ | 1.03 | 38,197 |

The controller expressed concern with the differences in the estimates, especially the differences between the estimates resulting from the high-low method and the estimates resulting from the scattergraph and least squares methods. The cost and production data used in developing these estimates are as follows:

| | Units Produced | Total Costs |
|---|---|---|
| January............. | 135,000 | $180,000 |
| February............. | 190,000 | 232,000 |
| March............... | 200,000 | 244,000 |
| April................ | 185,000 | 228,000 |
| May................. | 206,000 | 248,000 |
| June ............... | 197,000 | 238,000 |
| July ................ | 212,000 | 255,000 |
| August ............. | 223,000 | 272,000 |
| September........... | 218,000 | 266,000 |
| October ............ | 235,000 | 280,000 |

Instructions:

(1) Based on each of the preceding cost estimates for the high-low, scattergraph, and least squares methods, (a) compute the estimated total cost for 200,000 units of production, and (b) compute the differences between each of the total cost estimates in (a) and the actual cost of $244,000.

(2) Assuming that the January production and cost data are not typical of normal operations, recompute the variable cost per unit and the total fixed cost, using the high-low method.

(3) Based on (2), recompute the estimated total cost for 200,000 units of production, using the high-low method.

(4) Based on the total cost estimate computed in (3), what is the difference between this estimate and the actual cost of $244,000?

(5) Regardless of which cost estimation method is used, why should the estimated total cost be compared periodically with the actual cost?

**Problem 13-6A.** Tidmore Company began operations in January, 1984, and has decided to use the least squares method for estimating variable costs per unit and fixed costs. The following production and cost data have been gathered from the accounting and production records for the past 10 months:

|  | Units Produced | Total Costs |
|---|---|---|
| March . . . . . . . . . . . . . . . | 80,000 | $170,000 |
| April. . . . . . . . . . . . . . . . | 90,000 | 190,000 |
| May . . . . . . . . . . . . . . . . | 100,000 | 200,000 |
| June . . . . . . . . . . . . . . . | 110,000 | 220,000 |
| July . . . . . . . . . . . . . . . . | 120,000 | 224,000 |
| August . . . . . . . . . . . . . . | 115,000 | 218,000 |
| September. . . . . . . . . . . . | 110,000 | 210,000 |
| October . . . . . . . . . . . . . | 100,000 | 205,000 |
| November . . . . . . . . . . . . | 110,000 | 215,000 |
| December . . . . . . . . . . . . | 120,000 | 220,000 |

January and February cost and production data have been excluded, since operations during these months were in a start-up stage and were not typical.

Instructions:

(1) Prepare a computational table for the estimation of the variable cost per unit, using the following form. Do not include thousands in the table.

| Total Units Produced $(P_i)$ | Total Costs $(C_i)$ | $P_i^2$ | $P_i C_i$ |
|---|---|---|---|

(2) Determine the estimated variable cost per unit, using the table in (1) and the least squares formula on page 301. Round to the nearest cent.

(3) Determine the estimated fixed cost, using (1) and (2) and the least squares formula on page 302.

(4) Estimate the total cost of 100,000 units of production, using the results of (2) and (3).

**Mini-Case**

McDuffie Company has recently become concerned with the accuracy of its cost estimates because of large monthly differences between actual and estimated total costs. In the past, the senior cost accountant has used the high-low method to develop estimates of variable costs per unit and fixed costs. These cost estimates are as follows:

Variable cost per unit.............. $ 3
Fixed cost........................ 20,000

As a new junior cost accountant, the controller has asked you to determine whether the least squares method of cost estimation would provide more accurate estimates. The following twelve-month cost and production data have been gathered as a basis for developing the least squares cost estimates:

| | Units Produced | Total Costs |
|---|---|---|
| January ............. | 80,000 | $240,000 |
| February ........... | 60,000 | 196,000 |
| March.............. | 70,000 | 220,000 |
| April ............... | 50,000 | 175,000 |
| May ............... | 48,000 | 165,000 |
| June............... | 40,000 | 140,000 |
| July............... | 55,000 | 180,000 |
| August ............. | 68,000 | 212,000 |
| September ......... | 62,000 | 200,000 |
| October ............ | 75,000 | 230,000 |
| November........... | 82,000 | 245,000 |
| December.......... | 90,000 | 290,000 |

Instructions:

(1) Prepare a least squares computational table for the estimation of variable cost per unit, using the following form. Do not include thousands in the table.

| Total Units Produced $(P_i)$ | Total Costs $(C_i)$ | $P_i^2$ | $P_iC_i$ |
|---|---|---|---|

(2) Determine the estimated variable cost per unit, using the table in (1) and the least squares formula on page 301. Round to the nearest cent.
(3) Determine the estimated fixed cost, using (1) and (2) and the least squares formula on page 302.
(4) Prepare a table comparing the monthly differences between actual and estimated total costs for the high-low and least squares methods. Use the following headings:

| Month | Units Produced | Total Actual Costs | Total Estimated Costs High-Low Method | Least Squares Method | Monthly Differences High-Low Method | Least Squares Method |
|---|---|---|---|---|---|---|

(5) Which method is more accurate in estimating total costs? Explain.
(6) Which cost estimation method would you recommend to the controller?

# 14

CHAPTER

# Quantitative Techniques: Decision Making Under Uncertainty

## CHAPTER OBJECTIVES

*Describe and illustrate the use of the expected value concept for decision making under uncertainty.*

*Describe and illustrate the use of the maximin and maximax concepts for decision making under uncertainty.*

# 14

### CHAPTER

The preceding chapter described and illustrated the use of quantitative techniques by management, including methods used for inventory control and cost estimation. This chapter focuses on quantitative techniques useful to management in decision making under uncertainty, which is characteristic of the environment in which managers must make decisions. The managerial accountant can aid management in making decisions under uncertainty by providing data useful to management in assessing the chances that future events will occur and the impact of those events. One quantitative technique useful for this purpose is the expected value concept. Two alternative concepts that managers may find useful in special situations, the maximin and maximax concepts, are also discussed and illustrated.

MANAGERIAL
USE OF THE
EXPECTED
VALUE
CONCEPT

The concept of expected value involves identifying the possible outcomes from a decision and estimating the likelihood that each outcome will occur. By using the expected value concept, managers can better evaluate the uncertainty of the occurrence of predicted outcomes from decisions.

The likelihood that an outcome will occur from a decision is usually expressed in terms of a probability or chance of occurrence. For example, the probability or chance that, on the flip of a coin, a head will appear is .50 or 50%. Likewise, the probability or chance that the introduction of a new product will be successful might be expressed as .60 or 60%.

The expected value of a decision is the sum of the values that result when the dollar value of each outcome is multiplied by the probability or chance of its occurrence. Thus, expected value can be thought of as an average value. That is, each possible outcome is weighted by its chance of occurrence to obtain an average expected outcome. For example, assume that you are playing a game in which a coin is flipped. If a head appears, you win $10,000; if a tail appears, you lose $6,000. The expected value of this game is $2,000, computed as follows:

$$\text{Expected Value} = .50(\$10,000) + .50(-\$6,000)$$
$$\text{Expected Value} = \$5,000 - \$3,000$$
$$\text{Expected Value} = \$2,000$$

If you played the preceding game a large number of times, 50% of the time you would win $10,000, 50% of the time you would lose $6,000, and on the average you would win $2,000 per game. For example, if you played the game twice and won once and lost once, you would have won $10,000 and lost $6,000. Hence, you would have net winnings of $4,000 ($10,000 − $6,000). Since you played the game twice, your average winnings would be $2,000 per game ($4,000 ÷ 2). Consequently, the expected value of playing the game is $2,000.

To illustrate the expected value concept within a managerial context, assume that the management of Faxon Company is faced with deciding on a location for a new hotel. The search for the best site has been narrowed to two choices within a large metropolitan area. One site is in the center of the city. The accessibility to the city's business and entertainment district makes this site attractive for conventions. The other location is twenty miles from the center of the city at the intersection of two interstate highways. This site is attractive because of its proximity to the city's international airport. After the hotel is constructed, the management of Faxon Company plans to operate the hotel for one year and then sell the hotel for a profit. Over the past five years, Faxon has successfully constructed and sold four hotels in this fashion.

The estimated profit or loss at each site depends on whether the occupancy rate the first year is high or low. Based on marketing studies, the following profit and loss data have been estimated:

| City Site | Profit or Loss | Chance of Occurrence |
|---|---|---|
| High occupancy | $1,500,000 | 70% |
| Low occupancy | (500,000) | 30 |

| Interstate Site | Profit or Loss | Chance of Occurrence |
|---|---|---|
| High occupancy | $1,000,000 | 60% |
| Low occupancy | 100,000 | 40 |

The expected value of each site is computed by weighting each outcome by its chance of occurrence, as follows:

### City Site

Expected value = .7($1,500,000) + .3(−$500,000)
Expected value = $1,050,000 − $150,000
Expected value = $900,000

### Interstate Site

Expected value = .6($1,000,000) + .4($100,000)
Expected value = $600,000 + $40,000
Expected value = $640,000

Based on the expected values, the city site is more attractive than the interstate site because the city site has a higher expected value. Thus, on the average, the city site is expected to yield a higher profit than the interstate site.

The expected values for the city site and the interstate site of $900,000 and $640,000, respectively, will not actually occur. These values are weighted averages of the estimated profit or loss for each site. For the city site, the estimated outcome will be either a profit of $1,500,000 or a loss of $500,000. Likewise, for the interstate site, the estimated outcome will be either a profit of $1,000,000 or a profit of $100,000.

In the face of uncertainty, expected value is one of the most important pieces of information available to the manager for making a decision. Because expected value is an average concept, however, the range of possible outcomes (the variability of the outcomes) may also be valuable information for management's assessment of the uncertainty surrounding a decision. Although the city site in the preceding illustration has a higher expected value than the interstate site, the city site also has a wider range of possible outcomes (a profit of $1,500,000 or a loss of

$500,000) than does the interstate site (a profit of $1,000,000 or $100,000). Consequently, the management of Faxon Company might select the interstate site in order to minimize the variability of the possible outcomes from the site decision. As with many other decisions, management must exercise judgment after weighing all available data and analyses.

The use of the expected value concept by management can be facilitated through the use of payoff tables and decision trees. In addition, the expected value concept may be used by managers in assessing the value of collecting additional information before a decision is made. The remainder of this section describes and illustrates the use of payoff tables and decision trees and discusses the value of obtaining additional information.

**Payoff Tables**

A payoff table presents a summary of the possible outcomes of one or more decisions. A payoff table is especially useful in managerial decision making when a wide variety of possible outcomes exists. One such situation might involve a decision facing a store manager who must decide on the amount of merchandise to purchase for various levels of possible consumer demand. To illustrate, assume that the new manager of Grocery Wholesalers Inc. must decide how many pounds of a perishable product to purchase on Monday for sale during the week. The product is purchased in 100-pound units, and by the end of the week, any unsold product is spoiled and lost. In the past, the former manager had noted that the maximum weekly sales had been 900 pounds. Therefore, to be assured that all demand could be met, 1,000 pounds were purchased.

The variable cost of the product is $1.50 per pound, and the selling price is $1.80 per pound. Thus, for each pound sold, Grocery Wholesalers Inc. earns a contribution margin of $.30 ($1.80 selling price − $1.50 variable cost per pound) to cover fixed costs and earn a profit. For each pound unsold at the end of the week, the $1.50 variable cost per pound is lost.

Based on sales records, it was determined that sales during the past ten weeks were as follows:

| Number of Weeks | Actual Demand (Sales) |
|---|---|
| 2 | 700 lbs. |
| 5 | 800 |
| 3 | 900 |

The new manager must determine whether to purchase 700, 800, or 900 pounds. If the past ten weeks of sales data are used as an indication of future customer demand, the new manager should not purchase 1,000 pounds, since the recent sales data indicate that the maximum weekly demand (sales) has not exceeded 900 pounds.

The outcomes (payoffs) in terms of contribution margin for each of the possible purchase amounts and possible levels of customer demand are summarized in the following payoff table:

| | Possible | Contribution Margin of Purchases | | |
|---|---|---|---|---|
| PAYOFF TABLE OF POSSIBLE OUTCOMES | Demand | 700 lbs. | 800 lbs. | 900 lbs. |
| | 700 lbs. ........... | $210 | $ 60 | $ (90) |
| | 800 ............. | 210 | 240 | 90 |
| | 900 ............. | 210 | 240 | 270 |

The entries in the payoff table indicate that if 700 pounds are demanded and 700 pounds are purchased, for example, then 700 pounds will be sold and a total contribution margin of $210 (700 lbs. × $.30 per lb.) will result. If 700 pounds are demanded and 800 pounds are purchased, then 700 pounds will be sold and 100 pounds will spoil. In this case, the 700 pounds sold will generate a contribution margin of $210 (700 lbs. × $.30 per lb.), the 100 pounds that spoil will generate a loss of $150 (100 lbs. × $1.50 per lb.), and the net contribution margin will be $60 ($210 − $150). If 700 pounds are demanded and 900 pounds are purchased, then 700 pounds will be sold and 200 pounds will spoil. In this case, the 700 pounds sold will generate a contribution margin of $210 (700 lbs. × $.30 per lb.), the 200 pounds that spoil will generate a loss of $300 (200 lbs. × $1.50 per lb.), and the net contribution margin will be a loss of $90 ($210 − $300). If 800 pounds are demanded and 700 pounds are purchased, then 700 pounds will be sold and a total contribution margin of $210 (700 lbs. × $.30 per lb.) will result. The remaining entries in the payoff table are determined in a similar manner.

Based on the past ten weeks of sales data, the chances that the various levels of customer demand will occur can be estimated as follows:

| Possible Demand | Number of Weeks | Chance of Occurrence |
|---|---|---|
| 700 lbs. | 2 | 20% (2/10) |
| 800 | 5 | 50% (5/10) |
| 900 | 3 | 30% (3/10) |
| | 10 | |

A payoff table of expected values can now be constructed. Each entry in the payoff table of possible outcomes is multiplied by its chance of occurrence, as indicated above, to determine its expected value. The resulting amounts are entered in the following payoff table:

| | | Expected Value of Contribution Margin of Purchases | | |
|---|---|---|---|---|
| PAYOFF TABLE OF EXPECTED VALUE OF POSSIBLE OUTCOMES | Possible Demand | 700 lbs. | 800 lbs. | 900 lbs. |
| | 700 lbs. ........... | $ 42 | $ 12 | $ (18) |
| | 800............. | 105 | 120 | 45 |
| | 900............. | 63 | 72 | 81 |
| | Totals........... | $210 | $204 | $ 108 |

The expected value of the outcome that 700 pounds are demanded and 700 pounds are purchased is computed by multiplying the contribution margin of

$210 by the 20% chance that 700 pounds will be demanded. The resulting expected value is $42 ($210 × 20%). Likewise, the expected value of the outcome that 700 pounds are demanded and 800 pounds are purchased is computed by multiplying the contribution margin of $60 by the 20% chance that 700 pounds will be demanded. The resulting expected value is $12 ($60 × 20%). The expected value of the outcome that 700 pounds are demanded and 900 pounds are purchased is a loss of $18 (−$90 × 20%). Similarly, the expected value of the outcome that 800 pounds are demanded and 700 pounds are purchased is computed by multiplying the contribution margin of $210 by the 50% chance that 800 pounds will be demanded. The resulting expected value is $105 ($210 × 50%). The remaining entries in the payoff table are determined in a similar manner.

The total expected value of each possible purchase is determined by summing the individual expected values at each level of possible demand. In the above table, this total expected value is represented by the totals of each column. For example, the total expected value of a purchase of 700 pounds is equal to the sum of expected values of a purchase of 700 pounds and possible demand of 700 pounds ($42), a purchase of 700 pounds and possible demand of 800 pounds ($105), and a purchase of 700 pounds and possible demand of 900 pounds ($63). The resulting total expected value of purchasing 700 pounds is $210 (the total of the first column). Likewise, the total expected value of a purchase of 800 pounds is $204, and the total expected value of purchasing 900 pounds is $108.

Based solely on the above payoff table of expected values, the new manager should select that purchase with the highest total expected value. Thus, the best purchase decision, on the average, will be the purchase of 700 pounds, since its expected value of $210 is higher than any other purchase alternative. Even though this decision will result in lost sales in some weeks, on the average it will result in the largest possible profits.

## Decision Trees

Decision trees are graphical representations of decisions, possible outcomes, and chances that outcomes will occur. Decision trees are especially useful to managers who are choosing among alternatives when possible outcomes are dependent on several decisions. For example, if management decides to produce a new product, it must consider whether to offer the product in all consumer markets or only in specific markets, whether to offer special introductory rebates, whether to offer special warranties, and whether and how much to advertise. In this case, the expected profit from producing the new product depends on many decisions, each of which has an effect on the profitability of the new product.

To illustrate the use of decision trees, assume that Lampe Company is considering disposing of unimproved land. If the unimproved land is to be sold as is, its sales price would be $80,000. If the land is improved, however, there is a 40% chance that it can be rezoned for commercial development and sold for $120,000 more than the cost incurred in making improvements. There is a 60% chance that the improved land would be rezoned for residential use, in which case the land could be sold to a real estate developer for $70,000 more than the cost of improvements.

The decision tree for the preceding example can be diagrammed as follows:

DECISION TREE—
PROFIT FROM
SALE OF
UNIMPROVED OR
IMPROVED LAND

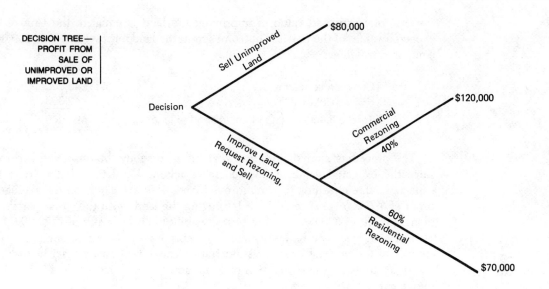

The expected values can be computed directly from the decision tree by tracing back through each branch of the decision tree and multiplying each of the possible outcomes by the chance of its occurrence. For example, the expected value of the land being rezoned for commercial use and sold for $120,000 is $48,000 ($120,000 × .4). The expected value of the residential rezoning is computed in a similar manner and is $42,000 ($70,000 × .6). Since there is no uncertainty concerning the selling of the unimproved land for $80,000, the expected value of selling the unimproved land is $80,000. These expected values are summarized in the following decision tree:

DECISION TREE
WITH EXPECTED
VALUES—PROFIT
FROM SALE OF
UNIMPROVED OR
IMPROVED LAND

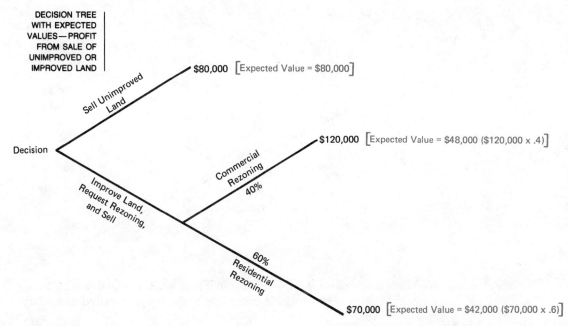

The total expected value of improving the land is equal to the sum of the expected values of the possible outcomes from the land improvement, or $90,000, computed as follows:

| | |
|---|---:|
| Commercial rezoning | $48,000 |
| Residential rezoning | 42,000 |
| Total expected value of improving the land | $90,000 |

The preceding analysis indicates that the land should be improved and sold, since the expected value of this course of action, $90,000, is higher than the expected value of selling the unimproved land, $80,000. Thus, on the average, a profit of $90,000 is expected from improving the land, with the worst possibility being a profit of $70,000 and the best possibility being a profit of $120,000.

Decision trees can be constructed to incorporate a large number of possible courses of action. The preceding illustration was intentionally brief in order to highlight the basic use of decision trees in aiding management's decision making under uncertainty.

**Value of Information**

In decision making, managers rarely have easy access to all the information they desire. In such cases, management must consider the information available and the value and the cost of seeking additional information relevant to the decision. If the expected value of acquiring additional information exceeds its expected cost, then the additional information should be acquired.

To illustrate, assume that an investment in Proposal A is expected to have a 60% chance of earning net income of $10,000 and a 40% chance of suffering a net loss of $5,000. This situation is diagrammed in the following decision tree:

DECISION TREE—
PROPOSAL A

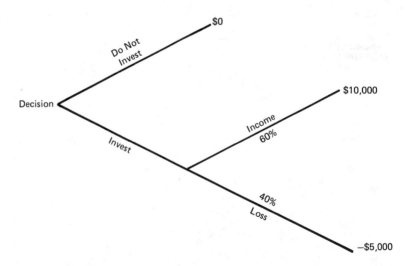

The expected value of investing in Proposal A is equal to the sum of the expected values of the possible outcomes, or $4,000, computed as follows:

Expected value of Proposal A = ($10,000 × .6) + (−$5,000 × .4)
Expected value of Proposal A = $6,000 − $2,000
Expected value of Proposal A = $4,000

Since the expected value of Proposal A is positive, the manager would normally invest in the proposal, even though there is a 40% chance of a loss of $5,000. Assume, however, that the manager could acquire additional information that would indicate with certainty whether Proposal A would earn the $10,000 income or suffer the loss of $5,000. How much would the manager be willing to pay for this additional (perfect) information?

The maximum amount (cost) that would be paid to obtain perfect information concerning a decision is termed the **value of perfect information**. It is the difference between (1) the expected value of a decision based on the perfect information and (2) the expected value of a decision based on existing information. To illustrate, the maximum amount that would be paid to obtain perfect information concerning Proposal A is determined by first computing the expected value of the proposal as if it is known beforehand whether the proposal would be successful or not. If the manager knows that the proposal will be successful, then a decision to invest would be made and income of $10,000 would be earned. If the manager knows that the proposal will be unsuccessful, then a decision not to invest would be made and no income or loss would result. For Proposal A, 60% of the time the perfect information will indicate that the proposal would be successful and therefore income of $10,000 would be earned. Also, 40% of the time the information will indicate that the proposal would be unsuccessful and therefore management would not invest. The expected value of perfect information is equal to the sum of the expected values of the possible outcomes, or **$6,000**, computed as follows:

Expected value of Proposal A,
   based on perfect information = ($10,000 × .6) + ($0 × .4)
Expected value of Proposal A,
   based on perfect information = $6,000

The value of perfect information concerning Proposal A is then determined by subtracting $4,000, the expected value of Proposal A, based on existing information, from the $6,000 computed above. Thus, as shown in the following computation, the manager would be willing to pay **$2,000** to obtain perfect information concerning Proposal A.

Expected value of Proposal A, based on perfect information . . . . . . . . $6,000
Less expected value of Proposal A, based on existing information . . .   4,000
Value of perfect information concerning Proposal A. . . . . . . . . . . . . . . . **$2,000**

**VARIANCE ANALYSIS USING EXPECTED VALUE**

When variances from standard costs occur, management must decide whether to investigate the causes and attempt corrective actions. To assist management in making this decision, the managerial accountant can use the expected value concept to focus on the expected costs relevant to the decision.

In prior illustrations, the use of the expected value concept focused on choosing among alternatives, so that the alternative with the highest expected value in terms of profit was chosen. Since management's primary focus in variance analysis is to minimize costs, however, the decision whether to investigate a variance is one of choosing that alternative with the lowest expected cost. In other words, in deciding whether to investigate a variance, management should compare the expected costs if an investigation is made with the expected costs if no investigation is made. It will then choose the alternative (investigate or not investigate) that provides the lowest expected costs.

To illustrate, assume that an unfavorable direct materials quantity variance of $1,000 has been reported for July and is expected to continue for one month if not corrected. Past experience indicates that 60% of the time the variance is caused by poor quality materials and can be eliminated (is controllable) by switching suppliers. On the other hand, 40% of the time the variance is caused by machine wear and tear and cannot be eliminated (is uncontrollable) without a major overhaul of the machinery. Due to sales commitments, production cannot be delayed for a machinery overhaul until the end of August, when regular maintenance is scheduled.

If the variance is not investigated, it will continue for August and the expected cost is the amount of the variance, $1,000. If the variance is investigated, using personnel who are available to conduct the investigation at no additional cost, the investigation may indicate that the variance is caused by poor quality materials and therefore is controllable. Management will then change suppliers and there will be no variance in August. If the investigation indicates that the variance is caused by machine wear and tear (and therefore is uncontrollable), the variance will continue for August at a cost of $1,000. However, the variance will be caused by machine wear and tear only 40% of the time, and thus the expected cost is $400 ($1,000 × 40%). These possible outcomes are diagrammed in the following decision tree:

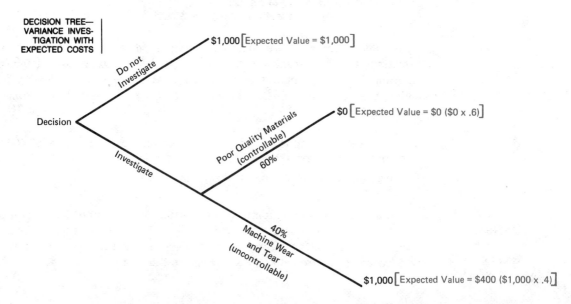

DECISION TREE—VARIANCE INVESTIGATION WITH EXPECTED COSTS

Decision

Do not Investigate — $1,000 [Expected Value = $1,000]

Investigate

Poor Quality Materials (controllable) 60% — $0 [Expected Value = $0 ($0 × .6)]

Machine Wear and Tear (uncontrollable) 40% — $1,000 [Expected Value = $400 ($1,000 × .4)]

The total expected cost if the variance is investigated is the sum of the expected costs of the two possible outcomes, as shown in the following computation:

| | |
|---|---:|
| Expected cost if variance is caused by poor quality materials (controllable) . . . | $   0 |
| Plus expected cost if variance is caused by machine wear | |
| and tear (uncontrollable) . . . . . . . . . . . . . . . . . . . . . . . . . . . . . . . . . . . . . . . . . | 400 |
| Total expected cost if variance is investigated . . . . . . . . . . . . . . . . . . . . . . . . . | $400 |

As indicated previously, management should select the alternative with the lowest expected cost. Since the total expected cost if the variance is investigated ($400) is less than the expected cost if no investigation is undertaken ($1,000), management should investigate the variance.

In this illustration, the cost of conducting the investigation was assumed to be zero. In practice, however, the cost may not be zero, and the important question therefore becomes: how much should management be willing to spend to investigate the variance? The answer for the direct materials variance illustration is $600, which is the difference between the total expected costs if (1) no investigation is undertaken and (2) an investigation is undertaken, as shown in the following computation:

| | |
|---|---:|
| Expected cost — no investigation . . . . . . . . . . . . . . . | $1,000 |
| Less expected cost — investigation. . . . . . . . . . . . . . | 400 |
| Value of conducting an investigation . . . . . . . . . . | $  600 |

In the above illustration, $600 is the maximum amount that management would spend to conduct an investigation of the direct materials variance. In other words, the value of conducting an investigation and obtaining perfect information concerning the cause of the variance is $600. Thus, if it is estimated that the cost to conduct an investigation would be $700, no investigation should be undertaken. If, on the other hand, the estimated cost to conduct an investigation is $500, the investigation should be undertaken. In the latter case, the expected cost savings would be $100, as shown in the following computation:

| | |
|---|---:|
| Value of conducting an investigation. . . . . . . . . . . . . . | $600 |
| Less cost of conducting the investigation . . . . . . . . . . | 500 |
| Expected cost savings from investigation . . . . . . . . | $100 |

**MAXIMIN AND MAXIMAX CONCEPTS OF DECISION MAKING UNDER UNCERTAINTY**

Alternate concepts to expected value are useful to management when it is extremely difficult to estimate the chances of occurrence of the various outcomes or when the potential loss or gain for a proposal is so great that management would ignore the expected value in making the decision. For example, management might be considering the possibility of introducing a revolutionary new product, which has a chance of earning extraordinarily large profits but which requires a total commitment of company resources. If the product is successful, the company will earn record profits; but if the product fails, the company may go bankrupt. In such a situation, the expected value concept may not be useful because management may not be willing to risk bankruptcy. The remainder of this chapter describes and illustrates two alternate concepts to expected value: (1) the maximin concept and (2) the maximax concept.

## Maximin Concept

The use of the maximin concept leads management to decide in favor of the alternative with the maximum (largest), minimum profit. The maximin concept is applied as follows:

1. The minimum (smallest) profit for each decision alternative is listed.
2. The decision alternative with the maximum (largest) profit from the list in (1) is chosen.

To illustrate, assume that the management of Hayes Company is considering building a condominium development in one of three locations. Because of limited funds, only one of the locations can be selected. The success of each location depends on demand. The estimated profit and loss from two levels of demand (low and high) for the condominium units for each location are as follows:

|              | Low Demand   | High Demand  |
|--------------|--------------|--------------|
| Location 1   | $(500,000)   | $4,000,000   |
| Location 2   | 100,000      | 1,200,000    |
| Location 3   | 150,000      | 800,000      |

In applying the maximin concept, the maximum, minimum profit (or loss) from each alternative is selected. In this illustration, the minimum profit (loss) for each location appears in the low demand column. For Hayes Company, the maximin concept indicates that Location 3 should be chosen, since under conditions of low demand, Location 3 will earn more than either Locations 1 or 2. In this way, management is assured that in the worst possible case (that of low demand), a maximum profit of $150,000 will be earned. By using the maximin concept, management has avoided the possibility of losing $500,000 from the selection of Location 1 and earning only $100,000 profit from the selection of Location 2. At the same time, however, management has also forgone the possibility of earning a maximum profit of $4,000,000 from the selection of Location 1 under the most favorable (high demand) condition.

The maximin concept is used by managers when the primary concern is minimizing the risk of any loss. In such situations, managers can be said to be risk averse.

## Maximax Concept

The use of the maximax concept leads management to decide in favor of the alternative with the maximum (largest) profit. The maximax concept is applied as follows:

1. The maximum (largest) profit for each decision alternative is listed.
2. The decision alternative with the maximum (largest) profit from the list in (1) is chosen.

To illustrate, assume the same facts as in the preceding illustration for Hayes Company. In applying the maximax concept, only the maximum (largest) profit for each location is considered. In this illustration, the maximum profit for each location appears in the high demand column on page 326. For Hayes Company, the maximax concept indicates that Location 1 should be selected, since under conditions of high demand, Location 1 will earn more than either Locations 2 or 3. In this way, management is assured that in the best possible case (that of high demand), the maximum profit of $4,000,000 will be earned. At the same time, however, management has also taken the risk of losing $500,000 from the selection of Location 1 under the worst (low demand) condition.

The maximax concept is used by managers when the primary concern is earning the largest possible profit, regardless of the risks. In such situations, managers can be said to be risk takers.

As illustrated by the Hayes Company, the maximin and maximax concepts depend on different philosophies of risk and thus lead to different decisions. The manager who uses the maximin concept is viewed as risk averse, while the manager who uses the maximax concept is viewed as a risk taker.

---

**Self-Examination Questions**
*(Answers in Appendix C.)*

1. The concept that involves identifying the possible outcomes from a decision and estimating the likelihood that each outcome will occur is the:
   A. maximin concept
   B. expected value concept
   C. maximax concept
   D. none of the above

2. Proposal R has a 60% chance of earning a profit of $80,000 and a 40% chance of incurring a loss of $60,000. What is the expected value of Proposal R?
   A. $24,000
   B. $48,000
   C. $72,000
   D. None of the above

3. Management's use of expected value can be facilitated through the use of payoff tables and:
   A. the maximax concept
   B. decision trees
   C. the maximin concept
   D. none of the above

4. The expected value of Proposal A, based on existing information, is $5,000, and the expected value of Proposal A, based on perfect information, is $8,000. What is the value of the perfect information concerning Proposal A?
   A. $3,000
   B. $5,000
   C. $8,000
   D. None of the above

5. The management of Freeman Co. is considering an investment in one of four real estate projects. The success of each project depends on whether demand is high or low. Based on the following data, which project would management select, using the maximin concept?

|  | Low Demand | High Demand |
|---|---|---|
| Project W . . . . . . . . . . | $120,000 | $600,000 |
| Project X . . . . . . . . . . | (40,000) | 800,000 |
| Project Y . . . . . . . . . . | 110,000 | 500,000 |
| Project Z . . . . . . . . . . | (60,000) | 900,000 |

A. Project W  
B. Project X

C. Project Y  
D. Project Z

## Discussion Questions

1. How can the managerial accountant aid management in making decisions under uncertainty?

2. What concept involves identifying possible outcomes from a decision and estimating the likelihood that each outcome will occur?

3. How is the expected value of a decision calculated?

4. Assume that you are playing a game in which a coin is flipped. If a head appears, you win $500, and if a tail appears, you lose $400. What is the expected value of playing this game?

5. Herrick Co. is considering an investment in a real estate project with the following outcomes and chances of occurrence. What is the expected value of the project?

| Profit | Chance of Occurrence |
|---|---|
| $1,200,000 | 30% |
| 400,000 | 70 |

6. What term is used to describe a table frequently used by managers to summarize the possible outcomes of one or more decisions?

7. The following data have been taken from the sales records of Kaufmann Co.:

| Number of Weeks | Actual Demand (Sales) |
|---|---|
| 4 | 1,000 units |
| 10 | 1,500 |
| 3 | 2,000 |
| 2 | 2,500 |
| 1 | 3,000 |

Estimate the chance that each sales level will reoccur.

8. Based on the following payoff table of expected values, what should be the amount of monthly purchases?

| Possible Demand | Expected Value of Contribution Margin of Purchases | |
|---|---|---|
| | 5,000 units | 10,000 units |
| 5,000 units.......... | $12,000 | $ 3,000 |
| 10,000.............. | 8,000 | 16,000 |
| Totals ............ | $20,000 | $19,000 |

9. What term is used to describe graphical representations of decisions, possible outcomes, and chances that outcomes will occur?

10. When are decision trees especially useful to managers in choosing among alternatives?

11. When should management acquire additional information before making a decision?

12. What term is used to describe the maximum amount that would be paid to obtain perfect information?

13. How is the value of perfect information computed?

14. Prete Co. is evaluating Proposal M as an investment. The expected value of Proposal M based on existing information is $10,000 and the expected value of Proposal M based on perfect information is $12,000. Prete Co. can obtain perfect information concerning Proposal M at a cost of $2,500. Should Prete Co. pay the $2,500 for the perfect information? Explain.

15. Using the expected value concept, how should management decide when to incur the costs necessary to investigate a variance?

16. What two alternate concepts to expected value can be used by management in making decisions under uncertainty?

17. When might the alternative concepts of maximax and maximin be more useful to management in decision making than the concept of expected value?

18. The president of Rosario Co. recently made the following statement concerning a proposed investment: "I don't care if the expected value is $1,500,000. I am not going to take the risk of losing $1,000,000 on Proposal Y. I'm selecting Proposal Z, with its expected value of $800,000, because its maximum possible loss is estimated to be $250,000." What decision-making concept was the president of Rosario Co. using?

19. Describe how the maximax concept of decision making is applied.

20. Would the use of the maximin and maximax concepts normally lead management to make the same decisions? Explain.

**Exercises**

**Exercise 14-1.** While on vacation in Las Vegas, you are offered the opportunity to play one game of chance in which a die is thrown. The die is numbered one through six, and each number has an equal chance of appearing on any throw of the die. The winnings and losses established for each number on a throw of the die are as follows:

| Number | Winnings (Losses) |
|--------|-------------------|
| 1 | $ 120 |
| 2 | 840 |
| 3 | (480) |
| 4 | (240) |
| 5 | (540) |
| 6 | 1,200 |

(a) Determine the expected value of playing the game. (b) If the cost of playing the game is $120, would you play? Explain.

**Exercise 14-2.** Based on a rumor that a new shopping mall will locate near its office complex, McElroy Company is considering exercising an option to purchase twenty acres of land surrounding its offices. If the shopping mall is constructed, the land should increase substantially in value and be sold for a profit. The chance that the shopping mall will be built near the McElroy Company office complex and the potential profits that could result are as follows:

| Outcome | Chance of Occurrence | Profit |
|---------|----------------------|--------|
| Shopping mall locates near office complex | 60% | $300,000 |
| Shopping mall locates elsewhere | 40 | 40,000 |

(a) Determine the expected value of exercising the option and purchasing the land. (b) Assuming that exercising the option is one of several investments being considered, briefly discuss how the expected values computed in (a) might be compared with the alternatives.

**Exercise 14-3.** The new manager of Erickson Grocery must decide how many pounds of a perishable product to purchase on Monday for sale during the week. The outcomes for each of the possible purchases and the possible levels of customer demand are summarized in the following payoff table of possible outcomes:

| Possible Demand | Contribution Margin of Purchases | | |
|-----------------|------------|----------|----------|
| | 100 lbs. | 200 lbs. | 300 lbs. |
| 100 lbs. . . . . . . . . . . . | $200 | $ 50 | $(100) |
| 200 . . . . . . . . . . . . . . | 200 | 400 | 250 |
| 300 . . . . . . . . . . . . . . | 200 | 400 | 600 |

The sales records for the past twenty weeks indicate the following levels of sales:

| Number of Weeks | Actual Demand (Sales) |
|-----------------|------------------------|
| 8 | 100 lbs. |
| 8 | 200 |
| 4 | 300 |

(a) Based on the sales data for the past twenty weeks, determine the chances that the various levels of customer demand (100 lbs., 200 lbs., 300 lbs.) will occur.

(b) Construct a payoff table of expected values of possible outcomes, using the format shown on page 319. (c) What should be the amount of purchases for Erickson Grocery?

**Exercise 14-4.** Sidwell Company is considering whether to offer a new product for sale in the South or in the West. Because of the uncertainty associated with introducing a new product, the decision will be made on the basis of expected annual income. The possible outcomes and chances of occurrence are summarized as follows:

| Customer Demand | Southern Region Annual Income | Southern Region Chance of Occurrence | Western Region Annual Income | Western Region Chance of Occurrence |
|---|---|---|---|---|
| High | $25,000,000 | 30% | $30,000,000 | 40% |
| Moderate | 10,000,000 | 40 | 6,000,000 | 20 |
| Low | 2,000,000 | 30 | 2,000,000 | 40 |

(a) To aid management in deciding in which region to offer the new product, prepare a decision tree with expected values. (b) Which region should be selected for the introduction of the new product, based on the expected value concept?

**Exercise 14-5.** The management of Newsome Company has the opportunity to invest in Proposal E, which is expected to have a 40% chance of earning income of $50,000 and a 60% chance of suffering a loss of $30,000. (a) What is the expected value of Proposal E, based on existing information? (b) What is the expected value of Proposal E, based on perfect information? (c) What is the value of perfect information concerning Proposal E? (d) If the management of Newsome Company could purchase perfect information concerning Proposal E for $10,000, should the perfect information be purchased?

**Exercise 14-6.** The controller of Zeigler Company must decide whether to investigate an unfavorable direct labor quantity variance of $4,000 for September. The variance is expected to continue for October if no investigation is undertaken. Based on past experience, there is an 80% chance that the variance is controllable and can be eliminated for October if an investigation is conducted. There is a 20% chance that the variance is uncontrollable and cannot be eliminated for October. (a) Determine the expected cost if the variance is investigated, assuming that no additional cost will be incurred in conducting the investigation. (b) How much should management be willing to spend to investigate the variance?

**Exercise 14-7.** Prepare a decision tree of expected values (costs) for (a) Exercise 14-5 and (b) Exercise 14-6.

**Exercise 14-8.** Ling Company is considering an investment in one of three projects. The success of each project depends on whether customer demand is low or high. The possible profit or loss for each project is summarized as follows:

|  | Low Demand | High Demand |
|---|---|---|
| Project A............ | $100,000 | $240,000 |
| Project B............ | (40,000) | 320,000 |
| Project C............ | (60,000) | 500,000 |

(a) Using the maximin concept, which project should management choose? (b) Using the maximax concept, which project should management choose? (c) Explain why the answers to (a) and (b) are not the same.

**Problems**
*(Problems in
Appendix B:
14-1B, 14-2B,
14-3B, 14-4B,
14-5B.)*

**Problem 14-1A.** Hudson Science Corporation is considering purchasing the rights to one of two laser patents for purposes of research and development. Patent A has potential developmental applications in the areas of medicine, computer science, pharmacology, and military weaponry. Patent B has potential developmental applications in the areas of mining, automobile manufacturing, telecommunications, and energy. Whichever patent rights are purchased, it is likely that only one of the potential applications will yield research and development results promising enough to market commercially. The estimated profit for each patent application and the estimated chances of occurrence are as follows:

**Patent A**

| Application | Estimated Profit | Chance of Occurrence |
|---|---|---|
| Medicine | $ 5,000,000 | 20% |
| Computer science | 6,500,000 | 40 |
| Pharmacology | 8,000,000 | 30 |
| Military weaponry | 12,000,000 | 10 |

**Patent B**

| Application | Estimated Profit | Chance of Occurrence |
|---|---|---|
| Mining | $ 3,000,000 | 10% |
| Automobile manufacturing | 5,000,000 | 30 |
| Telecommunications | 9,000,000 | 40 |
| Energy | 15,000,000 | 20 |

Instructions:

(1) Determine the expected value of each patent.
(2) Based on the results of (1), which patent rights should be purchased?

**Problem 14-2A.** Shiver News Distributors recently purchased a newsstand on the corner of 5th Avenue South and 2nd Street in downtown Clinton. The new manager of the newsstand must decide how many copies of the local newspaper to stock on a daily basis. The former manager had noted that the maximum daily sales, in the past, had been 175 papers, and to be assured that all demand could be met, 200 papers were purchased daily. The cost of the newspaper is $.20 per paper, and the paper is sold for $.30. Any papers remaining at the end of the day are worthless and are thrown away. The paper is published five days a week.

The records for the past month indicate the following sales:

| Number of Days | Actual Demand (Sales) |
|---|---|
| 2 | 100 papers |
| 8 | 125 |
| 6 | 150 |
| 4 | 175 |

Instructions:

(1) Prepare a payoff table of possible outcomes in terms of contribution margin, using the format shown on page 319.
(2) Based on the sales data for the past 20 days, estimate the chances of each level of possible demand for the newspaper.
(3) Prepare a payoff table of expected values of possible outcomes in terms of contribution margin, using the format shown on page 319.
(4) Based on (3), how many newspapers should be purchased? Explain.

**Problem 14-3A.** Tatum Mines Inc. is preparing to bid on the purchase of mining rights to one of two plats of federally owned land: Plat #1000 and Plat #1200. Both plats of land are known to contain deposits of uranium; however, the quality of the deposits will not be known until actual mining begins.

Preliminary estimates indicate that, for Plat #1000, there is a 60% chance that the deposit is of high quality and will yield total profits of $30,000,000. There is a 20% chance that the deposit is of moderate quality and will yield total profits of $16,000,000. Finally, there is a 20% chance that the deposit is of low quality and will yield total profits of $4,000,000.

Preliminary estimates indicate that, for Plat #1200, there is a 40% chance that the deposit is of high quality and will yield total profits of $50,000,000. There is a 40% chance that the deposit is of moderate quality and will yield total profits of $10,000,000. Finally, there is a 20% chance that the deposit is of low quality and will yield total profits of $500,000.

Instructions:

(1) Prepare a decision tree with expected values to aid management in deciding on which plat rights to bid.
(2) On which plat rights should the management of Tatum Mines Inc. bid?

**Problem 14-4A.** The controller of McFarland Company must decide whether to investigate an unfavorable direct labor time variance of $5,000 reported for March. The variance is expected to continue for April if not corrected. Past experience indicates that 70% of the time the variance is caused by lack of proper supervision and can be eliminated by reminding the supervisors of their responsibilities. On the other hand, 30% of the time the variance is caused by inexperienced personnel who lack proper training. Due to sales and production commitments, the appropriate training cannot be scheduled until the end of April.

Instructions:

(1) Assuming that no additional costs would be incurred in conducting an investigation, what is the expected cost of investigating the direct labor time variance?
(2) What is the value of conducting an investigation of the direct labor time variance?
(3) If the estimated cost to investigate the variance is $4,000, should the controller authorize an investigation? Explain.
(4) If the estimated cost to investigate the variance is $2,500, should the controller authorize an investigation? Explain.

**Problem 14-5A.** The management of Investors Diversified Inc. is considering a speculative investment in one of three oil and gas ventures. The success or failure of each venture depends on the quantity of oil and gas discovered. The estimated profit or loss for each venture is as follows:

| | Amount of Oil and Gas Discovered | | |
|---|---|---|---|
| | None | Moderate Quantities | Large Quantities |
| Venture A ...... | $(3,000,000) | $24,000,000 | $60,000,000 |
| Venture B ...... | (2,000,000) | 12,000,000 | 40,000,000 |
| Venture C ...... | (5,000,000) | 20,000,000 | 80,000,000 |

Instructions:

(1) If the management of Investors Diversified Inc. uses the maximin concept, which of the three ventures would be chosen?

(2) If the management of Investors Diversified Inc. uses the maximax concept, which of the three ventures would be chosen?

(3) Assuming that the Moderate Quantities column is the most likely estimate of profit from the oil and gas that will be discovered, what alternative decision concept can be used by Investors Diversified Inc.?

**Problem 14-6A.** Vickery Company is considering building a condominium development in one of three locations: a city location, a country club location, and a lakefront location. The success of each location depends on buyer demand. Based on marketing studies, the following profits and losses have been estimated for each location, along with the chances of occurrence:

| | High Buyer Demand | | Low Buyer Demand | |
|---|---|---|---|---|
| | Profit (Loss) | Chance of Occurrence | Profit (Loss) | Chance of Occurrence |
| City ......... | $25,000,000 | 75% | $(10,000,000) | 25% |
| Country club .. | 15,000,000 | 60 | (6,000,000) | 40 |
| Lakefront...... | 30,000,000 | 70 | (20,000,000) | 30 |

Instructions:

(1) Determine the expected value of each location.

(2) Which location should be chosen, using the expected value concept?

(3) Which location should be chosen, using the maximin concept?

(4) Which location should be chosen, using the maximax concept?

(5) Which location should be chosen if management's primary objective is to choose that location with the smallest range of possible outcomes?

(6) Which location would be chosen if management uses the concept of selecting that location with the highest chance of profit?

**Mini-Case**    Consolidated Oil Inc. must decide between two sites at which to drill for oil. At a desert site, there is a 75% chance that oil will be discovered, resulting in an estimated profit of $24,000,000. There is a 25% chance that no oil will be discovered at the desert site, resulting in an estimated loss of $4,000,000. At a mountain site, there is a 65% chance that oil will be discovered, resulting in an estimated profit of $30,000,000. There is a 35% chance that no oil will be discovered at the mountain site, resulting in an estimated loss of $10,000,000.

As a special summer intern serving in the capacity of assistant to the president, Deborah Keenan, you have been asked to analyze which site should be selected for drilling. In the past, Keenan has selected that site with the largest possible profit.

Instructions:

(1) What decision concept has Keenan used in the past?

(2) Using Keenan's concept identified in (1), which site should be selected?

(3) Prepare a decision tree with expected values to aid Keenan in the site selection decision.

(4) Based on the expected value concept, which site should be selected?

(5) Assuming that a new technology, using infrared photographs from satellites, can provide perfect information concerning the location of oil deposits, how much should Consolidated Oil Inc. be willing to pay for perfect information concerning (a) the desert site and (b) the mountain site?

(6) Assuming that the perfect information described in (5) costs $1,200,000 per site, should each site be analyzed at a cost of $1,200,000 per analysis to obtain perfect information?

(7) Assuming that Keenan agrees to use the expected value concept in the selection of a drilling site, prepare a final recommendation using the results of (3) through (6).

# 15

CHAPTER | # Financial Statement Analysis

**CHAPTER OBJECTIVES**

*Describe the usefulness of financial statement analysis
to management.*

*Describe basic financial statement analytical
procedures.*

*Illustrate the application of financial statement analysis
in assessing solvency and profitability.*

# PART 7 | Financial Analyses for Management Use

# 15

## CHAPTER

One of the primary objectives of accounting is to provide data to management for use in directing operations. In providing data to assist management, the accountant relies on a variety of concepts and techniques. Many of these concepts and techniques, such as budgeting, standard costs, differential analysis, break-even analysis, and variable costing, were discussed in preceding chapters. In this chapter, management's use of analyses of the data reported in the basic financial statements will be presented.

## USEFULNESS OF FINANCIAL STATEMENT ANALYSIS

The financial condition and the results of operations, as reported in the basic financial statements, are of interest to many groups external to the reporting enterprise. Since the basic statements will be evaluated by outsiders, such as creditors and owners, management is concerned with the basic financial statements and how they are viewed by these external parties. Management is also interested in the basic financial statements for other reasons. For example, the basic financial statements are used to assess the effectiveness of management in planning and controlling operations. In addition, management recognizes that the evaluation of past operations, as revealed by the analysis of the basic statements, represents a good starting point in planning future operations. Management uses financial statement analysis, therefore, as an important means of assessing past performance and in forecasting and planning future performance.

## TYPES OF FINANCIAL STATEMENT ANALYSIS

Most of the items in the basic statements are of limited significance when considered individually. Their usefulness can be enhanced through studying relationships and comparisons of items (1) within a single year's financial statements, (2) in a succession of financial statements, and (3) with other enterprises. The selection and the preparation of analytical aids are a part of the work of the accountant.

Certain aspects of financial condition or of operations are of greater importance to management than are other aspects. However, management is especially interested in the ability of a business to pay its debts as they come due and to earn a reasonable amount of income. These two aspects of the status of an enterprise are solvency and profitability. An enterprise that cannot meet its obligations to creditors on a timely basis is likely to experience difficulty in obtaining credit, and this may lead to a decline in profitability. Similarly, an enterprise whose earnings are less than those of its competitors is likely to be at a disadvantage in obtaining credit or new capital from stockholders. In this chapter, basic analytical procedures and various types of financial analysis useful in evaluating the solvency and profitability of an enterprise will be discussed.

## BASIC ANALYTICAL PROCEDURES

The analytical measures obtained from financial statements are usually expressed as ratios or percentages. For example, the relationship of $150,000 to $100,000 ($150,000/$100,000 or $150,000 : $100,000) may be expressed as 1.5, 1.5 : 1, or 150%. This ease of computation and simplicity of form for expressing financial relationships are major reasons for the widespread use of ratios and percentages in financial analysis.

Analytical procedures may be used to compare the amount of specific items on a current statement with the corresponding amounts on earlier statements. For example, in comparing cash of $150,000 on the current balance sheet with cash of $100,000 on the balance sheet of a year earlier, the current amount may be expressed as 1.5 or 150% of the earlier amount. The relationship may also be expressed in terms of change, that is, the increase of $50,000 may be stated as a 50% increase.

Analytical procedures are also widely used to show the relationships of individual items to each other and of individual items to totals on a single statement. To illustrate, assume that included in the total of $1,000,000 of assets on a balance sheet are cash of $50,000 and inventories of $250,000. In relative terms, the cash balance is 5% of total assets and the inventories represent 25% of total assets. Individual items in the current asset group could also be related to total current assets. Assuming that the total of current assets in the example is $500,000, cash represents 10% of the total and inventories represent 50% of the total.

Increases or decreases in items may be expressed in percentage terms only when the base figure is positive. If the base figure is zero or a negative value, the amount of change cannot be expressed as a percentage. For example, if comparative balance sheets indicate no liability for notes payable on the first, or base, date and a liability of $10,000 on the later date, the increase of $10,000 cannot be stated as a percent of zero. Similarly, if a net loss of $10,000 in a particular year is followed by a net income of $5,000 in the next year, the increase of $15,000 cannot be stated as a percent of the loss of the base year.

In the following discussion and illustrations of analytical procedures, the basic significance of the various measures will be emphasized. The measures developed are not ends in themselves; they are only guides to the evaluation of financial and operating data. Many other factors, such as trends in the industry, changes in price levels, and general economic conditions and prospects may also need consideration in order to arrive at sound conclusions.

## Horizontal Analysis

The percentage analysis of increases and decreases in corresponding items in comparative financial statements is called **horizontal analysis**. The amount of each item on the most recent statement is compared with the corresponding item on one or more earlier statements. The increase or decrease in the amount of the item is then listed, together with the percent of increase or decrease. When the comparison is made between two statements, the earlier statement is used as the base. If the analysis includes three or more statements, there are two alternatives in the selection of the base: the earliest date or period may be used as the basis for comparing all later dates or periods, or each statement may be compared with the immediately preceding statement. The two alternatives are illustrated as follows:

*Base: Earliest Year*

|  |  |  |  | Increase (Decrease*) | | | |
|  |  |  |  | 1984–85 | | 1984–86 | |
| Item | 1984 | 1985 | 1986 | Amount | Percent | Amount | Percent |
| A | $100,000 | $150,000 | $200,000 | $ 50,000 | 50% | $100,000 | 100% |
| B | 100,000 | 200,000 | 150,000 | 100,000 | 100% | 50,000 | 50% |

Base: Preceding Year

| | | | | Increase (Decrease*) | | | |
| | | | | 1984–85 | | 1985–86 | |
| Item | 1984 | 1985 | 1986 | Amount | Percent | Amount | Percent |
|---|---|---|---|---|---|---|---|
| A | $100,000 | $150,000 | $200,000 | $ 50,000 | 50% | $ 50,000 | 33% |
| B | 100,000 | 200,000 | 150,000 | 100,000 | 100% | 50,000* | 25%* |

Comparison of the amounts in the last two columns of the first analysis with the amounts in the corresponding columns of the second analysis reveals the effect of the base year on the direction of change and the amount and percent of change.

A condensed comparative balance sheet for two years, with horizontal analysis, is illustrated as follows:

COMPARATIVE
BALANCE SHEET—
HORIZONTAL
ANALYSIS

Chung Company<br>Comparative Balance Sheet<br>December 31, 1985 and 1984

| | 1985 | 1984 | Increase (Decrease*) | |
| | | | Amount | Percent |
|---|---|---|---|---|
| **Assets** | | | | |
| Current assets........... | $ 550,000 | $ 533,000 | $ 17,000 | 3.2% |
| Long-term investments .... | 95,000 | 177,500 | 82,500* | 46.5%* |
| Plant assets (net) ........ | 444,500 | 470,000 | 25,500* | 5.4%* |
| Intangible assets ........ | 50,000 | 50,000 | —— | |
| Total assets ............. | $1,139,500 | $1,230,500 | $ 91,000* | 7.4%* |
| **Liabilities** | | | | |
| Current liabilities.......... | $ 210,000 | $ 243,000 | $ 33,000* | 13.6%* |
| Long-term liabilities ....... | 100,000 | 200,000 | 100,000* | 50.0%* |
| Total liabilities ........... | $ 310,000 | $ 443,000 | $133,000* | 30.0%* |
| **Stockholders' Equity** | | | | |
| Preferred 6% stock, $100 par.................. | $ 150,000 | $ 150,000 | —— | —— |
| Common stock, $10 par ... | 500,000 | 500,000 | —— | —— |
| Retained earnings ........ | 179,500 | 137,500 | $ 42,000 | 30.5% |
| Total stockholders' equity .. | $ 829,500 | $ 787,500 | $ 42,000 | 5.3% |
| Total liab. & stockholders' equity ............... | $1,139,500 | $1,230,500 | $ 91,000* | 7.4%* |

The significance of the various increases and decreases in the items shown cannot be fully determined without additional information. Although total assets at the end of 1985 were $91,000 (7.4%) less than at the beginning of the year, liabilities were reduced by $133,000 (30%) and stockholders' equity increased $42,000 (5.3%). It would appear that the reduction of $100,000 in long-term liabilities was accomplished, for the most part, through the sale of long-term investments.

The foregoing balance sheet may be expanded to include the details of the various categories of assets and liabilities, or the details may be presented in separate schedules. Opinions differ as to which method presents the clearer picture. A supporting schedule with horizontal analysis is illustrated by the following comparative schedule of current assets:

COMPARATIVE
SCHEDULE OF
CURRENT
ASSETS—
HORIZONTAL
ANALYSIS

| | | | Increase (Decrease*) | |
|---|---|---|---|---|
| | 1985 | 1984 | Amount | Percent |
| Cash .................... | $ 90,500 | $ 64,700 | $25,800 | 39.9% |
| Marketable securities...... | 75,000 | 60,000 | 15,000 | 25.0% |
| Accounts receivable (net) .. | 115,000 | 120,000 | 5,000* | 4.2%* |
| Inventory................ | 264,000 | 283,000 | 19,000* | 6.7%* |
| Prepaid expenses........ | 5,500 | 5,300 | 200 | 3.8% |
| Total current assets ....... | $550,000 | $533,000 | $17,000 | 3.2% |

Chung Company
Comparative Schedule of Current Assets
December 31, 1985 and 1984

The changes in the current assets would appear to be favorable, particularly in view of the 24.8% increase in net sales, shown in the following comparative income statement with horizontal analysis:

COMPARATIVE
INCOME
STATEMENT—
HORIZONTAL
ANALYSIS

Chung Company
Comparative Income Statement
For Years Ended December 31, 1985 and 1984

| | | | Increase (Decrease*) | |
|---|---|---|---|---|
| | 1985 | 1984 | Amount | Percent |
| Sales .................... | $1,530,500 | $1,234,000 | $296,500 | 24.0% |
| Sales returns and allowances ................ | 32,500 | 34,000 | 1,500* | 4.4%* |
| Net sales ............... | $1,498,000 | $1,200,000 | $298,000 | 24.8% |
| Cost of goods sold........ | 1,043,000 | 820,000 | 223,000 | 27.2% |
| Gross profit ............. | $ 455,000 | $ 380,000 | $ 75,000 | 19.7% |
| Selling expenses ......... | $ 191,000 | $ 147,000 | $ 44,000 | 29.9% |
| General expenses ........ | 104,000 | 97,400 | 6,600 | 6.8% |
| Total operating expenses .. | $ 295,000 | $ 244,400 | $ 50,600 | 20.7% |
| Operating income......... | $ 160,000 | $ 135,600 | $ 24,400 | 18.0% |
| Other income............ | 8,500 | 11,000 | 2,500* | 22.7%* |
| | $ 168,500 | $ 146,600 | $ 21,900 | 14.9% |
| Other expense ........... | 6,000 | 12,000 | 6,000* | 50.0%* |
| Income before income tax .. | $ 162,500 | $ 134,600 | $ 27,900 | 20.7% |
| Income tax.............. | 71,500 | 58,100 | 13,400 | 23.1% |
| Net income ............. | $ 91,000 | $ 76,500 | $ 14,500 | 19.0% |

The reduction in accounts receivable may have come about through changes in credit terms or improved collection policies. Similarly, a reduction in the inventory during a period of increased sales probably indicates an improvement in the management of inventory.

An increase in net sales, considered alone, is not necessarily favorable. The increase in Chung Company's net sales was accompanied by a somewhat greater percentage increase in the cost of goods sold, which indicates a narrowing of the gross profit margin. Selling expenses increased markedly and general expenses increased slightly, making an overall increase in operating expenses of 20.7%, as contrasted with a 19.7% increase in gross profit.

Although the increase in operating income and in the final net income figure is favorable, it would be incorrect for management to conclude that its operations were at maximum efficiency. A study of the expenses and additional analysis and comparisons of individual expense accounts should be made.

The income statement illustrated is in condensed form. If desired, the statement may be expanded or supplemental schedules may be prepared to present details of the cost of goods sold, selling expenses, general expenses, other income, and other expense.

A comparative retained earnings statement with horizontal analysis is illustrated as follows:

COMPARATIVE RETAINED EARNINGS STATEMENT— HORIZONTAL ANALYSIS

Chung Company
Comparative Retained Earnings Statement
For Years Ended December 31, 1985 and 1984

| | 1985 | 1984 | Increase (Decrease*) Amount | Percent |
|---|---|---|---|---|
| Retained earnings, January 1 | $137,500 | $100,000 | $37,500 | 37.5% |
| Net income for year | 91,000 | 76,500 | 14,500 | 19.0% |
| Total | $228,500 | $176,500 | $52,000 | 29.5% |
| Dividends: | | | | |
| On preferred stock | $ 9,000 | $ 9,000 | —— | —— |
| On common stock | 40,000 | 30,000 | $10,000 | 33.3% |
| Total | $ 49,000 | $ 39,000 | $10,000 | 25.6% |
| Retained earnings, December 31 | $179,500 | $137,500 | $42,000 | 30.5% |

Examination of the statement reveals an increase of 30.5% in retained earnings for the year. The increase was attributable to the retention of $42,000 of the net income for the year ($91,000 net income − $49,000 dividends paid).

Vertical Analysis

Percentage analysis may also be used to show the relationship of the component parts to the total in a single statement. This type of analysis is called vertical analysis. As in horizontal analysis, the statements may be prepared in either detailed or condensed form. In the latter case, additional details of the changes in the various categories may be presented in supporting schedules. If such schedules are prepared, the percentage analysis may be based on either the total of the schedule or the balance sheet total. Although vertical analysis is confined within each individual statement, the significance of both the amounts and the percents is increased by preparing comparative statements.

In vertical analysis of the balance sheet, each asset item is stated as a percent of total assets, and each liability and stockholders' equity item is stated as a percent of total liabilities and stockholders' equity. A condensed comparative balance sheet with vertical analysis is illustrated as follows:

COMPARATIVE
BALANCE
SHEET—
VERTICAL
ANALYSIS

**Chung Company**
**Comparative Balance Sheet**
**December 31, 1985 and 1984**

|  | 1985 | | 1984 | |
|---|---|---|---|---|
|  | Amount | Percent | Amount | Percent |
| **Assets** | | | | |
| Current assets........... | $ 550,000 | 48.3% | $ 533,000 | 43.3% |
| Long-term investments .... | 95,000 | 8.3 | 177,500 | 14.4 |
| Plant assets (net) ........ | 444,500 | 39.0 | 470,000 | 38.2 |
| Intangible assets ........ | 50,000 | 4.4 | 50,000 | 4.1 |
| Total assets ............. | $1,139,500 | 100.0% | $1,230,500 | 100.0% |
| **Liabilities** | | | | |
| Current liabilities.......... | $ 210,000 | 18.4% | $ 243,000 | 19.7% |
| Long-term liabilities ....... | 100,000 | 8.8 | 200,000 | 16.3 |
| Total liabilities ........... | $ 310,000 | 27.2% | $ 443,000 | 36.0% |
| **Stockholders' Equity** | | | | |
| Preferred 6% stock ....... | $ 150,000 | 13.2% | $ 150,000 | 12.2% |
| Common stock .......... | 500,000 | 43.9 | 500,000 | 40.6 |
| Retained earnings ....... | 179,500 | 15.7 | 137,500 | 11.2 |
| Total stockholders' equity .. | $ 829,500 | 72.8% | $ 787,500 | 64.0% |
| Total liab. & stockholders' equity ................. | $1,139,500 | 100.0% | $1,230,500 | 100.0% |

The major relative changes in Chung Company's assets were in the current asset and long-term investment groups. In the lower half of the balance sheet, the greatest relative change was in long-term liabilities and retained earnings. Stockholders' equity increased from 64% of total liabilities and stockholders' equity at the end of 1984 to 72.8% at the end of 1985, with a corresponding decrease in the claims of creditors.

In vertical analysis of the income statement, each item is stated as a percent of net sales. A condensed comparative income statement with vertical analysis is illustrated as follows:

**Chung Company**
**Comparative Income Statement**
**For Years Ended December 31, 1985 and 1984**

|  | 1985 | | 1984 | |
|---|---|---|---|---|
|  | Amount | Percent | Amount | Percent |
| Sales | $1,530,500 | 102.2% | $1,234,000 | 102.8% |
| Sales returns and allowances | 32,500 | 2.2 | 34,000 | 2.8 |
| Net sales | $1,498,000 | 100.0% | $1,200,000 | 100.0% |
| Cost of goods sold | 1,043,000 | 69.6 | 820,000 | 68.3 |
| Gross profit | $ 455,000 | 30.4% | $ 380,000 | 31.7% |
| Selling expenses | $ 191,000 | 12.8% | $ 147,000 | 12.3% |
| General expenses | 104,000 | 6.9 | 97,400 | 8.1 |
| Total operating expenses | $ 295,000 | 19.7% | $ 244,400 | 20.4% |
| Operating income | $ 160,000 | 10.7% | $ 135,600 | 11.3% |
| Other income | 8,500 | .6 | 11,000 | .9 |
|  | $ 168,500 | 11.3% | $ 146,600 | 12.2% |
| Other expense | 6,000 | .4 | 12,000 | 1.0 |
| Income before income tax | $ 162,500 | 10.9% | $ 134,600 | 11.2% |
| Income tax | 71,500 | 4.8 | 58,100 | 4.8 |
| Net income | $ 91,000 | 6.1% | $ 76,500 | 6.4% |

Care must be used in judging the significance of differences between percentages for the two years. For example, the decline of the gross profit rate from 31.7% in 1984 to 30.4% in 1985 is only 1.3 percentage points. In terms of dollars of potential gross profit, however, it represents a decline of approximately $19,500 (1.3% × $1,498,000).

**Common-Size Statements**

Horizontal and vertical analyses with both dollar and percentage figures are helpful in disclosing relationships and trends in financial condition and operations of individual enterprises. Vertical analysis with both dollar and percentage figures is also useful in comparing one company with another or with industry averages. Such comparisons may be made easier by the use of common-size statements, in which all items are expressed only in relative terms.

Common-size statements may be prepared in order to compare percentages of a current period with past periods, to compare individual businesses, or to compare one business with industry percentages published by trade associations and financial information services. A comparative common-size income statement for two enterprises is illustrated as follows:

COMMON-SIZE
INCOME
STATEMENT

| Chung Company and Ross Corporation<br>Condensed Common-Size Income Statement<br>For Year Ended December 31, 1985 | | |
| --- | --- | --- |
| | Chung<br>Company | Ross<br>Corporation |
| Sales............................................. | 102.2% | 102.3% |
| Sales returns and allowances ................... | 2.2 | 2.3 |
| Net sales ....................................... | 100.0% | 100.0% |
| Cost of goods sold.............................. | 69.6 | 70.0 |
| Gross profit .................................... | 30.4% | 30.0% |
| Selling expenses................................ | 12.8% | 11.5% |
| General expenses ............................... | 6.9 | 4.1 |
| Total operating expenses ....................... | 19.7% | 15.6% |
| Operating income............................... | 10.7% | 14.4% |
| Other income................................... | .6 | .6 |
| | 11.3% | 15.0% |
| Other expense.................................. | .4 | .5 |
| Income before income tax ...................... | 10.9% | 14.5% |
| Income tax..................................... | 4.8 | 5.5 |
| Net income..................................... | 6.1% | 9.0% |

Examination of the statement reveals that although Chung Company has a slightly higher rate of gross profit than Ross Corporation, the advantage is more than offset by its higher percentage of both selling and general expenses. As a consequence, the operating income of Chung Company is 10.7% of net sales as compared with 14.4% for Ross Corporation, an unfavorable difference of 3.7 percentage points.

**Other Analytical Measures**

In addition to the percentage analyses discussed above, there are a number of other relationships that may be expressed in ratios and percentages. The items used in the measures are taken from the accounting statements of the current period and hence are a further development of vertical analysis. Comparison of the items with corresponding measures of earlier periods is an extension of horizontal analysis.

Some of the more important ratios useful in the evaluation of solvency and profitability are discussed in the sections that follow. The examples are based on the illustrative statements presented earlier. In a few instances, data from a company's statements of the preceding year and from other sources are also used.

SOLVENCY ANALYSIS

Solvency is the ability of a business to meet its financial obligations as they come due. Solvency analysis, therefore, focuses mainly on balance sheet relationships that indicate the ability to liquidate current and noncurrent liabilities. Major analyses used in assessing solvency include (1) current position analysis, (2) accounts receivable analysis, (3) inventory analysis, (4) the ratio of plant assets to long-term liabilities, and (5) the ratio of stockholders' equity to liabilities.

Current Position Analysis

To be useful, ratios relating to a firm's solvency must show the firm's ability to liquidate its liabilities. The use of ratios showing the ability to liquidate current liabilities is called **current position analysis** and is of particular interest to short-term creditors.

**Working Capital**

The excess of the current assets of an enterprise over its current liabilities at a certain moment of time is called working capital. The absolute amount of working capital and the flow of working capital during a period of time are often used in evaluating a company's ability to meet currently maturing obligations. Although useful for making intraperiod comparisons for a company, these absolute amounts are difficult to use in comparing companies of different sizes or in comparing such amounts with industry figures. For example, working capital of $250,000 may be very adequate for a small building contractor specializing in residential construction, but it may be completely inadequate for a large building contractor specializing in industrial and commercial construction.

**Current Ratio**

Another means of expressing the relationship between current assets and current liabilities is through the current ratio, sometimes referred to as the **working capital ratio** or **bankers' ratio.** The ratio is computed by dividing the total of current assets by the total of current liabilities. The determination of working capital and the current ratio for Chung Company is illustrated as follows:

|  | 1985 | 1984 |
|---|---|---|
| Current assets | $550,000 | $533,000 |
| Current liabilities | 210,000 | 243,000 |
| Working capital | $340,000 | $290,000 |
| Current ratio | 2.6 : 1 | 2.2 : 1 |

The current ratio is a more dependable indication of solvency than is working capital. To illustrate, assume that as of December 31, 1985, the working capital of a competing corporation is much greater than $340,000, but its current ratio is only 1.3 : 1. Considering these factors alone, the Chung Company, with its current ratio of 2.6 : 1, is in a more favorable position to obtain short-term credit than the corporation with the greater amount of working capital.

### Acid-Test Ratio

The amount of working capital and the current ratio are two solvency measures that indicate a company's ability to meet currently maturing obligations. However, these two measures do not take into account the composition of the current assets. To illustrate the significance of this additional factor, the following current position data for two companies are presented:

|  | Randall Corporation | Steward Company |
|---|---|---|
| Current assets: |  |  |
| Cash | $ 200,000 | $ 550,000 |
| Marketable securities | 100,000 | 100,000 |
| Receivables (net) | 200,000 | 200,000 |
| Inventories | 790,000 | 443,500 |
| Prepaid expenses | 10,000 | 6,500 |
| Total current assets | $1,300,000 | $1,300,000 |
| Current liabilities | 650,000 | 650,000 |
| Working capital | $ 650,000 | $ 650,000 |
| Current ratio | 2 : 1 | 2 : 1 |

Both companies have working capital of $650,000 and a current ratio of 2 to 1. But the ability of each company to meet its currently maturing debts is vastly different. Randall Corporation has a large part of its current assets in inventories, which must be sold and the receivables collected before the current liabilities can be paid in full. A considerable amount of time may be required to convert these inventories into cash. Declines in market prices and a reduction in demand could also impair the ability to pay current liabilities. Conversely, Steward Company has almost enough cash on hand to meet its current liabilities.

A ratio that measures the "instant" debt-paying ability of a company is called the acid-test ratio or **quick ratio.** It is the ratio of the sum of cash, receivables, and marketable securities, which are sometimes called quick assets, to current liabilities. The acid-test ratio data for Chung Company are as follows:

|  | 1985 | 1984 |
|---|---|---|
| Quick assets: |  |  |
| Cash | $ 90,500 | $ 64,700 |
| Marketable securities | 75,000 | 60,000 |
| Receivables (net) | 115,000 | 120,000 |
| Total | $280,500 | $244,700 |
| Current liabilities | $210,000 | $243,000 |
| Acid-test ratio | 1.3 : 1 | 1.0 : 1 |

A thorough analysis of a firm's current position would include the determination of the amount of working capital, the current ratio, and the acid-test ratio.

These ratios are most useful when viewed together and when compared with similar ratios for previous periods and with those of other firms in the industry.

**Accounts Receivable Analysis**

The size and composition of accounts receivable change continually during business operations. The amount is increased by sales on account and reduced by collections. Firms that grant long credit terms tend to have relatively greater amounts tied up in accounts receivable than those granting short credit terms. Increases or decreases in the volume of sales also affect the amount of outstanding accounts receivable.

Accounts receivable yield no revenue, hence it is desirable to keep the amount invested in them at a minimum. The cash made available by prompt collection of receivables improves solvency and may be used to purchase merchandise in larger quantities at a lower price, to pay dividends to stockholders, or for other purposes. Prompt collection also lessens the risk of loss from uncollectible accounts.

### Accounts Receivable Turnover

The relationship between credit sales and accounts receivable may be stated as the accounts receivable turnover. It is computed by dividing net sales on account by the average net accounts receivable. It is preferable to base the average on monthly balances, which gives effect to seasonal changes. When such data are not available, it is necessary to use the average of the balances at the beginning and the end of the year. If there are trade notes receivable as well as accounts, the two should be combined. The accounts receivable turnover data for Chung Company are as follows. All sales were made on account.

|  | 1985 | 1984 |
|---|---|---|
| Net sales on account | $1,498,000 | $1,200,000 |
| Accounts receivable (net): |  |  |
| Beginning of year | $ 120,000 | $ 140,000 |
| End of year | 115,000 | 120,000 |
| Total | $ 235,000 | $ 260,000 |
| Average | $ 117,500 | $ 130,000 |
| Accounts receivable turnover | 12.7 | 9.2 |

The increase in the accounts receivable turnover for 1985 indicates that there has been an acceleration in the collection of receivables, due perhaps to improvement in either the granting of credit or the collection practices used, or both.

### Number of Days' Sales in Receivables

Another means of expressing the relationship between credit sales and accounts receivable is the number of days' sales in receivables. This measure is determined by dividing the net accounts receivable at the end of the year by the average daily sales on account (net sales on account divided by 365), illustrated as follows for Chung Company:

| | 1985 | 1984 |
|---|---|---|
| Accounts receivable (net), end of year............ | $ 115,000 | $ 120,000 |
| Net sales on account .......................... | $1,498,000 | $1,200,000 |
| Average daily sales on account................. | $ 4,104 | $ 3,288 |
| Number of days' sales in receivables ............ | 28.0 | 36.5 |

The number of days' sales in receivables gives a rough measure of the length of time the accounts receivable have been outstanding. A comparison of this measure with the credit terms, with figures for comparable firms in the same industry, and with figures of Chung Company for prior years will help reveal the efficiency in collecting receivables and the trends in the management of credit.

**Inventory Analysis**

Although an enterprise must maintain sufficient inventory quantities to meet the demands of its operations, it is desirable to keep the amount invested in inventory to a minimum. Inventories in excess of the needs of business reduce solvency by tying up funds. Excess inventories may also cause increases in the amount of insurance, property taxes, storage, and other related expenses, further reducing funds that could be used to better advantage. There is also added risk of loss through price declines and deterioration or obsolescence of the inventory.

### Inventory Turnover

The relationship between the volume of goods sold and inventory may be stated as the inventory turnover. It is computed by dividing the cost of goods sold by the average inventory. If monthly data are not available, it is necessary to use the average of the inventories at the beginning and the end of the year. The inventory turnover data for Chung Company are as follows:

| | 1985 | 1984 |
|---|---|---|
| Cost of goods sold ........................... | $1,043,000 | $820,000 |
| Inventory: | | |
|   Beginning of year ........................... | $ 283,000 | $311,000 |
|   End of year................................. | 264,000 | 283,000 |
|   Total ..................................... | $ 547,000 | $594,000 |
|   Average.................................... | $ 273,500 | $297,000 |
| Inventory turnover ............................. | 3.8 | 2.8 |

The improvement in the turnover resulted from an increase in the cost of goods sold, combined with a decrease in average inventory. The variation in types of inventory is too great to permit any broad generalizations as to what is a satisfactory turnover. For example, a firm selling food should have a much higher turnover than one selling furniture or jewelry, and the perishable foods department of a supermarket should have a higher turnover than the soaps and cleansers department. However, for each business or each department within a business, there is a reasonable turnover rate. A turnover below this rate means that the company or the department is incurring extra expenses such as those for administration and storage, is increasing its risk of loss because of obsolescence and adverse price changes, is incurring interest charges in excess of those considered necessary, and is failing to free funds for other uses.

### Number of Days' Sales in Inventory

Another means of expressing the relationship between the cost of goods sold and inventory is the number of days' sales in inventory. This measure is determined by dividing the inventory at the end of the year by the average daily cost of goods sold (cost of goods sold divided by 365), illustrated as follows for Chung Company:

|  | 1985 | 1984 |
|---|---|---|
| Inventory, end of year | $ 264,000 | $283,000 |
| Cost of goods sold | $1,043,000 | $820,000 |
| Average daily cost of goods sold | $ 2,858 | $ 2,247 |
| Number of days' sales in inventory | 92.4 | 125.9 |

The number of days' sales in inventory gives a rough measure of the length of time it takes to acquire, sell, and then replace the average inventory. Although there was a substantial improvement in the second year, comparison of the measure with those of earlier years and of comparable firms is an essential element in judging the effectiveness of Chung Company's inventory control.

As with many attempts to analyze financial data, it is possible to determine more than one measure to express the relationship between the cost of goods sold and inventory. Both the inventory turnover and number of days' sales in inventory are useful for evaluating the efficiency in the management of inventory. Whether both measures are used or whether one measure is preferred over the other is a matter for the individual analyst to decide.

**Ratio of Plant Assets to Long-Term Liabilities**

Long-term notes and bonds are often secured by mortgages on plant assets. **The ratio of total plant assets to long-term liabilities** provides a solvency measure that shows the margin of safety of the noteholders or bondholders. It also gives an indication of the potential ability of the enterprise to borrow additional funds on a long-term basis. The ratio of plant assets to long-term liabilities of Chung Company is as follows:

|  | 1985 | 1984 |
|---|---|---|
| Plant assets (net) | $444,500 | $470,000 |
| Long-term liabilities | $100,000 | $200,000 |
| Ratio of plant assets to long-term liabilities | 4.4 : 1 | 2.4 : 1 |

The marked increase in the ratio at the end of 1985 was mainly due to the liquidation of one half of Chung Company's long-term liabilities. If the company should need to borrow additional funds on a long-term basis, it is in a stronger position to do so.

**Ratio of Stockholders' Equity to Liabilities**

Claims against the total assets of an enterprise are divided into two basic groups, those of the creditors and those of the owners. The relationship between the total claims of the two groups provides a solvency measure that indicates the margin of safety for the creditors and the ability of the enterprise to withstand adverse business conditions. If the claims of the creditors are large in proportion to the equity of the stockholders, there are likely to be substantial charges for interest payments. If earnings decline to the point where the company is unable to meet its interest payments, control of the business may pass to the creditors.

The relationship between stockholder and creditor equity is shown in the vertical analysis of the balance sheet. For example, the balance sheet of Chung Company presented on page 342 indicates that on December 31, 1985, stockholders' equity represented 72.8% and liabilities represented 27.2% of the sum of the liabilities and stockholders' equity (100.0%). Instead of expressing each item as a percent of the total, the relationship may be expressed as a ratio of one to the other, as follows:

|                                              | 1985      | 1984      |
| -------------------------------------------- | --------- | --------- |
| Total stockholders' equity                   | $829,500  | $787,500  |
| Total liabilities                            | $310,000  | $443,000  |
| Ratio of stockholders' equity to liabilities | 2.7 : 1   | 1.8 : 1   |

The balance sheet of Chung Company shows that the major factor affecting the change in the ratio was the $100,000 reduction in long-term liabilities during 1985. The ratio at both dates shows a large margin of safety for the creditors.

**PROFITABILITY ANALYSIS**

**Profitability** is the ability of an entity to earn income. It can be assessed by computing various relevant measures, including (1) the ratio of net sales to assets, (2) the rate earned on total assets, (3) the rate earned on stockholders' equity, (4) the rate earned on common stockholders' equity, (5) earnings per share on common stock, (6) the price-earnings ratio, and (7) dividend yield.

**Ratio of Net Sales to Assets**

The **ratio of net sales to assets** is a profitability measure that shows how effectively a firm utilizes its assets. Assume that two competing enterprises have equal amounts of assets, but the amount of the sales of one is double the amount of the sales of the other. Obviously, the former is making better use of its assets. In computing the ratio, any long-term investments should be excluded from total assets because they are wholly unrelated to sales of goods or services. Assets used in determining the ratio may be the total at the end of the year, the average at the beginning and the end of the year, or the average of the monthly totals. The basic data and the ratio of net sales to assets for Chung Company are as follows:

|  | 1985 | 1984 |
|---|---|---|
| Net sales | $1,498,000 | $1,200,000 |
| **Total assets (excluding long-term investments):** | | |
| Beginning of year | $1,053,000 | $1,010,000 |
| End of year | 1,044,500 | 1,053,000 |
| Total | $2,097,500 | $2,063,000 |
| Average | $1,048,750 | $1,031,500 |
| Ratio of net sales to assets | 1.4 : 1 | 1.2 : 1 |

The ratio improved to a minor degree in 1985, largely due to the increased sales volume. A comparison of the ratio with those of other enterprises in the same industry would be helpful in assessing Chung Company's effectiveness in the utilization of assets.

**Rate Earned on Total Assets**

The rate earned on total assets is a measure of the profitability of the assets, without regard to the equity of creditors and stockholders in the assets. The rate is therefore not affected by differences in methods of financing an enterprise.

The rate earned on total assets is derived by adding interest expense to net income and dividing this sum by total assets. By adding interest expense to net income, the profitability of the assets is determined without considering the means of financing the acquisition of the assets. The rate earned by Chung Company on total assets is determined as follows:

|  | 1985 | 1984 |
|---|---|---|
| Net income | $ 91,000 | $ 76,500 |
| Plus interest expense | 6,000 | 12,000 |
| Total | $ 97,000 | $ 88,500 |
| **Total assets:** | | |
| Beginning of year | $1,230,500 | $1,187,500 |
| End of year | 1,139,500 | 1,230,500 |
| Total | $2,370,000 | $2,418,000 |
| Average | $1,185,000 | $1,209,000 |
| Rate earned on total assets | 8.2% | 7.3% |

The rate earned on total assets of Chung Company for 1985 indicates an improvement over that for 1984. A comparison with other companies and with industry averages would also be useful in evaluating the effectiveness of management performance.

**Rate Earned on Stockholders' Equity**

Another relative measure of profitability is obtained by dividing net income by the total stockholders' equity. In contrast to the rate earned on total assets, the rate earned on stockholders' equity emphasizes the income yield in relationship to the amount invested by the stockholders.

The amount of the total stockholders' equity throughout the year varies for several reasons — the issuance of additional stock, the retirement of a class of stock, the payment of dividends, and the gradual accrual of net income. If monthly figures are not available, the average of the stockholders' equity at the beginning and the end of the year is used, as in the following illustration:

|  | 1985 | 1984 |
|---|---|---|
| Net income | $ 91,000 | $ 76,500 |
| Stockholders' equity: |  |  |
| Beginning of year | $ 787,500 | $ 750,000 |
| End of year | 829,500 | 787,500 |
| Total | $1,617,000 | $1,537,500 |
| Average | $ 808,500 | $ 768,750 |
| Rate earned on stockholders' equity | 11.3% | 10.0% |

The rate earned by a thriving enterprise on the equity of its stockholders is usually higher than the rate earned on total assets. The reason for the difference is that the amount earned on assets acquired through the use of funds provided by creditors is more than the interest charges paid to creditors. This tendency of the rate on stockholders' equity to vary disproportionately from the rate on total assets is sometimes called leverage. The Chung Company rate on stockholders' equity for 1985, 11.3%, compares favorably with the rate of 8.2% earned on total assets, as reported previously. The leverage factor of 3.1% (11.3% − 8.2%) for 1985 also compares favorably with the 2.7% (10.0% − 7.3%) differential for the preceding year.

**Rate Earned on Common Stockholders' Equity**

When a corporation has both preferred and common stock outstanding, the holders of the common stock have the residual claim on earnings. The rate earned on common stockholders' equity is the net income less preferred dividend requirements for the period, stated as a percent of the average equity of the common stockholders.

Chung Company has $150,000 of preferred 6% nonparticipating stock outstanding at both balance sheet dates, hence annual preferred dividends amount to $9,000. The common stockholders' equity is the total stockholders' equity, reduced by the par of the preferred stock ($150,000). The basic data and the rate earned on common stockholders' equity are as follows:

|  | 1985 | 1984 |
|---|---|---|
| Net income | $ 91,000 | $ 76,500 |
| Preferred dividends | 9,000 | 9,000 |
| Remainder—identified with common stock | $ 82,000 | $ 67,500 |
| Common stockholders' equity: |  |  |
| Beginning of year | $ 637,500 | $ 600,000 |
| End of year | 679,500 | 637,500 |
| Total | $1,317,000 | $1,237,500 |
| Average | $ 658,500 | $ 618,750 |
| Rate earned on common stockholders' equity | 12.5% | 10.9% |

The rate earned on common stockholders' equity differs from the rates earned by Chung Company on total assets and total stockholders' equity. This situation will occur if there are borrowed funds and also preferred stock outstanding, which rank ahead of the common shares in their claim on earnings. Thus the concept of leverage, as discussed in the preceding section, can be applied to the use of funds from the sale of preferred stock as well as from borrowing. Funds from both sources can be used in an attempt to increase the return on common stock-holders' equity.

**Earnings per Share on Common Stock**

One of the profitability measures most commonly quoted in the financial press and included in the income statement in corporate annual reports is earnings per share on common stock. If a company has issued only one class of stock, the earnings per share are determined by dividing net income by the number of shares of stock outstanding. If there are both preferred and common stock outstanding, the net income must be reduced first by the amount necessary to meet the preferred dividend requirements.

Any changes in the number of shares outstanding during the year, such as would result from stock dividends or stock splits, should be disclosed in quoting earnings per share on common stock. Also if there are any nonrecurring (extraordinary, etc.) items in the income statement, the income per share, before such items, should be reported along with net income per share. In addition, if there are convertible bonds or preferred stock outstanding, the amount reported as net income per share should be stated without considering the conversion privilege, followed by net income per share, assuming that conversion had occurred.

The data on the earnings per share of common stock for Chung Company are as follows:

|  | 1985 | 1984 |
|---|---|---|
| Net income | $91,000 | $76,500 |
| Preferred dividends | 9,000 | 9,000 |
| Remainder—identified with common stock | $82,000 | $67,500 |
| Shares of common stock outstanding | 50,000 | 50,000 |
| Earnings per share on common stock | $1.64 | $1.35 |

Earnings per share data can be presented in conjunction with dividends per share data to indicate the relationship between earnings and dividends and the extent to which the corporation is retaining its earnings for use in the business. The following chart shows this relationship for Chung Company:

CHART OF
EARNINGS AND
DIVIDENDS ON
COMMON STOCK

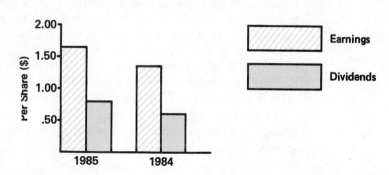

Price-Earnings
Ratio

A profitability measure commonly quoted in the financial press is the price-earnings (P/E) ratio on common stock. It is computed by dividing the market price per share of common stock at a specific date by the annual earnings per share. Assuming market prices per common share of 20½ at the end of 1985 and 13½ at the end of 1984, the price-earnings ratio on common stock of Chung Company is as follows:

|  | 1985 | 1984 |
|---|---|---|
| Market price per share of common stock................ | $20.50 | $13.50 |
| Earnings per share on common stock ................. | $ 1.64 | $ 1.35 |
| Price-earnings ratio on common stock ................. | 12.5 | 10.0 |

The price-earnings ratio indicates that a share of common stock of Chung Company was selling for 12.5 and 10 times the amount of earnings per share at the end of 1985 and 1984 respectively.

Dividend
Yield

The **dividend yield** on common stock is a profitability measure that shows the rate of return to common stockholders in terms of cash dividend distributions. The dividend yield is computed by dividing the annual dividends paid per share of common stock by the market price per share at a specific date. Assuming dividends of $.80 and $.60 per common share and market prices per common share of 20½ and 13½ at the end of 1985 and 1984 respectively, the dividend yield on common stock of Chung Company is as follows:

|  | 1985 | 1984 |
|---|---|---|
| Dividends per share on common stock ................. | $ .80 | $ .60 |
| Market price per share of common stock................ | $20.50 | $13.50 |
| Dividend yield on common stock ...................... | 3.9% | 4.4% |

SELECTION OF
ANALYTICAL
MEASURES

The analytical measures that have been discussed and illustrated are representative of many that can be developed for a medium-size business enterprise. Some of them might well be omitted in analyzing a specific firm, or additional measures could be developed. The type of business activity, the capital structure, and the size of the enterprise usually affect the measures used. For example, in analyzing railroads, public utilities, and other corporations with a high ratio of debt to stockholders' equity, it is customary to express the solvency measure that shows the relative risk of the bondholders in terms of the number of times the interest charges are earned during the year. The higher the ratio, the greater the assurance of continued interest payments in case of decreased earnings. The measure also provides an indication of general financial strength, which is of concern to stockholders and employees, as well as to creditors.

In the following data, the amount available to meet interest charges is not affected by taxes on income because interest is deductible in determining taxable income.

|                                                     | 1985        | 1984        |
|-----------------------------------------------------|-------------|-------------|
| Income before income tax.......................     | $ 900,000   | $ 800,000   |
| Add interest charges..........................      | 300,000     | 250,000     |
| Amount available to meet interest charges ......    | $1,200,000  | $1,050,000  |
| Number of times interest charges earned..........   | 4           | 4.2         |

Analyses like the above can be applied to dividends on preferred stock. In such cases, net income would be divided by the amount of preferred dividends to yield the number of times preferred dividends were earned. This measure gives an indication of the relative assurance of continued dividend payments to preferred stockholders.

Percentage analyses, ratios, turnovers, and other measures of financial position and operating results are useful analytical devices. They are helpful in appraising the present performance of an enterprise and in forecasting its future. They are not, however, a substitute for sound judgment nor do they provide definitive guides to action. In selecting and interpreting analytical indexes, proper consideration should be given to any conditions peculiar to the particular enterprise or to the industry of which the enterprise is a part. The possible influence of the general economic and business environment should also be weighed.

To determine trends, the interrelationship of the measures used in appraising a certain enterprise should be carefully studied, as should comparable indexes of earlier fiscal periods. Data from competing enterprises may also be compared in order to determine the relative efficiency of the firm being analyzed. In making such comparisons, however, it is essential to consider the potential effects of any significant differences in the accounting methods used by the enterprises. The following presentation is a summary of the analytical measures discussed in this chapter:

|                                          | Method of Computation                                                       | Use                                                                              |
|------------------------------------------|-----------------------------------------------------------------------------|----------------------------------------------------------------------------------|
| **Solvency measures**                    |                                                                             |                                                                                  |
| Working capital                          | Current assets − current liabilities                                        | To indicate the ability to meet currently maturing obligations                   |
| Current ratio                            | $\dfrac{\text{Current assets}}{\text{Current liabilities}}$                 |                                                                                  |
| Acid-test ratio                          | $\dfrac{\text{Quick assets}}{\text{Current liabilities}}$                   | To indicate instant debt-paying ability                                          |
| Accounts receivable turnover             | $\dfrac{\text{Net sales on account}}{\text{Average accounts receivable}}$   | To assess the efficiency in collecting receivables and in the management of credit |
| Number of days' sales in receivables     | $\dfrac{\text{Accounts receivable, end of year}}{\text{Average daily sales on account}}$ |                                                                     |
| Inventory turnover                       | $\dfrac{\text{Cost of goods sold}}{\text{Average inventory}}$               | To assess the efficiency in the management of inventory                          |
| Number of days' sales in inventory       | $\dfrac{\text{Inventory, end of year}}{\text{Average daily cost of goods sold}}$ |                                                                             |

| | Method of Computation | Use |
|---|---|---|
| Ratio of plant assets to long-term liabilities | $\dfrac{\text{Plant assets (net)}}{\text{Long-term liabilities}}$ | To indicate the margin of safety to long-term creditors |
| Ratio of stockholders' equity to liabilities | $\dfrac{\text{Total stockholders' equity}}{\text{Total liabilities}}$ | To indicate the margin of safety to creditors |

**Profitability measures**

| | | |
|---|---|---|
| Ratio of net sales to assets | $\dfrac{\text{Net sales}}{\text{Average total assets (excluding long-term investments)}}$ | To assess the effectiveness in the use of assets |
| Rate earned on total assets | $\dfrac{\text{Net income + interest expense}}{\text{Average total assets}}$ | To assess the profitability of the assets |
| Rate earned on stockholders' equity | $\dfrac{\text{Net income}}{\text{Average stockholders' equity}}$ | To assess the profitability of the investment by stockholders |
| Rate earned on common stockholders' equity | $\dfrac{\text{Net income − preferred dividends}}{\text{Average common stockholders' equity}}$ | To assess the profitability of the investment by common stockholders |
| Earnings per share on common stock | $\dfrac{\text{Net income − preferred dividends}}{\text{Shares of common stock outstanding}}$ | |
| Dividends per share of common stock | $\dfrac{\text{Dividends}}{\text{Shares of common stock outstanding}}$ | To indicate the extent to which earnings are being distributed to common stockholders |
| Price-earnings ratio | $\dfrac{\text{Market price per share of common stock}}{\text{Earnings per share on common stock}}$ | To indicate the relationship between market value of common stock and earnings |
| Dividend yield | $\dfrac{\text{Dividends per common share}}{\text{Market price per common share}}$ | To indicate the rate of return to common stockholders in terms of dividends |
| Number of times interest charges earned | $\dfrac{\text{Income before income tax + interest expense}}{\text{Interest expense}}$ | To assess the risk to bondholders in terms of number of times interest charges were earned |

1. What type of analysis is indicated by the following?

| | Amount | Percent |
|---|---|---|
| Current assets | $100,000 | 20% |
| Plant assets | 400,000 | 80 |
| Total assets | $500,000 | 100% |

A. Vertical analysis      C. Differential analysis
B. Horizontal analysis      D. None of the above

2. Which of the following measures is useful as an indication of the ability of a firm to liquidate current liabilities?
   A. Working capital
   B. Current ratio
   C. Acid-test ratio
   D. All of the above

3. The ratio determined by dividing total current assets by total current liabilities is:
   A. current ratio
   B. working capital ratio
   C. bankers' ratio
   D. all of the above

4. The ratio of the "quick assets" to current liabilities, which indicates the "instant" debt-paying ability of a firm, is:
   A. current ratio
   B. working capital ratio
   C. acid-test ratio
   D. none of the above

5. A measure useful in evaluating the efficiency in the management of inventory is:
   A. inventory turnover
   B. number of days' sales in inventory
   C. both A and B
   D. none of the above

**Discussion Questions**

1. In the analysis of the financial status of an enterprise, what is meant by *solvency* and *profitability*?

2. Illustrate (a) horizontal analysis and (b) vertical analysis, using the following data taken from a comparative balance sheet:

|  | Current Year | Preceding Year |
|---|---|---|
| Cash | $ 900,000 | $ 600,000 |
| Total current assets | 3,600,000 | 3,000,000 |

3. What is the advantage of using comparative statements for financial analysis rather than statements for a single date or period?

4. The current year's amount of net income (after income tax) is 15% larger than that of the preceding year. Does this indicate an improved operating performance? Discuss.

5. What are common-size financial statements?

6. (a) Name the major ratios useful in assessing solvency and profitability.
   (b) Why is it important not to rely on only one ratio or measure in assessing the solvency or profitability of an enterprise?

7. Identify the measure of current position analysis described by each of the following: (a) the excess of the current assets over current liabilities, (b) the ratio of current assets to current liabilities, (c) the ratio of quick assets to current liabilities.

8. The working capital for Robinson Company at the end of the current year is $60,000 greater than the working capital at the end of the preceding year, reported as follows. Does this mean that the current position has improved? Explain.

|  | Current Year | Preceding Year |
|---|---|---|
| Current assets: |  |  |
| Cash, marketable securities, and receivables...... | $288,000 | $240,000 |
| Inventory........................................ | 432,000 | 260,000 |
| Total current assets ........................... | $720,000 | $500,000 |
| Current liabilities................................ | 360,000 | 200,000 |
| Working capital................................. | $360,000 | $300,000 |

9. A company that grants terms of n/30 on all sales has an accounts receivable turnover for the year, based on monthly averages, of 6. Is this a satisfactory turnover? Discuss.

10. What does an increase in the number of days' sales in receivables ordinarily indicate about the credit and collection policy of the firm?

11. (a) Why is it advantageous to have a high inventory turnover? (b) Is it possible for inventory turnover to be too high? (c) Is it possible to have a high inventory turnover and a high number of days' sales in inventory? Discuss.

12. What does an increase in the ratio of stockholders' equity to liabilities indicate about the margin of safety for the firm's creditors and the ability of the firm to withstand adverse business conditions?

13. In computing the ratio of net sales to assets, why are long-term investments excluded in determining the amount of the total assets?

14. In determining the rate earned on total assets, why is interest expense added to net income before dividing by total assets?

15. (a) Why is the rate earned on stockholders' equity by a thriving enterprise ordinarily higher than the rate earned on total assets?
(b) Should the rate earned on common stockholders' equity normally be higher or lower than the rate earned on total stockholders' equity? Explain.

16. The net income (after income tax) of Morgan Company was $10 per common share in the latest year and $15 per common share for the preceding year. At the beginning of the latest year, the number of shares outstanding was doubled by a stock split. There were no other changes in the amount of stock outstanding. What were the earnings per share in the preceding year, adjusted to place them on a comparable basis with the latest year?

17. The price earnings ratio for common stock of Mura Company was 15 at June 30, the end of the current fiscal year. What does the ratio indicate about the selling price of common stock in relation to current earnings?

18. Why would the dividend yield differ significantly from the rate earned on common stockholders' equity?

19. Favorable business conditions may bring about certain seemingly unfavorable ratios, and unfavorable business operations may result in apparently favorable

ratios. For example, Almond Company increased its sales and net income substantially for the current year, yet the current ratio at the end of the year is lower than at the beginning of the year. Discuss some possible causes of the apparent weakening of the current position while sales and net income have increased substantially.

**Exercises**

**Exercise 15-1.** Revenue and expense data for Eastern Company are as follows:

|  | 1985 | 1984 |
|---|---|---|
| Sales | $900,000 | $800,000 |
| Cost of goods sold | 549,000 | 480,000 |
| Selling expense | 117,000 | 144,000 |
| General expense | 81,000 | 64,000 |
| Income tax | 63,000 | 48,000 |

(a) Prepare an income statement in comparative form, stating each item for both 1985 and 1984 as a percent of sales.
(b) Comment upon the significant changes disclosed by the comparative income statement.

**Exercise 15-2.** The following data were abstracted from the balance sheet of Valenzuela Company:

|  | Current Year | Preceding Year |
|---|---|---|
| Cash | $116,000 | $101,500 |
| Marketable securities | 55,000 | 40,000 |
| Accounts and notes receivable (net) | 159,000 | 152,500 |
| Inventory | 229,800 | 160,000 |
| Prepaid expenses | 10,200 | 8,000 |
| Accounts and notes payable (short-term) | 250,000 | 185,000 |
| Accrued liabilities | 50,000 | 25,000 |

(a) Determine for each year the (1) working capital, (2) current ratio, and (3) acid-test ratio. (Present figures used in your computations.)
(b) What conclusions can be drawn from these data as to the company's ability to meet its currently maturing debts?

**Exercise 15-3.** The following data are taken from the financial statements for Lasorta Company:

|  | Current Year | Preceding Year |
|---|---|---|
| Accounts receivable, end of year | $ 563,200 | $ 462,000 |
| Monthly average accounts receivable (net) | 522,500 | 423,500 |
| Net sales on account | 4,180,000 | 2,964,500 |

Terms of all sales are 1/10, n/60.
(a) Determine for each year (1) the accounts receivable turnover and (2) the number of days' sales in receivables.
(b) What conclusions can be drawn from these data concerning the composition of accounts receivable?

**Exercise 15-4.** The following data were abstracted from the income statement of Cowans Corporation:

|                     | Current Year | Preceding Year |
|---------------------|-------------:|---------------:|
| Sales               | $4,680,000   | $4,575,800     |
| Beginning inventory | 588,000      | 512,000        |
| Purchases           | 2,424,000    | 2,496,000      |
| Ending inventory    | 612,000      | 588,000        |

(a) Determine for each year (1) the inventory turnover and (2) the number of days' sales in inventory.

(b) What conclusions can be drawn from these data concerning the composition of the inventory?

**Exercise 15-5.** The following data were taken from the financial statements of John Concepcion and Co. for the current fiscal year:

| | |
|---|---:|
| Plant assets (net) | $1,104,000 |

Liabilities:

| | |
|---|---:|
| Current liabilities | $ 360,000 |
| Mortgage note payable, 10%, issued 1980, due 2000 | 480,000 |
| Total liabilities | $ 840,000 |

Stockholders' equity:

| | | | |
|---|---:|---:|---:|
| Preferred 9% stock, $100 par, cumulative, nonparticipating (no change during year) | | | $ 180,000 |
| Common stock, $10 par (no change during year) | | | 900,000 |
| Retained earnings: | | | |
|   Balance, beginning of year | $642,600 | | |
|   Net income | 198,000 | $840,600 | |
|   Preferred dividends | $ 16,200 | | |
|   Common dividends | 56,400 | 72,600 | |
|   Balance, end of year | | | 768,000 |
| Total stockholders' equity | | | $1,848,000 |

| | |
|---|---:|
| Net sales | $3,295,200 |
| Interest expense | 48,000 |

Assuming that long-term investments totaled $180,000 throughout the year and that total assets were $2,322,600 at the beginning of the year, determine the following, presenting figures used in your computations: (a) ratio of plant assets to long-term liabilities, (b) ratio of stockholders' equity to liabilities, (c) ratio of net sales to assets, (d) rate earned on total assets, (e) rate earned on stockholders' equity, (f) rate earned on common stockholders' equity.

**Exercise 15-6.** The net income reported on the income statement of A. B. Virgil Inc. was $2,200,000. There were 200,000 shares of $50 par common stock and 40,000 shares of $50 par 10% preferred stock outstanding throughout the current year. The income statement included two extraordinary items: a $900,000 gain from condemnation of property and a $700,000 loss arising from tornado damage, both after applicable income tax. Determine the per share figures for common stock for (a) income before extraordinary items and (b) net income.

**Exercise 15-7.** The balance sheet for Henderson Corporation at the end of the current fiscal year indicated the following:

Bonds payable, 11% (issued in 1980, due in 2000) . . . . . . . . . $2,000,000
Preferred 9% stock, $100 par . . . . . . . . . . . . . . . . . . . . . . . . . . . 500,000
Common stock, $20 par . . . . . . . . . . . . . . . . . . . . . . . . . . . . . . . 1,500,000

Income before income tax was $660,000 and income taxes were $300,000 for the current year. Cash dividends paid on common stock during the current year totaled $300,000. The common stock was selling for $42 per share at the end of the year. Determine each of the following: (a) number of times bond interest charges were earned, (b) number of times preferred dividends were earned, (c) earnings per share on common stock, (d) price-earnings ratio, and (e) dividend yield.

**Problems**
*(Problems in Appendix B: 15-1B, 15-3B, 15-5B.)*

**Problem 15-1A.** Data pertaining to the current position of R. Staub, Inc. are as follows:

Cash . . . . . . . . . . . . . . . . . . . . . . . . . . . . . . . . . . . . . . . $125,000
Marketable securities . . . . . . . . . . . . . . . . . . . . . . . 60,000
Accounts and notes receivable (net) . . . . . . . . . . 295,000
Inventory . . . . . . . . . . . . . . . . . . . . . . . . . . . . . . . . . . 487,000
Prepaid expenses . . . . . . . . . . . . . . . . . . . . . . . . . . 33,000
Accounts payable . . . . . . . . . . . . . . . . . . . . . . . . . . 270,000
Notes payable (short-term) . . . . . . . . . . . . . . . . . . 110,000
Accrued liabilities . . . . . . . . . . . . . . . . . . . . . . . . . . 20,000

Instructions:

(1) Compute (a) working capital, (b) current ratio, and (c) acid-test ratio.
(2) List the following captions on a sheet of paper:

| Transaction | Working Capital | Current Ratio | Acid-Test Ratio |
|---|---|---|---|

Compute the working capital, current ratio, and acid-test ratio after each of the following transactions, and record the results in the appropriate columns. Consider each transaction separately and assume that only that transaction affects the data given above.

(a) Paid accounts payable, $150,000.
(b) Received cash on account, $100,000.
(c) Purchased goods on account, $70,000.
(d) Paid notes payable, $100,000.
(e) Declared a cash dividend, $50,000.
(f) Declared a common stock dividend on common stock, $100,000.
(g) Borrowed cash from bank on a long-term note, $200,000.
(h) Sold marketable securities, $60,000.
(i) Issued additional shares of stock for cash, $150,000.
(j) Paid cash for store supplies, $40,000.

**Problem 15-2A.** Revenue and expense data for the current calendar year for Lopez Paper Company and for the paper industry are as follows. The Lopez Paper Company data are expressed in dollars; the paper industry averages are expressed in percentages.

| | Lopez Paper Company | Paper Industry Average |
|---|---|---|
| Sales | $7,070,000 | 100.5% |
| Sales returns and allowances | 70,000 | .5% |
| Cost of goods sold | 5,040,000 | 70.0% |
| Selling expenses | 574,000 | 9.2% |
| General expenses | 434,000 | 8.0% |
| Other income | 35,000 | .6% |
| Other expense | 84,000 | 1.4% |
| Income tax | 406,000 | 5.5% |

Instructions:

(1) Prepare a common-size income statement comparing the results of operations for Lopez Paper Company with the industry average.
(2) As far as the data permit, comment on significant relationships revealed by the comparisons.

**Problem 15-3A.** For 1985, Rose Company initiated an extensive sales promotion campaign that included the expenditure of an additional $40,000 for advertising. At the end of the year, Frank Rose, the president, is presented with the following condensed comparative income statement:

**Rose Company**
**Comparative Income Statement**
**For Years Ended December 31, 1985 and 1984**

| | 1985 | 1984 |
|---|---|---|
| Sales | $510,000 | $303,000 |
| Sales returns and allowances | 10,000 | 3,000 |
| Net sales | $500,000 | $300,000 |
| Cost of goods sold | 310,000 | 180,000 |
| Gross profit | $190,000 | $120,000 |
| Selling expenses | $ 90,000 | $ 48,000 |
| General expenses | 20,000 | 13,500 |
| Total operating expenses | $110,000 | $ 61,500 |
| Operating income | $ 80,000 | $ 58,500 |
| Other income | 2,000 | 900 |
| Income before income tax | $ 82,000 | $ 59,400 |
| Income tax | 20,000 | 15,000 |
| Net income | $ 62,000 | $ 44,400 |

Instructions:

(1) Prepare a comparative income statement for the two-year period, presenting an analysis of each item in relationship to net sales for each of the years.
(2) To the extent the data permit, comment on the significant relationships revealed by the vertical analysis prepared in (1).

**Problem 15-4A.** Prior to approving an application for a short-term loan, American National Bank required that Trillo Company provide evidence of working capital of at least $400,000, a current ratio of at least 1.5 : 1, and an acid-test ratio of at least 1.0 : 1. The chief accountant compiled the following data pertaining to the current position:

**Trillo Company**
**Schedule of Current Assets and Current Liabilities**
**December 31, 1984**

| | |
|---|---:|
| Current assets: | |
| Cash......................................................... | $ 52,750 |
| Accounts receivable .................................... | 262,250 |
| Notes receivable ........................................ | 200,000 |
| Interest receivable...................................... | 10,000 |
| Marketable securities .................................. | 150,000 |
| Inventory .................................................. | 205,000 |
| Supplies.................................................... | 20,000 |
|    Total .................................................... | $900,000 |
| | |
| Current liabilities: | |
| Accounts payable ....................................... | $250,000 |
| Notes payable ........................................... | 200,000 |
|    Total .................................................... | $450,000 |

Instructions:
(1) Compute (a) working capital, (b) current ratio, and (c) acid-test ratio.
(2) At the request of the bank, a firm of independent auditors was retained to examine data submitted with the loan application. This examination disclosed several errors. Prepare correcting entries for each of the following errors:
    (a) Accounts receivable of $42,250 are uncollectible and should be immediately written off. In addition, it was estimated that of the remaining receivables, 5% would eventually become uncollectible and an allowance should be made for these future uncollectible accounts.
    (b) Six months' interest had been accrued on the $200,000, 10%, six-month note receivable dated October 1, 1984.
    (c) The notes payable is a 12%, 90-day note dated October 17, 1984. No interest had been accrued on the note.
    (d) The marketable securities portfolio includes $100,000 of Porter Company stock that is held as a long-term investment.
    (e) A canceled check indicates that a bill for $25,000 for repairs on factory equipment had not been recorded in the accounts.
    (f) Accrued wages as of December 31, 1984, totaled $30,000.
    (g) Received a year's rent of $72,000 for warehouse space leased to Reese Inc., effective October 1, 1984. Upon receipt, rental income was credited for the full amount.
    (h) Supplies on hand at December 31, 1984, total $8,000.
(3) Consider each of the preceding errors separately and assume that only that error affects the current position of Trillo Company. Compute (a) working capital, (b) current ratio, and (c) acid-test ratio, giving effect to each of the preceding errors. Use the following column headings for recording your answers.

| Error | Working Capital | Current Ratio | Acid-Test Ratio |
|-------|-----------------|---------------|-----------------|

(4) Prepare a revised schedule of working capital as of December 31, 1984, and recompute the current ratio and acid-test ratio, giving effect to the corrections of all of the preceding errors.

(5) Discuss the action you would recommend the bank take regarding the pending loan application.

**Problem 15-5A.** The comparative financial statements of T. Rice Inc. are as follows. On December 31, 1985 and 1984, the market price of T. Rice Inc. common stock was $107.50 and $154 respectively.

T. Rice Inc.
Comparative Income Statement
For Years Ended December 31, 1985 and 1984

|  | 1985 | 1984 |
|---|---|---|
| Sales | $8,585,000 | $8,056,000 |
| Sales returns and allowances | 85,000 | 56,000 |
| Net sales | $8,500,000 | $8,000,000 |
| Cost of goods sold | 5,440,000 | 4,800,000 |
| Gross profit | $3,060,000 | $3,200,000 |
| Selling expenses | $1,380,000 | $1,250,000 |
| General expenses | 595,000 | 640,000 |
| Total operating expenses | $1,975,000 | $1,890,000 |
| Operating income | $1,085,000 | $1,310,000 |
| Other income | 119,500 | 120,000 |
|  | $1,204,500 | $1,430,000 |
| Other expense (interest) | 204,500 | 180,000 |
| Income before income tax | $1,000,000 | $1,250,000 |
| Income tax | 490,000 | 610,000 |
| Net income | $ 510,000 | $ 640,000 |

T. Rice Inc.
Comparative Retained Earnings Statement
For Years Ended December 31, 1985 and 1984

|  | 1985 | 1984 |
|---|---|---|
| Retained earnings, January 1 | $2,200,000 | $1,800,000 |
| Add net income for year | 510,000 | 640,000 |
| Total | $2,710,000 | $2,440,000 |
| Deduct dividends: |  |  |
| On preferred stock | $ 80,000 | $ 80,000 |
| On common stock | 175,000 | 160,000 |
| Total | $ 255,000 | $ 240,000 |
| Retained earnings, December 31 | $2,455,000 | $2,200,000 |

T. Rice Inc.
Comparative Balance Sheet
December 31, 1985 and 1984

| Assets | 1985 | 1984 |
|---|---|---|
| Current assets: | | |
| Cash | $ 375,000 | $ 330,000 |
| Marketable securities | 125,000 | 120,000 |
| Accounts receivable (net) | 500,000 | 450,000 |
| Inventory | 720,000 | 660,000 |
| Prepaid expenses | 80,000 | 40,000 |
| Total current assets | $1,800,000 | $1,600,000 |
| Long-term investments | 250,000 | 200,000 |
| Plant assets | 5,150,000 | 4,800,000 |
| Total assets | $7,200,000 | $6,600,000 |

| Liabilities | | |
|---|---|---|
| Current liabilities | $1,000,000 | $ 900,000 |
| Long-term liabilities: | | |
| Mortgage note payable, 10%, due 1990 | $ 245,000 | —— |
| Bonds payable, 12%, due 1999 | 1,500,000 | $1,500,000 |
| Total long-term liabilities | $1,745,000 | $1,500,000 |
| Total liabilities | $2,745,000 | $2,400,000 |

| Stockholders' Equity | | |
|---|---|---|
| Preferred 8% stock, $100 par | $1,000,000 | $1,000,000 |
| Common stock, $25 par | 1,000,000 | 1,000,000 |
| Retained earnings | 2,455,000 | 2,200,000 |
| Total stockholders' equity | $4,455,000 | $4,200,000 |
| Total liabilities and stockholders' equity | $7,200,000 | $6,600,000 |

Instructions:

Determine for 1985 the following ratios, turnovers, and other measures, presenting the figures used in your computations:
(1) Working capital.
(2) Current ratio.
(3) Acid-test ratio.
(4) Accounts receivable turnover.
(5) Number of days' sales in receivables.
(6) Inventory turnover.
(7) Number of days' sales in inventory.
(8) Ratio of plant assets to long-term liabilities.
(9) Ratio of stockholders' equity to liabilities.
(10) Ratio of net sales to assets.
(11) Rate earned on total assets.
(12) Rate earned on stockholders' equity.
(13) Rate earned on common stockholders' equity.
(14) Earnings per share on common stock.
(15) Price-earnings ratio.

*(continued)*

(16) Dividend yield.
(17) Number of times interest charges earned.
(18) Number of times preferred dividends earned.

**Problem 15-6A.** The controller of T. Rice Inc. is evaluating the operating results for 1985 for presentation at the next meeting of the Board of Directors. The company's comparative financial statements for 1985 and 1984 were given in Problem 15-5A. To assist in the evaluation of the company, the controller secured the following additional data taken from the balance sheet at December 31, 1983:

| | |
|---|---:|
| Accounts receivable (net) | $ 400,000 |
| Inventory | 600,000 |
| Long-term investments | 50,000 |
| Total assets | 6,500,000 |
| Total stockholders' equity (preferred and common stock outstanding same as in 1984) | 4,000,000 |

Instructions:

Prepare a report for the controller, based on an analysis of the financial data presented. In preparing your report, include all ratios and other data that will be useful to the controller in preparing for the presentation at the Board meeting.

**Mini-Case**

You and your brother are both presidents of companies in the same industry, CMR Inc. and IMR Inc., respectively. Both companies were originally operated as a single-family business; but shortly after your father's death in 1965, the business was divided into two companies. Your brother took over IMR Inc., located in Indianapolis, while you took over CMR Inc., located in Cincinnati.

During a recent family reunion, your brother referred to the much larger rate of return to his stockholders than was the case in your company and suggested that you consider rearranging the method of financing your corporation. Since 1965, the growth in your brother's company has been financed largely through borrowing and yours largely through the issuance of additional common stock. Both companies have about the same volume of sales, gross profit, operating income, and total assets.

In addition to the 1985 financial statements, the following data were taken from the balance sheets at December 31, 1984:

| | IMR Inc. | CMR Inc. |
|---|---:|---:|
| Total assets | $920,000 | $910,000 |
| Total stockholders' equity | 530,000 | 834,000 |

The income statements for both companies for the year ended December 31, 1985, and the balance sheets at December 31, 1985, are as follows:

| | IMR Inc. | CMR Inc. |
|---|---|---|
| Sales | $2,066,800 | $1,972,500 |
| Sales returns and allowances | 20,800 | 19,500 |
| Net sales | $2,046,000 | $1,953,000 |
| Cost of goods sold | 1,227,600 | 1,171,800 |
| Gross profit | $ 818,400 | $ 781,200 |
| Selling expenses | $ 375,800 | $ 340,400 |
| General expenses | 202,400 | 183,300 |
| Total operating expenses | $ 578,200 | $ 523,700 |
| Operating income | $ 240,200 | $ 257,500 |
| Interest expense | 35,200 | 7,500 |
| Income before income tax | $ 205,000 | $ 250,000 |
| Income tax | 82,000 | 100,400 |
| Net income | $ 123,000 | $ 149,600 |

| Assets | IMR Inc. | CMR Inc. |
|---|---|---|
| Current assets | $ 42,000 | $ 39,000 |
| Plant assets (net) | 880,000 | 906,000 |
| Intangible assets | 18,000 | 5,000 |
| Total assets | $940,000 | $950,000 |

| Liabilities | | |
|---|---|---|
| Current liabilities | $ 18,000 | $ 18,500 |
| Long-term liabilities | 352,000 | 75,500 |
| Total liabilities | $370,000 | $ 94,000 |

| Stockholders' Equity | | |
|---|---|---|
| Common stock ($10 par) | $100,000 | $500,000 |
| Retained earnings | 470,000 | 356,000 |
| Total stockholders' equity | $570,000 | $856,000 |
| Total liabilities and stockholders' equity | $940,000 | $950,000 |

Instructions:

(1) Determine for 1985 the following ratios and other measures for both companies:
  (a) ratio of plant assets to long-term liabilities,
  (b) ratio of stockholders' equity to liabilities,
  (c) ratio of net sales to assets,
  (d) rate earned on total assets, and
  (e) rate earned on stockholders' equity.
(2) For both IMR Inc. and CMR Inc., the rate earned on stockholders' equity is greater than the rate earned on total assets. Explain why.
(3) Why is the rate of return on stockholders' equity for IMR Inc. more than 25% greater than for CMR Inc.?
(4) Comment on your brother's suggestion for rearranging the financing of CMR Inc.

# 16

# Reporting Changes in Price Levels

**CHAPTER OBJECTIVES**

*Describe the effects of price-level changes on management decision making and reporting.*

*Describe and illustrate the effects of price-level changes on conventional financial statements.*

*Describe and illustrate constant dollar accounting for price-level changes.*

*Describe and illustrate current cost accounting for price-level changes.*

# 16

**CHAPTER**

The effects of business transactions are recorded and reported in terms of money. Other pertinent information of a nonfinancial nature may also be reported, such as a description of assets acquired, the terms of purchase and sale contracts, and the circumstances surrounding pending legal actions. However, it is only through the use of dollar amounts that the diverse transactions and activities of a business may be measured, reported, and periodically evaluated. Money is both the common factor of all business transactions and the only feasible unit of measurement that can be used to achieve uniformity of financial data.

As a unit of measurement, the dollar is far inferior to such quantitative standards as the kilogram, liter, or meter, which have remained unchanged for centuries. The value of the dollar changes over time, and such changes are called **price-level changes.** This instability of the purchasing power of the dollar is well known, and the disruptive effect of inflation on accounting reports is acknowledged by accountants. The discussion in this chapter focuses on approaches to presenting management with financial data that are modified for changes in the purchasing power of the dollar.

**INSTABILITY OF MONETARY UNIT AND MANAGEMENT**

Changes in the purchasing power of the dollar can affect almost all financial reporting and management decision making. To illustrate, assume that plant assets acquired by an enterprise for $1,000,000 ten years ago are now to be replaced with similar assets costing $2,000,000. Assume further that during the ten-year period, the plant assets had been fully depreciated and the net income of the enterprise had amounted to $5,000,000. Although the initial outlay of $1,000,000 for the plant assets was deducted as depreciation, this amount represents only one half of the cost of replacing the assets. Since $1,000,000 of the reported net income must be used to replace the assets, this $1,000,000 in income is, in a sense, illusory. Also, it is the $2,000,000 that is relevant in planning financing for the replacement of the assets.

In considering the effects of changing price levels, management might have annually compared depreciation expense based on the cost of the plant assets ($1,000,000) with depreciation based on the estimated replacement cost ($2,000,000). The difference between the two represents the estimated amount that should be provided for in order to maintain the productive capacity of the plant assets. If, for example, depreciation expense recorded in the accounts for a given year for the plant assets is $100,000 and depreciation based on the estimated replacement cost is $200,000, it would have been prudent to consider providing an additional $100,000 for "replacement of facilities." If a firm retains inadequate funds for asset replacements, other financing arrangements, such as stock issuance or borrowing, must be made.

Management must also consider the effects of price-level changes on other activities. For example, a failure to consider such effects on the budgetary process might result in adverse financial conditions, such as cash shortages. Significant changes in the price level can also impair the usefulness of the basic financial statements. Since the generally accepted accounting principles used in preparing the conventional statements assume the use of a stable monetary unit, the effect of price-level changes must be considered when such statements are used in evaluating management performance and in planning and controlling operations.

Accountants are in general agreement that the effects of price-level changes should be reported in supplemental statements, rather than in the conventional statements to which users are accustomed. The assumption of a stable monetary unit insures objectivity in the conventional statements. In addition, because they report transactions in terms of historical costs arising from arm's-length bargaining, the conventional statements can be independently verified.

**TYPES OF PRICE CHANGES**

The amount of goods or services that can be purchased with a given amount of money (number of dollars) changes over time. When prices in general are rising, a given number of dollars will buy less and less goods or services and it can be said that the value of the dollar is falling. During the past three decades, the purchasing power of the dollar has generally declined from year to year. Such periods are described as periods of inflation. When prices are falling, as was the case in the decades of the 1920's and 1930's, the value of the dollar is rising and the purchasing power of the dollar is increasing. Such periods are described as periods of deflation.

Two types of price changes can be identified as affecting business enterprises: (1) general price-level changes and (2) specific price-level changes. A general price-level change is the change over time in the amount of money (number of dollars) needed to purchase a general group or market basket of goods and services. To illustrate, assume that such a group of goods and services is composed of X, Y, and Z and that their individual prices and total price at December 31, 1985 and 1984, are as follows:

|  | December 31 | | Increase |
|  | 1985 | 1984 | (Decrease) |
|---|---|---|---|
| X | $ 6.40 | $ 5.00 | $ 1.40 |
| Y | 20.90 | 22.00 | (1.10) |
| Z | 17.10 | 10.00 | 7.10 |
| Total | $44.40 | $37.00 | $ 7.40 |

In this illustration, to purchase X, Y, and Z at December 31, 1985, would require an outlay of $7.40 more than would the same purchase at December 31, 1984. The general price level, as measured by the goods X, Y, and Z, has increased by 20% ($7.40 ÷ $37) during 1985. Correspondingly, the purchasing power of the dollar in terms of the amount of X, Y, and Z that can be purchased has decreased by 20%.

A specific price-level change is the change over time in the amount of money needed to purchase "individual" goods and services. Prices of individual items may change by a rate that differs from the rate for "general" prices. For example, in the preceding illustration, X increased by 28% ($1.40 ÷ $5) during 1985, Y decreased by 5% ($1.10 ÷ $22), and Z increased by 71% ($7.10 ÷ $10). The general price level for the total of X, Y, and Z increased by 20%.

The effects of general and specific price-level changes on conventional financial statements and two recommendations for reporting these effects are described and illustrated in the remainder of this chapter.

<table>
<tr><td>

**EFFECT OF GENERAL PRICE-LEVEL CHANGES ON FINANCIAL STATEMENTS**

</td><td>

The effect of general price-level changes on conventional financial statements depends on (1) the amount and direction of the change in the general purchasing power of the dollar and (2) the composition of the enterprise's assets and liabilities. The following paragraphs describe and illustrate the measurement of general price-level changes and the effect of these changes on different types of assets and liabilities.

</td></tr>
<tr><td>

**Measuring General Price-Level Changes**

</td><td>

Using a general price-level index, it is possible to convert conventional financial statement amounts to dollars of common purchasing power as of a given date. A **price-level index** is the ratio of the total cost of a group of goods prevailing at a particular time to the total cost of the same group of goods at an earlier base time. The total cost of the goods at the base time is given a value of 100 and the price-level indexes for all later times are expressed as a ratio to 100. For example, assume that the cost of a selected group of goods amounted to $12,000 at a particular time and $13,200 today. The price index for the earlier, or base, time becomes 100 and the current price index is 110 [($13,200 ÷ $12,000) × 100].

To illustrate the use of general price-level indexes, assume that land is purchased for $10,000 in 1978 when the general price-level index was 100, and that the index is 175 at the current date of December 31, 1984. Using these indexes, the original cost of the land can be restated in current dollars of purchasing power as follows:

</td></tr>
</table>

$$\frac{\text{Current Price Index}}{\text{Price Index at Date of Purchase}} \times \text{Original Cost} = \text{Restated Amount}$$

$$\frac{175}{100} \times \$10,000 = \$17,500$$

The computation results in a restated amount of $17,500. This $17,500 is the 1984 amount of money that is equivalent in purchasing power to the 1978 amount of $10,000.

<table>
<tr><td>

**Monetary and Nonmonetary Items**

</td><td>

The effect of general price-level changes on an enterprise's assets and liabilities depends on the type of asset or liability. For example, cash that is held by a business during a period of inflation always loses some of its purchasing power

</td></tr>
</table>

because the cash will purchase less goods and services at the end of the period than at the beginning. On the other hand, a plant asset, such as land, may increase in value and thus not lose some of its purchasing power during periods of inflation. In periods of inflation, a business gains purchasing power as a result of owing amounts, such as accounts payable, that it must settle in dollars. A gain results because the liability will be paid off in dollars which will purchase less than could have been purchased when the liability was incurred. Thus all assets and liabilities are not affected the same by changes in purchasing power.

For purposes of analyzing the effects of changes in purchasing power, the assets and liabilities of a business are classified as monetary or nonmonetary. A monetary item is money or a claim to receive money or an obligation to pay a fixed amount of money. Monetary assets are composed of cash and all claims which are to be settled in cash, such as accounts receivable and notes receivable. Monetary liabilities include virtually all debts, such as accounts payable, notes payable, and bonds payable, because settlement is usually to be made in cash.

All items that are not classified as monetary are classified as nonmonetary. The major nonmonetary items are inventories, plant assets, common stock, and retained earnings. Distinguishing monetary and nonmonetary items thus forms the basis for (1) restating nonmonetary items into dollars of current purchasing power and (2) recognizing purchasing power gains and losses related to the monetary items. In this way, the effects of general price-level changes on conventional financial statements are determined.

### Monetary Items

Holders of monetary assets and liabilities lose or gain general purchasing power during periods of inflation and deflation as a result of general price-level changes. These gains and losses are called purchasing power gains and losses. To illustrate, assume that as of January 1, 1984, a company had a cash balance of $50,000 which it kept throughout the year. If the general price-level index increased during the year from 125 to 150, then a purchasing power loss of $10,000 has occurred. This purchasing power loss is computed as follows:

| | |
|---|---|
| Amount needed to maintain the original purchasing power of cash ($50,000 × 150/125) | $60,000 |
| Actual amount of cash at end of year | 50,000 |
| Purchasing power loss | $10,000 |

When the general price-level index increased from 125 to 150 due to inflation, a dollar lost 20% (25/125) of its purchasing power. In this example, the amount of purchasing power loss was $10,000 ($50,000 × 20%). If the price-level index had decreased from 125 to 100, a purchasing power gain of $10,000 would have resulted.

The holding of noncash monetary assets and liabilities also results in purchasing power gains or losses. To illustrate, assume that ten years ago a $100,000 ten-year note receivable was acquired in connection with a sale of property, that the note is now due, and is paid in full.[1] Since the number of dollars received is exactly the same as the number of dollars loaned, it might appear that the lender has been restored to the original position (i.e., ten years earlier). This would be the case only if there had been no change in the general price level between the date of the note and the date of its repayment. If a 50% increase in the price level between the two dates is assumed, the holder of the note has incurred a purchasing power loss of $50,000 during the period. The amount of the loss is measured by the difference between the amount needed to maintain the original purchasing power and the actual amount of money received. The $50,000 purchasing power loss is computed as follows:

| | |
|---|---:|
| Amount needed to maintain original purchasing power of note receivable ($100,000 × 150%) | $150,000 |
| Actual amount of cash received | 100,000 |
| Purchasing power loss | $ 50,000 |

The effect of the assumed change in price level on the debtor would be the reverse of the effect on the creditor. During the ten-year period, the purchasing power of the $100,000 original liability increased to $150,000, but only $100,000 is needed to satisfy the obligation. Hence, a purchasing power gain of $50,000 is realized.

**Nonmonetary Items**

The purchasing power of nonmonetary items tends not to be affected by changes in the price level. For example, the sales price of a nonmonetary item, such as land, will tend to increase as the general price level increases and will therefore retain its purchasing power. Thus, in contrast to monetary items, no purchasing power gains or losses are recognized for nonmonetary items.

**CONSTANT DOLLAR STATEMENTS**

When historical costs reported in conventional financial statements are converted to dollars of common (or constant) purchasing power, the resulting financial statements are called constant dollar statements or **general price-level statements.** In the conversion process, the purchasing power gain or loss on monetary items is identified.

**Constant Dollar Balance Sheet**

For purposes of preparing the constant dollar balance sheet, the accounts must be classified into monetary and nonmonetary categories. Because general price-level changes affect monetary and nonmonetary items differently, these items must

---

[1]To simplify the illustration, the periodic interest payments will be excluded from consideration.

be classified correctly. The proper classification of common balance sheet accounts is as follows:

| Monetary | Nonmonetary |
|---|---|
| Cash | Inventory |
| Accounts Receivable | Land |
| Notes Receivable | Buildings |
| Accounts Payable | Accumulated Depreciation — Buildings |
| Notes Payable | Equipment |
| Bonds Payable | Accumulated Depreciation — Equipment |
| | Capital Stock |
| | Retained Earnings |

Monetary assets and liabilities are always stated in current purchasing power dollars and therefore need not be adjusted for price-level changes for the constant dollar balance sheet. However, the net purchasing power gain or loss on monetary items is reported on the constant dollar balance sheet as an adjustment of owners' equity. All other balance sheet accounts—the nonmonetary items—must be restated to constant (current) dollars for the constant dollar balance sheet. By restating the nonmonetary items, recognition is given to the effect of the changes that have occurred in the price level since the items were recorded in the accounts.

To illustrate the preparation of a constant dollar balance sheet, assume that Allen Company was organized on January 1, 1984, when the price-level index was 100. The company's balance sheet was as follows:

---

**Allen Company**
**Balance Sheet**
**January 1, 1984**

| Assets | | Stockholders' Equity | |
|---|---|---|---|
| Cash | $10,000 | Capital stock | $40,000 |
| Land | 30,000 | | |
| Total assets | $40,000 | Total stockholders' equity | $40,000 |

---

For purposes of illustration, assume that Allen Company intends to construct a warehouse on the land and then rent storage space to local businesses. However, because of delays in obtaining necessary construction permits, no transactions were completed during 1984 when the price-level index rose to 125. At December 31, 1984, the conventional balance sheet would appear as above, and the constant dollar balance sheet would appear as follows (the computations are inserted as an aid to understanding):

```
                        Allen Company
                  Constant Dollar Balance Sheet
                      December 31, 1984
────────────────────────────────────────────────────────────────
              Assets
Cash ...................   $10,000   (Monetary asset stated in constant
                                      dollars)
Land ...................    37,500   (Nonmonetary asset restated in
                                      constant dollars: $30,000 × 125/100)
                           ───────
Total assets ...........   $47,500

        Stockholders' Equity
Capital stock ...........  $50,000   (Nonmonetary item restated in
                                      constant dollars: $40,000 × 125/100)
Retained earnings (deficit) .  (2,500)  (Purchasing power loss on monetary
                                      asset: $10,000 × 125/100 less
                                      $10,000)
                           ───────
Total stockholders' equity ..  $47,500
```

The determination of the amount reported for each item of the constant dollar balance sheet is explained in the paragraphs that follow.

### Cash

The monetary assets are always stated in constant dollars in the accounts. Therefore, cash does not require adjustment for the general price-level change.

### Land

Land is a nonmonetary asset and the account amount is restated to end-of-the-year constant dollars by multiplying $30,000 by the ratio of the price-level index of 125 at the end of the year to the price-level index of 100 at the date the asset was purchased (the date the company was organized).

### Capital Stock

As a nonmonetary item, capital stock is restated to end-of-the-year constant dollars by multiplying $40,000 by the ratio of the price-level index of 125 at the end of the year to the price-level index of 100 at the date the stock was originally issued (the date the company was organized).

### Retained Earnings

Since no transactions were completed during the year, the constant dollar Retained Earnings balance contains only the purchasing power loss on the monetary assets held during the year. The only monetary item was cash, and the purchasing power loss of $2,500 is computed as follows:

Amount needed to maintain the original purchasing power of the
   monetary item (cash) $10,000 × 125/100 . . . . . . . . . . . . . . . . . . . .          $12,500
Actual amount of monetary item (cash) . . . . . . . . . . . . . . . . . . . . . . .           10,000

Purchasing power loss . . . . . . . . . . . . . . . . . . . . . . . . . . . . . . . . . . . . .       $ 2,500

The basic steps in preparing the constant dollar balance sheet can be summarized as follows:

1. List the monetary assets and liabilities at the account balance amounts because they are always stated in constant (current) dollars.
2. Restate the nonmonetary item account balances to constant dollar equivalents.
3. Reflect the purchasing power gain or loss on monetary items as an adjustment of owners' equity.

**Constant Dollar Income Statement**

For purposes of preparing the constant dollar income statement, all revenues and expenses are restated to end-of-the-year constant dollars by the use of a price-level index. The net purchasing power gain or loss on monetary items is then determined, and this amount is added or subtracted to arrive at the constant dollar net income or loss for the year.

To illustrate the preparation of a constant dollar income statement, assume that in January, 1985, Allen Company entered into a contract for the construction of a warehouse on the land at a cost of $63,000. The construction was completed and the warehouse was placed in service on June 30, 1985. In settlement of the construction contract, a 16%, two-year note payable, with interest payable monthly, was issued. All revenue during 1985 was for cash and all expenses, except depreciation, were paid in cash. The conventional income statement for the year ended December 31, 1985, and the conventional balance sheet on December 31, 1985, are as follows:

---

**Allen Company**
**Income Statement**
**For Year Ended December 31, 1985**

| | | |
|---|---|---|
| Revenues: | | |
| Rental revenue . . . . . . . . . . . . . . . . . | $43,500 | (Rents were collected uniformly during July–December; average price-level index during this period was 145) |
| Expenses: | | |
| Depreciation expense . . . | $ 2,100 | (The warehouse was placed in service when the price-level index was 140) |
| Other rental expenses . . . | 29,000 | (Expenses were paid uniformly during July–December; average price-level index during this period was 145) |
| Total expenses . . . . . . . . . . . . . . . | 31,100 | |
| Net income . . . . . . . . . . . . . . . . . . | $12,400 | |

Allen Company
Balance Sheet
December 31, 1985

**Assets**

| | | |
|---|---:|---:|
| Cash | | $ 24,500 |
| Land | | 30,000 |
| Building | $ 63,000 | |
| Less accumulated depreciation | 2,100 | 60,900 |
| Total assets | | $115,400 |

**Liabilities and Stockholders' Equity**

| | |
|---|---:|
| Notes payable | $ 63,000 |
| Capital stock | 40,000 |
| Retained earnings | 12,400 |
| Total liabilities and stockholders' equity | $115,400 |

If the price-level index at the end of the year was 150, the conventional income statement amounts would be restated to constant dollar equivalents and the constant dollar income statement would appear as follows (the computations are inserted as an aid to understanding):

Allen Company
Constant Dollar Income Statement
For Year Ended December 31, 1985

| | | | |
|---|---:|---:|---|
| Revenues: | | | |
| Rental revenue | | $45,000 | (Restated in constant dollars: $43,500 × 150/145) |
| Expenses: | | | |
| Depreciation expense | $ 2,250 | | (Restated in constant dollars: $2,100 × 150/140) |
| Other rental expenses | 30,000 | | (Restated in constant dollars: $29,000 × 150/145) |
| Total expenses | | 32,250 | |
| Income before purchasing power gain | | $12,750 | |
| Purchasing power gain | | 2,000 | (Computed on monetary items held during the year) |
| Net income | | $14,750 | |

The determination of the amount reported for each item on the constant dollar income statement is explained in the paragraphs that follow.

### Rental Revenue

Since the rents were collected uniformly over a period of time, they are restated to end-of-the-year constant dollars by multiplying $43,500 by the ratio of the price-level index of 150 at the end of the year to the average price-level index of 145 for the period July through December.

### Depreciation Expense

Since the warehouse was purchased when the price-level index was 140, the depreciation expense is restated to end-of-the-year constant dollars by multiplying $2,100 by the ratio of the price-level index of 150 at the end of the year to the price-level index of 140 at the date of the acquisition of the warehouse.

### Other Rental Expenses

As was the case for rental revenues, the other rental expenses, including interest on the note payable, were incurred uniformly throughout the period July through December. Hence, these expenses are restated to end-of-the-year constant dollars by multiplying $29,000 by the ratio of 150 to 145.

### Purchasing Power Gain

To determine the net purchasing power gain for the year, it is necessary to compute the purchasing power gains and losses on the monetary items held during the year. For Allen Company, the monetary items were (1) cash and (2) notes payable. The beginning balances and changes in these items during the year, along with the relevant price-level index for each, are summarized as follows:

|  | Amount | Price-Level Index |
|---|---|---|
| Monetary assets: |  |  |
| Cash, January 1, 1985 | $10,000 | 125 |
| Add rental revenue for 1985 | 43,500 | 145 |
| Deduct other rental expenses for 1985 | (29,000) | 145 |
| Cash, December 31, 1985 | $24,500 | 150 |
| Monetary liabilities: |  |  |
| Notes payable, January 1, 1985 | — | — |
| Issued during 1985 | $63,000 | 140 |
| Notes payable, December 31, 1985 | $63,000 | 150 |

The net purchasing power gain for the year related to the monetary items is $2,000 and is calculated as shown at the top of page 379.

For each monetary item, the January 1, 1985 balance and changes during 1985 are restated to December 31, 1985 constant dollar amounts. The purchasing power gain or loss on each monetary item is then computed by comparing the December 31, 1985 conventional and constant dollar balance sheet amounts. The sum of the

| | Conventional Balance Sheet Amount | Restatement Factor | Constant Dollar Balance Sheet Amount | Purchasing Power Gain (Loss) |
|---|---|---|---|---|
| Cash: | | | | |
| January 1 balance...... | $10,000 | 150/125 | $12,000 | |
| Add rental revenue for 1985 ............... | 43,500 | 150/145 | 45,000 | |
| Deduct other rental expenses for 1985 ...... | (29,000) | 150/145 | (30,000) | |
| December 31 balance .. | $24,500 | | $27,000 | $ (2,500) |
| Notes payable: | | | | |
| January 1 balance...... | — | — | — | |
| Issued during 1985 ..... | $63,000 | 150/140 | $67,500 | |
| December 31 balance .. | $63,000 | | $67,500 | 4,500 |
| Net purchasing power gain............................................. | | | | $ 2,000 |

purchasing power gains and losses for all monetary items held during 1985 determines the net purchasing power gain or loss for the year.

In the illustration, the January 1, 1985 cash balance is restated to December 31, 1985 constant dollars by multiplying $10,000 by the ratio of the price-level index of 150 at the end of the year to the price-level index of 125 at January 1, 1985. The restatement of cash received from rental revenue and cash paid for other rental expenses to December 31, 1985 constant dollars was described previously and reported on the constant dollar income statement. The $2,500 purchasing power loss from holding cash during 1985 is the difference between the December 31, 1985 constant dollar amount of $27,000 and the actual amount of cash on hand of $24,500 at December 31, 1985.

In a similar manner, the purchasing power gain of $4,500 related to the note payable is computed. The account amount of $63,000 is converted to the constant dollar amount of $67,500 by multiplying $63,000 by the ratio of the price-level index of 150 at the end of the year to the price-level index of 140 at the issuance date. The 1985 net purchasing power gain of $2,000 is the sum of the purchasing power loss of $2,500 from holding cash and the $4,500 purchasing power gain from owing the note payable.

The basic steps in preparing the constant dollar income statement can be summarized as follows:

1. Restate all revenue and expense accounts to constant dollar equivalents by the use of a price-level index.
2. Add or deduct the purchasing power gain or loss on monetary items.

**Constant Dollar Retained Earnings Statement**

For purposes of preparing a constant dollar retained earnings statement, the beginning balance of Retained Earnings, as reported at the end of the prior period in constant dollars, is restated to end-of-the-year constant dollars. The constant dollar net income or loss for the year is then added or subtracted. Finally, any dividends for the year are restated to end-of-the-year constant dollars and sub-tracted to arrive at the constant dollar retained earnings as of the end of the year.

To illustrate, Allen Company's conventional and constant dollar retained earn-ings statement for the year ended December 31, 1985, are as follows (the com-putations are inserted as an aid to understanding):

---

**Allen Company**
**Retained Earnings Statement**
**For Year Ended December 31, 1985**

Retained earnings, January 1, 1985. . . . . . . . . . . . . . . . . . . . . . .    —
Net income for the year. . . . . . . . . .    $12,400    (As reported on the 1985 income statement)

Retained earnings, December 31, 1985. . . . . . . . . . . . . . . . . . . . . . .    $12,400

---

**Allen Company**
**Constant Dollar Retained Earnings Statement**
**For Year Ended December 31, 1985**

Retained earnings, January 1, 1985. . . . . . . . . . . . . . . . . . . . . . .    $ (3,000)    (January 1, 1985 constant dollar retained earnings restated to De-cember 31, 1985 constant dol-lars: $2,500 × 150/125)

Constant dollar net income. . . . . . .    14,750    (As reported on the 1985 con-stant dollar income statement)

Retained earnings, December 31, 1985. . . . . . . . . . . . . . . . . . . . . . .    $11,750

---

Allen Company reported a constant dollar deficit of $2,500 on its December 31, 1984 constant dollar balance sheet (illustrated on page 375). This beginning-of-the-year amount must be restated to December 31, 1985 constant dollars by multi-plying the $2,500 deficit by the ratio of the price-level index of 150 at the end of the year to the beginning-of-the-year price-level index of 125. Since no dividends were declared in 1985, the December 31, 1985 constant dollar retained earnings of $11,750 is the result of adding the 1985 constant dollar net income of $14,750 to the restated beginning balance of Retained Earnings.

The basic steps in preparing the constant dollar retained earnings statement can be summarized as follows:

1. Restate the constant dollar beginning balance of Retained Earnings to end-of-the-year constant dollars.

2. Add or deduct the constant dollar net income or loss for the year.
3. Deduct constant dollar dividends for the year.

The December 31, 1985 constant dollar retained earnings of $11,750 would appear on the December 31, 1985 constant dollar balance sheet as follows (the computations are inserted as an aid to understanding):

---

**Allen Company**
**Constant Dollar Balance Sheet**
**December 31, 1985**

**Assets**

| | | |
|---|---|---|
| Cash | $ 24,500 | (Monetary asset stated in constant dollars) |
| Land | 45,000 | (Nonmonetary asset restated to constant dollars: $30,000 × 150/100) |
| Building | $67,500 | (Nonmonetary asset restated to constant dollars: $63,000 × 150/140) |
| Less accumulated depreciation | 2,250 | 65,250 | (Nonmonetary contra asset restated to constant dollars: $2,100 × 150/140) |
| Total assets | $134,750 | |

**Liabilities and Stockholders' Equity**

| | | |
|---|---|---|
| Notes payable | $ 63,000 | (Monetary asset stated in constant dollars) |
| Capital stock | 60,000 | (Nonmonetary item restated in constant dollars: $40,000 × 150/100) |
| Retained earnings | 11,750 | (As reported on the constant dollar retained earnings statement) |
| Total liabilities and stockholders' equity | $134,750 | |

---

**EFFECT OF SPECIFIC PRICE-LEVEL CHANGES ON FINANCIAL STATEMENTS**

The effect of specific price-level changes on conventional financial statements depends on (1) the amount and direction of the change in specific prices related to the enterprise's assets and liabilities and (2) the composition of the enterprise's assets and liabilities. The following paragraphs describe and illustrate the measurement of specific price-level changes and the effect of these changes on different types of assets and liabilities.

**Measuring Specific Price-Level Changes**

Accountants disagree concerning the best means to measure the impact of specific price-level changes on an enterprise's assets and liabilities. However, regardless of which of several suggested measures is used, the assets and liabilities are reported at amounts that approximate their current costs (values). The use of current costs permits the identification of gains and losses related to price-level changes for specific assets and liabilities held by an enterprise.

**Monetary and Nonmonetary Items**

The effect of specific price-level changes depends on the type of asset or liability. For purposes of analyzing the effects of changes in current costs, assets and liabilities of a business are classified as monetary or nonmonetary.

### Monetary Items

All monetary assets and liabilities are stated at current costs in the conventional financial statements. For example, since the current cost of a dollar is a dollar, cash is stated at current cost in the conventional balance sheet. Likewise, the current cost of other monetary items to be collected or paid in cash, such as receivables and liabilities, are also stated at current costs in the conventional balance sheet.

### Nonmonetary Items

The current cost of the nonmonetary assets, such as the plant assets, is the cost of replacing them with assets of the same age and the same operating capacity. Therefore, because the current cost of such nonmonetary assets tends to increase or decrease over time, the account balances need to be restated for current cost statements. By restating the nonmonetary asset to current cost amounts, it is possible to identify gains and losses that result when the current costs of these assets change. In other words, gains and losses that result from the holding of assets, often called holding gains and losses, are identified and reported in financial statements adjusted for current costs. In conventional financial statements, such holding gains and losses are not reported.

To illustrate the use of and reporting of current costs for nonmonetary assets, assume that land is purchased for $20,000 on January 1, 1985, and that its current cost on December 31, 1985, is $25,000. Restating the land to current costs would result in reporting it at $25,000 on the current-cost-adjusted balance sheet at December 31, 1985. The current-cost-adjusted income statement for the year ended December 31, 1985, would also report an "unrealized" holding gain of $5,000, which represents the increase of the current cost over the original cost of the land. It should be noted that the $5,000 holding gain is identified as "unrealized"; that is, since the land has not been sold, the gain has not been realized. If the land were sold for $25,000—for example, on January 1, 1986—the $5,000 of holding gain would then become realized.

**CURRENT COST STATEMENTS**

When historical costs reported in the conventional statements are adjusted for specific price-level changes, all elements of the financial statements are reported at their current costs. The resulting financial statements are called current cost statements or **specific price-level statements**. In the restatement process, the holding gains or losses on nonmonetary assets are identified.

To illustrate the basic concepts of preparing current cost financial statements, assume that Teasley Company was organized on December 31, 1984, by the sale of $150,000 of capital stock for cash. It leased store space and equipment and sold goods only for cash. During 1985, goods costing $295,000 were purchased, $140,000 of the goods were sold for $200,000, and operating expenses were $40,000. A comparative conventional balance sheet for the date of organization and one year later at December 31, 1985, is as follows:

**Teasley Company**
**Comparative Balance Sheet**
**December 31, 1985 and 1984**

| Assets | 1985 | 1984 |
|---|---|---|
| Cash | $ 25,000 | $150,000 |
| Inventory | 155,000 | —— |
| Total assets | $180,000 | $150,000 |
| **Liabilities and Stockholders' Equity** | | |
| Accounts payable | $ 10,000 | —— |
| Capital stock | 150,000 | $150,000 |
| Retained earnings | 20,000 | —— |
| Total liabilities and stockholders' equity | $180,000 | $150,000 |

The conventional income statement for the year ended December 31, 1985, is as follows:

**Teasley Company**
**Income Statement**
**For Year Ended December 31, 1985**

| | |
|---|---|
| Sales | $200,000 |
| Cost of goods sold | 140,000 |
| Gross profit | $ 60,000 |
| Operating expenses | 40,000 |
| Net income | $ 20,000 |

The relevant current cost amounts for the preceding financial statement items are as follows:

| | |
|---|---|
| Cash | $ 25,000 |
| Inventory | 162,000 |
| Accounts payable | 10,000 |
| Capital stock | 150,000 |
| Sales | 200,000 |
| Cost of goods sold | 154,000 |
| Operating expenses | 40,000 |

The conventional income statement of Teasley Company is converted to a current cost income statement by restating the revenues and expenses to current costs and by reporting realized and unrealized holding gains or losses. Revenues and expenses are restated to current costs as of the date each revenue and expense transaction takes place. In this way, current cost expenses are matched against current cost revenues. Most revenues are stated in the conventional income statement at amounts that represent the current values at the date the sales transactions occur. Likewise, most expenses which are directly paid for in cash also are stated in the conventional income statement at amounts that represent the current values at the transaction dates.

Based upon the preceding data, the current cost income statement for Teasley Company would appear as follows (the notations are inserted as an aid to understanding):

---

**Teasley Company**
**Current Cost Income Statement**
**For Year Ended December 31, 1985**

| | | |
|---|---|---|
| Sales......................... | $200,000 | (Stated at current cost at the transaction dates) |
| Cost of goods sold ............. | 154,000 | (Restated to current costs at the transaction dates) |
| Gross profit.................... | $ 46,000 | |
| Operating expenses ........... | 40,000 | (Stated at current costs at the transaction dates) |
| Operating income ............. | $ 6,000 | |
| Realized holding gain.......... | 14,000 | (Holding gain on cost of goods sold: $154,000 − $140,000) |
| Realized income................ | $ 20,000 | |
| Unrealized holding gain........ | 7,000 | (Holding gain on ending inventory: $162,000 − $155,000) |
| Net income ................... | $ 27,000 | |

---

The determination of the amount reported for each item on the current cost income statement is explained in the paragraphs that follow.

### Sales

Since sales are stated in the conventional income statement at amounts that represent the current values at the dates of the sales transactions, the sales amount does not require adjustment for the current cost income statement.

### Cost of Goods Sold

To determine the current cost of goods sold, the current cost of each item sold must be identified as of the date of sale. These current cost amounts are then accumulated throughout the year to determine the total current cost of goods sold during the year. The total current cost of goods sold is then deducted from the current value of sales to arrive at current cost gross profit. For Teasley Company, the accumulated current cost of goods sold was determined to be $154,000. Since the original cost of goods sold was $140,000, the amount of the realized holding gain was $14,000.

### Operating Expenses

The current cost for operating expenses of $40,000 is the cost of the resources consumed by Teasley Company as measured at the time the expenses were incurred. For this illustration, the conventional amount and the current cost amount is $40,000.[2]

### Realized Holding Gain

The $14,000 realized holding gain is the difference between the $154,000 current cost of goods sold and the $140,000 original cost of goods sold. This holding gain is reported as realized, since the goods have been sold.

### Unrealized Holding Gain

The $7,000 unrealized holding gain is the difference between the $162,000 current cost of inventory at the end of the year and its original cost of $155,000. This holding gain is classified as unrealized, since the goods have yet to be sold.

It should be noted that the current cost realized income of $20,000 for 1985 equals the conventional income statement net income for 1985. These two financial statement amounts will always be equal, because both the current cost realized income and the conventional financial statement net income include realized holding gains and losses from selling nonmonetary assets.

The basic steps in preparing the current cost income statement can be summarized as follows:

1. List revenues at their current cost amounts.
2. Restate the cost of goods sold and other expenses as reported on the conventional income statement to their current cost amounts.
3. Add or deduct the realized and unrealized holding gains and losses.

**Current Cost Balance Sheet**

For purposes of preparing the current cost balance sheet, the accounts must be classified into monetary and nonmonetary categories. The classification of common balance sheet accounts into monetary and nonmonetary categories was illustrated on page 374.

---

[2]To simplify this illustration, noncash expenses such as depreciation have been excluded from consideration. In current cost financial statements, depreciation would be restated, based upon the average current costs of the depreciable assets held during the year.

Monetary assets and liabilities are always stated in current costs and therefore need not be restated. All nonmonetary assets must be restated to current costs for the current cost balance sheet. By restating the nonmonetary assets, recognition is given to the effect of changes that have occurred in current costs since the assets were initially recorded in the accounts. These changes in current costs are shown in the current cost income statement as holding gains and losses.

Owners' equity accounts are nonmonetary items that must be analyzed separately. The accounts that show investments by stockholders, such as Capital Stock, are stated in the conventional financial statements at the amounts initially received from investors. These amounts represent the current costs of obtaining these funds and do not need to be restated. Other owners' equity accounts, such as Retained Earnings, must be restated to current costs. Retained Earnings is restated to current costs by restating the beginning-of-the-year balance to current costs, then adding current cost net income or subtracting current cost net loss, and subtracting any current cost dividends.

The current cost balance sheet for Teasley Company is as follows (the notations are inserted as an aid to understanding):

| Teasley Company Current Cost Balance Sheet December 31, 1985 | | |
|---|---|---|
| **Assets** | | |
| Cash......................... | $ 25,000 | (Monetary asset stated at current cost) |
| Inventory ...................... | 162,000 | (Nonmonetary asset restated to current cost) |
| Total assets.................... | $187,000 | |
| **Liabilities and Stockholders' Equity** | | |
| Accounts payable .............. | $ 10,000 | (Monetary liability stated at current cost) |
| Capital stock................... | 150,000 | (Nonmonetary capital stated at current cost) |
| Retained earnings ............. | 27,000 | (Nonmonetary capital restated to current cost) |
| Total liabilities and stockholders' equity........... | $187,000 | |

The determination of the amount reported for each item on the current cost balance sheet is explained in the paragraphs that follow.

### Cash and Accounts Payable

Monetary items are stated at current costs in conventional financial statements and therefore do not require restatement on the current cost balance sheet.

### Inventory

Inventory should be stated on the current cost balance sheet at its estimated current cost of $162,000.

### Capital Stock

Capital stock is reported in the conventional balance sheet at the amount initially received from investors. This amount represents the current cost of obtaining such funds and does not need to be restated.

### Retained Earnings

For Teasley Company, the current cost net income of $27,000 is equal to the December 31, 1985 current cost retained earnings. Preparation of a current cost retained earnings statement is described in the next section.

The basic steps in preparing the current cost balance sheet can be summarized as follows:

1. List the monetary assets and liabilities and capital stock account balances because they are always stated at current costs.
2. Restate the nonmonetary asset account balances to current costs.
3. Compute the current cost retained earnings by restating the beginning balance and changes during the year to current costs.

**Current Cost Retained Earnings Statement**

For purposes of preparing a current cost retained earnings statement, the beginning balance of Retained Earnings is restated to current costs by referring to the preceding year's current cost financial statements. The current cost net income or loss for the year is then added or subtracted and any current cost dividends are subtracted to arrive at the current cost retained earnings as of the end of the year.

To illustrate, the December 31, 1985 current cost retained earnings statement for Teasley Company is as follows (the notations are inserted as an aid to understanding):

---

Teasley Company
Current Cost Retained Earnings Statement
For Year Ended December 31, 1985

| | | |
|---|---|---|
| Retained earnings, January 1, 1985 .......................... | –0– | (The company was organized on December 31, 1984) |
| Current cost net income......... | $27,000 | (As reported in the 1985 current cost income statement) |
| Retained earnings, December 31, 1985 ......................... | $27,000 | |

Since Teasley Company was organized on December 31, 1984, current cost retained earnings as of January 1, 1985, is zero. No dividends were declared in 1985 and current cost net income is $27,000. The December 31, 1985 current cost retained earnings of $27,000 is reported on the December 31, 1985 current cost balance sheet shown on page 386.

The basic steps in preparing the current cost retained earnings statement are as follows:

1. Restate the beginning balance of retained earnings to current costs.
2. Add or deduct current cost net income or loss for the year.
3. Deduct any current cost dividends for the year.

**PRICE-LEVEL CHANGES AND MANAGEMENT POLICY**

Although management has no control over the price-level changes reported in the financial statements, it should be aware of the effect of such changes on operations and plan accordingly. For example, because management can control, to some extent, the relationship between monetary assets and liabilities, steps that minimize purchasing power losses on monetary items or maximize purchasing power gains on monetary items should be considered to the extent that other operating results will not be jeopardized. If a period of inflation is expected, the company should consider maintaining a position in which liabilities exceed monetary assets. If deflation is expected, monetary assets should exceed liabilities. As another example, management can use the current cost retained earnings statement in evaluating dividend policy. Because the statement indicates the effect that specific price-level changes have had on past operations, management is in a better position to evaluate the amount of dividends that can be paid without jeopardizing future operating capacity. Thus, reports that separate the effects of price-level changes from other factors enable management to better plan and control operations.

---

**Self-Examination Questions**
*(Answers in Appendix C.)*

1. A period when prices in general are rising is referred to as a period of:
   A. deflation
   B. inflation
   C. a purchasing power loss
   D. none of the above

2. If a $100,000 investment in stock was made at a time when the general price index was 100, what would be the restated constant dollar amount at a time when the index was 140?
   A. $40,000
   B. $100,000
   C. $140,000
   D. None of the above

3. During a period in which the general price level is rising, which of the following would create a purchasing power gain?
   A. Holding cash
   B. Holding a long-term bond payable
   C. Holding inventory
   D. Holding a note receivable

4. Which of the following is a monetary item?
   A. Cash
   B. Notes receivable
   C. Bonds payable
   D. All of the above

5. Land purchased for $30,000 on April 15, 1984, has a current cost of $40,000 at December 31, 1984. The $10,000 difference between the current cost and the original cost of the land is:
   A. a realized holding gain
   B. a purchasing power gain
   C. an unrealized holding gain
   D. none of the above

**Discussion Questions**

1. What term is used to refer to periods when the value of the dollar is rising and the purchasing power of the dollar is increasing?

2. Describe the difference between a general price-level change and a specific price-level change.

3. If equipment was purchased for $40,000 when the general price-level index was 220, and the general price-level index has risen to 242 in 1984, what is the original cost restated in current dollars?

4. (a) Describe the difference between monetary and nonmonetary items. (b) Describe a purchasing power gain.

5. Five years ago, Delaney Company accepted an $80,000 long-term note from Mintz Corporation. The note is now due. The general price level has increased by 32% during the five years. (a) What is Delaney Company's purchasing power gain or loss? (b) What is Mintz Corporation's purchasing power gain or loss?

6. During the current year, a mortgage note payable for $310,000, issued by Archer Corporation ten years ago, becomes due and is paid. Assuming that the general price level has increased by 100% during the ten-year period, did the loan result in an increase or decrease in Archer Corporation's purchasing power? Explain.

7. Indicate whether each of the following is a monetary or nonmonetary item:
   (a) Building
   (b) Notes Payable
   (c) Cash
   (d) Land
   (e) Accounts Payable
   (f) Capital Stock

8. During a period of inflation, would an enterprise gain in purchasing power if it held (a) monetary assets or (b) monetary liabilities?

9. Jesse Ward robbed a bank of $50,000 in cash in 1978. Before he was captured and sentenced to prison, he buried the money. In 1984, Ward was released on parole and promptly recovered the buried money. (a) If the general price-level index was 175 in 1978 and 210 in 1984, what was Ward's purchasing power loss while in prison? (b) How many dollars would be necessary in 1984 to equal the purchasing power of the $50,000 stolen in 1978?

10. Sales totaling $210,000 were made uniformly throughout the year. At what amount would sales be reported on the constant dollar income statement if the price-level index at the beginning of the year was 140, the average for the year was 160, and the index at the end of the year was 184?

11. When a constant dollar balance sheet is prepared, which of the following categories of items is restated in terms of constant dollars: (a) monetary items (b) nonmonetary items?

12. Describe the basic steps in preparing a constant dollar (a) balance sheet and (b) income statement.

13. Describe current cost for (a) a monetary asset and (b) a nonmonetary asset.

14. Distinguish between realized holding gains and losses and unrealized holding gains and losses.

15. Land was purchased for $128,000 on May 31, 1983. Subsequently, the current cost of the land was as follows:

> December 31, 1983........$130,000
> December 31, 1984........ 136,000
> December 31, 1985........ 135,000

(a) What is the unrealized holding gain or loss for each year ending on December 31? (b) If the land were sold on December 31, 1985, for $135,000, what is the realized holding gain or loss?

16. At what amount are sales normally reported on the current cost income statement?

17. When a current cost balance sheet is prepared, which of the following categories of items is restated in current costs: (a) monetary items, (b) nonmonetary assets, (c) paid-in capital accounts, (d) retained earnings?

18. If the current cost concept is used in preparing supplemental statements, what amounts would be reported for (a) land at December 31, 1984, and (b) unrealized gain from holding the land in 1984, based on the following data:

> Land, purchase price, January 2, 1984 ......... $60,000
> Land, current cost, December 31, 1984......... 78,000

19. What two amounts in a current cost income statement and a conventional income statement are always equal?

20. Identify two common methods for supplementing conventional financial statements and resolving the financial reporting problems created by increasing price levels?

**Exercises**

**Exercise 16-1.** Montgomery Enterprises purchased 3,000 shares of capital stock of Stein Company for $60,000 at a time when the price-level index was 120. On October 11 of the current year when the price-level index was 132, the stock was sold for $71,500.

    (a) Determine the amount of the gain that would be realized according to conventional accounting.

    (b) Indicate the amount of the gain (1) that may be attributed to the change in purchasing power and (2) that may be considered a true gain in terms of current dollars.

**Exercise 16-2.** Boyd Company was organized on April 1 of the current year. Capital stock was issued for $37,500 cash and land valued at $62,500. Assume that no transactions occurred during the year and that the price-level index was 125 on April 1 and 132 on March 31, the end of the current fiscal year.

(a) Prepare a conventional balance sheet in report form.

(b) Prepare a constant dollar balance sheet in report form.

**Exercise 16-3.** The following selected accounts were extracted from the records of Cordell Company at August 31, the end of the current fiscal year:

| | |
|---|---:|
| Depreciation expense on equipment. . . . . . . . . . | $ 7,000 |
| Fees earned . . . . . . . . . . . . . . . . . . . . . . . . . . . . | 112,500 |
| Miscellaneous expense . . . . . . . . . . . . . . . . . . . . | 2,250 |
| Rent and utilities expense . . . . . . . . . . . . . . . . . . | 27,000 |
| Supplies expense . . . . . . . . . . . . . . . . . . . . . . . . | 1,264 |
| Wages expense. . . . . . . . . . . . . . . . . . . . . . . . . . | 72,000 |

Fees earned, miscellaneous expense, rent and utilities expense, and wages expense occurred evenly throughout the year. Equipment was acquired when the price index was 140, and supplies were acquired when the price index was 158. The price index averaged 150 for the year and was 160 at the end of the year.

Prepare a constant dollar income statement for the current year. The purchasing power loss on monetary items was $6,090.

**Exercise 16-4.** The beginning balance and changes in cash for the year ended December 31, 1984, along with the relevant price-level indexes for DePew Company, are as follows:

| | Amount | Price-Level Index |
|---|---:|:---:|
| Cash, January 1, 1984 . . . . . . . . . . . . | $ 60,200 | 172 |
| Add revenue for 1984 . . . . . . . . . . . . . | 122,400 | 180 |
| Deduct expenses for 1984. . . . . . . . . | 104,400 | 180 |
| Cash, December 31, 1984. . . . . . . . . | $ 78,200 | 190 |

Calculate DePew Company's purchasing power loss from holding cash during 1984, using the format shown on page 379.

**Exercise 16-5.** Fisher Corporation was organized on January 1, 1982, and capital stock was issued for land valued at $60,000. Plans to construct several buildings and to begin operations were never finalized, and the land was sold on January 2, 1985, for $78,500. Assume that no other transactions were completed and that the current cost of the land was as follows:

| | |
|---|---:|
| December 31, 1982. . . . . . . . | $61,000 |
| December 31, 1983. . . . . . . . | 72,000 |
| December 31, 1984. . . . . . . . | 78,500 |

(a) Compute the conventional financial statement net income for the years ended December 31, 1982, 1983, and 1984.

(b) Compute the current cost net income for the years ended December 31, 1982, 1983, and 1984.

(c) Compute the conventional financial statement net income for the year ended December 31, 1985.

**Exercise 16-6.** Selby Company was organized on January 1, 1984, through the issuance of $50,000 capital stock for cash. The company leases store space and equipment and sells goods only for cash. During 1984, goods costing $368,600 were purchased, $301,450 of the goods were sold for $361,740, and operating expenses were $29,220. At December 31, 1984, the relevant current cost amounts are as follows:

| | |
|---|---:|
| Cash. | $ 22,850 |
| Inventory | 81,250 |
| Accounts payable | 8,930 |
| Capital stock | 50,000 |
| Sales | 361,740 |
| Cost of goods sold | 335,610 |
| Operating expenses | 29,220 |

For the year ended December 31, 1984, prepare (a) a conventional income statement and (b) a current cost income statement.

**Exercise 16-7.** Based on the data presented in Exercise 16-6, prepare as of December 31, 1984, (a) a conventional balance sheet in report form and (b) a current cost balance sheet in report form.

**Problems**
*(Problems in Appendix B: 16-1B, 16-2B, 16-3B, 16-4B.)*

**Problem 16-1A.** Hodges Company was organized on January 1, 1984, when the price-level index was 200. Capital stock of $140,000 was issued in exchange for cash of $45,000 and land valued at $105,000. The land was subject to property taxes of $10,000 due for the current year. No transactions occurred during 1984, and the price-level index at the end of the year was 210. The income statement for 1985 disclosed the following:

| | |
|---|---:|
| Sales (made uniformly during the year). | $347,600 |
| Cost of goods sold (purchased when price index was 218). | 272,500 |
| Depreciation expense (asset purchased when price index was 212). | 5,300 |
| Other expenses (incurred uniformly during the year). | 24,200 |

The average price-level index for 1985 was 220, and at the end of 1985 it was 240.

Instructions:
   (1) Prepare a conventional balance sheet at December 31, 1984, in report form.
   (2) Prepare a constant dollar balance sheet at December 31, 1984, in report form.
   (3) Prepare a constant dollar income statement for the year ended December 31, 1985. The purchasing power loss for the year was $6,140.

**Problem 16-2A.** The monetary items held by O'Brien Company throughout the fiscal year ended July 31, 1984, consisted of cash and accounts payable. The beginning balances and changes in these monetary items during the year, along with the relevant price-level index for each, are as follows:

| | Amount | Price-Level Index |
|---|---|---|
| Monetary asset: | | |
| Cash, August 1, 1983 | $ 31,500 | 210 |
| Add sales | 276,750 | 225 |
| Deduct expenses | 196,875 | 225 |
| Cash, July 31, 1984 | $111,375 | 240 |
| Monetary liability: | | |
| Accounts payable, August 1, 1983 | $ 16,800 | 210 |
| Add purchases on account | 170,550 | 225 |
| Deduct payments on account | 154,125 | 225 |
| Accounts payable, July 31, 1984 | $ 33,225 | 240 |

Instructions:

Calculate the purchasing power gain or loss for the year ended July 31, 1984, using the format shown on page 379.

**Problem 16-3A.** MZM Associates, a professional corporation, was organized with the issuance of $62,000 of capital stock on September 1, 1984, and began operations by leasing office space and office equipment. On December 1, 1984, MZM Associates acquired office equipment in exchange for a $12,300, 16%, three-year note payable with interest payable monthly. All services rendered were for cash, and all expenses, except for depreciation, were paid in cash. The conventional income statement for the year ended August 31, 1985, and the conventional balance sheet on August 31, 1985, are as follows:

**MZM Associates**
**Income Statement**
**For Year Ended August 31, 1985**

| | | |
|---|---|---|
| Revenues: | | |
| Professional fees | $143,650 | (Fees were collected uniformly during year; average price-level index was 170) |
| Expenses: | | |
| Depreciation expense | $ 1,640 | (The office equipment was purchased when the price-level index was 164) |
| Other operating expenses | 128,520 | (Expenses were paid uniformly during year; average price-level index was 170) |
| Total expenses | 130,160 | |
| Net income | $ 13,490 | |

MZM Associates
Balance Sheet
August 31, 1985

### Assets

| | | |
|---|---:|---:|
| Cash | | $77,130 |
| Office equipment | $12,300 | |
| Less accumulated depreciation | 1,640 | 10,660 |
| Total assets | | $87,790 |

### Liabilities and Stockholders' Equity

| | |
|---|---:|
| Notes payable | $12,300 |
| Capital stock | 62,000 |
| Retained earnings | 13,490 |
| Total liabilities and stockholders' equity | $87,790 |

The average general price-level index for the year ended August 31, 1985, was 170. During the year, the price-level index was as follows:

| | |
|---|---:|
| September 1, 1984 | 155 |
| December 1, 1984 | 164 |
| August 31, 1985 | 185 |

Instructions:
(1) Calculate the purchasing power gain or loss for the year ended August 31, 1985, using the format shown on page 379.
(2) Prepare a constant dollar income statement for the year ended August 31, 1985.
(3) Prepare a constant dollar retained earnings statement for the year ended August 31, 1985.
(4) Prepare a constant dollar balance sheet at August 31, 1985, in report form.

**Problem 16-4A.** Dunbar Wholesalers Inc. was organized on January 31, 1984, by the sale of $120,000 of capital stock for cash. It leased store space and equipment and sold goods only for cash. During 1984, goods costing $872,000 were purchased, $615,800 of the goods were sold for $862,120, and operating expenses were $182,600. The conventional income statement for the year ended December 31, 1984, and the conventional balance sheet at December 31, 1984, are as follows:

Dunbar Wholesalers Inc.
Income Statement
For Year Ended December 31, 1984

| | |
|---|---:|
| Sales | $862,120 |
| Cost of goods sold | 615,800 |
| Gross profit | $246,320 |
| Operating expenses | 182,600 |
| Net income | $ 63,720 |

Dunbar Wholesalers Inc.
Balance Sheet
December 31, 1984

### Assets

| | |
|---|---|
| Cash | $ 26,800 |
| Inventory | 256,200 |
| Total assets | $283,000 |

### Liabilities and Stockholders' Equity

| | |
|---|---|
| Accounts payable | $ 99,280 |
| Capital stock | 120,000 |
| Retained earnings | 63,720 |
| Total liabilities and stockholders' equity | $283,000 |

The relevant current cost amounts for the preceding financial statement items are as follows:

| | |
|---|---|
| Cash | $ 26,800 |
| Inventory | 279,450 |
| Accounts payable | 99,280 |
| Capital stock | 120,000 |
| Sales | 862,120 |
| Cost of goods sold | 660,500 |
| Operating expenses | 182,600 |

Instructions:

(1) Prepare a current cost income statement for the year ended December 31, 1984.

(2) Prepare a current cost retained earnings statement for the year ended December 31, 1984.

(3) Prepare a current cost balance sheet at December 31, 1984, in report form.

**Problem 16-5A.** Rowland Company's current cost income statement for the year ended December 31, 1984, and current cost balance sheet as of December 31, 1984, are as follows:

Rowland Company
Current Cost Income Statement
For Year Ended December 31, 1984

| | |
|---|---|
| Sales | $628,120 |
| Cost of goods sold | 471,090 |
| Gross profit | $157,030 |
| Operating expenses | 146,500 |
| Operating income | $ 10,530 |
| Realized holding gain | 30,850 |
| Realized income | $ 41,380 |
| Unrealized holding gain | 20,120 |
| Net income | $ 61,500 |

Rowland Company
Current Cost Balance Sheet
December 31, 1984

### Assets

| | |
|---|---:|
| Cash ......................................................... | $ 28,900 |
| Accounts receivable ......................................... | 54,750 |
| Inventory.................................................... | 118,150 |
| Land ........................................................ | 50,000 |
| Total assets ................................................ | $251,800 |

### Liabilities and Stockholders' Equity

| | |
|---|---:|
| Accounts payable............................................. | $ 48,230 |
| Capital stock ............................................... | 100,000 |
| Retained earnings ........................................... | 103,570 |
| Total liabilities and stockholders' equity................... | $251,800 |

The realized holding gain of $30,850 is identified entirely with the cost of goods sold, and $8,000 of the unrealized holding gain of $20,120 pertains to the land. Both the land and all of the ending inventory were purchased in 1984.

Instructions:

(1) Prepare a conventional income statement for the year ended December 31, 1984.

(2) Prepare a conventional balance sheet as of December 31, 1984.

**Mini-Case**

On January 2, 1976, Kreps Company, a small privately held company, purchased land for $108,000, paying cash of $16,200 and issuing a $91,800, 12%, 10-year note payable to the seller. The land was located near a proposed interstate highway and was to be used for the construction of a new warehouse and product distribution center. Because of changing business conditions, Kreps Company decided in 1978 to indefinitely defer the warehouse construction but keep the land as an investment. In late 1984, the local zoning commission rezoned the land from commercial use to residential use only. At the beginning of 1984, before the rezoning, the land had an estimated market value of $240,000. At the end of 1984, after the rezoning, the market value of the land dropped to $160,000. On January 4, 1985, Kreps Company sold the land to a real estate developer for $160,000 and paid off the $91,800 note. From January of 1976 to January of 1985, the general price level increased from 176 to 220.

Paul Shuford, a minority shareholder of Kreps Company, has been highly critical of the company's management for the past several years. Shuford has written a letter to Kreps Company's treasurer, questioning management's handling of the land transactions and its reporting of the gain from the sale of the land on the income statement. Excerpts from the letter are as follows:

(a) "Management used poor judgment in not selling the land before the rezoning, and this should be indicated in the 1984 financial statements by reporting an $80,000 ($240,000 − $160,000) loss for the drop in the market value of the land due to the rezoning."

(b) "The land restated in 1985 dollars for general price-level changes is $135,000 ($108,000 × 220/176). Therefore, the maximum gain on the sale of the land that should be reported in 1985 is $25,000 ($160,000 − $135,000) and not the $52,000 as reported on the income statement."

Instructions:

(1) The treasurer has asked you to draft a response to each of Shuford's allegations. How would you respond?

(2) While discussing the points raised in (1), the treasurer asked you the following questions. How would you respond to each?

(a) What is the total amount of purchasing power gain or loss from the issuance and subsequent payment of the note (ignore interest payments)?

(b) If current cost statements were prepared for 1984 and 1985, what would be the amount of realized and unrealized holding gains and losses from the land for each year?

# 17
CHAPTER

# Statement of Changes in Financial Position

**CHAPTER OBJECTIVES**

*Describe the usefulness of reporting changes in financial position.*

*Describe alternative concepts of funds.*

*Describe and illustrate the preparation and use by management of a statement of changes in financial position based upon (1) the working capital concept of funds and (2) the cash concept of funds.*

# 17

## CHAPTER

The preparation of various accounting reports for management's use has been described in previous chapters. This chapter is devoted to the statement of changes in financial position, a statement that is especially useful to management in evaluating past and planning future financing and investment activities. The statement of changes in financial position is one of the basic statements included in annual reports. Thus, the statement is useful not only to management but also to those external to the firm, such as investors and creditors, in evaluating past operations and future prospects.

The statement of changes in financial position reports a firm's significant financing and investing activities for a period. These activities are generally described in terms of the inflow and outflow of "funds", with funds defined as either "cash" or "working capital." The funds statement, then, can be said to provide a summary of the *sources* from which funds became available and the purposes for which the funds were *applied* during a period. Common inflows (sources) of funds include operations aimed at earning income, sale of long-term investments and plant assets, and issuance of bonds and capital stock. Typically, the funds obtained are used for such outflows (applications) as the purchase of long-term investments and plant assets, retirement of bonds, and declaration of cash dividends.

Both the acquisition and the subsequent use of funds can affect profitability and solvency. For example, the acquisition of funds by issuing bonds commits the firm not only to the payment of periodic interest expense (which affects profitability) but obligates the firm to make periodic interest payments and to redeem the bonds at maturity (which affect solvency). Thus, the statement of changes in financial position is useful in analyzing both past and future profitability and solvency of the firm.

Although the formal name of the statement is statement of changes in financial position, the term often used in discussing the statement is funds statement. This shorter term will often be used in the following discussion.

## CONCEPTS OF FUNDS

As indicated previously, funds can be interpreted broadly to mean working capital or, more narrowly, to mean cash. Two statements, one based on working capital and the other on cash, may be prepared for the use of management, but only one statement is usually presented in published financial reports.

Regardless of which of the concepts is used for a specific funds statement, financial position may also be affected by transactions that do not involve funds. If such transactions have occurred during the period, their effect, if significant, should be reported in the funds statement.

## WORKING CAPITAL CONCEPT OF FUNDS

The excess of an enterprise's total current assets over its total current liabilities at the same point in time may be termed its "net current assets" or working capital. To illustrate, assume that a corporate balance sheet lists current assets totaling $560,000 and current liabilities totaling $230,000. The working capital of the corporation at the balance sheet date is $330,000 ($560,000 − $230,000). The following comparative schedule includes the major categories of current assets and current liabilities:

|  | December 31 | | Increase |
|  | 1985 | 1984 | Decrease* |
| --- | --- | --- | --- |
| **Current assets:** | | | |
| Cash........................................ | $ 40,000 | $ 35,000 | $ 5,000 |
| Marketable securities ................... | 60,000 | 40,000 | 20,000 |
| Receivables (net)......................... | 100,000 | 115,000 | 15,000* |
| Inventories................................ | 350,000 | 295,000 | 55,000 |
| Prepaid expenses ....................... | 10,000 | 15,000 | 5,000* |
| Total .................................. | $560,000 | $500,000 | $60,000 |
| **Current liabilities:** | | | |
| Notes payable .......................... | $ 70,000 | $ 50,000 | $20,000 |
| Accounts payable ....................... | 125,000 | 145,000 | 20,000* |
| Income tax payable...................... | 10,000 | 20,000 | 10,000* |
| Dividends payable....................... | 25,000 | 25,000 | —— |
| Total ................................... | $230,000 | $240,000 | $10,000* |
| Working capital.......................... | $330,000 | $260,000 | $70,000 |

The increase or decrease in each item is reported in the third column of the schedule. The increase of $60,000 in total current assets during the year tended to increase working capital. The decrease of $10,000 in total current liabilities also tended to increase working capital. The combined effect was an increase of $70,000 in working capital. Note that working capital is a "net" concept. An increase or decrease in working capital cannot be determined solely by the amount of change in total current assets or solely by the amount of change in total current liabilities.

The amount of most of the items classified as current assets and current liabilities varies from one balance sheet date to another. Many of the items change daily. Inventories are increased by purchases on account, which also increase accounts payable. Accounts payable are reduced by payment, which also reduces cash. As merchandise is sold on account, inventories decrease and accounts receivable increase. In turn, the collections from customers increase cash and reduce accounts receivable. An understanding of this continuous interaction among the various current assets and current liabilities is essential to an understanding of the concept of working capital and analyses related to it. In the illustration, for example, the absence of increase or decrease in the amount of dividends payable between balance sheet dates should not be thought of as an indication that the account balance remained unchanged throughout the year. If dividends were paid quarterly, four separate liabilities would have been created and four would have been liquidated during the period. Also, the amount of working capital is neither increased nor decreased by a transaction (1) that affects only current assets (such as a purchase of marketable securities for cash), (2) that affects only current liabilities (such as issuance of a short-term note to a creditor on account), or (3) that affects only current assets and current liabilities (such as payment of an account payable).

**Working Capital Flow**

The working capital schedule on the preceding page shows an increase of $70,000 in working capital, which may be significant in evaluating financial position. However, the schedule gives no indication of the source of the increase. It could have resulted from the issuance of common stock, from the sale of treasury stock, from operating income, or from a combination of these and other sources. It is also possible that working capital would have increased by considerably more during the year had it not been for the purchase of plant assets, the retirement of bonded indebtedness, an adverse judgment as defendant in a damage suit, or other occurrences with a similar effect on working capital.

Both the inflow and the outflow of funds are reported in a funds statement. Those flowing into the enterprise, classified as to source, form the first section of the funds statement. Funds flowing out of the enterprise, classified according to the manner of their use or application, are reported in the second section of the statement. Ordinarily, the totals of the two sections are unequal. If the inflow (sources) has exceeded the outflow (applications), the excess is the amount of the increase in working capital. When the reverse situation occurs, the excess of outflow is a measure of the amount by which working capital has decreased. Accordingly, the difference between the total of the sources and the applications sections of the funds statement is identified as an increase or a decrease in working capital. The details of this balancing amount are presented in a subsidiary section of the statement or in a separate schedule.

Some of the data needed in preparing a funds statement can be obtained from comparing items on the current balance sheet with those on the preceding balance sheet. Information regarding net income may be obtained from the current income statement and dividend data are available in the retained earnings statement. However, there may be sources and applications of funds that are not disclosed by these statements. Some of the relevant data can be obtained only from an examination of accounts in the ledger or from journal entries.

Although there are many kinds of transactions that affect funds, consideration will be limited here to the most common sources and applications. As a matter of convenience in the discussion that follows, all asset accounts other than current assets will be referred to as "noncurrent assets" and all liability accounts other than current liabilities will be referred to as "noncurrent liabilities."

### Sources of Working Capital

The amount of inflow of working capital from various sources can be determined without reviewing and classifying every transaction that occurred during the period. There is also no need to determine the individual effects of a number of similar transactions; summary figures are sufficient. For purposes of discussion, transactions that provide working capital are classified in terms of their effect on noncurrent accounts, as follows:

1. Transactions that decrease noncurrent assets.
2. Transactions that increase noncurrent liabilities.
3. Transactions that increase stockholders' equity.

*Decreases in noncurrent assets.* The sale of long-term investments, equipment, buildings, land, patents, or other noncurrent assets for cash or on account provides working capital. However, the reduction in the balance of the noncurrent asset account between the beginning and end of the period is not necessarily the amount of working capital provided by the sale. For example, if a patent carried in the ledger at $30,000 is sold during the year for $70,000, the patents account will decrease by $30,000 but the funds provided by the transaction amounted to $70,000. Similarly, if the long-term investments carried at $120,000 at the beginning of the year are sold for $80,000 cash, the transaction provided funds of $80,000 instead of $120,000.

*Increases in noncurrent liabilities.* The issuance of bonds or long-term notes is a common source of working capital. For example, if bonds with a face value of $600,000 are sold at 100 for cash, the amount of funds provided by the transaction would be indicated by a $600,000 increase in the bonds payable account. If the bonds were issued at a price above or below 100, it would be necessary to refer to the bond premium or discount account, in addition to the bonds payable account, in order to determine the amount of funds provided by the transaction. For example, if the $600,000 of bonds had been issued at 90 instead of 100, the funds provided would have been $540,000 instead of $600,000.

*Increases in stockholders' equity.* Often the largest and most frequent source of working capital is profitable operations. Revenues realized from the sale of goods or services are accompanied by increases in working capital. Conversely, many of the expenses incurred are accompanied by decreases in working capital. Since the significant details of revenues and expenses appear in the income statement, they need not be repeated in the funds statement. However, the amount of income from operations reported on the income statement is not necessarily equivalent to the working capital actually provided by operations. Such expenses as depreciation of plant assets and amortization of patents are deducted from revenue but have no effect on current assets or current liabilities. Similarly, the amortization of premium on bonds payable, which decreases interest expense and therefore increases operating income, does not affect current assets or current liabilities. The amount reported on the income statement as income from operations must therefore be adjusted upward or downward to determine the amount of working capital so provided. If gains or losses are reported as "extraordinary" items on the income statement, they should be identified as such on the funds statement.

If capital stock is sold during the period, the amount of working capital provided will not necessarily coincide with the amount of the increase in the capital stock account. Consideration must be given to accompanying debits or credits to other paid-in capital accounts. There also may be entries in stockholders' equity accounts that do not affect working capital, such as a transfer of retained earnings to paid-in capital accounts in the issuance of a stock dividend. Similarly, transfers between the retained earnings account and appropriations accounts have no effect on working capital.

### Applications of Working Capital

As in the case of working capital sources, it is convenient to classify applications according to their effects on noncurrent accounts. Transactions affecting the outflow or applications of working capital may be described as follows:

1. Transactions that increase noncurrent assets.
2. Transactions that decrease noncurrent liabilities.
3. Transactions that decrease stockholders' equity.

*Increases in noncurrent assets.* Working capital may be applied to the purchase of equipment, buildings, land, long-term investments, patents, or other noncurrent assets. However, the amount of funds used for such purposes is not necessarily indicated by the net increases in the related accounts. For example, if the debits to the equipment account for acquisitions during the year totaled $160,000 and the credits to the same account for retirements amounted to $30,000, the net change in the account would be $130,000. Such facts can be determined only by reviewing the details in the account.

*Decreases in noncurrent liabilities.* The liquidation of bonds or long-term notes represents an application of working capital. However, the decrease in the balance of the liability account does not necessarily indicate the amount of working capital applied. For example, if callable bonds issued at their face value of $100,000 are redeemed at 105, the funds applied would be $105,000 instead of $100,000.

*Decreases in stockholders' equity.* Probably the most frequent application of working capital in decreases of stockholders' equity results from the declaration of cash dividends by the board of directors. Funds may also be applied to the redemption of preferred stock or to the purchase of treasury stock. As indicated earlier, the issuance of stock dividends does not affect working capital or financial position.

### Other Changes in Financial Position

According to the broadened concept of the funds statement, significant transactions affecting financial position should be reported even though they do not affect funds. For example, if an enterprise issues bonds or capital stock in exchange for land and buildings, the transaction has no effect on working capital. Nevertheless, because of the significant effect on financial position, both the increase in the plant assets and the increase in long-term liabilities or stockholders' equity should be reported on the statement. A complete catalog of the kinds of non-fund transactions that usually have a significant effect on financial position is beyond the scope of the discussion here. The following are illustrative of the many possibilities: preferred or common stock may be issued in liquidation of long-term debt, common stock may be issued in exchange for convertible preferred stock, long-term investments may be exchanged for machinery and equipment, and land and buildings may be received from a municipality as a gift.

Transactions of the type indicated in the preceding paragraph may be reported on the funds statement as though there were two transactions: (1) a source of funds and (2) an application of funds. The relationship of the source and the application should be disclosed by proper wording in the descriptive captions or by footnote. To illustrate, assume that common stock of $200,000 par is issued in exchange for $200,000 face amount of bonds payable, on which there is no unamortized discount or premium. The issuance of the common stock should be reported in the sources section of the statement somewhat as follows: "Issuance of common stock at par in retirement of bonds payable, $200,000." The other part of the transaction could be described in the applications section as follows: "Retirement of bonds payable by the issuance of common stock at par, $200,000."

**Assembling Data for the Funds Statement Based on Working Capital**

Much of the information on funds flow is obtained in the process of preparing the balance sheet, the income statement, and the retained earnings statement. When the volume of data is substantial, experienced accountants may first assemble all relevant facts in working papers designed for the purpose. Specialized working papers are not essential, however. Because of their complexity, they tend to obscure the basic concepts of funds analysis for anyone who is not already familiar with the subject. For this reason, special working papers will not be used in the following discussion. Instead, the emphasis will be on the basic analyses.[1]

In the illustration that follows, the necessary information will be obtained from (1) a comparative balance sheet and (2) the ledger accounts for noncurrent assets, noncurrent liabilities, and stockholders' equity. As each change in a noncurrent item is discussed, data from the related account(s) will be presented. Descriptive notations have been inserted in the accounts to facilitate the explanations. Otherwise, it would be necessary to refer to supportive journal entries to determine the complete effect of some of the transactions. The comparative balance sheet in simplified form is shown on page 405.

Since only the noncurrent accounts reveal sources and applications of funds, it is not necessary to examine the current asset accounts or the current liability accounts. The first of the noncurrent accounts listed on the comparative balance sheet of the T. R. Morgan Corporation is Investments.

### Investments

The comparative balance sheet indicates that investments decreased by $45,000. The notation in the following investments account indicates that the investments were sold for $75,000 in cash.

| ACCOUNT  INVESTMENTS | | | | | ACCOUNT NO. | |
|---|---|---|---|---|---|---|
| Date | | Item | Debit | Credit | Balance | |
| | | | | | Debit | Credit |
| 1985 Jan. | 1 | Balance | | | 45,000 | |
| June | 8 | Sold for $75,000 cash | | 45,000 | —— | —— |

---

[1]The use of a work sheet as an aid in assembling data for the funds statement is presented in Appendix E.

COMPARATIVE
BALANCE SHEET

| | T. R. Morgan Corporation<br>Comparative Balance Sheet<br>December 31, 1985 and 1984 | | |
|---|---|---|---|
| | 1985 | 1984 | Increase<br>Decrease* |
| **Assets** | | | |
| Cash | $ 49,000 | $ 26,000 | $ 23,000 |
| Trade receivables (net) | 74,000 | 65,000 | 9,000 |
| Inventories | 172,000 | 180,000 | 8,000* |
| Prepaid expenses | 4,000 | 3,000 | 1,000 |
| Investments (long-term) | —— | 45,000 | 45,000* |
| Land | 90,000 | 40,000 | 50,000 |
| Building | 200,000 | 200,000 | —— |
| Accumulated depreciation—building | (36,000) | (30,000) | (6,000) |
| Equipment | 180,000 | 142,000 | 38,000 |
| Accumulated depreciation—equipment | (43,000) | (40,000) | (3,000) |
| Total assets | $690,000 | $631,000 | $ 59,000 |
| **Liabilities** | | | |
| Accounts payable (merchandise creditors) | $ 50,000 | $ 32,000 | $ 18,000 |
| Income tax payable | 2,500 | 4,000 | 1,500* |
| Dividends payable | 15,000 | 8,000 | 7,000 |
| Bonds payable | 120,000 | 245,000 | 125,000* |
| Total liabilities | $187,500 | $289,000 | $101,500* |
| **Stockholders' Equity** | | | |
| Common stock | $280,000 | $230,000 | $ 50,000 |
| Retained earnings | 222,500 | 112,000 | 110,500 |
| Total stockholders' equity | $502,500 | $342,000 | $160,500 |
| Total liabilities and stockholders' equity | $690,000 | $631,000 | $ 59,000 |

The $30,000 gain on the sale is included in the net income reported on the income statement. It is necessary, of course, to report also the book value of the investments sold, as an additional source of working capital. To report the entire proceeds of $75,000 as a source of working capital would incorrectly include the gain reported in operating income. Accordingly, to avoid a double reporting of the $30,000 gain, the notation is as follows:

*Source of working capital:*
    Book value of investments sold (excludes $30,000 gain
      reported in net income)................................ $45,000

The proceeds from the sale of investments would appear on the funds statement in two places: (1) book value of investments sold, $45,000, and (2) gain on sale of investments as part of net income, $30,000.

## Land

The comparative balance sheet indicates that ~~land~~ increased by $50,000. The notation in the land account, as shown below, indicates that the land was acquired by issuance of common stock at par.

| ACCOUNT LAND | | | | | Balance | ACCOUNT NO. |
|---|---|---|---|---|---|---|
| Date | | Item | Debit | Credit | Debit | Credit |
| 1985 | | | | | | |
| Jan. | 1 | Balance | | | 40,000 | |
| Dec. | 28 | Acquired by issuance of common stock at par | 50,000 | | 90,000 | |

Although ~~working capital was not involved in this transaction~~, the acquisition represents a significant change in financial position, which may be noted as follows:

> Application of working capital:
> Purchase of land by issuance of common stock at par . . .    $50,000

## Building

According to the comparative balance sheet, there was no change in the $200,000 balance between the beginning and end of the year. Reference to the building account in the ledger confirms the absence of entries during the year and hence the account is not shown here. ~~The credit in the related accumulated depreciation account, shown below, reduced the investment in building, but working capital was not affected.~~

| ACCOUNT ACCUMULATED DEPRECIATION — BUILDING | | | | | Balance | ACCOUNT NO. |
|---|---|---|---|---|---|---|
| Date | | Item | Debit | Credit | Debit | Credit |
| 1985 | | | | | | |
| Jan. | 1 | Balance | | | | 30,000 |
| Dec. | 31 | Depreciation for year | | 6,000 | | 36,000 |

## Equipment

The comparative balance sheet indicates that the cost of equipment increased $38,000. The equipment account and the accumulated depreciation account illustrated below reveal that the net change of $38,000 was the result of two separate transactions, the discarding of equipment that had cost $9,000 and the purchase of equipment for $47,000. The equipment discarded had been fully depreciated, as indicated by the debit of $9,000 in the accumulated depreciation account, and no salvage was realized from its disposal. ~~Hence, the transaction had no effect on working capital and is not reported on the funds statement.~~

| ACCOUNT | EQUIPMENT | | | ACCOUNT NO. | |
|---|---|---|---|---|---|
| Date | Item | Debit | Credit | Balance | |
| | | | | Debit | Credit |
| 1985 | | | | | |
| Jan. 1 | Balance | | | 142,000 | |
| May 9 | Discarded, no salvage | | 9,000 | | |
| July 7 | Purchased for cash | 47,000 | | 180,000 | |

| ACCOUNT | ACCUMULATED DEPRECIATION — EQUIPMENT | | | ACCOUNT NO. | |
|---|---|---|---|---|---|
| Date | Item | Debit | Credit | Balance | |
| | | | | Debit | Credit |
| 1985 | | | | | |
| Jan. 1 | Balance | | | | 40,000 |
| May 9 | Discarded, no salvage | 9,000 | | | |
| Dec. 31 | Depreciation for year | | 12,000 | | 43,000 |

The effect on funds of the purchase of equipment for $47,000 was as follows:

✓ *Application of working capital:*
   Purchase of equipment............................... $47,000

The credit in the accumulated depreciation account had the effect of reducing the investment in equipment by $12,000 but caused no change in working capital. Further attention will be given to depreciation in a later paragraph.

## Bonds Payable

The next noncurrent item listed on the balance sheet, bonds payable, decreased $125,000 during the year. Examination of the bonds payable account, which appears below, indicates that $125,000 of the bonds payable were retired by payment of the face amount.

| ACCOUNT | BONDS PAYABLE | | | ACCOUNT NO. | |
|---|---|---|---|---|---|
| Date | Item | Debit | Credit | Balance | |
| | | | | Debit | Credit |
| 1985 | | | | | |
| Jan. 1 | Balance | | | | 245,000 |
| June 30 | Retired by payment of cash at face amount | 125,000 | | | 120,000 |

This transaction's effect on funds is noted as follows:

✓ *Application of working capital:*
   Retirement of bonds payable......................... $125,000

## Common Stock

The increase of $50,000 in the common stock account, as shown below, is identified as stock having been issued in exchange for land valued at $50,000.

| ACCOUNT COMMON STOCK | | | | ACCOUNT NO. | |
|---|---|---|---|---|---|
| Date | Item | Debit | Credit | Balance | |
| | | | | Debit | Credit |
| 1985 Jan. 1 | Balance | | | | 230,000 |
| Dec. 28 | Issued at par in exchange for land | | 50,000 | | 280,000 |

This change in financial position should be reported on the funds statement and may be noted as follows:

✓    *Source of working capital:*
       Issuance of common stock at par for land . . . . . . . . . . . . .    $50,000

## Retained Earnings

According to the comparative balance sheet, there was an increase of $110,500 in retained earnings during the year. The retained earnings account, as shown below, was credited for $140,500 of net income, which included the gain on sale of investments, and was debited for $30,000 of cash dividends.

| ACCOUNT RETAINED EARNINGS | | | | ACCOUNT NO. | |
|---|---|---|---|---|---|
| Date | Item | Debit | Credit | Balance | |
| | | | | Debit | Credit |
| 1985 Jan. 1 | Balance | | | | 112,000 |
| Dec. 31 | Net income | | 140,500 | | |
| 31 | Cash dividends | 30,000 | | | 222,500 |

The net income as reported on the income statement must usually be adjusted upward and/or downward to determine the amount of working capital provided by operations. Although most operating expenses either decrease current assets or increase current liabilities, thus affecting working capital, depreciation expense does not do so. The amount of net income understates the amount of working capital provided by operations to the extent that depreciation expense is deducted from revenue. Accordingly, the depreciation expense for the year on the equipment ($12,000) and the building ($6,000), totaling $18,000, must be added back to the $140,500 reported as net income.

The data to be reported as working capital provided by operations is noted as follows:

*Source of working capital:*
Operations during the year:
    Net income............................ $140,500
    Add deduction not decreasing working
    capital during the year:
        Depreciation ........................ 18,000 $158,500

Working capital is applied to cash dividends at the time the current liability is incurred, regardless of when the dividends are actually paid. The effect of the declaration of cash dividends of $30,000, recorded as a debit in the retained earnings account, is indicated as follows:

*Application of working capital:*
    Declaration of cash dividends........................ $30,000

**Form of the Funds Statement Based on Working Capital**

Although there are many possible variations in the form and the content of the funds statement, the first section is usually devoted to the source of funds, with income from operations presented as the first item. The second section is devoted to the application or use of funds. There may also be a third section in which changes in the amounts of the current assets and the current liabilities are reported.

The difference between the totals of the sources section and the applications section of the funds statement is identified as the increase or the decrease in working capital. The net change in the amount of working capital reported on the statement should be supported by details of the changes in each of the working capital components. The information may be presented in a third section of the statement, as in the illustration for T. R. Morgan Corporation on page 410, or it may be presented as a separate tabulation accompanying the statement. The data required in either case can be taken from the comparative balance sheet. The two amounts identified as the increase or decrease in working capital ($1,500 increase in the illustration) must agree.

An analysis of the funds statement for T. R. Morgan Corporation indicates that "operations" provided the majority of the funds during the year ($158,500). Because there are limits to the amount of funds that can be provided on a continuing basis from other sources, such as a sale of plant assets or an issuance of common stock, the amount of funds provided by operations is often the most significant source of funds. Therefore, this amount is most closely watched by management.

An analysis of the applications section indicates that $125,000 of bonds were retired, land and equipment were purchased for $97,000, and $30,000 of cash dividends were declared during the year, yet working capital increased by $1,500. The "changes in components of working capital" indicates that the current assets are more liquid at the end of the year than at the beginning. For example, the more liquid assets, cash and receivables, have increased, while the less liquid asset, inventories, has decreased. Also, the increase in the more liquid assets of cash and receivables ($32,000 increase) exceeds the increase in the current liabilities.

T. R. Morgan Corporation
Statement of Changes in Financial Position
For Year Ended December 31, 1985

Sources of working capital:
  Operations during the year:
    Net income.............................. $140,500
    Add deduction not decreasing working
    capital during the year:
      Depreciation ......................... 18,000 $158,500
  Book value of investments sold (excludes $30,000 gain re-
  ported in net income) ............................. 45,000
  Issuance of common stock at par for land ............. 50,000 $253,500

Applications of working capital:
  Purchase of land by issuance of common stock at par .. $ 50,000
  Purchase of equipment................................. 47,000
  Retirement of bonds payable.......................... 125,000
  Declaration of cash dividends........................ 30,000   252,000
Increase in working capital............................          $   1,500

Changes in components of working capital:
  Increase (decrease) in current assets:
    Cash ............................................. $ 23,000
    Trade receivables (net)............................   9,000
    Inventories .......................................  (8,000)
    Prepaid expenses...................................   1,000 $ 25,000
  Increase (decrease) in current liabilities:
    Accounts payable.................................. $ 18,000
    Income tax payable.................................  (1,500)
    Dividends payable..................................   7,000   23,500
Increase in working capital............................          $   1,500

## ANALYSIS OF CASH

When the cash concept of funds is used, the analysis is devoted to the movement of cash rather than to the inflow and outflow of working capital.[2] The portion of the statement devoted to operations may report the total revenue that provided cash, followed by deductions for operating costs and expenses requiring the outlay of cash. The usual practice, however, is to begin with net income from operations as was done in the preceding illustration. This basic amount is then adjusted for increases and decreases of all working capital items except cash, using the procedures demonstrated later in the chapter.

There has been much experimentation in the methodology of cash flow analysis and in the form of the related funds statement. The approach that will be used here

----

[2]The concept may be expanded to include temporary investments that are readily convertible into cash.

is patterned after the procedures used in the preceding discussion and illustrations. Although the working capital concept of funds discussed earlier is used more often, particularly in preparing funds statements for reports to stockholders, the cash concept is useful in evaluating financial policies and current cash position. It is especially useful to management in preparing cash budgets.

The format of a funds statement based on the cash concept may be quite similar to the format of a funds statement based on the working capital concept. It is usually divided into two main sections—sources of cash and applications of cash. The difference between the totals of the two sections is the cash increase or decrease for the period. The main parts of the report may be followed by a listing of the cash balance at the beginning of the period, at the end of the period, and the net change. An alternative is to begin the statement with the beginning cash balance, add the total of the sources section, subtract the total of the applications section, and conclude with the cash balance at the end of the period.

**Assembling Data for the Funds Statement Based on Cash**

The comparative balance sheet of T. R. Morgan Corporation on page 405 and the related accounts presented on the following pages will be used as the basis for illustration.[3] Reference to the earlier analysis discloses that the sale of investments yielded cash and that there were cash outlays for equipment and the retirement of bonds. These transactions may be noted as follows:

*Source of cash:*
　Book value of investments sold (excludes $30,000 gain
　　reported in net income)............................ $ 45,000
*Applications of cash:*
　Purchase of equipment.............................. $ 47,000
　Retirement of bonds payable........................ 125,000

The earlier analysis also indicated that land was acquired by the issuance of common stock. Although the transaction did not involve cash, it resulted in a significant change in financial position and should be reported on the statement. It is as if the common stock had been issued for cash and the cash received had then been expended for the parcel of land. The following notation indicates the manner in which the transaction is to be reported in the statement:

*Source of cash:*
　Issuance of common stock at par for land.............. $50,000
*Application of cash:*
　Purchase of land by issuance of common stock at par... $50,000

The amount of cash provided by operations usually differs from the amount of net income. The amount of cash used to pay dividends may also differ from the amount of cash dividends declared. The determination of these amounts is discussed in the paragraphs that follow.

---

[3]The use of a work sheet as an aid in assembling data for the funds statement is presented in Appendix E.

## Cash Provided by Operations

The starting point in the analysis of the effect of operations on cash is net income for the period. This amount was reported for T. R. Morgan Corporation on page 408 as $140,500. As in the earlier analysis, depreciation expense of $18,000 must be added to the $140,500 because depreciation expense did not decrease the amount of cash. In addition, it is necessary to recognize the relationship of the accrual method of accounting to the movement of cash. Usually, a part of some of the other costs and expenses reported on the income statement, as well as a part of the revenue earned, is not accompanied by cash outflow or inflow.

There is often a period of time between the accrual of a revenue and the receipt of the related cash. Perhaps the most common example is the sale of merchandise or a service on account, for which payment is received at a later point in time. Hence, the amount reported on the income statement as revenue from sales is not likely to correspond with the amount of the related cash inflow for the same period.

Timing differences between the incurrence of an expense and the related cash outflow must also be considered in determining the amount of cash provided by operations. For example, the amount reported on the income statement as insurance expense is the amount of insurance premiums expired rather than the amount of premiums paid during the period. Similarly, supplies paid for in one year may be used and thus converted to an expense in a later year. Conversely, a portion of some of the expenses incurred near the end of one period, such as wages and taxes, may not require a cash outlay until the following period.

The T. R. Morgan Corporation balance sheet (page 405) provides the following data that identify timing differences affecting the amount of cash inflow and outflow from operations:

| Accounts | December 31 | | Increase |
| | 1985 | 1984 | Decrease* |
| --- | --- | --- | --- |
| Trade receivables (net) .......................... | $ 74,000 | $ 65,000 | $ 9,000 |
| Inventories...................................... | 172,000 | 180,000 | 8,000* |
| Prepaid expenses ............................... | 4,000 | 3,000 | 1,000 |
| Accounts payable (merchandise creditors).......... | 50,000 | 32,000 | 18,000 |
| Income tax payable.............................. | 2,500 | 4,000 | 1,500* |

The effect of timing differences is indicated by the amount and the direction of change in the balances of the asset and liability accounts affected by operations. Decreases in such assets and increases in such liabilities during the period must be added to the amount reported as income from operations. Conversely, increases in such assets and decreases in such liabilities must be deducted from the amount reported as income from operations.

*Trade receivables (net) increase.* The additions to trade receivables for sales on account during the year were $9,000 more than the deductions for amounts collected from customers on account. The amount reported on the income statement as sales therefore included $9,000 that did not yield cash inflow during the year.

Accordingly, $9,000 must be deducted from income to determine the amount of cash provided by operations.

**Inventories decrease.** The $8,000 decrease in inventories indicates that the merchandise sold exceeded the cost of the merchandise purchased by $8,000. The amount reported on the income statement as a deduction from the revenue therefore included $8,000 that did not require cash outflow during the year. Accordingly, $8,000 must be added to income to determine the amount of cash provided by operations.

**Prepaid expenses increase.** The outlay of cash for prepaid expenses exceeded by $1,000 the amount deducted as an expense during the year. Hence, $1,000 must be deducted from income to determine the amount of cash provided by operations.

**Accounts payable increase.** The effect of the increase in the amount owed creditors for goods and services was to include in expired costs and expenses the sum of $18,000 for which there had been no cash outlay during the year. Income was thereby reduced by $18,000, though there was no cash outlay. Hence, $18,000 must be added to income to determine the amount of cash provided by operations.

**Income tax payable decrease.** The outlay of cash for income taxes exceeded by $1,500 the amount of income tax deducted as an expense during the period. Accordingly, $1,500 must be deducted from income to determine the amount of cash provided by operations.

The foregoing adjustments to income may be summarized as follows in a format suitable for the funds statement:

*Source of cash:*

| | | | |
|---|---|---|---|
| Operations during the year: | | | |
| Net income | | | $140,500 |
| Add deductions not decreasing cash during the year: | | | |
| Depreciation | | $18,000 | |
| Decrease in inventories | | 8,000 | |
| Increase in accounts payable | | 18,000 | 44,000 |
| | | | $184,500 |
| Deduct additions not increasing cash during the year: | | | |
| Increase in trade receivables | | $ 9,000 | |
| Increase in prepaid expenses | | 1,000 | |
| Decrease in income tax payable | | 1,500 | 11,500  $173,000 |

## Cash Applied to Payment of Dividends

According to the retained earnings account of T. R. Morgan Corporation (page 408), cash dividends of $30,000 were declared during the year. In the earlier funds flow analysis, this was noted as the amount of working capital applied to the declaration of cash dividends. However, the amounts reported as dividends payable on T. R. Morgan Corporation's comparative balance sheet (page 405) are $15,000 and $8,000 respectively, revealing a timing difference between declaration and payment.

According to the dividends payable account, shown below, dividend payments during the year totaled $23,000.

| ACCOUNT DIVIDENDS PAYABLE | | | | | ACCOUNT NO. | |
|---|---|---|---|---|---|---|
| Date | | Item | Debit | Credit | Balance | |
| | | | | | Debit | Credit |
| 1985 | | | | | | |
| Jan. | 1 | Balance | | | | 8,000 |
| | 10 | Cash paid | 8,000 | | — | — |
| June | 20 | Dividend declared | | 15,000 | | 15,000 |
| July | 10 | Cash paid | 15,000 | | — | — |
| Dec. | 20 | Dividend declared | | 15,000 | | 15,000 |

The amount of cash applied to dividend payments may be noted as follows:

> Application of cash:
> ✓  Cash dividends declared . . . . . . . . . . . . . . . . . . . .   $30,000
>    Deduct increase in dividends payable . . . . . . . .    7,000   $23,000

**Form of the Funds Statement Based on Cash**

The funds statement based on cash is comparable in form to the funds statement illustrated on page 410. The greatest difference between the two statements is in the section devoted to funds provided by operations. The statement shown at the top of page 415 is supported by a reconciliation of the change in cash, but a funds statement based on cash may conclude with the amount of increase or decrease in cash.

Analysis of the funds statement for T. R. Morgan Corporation indicates that the cash position has increased by $23,000 during the year. The principal source of cash was operations ($173,000), which indicates that most of the cash acquired during the year was generated internally. The principal uses of cash were the retirement of bonds payable ($125,000), the purchase of equipment ($47,000), and the payment of dividends ($23,000).

**CASH FLOW FROM OPERATIONS**

The term **cash flow** is sometimes encountered in reports to stockholders. It may be mentioned in a company president's letter to stockholders, in operating summaries, or elsewhere in the published financial report. Although there are variations in the method of determination, cash flow is approximately equivalent to income from operations plus depreciation, depletion, and any other expenses that had no effect on working capital during the period. Many terms have been used to describe the amount so determined, including "cash flow from operations," "cash income," "cash earnings," and "cash throw-off."

The amount of cash flow from operations for a period may be useful to internal financial management in considering the possibility of retiring long-term debt, in planning replacement of plant facilities, or in formulating dividend policies. However, when it is presented without reference to the funds statement and its importance stressed in reporting operations to stockholders, it is likely to be misunderstood. The reporting of so-called cash flow per share of stock may be even

STATEMENT OF
CHANGES IN
FINANCIAL
POSITION—BASED
ON CASH

**T. R. Morgan Corporation**
**Statement of Changes in Financial Position**
**For Year Ended December 31, 1985**

Sources of cash:
  Operations during the year:
    Net income.............................. $140,500
    Add deductions not decreasing cash during
    the year:
      Depreciation .................. $18,000
      Decrease in inventories......... 8,000
      Increase in accounts payable.... 18,000    44,000
                                              $184,500

    Deduct additions not increasing
    cash during the year:
      Increase in trade receivables .... $ 9,000
      Increase in prepaid expenses... 1,000
      Decrease in income tax payable .. 1,500   11,500  $173,000

  Book value of investments sold (excludes $30,000 gain re-
    ported in net income) .............................  45,000
  Issuance of common stock at par for land ............  50,000  $268,000

Applications of cash:
  Purchase of land by issuance of common stock at par ..  $ 50,000
  Purchase of equipment...............................  47,000
  Retirement of bonds payable.........................  125,000
  Payment of dividends:
    Cash dividends declared .................  $ 30,000
    Deduct increase in dividends payable .....  7,000   23,000   245,000
Increase in cash......................................         $ 23,000

Change in cash balance:
  Cash balance, December 31, 1985 ...................         $ 49,000
  Cash balance, December 31, 1984 ...................           26,000
Increase in cash......................................         $ 23,000

more misleading, particularly when the amount is larger, which it usually is, than the net income per share. Readers are quite likely to substitute cash flow for net income in appraising the relative success of operations.

1. If an enterprise's total current assets are $225,000 and its total current liabilities are $150,000, its working capital is:
   A. $75,000
   B. $225,000
   C. $375,000
   D. none of the above

2. Which of the following types of transactions would provide working capital?
   A. Transactions that decrease noncurrent assets
   B. Transactions that decrease noncurrent liabilities
   C. Transactions that decrease stockholders' equity
   D. None of the above

3. Which of the following transactions represents an application of working capital?
   A. Sale of common stock for cash
   B. Issuance of bonds payable for cash
   C. Acquisition of equipment for cash
   D. None of the above

4. The net income reported on the income statement for the year was $55,000 and depreciation on plant assets for the year was $22,000. The balances of the current asset and current liability accounts at the beginning and end of the year are as follows:

|                                            | End        | Beginning  |
|--------------------------------------------|------------|------------|
| Cash                                       | $ 65,000   | $ 70,000   |
| Trade receivables                          | 100,000    | 90,000     |
| Inventories                                | 145,000    | 150,000    |
| Prepaid expenses                           | 7,500      | 8,000      |
| Accounts payable (merchandise creditors)   | 51,000     | 58,000     |

   The total amount reported for working capital provided by operations in the statement of changes in financial position would be:
   A. $33,000                        C. $77,000
   B. $55,000                        D. none of the above

5. Based on the data presented in Question 4, the total amount reported for the cash provided by operations in the statement of changes in financial position would be:
   A. $33,000                        C. $77,000
   B. $55,000                        D. none of the above

**Discussion Questions**

1. What is the shorter term often employed in referring to the statement of changes in financial position?

2. What are the principal concepts of the term *funds,* as employed in referring to the statement of changes in financial position?

3. (a) What is meant by *working capital*? (b) Name another term, other than "funds," that has the same meaning.

4. State the effect of each of the following transactions, considered individually, on working capital:

(a) Purchased $5,000 of merchandise on account, terms 1/10, n/30.

(b) Sold, for $900 cash, merchandise that had cost $600.

(c) Issued 1,000 shares of $100 par preferred stock for $102 a share, receiving cash.

(d) Received $400 from a customer on account.

(e) Purchased office equipment for $1,750 on account.

(f) Issued a $2,000, 30-day non-interest-bearing note to a creditor in temporary settlement of an account payable.

(g) Borrowed $50,000 cash, issuing a 90-day, 12% note.

5. When the total of the applications section exceeds the total of the sources section on a statement of changes in financial position based on working capital, is this excess identified as an increase or as a decrease in working capital?

6. What is the effect on working capital of writing off $2,500 of uncollectible accounts against Allowance for Doubtful Accounts?

7. A corporation issued $1,000,000 of 20-year bonds for cash at 95. (a) Did the transaction provide funds or apply funds? (b) What was the amount of funds involved? (c) Was working capital affected? (d) Was cash affected?

8. Fully depreciated equipment costing $25,000 was discarded. What was the effect of the transaction on working capital if (a) $500 cash is received, (b) there is no salvage value?

9. A long-term investment in bonds with a cost of $90,000 was sold for $75,000 cash. (a) What was the gain or loss on the sale? (b) What was the effect of the transaction on working capital? (c) How should the transaction be reported in the funds statement?

10. The board of directors declared a cash dividend of $75,000 near the end of the fiscal year, which ends on December 31, payable in January. (a) What was the effect of the declaration on working capital? (b) Did the declaration represent a source or an application of working capital? (c) Did the payment of the dividend in January affect working capital, and if so, how?

11. (a) What is the effect on working capital of the declaration and issuance of a stock dividend? (b) Does the stock dividend represent a source or an application of working capital?

12. On its income statement for the current year, a company reported a net loss of $75,000 from operations. On its statement of changes in financial position, it reported an increase of $50,000 in working capital from operations. Explain the seeming contradiction between the loss and the increase in working capital.

13. What is the effect on working capital of an appropriation of retained earnings for plant expansion?

14. A net loss of $75,000 from operations is reported on the income statement. The only revenue or expense item reported that did not affect working capital was depreciation expense of $45,000. Will the change in financial position attributed to operations appear in the funds statement as a source or as an application of working capital, and at what amount?

15. Assume that a corporation has net income of $200,000 that included a charge of $5,000 for the amortization of bond discount and depreciation expense of $75,000. What amount should this corporation report on its funds statement for working capital provided by operations?

16. A corporation acquired as a long-term investment all of another corporation's capital stock, valued at $10,000,000, by the issuance of $10,000,000 of its own common stock. Where should the transaction be reported on the statement of changes in financial position (a) if the cash concept of funds is employed, and (b) if the working capital concept of funds is employed?

17. A retail enterprise, employing the accrual method of accounting, owed merchandise creditors (accounts payable) $275,000 at the beginning of the year and $240,000 at the end of the year. What adjustment for the $35,000 decrease must be made to income from operations in determining the amount of cash provided by operations? Explain.

18. If revenue from sales amounted to $975,000 for the year and trade receivables totaled $120,000 and $95,000 at the beginning and end of the year respectively, what was the amount of cash received from customers during the year?

19. If salaries payable was $75,000 and $65,000 at the beginning and end of the year respectively, should $10,000 be added to or deducted from income to determine the amount of cash provided by operations? Explain.

20. The board of directors declared cash dividends totaling $100,000 during the current year. The comparative balance sheet indicates dividends payable of $30,000 at the beginning of the year and $25,000 at the end of the year. What was the amount of cash disbursed to stockholders during the year?

**Exercises**

**Exercise 17-1.** Using the following schedule of current assets and current liabilities, prepare the section of the statement of changes in financial position entitled "Changes in components of working capital."

|  | End of Year | Beginning of Year |
|---|---|---|
| Cash | $ 49,500 | $ 45,400 |
| Trade receivables (net) | 55,500 | 60,000 |
| Inventories | 151,250 | 147,750 |
| Prepaid expenses | 4,700 | 4,550 |
| Accounts payable | 55,000 | 51,500 |
| Dividends payable | 15,000 | 12,500 |
| Salaries payable | 9,750 | 11,000 |

**Exercise 17-2.** The net income reported on an income statement for the current year was $79,250. Adjustments required to determine the amount of working capital provided by operations, as well as some other data used for the year-end adjusting entries, are described as follows:

(a) Uncollectible accounts expense, $6,100.
(b) Depreciation expense, $27,500.
(c) Amortization of patents, $4,500.
(d) Interest accrued on notes payable, $1,150.
(e) Income tax payable, $11,500.
(f) Wages accrued but not paid, $3,750.

Prepare the working-capital-provided-by-operations section of the statement of changes in financial position.

**Exercise 17-3.** On the basis of the details of the following plant asset account, indicate the items to be reported as a source of working capital and as an application of working capital on the statement of changes in financial position.

ACCOUNT LAND                                   ACCOUNT NO.

| Date | | Item | Debit | Credit | Balance Debit | Balance Credit |
|---|---|---|---|---|---|---|
| 19-- | | | | | | |
| Jan. | 1 | Balance | | | 650,000 | |
| Aug. | 29 | Purchased with long-term mortgage note | 200,000 | | | |
| Dec. | 9 | Purchased for cash | 75,000 | | 925,000 | |

**Exercise 17-4.** On the basis of the following stockholders' equity accounts, indicate the items, exclusive of net income, to be reported as a source of working capital and as an application of working capital on the statement of changes in financial position.

ACCOUNT COMMON STOCK, $20 PAR                       ACCOUNT NO.

| Date | | Item | Debit | Credit | Balance Debit | Balance Credit |
|---|---|---|---|---|---|---|
| 19-- | | | | | | |
| Jan. | 1 | Balance, 40,000 shares | | | | 800,000 |
| Feb. | 10 | 5,000 shares issued for cash | | 100,000 | | |
| July | 25 | 1,350 share stock dividend | | 27,000 | | 927,000 |

ACCOUNT PREMIUM ON COMMON STOCK                   ACCOUNT NO.

| Date | | Item | Debit | Credit | Balance Debit | Balance Credit |
|---|---|---|---|---|---|---|
| 19-- | | | | | | |
| Jan. | 1 | Balance | | | | 140,000 |
| Feb. | 10 | 5,000 shares issued for cash | | 50,000 | | |
| July | 25 | Stock dividend | | 13,500 | | 203,500 |

ACCOUNT RETAINED EARNINGS                          ACCOUNT NO.

| Date | | Item | Debit | Credit | Balance Debit | Balance Credit |
|---|---|---|---|---|---|---|
| 19-- | | | | | | |
| Jan. | 1 | Balance | | | | 425,000 |
| July | 25 | Stock dividend | 40,500 | | | |
| Dec. | 31 | Cash dividends | 91,350 | | | |
| | 31 | Net income | | 165,000 | | 458,150 |

**Exercise 17-5.** An analysis of the general ledger accounts indicated that delivery equipment, which had cost $35,000 and on which accumulated depreciation totaled

$29,750 on the date of sale, was sold for $7,000 during the year. Using this information, indicate the items to be reported as a source of working capital and as an application of working capital on the statement of changes in financial position.

**Exercise 17-6.** The net income reported on an income statement for the current year was $92,125. Depreciation recorded on equipment and building for the year amounted to $34,500. Balances of the current asset and current liability accounts at the beginning and end of the year are as follows:

|  | End | Beginning |
|---|---|---|
| Cash | $ 69,750 | $ 61,250 |
| Trade receivables | 80,500 | 75,000 |
| Inventories | 110,000 | 97,000 |
| Prepaid expenses | 6,900 | 7,400 |
| Accounts payable (merchandise creditors) | 69,700 | 72,700 |
| Salaries payable | 7,500 | 6,250 |

Prepare the cash-provided-by-operations section of a statement of changes in financial position.

**Exercise 17-7.** The following information was taken from the records of C. D. Collins Co.:

(a) Equipment and land were acquired for cash.
(b) There were no disposals of equipment during the year.
(c) The investments were sold for $80,000 cash.
(d) The common stock was issued for cash.
(e) There was a $76,750 credit to Retained Earnings for net income.
(f) There was a $45,000 debit to Retained Earnings for cash dividends declared.

Based on this information and the following comparative balance sheet, prepare a statement of changes in financial position, employing the working capital concept of funds.

|  | June 30 Current Year | June 30 Preceding Year |
|---|---|---|
| Cash | $ 64,200 | $ 49,900 |
| Trade receivables (net) | 91,500 | 80,000 |
| Inventories | 105,900 | 90,500 |
| Investments | — | 75,000 |
| Land | 85,000 | — |
| Equipment | 355,000 | 275,000 |
| Accumulated depreciation | (149,000) | (119,000) |
|  | $552,600 | $451,400 |
| Accounts payable (merchandise creditors) | $ 62,450 | $ 55,000 |
| Dividends payable | 12,000 | 10,000 |
| Common stock, $20 par | 300,000 | 250,000 |
| Premium on common stock | 22,000 | 12,000 |
| Retained earnings | 156,150 | 124,400 |
|  | $552,600 | $451,400 |

**Exercise 17-8.** From the data presented in Exercise 17-7, prepare a statement of changes in financial position, employing the cash concept of funds.

**Problems**
(*Problems in Appendix B: 17-1B, 17-2B, 17-3B, 17-4B, 17-5B.*)

**Problem 17-1A.** The comparative balance sheet of Chow Corporation at September 30 of the current year and the preceding year is as follows:

| Assets | Current Year | Preceding Year |
|---|---|---|
| Cash.......................................... | $ 39,600 | $ 52,000 |
| Accounts receivable (net) ......................... | 88,750 | 70,000 |
| Merchandise inventory ............................ | 149,550 | 130,750 |
| Prepaid expenses ................................. | 4,300 | 2,700 |
| Plant assets...................................... | 280,500 | 260,500 |
| Accumulated depreciation—plant assets ............ | (170,500) | (187,000) |
| | $392,200 | $328,950 |

| Liabilities and Stockholders' Equity | | |
|---|---|---|
| Accounts payable ................................. | $ 68,700 | $ 43,200 |
| Mortgage note payable ............................ | — | 75,000 |
| Common stock, $10 par........................... | 150,000 | 100,000 |
| Premium on common stock........................ | 40,000 | 25,000 |
| Retained earnings ................................ | 133,500 | 85,750 |
| | $392,200 | $328,950 |

Additional data obtained from the income statement and from an examination of the noncurrent asset, noncurrent liability, and stockholders' equity accounts in the ledger are as follows:
(a) Net income, $87,750.
(b) Depreciation reported on the income statement, $29,500.
(c) An addition to the building was constructed at a cost of $66,000, and fully depreciated equipment costing $46,000 was discarded, no salvage being realized.
(d) The mortgage note payable was not due until 1990, but the terms permitted earlier payment without penalty.
(e) 5,000 shares of common stock were issued at $13 for cash.
(f) Cash dividends declared, $40,000.

Instructions:

Prepare a statement of changes in financial position (working capital concept), including a section on changes in components of working capital.

**Problem 17-2A.** The comparative balance sheet of Wei Corporation at December 31 of the current year and the preceding year is as follows:

| Assets | Current Year | Preceding Year |
|---|---|---|
| Cash | $ 62,750 | $ 82,400 |
| Trade receivables (net) | 148,200 | 119,200 |
| Inventories | 216,350 | 236,100 |
| Prepaid expenses | 4,500 | 3,900 |
| Land | 100,000 | 100,000 |
| Buildings | 633,300 | 458,300 |
| Accumulated depreciation—buildings | (202,500) | (185,000) |
| Machinery and equipment | 250,000 | 250,000 |
| Accumulated depreciation—machinery and equipment | (130,600) | (108,400) |
| Patents | 50,000 | 62,500 |
|  | $1,132,000 | $1,019,000 |

| Liabilities and Stockholders' Equity | | |
|---|---|---|
| Accounts payable (merchandise creditors) | $ 36,280 | $ 51,780 |
| Dividends payable | 25,000 | 40,000 |
| Salaries payable | 18,480 | 12,480 |
| Mortgage note payable, due 1992 | 100,000 | —— |
| Bonds payable | —— | 80,000 |
| Common stock, $10 par | 450,000 | 400,000 |
| Premium on common stock | 80,000 | 50,000 |
| Retained earnings | 422,240 | 384,740 |
|  | $1,132,000 | $1,019,000 |

An examination of the income statement and the accounting records revealed the following additional information applicable to the current year:
- (a) Net income, $62,500.
- (b) Depreciation expense reported on the income statement: buildings, $17,500; machinery and equipment, $22,200.
- (c) Patent amortization reported on the income statement, $12,500.
- (d) A mortgage note for $100,000 was issued in connection with the construction of a building costing $175,000; the remainder was paid in cash.
- (e) 5,000 shares of common stock were issued at 16 in exchange for the bonds payable.
- (f) Cash dividends declared, $25,000.

Instructions:

Prepare a statement of changes in financial position (working capital concept), including a section for changes in components of working capital.

**Problem 17-3A.** The comparative balance sheet of Wei Corporation and other data necessary for the analysis of the corporation's funds flow are presented in Problem 17-2A.

Instructions:

Prepare a statement of changes in financial position (cash concept), including a summary of the change in cash balance.

**Problem 17-4A.** A comparative balance sheet of W. A. Sussman Inc., at December 31 of the current year and the preceding year, and the noncurrent asset accounts, the noncurrent liability accounts, and the stockholders' equity accounts for the current year, are as follows:

| Assets | Current Year | Preceding Year |
|---|---|---|
| Cash......................................... | $ 77,900 | $ 62,100 |
| Trade receivables (net)...................... | 128,800 | 109,200 |
| Income tax refund receivable ................. | 5,000 | —— |
| Inventories.................................. | 184,800 | 205,000 |
| Prepaid expenses ........................... | 7,450 | 8,150 |
| Investments................................. | 100,000 | 200,000 |
| Land........................................ | 56,000 | 100,000 |
| Buildings ................................... | 550,000 | 250,000 |
| Accumulated depreciation—buildings.......... | (73,100) | (61,500) |
| Equipment.................................... | 482,000 | 392,000 |
| Accumulated depreciation—equipment ........ | (181,620) | (156,420) |
| | $1,337,230 | $1,108,530 |

| Liabilities and Stockholders' Equity | | |
|---|---|---|
| Accounts payable (merchandise creditors)...... | $ 61,400 | $ 82,750 |
| Income tax payable........................... | —— | 9,000 |
| Notes payable ............................... | 355,000 | 30,000 |
| Discount on long-term notes payable ........... | (24,750) | (1,500) |
| Common stock, $20 par....................... | 515,000 | 500,000 |
| Premium on common stock.................... | 70,000 | 60,000 |
| Appropriation for contingencies ............... | 100,000 | 75,000 |
| Retained earnings ........................... | 260,580 | 353,280 |
| | $1,337,230 | $1,108,530 |

ACCOUNT  INVESTMENTS                                                        ACCOUNT NO.

| Date | | Item | Debit | Credit | Balance Debit | Balance Credit |
|---|---|---|---|---|---|---|
| 19-- | | | | | | |
| Jan. | 1 | Balance | | | 200,000 | |
| Feb. | 20 | Realized $91,000 cash from sale | | 100,000 | 100,000 | |

ACCOUNT  LAND                                                              ACCOUNT NO.

| Date | | Item | Debit | Credit | Balance Debit | Balance Credit |
|---|---|---|---|---|---|---|
| 19-- | | | | | | |
| Jan. | 1 | Balance | | | 100,000 | |
| May | 5 | Realized $60,000 from sale | | 44,000 | 56,000 | |

ACCOUNT BUILDINGS     ACCOUNT NO.

| Date | | Item | Debit | Credit | Balance Debit | Balance Credit |
|---|---|---|---|---|---|---|
| 19-- Jan. | 1 | Balance | | | 250,000 | |
| June | 30 | Acquired with notes payable | 300,000 | | 550,000 | |

ACCOUNT ACCUMULATED DEPRECIATION—BUILDINGS     ACCOUNT NO.

| Date | | Item | Debit | Credit | Balance Debit | Balance Credit |
|---|---|---|---|---|---|---|
| 19-- Jan. | 1 | Balance | | | | 61,500 |
| Dec. | 31 | Depreciation for year | | 11,600 | | 73,100 |

ACCOUNT EQUIPMENT     ACCOUNT NO.

| Date | | Item | Debit | Credit | Balance Debit | Balance Credit |
|---|---|---|---|---|---|---|
| 19-- Jan. | 1 | Balance | | | 392,000 | |
| Mar. | 19 | Discarded, no salvage | | 25,000 | | |
| June | 2 | Purchased for cash | 75,000 | | | |
| Oct. | 10 | Purchased for cash | 40,000 | | 482,000 | |

ACCOUNT ACCUMULATED DEPRECIATION—EQUIPMENT     ACCOUNT NO.

| Date | | Item | Debit | Credit | Balance Debit | Balance Credit |
|---|---|---|---|---|---|---|
| 19-- Jan. | 1 | Balance | | | | 156,420 |
| Mar. | 19 | Equipment discarded | 25,000 | | | |
| Dec. | 31 | Depreciation for year | | 50,200 | | 181,620 |

ACCOUNT LONG-TERM NOTES PAYABLE     ACCOUNT NO.

| Date | | Item | Debit | Credit | Balance Debit | Balance Credit |
|---|---|---|---|---|---|---|
| 19-- Jan. | 1 | Balance | | | | 30,000 |
| June | 30 | Issued 10-year notes | | 325,000 | | 355,000 |

ACCOUNT DISCOUNT ON LONG-TERM NOTES PAYABLE     ACCOUNT NO.

| Date | | Item | Debit | Credit | Balance Debit | Balance Credit |
|---|---|---|---|---|---|---|
| 19-- Jan. | 1 | Balance | | | 1,500 | |
| June | 30 | Notes issued | 25,000 | | 26,500 | |
| Dec. | 31 | Amortization—Jan. 1 Bal. | | 500 | | |
| | | June 30 Notes | | 1,250 | 24,750 | |

ACCOUNT COMMON STOCK, $20 PAR

ACCOUNT NO.

| Date | | Item | Debit | Credit | Balance | |
|---|---|---|---|---|---|---|
| | | | | | Debit | Credit |
| 19-- | | | | | | |
| Jan. | 1 | Balance | | | | 500,000 |
| Dec. | 1 | Stock dividend | | 15,000 | | 515,000 |

ACCOUNT PREMIUM ON COMMON STOCK

ACCOUNT NO.

| Date | | Item | Debit | Credit | Balance | |
|---|---|---|---|---|---|---|
| | | | | | Debit | Credit |
| 19-- | | | | | | |
| Jan. | 1 | Balance | | | | 60,000 |
| Dec. | 1 | Stock dividend | | 10,000 | | 70,000 |

ACCOUNT APPROPRIATION FOR CONTINGENCIES

ACCOUNT NO.

| Date | | Item | Debit | Credit | Balance | |
|---|---|---|---|---|---|---|
| | | | | | Debit | Credit |
| 19-- | | | | | | |
| Jan. | 1 | Balance | | | | 75,000 |
| Dec. | 31 | Appropriation | | 25,000 | | 100,000 |

ACCOUNT RETAINED EARNINGS

ACCOUNT NO.

| Date | | Item | Debit | Credit | Balance | |
|---|---|---|---|---|---|---|
| | | | | | Debit | Credit |
| 19-- | | | | | | |
| Jan. | 1 | Balance | | | | 353,280 |
| Dec. | 1 | Stock dividend | 25,000 | | | |
| | 31 | Net loss | 17,700 | | | |
| | 31 | Cash dividends | 25,000 | | | |
| | 31 | Appropriated | 25,000 | | | 260,580 |

Instructions:

Prepare a statement of changes in financial position (working capital concept), including a section for changes in components of working capital.

**Problem 17-5A.** The comparative balance sheet of W. A. Sussman Inc. and other data necessary for the analysis of the corporation's funds flow are presented in Problem 17-4A.

Instructions:

Prepare a statement of changes in financial position (cash concept), including a summary of the change in cash balance.

**Problem 17-6A.** A comparative balance sheet and an income statement of Mills Company are as follows:

Mills Company
Income Statement
For Current Year Ended December 31

| | | |
|---|---:|---:|
| Sales............................................................. | | $990,000 |
| Cost of merchandise sold................................ | | 615,000 |
| Gross profit.................................................. | | $375,000 |
| Operating expenses (including depreciation of $32,200) .. | | 250,700 |
| Income from operations ................................. | | $124,300 |
| Other income: | | |
|    Gain on sale of land................................ | $ 25,000 | |
|    Gain on sale of investments...................... | 3,500 | |
|    Interest income...................................... | 1,100 | 29,600 |
| | | $153,900 |
| Interest expense........................................... | | 18,000 |
| Income before income tax .............................. | | $135,900 |
| Income tax.................................................. | | 48,100 |
| Net income.................................................. | | $ 87,800 |

Mills Company
Comparative Balance Sheet
December 31, Current and Preceding Year

| Assets | Current Year | Preceding Year |
|---|---:|---:|
| Cash ............................................................. | $ 36,600 | $ 41,500 |
| Marketable securities..................................... | 32,100 | —— |
| Trade receivables (net).................................. | 110,000 | 83,000 |
| Inventories ................................................... | 168,600 | 147,100 |
| Prepaid expenses ......................................... | 3,750 | 4,100 |
| Investments .................................................. | —— | 80,000 |
| Land ............................................................ | 60,000 | 50,000 |
| Buildings....................................................... | 305,000 | 150,000 |
| Accumulated depreciation—buildings ................. | (87,000) | (79,000) |
| Equipment .................................................... | 402,500 | 350,000 |
| Accumulated depreciation—equipment................. | (145,300) | (121,100) |
| | $886,250 | $705,600 |

| Liabilities and Stockholders' Equity | | |
|---|---:|---:|
| Accounts payable (merchandise creditors) .............. | $ 67,250 | $ 52,900 |
| Income tax payable ....................................... | 5,000 | 11,500 |
| Dividends payable.......................................... | 25,000 | 15,000 |
| Mortgage note payable.................................... | 150,000 | —— |
| Bonds payable .............................................. | 100,000 | 150,000 |
| Common stock, $10 par .................................. | 340,000 | 300,000 |
| Premium on common stock ............................. | 65,000 | 55,000 |
| Retained earnings ......................................... | 134,000 | 121,200 |
| | $886,250 | $705,600 |

The following additional information on funds flow during the year was obtained from an examination of the ledger:
(a) Marketable securities were purchased for $32,100.
(b) Investments (long-term) were sold for $83,500.
(c) Equipment was purchased for $52,500. There were no disposals.
(d) A building valued at $155,000 and land valued at $45,000 were acquired by a cash payment of $50,000 and issuance of a five-year mortgage note payable for the balance.
(e) Land which cost $35,000 was sold for $60,000 cash.
(f) Bonds payable of $50,000 were retired by the payment of their face amount.
(g) 4,000 shares of common stock were issued for cash at 12½.
(h) Cash dividends of $75,000 were declared.

Instructions:
(1) Prepare a statement of changes in financial position (working capital concept), including a section for changes in components of working capital.
(2) Prepare a statement of changes in financial position (cash concept), including a summary of the change in cash balance.

**Mini-Case**

Robert Pickett is the president and majority shareholder of Variety Stores Inc., a small retail store chain. Recently, Pickett submitted a loan application for Variety Stores Inc. to Arcadia State Bank for a $100,000, 14%, 10-year loan to finance the purchase of land and buildings in Clinton, where the company plans to open a new store. The bank's loan officer requested a statement of changes in financial position (based on the working capital concept) in addition to the most recent income statement, balance sheet, and retained earnings statement that Pickett had submitted with the loan application.

As a close family friend, Pickett asked you to prepare a statement of changes in financial position. Using Variety Stores' records, you prepared the statement shown on page 428.

After reviewing the statement, Pickett telephoned you and commented, "Are you sure this statement is right?" Pickett then raised the following questions:
(a) "How can depreciation be a source of working capital?"
(b) "The issuance of common stock for the land is listed both as a source and an application of working capital. This transaction had nothing to do with working capital! Shouldn't the two items related to this transaction be eliminated from both the sources and applications sections?"
(c) "Why did you list only the $27,000 book value of the investments sold, excluding the gain of $5,000, as a source of funds? We actually received cash of $32,000 from the sale. Shouldn't the $32,000 be included as a source of working capital?"
(d) "Why not eliminate the 'changes in components of working capital' section of the statement? Since the amount of increase in working capital is already shown in the upper portion of the statement, this section adds nothing."
(e) "Why does the bank need this statement anyway? They can compute the increase in working capital from the balance sheets for the last two years."

After jotting down Pickett's questions, you assured him that this statement was "right". However, to alleviate Pickett's concern, you arranged a meeting for the following day.

Variety Stores Inc.
Statement of Changes in Financial Position
For Year Ended December 31, 19--

Sources of working capital:
  Operations during the year:
    Net income......................... $ 80,000
    Add deduction not decreasing work-
      ing capital during the year:
      Depreciation.....................   20,000 $100,000
  Book value of investments sold (ex-
    cludes $5,000 gain)................            27,000
  Issuance of common stock at par for
    land ............................             50,000 $177,000

Applications of working capital:
  Purchase of land by issuance of com-
    mon stock at par....................  $ 50,000
  Purchase of store equipment ..........    25,000
  Declaration of cash dividends.........    20,000    95,000
  Increase in working capital .............          $ 82,000

Changes in components of working capital:
  Increase (decrease) in current assets:
    Cash.............................     $ 16,300
    Trade receivables (net) ............    24,600
    Inventories ........................    53,600
    Prepaid expenses .................      (2,500) $ 92,000

  Increase (decrease) in current liabilities:
    Accounts payable ..................   $ 12,400
    Income tax payable.................      2,600
    Dividends payable..................     (5,000)   10,000
  Increase in working capital .............          $ 82,000

Instructions:
  (1) How would you respond to each of Pickett's questions?
  (2) Do you think that the statement of changes in financial position enhances
      Variety Stores' chances of receiving the loan? Discuss.

# 18

CHAPTER

# Nonprofit Organizations

## CHAPTER OBJECTIVES

*Describe the characteristics of nonprofit organizations.*

*Describe and illustrate accounting concepts useful to management in planning and controlling operations of nonprofit organizations.*

# PART 8

## Managerial Aids for Nonprofit Organizations

# 18

## CHAPTER

Entities engaged in business transactions may be classified as profit making or nonprofit. Profit-making organizations respond to a demand for a product or a service, with the objective of earning net income. The accounting concepts and their use by management of such organizations were discussed in preceding chapters.

Nonprofit organizations provide goods or services that fulfill a social need, often for those who do not have the purchasing power to acquire these goods or services for themselves. These organizations are usually operated as informal associations or as corporations in accordance with the applicable laws and regulations. Nonprofit organizations may be classified as either (1) governmental units or (2) charitable, religious, or philanthropic units (hereafter referred to simply as "charitable"). Governmental organizations include the United States, states, cities, and counties. The second category includes churches, hospitals, private schools and universities, medical research facilities, and many other types of organizations that are financed wholly or in part by donations.

As the sense of social responsibility to society has increased in recent years, there has been a corresponding increase in the number of nonprofit organizations and in the volume of their activities. Approximately one third of the volume of business in the United States is conducted by approximately 750,000 governmental units and charitable organizations with annual spending of approximately one trillion dollars ($1,000,000,000,000).

As nonprofit organizations play an increasingly significant role, managers of such organizations have as much need for accounting information to assist them in planning and controlling operations and in decision making as do managers of profit-making organizations. This chapter is devoted to the accounting concepts applicable to nonprofit organizations and their use by management.

## CHARACTER-ISTICS OF NONPROFIT ORGANIZA-TIONS

Profit-making organizations are characterized by (1) the private ownership of the organization's assets and (2) the objective of earning net income for the private ownership interests, whether these interests are represented by sole proprietors, partners, or stockholders. The distinguishing characteristics of nonprofit organizations are: (1) no individuals own any equity shares or interests; (2) there is neither a conscious profit motive nor an expectation of earning net income; (3) no part of any excess of revenues over expenditures is distributed to those who contributed support through taxes or voluntary donations; and (4) any excess of revenues over expenditures that results from operations in the short run is ordinarily used in later years to further the purposes of the organization.

Some nonprofit organizations, such as a government-owned electric utility or a public transportation company, are created to provide services to the citizens of the area for a fee that is close to the cost of providing the service. After the initial investment, they tend to be self-sustaining; that is, the revenues earned support their operations. Because the activities of such organizations are financed mainly by charges to the customers using the services, the accounting concepts used are those appropriate to a commercial enterprise. Most nonprofit organizations, however, are established to provide a service to society without levying against the user a direct charge equal to the full cost of the service.

FUND
ACCOUNTING

The accounting systems for all nonprofit organizations must provide financial data to management for use in planning and controlling operations as well as for reporting to external parties, such as taxpayers and donors, for their use in determining the effectiveness of operations. Therefore, most of the basics of accounting for profit-making enterprises are essential for nonprofit organizations. In addition, accounting systems for nonprofit organizations should include mechanisms (1) to ensure that management observes the restrictions imposed upon it by law, charter, by-laws, etc., and (2) to provide for reports to taxpayers and donors that such restrictions have been respected. For these reasons, a nonprofit organization often applies the concept of "fund accounting" in conjunction with a budget and appropriations technique to account for the assets received by the organization and to ensure that expenditures are made only for authorized purposes.

The term "fund" was used in the preceding chapter in the context of the funds statement, where funds can be interpreted broadly to mean "working capital" or more narrowly to mean "cash." The term fund, as used in accounting for nonprofit organizations, is defined as an accounting entity with accounts maintained for recording assets, liabilities, capital (usually called **fund balance**), revenues, and expenditures for a particular purpose according to specified restrictions or limitations. Funds may be established by law, provisions of a charter, administrative action, or by a special contribution to a charitable organization. For example, cities usually maintain a "General Fund" for recording transactions related to many community services, such as fire and police protection, street lighting and repairs, and maintenance of water and sewer mains. Additional funds may be maintained for special tax assessments, bond redemption, and for other specified purposes.

The fundamentals of fund accounting are similar to the accounting principles for profit-making organizations. Most nonprofit organizations use the concepts of budgetary control described in preceding chapters, although the manner in which these concepts are applied is modified somewhat to make them more useful for planning and controlling nonprofit operations. Accountants for nonprofit organizations also provide various management reports and special analyses to assist management in making decisions. In the following paragraphs, the fund accounting principles of budgeting and management reports and special analyses are discussed, and the basic fund accounting system is illustrated.

Budgeting

The essentials of budgeting are the same for both profit and nonprofit organizations. In both cases, the budget is prepared by management and subsequently reviewed, revised, and approved by the appropriate body. For the nonprofit organization, the budget is approved by the governing body (council, directors, or trustees) of the organization. The concept of zero-base budgeting can also be applied in developing the budget estimates for both types of organizations. (The zero-base budgeting concept requires all levels of management to start from zero and estimate revenues and expenditures as if there had been no previous activities in their unit.)

The budgeting process in profit-oriented organizations generally starts with the preparation of the sales or revenue budget. In nonprofit organizations, however, the budgeting process often begins with the estimation of the expenditures for the various programs provided by the organization. The organization then seeks means of financing these programs or, if adequate financing cannot be provided, the expenditures are reduced to levels that can be financed from expected revenues. For example, a hospital, a church, or a governmental organization proposes specific programs and activities and the related expenditures for the coming year. Then the organization seeks financing from such sources as donations or taxes. For the final budget, the proposed expenditures should not exceed the estimated revenues. In many cases, this restriction requires a downward revision of the original estimates for expenditures.

Since the main function of most nonprofit organizations is to provide nonrevenue-producing goods or services, the most critical element in the budgetary control process is the control of expenditures. Therefore, in an attempt to make the budgetary process more useful in controlling expenditures and operations, budget performance reporting has received increased attention in recent years by nonprofit organizations. The manner of identifying expenditures has become the focus of the budget format, which may follow one of three basic types: (1) line budget, (2) program budget, and (3) combined line-program budget.

## Line Budgets

The line, or **functional**, budget is very popular because its format closely parallels that of the profit-making organization. In the line budget, items of expenditure are presented by the "object" of the expenditure, that is, by the "reason" for the expenditure. Objects of expenditures for a nonprofit organization would include salaries, supplies, and travel, just as wages, power and light, and maintenance would be identified for the factory overhead cost budget for a profit-making organization. A budget in the line format, severely condensed to focus on the basic concept of the format, is illustrated as follows:

LINE
BUDGET

### Gates Community College
### Budget of Expenditures
### For Year Ending June 30, 19--

| | |
|---|---:|
| Faculty salaries | $ 6,270,000 |
| Administrative salaries | 1,862,000 |
| Maintenance salaries | 990,000 |
| Supplies | 695,000 |
| Utilities | 655,000 |
| Miscellaneous | 553,000 |
| Total expenditures | $11,025,000 |

## Program Budgets

The program budget focuses on the services or programs provided by the nonprofit organization. For example, the budget of expenditures for a small community college may focus on such programs as basic education, adult education, athletic programs, and community service programs, as illustrated in the following budget:

PROGRAM
BUDGET

Gates Community College
Budget of Expenditures
For Year Ending June 30, 19--

| | Basic Education | Adult Education | Athletic Programs | Community Service Programs |
|---|---|---|---|---|
| Faculty salaries ........... | $5,200,000 | $ 850,000 | $120,000 | $100,000 |
| Administrative salaries ...... | 1,750,000 | 85,000 | 15,000 | 12,000 |
| Maintenance salaries ....... | 900,000 | 65,000 | 15,000 | 10,000 |
| Supplies................... | 640,000 | 37,000 | 10,000 | 8,000 |
| Utilities .................. | 600,000 | 35,000 | 10,000 | 10,000 |
| Miscellaneous.............. | 510,000 | 28,000 | 5,000 | 10,000 |
| Total expenditures......... | $9,600,000 | $1,100,000 | $175,000 | $150,000 |

Since the program budget requires management to identify the programs to be provided and their related costs, the principal advantage of the program budget is that the effectiveness of the program can be easily evaluated in terms of the benefits provided and the expenditures made on each program.

### Combined Line-Program Budgets

The advantages of both the line and program budget can be achieved by adding a total column to the program budget. In effect, this combined line-program budget adds the features of the line budget to the program budget, as shown in the following illustration:

COMBINED
LINE-PROGRAM
BUDGET

Gates Community College
Budget of Expenditures
For Year Ending June 30, 19--

| | Basic Education | Adult Education | Athletic Programs | Community Service Programs | Total |
|---|---|---|---|---|---|
| Faculty salaries....... | $5,200,000 | $ 850,000 | $120,000 | $100,000 | $ 6,270,000 |
| Administrative salaries.. | 1,750,000 | 85,000 | 15,000 | 12,000 | 1,862,000 |
| Maintenance salaries.. | 900,000 | 65,000 | 15,000 | 10,000 | 990,000 |
| Supplies............. | 640,000 | 37,000 | 10,000 | 8,000 | 695,000 |
| Utilities ............. | 600,000 | 35,000 | 10,000 | 10,000 | 655,000 |
| Miscellaneous........ | 510,000 | 28,000 | 5,000 | 10,000 | 553,000 |
| Total expenditures .... | $9,600,000 | $1,100,000 | $175,000 | $150,000 | $11,025,000 |

Management
Reports and
Special Analyses

Some of the reports and special analyses discussed in preceding chapters relate specifically to the profit motive and thus, in general, are not applicable to nonprofit organizations. Such analyses would include gross profit analysis and differential analysis for evaluating a proposal to discontinue an unprofitable segment. Many of the profit-making concepts, however, are applicable to the nonprofit organization. As mentioned previously, for example, budget performance reports that compare actual results with budgeted figures can be helpful in controlling the costs and operations of a nonprofit organization. A nonprofit organization may use the differential analysis concepts described in preceding chapters in evaluating a proposal either to lease equipment or to purchase it. Likewise, a proposal to replace old equipment with new and more efficient equipment could be evaluated in terms of the differential costs associated with both the old and new equipment. Similarly, the basic concept of economic order quantities would be equally applicable to nonprofit and profit-making organizations.

**Basic Fund Accounting System**     The basic double-entry system, the determination of financial position, and the reporting of financial position and results of operations are essential for the planning and controlling of the activities of nonprofit organizations. In addition, the integration of budgetary data into the system and the extensive use of other control techniques, such as subsidiary ledgers, increases the effectiveness of the accounting system in aiding management's control of expenditures and operations. The fundamentals of the basic fund accounting system and its use in providing data for management are discussed in the remainder of the chapter.

### Estimated Revenues and Appropriations

Budgeting is an important part of an accounting system for nonprofit organizations. The official budget sets the specific goals for the fiscal period. Through appropriations (authorization to spend the budgeted expenditures), the budget designates the manner in which the revenues of each fund are to be used to accomplish the organization's goals. The estimated revenues may be viewed as potential assets and the appropriations as potential liabilities.

By integrating the budget amounts into the accounting system, the comparison of these budgeted amounts with actual amounts assists management in controlling operations. Therefore, after the budget for the general fund has been approved by the governing body, the estimated revenues and appropriations are entered into the accounting system by an entry such as the following:

| | | |
|---|---|---|
| Estimated Revenues | 1,900,000 | |
| Appropriations | | 1,850,000 |
| Fund Balance | | 50,000 |

The effect of the recording of the budgeted amounts in the general fund accounts is presented in the following diagram:

### General Fund Accounts

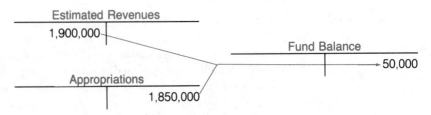

When the budget shows an excess of estimated revenues over appropriations, as in the illustration, the account Fund Balance is credited. The amount in Fund

Balance represents the estimated accumulated capital of the general fund. If the budget had shown an excess of appropriations over estimated revenues, the excess would be debited to the account Fund Balance. The subsidiary ledgers for Estimated Revenues and Appropriations contain accounts for the various sources of expected revenue (property taxes, sales taxes, etc.) and the various purposes of appropriations (general government, streets and roads, libraries, etc.). By recording this budgetary information in the accounts, periodic reports comparing actual with budget can be prepared readily.

### Revenues

The realization of revenues requires an entry debiting accounts for the assets acquired and crediting the revenues account. For example, a portion of the estimated revenues from property taxes, sales taxes, etc., may be realized in the form of cash during the first month of the fiscal year. To summarize these receipts, an entry would be made as follows, in general journal form:

```
Cash...............................................  152,500
    Revenues......................................            152,500
```

Revenues is a controlling account. In practice, it is customary to use a single subsidiary ledger, called the revenue ledger, for both Estimated Revenues and Revenues. Each subsidiary account is used for recording the estimated revenues and the actual revenues. The relationship between the general ledger accounts and the subsidiary revenue ledger is illustrated in the following diagram:

### General Ledger Accounts

| Estimated Revenues | Revenues |
|---|---|
| 1,900,000 | 152,500 |

### Revenue Ledger

Property Taxes Revenue

| | |
|---|---|
| 1,145,000 | 102,000 |

Sales Taxes Revenue

| | |
|---|---|
| 395,000 | 32,500 |

Miscellaneous Revenue

| | |
|---|---|
| 360,000 | 18,000 |

At any point in time, the difference between the two general ledger controlling accounts, Estimated Revenues and Revenues, would be equal to the sum of the balances of the accounts in the subsidiary revenue ledger. A debit balance in a subsidiary ledger account indicates the amount of the excess of estimated revenues over actual revenues. If actual revenues exceed the amount estimated, the account balance would be a credit.

## Expenditures

As regularly recurring expenditures, such as payrolls, are incurred, the account Expenditures is debited and the appropriate liability accounts or Cash are credited. For example, the entry for the biweekly payroll would be as follows:

| | | |
|---|---|---|
| Expenditures...................................... | 31,200 | |
| Wages Payable ................................ | | 31,200 |

## Encumbrances

There is usually a lapse of time between the placing of an order and delivery of the goods or services ordered. When contracts such as those for road or building construction are executed, the time lag may extend over relatively long periods. All legally binding commitments to pay money eventually become expenditures. These commitments, called encumbrances, should be recorded in the accounts when a contract is entered into in order to ensure that expenditures do not exceed amounts appropriated. The means of preventing overexpenditures is illustrated by the following entry:

| | | |
|---|---|---|
| Encumbrances..................................... | 10,000 | |
| Reserve for Encumbrances....................... | | 10,000 |

When orders are filled or contracts completed for amounts encumbered, the entry that recorded the encumbrance is reversed and the expenditure is recorded, as illustrated by the following entries:

| | | |
|---|---|---|
| Reserve for Encumbrances......................... | 10,000 | |
| Encumbrances.................................. | | 10,000 |
| Expenditures...................................... | 10,000 | |
| Accounts Payable .............................. | | 10,000 |

The effect of these two entries is to (1) cancel the original entry in which the encumbrance was recorded and (2) record the expenditure and the related liability.

When encumbrances are recorded, the sum of the balances of the accounts Encumbrances and Expenditures can be viewed as offsets to the account Appropriations. The difference obtained by subtracting the balance of Encumbrances and Expenditures from the amount of Appropriations is the amount of commitments that can still be made. For example, if appropriations of $1,850,000 were approved when the budget was adopted and $1,500,000 and $240,000 have been recorded in Expenditures and Encumbrances, respectively, only $110,000 is available for commitment during the remainder of the fiscal year.

## Expenditure Ledger

Appropriations, Encumbrances, and Expenditures are controlling accounts. In practice, it is customary to use a single subsidiary ledger, called the expenditure ledger, in which each account indicates appropriations, encumbrances, and expenditures.

When a budget is approved, appropriations are recorded in the proper accounts in the expenditure ledger to indicate the uncommitted balance. As order commitments are made, the amounts of the encumbrances are recorded in the proper expenditure ledger account (by a debit) and the uncommitted balance is adjusted accordingly. When orders are filled, the expenditure and the credit to encumbrances are recorded in the proper columns. At any point in time, the accounts in the expenditure ledger indicate the balance of the encumbrances outstanding and the uncommitted balance.

In the following illustration of an account in the expenditure ledger, the budget appropriation for police department supplies is $250,000 as of July 1. On July 5, a purchase order that encumbered $10,000 was recorded and the encumbrances balance of $10,000 and the uncommitted balance of $240,000 were recorded. When the invoice of $10,000 was received on July 17, the encumbrances balance was reduced to zero and the $10,000 expenditure was recorded.

| ACCOUNT POLICE DEPARTMENT—SUPPLIES | | | | | | | | ACCOUNT NO. 200-21 |
|---|---|---|---|---|---|---|---|---|
| Date | | Item | Encumbrances | | | Expenditures | | Uncommitted Balance |
| | | | Debit | Credit | Balance | Item | Total | |
| July | 1 | Budget appropriation | | | | | | 250,000 |
| | 5 | Purchase order | 10,000 | | 10,000 | | | 240,000 |
| | 17 | Invoice | | 10,000 | —— | 10,000 | 10,000 | 240,000 |
| | 30 | Purchase order | 7,500 | | 7,500 | | | 232,500 |

## Long-Lived Assets

When long-lived assets are purchased, they are usually recorded as debits to the account Expenditures in the same manner as supplies and other ordinary expenses. A separate record of the individual assets can be maintained for the purpose of assigning responsibility for the custody and use of these assets.

The practice of recording the purchase of long-lived assets as an expenditure and the related failure to record depreciation expense has been severely criticized for many years. Most governmental units and charitable organizations still fail to differentiate between long-lived assets and ordinary recurring expenses. This practice is supported by the fact that the acquisition of plant assets is often authorized by a special appropriation, perhaps financed by a bond issue for a local government unit or by donations or special fund-raising drives for a charitable organization.

**Periodic Reporting** | A nonprofit organization should prepare interim statements comparing actual revenues and expenditures with the related budgeted amounts. Variations between the two should be investigated immediately to determine their cause and to consider possible corrective actions.

At the end of the fiscal year, closing entries are recorded and the operating data are summarized and reported. The entry to close the revenues and estimated revenues accounts is illustrated as follows:

Revenues. . . . . . . . . . . . . . . . . . . . . . . . . . . . . . . . . . . . . . . . . . . 1,920,000
    Estimated Revenues . . . . . . . . . . . . . . . . . . . . . . . . . . . . .                1,900,000
    Fund Balance . . . . . . . . . . . . . . . . . . . . . . . . . . . . . . . . . .                20,000

In the illustration, actual revenues exceeded the amount estimated. If the actual revenues had been less than the amount estimated, the capital account, Fund Balance, would have been decreased by a debit. The effect of this entry is to adjust Fund Balance to the actual amount of the revenues for the period.

The entry to close the appropriations and expenditures accounts is illustrated as follows:

Appropriations . . . . . . . . . . . . . . . . . . . . . . . . . . . . . . . . . . . . 1,850,000
    Expenditures. . . . . . . . . . . . . . . . . . . . . . . . . . . . . . . . . . .                1,825,000
    Fund Balance . . . . . . . . . . . . . . . . . . . . . . . . . . . . . . . . . .                25,000

In the illustration, appropriations exceeded the actual expenditures. If the appropriations had been less than the actual expenditures, the capital account, Fund Balance, would have been decreased by a debit. The effect of this entry is to adjust Fund Balance to the actual amount of the expenditures for the period.

The entry to close the encumbrances account, which represents the commitments outstanding at the end of the year, is illustrated as follows:

Fund Balance . . . . . . . . . . . . . . . . . . . . . . . . . . . . . . . . . . . .                20,000
    Encumbrances . . . . . . . . . . . . . . . . . . . . . . . . . . . . . . . . .                20,000

Inevitably, some orders placed during the year will remain unfilled at the end of the year. To indicate the commitment to pay for these orders, Reserve for Encumbrances is not closed and is included in the year-end balance sheet. When the orders are filled in the next year, Reserve for Encumbrances will be debited and Accounts Payable credited.

Financial statements for each fund and combined financial statements for all funds should be prepared periodically. These statements should also be accompanied by adequate disclosures, including a summary of significant accounting policies.

The principal financial statements prepared at the end of each fiscal year are: (1) statement of revenues and expenditures — budget and actual, (2) balance sheet, and (3) statement of changes in fund balance. Because of the absence of the profit motive and the presence of controls imposed upon nonprofit organizations by law or dictate of donors, the operating statement shows budgeted and actual results instead of a net income figure. The balance sheet is similar to a balance sheet for commercial enterprises. A statement of changes in fund balance, although similar to the retained earnings statement for a commercial enterprise, has a unique format. These statements are illustrated in the following section.

**ILLUSTRATION OF NONPROFIT ACCOUNTING**

To illustrate further the concepts and procedures that have been described, assume that the trial balance of the General Fund of the City of Lewiston, as of July 1, the beginning of the fiscal year, is as follows:

City of Lewiston—General Fund
Trial Balance
July 1, 19--

| | | |
|---|---:|---:|
| Cash ............................................. | 242,500 | |
| Savings Accounts.................................. | 250,000 | |
| Property Taxes Receivable......................... | 185,000 | |
| Investment in U.S. Treasury Notes ................. | 350,000 | |
| Accounts Payable.................................. | | 162,600 |
| Wages Payable..................................... | | 30,000 |
| Fund Balance ..................................... | | 834,900 |
| | 1,027,500 | 1,027,500 |

The transactions completed during the year for the General Fund are summarized and recorded as follows, in general journal form. In practice, the transactions would be recorded from day to day in various journals.

*(a) Estimated revenues and appropriations.*

    *Entry:* Estimated Revenues...................... 9,100,000

            Appropriations......................... 9,070,000

            Fund Balance......................... 30,000

*(b) Revenues from property tax levy.*

    *Entry:* Property Taxes Receivable ............... 6,500,000

            Revenues ........................... 6,500,000

*(c) Collection of property taxes and other taxes on a cash basis, such as sales taxes, motor vehicle license fees, municipal court fines, etc.*

    *Entry:* Cash ................................... 9,105,000

            Property Taxes Receivable.............. 6,470,000

            Revenues ........................... 2,635,000

*(d) Expenditures for payrolls.*

    *Entry:* Expenditures........................... 3,280,000

            Wages Payable....................... 3,280,000

*(e) Expenditures encumbered.*

    *Entry:* Encumbrances........................... 5,800,000

            Reserve for Encumbrances ............. 5,800,000

*(f) Liquidation of encumbrances and receipt of invoices.*

    *Entry:* Reserve for Encumbrances ............... 5,785,000

            Encumbrances........................ 5,785,000

            Expenditures .......................... 5,785,000

            Accounts Payable...................... 5,785,000

*(g) Cash disbursed.*

    *Entry:*    Accounts Payable ........................ 5,800,000
                 Wages Payable.......................... 3,270,000
                 Cash ...............................            9,070,000

*(h) Revenues and estimated revenues accounts closed.*

    *Entry:*    Revenues ............................. 9,135,000
                 Estimated Revenues...................            9,100,000
                 Fund Balance........................            35,000

*(i) Appropriations and expenditures accounts closed.*

    *Entry:*    Appropriations.......................... 9,070,000
                 Expenditures .......................            9,065,000
                 Fund Balance........................            5,000

*(j) Encumbrances account closed.*

    *Entry:*    Fund Balance ......................... 15,000
                 Encumbrances.......................            15,000

After the foregoing entries have been posted, the general ledger accounts, the trial balance, and the balance sheet for the General Fund appear as follows. Entries in the accounts are identified by letters to facilitate comparison with the summary journal entries.

**Cash**

| | | | | | |
|---|---|---|---|---|---|
| Balance | 242,500 | (g) | 9,070,000 | | |
| (c) | 9,105,000 | Balance | 277,500 | | |
| | 9,347,500 | | 9,347,500 | | |
| Balance | 277,500 | | | | |

**Accounts Payable**

| | | | |
|---|---|---|---|
| (g) | 5,800,000 | Balance | 162,600 |
| Balance | 147,600 | (f) | 5,785,000 |
| | 5,947,600 | | 5,947,600 |
| | | Balance | 147,600 |

**Savings Accounts**

| | |
|---|---|
| Balance | 250,000 |

**Wages Payable**

| | | | |
|---|---|---|---|
| (g) | 3,270,000 | Balance | 30,000 |
| Balance | 40,000 | (d) | 3,280,000 |
| | 3,310,000 | | 3,310,000 |
| | | Balance | 40,000 |

**Property Taxes Receivable**

| | | | |
|---|---|---|---|
| Balance | 185,000 | (c) | 6,470,000 |
| (b) | 6,500,000 | Balance | 215,000 |
| | 6,685,000 | | 6,685,000 |
| Balance | 215,000 | | |

**Reserve for Encumbrances**

| | | | |
|---|---|---|---|
| (f) | 5,785,000 | (e) | 5,800,000 |
| Balance | 15,000 | | |
| | 5,800,000 | | 5,800,000 |
| | | Balance | 15,000 |

**Investment in U.S. Treasury Notes**

| | |
|---|---|
| Balance | 350,000 |

|  | Fund Balance |  |  |  | Appropriations |  |  |
|---|---|---|---|---|---|---|---|
| (j) | 15,000 | Balance | 834,900 | (i) | 9,070,000 | (a) | 9,070,000 |
| Balance | 889,900 | (a) | 30,000 |  |  |  |  |
|  |  | (h) | 35,000 |  |  |  |  |
|  | 904,900 | (i) | 5,000 |  | Expenditures |  |  |
|  |  |  | 904,900 | (d) | 3,280,000 | (i) | 9,065,000 |
|  |  | Balance | 889,900 | (f) | 5,785,000 |  |  |
|  |  |  |  |  | 9,065,000 |  | 9,065,000 |

|  | Estimated Revenues |  |  |
|---|---|---|---|
| (a) | 9,100,000 | (h) | 9,100,000 |

|  | Encumbrances |  |  |
|---|---|---|---|
| (e) | 5,800,000 | (f) | 5,785,000 |
|  |  | (j) | 15,000 |
|  | 5,800,000 |  | 5,800,000 |

|  | Revenues |  |  |
|---|---|---|---|
| (h) | 9,135,000 | (b) | 6,500,000 |
|  |  | (c) | 2,635,000 |
|  | 9,135,000 |  | 9,135,000 |

**City of Lewiston—General Fund**
**Trial Balance**
**June 30, 19--**

| | | |
|---|---|---|
| Cash................................................ | 277,500 | |
| Savings Accounts.................................... | 250,000 | |
| Property Taxes Receivable........................... | 215,000 | |
| Investment in U.S. Treasury Notes ................... | 350,000 | |
| Accounts Payable.................................... | | 147,600 |
| Wages Payable....................................... | | 40,000 |
| Reserve for Encumbrances ........................... | | 15,000 |
| Fund Balance ....................................... | | 889,900 |
| | 1,092,500 | 1,092,500 |

BALANCE
SHEET

**City of Lewiston—General Fund**
**Balance Sheet**
**June 30, 19--**

### Assets

| | |
|---|---|
| Cash..................................................... | $ 277,500 |
| Savings accounts......................................... | 250,000 |
| Property taxes receivable................................ | 215,000 |
| Investment in U.S. Treasury notes ....................... | 350,000 |
| Total assets............................................. | $1,092,500 |

### Liabilities and Fund Balance

| | |
|---|---|
| Accounts payable......................................... | $ 147,600 |
| Wages payable............................................ | 40,000 |
| Reserve for encumbrances ................................ | 15,000 |
| Fund balance ............................................ | 889,900 |
| Total liabilities and fund balance....................... | $1,092,500 |

To simplify the illustration, the subsidiary ledgers were not presented. Such ledgers provide data for the following statement of revenues and expenditures — budget and actual.

**City of Lewiston — General Fund**
**Statement of Revenues and Expenditures — Budget and Actual**
**For Year Ended June 30, 19--**

| | Budget | Actual | Over | Under |
|---|---|---|---|---|
| **Revenues:** | | | | |
| General property taxes | $6,480,000 | $6,500,000 | $20,000 | |
| Sales taxes | 1,835,500 | 1,850,500 | 15,000 | |
| Motor vehicle licenses | 312,250 | 310,250 | | $ 2,000 |
| Municipal court fines | 257,000 | 255,750 | | 1,250 |
| Interest | 35,000 | 35,000 | | |
| Building permits | 27,100 | 27,500 | 400 | |
| Miscellaneous | 153,150 | 156,000 | 2,850 | |
| Total revenues | $9,100,000 | $9,135,000 | $38,250 | $ 3,250 |
| **Expenditures:** | | | | |
| General government | $2,450,000 | $2,465,250 | $15,250 | |
| Police department — personnel services | 1,250,000 | 1,256,000 | 6,000 | |
| Police department — supplies | 299,000 | 290,500 | | $ 8,500 |
| Police department — equipment | 190,000 | 182,750 | | 7,250 |
| Police department — other charges | 30,000 | 27,500 | | 2,500 |
| Fire department — personnel services | 1,035,000 | 1,039,000 | 4,000 | |
| Fire department — supplies | 320,600 | 315,600 | | 5,000 |
| Fire department — equipment | 200,500 | 197,750 | | 2,750 |
| Fire department — other charges | 16,400 | 18,200 | 1,800 | |
| Streets and roads | 1,530,000 | 1,521,850 | | 8,150 |
| Sanitation | 741,000 | 739,500 | | 1,500 |
| Public welfare | 630,000 | 632,600 | 2,600 | |
| Libraries | 377,500 | 378,500 | 1,000 | |
| Total expenditures | $9,070,000 | $9,065,000 | $30,650 | $35,650 |
| Excess of revenues over expenditures | $ 30,000 | $ 70,000 | | |

Although there are many variations in form, the following statement of changes in fund balance has the advantages of indicating (1) the excess of estimated revenues over appropriations, (2) the excess of revenues over estimated revenues, (3) the excess of appropriations over expenditures, and (4) the encumbrances outstanding at the end of the year. These four items represent the effect of the four entries made in the fund account during the year.

STATEMENT OF
CHANGES IN FUND
BALANCE

**City of Lewiston—General Fund**
**Statement of Changes in Fund Balance**
**For Year Ended June 30, 19--**

| | | | |
|---|---|---|---|
| Balance, July 1, 19-- ........................ | | | $834,900 |
| Add: | | | |
| Excess of estimated revenues over appropriations: | | | |
| Estimated revenues .................. | $9,100,000 | | |
| Appropriations....................... | 9,070,000 | $30,000 | |
| Excess of revenues over estimated revenues: | | | |
| Revenues .......................... | $9,135,000 | | |
| Estimated revenues .................. | 9,100,000 | 35,000 | |
| Excess of appropriations over expenditures: | | | |
| Appropriations ..................... | $9,070,000 | | |
| Expenditures ...................... | 9,065,000 | 5,000 | 70,000 |
| | | | $904,900 |
| Deduct: | | | |
| Encumbrances, June 30, 19-- .................... | | | 15,000 |
| Balance, June 30, 19-- .............................. | | | $889,900 |

Self-
Examination
Questions
*(Answers in
Appendix C.)*

1. In accounting for nonprofit organizations, the term employed to represent an accounting entity with accounts for assets, liabilities, capital, revenues, and expenditures for a particular purpose is:
   A. fund                     C. encumbrance
   B. appropriation            D. none of the above

2. The budget format that focuses on the programs to be provided by the nonprofit organization and their related costs is:
   A. line budget              C. zero-base budget
   B. program budget           D. none of the above

3. In accounting for nonprofit organizations, the account that represents the capital of an accounting entity is:
   A. Retained Earnings        C. Fund Balance
   B. Accumulated Earnings     D. none of the above

4. Each account in the expenditures ledger indicates:
   A. appropriations           C. expenditures
   B. encumbrances             D. all of the above

5. The financial statement for a nonprofit organization that is similar to the retained earnings statement for a commercial enterprise is:
   A. statement of changes in fund balance
   B. trial balance
   C. balance sheet
   D. none of the above

**Discussion Questions**

1. (a) What types of organizations are classified as nonprofit? (b) Give three examples of nonprofit organizations.
2. What characteristics distinguish commercial enterprises from nonprofit organizations?
3. As the term is used in reference to accounting for nonprofit organizations, what is meant by "fund accounting"?
4. What concept requires all levels of management of a governmental unit to start from zero and estimate revenues and appropriations as if there had been no previous activities in their unit?
5. How are expenditures presented in a line budget?
6. What is the principal advantage of the program budget format?
7. In recording estimated revenues and appropriations as expressed in the budget, would Fund Balance be debited or credited if estimated revenues exceed appropriations?
8. If an account in the revenue ledger indicated that revenues exceeded estimated revenues, will the account have a debit or a credit balance?
9. What is the purpose of recording encumbrances in the accounts?
10. If the appropriations, expenditures, and encumbrances accounts have balances of $900,000, $600,000, and $250,000 respectively, what amount is available for commitments during the remainder of the fiscal year?
11. In the subsidiary expenditure ledger, the libraries account shows an uncommitted balance. Does this balance indicate that appropriations for the year exceed the sum of encumbrances outstanding and expenditures incurred to date?
12. (a) What account in the general ledger of a nonprofit organization is debited for purchases of long-lived assets? (b) Is depreciation generally recorded on such assets?
13. When the closing entry for the appropriations and expenditures accounts is prepared, in what account is the difference between the balances in the two accounts recorded?
14. In which financial statement will the year-end balance of the following accounts appear: (a) Reserve for Encumbrances and (b) Encumbrances?
15. What statement for a commercial corporate enterprise is similar to the statement of changes in fund balance that is prepared for each fund of a nonprofit organization?

**Exercises**

**Exercise 18-1.** The estimates of the expenditures of the Parks and Recreation Department of the City of Urbana, as submitted by the departmental supervisors for the fiscal year ending June 30, 19--, are as follows:

Parks:

| | |
|---|---|
| Supervisory salaries | $200,000 |
| Maintenance salaries | 175,000 |
| Clerical salaries | 150,000 |
| Utilities | 147,500 |
| Payroll taxes | 47,500 |
| Maintenance | 40,000 |
| Equipment purchases | 40,000 |
| Miscellaneous | 25,000 |

Recreation:

| | |
|---|---|
| Supervisory salaries | $155,000 |
| Utilities | 125,000 |
| Lifeguard salaries | 90,000 |
| Instructors' salaries | 90,000 |
| Clerical salaries | 75,000 |
| Maintenance | 70,000 |
| Payroll taxes | 37,000 |
| Equipment purchases | 30,000 |
| Miscellaneous | 20,000 |

Prepare a combined line-program budget.

**Exercise 18-2.** The budget approved for the fiscal year by the city council of Spirit Lake for the general fund indicated appropriations of $2,715,000 and estimated revenues of $2,760,000. Present the general journal entry to record the financial data indicated by the budget.

**Exercise 18-3.** An order was placed by a nonprofit organization for $19,250 of supplies. Subsequently, $16,850 of the supplies were received and $2,400 were back ordered. Present entries to record (a) the placement of the order and (b) the receipt of the supplies and the invoice for $16,850, terms n/30.

**Exercise 18-4.** Selected account balances from the general fund ledger of Truesdell Foundation at the end of the current fiscal year are as follows:

| | |
|---|---|
| Appropriations | $676,000 |
| Encumbrances | 10,000 |
| Estimated Revenues | 672,000 |
| Expenditures | 664,000 |
| Fund Balance | 92,400 |
| Reserve for Encumbrances | 10,000 |
| Revenues | 680,000 |

Prepare the appropriate closing entries.

**Exercise 18-5.** Selected account balances from the ledger of the University of Amarillo Alumni Association—General Fund are as follows:

| | |
|---|---:|
| Accounts Payable | $ 2,730 |
| Cash in Bank | 8,330 |
| Fund Balance | 80,780 |
| Marketable Securities | 35,000 |
| Petty Cash | 280 |
| Reserve for Encumbrances | 2,100 |
| Savings Accounts | 42,000 |

Prepare a balance sheet as of August 31.

**Exercise 18-6.** Data from two subsidiary ledgers of Dexter College—Intercollegiate Athletics Fund, at June 30, are as follows:

**Revenue Ledger**

| | Debits | Credits |
|---|---:|---:|
| Basketball | 87,500 | 86,250 |
| Football | 275,000 | 279,000 |
| Other | 7,500 | 8,550 |

**Expenditure Ledger**

| | Expenditures | Budget Appropriations |
|---|---:|---:|
| Administration | 43,000 | 42,000 |
| Basketball | 58,200 | 60,800 |
| Football | 185,900 | 187,600 |
| Maintenance of facilities | 31,800 | 33,600 |
| Publicity | 11,400 | 11,000 |
| Other | 27,700 | 25,000 |

Prepare a statement of revenues and expenditures—budget and actual for the fiscal year ended June 30.

**Exercise 18-7.** Selected account balances before closing on June 30, the end of the current fiscal year for C. R. Corbin Foundation—General Fund, are as follows. The fund balance account had a balance of $792,800 on July 1, the beginning of the current year.

| | |
|---|---:|
| Appropriations | $4,160,000 |
| Encumbrances | 20,000 |
| Estimated Revenues | 4,240,000 |
| Expenditures | 4,016,000 |
| Revenues | 4,120,000 |

Prepare a statement of changes in fund balance.

**Problems**
*(Problems in
Appendix B:
18-1B, 18-2B,
18-3B.)*

**Problem 18-1A.** The Mulberry Police Department prepared the following line budget for the current fiscal year:

Mulberry Police Department
Budget of Expenditures
For Year Ending June 30, 19--

| | |
|---|---:|
| Salaries | $ 950,000 |
| Patrol cars | 300,000 |
| Utilities | 240,000 |
| Building maintenance | 150,000 |
| Supplies | 125,000 |
| Miscellaneous | 50,000 |
| Total expenditures | $1,815,000 |

Estimates of the percent of each line item for each of the three principal programs of the police department are as follows:

| | Percent of Cost by Program | | |
|---|---|---|---|
| | Crime Prevention | Criminal Investigation | Community Education |
| Salaries | 55% | 35% | 10% |
| Patrol cars | 70 | 25 | 5 |
| Utilities | 30 | 60 | 10 |
| Building maintenance | 40 | 55 | 5 |
| Supplies | 60 | 25 | 15 |
| Miscellaneous | 40 | 40 | 20 |

Instructions:

Prepare a combined line-program budget for the current year.

*(If the working papers correlating with the textbook are not used, omit Problem 18-2A.)*

**Problem 18-2A.** After the closing entries were posted, the account balances in the ledger of the general fund for Woodbury on June 30, the end of the current year, are as follows:

| | |
|---|---:|
| Accounts Payable | $114,300 |
| Cash in Bank | 162,900 |
| Cash on Hand | 23,500 |
| Fund Balance | 654,700 |
| Investments in Marketable Securities | 240,000 |
| Property Taxes Receivable | 213,000 |
| Reserve for Encumbrances | 21,300 |
| Savings Accounts | 180,000 |
| Wages Payable | 29,100 |

Estimated revenues, revenues, appropriations, encumbrances, and expenditures from the respective subsidiary ledgers have been entered in the statement of revenues and expenditures—budget and actual in the working papers. The fund balance account had a balance of $631,400 on July 1, the beginning of the current year.

Instructions:

(1) Complete the statement of revenues and expenditures—budget and actual.
(2) Prepare a statement of changes in fund balance.
(3) Prepare a balance sheet.

**Problem 18-3A.** The trial balance for the City of Covington—General Fund at the beginning of the current year is as follows:

City of Covington—General Fund
Trial Balance
July 1, 19--

| | | |
|---|---:|---:|
| Cash | 455,000 | |
| Savings Accounts | 140,000 | |
| Property Taxes Receivable | 245,000 | |
| Investment in U.S. Treasury Notes | 280,000 | |
| Accounts Payable | | 245,000 |
| Wages Payable | | 38,500 |
| Fund Balance | | 836,500 |
| | 1,120,000 | 1,120,000 |

The following data summarize the operations for the current year.

(a) Estimated revenues, $6,370,000; appropriations, $6,300,000.
(b) Revenues from property tax levy, $4,900,000.
(c) Cash received from property taxes, $5,000,000; other revenues, $1,540,000.
(d) Expenditures for payrolls, $2,870,000.
(e) Expenditures encumbered and evidenced by purchase orders, $3,535,000.
(f) Liquidation of encumbrances and vouchers prepared, $3,510,000.
(g) Cash disbursed for vouchers, $3,515,000; for payment of wages, $2,880,000; for savings accounts, $100,000.

Instructions:

(1) Prepare entries in general journal form to record the foregoing summarized operations.
(2) Open T accounts for the accounts appearing in the trial balance and enter the balances as of July 1, identifying them as "Bal."
(3) Open T accounts for Reserve for Encumbrances, Estimated Revenues, Revenues, Appropriations, Expenditures, and Encumbrances. Post the entries recorded in (1) to the accounts, using the identifying letters in place of dates.
(4) Prepare the appropriate entries to close the accounts as of June 30 and post to the accounts, using the letter "C" to identify the postings.
(5) Prepare a trial balance as of June 30.

**Problem 18-4A.** The account balances in the general fund ledger of the City of Tallulah Falls on June 30, the end of the current fiscal year, are as follows:

| | | |
|---|---|---:|
| Cash on Hand | $ | 3,000 |
| Cash in Bank | | 204,600 |
| Savings Accounts | | 250,000 |

| | |
|---|---:|
| Property Taxes Receivable | $ 100,000 |
| Accounts Payable | 40,200 |
| Wages Payable | 25,800 |
| Reserve for Encumbrances | 11,200 |
| Estimated Revenues | 3,375,000 |
| Revenues | 3,390,000 |
| Appropriations | 3,350,000 |
| Expenditures | 3,353,500 |
| Encumbrances | 11,200 |

The total of the debits and credits in the revenue ledger are as follows:

| | Debits | Credits |
|---|---:|---:|
| General property taxes | 2,580,000 | 2,600,000 |
| Sales taxes | 612,000 | 601,000 |
| Motor vehicle licenses | 116,000 | 118,000 |
| Interest on savings accounts | 25,000 | 26,500 |
| Miscellaneous | 42,000 | 44,500 |

Data from the expenditure ledger are as follows:

| | Expenditures | Budget Appropriations |
|---|---:|---:|
| General government | 1,123,500 | 1,110,000 |
| Police department | 660,000 | 666,000 |
| Fire department | 514,900 | 528,000 |
| Streets and roads | 498,000 | 482,000 |
| Sanitation | 353,100 | 354,000 |
| Public welfare | 204,000 | 210,000 |

The encumbrances balances in the expenditure ledger are as follows:

| | |
|---|---:|
| General government | 4,300 |
| Fire department | 2,500 |
| Sanitation | 4,400 |

Instructions:

(1) Prepare a statement of revenues and expenditures—budget and actual.
(2) Prepare a statement of changes in fund balance. The fund balance account had a balance of $455,100 on July 1, the beginning of the current fiscal year.
(3) Prepare a balance sheet.

**Mini-Case**

During a recent visit with your parents over Thanksgiving vacation, your mother was discussing her recent election to the Unit 4 School Board. At the first board meeting, she was presented with the following operating budget for the current year:

Unit 4 School District
Budget of Expenditures
For Year Ending June 30, 19--

| | |
|---|---|
| Teachers' salaries | $4,250,000 |
| Administrative salaries | 1,150,000 |
| Transportation | 1,000,000 |
| Utilities | 900,000 |
| Maintenance | 850,000 |
| Equipment purchases | 750,000 |
| Supplies | 200,000 |
| Miscellaneous | 400,000 |
| Total expenditures | $9,500,000 |

The school district, like all public school districts, has limited resources available to conduct its programs. These resources are generally from taxes, and knowing that the likelihood of tax increases is almost nil in the near future, your mother is especially interested in studying the allocation of these scarce resources among the various district programs. These programs have been classified as Primary Education, Secondary Education, Adult Education, Community Service Programs, and Extra-curricular Programs. Your mother has asked you whether or not future budgets can be presented in a format that would be more useful in evaluating the programs.

Instructions:

(1) Briefly indicate the advantages and disadvantages of the current budget format for use in evaluating the district programs.
(2) Suggest a budget format that might be more useful in the evaluation of the district programs. Include an illustration of the recommended budget.
(3) Suggest factors other than proposed expenditures that might be considered in evaluating the district programs.

APPENDIX

# Glossary

## A

**Absorption costing.** The concept that considers the cost of manufactured products to be composed of direct materials, direct labor, and factory overhead.

**Accelerated Cost Recovery System (ACRS).** The system described in the Internal Revenue Code for determining depreciation (cost recovery) of plant asset acquisitions.

**Accounting.** The process of identifying, measuring, and communicating economic information to permit informed judgments and decisions by users of the information.

**Accounts receivable turnover.** The relationship between credit sales and accounts receivable, computed by dividing net sales on account by the average net accounts receivable.

**Acid-test ratio.** The ratio of the sum of cash, receivables, and marketable securities to current liabilities.

**Annuity.** A series of equal cash flows at fixed intervals.

**Appropriation.** A designated use of revenues for which a potential liability is recognized by nonprofit organizations.

**Average rate of return.** A method of evaluating capital investment proposals that focuses on the expected profitability of the investment.

## B

**Break-even point.** The point in the operations of an enterprise at which revenues and expired costs are equal.

**Budget.** A formal written statement of management's plans for the future, expressed in financial terms.

**Budget performance report.** A report comparing actual results with budget figures.

**By-product.** A product resulting from a manufacturing process and having little value in relation to the principal product or joint products.

## C

**Capital expenditures budget.** The budget summarizing future plans for acquisition of plant facilities and equipment.

**Capital gain or loss.** A gain or loss resulting from the sale or exchange of a capital asset, as defined by the Internal Revenue Code and given special treatment for federal income tax purposes.

**Capital investment analysis.** The process by which management plans, evaluates, and controls long-term capital investments involving property, plant, and equipment.

**Capital rationing.** The process by which management allocates available investment funds among competing capital investment proposals.

**Cash payback period.** The expected period of time that will elapse between the date of a capital investment and the complete recovery in cash (or equivalent) of the amount invested.

**Clock cards.** The form on which the amount of time spent by an employee in the factory is recorded.

**Combined line-program budget.** A budget that combines the advantages of both the line and program budget by adding a total column to the program budget.

Common-size statement. A financial statement in which all items are expressed only in relative terms.

Completed-contract method. The method that recognizes revenue from long-term construction contracts when the project is completed.

Constant dollar statements. The financial statements that result when historical costs reported in conventional statements are converted to dollars of common (or constant) purchasing power.

Continuous budgeting. A method of budgeting that provides for maintenance of a twelve-month projection into the future.

Contribution margin. Sales less variable cost of goods sold and variable selling and general expenses.

Contribution margin ratio. The percentage of each sales dollar that is available to cover the fixed expenses and provide an operating income.

Control. The process of directing operations to achieve the organization's goals and plans.

Controller. The chief managerial accountant of an organization.

Cost center. A decentralized unit in which the responsibility for control of costs incurred and the authority to make decisions that affect these costs is the responsibility of the unit's manager.

Cost ledger. A subsidiary ledger employed in a job order cost system and which contains an account for each job order.

Cost of goods sold. The cost of the manufactured product sold.

Cost of production report. A report prepared periodically by a processing department, summarizing (1) the units for which the department is accountable and the disposition of these units and (2) the costs charged to the department and the allocation of these costs.

Cost price approach. An approach to transfer pricing that uses cost as the basis for setting the transfer price.

Cost-volume-profit analysis. The systematic examination of the interrelationships between selling prices, volume of sales and production, costs, expenses, and profits.

Cost-volume-profit chart. A chart used to assist management in understanding the relationships between costs, expenses, sales, and operating profit or loss.

Current cost statements. The financial statements that result when historical costs reported in conventional statements are adjusted for specific price-level changes, so that all elements of the statements are reported at their current costs.

Currently attainable standards. Standards which represent levels of operation that can be attained with reasonable effort.

Current ratio. The ratio of current assets to current liabilities.

## D

Decentralization. The separation of a business into more manageable units.

Decision tree. A graphical representation of decisions, possible outcomes, and chances that outcomes will occur.

Deflation. A period when prices in general are falling and the purchasing power of money is increasing.

Departmental margin. Departmental gross profit less direct departmental expenses.

Differential analysis. The area of accounting concerned with the effect of alternative courses of action on revenues and costs.

Differential cost. The amount of increase or decrease in cost that is expected from a particular course of action compared with an alternative.

Differential revenue. The amount of increase or decrease in revenue expected from a particular course of action as compared with an alternative.

Direct expense. An expense directly traceable to or incurred for the sole benefit of a specific department and ordinarily subject to the control of the department manager.

Direct labor. Wages of factory workers who convert materials into a finished product.

Direct labor rate variance. The cost associated with the difference between the actual rate paid for direct labor used in producing a commodity and the standard rate for the commodity.

Direct labor time variance. The cost associated with the difference between the actual direct labor hours spent producing a commodity and the standard hours for the commodity.

Direct materials. The cost of materials that enter directly into the finished product.

Direct materials price variance. The cost associated with the difference between the actual price of direct materials used in producing a commodity and the standard price for the commodity.

Direct materials quantity variance. The cost associated with the difference between the actual quantity of direct materials used in producing a commodity and the standard quantity for the commodity.

Discounted cash flow method. A method of analysis of proposed capital investments that focuses on the present value of the cash flows expected from the investment.

Discounted internal rate of return method. A method of analysis of proposed capital investments that focuses on using present value concepts to compute the rate of return from the net cash flows expected from the investment.

E

Earnings per share (EPS) on common stock. The profitability ratio of net income available to common shareholders to the number of common shares outstanding.

Economic order quantity (EOQ). The optimum quantity of specified inventoriable materials to be ordered at one time.

Economies of scale. An economic concept that implies that, for a given amount of facilities, it is more efficient to produce and sell large quantities than small quantities.

Encumbrance. A commitment by a nonprofit organization to incur expenditures in the future.

Equivalent units of production. The number of units that could have been manufactured from start to finish during a period.

Expected value. A concept useful for managers in decision making which involves identifying the possible outcomes from a decision and estimating the likelihood that each outcome will occur.

F

Factory overhead. All of the costs of operating the factory except for direct materials and direct labor.

Factory overhead controllable variance. The difference between the actual amount of factory overhead cost incurred and the amount of factory overhead budgeted for the level of operations achieved.

Factory overhead volume variance. The cost or benefit associated with operating at a level above or below 100% of productive capacity.

Financial accounting. The branch of accounting that is concerned with the recording of transactions using generally accepted accounting principles (GAAP) for a business enterprise or other economic unit and with a periodic preparation of various statements from such records.

Finished goods. Goods in the state in which they are to be sold.

Finished goods ledger. The subsidiary ledger that contains the individual accounts for each kind of commodity produced.

Fixed expense (cost). An expense (cost) that tends to remain constant in amount regardless of variations in volume of activity.

Flexible budget. A series of budgets for varying rates of activity.

Fund. A term with multiple meanings, including (1) segregations of cash for a special purpose, (2) working capital or cash as reported in the funds statement, (3) in accounting for nonprofit organizations, an accounting entity with accounts maintained for recording assets, liabilities, capital (called fund balance), revenues, and expenditures for a particular purpose.

Funds statement. The statement of changes in financial position.

## G

Generally accepted accounting principles. Generally accepted guidelines for the preparation of financial statements.

General price-level change. The change over time in the amount of money needed to purchase a general group of goods and services.

Gross profit analysis. The procedure used to develop information concerning the effect of changes in quantities and unit prices on sales and cost of goods sold.

## H

High-low method. A method used to estimate total cost as well as variable and fixed components by using the highest and lowest total costs revealed by past cost patterns.

Holding gains and losses. Gains and losses that result from the holding of nonmonetary assets.

Horizontal analysis. The percentage analysis of increases and decreases in corresponding items in comparative financial statements.

## I

Indirect expense. An expense that is incurred for an entire business enterprise as a unit and that is not subject to the control of individual department managers.

Inflation. A period when prices in general are rising and the purchasing power of money is declining.

Installment method. The method of recognizing revenue, whereby each receipt of cash from installment sales is considered to be composed of partial payment of cost of merchandise sold and gross profit.

Internal Revenue Code (IRC). The codification of current federal tax statutes.

Inventory order point. The level to which inventory is allowed to fall before an order for additional inventory is placed.

Inventory turnover. The relationship between the volume of goods sold and inventory, computed by dividing the cost of goods sold by the average inventory.

Investment center. A decentralized unit in which the manager has the responsibility and authority to make decisions that affect not only cost and revenues, but also the plant assets available to the center.

Investment tax credit. An income tax credit allowed for the purchase of capital assets which reduces the amount of federal income tax payable.

Investment turnover. A component of the rate of return on investment, computed as the ratio of sales to invested assets.

## J

Job cost sheet. An account in the cost ledger in which the costs charged to a particular job order are recorded.

Job order cost system. A type of cost system that provides for a separate record of the cost of each particular quantity of product that passes through the factory.

Joint cost. The cost common to the manufacture of two or more products (joint products).

Joint products. Two or more commodities of significant value produced from a single principal direct material.

## L

Lead time. The time, usually expressed in days, that it takes to receive an order for inventory.

Learning effect (learning curve). The effect on costs determined by how rapidly new employees learn their jobs or by how rapidly experienced employees learn new job assignments.

Least squares method. A method that uses statistics to estimate total cost and the fixed and variable cost components.

**Leverage.** The tendency of the rate earned on stockholders' equity to vary from the rate earned on total assets because the amount earned on assets acquired through the use of funds provided by creditors varies from the interest paid to these creditors.

**Line budget.** A budget in which items of expenditure are presented by the "object" of the expenditure, that is, by the "reason" for the expenditure.

**Linear programming.** A quantitative method that can be used in providing data for solving a variety of business problems in which management's objective is to minimize cost or maximize profits, subject to several limiting factors.

## M

**Management.** Individuals who are charged with the responsibility of directing the operations of enterprises.

**Managerial accounting.** The branch of accounting that uses both historical and estimated data in providing information which management uses in conducting daily operations and in planning future operations.

**Manufacturing margin.** Sales less variable cost of goods sold.

**Marginal cost.** The increase in total cost of producing and selling an additional unit of product.

**Marginal revenue.** The increase (or decrease) in total revenue realized from the sale of an additional unit of product.

**Marginal tax rate.** The highest rate applied to the income of any particular taxpayer.

**Margin of safety.** The difference between current sales revenue and the sales at the break-even point.

**Market price approach.** An approach to transfer pricing that uses the price at which the product or service transferred could be sold to outside buyers as the transfer price.

**Market (sales) value method.** A method of allocating joint costs among products according to their relative sales values.

**Markup.** An amount which is added to a "cost" amount to determine product price.

**Master budget.** The comprehensive budget plan encompassing all the individual budgets related to sales, cost of goods sold, operating expenses, capital expenditures, and cash.

**Materials.** Goods in the state in which they were acquired for use in manufacturing operations.

**Materials ledger.** The subsidiary ledger containing the individual accounts for each type of material.

**Materials requisition.** The form used by the appropriate manufacturing department to authorize the issuance of materials from the storeroom.

**Maximax concept.** A concept useful for managerial decision making, which leads management to decide in favor of that alternative with the maximum (largest) profit.

**Maximin concept.** A concept useful for managerial decision making, which leads management to decide in favor of that alternative with the maximum (largest) minimum profit.

**Mixed cost.** A cost with both variable and fixed characteristics, sometimes referred to as semivariable or semifixed cost.

**Monetary items.** Money or a claim to receive money or an obligation to pay a fixed amount of money.

## N

**Negotiated price approach.** An approach to transfer pricing that allows the managers of decentralized units to agree (negotiate) among themselves as to the proper transfer price.

**Nonmonetary items.** All items, such as inventories, plant assets, common stock, and retained earnings, that are not classified as monetary items.

**Number of days' sales in inventory.** The relationship between the volume of goods sold and inventory, computed by dividing the inventory at the end of the year by the average daily cost of goods sold.

**Number of days' sales in receivables.** The relationship between credit sales and accounts receivable, computed by dividing the net accounts receivable at the end of the year by the average daily sales on account.

## O-Q

Opportunity cost. The amount of income that would result from the best available alternative to a proposed use of cash or its equivalent.

Overapplied factory overhead. The amount of factory overhead applied in excess of the actual factory overhead costs incurred for production during a period.

Payoff table. A table that summarizes the possible outcomes of one or more decisions for management's use in decision making.

Percentage-of-completion method. The method of recognizing revenue from long-term contracts over the entire life of the contract.

Planning. The process of setting goals for the use of an organization's resources and developing ways to achieve these goals.

Predetermined factory overhead rate. The rate used to apply factory overhead costs to the goods manufactured.

Present value. The estimated present worth of an amount of cash to be received (or paid) in the future.

Present value index. An index computed by dividing the total present value of the net cash flow to be received from a proposed capital investment by the amount to be invested.

Present value of an annuity. The sum of the present values of a series of equal cash flows to be received at fixed intervals.

Price-earnings (P/E) ratio. The ratio of the market price per share of common stock, at a specific date, to the annual earnings per share.

Price graph. A graph used to determine the price-cost combination that maximizes the total profit of an enterprise by plotting the marginal revenues and marginal costs.

Price theory. A separate discipline in the area of microeconomics which studies the setting of product prices.

Process cost system. A type of cost system that accumulates costs for each of the various departments or processes within a factory.

Processing cost. The direct labor and factory overhead costs associated with the manufacture of a product.

Product cost concept. A concept used in applying the cost-plus approach to product pricing in which only the costs of manufacturing the product, termed the product cost, are included in the cost amount to which the markup is added.

Profitability. The ability of a firm to earn income.

Profit center. A decentralized unit in which the manager has the responsibility and the authority to make decisions that affect both cost and revenues (and thus profits).

Profit margin. A component of the rate of return on investment, computed as the ratio of operating income to sales.

Profit-volume chart. A chart used to assist management in understanding the relationship between profit and volume.

Program budget. A budget in which items of expenditure are presented by the services or programs provided by the nonprofit organization.

Purchase order. The form issued by the purchasing department to suppliers, requesting the delivery of materials.

Purchase requisition. The form used to inform the purchasing department that items are needed by a business.

Purchasing power gains and losses. Gains and losses that result from holding monetary items during periods of price-level change.

Quick assets. The sum of cash, receivables, and marketable securities.

## R

Rate earned on common stockholders' equity. A measure of profitability computed by dividing net income, reduced by preferred dividend requirements, by common stockholders' equity.

Rate earned on stockholders' equity. A measure of profitability computed by dividing net income by total stockholders' equity.

Rate earned on total assets. A measure of the profitability of assets, without regard to the equity of creditors and stockholders in the assets.

Rate of return on investment (ROI). A measure of managerial efficiency in the use of investments in assets.

Receiving report. The form used by the receiving department to indicate that materials have been received and inspected.

Residual income. The excess of divisional operating income over a "minimum" amount of desired operating income.

Responsibility accounting. The process of measuring and reporting operating data by areas of responsibility.


**S**

Safety stock. The amount of inventory that serves as a reserve for unforeseen circumstances, and therefore is not normally used in regular operations.

Sales mix. The relative distribution of sales among the various products available for sale.

Scattergraph method. A method that uses a graph to estimate total cost and the fixed and variable cost components.

Service department. A factory department that does not process materials directly but renders services for the benefit of production departments.

Simplex method. A mathematical equation approach to linear programming, which is often used more practically with a computer.

Solvency. The ability of a firm to pay its debts as they come due.

Specific price-level change. The change over time in the amount of money needed to purchase individual goods and services.

Standard costs. Detailed estimates of what a product should cost.

Standard cost system. An accounting system that uses standards for each element of manufacturing costs entering into the finished product.

Statement of changes in financial position. A basic financial statement devoted exclusively to reporting changes in financial position for a specified period of time.

Statement of changes in fund balance. The statement for a nonprofit enterprise that is similar to the retained earnings statement for a commercial enterprise.

Statement of cost of goods manufactured. A separate statement for a manufacturer that reports the cost of goods manufactured during a period.

Strategic planning. The process of establishing long-term goals for an enterprise and developing ways to achieve these goals.

Sunk cost. A cost that is not affected by subsequent decisions.


**T**

Taxable income. The base on which the amount of income tax is determined.

Theoretical standards. Standards that represent levels of performance that can be achieved only under perfect operating conditions, such as no idle time, no machine breakdowns, and no materials spoilage.

Time tickets. The form on which the amount of time spent by each employee and the labor cost incurred for each individual job, or for factory overhead, are recorded.

Total cost concept. A concept used in applying the cost-plus approach to product pricing in which all costs of manufacturing a product plus the selling and general expenses are included in the cost amount to which the markup is added.

Transfer price. The price charged one decentralized unit by another for the goods or services provided.

## U-V

**Underapplied factory overhead.** The amount of actual factory overhead in excess of the factory overhead applied to production during a period.

**Value of perfect information.** The maximum amount (cost) that will be paid to obtain perfect information concerning a decision.

**Variable cost concept.** A concept used in applying the cost-plus approach to product pricing in which only variable costs and expenses are included in the cost amount to which the markup is added.

**Variable costing.** The concept that considers the cost of products manufactured to be composed only of those manufacturing costs that increase or decrease as the volume of production rises or falls (direct materials, direct labor, and variable factory overhead).

**Variable expense (cost).** An expense (cost) that tends to fluctuate in amount in accordance with variations in volume of activity.

**Variances from standard.** Difference between standard cost and actual cost.

**Vertical analysis.** The percentage analysis of component parts in relation to the total of the parts in a single financial statement.

## W-Z

**Working capital.** The excess of total current assets over total current liabilities at some point in time.

**Work in process.** Goods in the process of manufacture.

**Zero-base budgeting.** A concept of budgeting that requires all levels of management to start from zero and estimate budget data as if there had been no previous activities in their unit.

# Series B Problems

**CHAPTER 2** | **Problem 2-1B.** Pendaflex Printing Company uses a job order cost system. The following data summarize the operations related to production for September, the first month of operations:

(a) Materials purchased on account, $47,850.

(b) Materials requisitioned and factory labor used:

|  | Materials | Factory Labor |
|---|---|---|
| Job 1001 | $9,720 | $7,630 |
| Job 1002 | 2,780 | 1,640 |
| Job 1003 | 7,100 | 3,910 |
| Job 1004 | 3,570 | 1,580 |
| Job 1005 | 5,680 | 2,410 |
| Job 1006 | 5,150 | 3,850 |
| For general factory use | 1,540 | 2,380 |

(c) Factory overhead costs incurred on account, $9,390.

(d) Depreciation of machinery and equipment, $4,510.

(e) The factory overhead rate is 60% of direct labor cost.

(f) Jobs completed: 1001, 1002, 1003, and 1004.

(g) Jobs 1001, 1002, and 1004 were shipped and customers were billed for $30,100, $7,300, and $8,500 respectively.

Instructions:

(1) Prepare entries in general journal form to record the foregoing summarized operations.

(2) Open T accounts for Work in Process and Finished Goods and post the appropriate entries, using the identifying letters as dates. Insert memorandum account balances as of the end of the month.

(3) Prepare a schedule of unfinished jobs to support the balance in the work in process account.

(4) Prepare a schedule of completed jobs on hand to support the balance in the finished goods account.

*(If the working papers correlating with the textbook are not used, omit Problem 2-2B.)*

**Problem 2-2B.** Rubinstein Furniture Company repairs, refinishes, and reupholsters furniture. A job order cost system was installed recently to facilitate (1) the determination of price quotations to prospective customers, (2) the determination of actual costs incurred on each job, and (3) cost reductions.

In response to a prospective customer's request for a price quotation on a job, the estimated cost data are inserted on an unnumbered job cost sheet. If the offer is accepted, a number is assigned to the job and the costs incurred are recorded in the usual manner on the job cost sheet. After the job is completed, reasons for the variances between the estimated and actual costs are noted on the sheet. The data are then available to management in evaluating the efficiency of operations and in preparing quotations on future jobs.

On November 18, an estimate of $742 for reupholstering a chair and couch was given to Chris Joel. The estimate was based upon the following data:

| | |
|---|---|
| Estimated direct materials: | |
| 20 meters at $16 per meter.............................. | $320 |
| Estimated direct labor: | |
| 14 hours at $10 per hour................................. | 140 |
| Estimated factory overhead (50% of direct labor cost)........... | 70 |
| Total estimated costs ...................................... | $530 |
| Markup (40% of production costs) ......................... | 212 |
| Total estimate........................................... | $742 |

On November 21, the chair and couch were picked up from the residence of Chris Joel, 4810 Beekman Place, Racine, with a commitment to return it on November 30. The job was completed on November 28.

The related materials requisitions and time tickets are summarized as follows:

| Materials Requisition No. | Description | Amount |
|---|---|---|
| 715 | 6 meters at $16 | $ 96 |
| 718 | 10 meters at $16 | 160 |
| 723 | 6 meters at $16 | 96 |

| Time Ticket No. | Description | Amount |
|---|---|---|
| 471 | 4 hours at $10 | $ 40 |
| 478 | 8 hours at $10 | 80 |
| 481 | 3 hours at $10 | 30 |

Instructions:

(1) Complete that portion of the job order cost sheet that would be completed when the estimate is given to the customer.
(2) Assign number 85-11-8 to the job, record the costs incurred, and complete the job order cost sheet. In commenting upon the variances between actual costs and estimated costs, assume that 2 meters of materials were spoiled, the factory overhead rate has been proved to be satisfactory, and an inexperienced employee performed the work.

**Problem 2-4B.** The trial balance of the general ledger of J. J. Koehn Co. as of July 31, the end of the first month of the current fiscal year, is as follows:

**J. J. Koehn Co.**
**Trial Balance**
**July 31, 19--**

| | | |
|---|---|---|
| Cash | 45,700 | |
| Accounts Receivable | 92,650 | |
| Finished Goods | 88,650 | |
| Work in Process | 30,700 | |
| Materials | 36,900 | |
| Plant Assets | 395,500 | |
| Accumulated Depreciation—Plant Assets | | 176,450 |
| Accounts Payable | | 66,485 |
| Wages Payable | | 7,500 |
| Capital Stock | | 300,000 |
| Retained Earnings | | 125,325 |
| Sales | | 132,700 |
| Cost of Goods Sold | 98,400 | |
| Factory Overhead | 460 | |
| Selling and General Expenses | 19,500 | |
| | 808,460 | 808,460 |

As of the same date, balances in the accounts of selected subsidiary ledgers are as follows:

Finished goods ledger:
  Commodity A, 1,100 units, $9,900; Commodity B, 2,500 units, $55,000; Commodity C, 1,250 units, $23,750.

Cost ledger:
  Job 915, $30,700.

Materials ledger:
  Material X, $20,200; Material Y, $15,800; Material Z, $900.

The transactions completed during August are summarized as follows:

(a) Materials were purchased on account as follows:
  Material X ......... $27,500
  Material Y ......... 19,250
  Material Z ......... 750
(b) Materials were requisitioned from stores as follows:
  Job 915, Material X, $10,600; Material Y, $8,400 ......... $19,000
  Job 916, Material X, $13,500; Material Y, $11,900 ......... 25,400
  Job 917, Material X, $6,900; Material Y, $2,800 ......... 9,700
  For general factory use, Material Z ......... 800
(c) Time tickets for the month were chargeable as follows:
  Job 915 ......... $9,800    Job 917 ......... $8,200
  Job 916 ......... 8,400    Indirect labor ......... 3,000
(d) Factory payroll checks for $29,700 were issued.
(e) Various factory overhead charges of $4,940 were incurred on account.
(f) Selling and general expenses of $19,100 were incurred on account.
(g) Payments on account were $71,500.
(h) Depreciation of $4,500 on factory plant and equipment was recorded.

(i) Factory overhead was applied to jobs at 50% of direct labor cost.

(j) Jobs completed during the month were as follows: Job 915 produced 2,800 units of Commodity B; Job 916 produced 2,000 units of Commodity C.

(k) Total sales on account were $122,950. The goods sold were as follows (use first-in, first-out method): 500 units of Commodity A; 2,700 units of Commodity B; 1,500 units of Commodity C.

(l) Cash of $125,500 was received on accounts receivable.

Instructions:

(1) Open T accounts for the general ledger, the finished goods ledger, the cost ledger, and the materials ledger. Record directly in these accounts the balances as of July 31, identifying them as "Bal." Record the quantities as well as the dollar amounts in the finished goods ledger.

(2) Prepare entries in general journal form to record the August transactions. After recording each transaction, post to the T accounts, using the identifying letters as dates. When posting to the finished goods ledger, record quantities as well as dollar amounts.

(3) Prepare a trial balance.

(4) Prepare schedules of the account balances in the finished goods ledger, the cost ledger, and the materials ledger.

(5) Prepare an income statement for the two months ended August 31.

**Problem 2-5B.** Following are selected accounts for Gould Industrial Products. For the purposes of this problem, some of the debits and credits have been omitted.

### Accounts Receivable

| | | | | |
|---|---|---|---|---|
| Aug. | 1 Balance | 40,800 | Aug. 31 Collections | 60,175 |
| | 31 Sales | (A) | | |

### Materials

| | | | | |
|---|---|---|---|---|
| Aug. | 1 Balance | 10,050 | Aug. 31 Requisitions | (B) |
| | 31 Purchases | 15,190 | | |

### Work in Process

| | | | | |
|---|---|---|---|---|
| Aug. | 1 Balance | 11,775 | Aug. 31 Goods finished | (E) |
| | 31 Direct materials | (C) | | |
| | 31 Direct labor | 24,000 | | |
| | 31 Factory overhead | (D) | | |

### Finished Goods

| | | | | |
|---|---|---|---|---|
| Aug. | 1 Balance | 5,585 | Aug. 31 Cost of goods sold | (G) |
| | 31 Goods finished | (F) | | |

### Factory Overhead

| | | | | |
|---|---|---|---|---|
| Aug. | 1 Balance | 200 | Aug. 31 Applied (80% of | |
| | 1–31 Costs incurred | 18,790 | direct labor cost) | (H) |

| Cost of Goods Sold | | |
| --- | --- | --- |
| Aug. 31 | (I) | |

| Sales | | |
| --- | --- | --- |
| | Aug. 31 | (J) |

Selected balances at August 31:

| | |
| --- | --- |
| Accounts receivable | $44,375 |
| Finished goods | 11,195 |
| Work in process | 14,070 |
| Materials | 7,620 |

Materials requisitions for August included $750 of materials issued for general factory use. All sales are made on account, terms n/30.

Instructions:

(1) Determine the amounts represented by the letters (A) through (J), presenting your computations.

(2) Determine the amount of factory overhead overapplied or underapplied as of August 31.

**CHAPTER 3** | **Problem 3-1B.** Rutherford Company manufactures Product G. Material A is placed in process in Department 1, where it is ground and partially refined. The output of Department 1 is transferred to Department 2, where Material B is added at the beginning of the process and the refining is completed. On March 1, Rutherford Company had the following inventories:

| | |
| --- | --- |
| Finished goods (4,100 units) | $71,750 |
| Work in process — Department 1 | — |
| Work in process — Department 2 (2,100 units, ⅔ completed) | 34,230 |
| Materials | 40,980 |

Departmental accounts are maintained for factory overhead and there is one service department, Factory Office. Manufacturing operations for March are summarized as follows:

| | | |
| --- | --- | --- |
| (a) | Materials purchased on account | $21,800 |
| (b) | Materials requisitioned for use: | |
| | Material A | $34,470 |
| | Material B | 6,560 |
| | Indirect materials — Department 1 | 1,440 |
| | Indirect materials — Department 2 | 360 |
| (c) | Labor used: | |
| | Direct labor — Department 1 | $48,700 |
| | Direct labor — Department 2 | 20,500 |
| | Indirect labor — Department 1 | 2,800 |
| | Indirect labor — Department 2 | 1,280 |
| | Factory Office | 2,300 |
| (d) | Depreciation charged on plant assets: | |
| | Department 1 | $19,900 |
| | Department 2 | 9,600 |
| | Factory Office | 1,100 |

(e) Miscellaneous costs incurred on account:
    Department 1............................................... $ 3,690
    Department 2...............................................     2,310
    Factory Office .............................................     1,200

(f) Expiration of prepaid expenses:
    Department 1............................................... $ 2,280
    Department 2...............................................       490
    Factory Office .............................................       750

(g) Distribution of Factory Office costs:
    Department 1...................... 60% of total Factory Office costs
    Department 2...................... 40% of total Factory Office costs

(h) Application of factory overhead costs:
    Department 1.............................. 70% of direct labor cost
    Department 2.............................. 80% of direct labor cost

(i) Production costs transferred from Department 1 to Department 2:
    8,200 units were fully processed and there was no inventory of work in process in Department 1 at March 31.

(j) Production costs transferred from Department 2 to finished goods:
    7,500 units, including the inventory at March 1, were fully processed. There were 2,800 units ¾ completed at March 31.

(k) Cost of goods sold during March:
    8,000 units (use the first-in, first-out method in crediting the finished goods account).

Instructions:

(1) Prepare entries in general journal form to record the foregoing operations. Identify each entry by letter.

(2) Compute the March 31 work in process inventory for Department 2.

**Problem 3-4B.** Pugh Company manufactures Product J by a series of four processes, all materials being introduced in Department 1. From Department 1, the materials pass through Departments 2, 3, and 4, emerging as finished Product J. All inventories are priced at cost by the first-in, first-out method.

The balances in the accounts Work in Process—Department 4 and Finished Goods were as follows on March 1:

Work in Process—Department 4 (4,000 units, ¾ completed)......... $40,400
Finished Goods (7,200 units at $12.50 a unit) .....................   90,000

The following costs were charged to Work in Process—Department 4 during March:

Direct materials transferred from Department 3: 24,000 units
  at $4.80 a unit.......................................... $115,200
Direct labor...............................................   127,260
Factory overhead...........................................    42,420

During March, 21,600 units of J were completed and 20,800 units were sold. Inventories on March 31 were as follows:

Work in Process—Department 4: 6,400 units, ¼ completed
Finished Goods: 8,000 units

Instructions:

(1) Determine the following, presenting computations in good order:
    (a) Equivalent units of production for Department 4 during March.

(b) Unit processing cost for Department 4 for March.
(c) Total and unit cost of Product J started in a prior period and finished in March.
(d) Total and unit cost of Product J started and finished in March.
(e) Total cost of goods transferred to finished goods.
(f) Work in process inventory for Department 4, March 31.
(g) Cost of goods sold (indicate number of units and unit costs).
(h) Finished goods inventory, March 31.
(2) Prepare a cost of production report for Department 4 for March.

**Problem 3-6B.** A process cost system is used to record the costs of manufacturing Product CE5, which requires a series of three processes. The inventory of Work in Process—Department 3 on August 1 and debits to the account during August were as follows:

| | |
|---|---:|
| Balance, 2,400 units, ⅔ completed | $ 23,280 |
| From Department 2, 10,500 units | 18,900 |
| Direct labor | 101,352 |
| Factory overhead | 25,338 |

During August, the 2,400 units in process on August 1 were completed, and of the 10,500 units entering the department, all were completed except 4,000 units, which were ¾ completed.

Charges to Work in Process—Department 3 for September were as follows:

| | |
|---|---:|
| From Department 2, 12,200 units | $ 21,350 |
| Direct labor | 127,000 |
| Factory overhead | 31,750 |

During September, the units in process at the beginning of the month were completed, and of the 12,200 units entering the department, all were completed except 1,500 units, which were ⅔ completed.

Instructions:
(1) Set up an account for Work in Process—Department 3. Enter the balance as of August 1 and record the debits and the credits in the account for August. Present computations for the determination of (a) equivalent units of production, (b) unit processing cost, (c) cost of goods finished, differentiating between units started in the prior period and units started and finished in August, and (d) work in process inventory.
(2) Record the transactions for September in the account. Present the computations listed in instruction (1).
(3) Determine the difference in unit cost between the product started and completed in August and the product started and completed in September. Determine also the amount of the difference attributable collectively to operations in Departments 1 and 2 and the amount attributable to operations in Department 3.

**CHAPTER 4 ı Problem 4-1B.** Alliance Company prepared the following factory overhead cost budget for November of the current year for 21,250 units of product:

Alliance Company
Factory Overhead Cost Budget
For Month Ending November 30, 19--

| | | |
|---|---:|---:|
| Variable cost: | | |
| Indirect factory wages | $17,000 | |
| Indirect materials | 10,540 | |
| Power and light | 7,480 | |
| Total variable cost | | $ 35,020 |
| Fixed cost: | | |
| Supervisory salaries | $23,640 | |
| Indirect factory wages | 8,730 | |
| Depreciation of plant and equipment | 16,200 | |
| Insurance | 14,400 | |
| Power and light | 7,530 | |
| Property taxes | 9,800 | |
| Total fixed cost | | 80,300 |
| Total factory overhead cost | | $115,320 |

The following factory overhead costs were incurred in producing 18,750 units in November:

| | |
|---|---:|
| Indirect factory wages | $ 23,230 |
| Supervisory salaries | 23,640 |
| Indirect materials | 9,275 |
| Power and light | 14,680 |
| Depreciation of plant and equipment | 16,200 |
| Insurance | 14,400 |
| Property taxes | 9,800 |
| Total factory overhead cost incurred | $111,225 |

Instructions:

(1) Prepare a flexible factory overhead cost budget for November, indicating capacities of 18,750, 21,250, 25,000 and 30,000 units of product.
(2) Prepare a budget performance report for November.

**Problem 4-3B.** Trane Company prepared the sales budget on page 467 for the current year.

At the end of September, 1985, the following unit sales data were reported for the first nine months of the year:

| | Unit Sales | |
|---|---|---|
| | Product A | Product B |
| East | 32,400 | 28,350 |
| Central | 14,850 | 24,750 |
| West | 18,000 | 33,750 |

Trane Company
Sales Budget
For Year Ending December 31, 1985

| Product and Area | Unit Sales Volume | Unit Selling Price | Total Sales |
|---|---|---|---|
| Product A: | | | |
| East.......................... | 36,000 | $10.00 | $ 360,000 |
| Central ...................... | 18,000 | 10.00 | 180,000 |
| West ........................ | 24,000 | 10.00 | 240,000 |
| Total .................... | 78,000 | | $ 780,000 |
| | | | |
| Product B: | | | |
| East.......................... | 42,000 | $15.00 | $ 630,000 |
| Central ...................... | 30,000 | 15.00 | 450,000 |
| West ........................ | 45,000 | 15.00 | 675,000 |
| Total .................... | 117,000 | | $1,755,000 |
| Total revenue from sales ......... | | | $2,535,000 |

For the year ending December 31, 1986, unit sales are expected to follow the patterns established during the first nine months of the year ending December 31, 1985. The unit selling price for Product A is expected to be increased to $11, effective January 1, 1986, and the unit selling price for Product B is not expected to change.

Instructions:

(1) Compute the increase or decrease of actual *unit* sales for the nine months ended September 30, 1985, over expectations for this nine-month period. Since sales have historically occurred evenly throughout the year, budgeted sales for the first nine months of a year would be 75% of the year's budgeted sales. Comparison of this amount with actual sales will indicate the percentage increase or decrease of actual sales for the nine months over budgeted sales for the nine months. Place your answers in a columnar table with the following format:

| | Unit Budgeted Sales | | Actual Sales for Nine Months | Increase (Decrease) | |
|---|---|---|---|---|---|
| | Year | Nine Months | | Amount | Percent |
| Product A | | | | | |
| East | | | | | |
| Central | | | | | |
| West | | | | | |
| | | | | | |
| Product B | | | | | |
| East | | | | | |
| Central | | | | | |
| West | | | | | |

(2) Assuming that the trend of sales indicated in (1) is to continue in 1986, compute the unit sales volume to be used for preparing the sales budget for the year ending December 31, 1986. Place your answers in a columnar table with the following format:

| | 1985 Budgeted Units | Percentage Increase (Decrease) | 1986 Budgeted Units |
|---|---|---|---|
| **Product A** | | | |
| East | | | |
| Central | | | |
| West | | | |
| | | | |
| **Product B** | | | |
| East | | | |
| Central | | | |
| West | | | |

(3) Prepare a sales budget for the year ending December 31, 1986.

**Problem 4-4B.** The treasurer of Donovan Company instructs you to prepare a monthly cash budget for the next three months. You are presented with the following budget information:

| | May | June | July |
|---|---|---|---|
| Sales ............................. | $300,000 | $245,000 | $350,000 |
| Manufacturing costs.................. | 195,000 | 160,000 | 227,000 |
| Operating expenses.................. | 45,000 | 37,000 | 56,000 |
| Capital expenditures ................ | — | 100,000 | — |

The company expects to sell about 20% of its merchandise for cash. Of sales on account, 75% are expected to be collected in full in the month following the sale and the remainder the following month. Depreciation, insurance, and property taxes represent $15,000 of the estimated monthly manufacturing costs and $3,000 of the probable monthly operating expenses. Insurance and property taxes are paid in March and August respectively. Of the remainder of the manufacturing costs and operating expenses, 70% are expected to be paid in the month in which they are incurred and the balance in the following month.

Current assets as of May 1 are composed of cash of $31,000, marketable securities of $20,000, and accounts receivable of $265,000 ($220,000 from April sales and $45,000 from March sales). Current liabilities as of May 1 are composed of a $30,000, 14%, 120-day note payable due June 10, $60,400 of accounts payable incurred in April for manufacturing costs, and accrued liabilities of $14,100 incurred in April for operating expenses.

It is expected that $2,200 in dividends will be received in June. An estimated income tax payment of $12,500 will be made in June. Donovan Company's regular quarterly dividend of $5,000 is expected to be declared in June and paid in July. Management desires to maintain a minimum cash balance of $35,000.

Instructions:
(1) Prepare a monthly cash budget for May, June, and July.
(2) On the basis of the cash budget prepared in (1), what recommendation should be made to the treasurer?

**CHAPTER 5** | **Problem 5-1B.** Standard costs and actual costs for direct materials, direct labor, and factory overhead incurred for the manufacture of 1,000 units of product were as follows:

|  | Standard Costs | Actual Costs |
|---|---|---|
| Direct materials . . . . . . . . | 1,000 pounds at $75 | 980 pounds at $75.50 |
| Direct labor . . . . . . . . . . . | 12,500 hours at $9 | 12,600 hours at $8.95 |
| Factory overhead . . . . . . . | Rates per direct labor hour, based on 100% of capacity of 15,000 labor hours: |  |
|  | Variable cost, $3.50 | $44,150 variable cost |
|  | Fixed cost, $1.00 | $15,000 fixed cost |

Instructions:

Determine (a) the quantity variance, price variance, and total direct materials cost variance; (b) the time variance, rate variance, and total direct labor cost variance; and (c) the volume variance, controllable variance, and total factory overhead cost variance.

**Problem 5-3B.** Barnes Inc. prepared the following factory overhead cost budget for the Painting Department for January of the current year:

Barnes Inc.
Factory Overhead Cost Budget—Painting Department
For Month Ending January 31, 19--

| Direct labor hours: |  |  |
|---|---|---|
| Productive capacity of 100% . . . . . . . . . . . . . . . . . . . . . . . . |  | 24,000 |
| Hours budgeted . . . . . . . . . . . . . . . . . . . . . . . . . . . . . . . . . |  | 21,600 |
| Variable cost: |  |  |
| Indirect factory wages . . . . . . . . . . . . . . . . . . . . . . . . . . . . . | $13,905 |  |
| Indirect materials . . . . . . . . . . . . . . . . . . . . . . . . . . . . . . . | 10,935 |  |
| Power and light . . . . . . . . . . . . . . . . . . . . . . . . . . . . . . . . . | 9,720 |  |
|     Total variable cost . . . . . . . . . . . . . . . . . . . . . . . . . . . . . |  | $34,560 |
| Fixed cost: |  |  |
| Supervisory salaries . . . . . . . . . . . . . . . . . . . . . . . . . . . . . . | $12,950 |  |
| Indirect factory wages . . . . . . . . . . . . . . . . . . . . . . . . . . . . . | 4,820 |  |
| Depreciation of plant and equipment . . . . . . . . . . . . . . . . . | 4,460 |  |
| Insurance . . . . . . . . . . . . . . . . . . . . . . . . . . . . . . . . . . . . | 2,600 |  |
| Power and light . . . . . . . . . . . . . . . . . . . . . . . . . . . . . . . . | 2,350 |  |
| Property taxes . . . . . . . . . . . . . . . . . . . . . . . . . . . . . . . . . | 1,620 |  |
|     Total fixed cost . . . . . . . . . . . . . . . . . . . . . . . . . . . . . . . |  | 28,800 |
| Total factory overhead cost . . . . . . . . . . . . . . . . . . . . . . . . |  | $63,360 |

During January, the Painting Department was operated for 21,600 direct labor hours and the following factory overhead costs were incurred:

| | |
|---|---|
| Indirect factory wages | $19,120 |
| Supervisory salaries | 12,950 |
| Power and light | 13,050 |
| Indirect materials | 10,600 |
| Depreciation of plant and equipment | 4,460 |
| Insurance | 2,600 |
| Property taxes | 1,620 |
| Total factory overhead cost incurred | $64,400 |

Instructions:
(1) Prepare a flexible budget for January, indicating capacities of 19,200, 21,600, 24,000, and 26,400 direct labor hours and the determination of a standard factory overhead rate per direct labor hour.
(2) Prepare a standard factory overhead cost variance report for January.

Problem 5-5B. McCloskey Inc. maintains perpetual inventory accounts for materials, work in process, and finished goods and uses a standard cost system based on the following data:

| | Standard Cost per Unit |
|---|---|
| Direct materials: 5 kilograms at $2.80 per kg | $14 |
| Direct labor: 2 hours at $18 per hour | 36 |
| Factory overhead: $2.50 per direct labor hour | 5 |
| Total | $55 |

There was no inventory of work in process at the beginning or end of August, the first month of the current fiscal year. The transactions relating to production completed during August are summarized as follows:
(a) Materials purchased on account, $89,600.
(b) Direct materials used, $92,220. This represented 31 800 kilograms at $2.90 per kilogram.
(c) Direct labor paid, $227,500. This represented 13,000 hours at $17.50 per hour. There were no accruals at either the beginning or the end of the period.
(d) Factory overhead incurred during the month was composed of depreciation on plant and equipment, $14,600; indirect labor, $11,750; insurance, $3,000; and miscellaneous factory costs, $5,500. The indirect labor and miscellaneous factory costs were paid during the period, and the insurance represents an expiration of prepaid insurance. Of the total factory overhead of $34,850, fixed costs amounted to $19,600 and variable costs were $15,250.
(e) Goods finished during the period, 6,400 units.

Instructions:
(1) Prepare entries in general journal form to record the transactions, assuming that the work in process account is debited for actual production costs and credited with standard costs for goods finished.
(2) Prepare a T account for Work in Process and post to the account, using the identifying letters as dates.
(3) Prepare schedules of variances for direct materials cost, direct labor cost, and factory overhead cost. Productive capacity for the plant is 14,000 direct labor hours.
(4) Total the amount of the standard cost variances and compare this total with the balance of the work in process account.

**CHAPTER 6** | **Problem 6-1B.** Maloney Company manufactures only one product. In 1984, the plant operated at full capacity. At a meeting of the board of directors on December 12, 1984, it was decided to raise the price of this product from $16, which had prevailed for the past few years, to $18, effective January 1, 1985. Although the cost price was expected to rise about $1.20 per unit in 1985 because of a direct materials and direct labor wage increase, the increase in selling price was expected to cover this increase and also add to operating income. The comparative income statement for 1984 and 1985 is as follows:

|  | 1985 | | 1984 | |
|---|---:|---:|---:|---:|
| Sales............................................ | | $612,000 | | $640,000 |
| Cost of goods sold: variable.............. | $289,000 | | $292,000 | |
| fixed ............... | 136,000 | 425,000 | 136,000 | 428,000 |
| Gross profit............................... | | $187,000 | | $212,000 |
| Operating expenses: variable............. | $ 71,400 | | $ 72,000 | |
| fixed ............... | 36,000 | 107,400 | 36,000 | 108,000 |
| Operating income ...................... | | $ 79,600 | | $104,000 |

Instructions:

(1) Prepare a gross profit analysis report for 1985.
(2) At a meeting of the board of directors on February 3, 1986, the president, after reading the gross profit analysis report, made the following comment:

"It looks as if the increase in unit cost price was $1.80 and not the anticipated $1.20. The failure of operating management to keep these costs within the bounds of those in 1984, except for the anticipated $1.20 increase in direct materials and direct labor cost, was a major factor in the decrease in gross profit."

Do you agree with this analysis of the increase in unit cost price? Explain.

**Problem 6-2B.** During the first month of operations ended January 31, Lorenz Company manufactured 24,000 units, of which 20,000 were sold. Operating data for the month are summarized as follows:

| Sales ............................................... | | $800,000 |
|---|---:|---:|
| Manufacturing costs: | | |
| Direct materials ................................ | $320,000 | |
| Direct labor.................................... | 160,000 | |
| Variable factory overhead ........................ | 96,000 | |
| Fixed factory overhead ........................... | 120,000 | 696,000 |
| | | |
| Selling and general expenses: | | |
| Variable........................................ | $100,000 | |
| Fixed ......................................... | 50,000 | 150,000 |

Instructions:

(1) Prepare an income statement based on the absorption costing concept.
(2) Prepare an income statement based on the variable costing concept.
(3) Explain the reason for the difference in the amount of operating income reported in (1) and (2).

**Problem 6-3B.** The demand for Product G, one of numerous products manufactured by Bolton Inc., has dropped sharply because of recent competition from a similar product. The company's chemists are currently completing tests of various new formulas, and it is anticipated that the manufacture of a superior product can be started on May 1, one month hence. No changes will be needed in the present production facilities to manufacture the new product because only the mixture of the various materials will be changed.

The controller has been asked by the president of the company for advice on whether to continue production during April or to suspend the manufacture of Product G until May 1. The controller has assembled the following pertinent data:

Bolton Inc.
Estimated Income Statement—Product G
For Month Ending March 31, 19--

| | |
|---|---:|
| Sales (20,000 units) | $320,000 |
| Cost of goods sold | 280,000 |
| Gross profit | $ 40,000 |
| Selling and general expenses | 75,000 |
| Loss from operations | $ 35,000 |

The estimated production costs and selling and general expenses, based on a production of 20,000 units, are as follows:

| | |
|---|---|
| Direct materials | $3.40 per unit |
| Direct labor | 6.50 per unit |
| Variable factory overhead | .80 per unit |
| Variable selling and general expenses | 2.20 per unit |
| Fixed factory overhead | $66,000 for March |
| Fixed selling and general expenses | $31,000 for March |

Sales for April are expected to drop about 30% below those of the preceding month. No significant changes are anticipated in the production costs or operating expenses. No extra costs will be incurred in discontinuing operations in the portion of the plant associated with Product G. The inventory of Product G at the beginning and end of April is expected to be inconsequential.

Instructions:
(1) Prepare an estimated income statement in absorption costing form for April for Product G, assuming that production continues during the month.
(2) Prepare an estimated income statement in variable costing form for April for Product G, assuming that production continues during the month.
(3) State the estimated operating loss arising from the activities associated with Product G for April if production is temporarily suspended.
(4) Prepare a brief statement of the advice the controller should give.

**CHAPTER 7** | **Problem 7-1B.** For the coming year, Wooten Company anticipates fixed costs of $120,000 and variable costs equal to 70% of sales.

Instructions:

    (1) Compute the anticipated break-even point.

    (2) Compute the sales required to realize operating profit of $60,000.

    (3) Construct a cost-volume-profit chart, assuming sales of $1,000,000 at full capacity.

    (4) Determine the probable operating profit if sales total $800,000.

**Problem 7-2B.** Rose Company operated at 60% of capacity last year, when sales totaled $3,000,000. Fixed costs were $1,000,000, and variable costs were 60% of sales. Rose Company is considering a proposal to spend an additional $200,000 on billboard advertising during the current year in an attempt to increase sales and utilize additional capacity.

Instructions:

    (1) Construct a cost-volume-profit chart indicating the break-even point for last year.

    (2) Using the cost-volume-profit chart prepared in (1), determine (a) the operating profit for last year and (b) the maximum operating profit that could have been realized during the year.

    (3) Construct a cost-volume-profit chart indicating the break-even point for the current year, assuming that a noncancelable contract is signed for the additional billboard advertising. No changes are expected in unit selling price or other costs.

    (4) Using the cost-volume-profit chart prepared in (3), determine (a) the operating profit if sales total $3,000,000 and (b) the maximum operating profit that could be realized during the year.

**Problem 7-3B.** Last year, Perez Company had sales of $800,000, fixed costs of $200,000, and variable costs of $400,000. Perez Company is considering a proposal to spend $50,000 to hire a public relations firm, hoping that the company's image can be improved and sales increased. Maximum operating capacity is $1,000,000 of sales.

Instructions:

    (1) Construct a profit-volume chart for last year.

    (2) Using the profit-volume chart prepared in (1), determine for last year (a) the break-even point, (b) the operating profit, and (c) the maximum operating profit that could have been realized.

    (3) Construct a profit-volume chart for the current year, assuming that the additional $50,000 expenditure is made and there is no change in unit selling price or other costs.

    (4) Using the profit-volume chart prepared in (3), determine (a) the break-even point, (b) the operating profit if sales total $800,000, and (c) the maximum operating profit that could be realized.

**Problem 7-5B.** W. F. Epstein Company expects to maintain the same inventories at the end of 1985 as at the beginning of the year. The total of all production costs for the year is therefore assumed to be equal to the cost of goods sold. With this in mind, the various department heads were asked to submit estimates of the expenses for their departments during 1985. A summary report of these estimates is as follows:

| | Estimated Fixed Expense | Estimated Variable Expense (per unit sold) |
|---|---|---|
| Production costs: | | |
| Direct materials .......................... | — | $ 9.20 |
| Direct labor............................. | — | 4.80 |
| Factory overhead......................... | $174,000 | 2.00 |
| Selling expenses: | | |
| Sales salaries and commissions............. | 80,400 | 1.20 |
| Advertising ............................. | 21,600 | — |
| Travel .................................. | 3,600 | — |
| Miscellaneous selling expense ............. | 2,400 | .48 |
| General expenses: | | |
| Office and officers' salaries................ | 70,500 | — |
| Supplies................................ | 4,500 | .24 |
| Miscellaneous general expense ............ | 3,000 | .08 |
| | $360,000 | $18.00 |

It is expected that 70,000 units will be sold at a selling price of $24 a unit. Capacity output is 75,000 units.

Instructions:

(1) Determine the break-even point (a) in dollars of sales, (b) in units, and (c) in terms of capacity.
(2) Prepare an estimated income statement for 1985.
(3) Construct a cost-volume-profit chart, indicating the break-even point in dollars of sales.
(4) What is the expected margin of safety?
(5) What is the expected contribution margin ratio?

CHAPTER 8 | Problem 8-1B. On November 1, Levy Company is considering leasing a building and purchasing the necessary equipment to operate a public warehouse. The project would be financed by selling $800,000 of 12% U.S. Treasury bonds that mature in 20 years. The bonds were purchased at face value and are currently selling at face value. The following data have been assembled:

| | |
|---|---|
| Cost of equipment......................................... | $800,000 |
| Life of equipment......................................... | 20 years |
| Estimated residual value of equipment......................... | $120,000 |
| Yearly costs to operate the warehouse, in addition to depreciation of equipment............................................ | $ 75,000 |
| Yearly expected revenues—first 10 years...................... | $200,000 |
| Yearly expected revenues—next 5 years ...................... | $220,000 |
| Yearly expected revenues—last 5 years....................... | $250,000 |

Instructions:

(1) Prepare a differential analysis report representing the differential revenue and the differential cost associated with the proposed operation of the warehouse for the 20 years as compared with present conditions.
(2) Based on the results disclosed by the differential analysis, should the proposal be accepted?

(3) If the proposal is accepted, what is the total estimated income from operation of the warehouse for the 20 years?

**Problem 8-2B.** Fedder Company is considering the replacement of a machine that has been used in its factory for two years. Relevant data associated with the operations of the old machine and the new machine, neither of which has any residual value, are as follows:

### Old Machine

| | |
|---|---|
| Cost of machine, 8-year life | $224,000 |
| Annual depreciation | 28,000 |
| Annual manufacturing costs, exclusive of depreciation | 372,000 |
| Related annual operating expenses | 193,600 |
| Associated annual revenue | 600,000 |
| Estimated selling price of old machine | 116,000 |

### New Machine

| | |
|---|---|
| Cost of machine, 6-year life | $384,000 |
| Annual depreciation | 64,000 |
| Estimated annual manufacturing costs, exclusive of depreciation | 300,000 |

Annual operating expenses and revenue are not expected to be affected by purchase of the new machine.

Instructions:

(1) Prepare a differential analysis report as of January 3 of the current year, comparing operations utilizing the new machine with operations using the present equipment. The analysis should indicate the total differential decrease or increase in costs that would result over the 6-year period if the new machine is acquired.

(2) List other factors that should be considered before a final decision is reached.

**Problem 8-5B.** Ladner Refining Inc. refines Product X in batches of 200,000 gallons, which it sells for $3.20 per gallon. The associated unit costs and expenses are currently as follows:

| | |
|---|---|
| Direct materials | $1.84 per gallon |
| Direct labor | .48 |
| Variable factory overhead | .18 |
| Fixed factory overhead | .12 |
| Sales commissions | .16 |
| Fixed selling and general expenses | .08 |

The company is presently considering a proposal to put Product X through several additional processes to yield Products X and Z. Although the company had determined such further processing to be unwise, new processing methods have now been developed. Existing facilities can be used for the additional processing, but since the factory is operating at full 8-hour-day capacity, the processing would have to be performed at night. Additional costs of processing would be $11,650 per batch and there would be an evaporation loss of 8%, with 70% of the processed material evolving as Product X and 22% as Product Z. The selling price of Product Z is $4.80 per gallon. Sales commissions are a uniform percentage based on the sales price.

Instructions:

(1) Prepare a differential analysis report as of November 12, presenting the differential revenue and the differential cost per batch associated with the processing to produce Products X and Z, compared with processing to produce Product X only.

(2) Briefly report your recommendations.

**Problem 8-6B.** Ahearn Company recently began production of a new product, G, which required the investment of $1,000,000 in assets. The costs and expenses of producing and selling 50,000 units of Product G are as follows:

| | |
|---|---|
| Variable costs and expenses: | |
| Direct materials ..................... | $ 2.40 per unit |
| Direct labor.......................... | 4.80 |
| Factory overhead .................... | .80 |
| Selling and general expenses ......... | 2.00 |
| Total............................. | $10.00 per unit |

| | |
|---|---|
| Fixed costs and expenses: | |
| Factory overhead .................... | $70,000 |
| Selling and general expenses ......... | 30,000 |

Ahearn Company is currently considering the establishment of a selling price for Product G. The President of Ahearn Company has decided to use the cost-plus approach to product pricing and has indicated that Product G must earn a 12% rate of return on invested assets.

Instructions:

(1) Determine the amount of desired profit from the production and sale of Product G.

(2) Assuming that the total cost concept is used, determine (a) the cost amount per unit, (b) the markup percentage, and (c) the selling price of Product G.

(3) Assuming that the product cost concept is used, determine (a) the cost amount per unit, (b) the markup percentage, and (c) the selling price of Product G. Round to the nearest cent.

(4) Assuming that the variable cost concept is used, determine (a) the cost amount per unit, (b) the markup percentage, and (c) the selling price of Product G.

(5) Comment on any additional considerations that could influence the establishment of the selling price for Product G.

**CHAPTER 9** | **Problem 9-1B.** The capital investments budget committee is considering two projects. The estimated operating income and net cash flows from each project are shown on page 477.

Each project requires an investment of $160,000, with no residual value expected. The committee has selected a rate of 15% for purposes of the discounted cash flow analysis.

| | Project A | | Project B | |
|---|---|---|---|---|
| Year | Operating Income | Net Cash Flow | Operating Income | Net Cash Flow |
| 1 | $19,950 | $ 60,000 | $28,000 | $ 75,000 |
| 2 | 13,300 | 60,000 | 14,000 | 75,000 |
| 3 | 13,300 | 50,000 | 14,000 | 50,000 |
| 4 | 13,300 | 30,000 | 7,000 | 20,000 |
| 5 | 10,150 | 30,000 | 7,000 | 10,000 |
| Total | $70,000 | $230,000 | $70,000 | $230,000 |

Instructions:

(1) Compute the following:
    (a) The average rate of return for each project, giving effect to straight-line depreciation on the investment.
    (b) The excess (deficiency) of present value over the amount to be invested, as determined by the discounted cash flow method for each project. Use the present value of 1 table appearing in this chapter.
(2) Prepare a brief report for the budget committee, advising it on the relative merits of the two projects.

**Problem 9-2B.** Berra Company is considering two projects. The estimated net cash flows from each project are as follows:

| Year | Project X | Project Y |
|---|---|---|
| 1 | $ 25,000 | $100,000 |
| 2 | 75,000 | 100,000 |
| 3 | 150,000 | 50,000 |
| 4 | 50,000 | 50,000 |
| 5 | 50,000 | 50,000 |
| Total | $350,000 | $350,000 |

Each project requires an investment of $250,000, with no residual value expected. A rate of 12% has been selected for the discounted cash flow analysis.

Instructions:

(1) Compute the following for each project:
    (a) Cash payback period.
    (b) The excess (deficiency) of present value over the amount to be invested, as determined by the discounted cash flow method. Use the present value of 1 table appearing in this chapter.
(2) Prepare a brief report advising management on the relative merits of each of the two projects.

**Problem 9-3B.** W. J. Atlantis Company is evaluating three capital investment projects by using the discounted cash flow method. Relevant data related to the projects are summarized as follows:

|                          | Project A | Project B | Project C |
|--------------------------|-----------|-----------|-----------|
| Amount to be invested..... | $400,000 | $800,000 | $400,000 |
| Annual net cash flows:   |           |           |           |
| Year 1 ................. | 300,000 | 500,000 | 100,000 |
| Year 2 ................. | 200,000 | 400,000 | 200,000 |
| Year 3 ................. | 100,000 | 300,000 | 300,000 |

Instructions:

(1) Assuming that the desired rate of return is 20%, prepare a discounted cash flow analysis for each project. Use the present value of 1 table appearing in this chapter.
(2) Determine a present value index for each project.
(3) Which project offers the largest amount of present value per dollar of investment? Explain.

**Problem 9-4B.** Management is considering two capital investment projects. The estimated net cash flows from each project are as follows:

| Year | Project A | Project B |
|------|-----------|-----------|
| 1 | $60,000 | $180,000 |
| 2 | 60,000 | 180,000 |
| 3 | 60,000 | 180,000 |
| 4 | 60,000 | 180,000 |

Project A requires an investment of $171,300, while project B requires an investment of $546,600. No residual value is expected from either project.

Instructions:

(1) Compute the following for each project:
   (a) The excess (deficiency) of present value over the amount to be invested, as determined by the discounted cash flow method. Use a rate of 10% and the present value of 1 table appearing in this chapter.
   (b) A present value index.
(2) Determine the discounted internal rate of return for each project by (a) computing a "present value factor for an annuity of 1" and (b) using the present value of an annuity of 1 table appearing in this chapter.
(3) What advantage does the discounted internal rate of return method have over the discounted cash flow method in comparing projects?

**CHAPTER 10 | Problem 10-3B.** Benny Golf Carts sold 150 electric golf carts for $1,500 each during the first year of operations. Data related to purchases during the year are as follows:

|              | Quantity | Unit Cost |
|--------------|----------|-----------|
| February 1.............. | 25 | $1,200 |
| April 20................. | 45 | 1,225 |
| June 1 ................. | 50 | 1,250 |
| August 15 .............. | 25 | 1,250 |
| November 1 ............. | 25 | 1,280 |

Sales of electric golf carts are the company's only source of income, and operating expenses for the current year are $15,500.

Instructions:

(1) Determine the net income for the current year, using the lifo method (last-in, first-out) inventory method.
(2) Determine the net income for the current year, using the fifo (first-in, first-out) inventory method.
(3) Which method of inventory costing, lifo or fifo, would you recommend for tax purposes? Discuss.

**Problem 10-4B.** Cosell Company began construction on three contracts during 1984. The contract prices and construction activities for 1984, 1985, and 1986 were as follows:

| | | 1984 | | 1985 | | 1986 | |
|---|---|---|---|---|---|---|---|
| Contract | Contract Price | Costs Incurred | Percent Completed | Costs Incurred | Percent Completed | Costs Incurred | Percent Completed |
| 1 | $6,000,000 | $2,150,000 | 40% | $3,250,000 | 60% | — | — |
| 2 | 3,000,000 | 525,000 | 20 | 1,075,000 | 40 | $1,100,000 | 40% |
| 3 | 3,500,000 | 305,000 | 10 | 985,000 | 30 | 1,675,000 | 50 |

Instructions:

(1) Determine the amount of income to be recognized from the contracts in 1984, 1985, and 1986 by using (a) the percentage-of-completion method and (b) the completed-contract method. Present computations in good order.
(2) Would the total amount of income to be recognized by using the percentage-of-completion method for each contract be the same as the total amount recognized by using the completed-contract method?
(3) What is the principal advantage for tax purposes of using the completed-contract method of recognizing income from long-term contracts?

**Problem 10-5B.** The board of directors of Mickelsen Inc. is planning an expansion of plant facilities expected to cost $5,000,000. The board is undecided about the method of financing this expansion and is considering two plans:

Plan 1. Issue 50,000 shares of $100, 8% cumulative preferred stock at par.
Plan 2. Issue $5,000,000 of 20-year, 10% bonds at face amount.

The condensed balance sheet of the corporation at the end of the most recent fiscal year is presented as follows:

Mickelsen Inc.
Balance Sheet
December 31, 19--

| Assets | | Liabilities and Capital | |
|---|---|---|---|
| Current assets ...... | $ 6,000,000 | Current liabilities......... | $ 3,000,000 |
| Plant assets......... | 34,000,000 | Common stock, $10 par.. | 10,000,000 |
| | | Premium on common | |
| | | stock................ | 2,000,000 |
| | | Retained earnings ....... | 25,000,000 |
| Total assets......... | $40,000,000 | Total liabilities and capital | $40,000,000 |

Net income has remained relatively constant over the past several years. As a result of the expansion program, yearly income after tax but before bond interest and related income tax is expected to increase to $3,000,000.

Instructions:

(1) Prepare a tabulation indicating the net annual outlay (dividends and interest after tax) for financing under each plan. (Use the income tax rates indicated in the chapter.)
(2) Prepare a tabulation indicating the expected earnings per share on common stock under each plan.
(3) List factors other than the net cost of financing and earnings per share that the board should consider in evaluating the two plans.

**CHAPTER 11**
*(If the working papers correlating with the textbook are not used, omit Problem 11-1B.)*

**Problem 11-1B.** The organization chart for manufacturing operations for Carlos Inc. is presented in the working papers. Also presented are the budget performance reports for the three departments in Plant 3 and a partially completed budget performance report prepared for the vice-president in charge of production.

In response to an inquiry into the cause of the direct labor variance in the Plating Shop-Plant 3, the following data were accumulated:

| Job No. | Budgeted Hours | Actual Hours | Hourly Rate |
|---------|----------------|--------------|-------------|
| 940 | 70 | 75 | $16.00 |
| 942 | 120 | 113 | 17.00 |
| 944 | 115 | 119 | 16.50 |
| 945 | 90 | 105 | 18.00 |
| 950 | 80 | 80 | 17.20 |
| 951 | 119 | 128 | 17.00 |
| 952 | 100 | 94 | 15.50 |
| 958 | 65 | 67 | 16.50 |

The significant variations from budgeted hours were attributed to the fact that Job 945 was of a type that was being done for the first time, to machine breakdown on Jobs 940, 944, and 958, and to an inexperienced operator on Job 951. Experienced operators were assigned to Jobs 942 and 952.

Instructions:

(1) Prepare a direct labor time variance report for the Plating Shop-Plant 3.
(2) Prepare a budget performance report for the use of the manager of Plant 3, detailing the relevant data from the three departments in the plant. Assume that the budgeted and actual administration expenses for the plant were $12,400 and $12,210, respectively.
(3) Complete the budget performance report for the vice-president in charge of production.

**Problem 11-2B.** Lawson Appliances operates two sales departments: Department A for small appliances, such as radios and televisions, and Department B for large appliances, such as refrigerators and washing machines. The trial balance on page 481 was prepared at the end of the current fiscal year, after all adjustments, including the adjustments for merchandise inventory, were recorded and posted.

Lawson Appliances
Trial Balance
July 31, 19--

| | | |
|---|---:|---:|
| Cash | 29,300 | |
| Accounts Receivable | 84,500 | |
| Merchandise Inventory — Department A | 20,300 | |
| Merchandise Inventory — Department B | 70,500 | |
| Prepaid Insurance | 600 | |
| Store Supplies | 550 | |
| Store Equipment | 92,200 | |
| Accumulated Depreciation — Store Equipment | | 21,280 |
| Accounts Payable | | 17,700 |
| Income Tax Payable | | 5,525 |
| Common Stock | | 100,000 |
| Retained Earnings | | 98,491 |
| Cash Dividends | 10,000 | |
| Income Summary | 89,200 | 90,800 |
| Sales — Department A | | 197,080 |
| Sales — Department B | | 560,920 |
| Sales Returns and Allowances — Department A | 2,780 | |
| Sales Returns and Allowances — Department B | 6,800 | |
| Purchases — Department A | 109,884 | |
| Purchases — Department B | 369,232 | |
| Sales Salaries Expense | 56,500 | |
| Advertising Expense | 14,350 | |
| Depreciation Expense — Store Equipment | 6,100 | |
| Store Supplies Expense | 2,700 | |
| Miscellaneous Selling Expense | 4,450 | |
| Office Salaries Expense | 48,000 | |
| Rent Expense | 18,000 | |
| Heating and Lighting Expense | 16,800 | |
| Property Tax Expense | 6,200 | |
| Insurance Expense | 2,400 | |
| Uncollectible Accounts Expense | 2,200 | |
| Miscellaneous General Expense | 3,150 | |
| Interest Expense | 3,000 | |
| Income Tax | 22,100 | |
| | 1,091,796 | 1,091,796 |

Merchandise inventories at the beginning of the year were as follows: Department A, $26,400; Department B, $62,800.

The bases to be used in apportioning expenses, together with other essential information, are as follows:

Sales salaries expense — payroll records: Department A, $12,900; Department B, $43,600.

Advertising expense — usage: Department A, $5,600; Department B, $8,750.

Depreciation expense—average cost of equipment. Balances at beginning of year: Department A, $18,600; Department B, $59,200. Balances at end of year: Department A, $22,200; Department B, $70,000.

Store supplies expense—requisitions: Department A, $1,200; Department B, $1,500.

Office salaries expense—Department A, 30%; Department B, 70%.

Rent expense and heating and lighting expense—floor space: Department A, 4,800 sq. ft.; Department B, 7,200 sq. ft.

Property tax expense and insurance expense—average cost of equipment plus average cost of merchandise inventory.

Uncollectible accounts expense, miscellaneous selling expense, and miscellaneous general expense—volume of gross sales.

Instructions:

Prepare an income statement departmentalized through income from operations.

**Problem 11-3B.** R. W. Miller Company is considering discontinuance of one of its twelve departments. If operations in Department L are discontinued, it is estimated that the indirect operating expenses and the level of operations in the other departments will not be affected.

Data from the income statement for the past year ended December 31, which is considered to be a typical year, are as follows:

|  | | Department L | | Other Departments |
|---|---|---|---|---|
| Sales ........................... | | $44,000 | | $765,000 |
| Cost of merchandise sold......... | | 23,500 | | 420,750 |
| Gross profit .................... | | $20,500 | | $344,250 |
| Operating expenses: | | | | |
| Direct expenses .............. | $16,500 | | $192,500 | |
| Indirect expenses............. | 9,000 | 25,500 | 99,000 | 291,500 |
| Income (loss) before income tax... | | $ (5,000) | | $ 52,750 |

Instructions:

(1) Prepare an estimated income statement for the current year ending December 31, assuming the discontinuance of Department L.

(2) On the basis of the data presented, would it be advisable to retain Department L?

**Problem 11-4B.** Kearney Fashions has 16 departments. Those with the least sales volume are Department 13 and Department 15, which were established about eighteen months ago on a trial basis. The board of directors believes that it is now time to consider the retention or the termination of these two departments. The following adjusted trial balance as of August 31, the end of the first month of the current fiscal year, is severely condensed. August is considered to be a typical month. The income tax accrual has no bearing on the decision and is excluded from consideration.

Kearney Fashions
Trial Balance
August 31, 19--

| | | |
|---|---:|---:|
| Current Assets. | 236,200 | |
| Plant Assets. | 672,400 | |
| Accumulated Depreciation—Plant Assets | | 168,100 |
| Current Liabilities | | 118,100 |
| Common Stock | | 200,000 |
| Retained Earnings | | 403,304 |
| Cash Dividends. | 30,000 | |
| Sales—Department 13 | | 32,500 |
| Sales—Department 15 | | 21,400 |
| Sales—Other Departments | | 948,600 |
| Cost of Merchandise Sold—Department 13 | 21,125 | |
| Cost of Merchandise Sold—Department 15 | 14,980 | |
| Cost of Merchandise Sold—Other Departments. | 569,160 | |
| Direct Expenses—Department 13 | 8,125 | |
| Direct Expenses—Department 15 | 7,490 | |
| Direct Expenses—Other Departments | 227,664 | |
| Indirect Expenses. | 94,860 | |
| Interest Expense. | 10,000 | |
| | 1,892,004 | 1,892,004 |

Instructions:

(1) Prepare an income statement for August, departmentalized through departmental margin.

(2) State your recommendations concerning the retention of Departments 13 and 15, giving reasons.

**CHAPTER 12** | **Problem 12-1B.** Barrow Company is a diversified company with three operating divisions organized as investment centers. Condensed data taken from the records of the three divisions for the year ended December 31 are as follows:

| | Division R | Division S | Division T |
|---|---:|---:|---:|
| Sales | $1,200,000 | $750,000 | $1,800,000 |
| Cost of goods sold | 950,000 | 600,000 | 1,300,000 |
| Operating expenses | 130,000 | 60,000 | 275,000 |
| Invested assets | 750,000 | 500,000 | 1,500,000 |

The management of Barrow Company is evaluating each division as a basis for planning a future expansion of operations.

Instructions:

(1) Prepare condensed divisional income statements for Divisions R, S, and T.

(2) Using the expanded expression, compute the profit margin, investment turnover, and rate of return on investment for each division.

(3) If available funds permit the expansion of operations of only one division, which of the divisions would you recommend for expansion, based on (1) and (2)?

**Problem 12-3B.** Data for Divisions P, Q, R, S, and T of Fawcett Company are as follows:

| | Sales | Operating Income | Invested Assets | Rate of Return on Investment | Profit Margin | Investment Turnover |
|---|---|---|---|---|---|---|
| Division P ... | (a) | (b) | $400,000 | 17% | 13.6% | (c) |
| Division Q ... | $2,200,000 | $176,000 | (d) | (e) | (f) | 2.75 |
| Division R ... | (g) | $135,000 | (h) | (i) | 15% | 1.20 |
| Division S ... | $ 840,000 | (j) | $600,000 | 14% | (k) | (l) |
| Division T ... | $ 704,000 | (m) | (n) | (o) | 12.5% | 1.28 |

Instructions:

(1) Determine the missing items, identifying each by letters (a) through (o).
(2) Determine the residual income for each division, assuming that the minimum rate of return established by management is 12%.
(3) Which division is the most profitable?

**Problem 12-4B.** The vice-president of operations of Gustafson Company is evaluating the performance of two divisions organized as investment centers. Division L has the highest rate of return on investment, but generates the smallest amount of operating income. Division M generates the largest operating income, but has the lowest rate of return on investment. Invested assets and condensed income statement data for the past year for each division are as follows:

| | Division L | Division M |
|---|---|---|
| Sales..................... | $3,125,000 | $5,100,000 |
| Cost of goods sold ......... | 2,500,000 | 4,000,000 |
| Operating expenses ........ | 150,000 | 590,000 |
| Invested assets ........... | 2,500,000 | 3,000,000 |

Instructions:

(1) Prepare condensed income statements for the past year for each division.
(2) Using the expanded expression, determine the profit margin, investment turnover, and rate of return on investment for each division.
(3) If management desires a minimum rate of return of 12%, determine the residual income for each division.
(4) Discuss the evaluation of Divisions L and M, using the performance measures determined in (1), (2), and (3).

**Problem 12-5B.** Bradford Company is diversified, with two operating divisions, X and Y. Condensed divisional income statements, which involve no intracompany transfers and which include a breakdown of expenses into variable and fixed components, are shown on page 485.

Division X is operating at three fourths of capacity of 200,000 units. Materials used in producing Division Y's product are currently purchased from outside suppliers at a price of $40 per unit. The materials used by Division Y are produced by Division X. Except for the possible transfer of materials between divisions, no changes are expected in sales and expenses.

**Bradford Company**
**Divisional Income Statements**
**For Year Ended December 31, 19--**

| | Division X | Division Y | Total |
|---|---|---|---|
| Sales: | | | |
| 150,000 units × $60 per unit...... | $9,000,000 | | $ 9,000,000 |
| 50,000 units × $80 per unit....... | | $4,000,000 | 4,000,000 |
| | | | $13,000,000 |
| Expenses: | | | |
| Variable: | | | |
| 150,000 units × $30 per unit.... | $4,500,000 | | $ 4,500,000 |
| 50,000 units × $50* per unit.... | | $2,500,000 | 2,500,000 |
| Fixed......................... | 3,000,000 | 1,000,000 | 4,000,000 |
| Total expenses............... | $7,500,000 | $3,500,000 | $11,000,000 |
| Operating income ............... | $1,500,000 | $ 500,000 | $ 2,000,000 |

*$40 of the $50 per unit represents materials costs, and the remaining $10 per unit represents other expenses incurred within Division Y.

Instructions:

(1) Would the market price of $40 per unit be an appropriate transfer price for Bradford Company? Explain.

(2) If Division Y purchases 50,000 units from Division X and a transfer price of $35 per unit is negotiated between the managers of Divisions X and Y, how much would the operating income of each division and total company operating income increase?

(3) Prepare condensed divisional income statements for Bradford Company, based on the data in (2).

(4) If a transfer price of $34 per unit is negotiated, how much would the operating income of each division and total company income increase?

(5) (a) What is the range of possible negotiated transfer prices that would be acceptable for Bradford Company?

(b) Assume that the division managers of X and Y cannot agree on a transfer price, what price would you suggest as the transfer price?

**CHAPTER 13** | **Problem 13-1B.** Strauss Company has recently decided to implement a policy designed to control inventory better. Based on past experience, the following data have been gathered for materials, which are used at a uniform rate throughout the year:

| | |
|---|---|
| Units required during the year.............. | 4,800 |
| Ordering cost, per order placed ............ | $40.00 |
| Storage cost, per unit...................... | .60 |

Instructions:
  (1) Complete the following table for "number of orders" of 1 through 8. Round to the nearest dollar.

| Number of Orders | Number of Units per Order | Average Units in Inventory | Order and Storage Costs | | |
|---|---|---|---|---|---|
| | | | Order Cost | Storage Cost | Combined Cost |
| 1 | 4,800 | 2,400 | $40 | $1,440 | $1,480 |

  (2) Determine the economic order quantity, based on the table completed in (1).
  (3) Determine the economic order quantity, using the formula in Chapter 13.

**Problem 13-3B.** Hansen Company purchases Part M for use at both its Akron and Tifton branches. Part M is available in limited quantities from two suppliers. The relevant data are as follows:

Units required:
  Akron Branch..................... 200
  Tifton Branch..................... 300

Supplier X:
  Units available................... 300
  Unit cost delivered to:
    Akron Branch................... $60
    Tifton Branch.................. $80

Supplier Y:
  Units available................... 300
  Unit cost delivered to:
    Akron Branch................... $75
    Tifton Branch.................. $70

The manager of the purchasing department has prepared the following purchase plan for the Akron and Tifton branches:
  (1) Purchase all units for Akron Branch from Supplier X.
  (2) Purchase remaining available units of Supplier X for the Tifton Branch.
  (3) Purchase any additional units required by the Tifton Branch from Supplier Y.

Instructions:
  (1) Construct a linear programming graph for units to be purchased from Supplier X. Plot the units for the Akron Branch along the horizontal axis.
  (2) Identify the four corners at which an economical purchase plan might be identified on the linear programming graph. Label the corners A through D, as shown in the illustration on page 294.
  (3) For each corner in (2), indicate purchases from Suppliers X and Y for the Akron and Tifton branches. Identify Plan 1 with Corner A, Plan 2 with Corner B, Plan 3 with Corner C, and Plan 4 with Corner D.
  (4) Determine the most economical purchase plan by computing the total cost of purchases for each plan identified in (3).
  (5) Was the purchasing department manager's plan the most economical? Explain.

**Problem 13-4B.** The controller for Barrentine Company is preparing some preliminary cost projections for the 1985 budget and has accumulated the following cost and production data for 1984:

|  | Units Produced | Total Costs |
|---|---|---|
| January.............. | 15,000 | $40,000 |
| February............. | 20,000 | 41,500 |
| March............... | 26,000 | 46,000 |
| April................ | 35,000 | 52,000 |
| May................. | 48,000 | 59,000 |
| June ............... | 54,000 | 62,000 |
| July ................ | 60,000 | 65,200 |
| August .............. | 45,000 | 57,000 |
| September........... | 31,000 | 48,000 |
| October ............. | 21,000 | 42,000 |
| November ........... | 10,000 | 34,200 |
| December ........... | 12,000 | 37,000 |

Instructions:

(1) Estimate the variable cost per unit and the total fixed cost, using the high-low method of cost estimation.
(2) Construct a scattergraph, including the total cost line.
(3) Based on the scattergraph in (2), estimate the variable cost per unit and the total fixed cost at 20,000 units of production.
(4) Why are there differences between the estimates in (1) and (3)?

**Problem 13-6B.** The management of Mathis Company has decided to use the least squares method for estimating variable costs per unit and fixed costs. The following production and cost data have been gathered from the accounting and production records.

|  | Units Produced | Total Costs |
|---|---|---|
| January.............. | 60,000 | $160,000 |
| February............. | 70,000 | 180,000 |
| March............... | 80,000 | 200,000 |
| April................ | 90,000 | 220,000 |
| May................. | 100,000 | 238,000 |
| June ............... | 95,000 | 226,000 |
| July ................ | 110,000 | 260,000 |
| August .............. | 120,000 | 282,000 |
| September........... | 105,000 | 249,000 |
| October ............. | 85,000 | 212,000 |

Cost and production data for November and December have been excluded, since operations during these months were not typical.

Instructions:

(1) Prepare a computational table for the estimation of the variable cost per unit, using the following form. Do not include thousands in the table.

| Total Units Produced (P$_i$) | Total Costs (C$_i$) | P$_i^2$ | P$_i$C$_i$ |
|---|---|---|---|

(2) Determine the estimated variable cost per unit, using the table in (1) and the least squares formula in Chapter 13. Round to the nearest cent.

(3) Determine the estimated fixed cost, using (1) and (2) and the least squares formula in Chapter 13.

(4) Estimate the total cost of 80,000 units of production, using the results of (2) and (3).

**CHAPTER 14** | **Problem 14-1B.** International Films Inc. is considering purchasing the rights to one of two autobiographies for the purposes of producing and marketing a motion picture. Each autobiography has the potential for development and sale as one of the following: (1) a cable TV movie, (2) a network (noncable) TV movie, (3) a weekly TV series, or (4) a commercial theater movie. The estimated profit for development and sale of each autobiography and the estimated chances of occurrence are as follows:

**Autobiography E**

|  | Estimated Profit | Chance of Occurrence |
|---|---|---|
| Cable TV movie............ | $10,000,000 | 15% |
| Network TV movie.......... | 8,000,000 | 30 |
| Weekly TV series........... | 6,000,000 | 35 |
| Theater movie ............. | 12,000,000 | 20 |

**Autobiography F**

|  | Estimated Profit | Chance of Occurrence |
|---|---|---|
| Cable TV movie............ | $20,000,000 | 30% |
| Network TV movie.......... | 6,000,000 | 40 |
| Weekly TV series........... | 2,000,000 | 10 |
| Theater movie ............. | 10,000,000 | 20 |

Instructions:

(1) Determine the expected value of each autobiography.

(2) Based on the results of (1), which autobiography rights should be purchased?

**Problem 14-2B.** Pfeiffer News Distributors recently purchased a newsstand on the corner of Elm Street and Hubbard Avenue in downtown Whitlock. The new manager of the newsstand must decide how many copies of a magazine to stock on a weekly basis. The magazine is published locally and features local civic and social events and has a large classified advertising section. The former manager had noted that the maximum weekly sales, in the past, had been 100 magazines, and to be assured that all demand could be met, 120 magazines were purchased. The cost of the magazine is $30 for quantities of 20 ($1.50 per magazine), and the magazine is sold for $3.50. Any magazines remaining at the end of the week are worthless and are thrown away.

The records for the past ten weeks indicate the following sales:

| Number of Weeks | Actual Demand (Sales) |
|---|---|
| 2 | 40 magazines |
| 3 | 60 |
| 4 | 80 |
| 1 | 100 |

Instructions:

(1) Prepare a payoff table of possible outcomes in terms of contribution margin, using the format shown on page 319.

(2) Based on the sales data for the past ten weeks, estimate the chances of each level of possible demand for the magazine.

(3) Prepare a payoff table of expected values of possible outcomes in terms of contribution margin, using the format shown on page 319.

(4) Based on (3), how many magazines should be purchased? Explain.

**Problem 14-3B.** Davies Mines Inc. is preparing to bid on the purchase of mining rights to one of two plats of federally owned land: Plat #2400 and Plat #3100. Both plats of land are known to contain deposits of coal; however, the quality of the deposits will not be known until actual mining begins.

Preliminary estimates indicate that, for Plat #2400, there is a 60% chance that the deposit is of high quality and will yield total profits of $22,000,000. There is a 25% chance that the deposit is of moderate quality and will yield total profits of $5,000,000. Finally, there is a 15% chance that the deposit is of low quality and will yield total profits of $1,000,000.

Preliminary estimates indicate that, for Plat #3100, there is an 80% chance that the deposit is of high quality and will yield total profits of $16,000,000. There is a 15% chance that the deposit is of moderate quality and will yield total profits of $8,000,000. Finally, there is a 5% chance that the deposit is of low quality and will yield total profits of $2,000,000.

Instructions:

(1) Prepare a decision tree with expected values to aid management in deciding on which plat rights to bid.

(2) On which plat rights should the management of Davies Mines Inc. bid?

**Problem 14-4B.** The controller of Yung Company must decide whether to investigate an unfavorable direct labor rate variance of $10,000 reported for June. The variance is expected to continue for July if not corrected. Past experience indicates that 60% of the time the variance is caused by use of more experienced, higher paid employees in jobs budgeted for less experienced, lower paid employees. In this case, the variance can be eliminated by the rescheduling of job assignments. On the other hand, 40% of the time the variance is caused by overtime created by production commitments in excess of normal operations. If production demands continue additional employees will be hired. However, because of training commitments, any new employees would not be available for assignment to normal operations until the end of July.

Instructions:

(1) Assuming that no additional costs would be incurred in conducting an investigation, what is the expected cost of investigating the direct labor rate variance?

(2) What is the value of conducting an investigation of the direct labor rate variance?

(3) If the estimated cost to investigate the variance is $4,500, should the controller authorize an investigation? Explain.

(4) If the estimated cost to investigate the variance is $6,500, should the controller authorize an investigation? Explain.

**Problem 14-5B.** The management of Inwood Realty Corporation is considering an investment in one of three real estate projects. The first project involves the construction of a medical office complex which will be sold to a group of practicing physicians.

The second project involves the construction of a professional office building in which space will be sold to nonmedical professional businesses, such as law firms and insurance agencies. The third project is the construction of a small shopping mall in which space will be sold to small businesses. The success of each project depends on whether demand for the constructed space is high, moderate, or low. The estimated profit or loss for each project is as follows:

|                          | Demand for Space | | |
| --- | --- | --- | --- |
| Project | High | Moderate | Low |
| Medical office complex....... | $5,000,000 | $2,000,000 | $(2,000,000) |
| Professional office complex... | 4,000,000 | 2,500,000 | (1,000,000) |
| Shopping mall.............. | 3,000,000 | 1,500,000 | (500,000) |

Instructions:

(1) If the management of Inwood Realty Corporation uses the maximin concept, which of the three projects would be chosen?

(2) If the management of Inwood Realty Corporation uses the maximax concept, which of the three projects would be chosen?

(3) Assuming that the Moderate column is the most likely estimate of profit for each of the projects, what alternative decision concept can be used by Inwood Realty Corporation?

**CHAPTER 15 | Problem 15-1B.** Data pertaining to the current position of Carol Cavitt and Company are as follows:

| | |
| --- | --- |
| Cash..................................... | $120,000 |
| Marketable securities ........................ | 50,000 |
| Accounts and notes receivable (net).......... | 130,000 |
| Inventory .................................. | 275,000 |
| Prepaid expenses .......................... | 25,000 |
| Accounts payable .......................... | 165,000 |
| Notes payable (short-term) .................. | 100,000 |
| Accrued liabilities........................... | 35,000 |

Instructions:
    (1) Compute (a) working capital, (b) current ratio, and (c) acid-test ratio.
    (2) List the following captions on a sheet of paper:

| Transaction | Working Capital | Current Ratio | Acid-Test Ratio |
|---|---|---|---|

Compute the working capital, current ratio, and acid-test ratio after each of the following transactions, and record the results in the appropriate columns. Consider each transaction separately and assume that only that transaction affects the data given above.
    (a) Declared a cash dividend, $50,000.
    (b) Issued additional shares of stock for cash, $100,000.
    (c) Purchased goods on account, $40,000.
    (d) Paid accounts payable, $60,000.
    (e) Borrowed cash from bank on a long-term note, $50,000.
    (f) Paid cash for office supplies, $25,000.
    (g) Received cash on account, $75,000.
    (h) Paid notes payable, $100,000.
    (i) Declared a common stock dividend on common stock, $150,000.
    (j) Sold marketable securities, $50,000.

**Problem 15-3B.** For 1985, Chapman Company initiated an extensive sales promotion campaign that included the expenditure of an additional $75,000 for advertising. At the end of the year, Susan Chapman, the president, is presented with the following condensed comparative income statement:

Chapman Company
Comparative Income Statement
For Years Ended December 31, 1985 and 1984

|  | 1985 | 1984 |
|---|---|---|
| Sales | $845,625 | $689,520 |
| Sales returns and allowances | 20,625 | 9,520 |
| Net sales | $825,000 | $680,000 |
| Cost of goods sold | 528,000 | 442,000 |
| Gross profit | $297,000 | $238,000 |
| Selling expenses | $198,000 | $102,000 |
| General expenses | 36,300 | 40,800 |
| Total operating expenses | $234,300 | $142,800 |
| Operating income | $ 62,700 | $ 95,200 |
| Other expense | 3,300 | 3,400 |
| Income before income tax | $ 59,400 | $ 91,800 |
| Income tax | 14,025 | 23,800 |
| Net income | $ 45,375 | $ 68,000 |

Instructions:

(1) Prepare a comparative income statement for the two-year period, presenting an analysis of each item in relationship to net sales for each of the years.
(2) To the extent the data permit, comment on the significant relationships revealed by the vertical analysis prepared in (1).

**Problem 15-5B.** The comparative financial statements of R. C. Jain Company are as follows. On December 31, 1985 and 1984, the market price of R. C. Jain Company common stock was $60 and $47 respectively.

R. C. Jain Company
Comparative Income Statement
For Years Ended December 31, 1985 and 1984

|  | 1985 | 1984 |
|---|---|---|
| Sales | $4,590,000 | $3,272,500 |
| Sales returns and allowances | 90,000 | 72,500 |
| Net sales | $4,500,000 | $3,200,000 |
| Cost of goods sold | 3,060,000 | 2,080,000 |
| Gross profit | $1,440,000 | $1,120,000 |
| Selling expenses | $ 585,000 | $ 464,000 |
| General expenses | 292,500 | 224,000 |
| Total operating expenses | $ 877,500 | $ 688,000 |
| Operating income | $ 562,500 | $ 432,000 |
| Other income | 22,500 | 19,200 |
|  | $ 585,000 | $ 451,200 |
| Other expense (interest) | 129,200 | 110,000 |
| Income before income tax | $ 455,800 | $ 341,200 |
| Income tax | 210,800 | 150,200 |
| Net income | $ 245,000 | $ 191,000 |

R. C. Jain Company
Comparative Retained Earnings Statement
For Years Ended December 31, 1985 and 1984

|  | 1985 | 1984 |
|---|---|---|
| Retained earnings, January 1 | $723,000 | $602,000 |
| Add net income for year | 245,000 | 191,000 |
| Total | $968,000 | $793,000 |
| Deduct dividends: |  |  |
| On preferred stock | $ 40,000 | $ 40,000 |
| On common stock | 45,000 | 30,000 |
| Total | $ 85,000 | $ 70,000 |
| Retained earnings, December 31 | $883,000 | $723,000 |

R. C. Jain Company
Comparative Balance Sheet
December 31, 1985 and 1984

| Assets | 1985 | 1984 |
|---|---|---|
| Current assets: | | |
| Cash | $ 225,000 | $ 175,000 |
| Marketable securities | 100,000 | — |
| Accounts receivable (net) | 425,000 | 325,000 |
| Inventory | 720,000 | 480,000 |
| Prepaid expenses | 30,000 | 20,000 |
| Total current assets | $1,500,000 | $1,000,000 |
| Long-term investments | 250,000 | 225,000 |
| Plant assets | 2,093,000 | 1,948,000 |
| Total assets | $3,843,000 | $3,173,000 |

| Liabilities | | |
|---|---|---|
| Current liabilities | $ 750,000 | $ 650,000 |
| Long-term liabilities: | | |
| Mortgage note payable, 12%, due 1989 | $ 410,000 | — |
| Bonds payable, 10%, due 1995 | 800,000 | $ 800,000 |
| Total long-term liabilities | $1,210,000 | $ 800,000 |
| Total liabilities | $1,960,000 | $1,450,000 |

| Stockholders' Equity | | |
|---|---|---|
| Preferred $4 stock, $50 par | $ 500,000 | $ 500,000 |
| Common stock, $20 par | 500,000 | 500,000 |
| Retained earnings | 883,000 | 723,000 |
| Total stockholders' equity | $1,883,000 | $1,723,000 |
| Total liabilities and stockholders' equity | $3,843,000 | $3,173,000 |

Instructions:

Determine for 1985 the following ratios, turnovers, and other measures, presenting the figures used in your computations:
(1) Working capital.
(2) Current ratio.
(3) Acid-test ratio.
(4) Accounts receivable turnover.
(5) Number of days' sales in receivables.
(6) Inventory turnover.
(7) Number of days' sales in inventory.
(8) Ratio of plant assets to long-term liabilities.
(9) Ratio of stockholders' equity to liabilities.
(10) Ratio of net sales to assets.
(11) Rate earned on total assets.
(12) Rate earned on stockholders' equity.
(13) Rate earned on common stockholders' equity.
(14) Earnings per share on common stock.

*(continued)*

(15) Price-earnings ratio.
(16) Dividend yield.
(17) Number of times interest charges earned.
(18) Number of times preferred dividends earned.

**CHAPTER 16** | **Problem 16-1B.** Lin Chin Company was organized on March 1, 1984, when the price-level index was 140. Capital stock of $98,000 was issued in exchange for cash of $25,000 and land valued at $81,200. The land was subject to property taxes of $8,200 due for the current year. No transactions occurred in the year ended April 30, 1985, and the price-level index at the end of the year was 154. The income statement for the year ended April 30, 1986, disclosed the following:

| | |
|---|---|
| Sales (made uniformly during the year) | $196,800 |
| Cost of goods sold (purchased when price index was 162) | 129,600 |
| Depreciation expense (asset purchased when price index was 156) | 9,672 |
| Other expenses (incurred uniformly during the year) | 36,080 |

The average price-level index for the year ended April 30, 1986, was 164, and at the end of the year it was 172.

Instructions:
(1) Prepare a conventional balance sheet at April 30, 1985, in report form.
(2) Prepare a constant dollar balance sheet at April 30, 1985, in report form.
(3) Prepare a constant dollar income statement for the year ended April 30, 1986. The purchasing power gain for the year was $2,680.

**Problem 16-2B.** The monetary items held by Melton Company throughout 1984 consisted of cash and accounts payable. The beginning balances and changes in these monetary items during the year, along with the relevant price-level index for each, are as follows:

| | Amount | Price-Level Index |
|---|---|---|
| Monetary asset: | | |
| Cash, January 1, 1984 | $ 47,500 | 190 |
| Add sales | 175,480 | 205 |
| Deduct expenses | 154,775 | 205 |
| Cash, December 31, 1984 | $ 68,205 | 220 |
| Monetary liability: | | |
| Accounts payable, January 1, 1984 | $ 29,640 | 190 |
| Add purchases on account | 135,300 | 205 |
| Deduct payments on account | 136,325 | 205 |
| Accounts payable, December 31, 1984 | $ 28,615 | 220 |

Instructions:
Calculate the purchasing power gain or loss for the year ended December 31, 1984, using the format shown on page 379.

**Problem 16-3B.** P. R. Murray & Associates, a professional corporation, was organized with the issuance of $30,000 of capital stock on January 1, 1984, and began operations by leasing office space and office equipment. On April 30, 1984, P. R. Murray & Associates acquired office equipment in exchange for a $25,000, 18%, three-year note payable with interest payable monthly. All services rendered were for cash, and all expenses, except for depreciation, were paid in cash. The conventional income statement for the year ended December 31, 1984, and the conventional balance sheet on December 31, 1984, are as follows:

**P. R. Murray & Associates**
**Income Statement**
**For Year Ended December 31, 1984**

| | | |
|---|---|---|
| Revenues: | | |
| Professional fees............$132,300 | | (Fees were collected uniformly during year; average price-level index was 252) |
| Expenses: | | |
| Depreciation | | |
| expense........ $  3,000 | | (The office equipment was purchased when the price-level index was 250) |
| Other operating | | |
| expenses.......  114,030 | | (Expenses were paid uniformly during year; average price-level index was 252) |
| Total expenses .............  117,030 | | |
| Net income.................. $ 15,270 | | |

**P. R. Murray & Associates**
**Balance Sheet**
**December 31, 1984**

**Assets**

| | | |
|---|---:|---:|
| Cash ...................................................... | | $48,270 |
| Office equipment ...................................... | $25,000 | |
| Less accumulated depreciation ..................... | 3,000 | 22,000 |
| Total assets ............................................. | | $70,270 |

**Liabilities and Stockholders' Equity**

| | |
|---|---:|
| Notes payable........................................... | $25,000 |
| Capital stock ............................................ | 30,000 |
| Retained earnings ...................................... | 15,270 |
| Total liabilities and stockholders' equity........... | $70,270 |

The average general price-level index for 1984 was 252. During the year, the price-level index was as follows:

| | |
|---|---|
| January 1, 1984........... | 240 |
| April 30, 1984............. | 250 |
| December 31, 1984........ | 264 |

Instructions:

    (1) Calculate the purchasing power gain or loss for the year ended December 31, 1984, using the format shown on page 379.

    (2) Prepare a constant dollar income statement for the year ended December 31, 1984.

    (3) Prepare a constant dollar retained earnings statement for the year ended December 31, 1984.

    (4) Prepare a constant dollar balance sheet at December 31, 1984, in report form.

**Problem 16-4B.** Waller Company was organized on July 1, 1984, by the sale of $80,000 of capital stock for cash. It leased store space and equipment and sold goods only for cash. During the year ended June 30, 1985, goods costing $248,500 were purchased, $201,650 of the goods were sold for $262,145, and operating expenses were $31,261. The conventional income statement for the year ended June 30, 1985, and the conventional balance sheet at June 30, 1985, are as follows:

**Waller Company**
**Income Statement**
**For Year Ended June 30, 1985**

| | |
|---|---:|
| Sales | $262,145 |
| Cost of goods sold | 201,650 |
| Gross profit | $ 60,495 |
| Operating expenses | 31,261 |
| Net income | $ 29,234 |

**Waller Company**
**Balance Sheet**
**June 30, 1985**

**Assets**

| | |
|---|---:|
| Cash | $104,895 |
| Inventory | 46,850 |
| Total assets | $151,745 |

**Liabilities and Stockholders' Equity**

| | |
|---|---:|
| Accounts payable | $ 42,511 |
| Capital stock | 80,000 |
| Retained earnings | 29,234 |
| Total liabilities and stockholders' equity | $151,745 |

    The relevant current cost amounts for the preceding financial statement items are as follows:

| | |
|---|---:|
| Cash | $104,895 |
| Inventory | 68,650 |
| Accounts payable | 42,511 |
| Capital stock | 80,000 |

| | |
|---|---:|
| Sales.......................... | $262,145 |
| Cost of goods sold............. | 234,150 |
| Operating expenses............ | 31,261 |

Instructions:
- (1) Prepare a current cost income statement for the year ended June 30, 1985.
- (2) Prepare a current cost retained earnings statement for the year ended June 30, 1985.
- (3) Prepare a current cost balance sheet at June 30, 1985, in report form.

CHAPTER 17 | **Problem 17-1B.** The comparative balance sheet of Meyers Corporation at June 30 of the current year and the preceding year is as follows:

| Assets | Current Year | Preceding Year |
|---|---:|---:|
| Cash ......................................... | $ 47,300 | $ 45,300 |
| Accounts receivable (net)........................... | 59,400 | 58,500 |
| Merchandise inventory ............................. | 77,250 | 91,850 |
| Prepaid expenses.................................. | 5,600 | 4,950 |
| Plant assets...................................... | 375,000 | 310,000 |
| Accumulated depreciation — plant assets............. | (117,500) | (125,000) |
| | $447,050 | $385,600 |

| Liabilities and Stockholders' Equity | | |
|---|---:|---:|
| Accounts payable................................. | $ 55,250 | $ 38,800 |
| Mortgage note payable............................ | — | 50,000 |
| Common stock, $25 par ........................... | 250,000 | 200,000 |
| Premium on common stock ........................ | 35,000 | 25,000 |
| Retained earnings ................................ | 106,800 | 71,800 |
| | $447,050 | $385,600 |

Additional data obtained from the income statement and from an examination of the noncurrent asset, noncurrent liability, and stockholders' equity accounts in the ledger are as follows:
- (a) Net income, $75,000.
- (b) Depreciation reported on the income statement, $27,500.
- (c) An addition to the building was constructed at a cost of $100,000, and fully depreciated equipment costing $35,000 was discarded, no salvage being realized.
- (d) The mortgage note payable was not due until 1989, but the terms permitted earlier payment without penalty.
- (e) 2,000 shares of common stock were issued at $30 for cash.
- (f) Cash dividends declared, $40,000.

Instructions:
Prepare a statement of changes in financial position (working capital concept), including a section on changes in components of working capital.

**Problem 17-2B.** The comparative balance sheet of Brown Corporation at December 31 of the current year and the preceding year is as follows:

| Assets | Current Year | Preceding Year |
|---|---|---|
| Cash | $ 55,100 | $ 42,500 |
| Trade receivables (net) | 91,350 | 61,150 |
| Inventories | 104,500 | 109,500 |
| Prepaid expenses | 3,600 | 2,700 |
| Land | 50,000 | 50,000 |
| Buildings | 325,000 | 245,000 |
| Accumulated depreciation—buildings | (120,600) | (110,400) |
| Machinery and equipment | 255,000 | 255,000 |
| Accumulated depreciation—machinery and equipment | ( 92,000) | ( 65,000) |
| Patents | 35,000 | 40,000 |
|  | $706,950 | $630,450 |

| Liabilities and Stockholders' Equity | | |
|---|---|---|
| Accounts payable (merchandise creditors) | $ 61,150 | $ 75,000 |
| Dividends payable | 15,000 | 10,000 |
| Salaries payable | 6,650 | 7,550 |
| Mortgage note payable, due 1990 | 50,000 | — |
| Bonds payable | — | 75,000 |
| Common stock, $20 par | 300,000 | 250,000 |
| Premium on common stock | 100,000 | 75,000 |
| Retained earnings | 174,150 | 137,900 |
|  | $706,950 | $630,450 |

An examination of the income statement and the accounting records revealed the following additional information applicable to the current year:
  (a) Net income, $96,250.
  (b) Depreciation expense reported on the income statement: buildings, $10,200; machinery and equipment, $27,000.
  (c) Patent amortization reported on the income statement, $5,000.
  (d) A mortgage note for $50,000 was issued in connection with the construction of a building costing $80,000; the remainder was paid in cash.
  (e) 2,500 shares of common stock were issued at 30 in exchange for the bonds payable.
  (f) Cash dividends declared, $60,000.

Instructions:
  Prepare a statement of changes in financial position (working capital concept), including a section for changes in components of working capital.

**Problem 17-3B.** The comparative balance sheet of Brown Corporation and other data necessary for the analysis of the corporation's funds flow are presented in Problem 17-2B.

Instructions:

Prepare a statement of changes in financial position (cash concept), including a summary of the change in cash balance.

**Problem 17-4B.** The comparative balance sheet of D. A. Ruiz Inc., at December 31 of the current year and the preceding year, and the noncurrent asset accounts, the noncurrent liability accounts, and the stockholders' equity accounts for the current year, are as follows:

| Assets | Current Year | Preceding Year |
|---|---|---|
| Cash . . . . . . . . . . . . . . . . . . . . . . . . . . . . . . . . . . . . . . . . . . . . . . . . . . . | $ 58,000 | $ 64,500 |
| Trade receivables (net) . . . . . . . . . . . . . . . . . . . . . . . . . . . . . | 103,325 | 91,725 |
| Inventories . . . . . . . . . . . . . . . . . . . . . . . . . . . . . . . . . . . . . . . . . | 208,100 | 188,000 |
| Prepaid expenses. . . . . . . . . . . . . . . . . . . . . . . . . . . . . . . . . . . . | 6,850 | 7,100 |
| Investments . . . . . . . . . . . . . . . . . . . . . . . . . . . . . . . . . . . . . . . . . | — | 50,000 |
| Land . . . . . . . . . . . . . . . . . . . . . . . . . . . . . . . . . . . . . . . . . . . . . . . . | 65,000 | 65,000 |
| Buildings. . . . . . . . . . . . . . . . . . . . . . . . . . . . . . . . . . . . . . . . . . . . | 285,000 | 185,000 |
| Accumulated depreciation — buildings . . . . . . . . . . . . . . . . | ( 76,400) | ( 69,000) |
| Equipment . . . . . . . . . . . . . . . . . . . . . . . . . . . . . . . . . . . . . . . . . . | 480,500 | 410,500 |
| Accumulated depreciation — equipment. . . . . . . . . . . . . . . | (143,500) | (129,000) |
| | $986,875 | $863,825 |

| Liabilities and Stockholders' Equity | | |
|---|---|---|
| Accounts payable (merchandise creditors) . . . . . . . . . . . . | $ 60,075 | $ 77,600 |
| Income tax payable. . . . . . . . . . . . . . . . . . . . . . . . . . . . . . . . . . | 5,500 | 2,800 |
| Notes payable. . . . . . . . . . . . . . . . . . . . . . . . . . . . . . . . . . . . . . | 105,000 | — |
| Discount on long-term notes payable . . . . . . . . . . . . . . . . . | (4,625) | — |
| Common stock, $20 par . . . . . . . . . . . . . . . . . . . . . . . . . . . . . | 624,000 | 600,000 |
| Premium on common stock . . . . . . . . . . . . . . . . . . . . . . . . . . | 67,000 | 55,000 |
| Appropriation for contingencies . . . . . . . . . . . . . . . . . . . . . . | 35,000 | 25,000 |
| Retained earnings . . . . . . . . . . . . . . . . . . . . . . . . . . . . . . . . . . | 94,925 | 103,425 |
| | $986,875 | $863,825 |

ACCOUNT INVESTMENTS                                                      ACCOUNT NO.

| Date | | Item | Debit | Credit | Balance Debit | Balance Credit |
|---|---|---|---|---|---|---|
| 19-- | | | | | | |
| Jan. | 1 | Balance | | | 50,000 | |
| June | 29 | Realized $57,500 cash from sale | | 50,000 | — | — |

ACCOUNT LAND                                                             ACCOUNT NO.

| Date | | Item | Debit | Credit | Balance Debit | Balance Credit |
|---|---|---|---|---|---|---|
| 19-- | | | | | | |
| Jan. | 1 | Balance | | | 65,000 | |

ACCOUNT  BUILDINGS                                                      ACCOUNT NO.

| Date | | Item | Debit | Credit | Balance Debit | Balance Credit |
|---|---|---|---|---|---|---|
| 19-- | | | | | | |
| Jan. | 1 | Balance | | | 185,000 | |
| Apr. | 1 | Acquired with notes payable | 100,000 | | 285,000 | |

ACCOUNT  ACCUMULATED DEPRECIATION — BUILDINGS                          ACCOUNT NO.

| Date | | Item | Debit | Credit | Balance Debit | Balance Credit |
|---|---|---|---|---|---|---|
| 19-- | | | | | | |
| Jan. | 1 | Balance | | | | 69,000 |
| Dec. | 31 | Depreciation for year | | 7,400 | | 76,400 |

ACCOUNT  EQUIPMENT                                                      ACCOUNT NO.

| Date | | Item | Debit | Credit | Balance Debit | Balance Credit |
|---|---|---|---|---|---|---|
| 19-- | | | | | | |
| Jan. | 1 | Balance | | | 410,500 | |
| Feb. | 8 | Discarded, no salvage | | 35,000 | | |
| July | 2 | Purchased for cash | 60,000 | | | |
| Nov. | 1 | Purchased for cash | 45,000 | | 480,500 | |

ACCOUNT  ACCUMULATED DEPRECIATION — EQUIPMENT                          ACCOUNT NO.

| Date | | Item | Debit | Credit | Balance Debit | Balance Credit |
|---|---|---|---|---|---|---|
| 19-- | | | | | | |
| Jan. | 1 | Balance | | | | 129,000 |
| Feb. | 8 | Equipment discarded | 35,000 | | | |
| Dec. | 31 | Depreciation for year | | 49,500 | | 143,500 |

ACCOUNT  LONG-TERM NOTES PAYABLE                                        ACCOUNT NO.

| Date | | Item | Debit | Credit | Balance Debit | Balance Credit |
|---|---|---|---|---|---|---|
| 19-- | | | | | | |
| Apr. | 1 | Issued 10-year notes | | 105,000 | | 105,000 |

ACCOUNT  DISCOUNT ON LONG-TERM NOTES PAYABLE                           ACCOUNT NO.

| Date | | Item | Debit | Credit | Balance Debit | Balance Credit |
|---|---|---|---|---|---|---|
| 19-- | | | | | | |
| Apr. | 1 | Notes issued | 5,000 | | 5,000 | |
| Dec. | 31 | Amortization | | 375 | 4,625 | |

ACCOUNT  COMMON STOCK, $20 PAR                                    ACCOUNT NO.

| Date | | Item | Debit | Credit | Balance | |
|------|---|------|-------|--------|---------|---|
| | | | | | Debit | Credit |
| 19-- | | | | | | |
| Jan. | 1 | Balance | | | | 600,000 |
| July | 10 | Stock dividend | | 24,000 | | 624,000 |

ACCOUNT  PREMIUM ON COMMON STOCK                                 ACCOUNT NO.

| Date | | Item | Debit | Credit | Balance | |
|------|---|------|-------|--------|---------|---|
| | | | | | Debit | Credit |
| 19-- | | | | | | |
| Jan. | 1 | Balance | | | | 55,000 |
| July | 10 | Stock dividend | | 12,000 | | 67,000 |

ACCOUNT  APPROPRIATION FOR CONTINGENCIES                         ACCOUNT NO.

| Date | | Item | Debit | Credit | Balance | |
|------|---|------|-------|--------|---------|---|
| | | | | | Debit | Credit |
| 19-- | | | | | | |
| Jan. | 1 | Balance | | | | 25,000 |
| Dec. | 31 | Appropriation | | 10,000 | | 35,000 |

ACCOUNT  RETAINED EARNINGS                                       ACCOUNT NO.

| Date | | Item | Debit | Credit | Balance | |
|------|---|------|-------|--------|---------|---|
| | | | | | Debit | Credit |
| 19-- | | | | | | |
| Jan. | 1 | Balance | | | | 103,425 |
| July | 10 | Stock dividend | 36,000 | | | |
| Dec. | 31 | Net income | | 127,500 | | |
| | 31 | Cash dividends | 90,000 | | | |
| | 31 | Appropriated | 10,000 | | | 94,925 |

Instructions:

Prepare a statement of changes in financial position (working capital concept), including a section for changes in components of working capital.

**Problem 17-5B.** The comparative balance sheet of D. A. Ruiz Inc. and other data necessary for the analysis of the corporation's funds flow are presented in Problem 17-4B.

Instructions:

Prepare a statement of changes in financial position (cash concept), including a summary of the change in cash balance.

**CHAPTER 18** | **Problem 18-1B.** The Savoy Police Department prepared the following line budget for the current fiscal year:

Savoy Police Department
Budget of Expenditures
For Year Ending June 30, 19--

| | |
|---|---|
| Salaries | $1,100,000 |
| Patrol cars | 400,000 |
| Utilities | 280,000 |
| Building maintenance | 190,000 |
| Supplies | 150,000 |
| Miscellaneous | 60,000 |
| Total expenditures | $2,180,000 |

Estimates of the percent of each line item for each of the three principal programs of the police department are as follows:

| | Crime Prevention | Criminal Investigation | Community Education |
|---|---|---|---|
| Salaries | 60% | 30% | 10% |
| Patrol cars | 65 | 30 | 5 |
| Utilities | 40 | 50 | 10 |
| Building maintenance | 45 | 50 | 5 |
| Supplies | 50 | 30 | 20 |
| Miscellaneous | 40 | 40 | 20 |

Percent of Cost by Program

Instructions:

Prepare a combined line-program budget for the current year.

*(If the working papers correlating with the textbook are not used, omit Problem 18-2B.)*

**Problem 18-2B.** After the closing entries were posted, the accounts in the ledger of the general fund for Woodbury on June 30, the end of the current year, are as follows:

| | |
|---|---|
| Accounts Payable | $ 52,500 |
| Cash in Bank | 18,400 |
| Savings Accounts | 50,000 |
| Cash on Hand | 5,600 |
| Fund Balance | 170,750 |
| Investments in Marketable Securities | 150,000 |
| Property Taxes Receivable | 72,650 |
| Reserve for Encumbrances | 41,000 |
| Wages Payable | 32,400 |

Estimated revenues, revenues, appropriations, encumbrances, and expenditures from the respective subsidiary ledgers have been entered in the statement of revenues and expenditures—budget and actual in the working papers. The fund balance account had a balance of $167,150 on July 1, the beginning of the current year.

Instructions:

(1) Complete the statement of revenues and expenditures—budget and actual.
(2) Prepare a statement of changes in fund balance.
(3) Prepare a balance sheet.

**Problem 18-3B.** The trial balance for the City of Waycross—General Fund at the beginning of the current year is as follows:

City of Waycross—General Fund
Trial Balance
July 1, 19--

| | | |
|---|---|---|
| Cash | 72,600 | |
| Savings Accounts | 220,000 | |
| Property Taxes Receivable | 190,600 | |
| Investment in U. S. Treasury Notes | 80,000 | |
| Accounts Payable | | 81,700 |
| Wages Payable | | 26,120 |
| Fund Balance | | 455,380 |
| | 563,200 | 563,200 |

The following data summarize the operations for the current year.
(a) Estimated revenues, $4,600,000; appropriations, $4,560,000.
(b) Revenues from property tax levy, $3,320,000.
(c) Cash received from property taxes, $3,040,000; other revenues, $1,320,000.
(d) Expenditures encumbered and evidenced by purchase orders, $2,660,000.
(e) Expenditures for payrolls, $1,850,000.
(f) Liquidation of encumbrances and vouchers prepared, $2,600,000.
(g) Cash disbursed for vouchers, $2,530,000; for payment of wages, $1,840,000; for savings accounts, $50,000.

Instructions:

(1) Prepare entries in general journal form to record the foregoing summarized operations.
(2) Open T accounts for the accounts appearing in the trial balance and enter the balances as of July 1, identifying them as "Bal."
(3) Open T accounts for Reserve for Encumbrances, Estimated Revenues, Revenues, Appropriations, Expenditures, and Encumbrances. Post the entries recorded in (1) to the accounts, using the identifying letters in place of dates.
(4) Prepare the appropriate entries to close the accounts as of June 30 and post to the accounts, using the letter "C" to identify the postings.
(5) Prepare a trial balance as of June 30.

# Answers to Self-Examination Questions

## CHAPTER 2

1. **D** Factory overhead includes all manufacturing costs except direct materials and direct labor. Gloves for factory workers (answer A), salaries for factory plant supervisors (answer B), and salaries for material handlers (answer C) are examples of factory overhead items.

2. **A** Job order cost systems are best suited to businesses manufacturing for special orders from customers, such as would be the case for a repair shop for antique furniture (answer A). A process cost system is best suited for manufacturers of homogeneous units of product, such as rubber (answer B) and coal (answer C).

3. **D** Materials are transferred from the storeroom to the factory in response to materials requisitions (answer D). Materials needed for production are requested by the department responsible by issuing purchase requisitions (answer A), which serve as the basis for the purchasing department to order the goods by issuing purchase orders (answer B). When the goods are received, the receiving department personnel prepare receiving reports (answer C).

4. **B** If the amount of factory overhead applied during a particular period exceeds the actual overhead costs, the factory overhead account will have a credit balance and is said to be overapplied (answer B) or overabsorbed. If the amount applied is less than the actual costs, the account will have a debit balance and is said to be underapplied (answer A) or underabsorbed (answer C).

5. **A** The subsidiary ledger containing the details of each job order is the cost ledger (answer A), while each account in the cost ledger is called a job cost sheet (answer B). The stock ledger (answer C), also called the finished goods ledger, is the subsidiary ledger for the finished goods account and contains an account for each kind of finished product.

## CHAPTER 3

1. **C** The process cost system is most appropriate for a business where manufacturing is conducted by continuous operations and involves a series of uniform production processes, such as the processing of crude oil (answer C). The job order cost system is most appropriate for a business where the product is made to customers' specifications, such as custom furniture manufacturing (answer A) and commercial building construction (answer B).

2. **C** The manufacturing costs that are necessary to convert direct materials into finished products are referred to as processing costs. The processing costs include direct labor and factory overhead (answer C).

3. **B** The number of units that could have been produced from start to finish during a period is termed equivalent units. The 4,875 equivalent units (answer B) is determined as follows:

| | |
|---|---:|
| To process units in inventory on May 1: | |
| 1,000 units × ¼ . . . . . . . . . . . . . . . . . . . . . | 250 |
| To process units started and completed in | |
| May: 5,500 units − 1,000 units . . . . . . . . . | 4,500 |
| To process units in inventory on May 31: | |
| 500 units × ¼ . . . . . . . . . . . . . . . . . . . . . . . | 125 |
| Equivalent units of production in May . . . . . | 4,875 |

4. **A** The processing costs (direct labor and factory overhead) totaling $48,750 are divided by the number of equivalent units (4,875) to

determine the unit processing cost of $10 (answer A).

5. **B** The product resulting from a process that has little value in relation to the principal product or joint products is known as a by-product (answer B). When two or more commodities of significant value are produced from a single direct material, the products are termed joint products (answer A). The raw material that enters directly into the finished product is termed direct material (answer C).

## CHAPTER 4

1. **C** Continuous budgeting (answer C) is a type of budgeting that continually provides for maintenance of a twelve-month projection into the future.

2. **C** The capital expenditures budget (answer C) summarizes the plans for the acquisition of plant facilities and equipment for a number of years into the future. The cash budget (answer A) presents the expected inflow and outflow of cash for a budget period, and the sales budget (answer B) presents the expected sales for the budget period.

3. **B** A budget performance report (answer B) compares actual results with budgeted figures.

4. **A** Costs that tend to remain constant in amount, regardless of variations in volume of activity, are called fixed costs (answer A). Costs that tend to fluctuate in amount in accordance with variations in volume are called variable costs (answer B). Costs that have both fixed and variable characteristics are called semi-fixed costs (answer C) or semivariable costs (answer D).

5. **C** Flexible budgeting (answer C) provides a series of budgets for varying rates of activity and thereby builds into the budgeting system the effect of fluctuations in volume of activity. Budget performance reporting (answer A) is a system of reports that compares actual results with budgeted figures. Continuous budgeting (answer B) is a variant of fiscal-year budgeting that provides for continuous twelve-month projections into the future. This is achieved by periodically deleting from the current budget the data for the elapsed period and adding newly estimated budget data for the same period next year.

## CHAPTER 5

1. **B** The unfavorable direct materials price variance of $2,550 (answer B) is determined as follows:

| | |
|---|---:|
| Actual price | $5.05 per pound |
| Standard price | 5.00 per pound |
| Price variance—unfavorable | $ .05 per pound |

$.05 × 51,000 actual quantity = $2,550

2. **C** The favorable direct labor cost time variance of $110 (answer C) is determined as follows:

| | |
|---|---:|
| Actual time | 990 hours |
| Standard time | 1,000 hours |
| Time variance—favorable | 10 hours |

10 hours × $11 standard ........ $110

3. **B** The unfavorable factory overhead volume variance of $2,000 (answer B) is determined as follows:

| | |
|---|---:|
| Productive capacity not used | 1,000 hours |
| Standard fixed factory overhead cost rate | × $2 |
| Factory overhead volume variance —unfavorable | $2,000 |

4. **A** The favorable factory overhead controllable variance of $3,500 (answer A) is determined as follows:

| | |
|---|---:|
| Actual factory overhead cost incurred | $112,500 |
| Budgeted factory overhead for standard product produced [(19,000 hours at $4 variable) + (20,000 hours at $2 fixed)] | 116,000 |
| Factory overhead controllable variance —favorable | $ 3,500 |

5. **D** Since variances from standard costs represent the differences between the standard cost of manufacturing a product and the actual costs incurred, the variances relate to the product. Therefore, they should be reported on interim income statements as an adjustment to gross profit—at standard.

## CHAPTER 6

1. **C** A change in sales from one period to another can be attributed to (1) a change in the number of units sold—quantity factor and (2) a change in the unit price—price factor.

The $45,000 decrease (answer C) attributed to the quantity factor is determined as follows:

Decrease in number of units sold in
current year . . . . . . . . . . . . . . . . . . . . . .    5,000
Unit sales price in preceding year . . . . . . .   × $9
Quantity factor—decrease. . . . . . . . . . . .   $45,000

The price factor can be determined as follows:

Increase in unit sales price in current
year . . . . . . . . . . . . . . . . . . . . . . . . . . . .      $1
Number of units sold in current year . . . .  ×80,000
Price factor—increase . . . . . . . . . . . . . .   $80,000

The increase of $80,000 attributed to the price factor less the decrease of $45,000 attributed to the quantity factor accounts for the $35,000 increase in total sales for the current year.

2. B Under the variable costing concept (answer B), the cost of products manufactured are composed of only those manufacturing costs that increase or decrease as the volume of production rises or falls. These costs include direct materials, direct labor, and variable factory overhead. Under the absorption costing concept (answer A), all manufacturing costs become a part of the cost of the products manufactured. The absorption costing concept is required in the determination of historical cost and taxable income. The variable costing concept is often useful to management in making decisions.

3. C In the variable costing income statement, the deduction of the variable cost of goods sold from sales yields the manufacturing margin (answer C). Deduction of the variable selling and general expenses from manufacturing margin yields the contribution margin (answer B).

4. B The contribution margin of $260,000 (answer B) is determined by deducting all of the variable costs and expenses ($400,000 + $90,000) from sales ($750,000).

5. A In a period in which the number of units manufactured exceeds the number of units sold, the operating income reported under the absorption costing concept is larger than the operating income reported under the variable costing concept (answer A) because fixed manufacturing costs are deferred when the absorption costing concept is used. This deferment has the effect of excluding fixed manufacturing costs from the current cost of goods sold.

## CHAPTER 7

1. A Variable costs change in total as the volume of activity changes (answer A) or, expressed in another way, the unit variable cost remains constant with changes in volume.

2. C The break-even point of $400,000 (answer C) is that point in operations at which revenue and expired costs are exactly equal and is determined as follows:

$$\underset{\text{(in \$)}}{\text{Break-Even Sales}} = \underset{\text{(in \$)}}{\text{Fixed Costs}} + \underset{\text{(as \% of Sales)}}{\text{Variable Costs}}$$
$$S = \$240,000 + 40\%S$$
$$60\%S = \$240,000$$
$$S = \$400,000$$

3. B $450,000 of sales would be required to realize operating profit of $30,000, computed as follows:

$$\underset{\text{(in \$)}}{\text{Sales}} = \underset{\text{(in \$)}}{\text{Fixed Costs}} + \underset{\text{(as \% of Sales)}}{\text{Variable Costs}} + \underset{\text{Profit}}{\text{Desired}}$$
$$S = \$240,000 + 40\%S + \$30,000$$
$$60\%S = \$270,000$$
$$S = \$450,000$$

4. A The margin of safety of 20% (answer A) represents the possible decrease in sales revenue that may occur before an operating loss results and is determined as follows:

$$\text{Margin of Safety} = \frac{\text{Sales} - \text{Sales at Break-Even Point}}{\text{Sales}}$$

$$\text{Margin of Safety} = \frac{\$500,000 - \$400,000}{\$500,000}$$
$$= 20\%$$

The margin of safety can also be expressed in terms of dollars and would amount to $100,000, determined as follows:

Sales . . . . . . . . . . . . . . . . . . . . . . . . . . . . . . .   $500,000
Less sales at break-even point . . . . . . . .    400,000
Margin of safety . . . . . . . . . . . . . . . . . . .   $100,000

5. D The contribution margin ratio indicates the percentage of each sales dollar available to cover the fixed expenses and provide operating income and is determined as follows:

$$\text{Contribution Margin Ratio} = \frac{\text{Sales} - \text{Variable Expenses}}{\text{Sales}}$$

$$\text{Contribution Margin Ratio} = \frac{\$500,000 - \$200,000}{\$500,000}$$

$$= 60\%$$

# CHAPTER 8

1.  **A** Differential cost (answer A) is the amount of increase or decrease in cost that is expected from a particular course of action compared with an alternative. Replacement cost (answer B) is the cost of replacing an asset at current market prices, and sunk cost (answer C) is a past cost that will not be affected by subsequent decisions.

2.  **A** A sunk cost is not affected by later decisions. For Victor Company, the sunk cost is the $50,000 (answer A) book value of the equipment, which is equal to the original cost of $200,000 (answer C) less the accumulated depreciation of $150,000 (answer B).

3.  **C** The amount of income that could have been earned from the best available alternative to a proposed use of cash is called opportunity cost (answer C). Actual cost (answer A) or historical cost (answer B) is the cash or equivalent outlay for goods or services actually acquired.

4.  **C** Under the variable cost concept of product pricing (answer C), fixed manufacturing costs, fixed general and selling expenses, and desired profit are allowed for in the determination of the markup. Only desired profit is allowed for in the markup under the total cost concept (answer A). Under the product cost concept (answer B), total selling and general expenses, and desired profit are allowed for in the determination of markup.

5.  **A** Microeconomic theory indicates that profits of a business enterprise will be maximized at the point where marginal revenue equals marginal cost (answer A). At lower levels of production and sales, the change in total revenue is greater than the change in total cost (answer B); hence, more profit can be achieved by manufacturing and selling more units. At higher levels of production and sales, the change in total cost is greater than the change in total revenue (answer C); hence, less profit will be achieved by manufacturing and selling more units.

# CHAPTER 9

1.  **C** Methods of evaluating capital investment proposals that ignore the time value of money are categorized as methods that ignore present value. This category includes the average rate of return method (answer A) and the cash payback method (answer B).

2.  **B** The average rate of return is 24% (answer B), determined by dividing the expected average annual earnings by the average investment, as indicated below:

$$\frac{\$60,000 \div 5}{(\$100,000 + \$0) \div 2} = 24\%$$

3.  **B** Of the three methods of analyzing proposals for capital investments, the cash payback method (answer B) refers to the expected period of time required to recover the amount of cash to be invested. The average rate of return method (answer A) is a measure of the anticipated profitability of a proposal. The discounted cash flow method (answer C) reduces the expected future net cash flows originating from a proposal to their present values.

4.  **C** The discounted cash flow method (answer C) uses the concept of present value to determine the total present value of the cash flows expected from a proposal and compares this value with the amount to be invested. The average rate of return method (answer A) and the cash payback method (answer B) ignore present value. The discounted internal rate of return method (answer D) uses the present value concept to determine the discounted internal rate of return expected from the proposal.

5.  **A** Capital rationing (answer A) is the process by which management allocates available investment funds among competing capital investment proposals. Capital expenditure budgeting (answer B) is the process of summarizing the decisions that have been made for the acquisition of plant assets and preparing a capital expenditures budget to reflect these decisions. Leasing (answer C) is an alternative that management should consider before making a final decision on the acquisition of assets.

## CHAPTER 10

1. C Corporations are taxable entities (answer C), while individuals practicing as sole proprietors (answer A) and as partners in partnerships (answer B) report their income in their individual tax returns.
2. B The federal income tax is a progressive tax; that is, it provides for a graduated series of tax rates, with successively higher rates being applied to successively higher segments of taxable income. The highest tax rate applied to the income of any particular taxpayer is called the taxpayer's marginal tax rate (answer B).
3. D In periods of rising prices, the use of lifo rather than fifo results in a higher cost of goods sold (answer A), lower net income (answer B), and lower income tax (answer C) because the last goods purchased (which are the most costly) are considered to be the first sold. Thus, since the most costly goods are considered to be sold, the result is a higher cost of goods sold, lower net income, and lower income tax.
4. C By using both the installment method of reporting sales (answer A) and the completed-contract method of reporting income on long-term construction projects (answer B), a taxpayer may postpone the payment of a portion of the income tax. Although the same amount of tax is eventually due in both cases, the delay of cash payments means that the taxpayer can retain cash longer, and this cash can be invested to earn income or to reduce debt and thus save on interest costs.
5. B Net long-term capital gains for both individual and corporate taxpayers are given preferential treatment, with the maximum tax rate for corporations being 28% (answer B).

## CHAPTER 11

1. B The manager of a profit center (answer B) has responsibility for and authority over costs and revenues. If the manager has responsibility and authority for only costs, the department is referred to as a cost center (answer A). If the responsibility and authority extend to the investment in assets as well as costs and revenues, it is referred to as an investment center (answer C).

2. B Operating expenses should be apportioned to the various departments as nearly as possible in accordance with the cost of services rendered to them. For rent expense, generally the most appropriate basis is the floor space devoted to each department (answer B).
3. C When the departmental margin approach to income reporting is employed, the direct departmental expenses for each department are deducted from the gross profit for each department to yield departmental margin for each department (answer C). The indirect expenses are deducted from the total departmental margin to yield income from operations (answer A). The final total income is identified as net income (answer B).
4. A Operating expenses traceable to or incurred for the sole benefit of a specific department, such as sales commissions expense, are termed direct expenses (answer A) and should be so reported on the income statement departmentalized through departmental margin.
5. B Operating expenses incurred for the entire enterprise as a unit and hence not subject to the control of individual department managers, such as office salaries, are termed indirect expenses (answer B) and should be so reported on the income statement departmentalized through departmental margin.

## CHAPTER 12

1. C Managers of investment centers (answer C) have authority and responsibility for revenues, expenses, and assets. Managers of profit centers (answer A) have authority and responsibility for revenues and expenses. Managers of cost centers (answer B) have authority and responsibility for costs.
2. A The rate of return on investment for Division A is 20% (answer A), computed as follows:

$$\text{Rate of Return on Investment (ROI)} = \frac{\text{Operating Income}}{\text{Invested Assets}}$$

$$\text{ROI} = \frac{\$350,000 - \$200,000 - \$30,000}{\$600,000}$$

$$\text{ROI} = \frac{\$120,000}{\$600,000}$$

$$\text{ROI} = 20\%$$

3. C Investment turnover is the ratio of sales to invested assets (answer C). The ratio of operating income to sales is the profit margin (answer A). The ratio of operating income to invested assets is the rate of return on investment (answer B).

4. B The profit margin for Division L of Liddy Co. is 15% (answer B), computed as follows:

$$\frac{\text{Rate of Return on}}{\text{Investment (ROI)}} = \frac{\text{Profit Margin} \times}{\text{Investment Turnover}}$$
$$24\% = \text{Profit Margin} \times 1.6$$
$$15\% = \text{Profit Margin}$$

5. C The market price approach (answer C) to transfer pricing uses the price at which the product or service transferred could be sold to outside buyers as the transfer price. The cost price approach (answer A) uses cost as the basis for setting transfer prices. The negotiated price approach (answer B) allows managers of decentralized units to agree (negotiate) among themselves as to the proper transfer price.

## CHAPTER 13

1. B Linear programming (answer B) is a quantitative technique that can be useful to management in solving problems in which the objective is to minimize cost or maximize profits, subject to several limiting factors. The economic order quantity (answer A) is useful to management in determining the optimum quantity of inventory to be ordered at one time. The least squares (answer C) and high-low (answer D) methods are useful to management in cost estimation.

2. D Storage cost per unit (answer A), annual units required (answer B), and cost per order (answer C) are all important in the determination of economic order quantity.

3. B The point at which the total cost line intersects the vertical axis of the scattergraph indicates the estimated total fixed cost of production (answer B). The total variable cost (answer A) for any level of production is the difference between the estimated total cost indicated on the scattergraph and the estimated total fixed cost. The estimated variable cost per unit (answer C) can be computed by dividing the total variable cost by the total units of production for a given level of production.

4. C The least squares method (answer C) uses statistical formulas to estimate the total cost and the variable and fixed cost components. The high-low method (answer A) uses only data for the highest and lowest levels of production in estimating costs. The scattergraph method (answer D) uses a graph to estimate costs. The linear programming method (answer B) is not a cost estimation method.

5. A The high-low method (answer A) is normally considered the least accurate method of estimating costs because it uses data for only the highest and lowest levels of production. On the other hand, the scattergraph method (answer B) and the least squares method (answer C) both utilize data for all the observed levels of production. Linear programming (answer D) is not a cost estimation method.

## CHAPTER 14

1. B The expected value concept (answer B) involves identifying the possible outcomes from a decision and estimating the likelihood that each outcome will occur. The maximin concept (answer A) leads management to decide in favor of that alternative with the maximum (largest) minimum profit. The maximax concept (answer C) leads management to decide in favor of that alternative with the maximum (largest) profit.

2. A The expected value of Proposal R is $24,000 (answer A), computed as follows:

Expected Value = .60($80,000) + .40(−$60,000)
Expected Value = $48,000 − $24,000
Expected Value = $24,000

3. B Management's use of expected value can be facilitated through the use of payoff tables and decision trees (answer B). The maximax concept (answer A) and the maximin concept (answer C) do not use expected values.

4. A The value of perfect information concerning Proposal A is $3,000 (answer A), which is the difference between (1) the expected value of Proposal A based on perfect information, $8,000 (answer C), and (2) the expected value of a decision based on existing information, $5,000 (answer B).

5. A The maximin concept leads management to decide in favor of that alternative with the maximum, minimum profit. For Freeman Co., the

minimum profit (loss) for each alternative appears in the low demand column. This column indicates that Project W (answer A) has the highest minimum profit ($120,000) of the four alternatives.

## CHAPTER 15

1.  A Percentage analysis indicating the relationship of the component parts to the total in a financial statement, such as the relationship of current assets to total assets (20% to 100%) in the question, is called vertical analysis (answer A). Percentage analysis of increases and decreases in corresponding items in comparative financial statements is called horizontal analysis (answer B). An example of horizontal analysis would be the presentation of the amount of current assets in the preceding balance sheet along with the amount of current assets for the current year, with the increase or decrease in current assets between the periods expressed as a percentage. Differential analysis (answer C), as discussed in Chapter 8, is the area of accounting concerned with the effect of alternative courses of action on revenue and expenses.

2.  D Various solvency measures, categorized as current position analysis, indicate a firm's ability to meet currently maturing obligations. Each measure contributes in the analysis of a firm's current position and is most useful when viewed with other measures and when compared with similar measures for other periods and for other firms. Working capital (answer A) is the excess of current assets over current liabilities; the current ratio (answer B) is the ratio of current assets to current liabilities; and the acid-test ratio (answer C) is the ratio of the sum of cash, receivables, and marketable securities to current liabilities.

3.  D The ratio of current assets to current liabilities is usually referred to as the current ratio (answer A) and is sometimes referred to as the working capital ratio (answer B) or bankers' ratio (answer C).

4.  C The ratio of the sum of cash, receivables, and marketable securities (sometimes called "quick assets") to current liabilities is called the acid-test ratio (answer C) or quick ratio. The current ratio (answer A) and working capital ratio (answer B) are two terms that describe the ratio of current assets to current liabilities.

5.  C As with many attempts at analyzing financial data, it is possible to determine more than one measure that is useful for evaluating the efficiency in the management of inventory. Both the inventory turnover (answer A), which is determined by dividing the cost of goods sold by the average inventory, and the number of days' sales in inventory (answer B), which is determined by dividing the inventory at the end of the year by the average daily cost of goods sold, express the relationship between the cost of goods sold and inventory.

## CHAPTER 16

1.  B A decline in the general purchasing power caused by rising prices is termed inflation (answer B), while an increase in general purchasing power caused by declining prices is deflation (answer A). A purchasing power loss (answer C) is created by holding monetary items during periods of inflation or deflation.

2.  C The restated constant dollar amount would be $140,000 (answer C), determined as follows:

$$\frac{140}{100} \times \$100,000 = \$140,000$$

3.  B Purchasing power gains are created by holding monetary liabilities such as bonds payable (answer B) during periods in which the general price level is rising. Cash (answer A) and notes receivable (answer D) are monetary assets which, if held during periods of increasing general price levels, create purchasing power losses. Inventory (answer C) is a nonmonetary asset. Nonmonetary assets do not create purchasing power gains or losses.

4.  D Cash (answer A), notes receivable (answer B), and bonds payable (answer C) are all monetary items representing cash or claims to a fixed amount of cash.

5.  C An increase in the current cost of the land over the original cost is termed an unrealized holding gain (answer C). When the land is sold, the gain becomes a realized holding gain (answer A). A purchasing power gain (answer B) is created by holding monetary items during periods of general price-level changes.

## CHAPTER 17

1.  A Working capital is the excess of total current assets over total current liabilities; that is,

$225,000 less $150,000, or $75,000 (answer A) in the question.

2. **A** Working capital is provided by transactions that decrease noncurrent assets (answer A), such as the sale of a plant asset for cash. Transactions that decrease noncurrent liabilities (answer B), such as the redemption of long-term liabilities for cash, and transactions that decrease stockholders' equity (answer C), such as the declaration of cash dividends, are applications of working capital.

3. **C** The acquisition of equipment for cash (answer C) decreases cash and working capital and is therefore an application of working capital. The sale of common stock for cash (answer A) and the issuance of bonds payable for cash (answer B) both increase cash and working capital and therefore are sources of working capital.

4. **C** The operations section of the statement of changes in financial position would report a total of $77,000 (answer C) for the working capital provided by operations, determined as follows:

| | | |
|---|---:|---:|
| Operations during the year: | | |
| Net income.................. | $55,000 | |
| Add deduction not decreasing working capital during the year: | | |
| Depreciation............. | 22,000 | $77,000 |

5. **D** The operations section of the statement of changes in financial position would report a total of $65,500 for the cash provided by operations, determined as follows:

| | | |
|---|---:|---:|
| Operations during the year: | | |
| Net income................. | | $55,000 |
| Add deductions not decreasing cash during the year: | | |
| Depreciation............. | $22,000 | |
| Decrease in inventories.... | 5,000 | |
| Decrease in prepaid expenses ............... | 500 | 27,500 |
| | | $82,500 |
| Deduct additions not increasing cash during the year: | | |
| Increase in trade receivables.............. | $10,000 | |
| Decrease in accounts payable................. | 7,000 | 17,000 |
| | | $65,500 |

## CHAPTER 18

1. **A** In accounting for nonprofit organizations, the term used to represent an accounting entity with appropriate accounts for a particular purpose is "fund" (answer A). Potential liabilities of a fund are referred to as appropriations (answer B), and a fund's binding commitments to pay money eventually are referred to as encumbrances (answer C).

2. **B** The program format (answer B) focuses on programs and their related costs. A line format (answer A) presents expenditures by object of the expenditure or by the reason for the expenditure. Zero-base budgeting (answer C) is a concept that requires all levels of management to start from zero and estimate revenues and expenditures as if there had been no previous activities in their unit.

3. **C** The account that represents the capital for a nonprofit organization is termed Fund Balance (answer C). For a commercial enterprise, the capital resulting from earnings retained in the enterprise is referred to by various terms, including Retained Earnings (answer A) and Accumulated Earnings (answer B).

4. **D** Each account in the subsidiary expenditure ledger indicates appropriations (answer A), encumbrances (answer B), and expenditures (answer C).

5. **A** A statement of changes in fund balance (answer A), although similar to the retained earnings statement of a commercial enterprise, has a unique format. It indicates the balance at the beginning of the year in fund balance, plus or minus, as appropriate, the difference for the fiscal year of (1) estimated revenues and appropriations, (2) revenues and estimated revenues, and (3) appropriations and expenditures. Finally, the encumbrances outstanding at the end of the year are deducted to arrive at the end-of-the year balance of the fund balance account. The trial balance (answer B) and balance sheet (answer C) for nonprofit organizations are similar to such statements for commercial enterprises.

# D
APPENDIX

# General Accounting Systems for Manufacturing Operations

A general accounting system for manufacturing operations is essentially an extension of the periodic inventory procedures commonly used by merchandising enterprises. A general accounting system is fairly simple and may be used when only a single product or several similar products are manufactured and the manufacturing processes are neither complicated nor numerous. Such a situation will be assumed in the following discussion.

STATEMENT OF<br>COST OF<br>GOODS<br>MANUFAC-<br>TURED

Since manufacturing activities differ greatly from selling and general administration activities, it is customary to separate the two groups of accounts in the summarizing process at the end of an accounting period. In addition, the manufacturing group is usually reported in a separate statement of cost of goods manufactured in order to avoid a long, complicated income statement. An income statement and its supporting statement of cost of goods manufactured are illustrated on page 513.

In the statement of cost of goods manufactured, the amount listed for the work in process inventory at the beginning of the period is composed of the estimated cost of the direct materials, the direct labor, and the factory overhead applicable to the inventory of partially processed products at the end of the preceding period. The cost of the direct materials placed in production is determined by adding to the beginning inventory of materials the net cost of the direct materials purchased and deducting the ending inventory. The amount listed for direct labor is determined by referring to the direct labor account. The factory overhead costs, which are determined by referring to the ledger, can be listed individually in the statement of cost of goods manufactured or reported in a separate schedule, as was assumed for the illustration. The sum of the costs of direct materials placed in production, the direct labor, and the factory overhead represents the total manufacturing costs incurred during the period. Addition of this amount to the beginning inventory of work in process yields the total cost of the work that has been in process during the period. The estimated cost of the ending inventory of work in process is then deducted to yield the cost of goods manufactured. The "cost of goods manufactured" reported in the statement of cost of goods manufactured and income statement is comparable to the "purchases" reported by a merchandising enterprise.

INCOME
STATEMENT

**Cox Manufacturing Company**
**Income Statement**
**For Year Ended December 31, 1985**

| | | |
|---|---:|---:|
| Sales | | $821,400 |
| Cost of goods sold: | | |
| Finished goods inventory, January 1, 1985 | $ 71,250 | |
| Cost of goods manufactured | 462,750 | |
| Cost of finished goods available for sale | $534,000 | |
| Less finished goods inventory, December 31, 1985 | 80,500 | |
| Cost of goods sold | | 453,500 |

STATEMENT OF
COST OF GOODS
MANUFACTURED

**Cox Manufacturing Company**
**Statement of Cost of Goods Manufactured**
**For Year Ended December 31, 1985**

| | | |
|---|---:|---:|
| Work in process inventory, January 1, 1985 | | $ 47,500 |
| Direct materials: | | |
| Inventory, January 1, 1985 | $ 50,750 | |
| Purchases | 195,000 | |
| Cost of materials available for use | $245,750 | |
| Less inventory, December 31, 1985 | 48,250 | |
| Cost of materials placed in production | $197,500 | |
| Direct labor | 145,500 | |
| Factory overhead | 116,400 | |
| Total manufacturing costs | | 459,400 |
| Total work in process during period | | $506,900 |
| Less work in process inventory, December 31, 1985 | | 44,150 |
| Cost of goods manufactured | | $462,750 |

**PERIODIC INVENTORY PROCEDURES**

The process of adjusting the periodic inventory and other accounts of a manufacturing business is like that for a merchandising enterprise. Adjustments to the merchandise inventory account are replaced by adjusting entries for the three inventory accounts: Finished Goods, Work in Process, and Materials. The first account (Finished Goods) is adjusted through Income Summary, and the other two accounts (Work in Process and Materials) are adjusted through Manufacturing Summary.

At the end of the accounting period, the temporary accounts that appear in the statement of cost of goods manufactured are closed to Manufacturing Summary. This account's final balance, which represents the cost of goods manufactured during the period, is then closed to Income Summary. The remaining temporary accounts (Sales, Expenses, etc.) are then closed to Income Summary in the usual manner.

The relationship of the manufacturing summary account to the income summary account is illustrated as follows:

Manufacturing Summary

| | | | | |
|---|---|---|---|---|
| Dec. 31 Work in process inventory, Jan. 1 | 47,500 | Dec. 31 Work in process inventory, Dec. 31 | 44,150 |
| 31 Direct materials inventory, Jan. 1 | 50,750 | 31 Direct materials inventory, Dec. 31 | 48,250 |
| 31 Direct materials purchases | 195,000 | 31 To Income Summary | 462,750 |
| 31 Direct labor | 145,500 | | |
| 31 Factory overhead | 116,400 | | |
| | 555,150 | | 555,150 |

Income Summary

| | | | |
|---|---|---|---|
| Dec. 31 Finished goods inventory, Jan. 1 | 71,250 | Dec. 31 Finished goods inventory, Dec. 31 | 80,500 |
| 31 From Manufacturing Summary | 462,750 | | |

COST OF GOODS MANUFACTURED CLOSED TO INCOME SUMMARY

To simplify the illustration, the individual overhead accounts are presented as a total. Note that the balance transferred from the manufacturing summary account to the income summary account, $462,750, is the same as the final figure reported on the statement of cost of goods manufactured.

**MANUFAC-TURING WORK SHEET**

Many accountants use a work sheet to assist them in adjusting the inventory and other accounts and in the preparation of the financial statements. The work sheet used for manufacturing enterprises using periodic inventory procedures includes a column for account titles and ten money columns, arranged in five pairs of debit and credit columns. The principal headings of the five sets of money columns are as follows:

1. Trial Balance
2. Adjustments
3. Cost of Goods Manufactured
4. Income Statement
5. Balance Sheet

The following sections describe and illustrate the use of a work sheet for the manufacturing operations of Ming Manufacturing Company.

**Trial Balance and Adjustments on the Work Sheet**

The trial balance for Ming Manufacturing Company as of December 31, 1985, appears on the work sheet presented on pages 516-517. The data needed for year-end adjustments on December 31, 1985, are summarized as follows:

Wages payable on December 31, 1985:
Direct labor . . . . . . . . . . . . . . . . . . . . . . . . . . . . . . . . . . . . . . . . $ 4,500
Indirect labor . . . . . . . . . . . . . . . . . . . . . . . . . . . . . . . . . . . . . . . 950

Depreciation for the year:
Factory equipment . . . . . . . . . . . . . . . . . . . . . . . . . . . . . . . . . . 22,300
Factory buildings . . . . . . . . . . . . . . . . . . . . . . . . . . . . . . . . . . . . 6,000

Inventories on December 31, 1985:
Factory supplies . . . . . . . . . . . . . . . . . . . . . . . . . . . . . . . . . . . . . 1,800
Finished goods . . . . . . . . . . . . . . . . . . . . . . . . . . . . . . . . . . . . . . 91,000
Work in process . . . . . . . . . . . . . . . . . . . . . . . . . . . . . . . . . . . . . 65,800
Direct materials . . . . . . . . . . . . . . . . . . . . . . . . . . . . . . . . . . . . . 58,725

Explanations of the adjusting entries in the work sheet are given in the paragraphs that follow.

### Wages Payable

The liability for the wages earned by employees but not yet paid is recorded by a credit of $5,450 to Wages and Salaries Payable and debit to Direct Labor and Indirect Factory Labor of $4,500 and $950 respectively (entry (a) on the work sheet).

### Depreciation

The adjustment for depreciation expense of factory equipment is recorded by a debit to Depreciation — Factory Equipment for $22,300 and a credit to Accumulated Depreciation — Factory Equipment for $22,300 (entry (b) on the work sheet). The adjustment for depreciation expense of factory buildings is recorded by a debit to Depreciation — Factory Buildings for $6,000 and a credit to Accumulated Depreciation — Factory Buildings for $6,000 (entry (c) on the work sheet).

### Factory Supplies

The $4,700 balance of factory supplies in the trial balance is the cost of supplies on hand at the beginning of the year and the cost of supplies purchased during the year. The amount on hand at the end of the year (inventory) is $1,800. The excess of $2,900 over the inventory of $1,800 represents the supplies used, and the adjustment is a debit to Factory Supplies Expense and a credit to Factory Supplies for $2,900 (entry (d) on the work sheet).

### Finished Goods Inventory

The finished goods inventory account is adjusted through the income summary account. The beginning finished goods inventory is transferred to the income summary account by crediting Finished Goods and debiting Income Summary for $78,500 (entry (e) on the work sheet). The ending finished goods inventory is recorded by debiting Finished Goods and crediting Income Summary for $91,000 (entry (f) on the work sheet).

### Work in Process Inventory

As explained in a preceding section, the work in process inventory account is adjusted through Manufacturing Summary. The inventory of work in process at the beginning of the period is transferred to the manufacturing summary account by crediting Work in Process and debiting Manufacturing Summary for $55,000 (entry (g) on the work sheet). The ending work in process inventory is recorded by debiting Work in Process and crediting Manufacturing Summary for $65,800 (entry (h) on the work sheet).

### Direct Materials Inventory

Like the work in process inventory, the direct materials inventory at the beginning of the fiscal period is transferred to the manufacturing summary account by crediting Direct Materials and debiting Manufacturing Summary for $62,000 (entry (i) on the work sheet). The direct materials inventory at the end of the period is recorded by debiting Direct Materials and crediting Manufacturing Summary for $58,725 (entry (j) on the work sheet).

**Completing the Work Sheet**

After all the adjustments have been entered on the work sheet, each account balance, as adjusted, is then extended to the proper financial statement columns. The temporary accounts that appear in the statement of cost of goods manufactured are extended to the statement of cost of goods manufactured columns. The other accounts are extended to the income statement and balance sheet columns as appropriate. Note that the beginning and ending inventory amounts appearing

MING MANUFACTURING
Work
For Year Ended

| ACCOUNT TITLE | TRIAL BALANCE | | ADJUSTMENTS | |
|---|---|---|---|---|
| | DEBIT | CREDIT | DEBIT | CREDIT |
| Cash............................................... | 18,200 | | | |
| Accounts Receivable.......................... | 66,100 | | | |
| Allowance for Doubtful Accounts ................... | | 1,500 | | |
| Finished Goods ................................ | 78,500 | | (f) 91,000 | (e) 78,500 |
| Work in Process................................ | 55,000 | | (h) 65,800 | (g) 55,000 |
| Direct Materials................................ | 62,000 | | (j) 58,725 | (i) 62,000 |
| Factory Supplies................................ | 4,700 | | | (d) 2,900 |
| Prepaid Insurance ............................. | 1,250 | | | |
| Land............................................ | 50,000 | | | |
| Factory Buildings .............................. | 240,000 | | | |
| Accumulated Depreciation—Factory Buildings........ | | 30,000 | | (c) 6,000 |
| Factory Equipment.............................. | 446,000 | | | |
| Accumulated Depreciation—Factory Equipment....... | | 111,500 | | (b) 22,300 |
| Accounts Payable ............................. | | 45,600 | | |
| Wages and Salaries Payable....................... | | | | (a) 5,450 |
| Income Tax Payable ........................... | | 13,200 | | |
| Common Stock ($10 par)........................ | | 200,000 | | |
| Retained Earnings ............................. | | 537,325 | | |
| Dividends...................................... | 40,000 | | | |
| Income Summary............................... | | | (e) 78,500 | (f) 91,000 |
| Manufacturing Summary........................... | | | (g) 55,000 | (h) 65,800 |
| | | | (i) 62,000 | (j) 58,725 |
| Sales........................................... | | 915,800 | | |
| Direct Materials Purchases ........................ | 220,800 | | | |
| Direct Labor.................................... | 214,250 | | (a) 4,500 | |
| Indirect Factory Labor............................ | 48,350 | | (a) 950 | |
| Depreciation—Factory Equipment................... | | | (b) 22,300 | |
| Factory Heat, Light, and Power..................... | 21,800 | | | |
| Factory Property Taxes............................ | 9,750 | | | |
| Depreciation—Factory Buildings .................... | | | (c) 6,000 | |
| Insurance Expense—Factory ...................... | 4,750 | | | |
| Factory Supplies Expense ......................... | | | (d) 2,900 | |
| Miscellaneous Factory Expense ..................... | 2,050 | | | |
| Selling Expenses ............................... | 130,500 | | | |
| General Expenses............................... | 88,700 | | | |
| Income Tax..................................... | 52,225 | | | |
| | 1,854,925 | 1,854,925 | 447,675 | 447,675 |
| Cost of Goods Manufactured...................... | | | | |
| Net Income ..................................... | | | | |

opposite Income Summary and Manufacturing Summary in the adjustments column are extended individually rather than as the net figure, since both amounts will be used in preparing the statements.

After all of the amounts have been extended to the appropriate columns, the work sheet is completed in the following manner:

(1) The statement of cost of goods manufactured columns are totaled. In the illustration, the total of the debit column is $675,400 and the total of the credit column is $124,525.

(2) The amount of the difference between the two statement of cost of goods manufactured columns is determined and entered in the statement of cost of goods manufactured credit column and the income statement debit column.

COMPANY
Sheet
December 31, 1985

| STATEMENT OF COST OF GOODS MANUFACTURED | | INCOME STATEMENT | | BALANCE SHEET | |
|---|---|---|---|---|---|
| DEBIT | CREDIT | DEBIT | CREDIT | DEBIT | CREDIT |
| | | | | 18,200 | |
| | | | | 66,100 | |
| | | | | | 1,500 |
| | | | | 91,000 | |
| | | | | 65,800 | |
| | | | | 58,725 | |
| | | | | 1,800 | |
| | | | | 1,250 | |
| | | | | 50,000 | |
| | | | | 240,000 | |
| | | | | | 36,000 |
| | | | | 446,000 | |
| | | | | | 133,800 |
| | | | | | 45,600 |
| | | | | | 5,450 |
| | | | | | 13,200 |
| | | | | | 200,000 |
| | | | | | 537,325 |
| | | | | 40,000 | |
| | | 78,500 | 91,000 | | |
| 55,000 | 65,800 | | | | |
| 62,000 | 58,725 | | 915,800 | | |
| 220,800 | | | | | |
| 218,750 | | | | | |
| 49,300 | | | | | |
| 22,300 | | | | | |
| 21,800 | | | | | |
| 9,750 | | | | | |
| 6,000 | | | | | |
| 4,750 | | | | | |
| 2,900 | | | | | |
| 2,050 | | | | | |
| | | 130,500 | | | |
| | | 88,700 | | | |
| | | 52,225 | | | |
| 675,400 | 124,525 | | | | |
| | 550,875 | 550,875 | | | |
| 675,400 | 675,400 | 900,800 | 1,006,800 | 1,078,875 | 972,875 |
| | | 106,000 | | | 106,000 |
| | | 1,006,800 | 1,006,800 | 1,078,875 | 1,078,875 |

This amount ($550,875 in the illustration) is the cost of goods manufactured for the period.

(3) The totals of the statement of cost of goods manufactured columns are then entered. The columns should now be in balance.

(4) The income statement columns and the balance sheet columns are totaled. The difference between the debits and credits in each of the two sets of columns is the amount of net income or loss for the period. This amount (net income of $106,000 in the illustration) is then entered as a balancing figure on the work sheet. For Ming Manufacturing Company, the net income of $106,000 is entered in the income statement debit column and in the balance sheet credit column.

(5) The totals of the last four columns, which should now be in balance, are entered.

**FINANCIAL STATEMENTS**    The completed work sheet provides the information necessary for preparing the financial statements. For Ming Manufacturing Company, the income statement, statement of cost of goods manufactured, retained earnings statement, and balance sheet are shown below and on pages 519-520. It should be noted that the factory overhead items are listed separately in the statement of cost of goods manufactured. An alternative would be to report the items in a separate schedule and list only the total in the statement of cost of goods manufactured.

**INCOME STATEMENT**

Ming Manufacturing Company
Income Statement
For Year Ended December 31, 1985

| | | |
|---|---:|---:|
| Sales | | $915,800 |
| Cost of goods sold: | | |
| Finished goods inventory, January 1, 1985 | $ 78,500 | |
| Cost of goods manufactured | 550,875 | |
| Cost of finished goods available for sale | $629,375 | |
| Less finished goods inventory, December 31, 1985 | 91,000 | |
| Cost of goods sold | | 538,375 |
| Gross profit | | $377,425 |
| Operating expenses: | | |
| Selling expenses | $130,500 | |
| General expenses | 88,700 | |
| Total operating expenses | | 219,200 |
| Income before income tax | | $158,225 |
| Income tax | | 52,225 |
| Net income (per share, $5.30) | | $106,000 |

STATEMENT OF
COST OF GOODS
MANUFACTURED

**Ming Manufacturing Company**
**Statement of Cost of Goods Manufactured**
**For Year Ended December 31, 1985**

| | | |
|---|---:|---:|
| Work in process inventory, January 1, 1985..... | | $ 55,000 |
| Direct materials: | | |
|     Inventory, January 1, 1985.................. | $ 62,000 | |
|     Purchases.................................. | 220,800 | |
|     Cost of materials available for use........... | $282,800 | |
|     Less inventory, December 31, 1985.......... | 58,725 | |
|       Cost of materials placed in production..... | $224,075 | |
| Direct labor.................................... | 218,750 | |
| Factory overhead: | | |
|     Indirect labor............................. | $49,300 | |
|     Depreciation of factory equipment........... | 22,300 | |
|     Heat, light, and power...................... | 21,800 | |
|     Property taxes............................. | 9,750 | |
|     Depreciation on buildings................... | 6,000 | |
|     Insurance expired.......................... | 4,750 | |
|     Factory supplies used...................... | 2,900 | |
|     Miscellaneous factory costs................ | 2,050 | |
|       Total factory overhead.................... | 118,850 | |
| Total manufacturing costs..................... | | 561,675 |
| Total work in process during period........... | | $616,675 |
| Less work in process inventory, December 31, | | |
|   1985...................................... | | 65,800 |
| Cost of goods manufactured.................. | | $550,875 |

RETAINED EARNINGS
STATEMENT

**Ming Manufacturing Company**
**Retained Earnings Statement**
**For Year Ended December 31, 1985**

| | | |
|---|---:|---:|
| Retained earnings, January 1, 1985 .................. | | $537,325 |
| Net income for year................................ | $106,000 | |
| Less dividends..................................... | 40,000 | |
| Increase in retained earnings ........................ | | 66,000 |
| Retained earnings, December 31, 1985................ | | $603,325 |

BALANCE
SHEET

**Ming Manufacturing Company**
**Balance Sheet**
**December 31, 1985**

## Assets

Current assets:

| | | | |
|---|---|---:|---:|
| Cash | | | $ 18,200 |
| Accounts receivable | | $ 66,100 | |
|   Less allowance for doubtful accounts | | 1,500 | 64,600 |
| Inventories: | | | |
|   Finished goods | | $ 91,000 | |
|   Work in process | | 65,800 | |
|   Direct materials | | 58,725 | 215,525 |
| Factory supplies | | | 1,800 |
| Prepaid insurance | | | 1,250 |
| Total current assets | | | $301,375 |
| Plant assets: | | | |
| Land | | | $ 50,000 |
| Buildings | | $240,000 | |
|   Less accumulated depreciation | | 36,000 | 204,000 |
| Factory equipment | | $446,000 | |
|   Less accumulated depreciation | | 133,800 | 312,200 |
| Total plant assets | | | 566,200 |
| Total assets | | | $867,575 |

## Liabilities

Current liabilities:

| | | |
|---|---:|---:|
| Accounts payable | $ 45,600 | |
| Wages and salaries payable | 5,450 | |
| Income tax payable | 13,200 | |
| Total current liabilities | | $ 64,250 |

## Stockholders' Equity

| | | |
|---|---:|---:|
| Common stock, $10 par | $200,000 | |
| Retained earnings | 603,325 | |
| Total stockholders' equity | | 803,325 |
| Total liabilities and stockholders' equity | | $867,575 |

ADJUSTING
ENTRIES

    At the end of the accounting period, the adjusting entries appearing in the work sheet are recorded in the journal and posted to the ledger, bringing the ledger into agreement with the data reported in the financial statements. The adjusting entries for Ming Manufacturing Company are as follows:

Adjusting Entries

(a)  Direct Labor . . . . . . . . . . . . . . . . . . . . . . . . . . . . . . . . . . . . . . .          4,500
     Indirect Factory Labor. . . . . . . . . . . . . . . . . . . . . . . . . . . . . . . . .            950
          Wages and Salaries Payable. . . . . . . . . . . . . . . . . . . . . . . . . .                        5,450

(b)  Depreciation — Factory Equipment. . . . . . . . . . . . . . . . . . . . . . .         22,300
          Accumulated Depreciation — Factory Equipment . . . . . . . . . .                       22,300

(c)  Depreciation — Factory Buildings. . . . . . . . . . . . . . . . . . . . . . . . .          6,000
          Accumulated Depreciation — Factory Buildings . . . . . . . . . . .                       6,000

(d)  Factory Supplies Expense . . . . . . . . . . . . . . . . . . . . . . . . . . . . . .          2,900
          Factory Supplies. . . . . . . . . . . . . . . . . . . . . . . . . . . . . . . . . . .                       2,900

(e)  Income Summary. . . . . . . . . . . . . . . . . . . . . . . . . . . . . . . . . . . . .         78,500
          Finished Goods . . . . . . . . . . . . . . . . . . . . . . . . . . . . . . . . . . .                       78,500

(f)  Finished Goods . . . . . . . . . . . . . . . . . . . . . . . . . . . . . . . . . . . . . .         91,000
          Income Summary. . . . . . . . . . . . . . . . . . . . . . . . . . . . . . . . . .                       91,000

(g)  Manufacturing Summary. . . . . . . . . . . . . . . . . . . . . . . . . . . . . . .         55,000
          Work in Process . . . . . . . . . . . . . . . . . . . . . . . . . . . . . . . . . . .                       55,000

(h)  Work in Process . . . . . . . . . . . . . . . . . . . . . . . . . . . . . . . . . . . . .         65,800
          Manufacturing Summary. . . . . . . . . . . . . . . . . . . . . . . . . . . . .                       65,800

(i)  Manufacturing Summary. . . . . . . . . . . . . . . . . . . . . . . . . . . . . . .         62,000
          Direct Materials. . . . . . . . . . . . . . . . . . . . . . . . . . . . . . . . . . .                       62,000

(j)  Direct Materials. . . . . . . . . . . . . . . . . . . . . . . . . . . . . . . . . . . . . .         58,725
          Manufacturing Summary. . . . . . . . . . . . . . . . . . . . . . . . . . . . .                       58,725

**CLOSING ENTRIES**    The closing entries are recorded in the general journal immediately following the adjusting entries, illustrated as follows:

Closing Entries

Manufacturing Summary . . . . . . . . . . . . . . . . . . . . . . . . . . . . . . . . . .         558,400
     Direct Materials Purchases. . . . . . . . . . . . . . . . . . . . . . . . . . . . . .                     220,800
     Direct Labor. . . . . . . . . . . . . . . . . . . . . . . . . . . . . . . . . . . . . . . . .                     218,750
     Indirect Factory Labor . . . . . . . . . . . . . . . . . . . . . . . . . . . . . . . . .                      49,300
     Depreciation — Factory Equipment . . . . . . . . . . . . . . . . . . . . . . .                      22,300
     Factory Heat, Light, and Power . . . . . . . . . . . . . . . . . . . . . . . . . .                      21,800
     Factory Property Taxes . . . . . . . . . . . . . . . . . . . . . . . . . . . . . . . .                       9,750
     Depreciation — Factory Buildings . . . . . . . . . . . . . . . . . . . . . . . .                       6,000
     Insurance Expense — Factory. . . . . . . . . . . . . . . . . . . . . . . . . . . .                       4,750
     Factory Supplies Expense. . . . . . . . . . . . . . . . . . . . . . . . . . . . . .                       2,900
     Miscellaneous Factory Expense. . . . . . . . . . . . . . . . . . . . . . . . . .                       2,050

| | | |
|---|---:|---:|
| Sales . . . . . . . . . . . . . . . . . . . . . . . . . . . . . . . . . . . . . . . . . . . . . . . . . . . . . | 915,800 | |
|    Income Summary . . . . . . . . . . . . . . . . . . . . . . . . . . . . . . . . . . . . . . | | 915,800 |
| | | |
| Income Summary . . . . . . . . . . . . . . . . . . . . . . . . . . . . . . . . . . . . . . . . . | 822,300 | |
|    Selling Expenses. . . . . . . . . . . . . . . . . . . . . . . . . . . . . . . . . . . . . . . | | 130,500 |
|    General Expenses. . . . . . . . . . . . . . . . . . . . . . . . . . . . . . . . . . . . . . | | 88,700 |
|    Income Tax. . . . . . . . . . . . . . . . . . . . . . . . . . . . . . . . . . . . . . . . . . . | | 52,225 |
|    Manufacturing Summary . . . . . . . . . . . . . . . . . . . . . . . . . . . . . . | | 550,875 |
| | | |
| Income Summary . . . . . . . . . . . . . . . . . . . . . . . . . . . . . . . . . . . . . . . . . | 106,000 | |
|    Retained Earnings. . . . . . . . . . . . . . . . . . . . . . . . . . . . . . . . . . . . . | | 106,000 |
| | | |
| Retained Earnings. . . . . . . . . . . . . . . . . . . . . . . . . . . . . . . . . . . . . . . . . | 40,000 | |
|    Dividends . . . . . . . . . . . . . . . . . . . . . . . . . . . . . . . . . . . . . . . . . . . . | | 40,000 |

The manufacturing accounts are closed to Manufacturing Summary. The revenue account, Sales, is closed to Income Summary. The expense accounts, including the balance in Manufacturing Summary ($550,875, which represents the cost of goods manufactured), are also closed to Income Summary. The final steps in the closing process are to close the balance in Income Summary (representing the net income) and Dividends to Retained Earnings.

**Problems**

**Problem D-1.** The following accounts related to manufacturing operations were selected from the pre-closing trial balance of Thomas Co. at December 31, the end of the current fiscal year:

| | |
|---|---:|
| Depreciation of Factory Buildings | $ 19,000 |
| Depreciation of Factory Equipment | 30,000 |
| Direct Labor | 210,600 |
| Direct Materials Inventory | 59,100 |
| Direct Materials Purchases | 290,500 |
| Factory Supplies Expense | 5,150 |
| Finished Goods Inventory | 87,750 |
| Heat, Light, and Power Expense | 29,750 |
| Indirect Labor | 47,250 |
| Insurance Expense | 9,000 |
| Miscellaneous Factory Costs | 4,850 |
| Property Taxes Expense | 12,500 |
| Work in Process Inventory | 61,500 |

Inventories at December 31 were as follows:

| | |
|---|---:|
| Finished Goods | $ 90,000 |
| Work in Process | 72,000 |
| Direct Materials | 70,500 |

Instructions:

(1) Prepare a statement of cost of goods manufactured.
(2) Prepare journal entries to adjust the work in process and direct materials inventories.
(3) Prepare journal entries to close the appropriate accounts to Manufacturing Summary.
(4) Prepare the journal entry to close Manufacturing Summary.

*(If the working papers correlating with the textbook are not used, omit Problem D-2.)*

**Problem D-2.** The work sheet for Centennial Manufacturing Company, for the current year ended August 31, 1985, is presented in the working papers. Data concerning account titles, trial balance amounts, and selected adjustments have been entered on the work sheet.

Instructions:

(1) Enter the six adjustments required for the inventories on the work sheet. Additional adjustment data are:

| | |
|---|---:|
| Finished goods inventory at August 31 | $109,200 |
| Work in process inventory at August 31 | 78,960 |
| Direct materials inventory at August 31 | 70,470 |

(2) Complete the work sheet.
(3) Prepare a statement of cost of goods manufactured.
(4) Prepare an income statement.
(5) Prepare a retained earnings statement.
(6) Prepare a balance sheet.

**Problem D-3.** The chief accountant for Adams Co. prepared the following manufacturing work sheet for the current year:

ADAMS
Work
For Year Ended

| ACCOUNT TITLE | TRIAL BALANCE | | ADJUSTMENTS | |
|---|---|---|---|---|
| | DEBIT | CREDIT | DEBIT | CREDIT |
| Cash.......................................... | 20,450 | | | |
| Accounts Receivable......................... | 75,500 | | | |
| Allowance for Doubtful Accounts .................... | | 1,800 | | |
| Finished Goods ............................... | 88,500 | | (f) 99,000 | (e) 88,500 |
| Work in Process............................... | 75,000 | | (h) 65,800 | (g) 75,000 |
| Direct Materials............................... | 62,800 | | (j) 58,725 | (i) 62,800 |
| Prepaid Insurance ............................ | 8,700 | | | (k) 5,900 |
| Factory Supplies............................... | 8,250 | | | (d) 5,250 |
| Land ......................................... | 75,000 | | | |
| Factory Buildings ............................. | 290,000 | | | |
| Accumulated Depreciation—Factory Buildings........ | | 170,000 | | (c) 16,000 |
| Factory Equipment.............................. | 446,000 | | | |
| Accumulated Depreciation—Factory Equipment ...... | | 211,500 | | (b) 22,300 |
| Accounts Payable ............................. | | 55,900 | | |
| Wages Payable ............................... | | | | (a) 4,550 |
| Income Tax Payable .......................... | | 8,200 | | |
| Common Stock ($20 par)....................... | | 300,000 | | |
| Retained Earnings ............................ | | 331,025 | | |
| Dividends..................................... | 60,000 | | | |
| Income Summary.............................. | | | (e) 88,500 | (f) 99,000 |
| Manufacturing Summary........................ | | | (g) 75,000 | (h) 65,800 |
| | | | (i) 62,800 | (j) 58,725 |
| Sales......................................... | | 785,500 | | |
| Direct Materials Purchases .................... | 184,800 | | | |
| Direct Labor................................... | 174,250 | | (a) 3,800 | |
| Indirect Factory Labor......................... | 47,250 | | (a) 750 | |
| Depreciation—Factory Equipment.................. | | | (b) 22,300 | |
| Factory Heat, Light, Power...................... | 31,800 | | | |
| Factory Property Taxes......................... | 12,750 | | | |
| Depreciation—Factory Buildings ................. | | | (c) 16,000 | |
| Insurance Expense—Factory .................... | | | (k) 5,900 | |
| Factory Supplies Expense ..................... | | | (d) 5,250 | |
| Miscellaneous Factory Expense .................... | 3,650 | | | |
| Selling Expenses .............................. | 100,500 | | | |
| General Expenses............................. | 58,500 | | | |
| Income Tax................................... | 40,225 | | | |
| | 1,863,925 | 1,863,925 | 503,825 | 503,825 |
| Cost of Goods Manufactured...................... | | | | |
| Net Income ................................... | | | | |

Instructions:

(1) Prepare a statement of cost of goods manufactured.
(2) Prepare an income statement.
(3) Prepare a retained earnings statement.
(4) Prepare a balance sheet.

CO.
Sheet
December 31, 19--

| STATEMENT OF COST OF GOODS MANUFACTURED | | INCOME STATEMENT | | BALANCE SHEET | |
|---|---|---|---|---|---|
| DEBIT | CREDIT | DEBIT | CREDIT | DEBIT | CREDIT |
| | | | | 20,450 | |
| | | | | 75,500 | |
| | | | | | 1,800 |
| | | | | 99,000 | |
| | | | | 65,800 | |
| | | | | 58,725 | |
| | | | | 2,800 | |
| | | | | 3,000 | |
| | | | | 75,000 | |
| | | | | 290,000 | |
| | | | | | 186,000 |
| | | | | 446,000 | |
| | | | | | 233,800 |
| | | | | | 55,900 |
| | | | | | 4,550 |
| | | | | | 8,200 |
| | | | | | 300,000 |
| | | | | | 331,025 |
| | | | | 60,000 | |
| | | 88,500 | 99,000 | | |
| 75,000 | 65,800 | | | | |
| 62,800 | 58,725 | | 785,500 | | |
| 184,800 | | | | | |
| 178,050 | | | | | |
| 48,000 | | | | | |
| 22,300 | | | | | |
| 31,800 | | | | | |
| 12,750 | | | | | |
| 16,000 | | | | | |
| 5,900 | | | | | |
| 5,250 | | | | | |
| 3,650 | | | | | |
| | | 100,500 | | | |
| | | 58,500 | | | |
| | | 40,225 | | | |
| 646,300 | 124,525 | | | | |
| | 521,775 | 521,775 | | | |
| 646,300 | 646,300 | 809,500 | 884,500 | 1,196,275 | 1,121,275 |
| | | 75,000 | | | 75,000 |
| | | 884,500 | 884,500 | 1,196,275 | 1,196,275 |

**Problem D-4.** The accounts in the ledger of Payne Manufacturing Inc., with unadjusted balances on December 31, the end of the current year, are as follows:

| | |
|---|---:|
| Cash | 30,550 |
| Accounts Receivable | 47,450 |
| Allowance for Doubtful Accounts | 900 |
| Finished Goods | 53,150 |
| Work in Process | 36,500 |
| Direct Materials | 34,100 |
| Prepaid Expenses (Controlling) | 10,000 |
| Land | 50,000 |
| Factory Buildings | 260,000 |
| Accumulated Depreciation—Factory Buildings | 90,000 |
| Factory Equipment | 172,650 |
| Accumulated Depreciation—Factory Equipment | 97,950 |
| Office Equipment | 30,000 |
| Accumulated Depreciation—Office Equipment | 10,000 |
| Accounts Payable | 40,400 |
| Income Tax Payable | — |
| Wages Payable | — |
| Common Stock ($25 par) | 300,000 |
| Retained Earnings | 120,300 |
| Dividends | 20,000 |
| Income Summary | — |
| Manufacturing Summary | — |
| Sales | 668,500 |
| Direct Materials Purchases | 197,000 |
| Direct Labor | 178,900 |
| Factory Overhead (Controlling) | 65,150 |
| Selling Expenses (Controlling) | 70,275 |
| General Expenses (Controlling) | 45,825 |
| Interest Expense | 3,500 |
| Income Tax | 23,000 |

The data needed for the year-end adjustments on December 31 are as follows:

| | | |
|---|---:|---:|
| Doubtful accounts at December 31 from analysis of accounts receivable | | $ 2,400 |
| Prepaid insurance expired during year: | | |
|    Factory overhead | $ 4,800 | |
|    General expenses | 1,100 | 5,900 |
| Accrued wages at December 31: | | |
|    Direct labor | $ 2,900 | |
|    Indirect labor | 500 | 3,400 |
| Depreciation expense for year: | | |
|    Factory building | $ 8,000 | |
|    Factory equipment | 16,700 | |
|    Office equipment | 2,600 | 27,300 |
| Income tax owed at December 31 | | 8,500 |

Inventories on December 31:

| | | |
|---|---|---|
| Finished goods | $55,000 | |
| Work in process | 38,500 | |
| Direct materials | 33,150 | $126,650 |

Instructions:

(1) Prepare a manufacturing work sheet. (Leave one extra line after Manufacturing Summary and two extra lines after Factory Overhead and General Expenses for use in recording the adjusting entries.)

(2) Prepare a statement of cost of goods manufactured.

(3) Prepare an income statement.

(4) Prepare a retained earnings statement.

(5) Prepare a balance sheet.

# Work Sheet for Statement of Changes in Financial Position

Some accountants prefer to use a work sheet to assist them in assembling data for the statement of changes in financial position (funds statement). Although a work sheet is not essential, it is especially useful when a large number of transactions must be analyzed. Also, whether or not a work sheet is used, the concepts of funds and the funds statement are not affected.

The following sections describe and illustrate the use of the work sheet. Attention is directed to its use in preparing the funds statement (1) based on working capital and (2) based on cash. The data that appear in Chapter 17 for T. R. Morgan Corporation are used for the illustrations.

**WORK SHEET PROCEDURES FOR FUNDS STATEMENT BASED ON WORKING CAPITAL**

The comparative balance sheet and additional data obtained from the accounts of T. R. Morgan Corporation are presented on page 529. The work sheet prepared from these data is presented on page 530.

The procedures to prepare the work sheet for the funds statement based on working capital are outlined as follows:

1. List the title of each noncurrent account in the Description column. For each account, enter that debit or credit representing the change (increase or decrease) in the account balance for the year in the Change During Year column.
2. Add the debits and credits in the Change During Year column and determine the subtotals. Enter the change (increase or decrease) in working capital during the year in the appropriate column to balance the totals of the debits and credits.
3. Provide space in the bottom portion of the work sheet for later use in identifying the various (1) sources of working capital and (2) applications of working capital.
4. Analyze the change during the year in each noncurrent account in order to determine the sources and/or applications of working capital related to the transactions recorded in each account. Record these sources and applications

in the bottom portion of the work sheet by means of entries in the Work Sheet Entries columns.

5. Complete the work sheet.

These procedures are explained in detail in the following paragraphs.

COMPARATIVE
BALANCE SHEET

**T. R. Morgan Corporation**
**Comparative Balance Sheet**
**December 31, 1985 and 1984**

| | 1985 | 1984 | Increase Decrease* |
|---|---|---|---|
| **Assets** | | | |
| Cash .................................... | $ 49,000 | $ 26,000 | $ 23,000 |
| Trade receivables (net) .................... | 74,000 | 65,000 | 9,000 |
| Inventories ............................... | 172,000 | 180,000 | 8,000* |
| Prepaid expenses......................... | 4,000 | 3,000 | 1,000 |
| Investments (long-term)................... | — | 45,000 | 45,000* |
| Land ..................................... | 90,000 | 40,000 | 50,000 |
| Building.................................. | 200,000 | 200,000 | — |
| Accumulated depreciation — building ....... | (36,000) | (30,000) | (6,000) |
| Equipment ............................... | 180,000 | 142,000 | 38,000 |
| Accumulated depreciation — equipment..... | (43,000) | (40,000) | (3,000) |
| Total assets ............................. | $690,000 | $631,000 | $ 59,000 |
| | | | |
| **Liabilities** | | | |
| Accounts payable (merchandise creditors) .. | $ 50,000 | $ 32,000 | $ 18,000 |
| Income tax payable........................ | 2,500 | 4,000 | 1,500* |
| Dividends payable......................... | 15,000 | 8,000 | 7,000 |
| Bonds payable ........................... | 120,000 | 245,000 | 125,000* |
| Total liabilities .......................... | $187,500 | $289,000 | $101,500* |
| | | | |
| **Stockholders' Equity** | | | |
| Common stock ........................... | $280,000 | $230,000 | $ 50,000 |
| Retained earnings ........................ | 222,500 | 112,000 | 110,500 |
| Total stockholders' equity ................. | $502,500 | $342,000 | $160,500 |
| Total liabilities and stockholders' equity...... | $690,000 | $631,000 | $ 59,000 |

Additional data:

(1) Net income, $140,500.
(2) Cash dividends declared, $30,000.
(3) Common stock issued at par for land, $50,000.
(4) Bonds payable retired for cash, $125,000.
(5) Depreciation for year: equipment, $12,000; building, $6,000.
(6) Fully depreciated equipment discarded, $9,000.
(7) Equipment purchased for cash, $47,000.
(8) Book value of investments sold for $75,000 cash, $45,000.

WORK SHEET FOR
STATEMENT OF CHANGES IN
FINANCIAL
POSITION—BASED ON
WORKING CAPITAL

**T. R. Morgan Corporation**
**Work Sheet for Statement of Changes in Financial Position**
**For Year Ended December 31, 1985**

| Description | Change During Year | | Work Sheet Entries | |
|---|---|---|---|---|
| | Debit | Credit | Debit | Credit |
| Investments . . . . . . . . . . . . . . . . . . | | 45,000 | (j)  45,000 | |
| Land . . . . . . . . . . . . . . . . . . . . . . . . | 50,000 | | | (i)  50,000 |
| Building. . . . . . . . . . . . . . . . . . . . . . | — | — | | |
| Accumulated depreciation— building. . . . . . . . . . . . . . . . . . . . | | 6,000 | (h)  6,000 | |
| Equipment . . . . . . . . . . . . . . . . . . . | 38,000 | | (f)  9,000 | (g)  47,000 |
| Accumulated depreciation— equipment . . . . . . . . . . . . . . . . . . | | 3,000 | (e)  12,000 | (f)  9,000 |
| Bonds payable . . . . . . . . . . . . . . . | 125,000 | | | (d) 125,000 |
| Common stock . . . . . . . . . . . . . . . . | | 50,000 | (c)  50,000 | |
| Retained earnings . . . . . . . . . . . . . | | 110,500 | (a) 140,500 | (b)  30,000 |
| | 213,000 | 214,500 | | |
| Increase in working capital . . . . . . . | 1,500 | | | |
| Totals. . . . . . . . . . . . . . . . . . . . . . . . | 214,500 | 214,500 | | |
| Sources of working capital: | | | | |
| Operations: | | | | |
| Net income . . . . . . . . . . . . . . . . . . . . . . . . . . . . . . . . . | | | | (a) 140,500 |
| Depreciation of equipment. . . . . . . . . . . . . . . . . . . . | | | | (e)  12,000 |
| Depreciation of building . . . . . . . . . . . . . . . . . . . . . . | | | | (h)  6,000 |
| Issuance of common stock for land . . . . . . . . . . . . . | | | | (c)  50,000 |
| Book value of investments sold. . . . . . . . . . . . . . . . . | | | | (j)  45,000 |
| Applications of working capital: | | | | |
| Declaration of cash dividends. . . . . . . . . . . . . . . . . . | | | (b)  30,000 | |
| Retirement of bonds. . . . . . . . . . . . . . . . . . . . . . . . . . | | | (d) 125,000 | |
| Purchase of equipment. . . . . . . . . . . . . . . . . . . . . . . | | | (g)  47,000 | |
| Purchase of land by issuance of common stock. . . | | | (i)  50,000 | |
| Totals. . . . . . . . . . . . . . . . . . . . . . . . . . . . . . . . . . . . . . | | | 514,500 | 514,500 |

Noncurrent
Accounts

Since the analysis of transactions recorded in the noncurrent accounts reveals the sources and applications of working capital, the work sheet focuses on the noncurrent accounts. For this purpose, the titles of the noncurrent accounts are entered in the Description column. Next, the debit or credit change for the year in each account balance is entered in the Change During Year column. For example, the beginning and ending balances of Investments were $45,000 and zero, respectively. Thus, the change for the year was a decrease, or credit, of $45,000. The beginning and ending balances of Land were $40,000 and $90,000, respectively. Thus, the change for the year was an increase, or debit, of $50,000. The changes in the other accounts are determined in a like manner.

Change in
Working Capital

Since transactions that result in changes in working capital (the current accounts) also result in changes in the noncurrent accounts, the change in working capital for the period will equal the change in the noncurrent accounts for the period. Thus, if a subtotal of the debits and credits for the noncurrent accounts (as indicated in the Change During Year column) is determined, the increase or decrease in working capital for the period can be inserted in the appropriate column and the two columns will balance. In the illustration, the subtotal of the credit column ($214,500) exceeds the subtotal of the debit column ($213,000) by $1,500, which is identified as the increase in working capital. By entering the $1,500 as a debit in the Change During Year column, the debit and credit columns are balanced. This $1,500 increase in working capital will be reported on the funds statement as the difference between the total of the sources section and the total of the applications section. This change is supported by details of the change in each of the working capital components, as follows:

CHANGES IN
COMPONENTS OF
WORKING CAPITAL

| Changes in components of working capital: | | |
|---|---|---|
| Increase (decrease) in current assets: | | |
| Cash | $23,000 | |
| Trade receivables (net) | 9,000 | |
| Inventories | (8,000) | |
| Prepaid expenses | 1,000 | $25,000 |
| Increase (decrease) in current liabilities: | | |
| Accounts payable | $18,000 | |
| Income tax payable | (1,500) | |
| Dividends payable | 7,000 | 23,500 |
| Increase in working capital | | $ 1,500 |

If the subtotals in the Change During Year columns indicate that the debits exceed the credits, the balancing figure would be identified as a decrease in working capital.

Sources and
Applications
Sections

After the Change During Year columns are totaled and ruled, "Sources of working capital" is written in the Description column. Several lines are skipped, so that at a later time the various sources of working capital can be entered, and "Applications of working capital" is written in the Description column. When the work sheet is completed, this bottom portion will contain the data necessary to prepare the sources section and the applications section of the funds statement.

Analysis
of Noncurrent
Accounts

As was discussed on pages 401-403, transactions that result in sources and applications of working capital can be classified in terms of their effect on the noncurrent accounts. Therefore, to determine the various sources and applications for the year, the changes in the noncurrent accounts are analyzed. As each account is analyzed, entries made in the work sheet relate specific sources or applications of working capital to the noncurrent account. It should be noted that the work sheet entries are not entered into the accounts. They are, as is the entire work sheet, strictly an aid in assembling the data for later use in preparing the funds statement.

The sequence in which the noncurrent accounts are analyzed is unimportant. However, because it is more convenient and efficient, and the chance for errors is reduced, the analysis illustrated will begin with the retained earnings account and proceed upward in the listing in sequential order.

### Retained Earnings

The work sheet indicates that there was an increase of $110,500 in retained earnings for the year. The additional data, taken from an examination of the account, indicate that the increase was the result of two factors: (1) net income of $140,500 and (2) declaration of cash dividends of $30,000. To identify the sources and applications of working capital, two entries are made on the work sheet. These entries also serve to account for, or explain, the increase of $110,500.

*Net income.* In closing the accounts at the end of the year, the retained earnings account was credited for $140,500, representing the net income. The $140,500 is also reported on the funds statement as a source of working capital. An entry on the work sheet to debit retained earnings and to credit "Sources of working capital — operations: net income" accomplishes the following: (1) the credit portion of the closing entry (to retained earnings) is accounted for, or in effect canceled, and (2) the source of working capital is identified in the bottom portion of the work sheet. The entry on the work sheet is as follows:

| | | |
|---|---|---|
| (a) Retained Earnings.............................. | 140,500 | |
| Sources of Working Capital — Operations: | | |
| Net Income.................................. | | 140,500 |

*Dividends.* In closing the accounts at the end of the year, the retained earnings account was debited for $30,000, representing the cash dividends declared. The $30,000 is also reported on the funds statement as an application of working capital. An entry on the work sheet to debit "Applications of working capital — declaration of cash dividends" and to credit retained earnings accomplishes the following: (1) the debit portion of the closing entry (to retained earnings) is accounted for, or in effect canceled, and (2) the application of working capital is identified in the bottom portion of the work sheet. The entry on the work sheet is as follows:

| | | |
|---|---|---|
| (b) Applications of Working Capital — Declaration | | |
| of Cash Dividends ............................ | 30,000 | |
| Retained Earnings............................ | | 30,000 |

### Common Stock

The next noncurrent item on the work sheet, common stock, increased by $50,000 during the year. The additional data, taken from an examination of the account, indicate that the stock was exchanged for land. The work sheet entry to account for this increase and to identify the source of working capital is as follows:

```
(c) Common Stock ...............................    50,000
        Sources of Working Capital—Issuance of
        Common Stock for Land ......................          50,000
```

It should be noted that the effect of the exchange will also be analyzed when the land account is examined.

**Bonds Payable**

The decrease of $125,000 in the bonds payable account during the year resulted from the retirement of the bonds for cash. The work sheet entry to record the effect of this transaction on working capital is as follows:

```
(d) Applications of Working Capital—Retirement of
        Bonds Payable. ................................    125,000
        Bonds Payable. ...............................           125,000
```

**Accumulated Depreciation—Equipment**

The work sheet indicates that the accumulated depreciation—equipment account increased by $3,000 during the year. The additional data indicate that the increase resulted from (1) depreciation expense of $12,000 (credit) for the year and (2) discarding $9,000 (debit) of fully depreciated equipment. Since depreciation expense does not affect working capital but does decrease the amount of net income, it should be added to net income to determine the amount of working capital from operations. This effect is indicated on the work sheet by the following entry:

```
(e) Accumulated Depreciation—Equipment. ..........    12,000
        Sources of Working Capital—Operations:
        Depreciation of Equipment ....................           12,000
```

It should be noted that the notation in the Description column is placed so that the $12,000 can be added to "Sources of working capital—operations: net income."

Since the discarding of the fully depreciated equipment did not affect working capital, the following entry is made on the work sheet in order to fully account for the change of $3,000 in the accumulated depreciation—equipment account:

```
(f) Equipment .......................................    9,000
        Accumulated Depreciation—Equipment. ..........            9,000
```

It should be noted that this entry, like the transaction that was recorded in the accounts, does not affect working capital. It serves only to complete the accounting for all transactions that resulted in the change in the account during the year and thus helps assure that no transactions affecting working capital are overlooked in the analysis.

## Equipment

The work sheet indicated that the equipment account increased by $38,000 during the year. The additional data, determined from an examination of the ledger account, indicated that the increase resulted from (1) discarding $9,000 of fully depreciated equipment and (2) purchasing $47,000 of equipment. The discarding of the equipment was included in, or accounted for, in (f) and needs no additional attention. The application of working capital to the purchase of equipment is recognized by the following entry on the work sheet:

(g) Applications of Working Capital—Purchase
    of Equipment . . . . . . . . . . . . . . . . . . . . . . . . . . . . . . . . . . . .    47,000
        Equipment . . . . . . . . . . . . . . . . . . . . . . . . . . . . . . . . .                47,000

## Accumulated Depreciation—Building

The $6,000 increase in the accumulated depreciation—building account during the year resulted from the entry to record depreciation expense. Since depreciation expense does not affect working capital but does decrease the amount of net income, it should be added to net income to determine the amount of working capital from operations. This effect is accomplished by the following entry on the work sheet:

(h) Accumulated Depreciation—Building . . . . . . . . . . . . . . .    6,000
        Sources of Working Capital—Operations:
        Depreciation of Building . . . . . . . . . . . . . . . . . . . . . . . .                6,000

## Building

There was no change in the beginning and ending balances of the building account and reference to the account confirms that no entries were made in it during the year. Hence, no entry is necessary on the work sheet.

## Land

As indicated in the analysis of the common stock account, the $50,000 increase in land resulted from a purchase by issuance of common stock. The work sheet entry to indicate this application of working capital is as follows:

(i) Applications of Working Capital—Purchase of
    Land by Issuance of Common Stock . . . . . . . . . . . . . .    50,000
        Land. . . . . . . . . . . . . . . . . . . . . . . . . . . . . . . . . . . . . . .                50,000

## Investments

The work sheet indicates that investments decreased by $45,000. The examination of the ledger account indicates that investments were sold for $75,000. As was explained on page 405, the $30,000 gain on the sale is already included in net income and consequently has already been accounted for as a source of working capital. Only the $45,000 book value of the investments sold would be reported as a source of working capital. To indicate this source on the work sheet, the following entry is made:

| | |
|---|---|
| (j) Investments ...................................... | 45,000 |
| Sources of Working Capital—Book Value of | |
| Investments Sold............................ | 45,000 |

**Completing the Work Sheet**

After all of the noncurrent accounts have been analyzed, all of the sources and applications are identified in the bottom portion of the work sheet. To assure the equality of the work sheet entries, the last step is to total the Work Sheet Entries columns.

**Preparation of the Funds Statement**

The data for the sources section and the applications section of the funds statement are obtained from the bottom portion of the work sheet. Some modifications are made to the work sheet data for presentation on the statement. For example, in presenting the working capital provided by operations, the additions to net income are labeled "Add deductions not decreasing working capital during the year." Another example is the reporting of the total depreciation expense ($18,000) instead of the two separate amounts ($12,000 and $6,000).

The increase (or decrease) in working capital that is reported on the statement is also identified on the work sheet. The funds statement prepared from the work sheet, including the details of the changes in each working capital component, is presented on page 536.

**WORK SHEET PROCEDURES FOR FUNDS STATEMENT BASED ON CASH**

The work sheet used to assemble the data for the funds statement based on working capital is also used to assemble data for the funds statement based on cash. The procedures differ in that the focus for the statement based on cash is on the analysis of the *noncash* accounts instead of the *noncurrent* accounts, as was the case when the statement was based on working capital. In other words, *in addition* to analyzing the changes in the noncurrent accounts, all of the current accounts *except cash* are analyzed in preparing the work sheet for the funds statement based on cash. To illustrate such a work sheet, the data for T. R. Morgan Corporation presented on page 529 are used. The work sheet prepared from these data is presented on page 537.

The procedures to prepare the work sheet for the funds statement based on cash are outlined as follows:

1. List the title of each *noncash* account in the Description column. For each account, enter the debit or credit representing the change (increase or decrease) in the account balance for the year in the Change During Year column.
2. Add the debits and credits in the Change During Year column and determine the subtotals. Enter the change (increase or decrease) in cash during the year in the appropriate column to balance the totals of the debits and credits.

**T. R. Morgan Corporation**
**Statement of Changes in Financial Position**
**For Year Ended December 31, 1985**

Sources of working capital:
  Operations during the year:
    Net income............................. $140,500
    Add deduction not decreasing working
    capital during the year:
      Depreciation ...................... 18,000 $158,500
  Issuance of common stock at par for land.......... 50,000
  Book value of investments sold (excludes $30,000
    gain reported in net income) .................... 45,000 $253,500

Applications of working capital:
  Declaration of cash dividends.................... $ 30,000
  Retirement of bonds payable..................... 125,000
  Purchase of equipment.......................... 47,000
  Purchase of land by issuance of common stock
    at par....................................... 50,000 252,000
Increase in working capital......................... $ 1,500

Changes in components of working capital:
  Increase (decrease) in current assets:
    Cash ....................................... $ 23,000
    Trade receivables (net)....................... 9,000
    Inventories ................................. (8,000)
    Prepaid expenses............................ 1,000 $ 25,000
  Increase (decrease) in current liabilities:
    Accounts payable............................ $ 18,000
    Income tax payable.......................... (1,500)
    Dividends payable........................... 7,000 23,500
Increase in working capital......................... $ 1,500

3. Provide space in the bottom portion of the work sheet for later use in identifying the various (1) sources of cash and (2) applications of cash.
4. Analyze the change during the year in each noncash account to determine the sources and/or applications of cash related to the transactions recorded in each account. Record these sources and applications in the bottom portion of the work sheet by means of entries in the Work Sheet Entries columns.
5. Complete the work sheet.

These procedures are explained in detail in the following paragraphs.

**Noncash Accounts**

Since the analysis of transactions recorded in the noncash accounts reveals the sources and applications of cash, the work sheet focuses on noncash accounts. For this purpose, the titles of the noncash accounts are entered in the Description

T. R. Morgan Corporation
Work Sheet for Statement of Changes in Financial Position
For Year Ended December 31, 1985

| Description | Change During Year Debit | Change During Year Credit | Work Sheet Entries Debit | Work Sheet Entries Credit |
|---|---|---|---|---|
| Trade receivables .................. | 9,000 | | | (p)   9,000 |
| Inventories...................... | | 8,000 | (o)   8,000 | |
| Prepaid expenses ................. | 1,000 | | | (n)   1,000 |
| Accounts payable ................. | | 18,000 | (m) 18,000 | |
| Income tax payable................ | 1,500 | | | (l)   1,500 |
| Dividends payable................. | | 7,000 | (k)   7,000 | |
| Investments...................... | | 45,000 | (j) 45,000 | |
| Land............................. | 50,000 | | | (i) 50,000 |
| Building ......................... | — | — | | |
| Accumulated depreciation — building.. | | 6,000 | (h)   6,000 | |
| Equipment........................ | 38,000 | | (f)   9,000 | (g) 47,000 |
| Accumulated depreciation — equipment......................... | | 3,000 | (e) 12,000 | (f)   9,000 |
| Bonds payable.................... | 125,000 | | | (d) 125,000 |
| Common stock.................... | | 50,000 | (c) 50,000 | |
| Retained earnings ................ | | 110,500 | (a) 140,500 | (b) 30,000 |
| | 224,500 | 247,500 | | |
| Increase in cash.................. | 23,000 | | | |
| Totals .......................... | 247,500 | 247,500 | | |

Sources of cash:
  Operations:

| | | |
|---|---|---|
| Net income ....................................... | | (a) 140,500 |
| Depreciation of equipment ....................... | | (e)   12,000 |
| Depreciation of building.......................... | | (h)     6,000 |
| Decrease in income tax payable .................. | (l)   1,500 | |
| Increase in accounts payable..................... | | (m)   18,000 |
| Increase in prepaid expenses .................... | (n)   1,000 | |
| Decrease in inventories .......................... | | (o)     8,000 |
| Increase in trade receivables .................... | (p)   9,000 | |
| Issuance of common stock for land................. | | (c)   50,000 |
| Book value of investments sold ..................... | | (j)   45,000 |
| Applications of cash: | | |
| Declaration of cash dividends...................... | (b) 30,000 | |
| Increase in dividends payable ..................... | | (k)     7,000 |
| Retirement of bonds .............................. | (d) 125,000 | |
| Purchase of equipment............................ | (g) 47,000 | |
| Purchase of land by issuance of common stock ....... | (i) 50,000 | |
| Totals .......................................... | 559,000 | 559,000 |

column. To facilitate reference in the illustration, noncash current accounts are listed first, followed by the noncurrent accounts. The order of the listing is not important.

The debit or credit change for the year in each account balance is entered in the Change During Year column. For example, the beginning and ending balances of Trade Receivables were $65,000 and $74,000, respectively. Thus, the change for the year was an increase, or debit, of $9,000. The changes in the other accounts are determined in a like manner.

Change in Cash

Since transactions that result in changes in cash also result in changes in the noncash accounts, the change in cash for the period will equal the change in the noncash accounts for the period. Thus, if a subtotal of the debits and credits for the noncash accounts (as indicated in the Change During Year column) is determined, the increase or decrease in cash for the period can be inserted in the appropriate column and the two columns will balance. In the illustration, the subtotal of the credit column ($247,500) exceeds the subtotal of the debit column ($224,500) by $23,000, which is identified as the increase in cash. By entering the $23,000 as a debit in the Change During Year column, the debit and credit columns are balanced. This $23,000 increase in cash will be reported on the funds statement as the difference between the total of the sources section and the total of the applications section.

If the subtotals in the Change During Year columns indicate that the debits exceed the credits, the balancing figure would be identified as a decrease in cash.

Sources and Applications of Cash

After the Change During Year columns are totaled and ruled, "Sources of cash" is written in the Description column. Several lines are skipped, so that at a later time the various sources of cash can be entered, and "Applications of cash" is written in the Description column. When the work sheet is completed, this bottom portion will contain the data necessary to prepare the sources section and the applications section of the funds statement.

To determine the various sources and applications of cash for the year, the changes in the noncash accounts are analyzed. As each account is analyzed, entries made in the work sheet relate specific sources or applications of cash to the noncash accounts. For purposes of discussion, the noncash accounts can be classified as (1) noncurrent accounts and (2) current accounts (except cash).

The analysis of the noncurrent accounts for T. R. Morgan Corporation, discussed on pages 401-403, revealed (as does the additional data presented on page 529) that the sale of investments yielded cash, that there were cash outlays for equipment and the retirement of bonds, and that land was acquired by the issuance of common stock. The effect of these transactions on both cash and working capital is therefore the same. For the statement based on cash, it is necessary to add the analysis of the current accounts (except cash).

Analysis of Noncurrent Accounts

The entries resulting from the analysis of the noncurrent accounts are summarized as follows (the letters refer to those used on the work sheet to identify the entries). These entries are identical to the entries shown on pages 532-535, except that they have been adjusted to reflect the cash concept.

| | | |
|---|---:|---:|
| (a) Retained Earnings. . . . . . . . . . . . . . . . . . . . . . . . . . . . . . | 140,500 | |
|     Sources of Cash—Operations: Net Income . . . . . . | | 140,500 |
| (b) Applications of Cash—Declaration of Cash | | |
|     Dividends . . . . . . . . . . . . . . . . . . . . . . . . . . . . . . . . . | 30,000 | |
|     Retained Earnings. . . . . . . . . . . . . . . . . . . . . . . . . . | | 30,000 |
| (c) Common Stock . . . . . . . . . . . . . . . . . . . . . . . . . . . . . | 50,000 | |
|     Sources of Cash—Issuance of Common Stock | | |
|     for Land. . . . . . . . . . . . . . . . . . . . . . . . . . . . . . . . . . . | | 50,000 |
| (d) Applications of Cash—Retirement of Bonds | | |
|     Payable . . . . . . . . . . . . . . . . . . . . . . . . . . . . . . . . . . . | 125,000 | |
|     Bonds Payable. . . . . . . . . . . . . . . . . . . . . . . . . . . . | | 125,000 |
| (e) Accumulated Depreciation—Equipment. . . . . . . . . . | 12,000 | |
|     Sources of Cash—Operations: Depreciation | | |
|     of Equipment . . . . . . . . . . . . . . . . . . . . . . . . . . . . . . | | 12,000 |
| (f) Equipment . . . . . . . . . . . . . . . . . . . . . . . . . . . . . . . . . | 9,000 | |
|     Accumulated Depreciation—Equipment. . . . . . . . | | 9,000 |
| (g) Applications of Cash—Purchase of Equipment. . . . . | 47,000 | |
|     Equipment . . . . . . . . . . . . . . . . . . . . . . . . . . . . . . . . | | 47,000 |
| (h) Accumulated Depreciation—Building . . . . . . . . . . . . | 6,000 | |
|     Sources of Cash—Operations: Depreciation | | |
|     of Building . . . . . . . . . . . . . . . . . . . . . . . . . . . . . . . . | | 6,000 |
| (i) Applications of Cash—Purchase of Land by | | |
|     Issuance of Common Stock . . . . . . . . . . . . . . . . . . . | 50,000 | |
|     Land. . . . . . . . . . . . . . . . . . . . . . . . . . . . . . . . . . . . . | | 50,000 |
| (j) Investments . . . . . . . . . . . . . . . . . . . . . . . . . . . . . . . . | 45,000 | |
|     Sources of Cash—Book Value of Investments | | |
|     Sold . . . . . . . . . . . . . . . . . . . . . . . . . . . . . . . . . . . . . | | 45,000 |

**Analysis of Current Accounts (Except Cash)**

The amount of cash used to pay dividends may differ from the amount of cash dividends declared. Timing differences between the incurrence of an expense and the related cash outflow and the recognition of revenue and the receipt of cash must be considered in determining the amount of cash provided by operations. Therefore, the current accounts (other than cash) are analyzed to determine (1) cash applied to payment of dividends and (2) cash provided by operations.

### Cash Applied to Payment of Dividends

The additional data indicate that $30,000 of dividends had been declared, which was identified as an application in entry (b). The $7,000 credit in the Change During Year column of the work sheet for Dividends Payable reveals a timing difference between the declaration and the payment. In other words, the $7,000 increase in Dividends Payable for the year indicates that dividends paid were $7,000 less than dividends declared. The work sheet entry to adjust the dividends declared of $30,000 to reflect the dividends paid of $23,000 is as follows:

(k) Dividends Payable .................................  7,000
    Applications of Cash—Declaration of Cash
    Dividends: Increase in Dividends Payable..........                7,000

When the $7,000, which represents the increase in dividends payable, is deducted from the $30,000 of "application of cash—declaration of cash dividends," $23,000 is subsequently reported on the funds statement as an application of cash.

### Cash Provided by Operations

The starting point in the analysis of the effect of operations on cash is net income for the period. The effect of this amount, $140,500, is indicated by entry (a). As in the earlier analysis, depreciation expense of $18,000 must be added [(e) and (h)] to the $140,500 because depreciation expense did not decrease the amount of cash. In addition, it is necessary to recognize the relationship of the accrual method of accounting to the movement of cash. Ordinarily, a portion of some of the other costs and expenses reported on the income statement, as well as a portion of the revenue earned, is not accompanied by cash outflow or inflow.

The effect of timing differences is indicated by the amount and the direction of change in the balances of the asset and liability accounts affected by operations. Decreases in such assets and increases in such liabilities during the period must be added to the amount reported as net income to determine the amount of cash provided by operations. Conversely, increases in such assets and decreases in such liabilities must be deducted from the amount reported as net income.

The noncash current accounts (except Dividends Payable) provide the following data that indicate the effect of timing differences on the amount of cash inflow and outflow from operations:

| Accounts | Increase Decrease* |
|---|---|
| Trade receivables (net)..................................... | $ 9,000 |
| Inventories............................................... | 8,000* |
| Prepaid expenses ........................................ | 1,000 |
| Accounts payable (merchandise creditors).................... | 18,000 |
| Income tax payable....................................... | 1,500* |

The sequence in which the noncash current accounts are analyzed is unimportant. However, to continue the sequence used in analyzing preceding accounts, the analysis illustrated will begin with the income tax payable account and proceed upward in the listing in sequential order.

*Income tax payable decrease.* The outlay of cash for income taxes exceeded by $1,500 the amount of income tax deducted as an expense during the period. Accordingly, $1,500 must be deducted from income to determine the amount of cash provided by operations. This procedure is indicated on the work sheet by the following entry:

(l) Sources of Cash—Operations: Decrease in Income
    Tax Payable....................................  1,500
      Income Tax Payable ..........................                1,500

*Accounts payable increase.* The effect of the increase in the amount owed creditors for goods and services was to include in expired costs and expenses the sum of $18,000. Income was thereby reduced by $18,000, for which there had been no cash outlay during the year. Hence, $18,000 must be added to income to determine the amount of cash provided by operations. The work sheet entry is as follows:

| | | | |
|---|---|---|---|
| (m) | Accounts Payable ........................... | 18,000 | |
| | Sources of Cash—Operations: Increase in | | |
| | Accounts Payable .......................... | | 18,000 |

*Prepaid expenses increase.* The outlay of cash for prepaid expenses exceeded by $1,000 the amount deducted as an expense during the year. Hence, $1,000 must be deducted from income to determine the amount of cash provided by operations. The work sheet entry is as follows:

| | | | |
|---|---|---|---|
| (n) | Sources of Cash—Operations: Increase in Prepaid | | |
| | Expenses..................................... | 1,000 | |
| | Prepaid Expenses ............................ | | 1,000 |

*Inventories decrease.* The $8,000 decrease in inventories indicates that the merchandise sold exceeded the cost of the merchandise purchased by $8,000. The amount reported on the income statement as a deduction from the revenue therefore included $8,000 that did not require cash outflow during the year. Accordingly, $8,000 must be added to income to determine the amount of cash provided by operations. The work sheet entry is as follows:

| | | | |
|---|---|---|---|
| (o) | Inventories..................................... | 8,000 | |
| | Sources of Cash—Operations: Decrease in | | |
| | Inventories..................................... | | 8,000 |

*Trade receivables (net) increase.* The additions to trade receivables for sales on account during the year exceeded by $9,000 the deductions for amounts collected from customers on account. The amount reported on the income statement as sales therefore included $9,000 that did not yield cash inflow during the year. Accordingly, $9,000 must be deducted from income to determine the amount of cash provided by operations. The work sheet entry is as follows:

| | | | |
|---|---|---|---|
| (p) | Sources of Cash—Operations: Increase in Trade | | |
| | Receivables.................................... | 9,000 | |
| | Trade Receivables............................. | | 9,000 |

**Completing the Work Sheet**

After all of the noncash accounts have been analyzed, all of the sources and applications are identified in the bottom portion of the work sheet. To assure the equality of the work sheet entries, the last step is to total the Work Sheet Entries columns.

**Preparation of the Funds Statement**

The data for the sources section and the applications section of the funds statement are obtained from the bottom portion of the work sheet. The increase (or decrease) in cash that is reported on the statement is also identified on the work sheet. The funds statement prepared from the work sheet, including the details of the changes in the cash account, is as follows:

STATEMENT OF CHANGES IN FINANCIAL POSITION—BASED ON CASH

---

**T. R. Morgan Corporation**
**Statement of Changes in Financial Position**
**For Year Ended December 31, 1985**

Sources of cash:
  Operations during the year:
    Net income................................ $140,500
    Add deductions not decreasing cash
    during the year:
      Depreciation .................. $18,000
      Increase in accounts payable ... 18,000
      Decrease in inventories......... 8,000   44,000
                                     $184,500

    Deduct additions not increasing
    cash during the year:
      Decrease in income tax payable . $ 1,500
      Increase in prepaid expenses... 1,000
      Increase in trade receivables.... 9,000   11,500 $173,000
  Issuance of common stock at par for land............. 50,000
  Book value of investments sold (excludes $30,000 gain
    reported in net income)........................... 45,000 $268,000

Applications of cash:
  Payment of dividends:
    Cash dividends declared ................. $ 30,000
    Deduct increase in dividends payable ..... 7,000 $ 23,000
  Retirement of bonds payable....................... 125,000
  Purchase of equipment............................ 47,000
  Purchase of land by issuance of common stock at par .. 50,000  245,000

Increase in cash...................................... $ 23,000

Change in cash balance:
  Cash balance, December 31, 1985 ................... $ 49,000
  Cash balance, December 31, 1984 .................. 26,000

Increase in cash...................................... $ 23,000

APPENDIX

# Specimen Financial Statements

*This appendix contains financial statements based on the actual statements of a small, privately held manufacturing company, the complete financial section of the annual report of The Coca Cola Company, and selected statements and notes for other companies. Because privately held companies are not required to release their financial statements to the public, the Carter Manufacturing Company statements were modified to protect the confidentiality of the company. We are grateful for the assistance of the public accounting firm of Deloitte Haskins & Sells and Mr. Mark Young in developing these statements.*

## AUDITORS' OPINION

Carter Manufacturing Company:

We have examined the balance sheets of Carter Manufacturing Company as of December 31, 1982 and 1981, and the related statements of income and retained earnings and of changes in financial position for the years then ended. Our examinations were made in accordance with generally accepted auditing standards and, accordingly, included such tests of the accounting records and such other auditing procedures as we considered necessary in the circumstances.

In our opinion, the accompanying financial statements present fairly the financial position of Carter Manufacturing Company as of December 31, 1982 and 1981, and the results of its operations and the changes in its financial position for the years then ended, in conformity with generally accepted accounting principles consistently applied.

*Masters & Young*

February 22, 1983
Atlanta, Georgia

# CARTER MANUFACTURING COMPANY

## BALANCE SHEETS, DECEMBER 31, 1982 and 1981

| ASSETS | NOTES | 1982 | 1981 |
|---|---|---|---|
| **CURRENT ASSETS:** | | | |
| Cash: | | | |
| Cash in bank.......................... | | $ 38,526 | $ 88,443 |
| Petty cash .............................. | | 7,650 | 12,300 |
| Savings certificates ...................... | | 375,000 | 235,344 |
| Marketable securities ..................... | 2,5 | 332,238 | 361,842 |
| Receivables: | | | |
| Customers—less allowance for doubtful accounts of $486,000 in 1982 and $45,000 in 1981 ..................... | 3 | 2,979,197 | 2,809,352 |
| Dividends............................. | | 2,157 | 2,091 |
| Interest................................ | | 16,680 | 6,288 |
| Other................................. | | 20,736 | 8,034 |
| Inventories............................. | 4 | 5,927,631 | 6,033,126 |
| Prepaid insurance ........................ | | 38,604 | 45,234 |
| Other prepayments ....................... | | 22,566 | 32,586 |
| Total current assets....................... | | 9,760,985 | 9,634,640 |
| **PLANT AND EQUIPMENT:** | | | |
| Machinery and equipment ................. | | 2,901,148 | 2,788,225 |
| Delivery equipment ....................... | | 745,893 | 771,873 |
| Furniture and fixtures ..................... | | 214,119 | 214,437 |
| Leasehold improvements ................... | | 97,758 | 94,011 |
| Total..................................... | | 3,958,918 | 3,868,546 |
| Less accumulated depreciation and amortization........................... | | 2,172,171 | 2,085,417 |
| Plant and equipment—net................. | | 1,786,747 | 1,783,129 |
| TOTAL ASSETS.......................... | | $11,547,732 | $11,417,769 |

See notes to financial statements.

| LIABILITIES AND SHAREHOLDERS' EQUITY | NOTES | 1982 | 1981 |
|---|---|---|---|
| **CURRENT LIABILITIES:** | | | |
| Trade accounts payable . . . . . . . . . . . . . . . . . . . . | | $ 1,804,807 | $ 1,700,652 |
| Due under line of credit . . . . . . . . . . . . . . . . . | 5 | 120,000 | 180,000 |
| Current portion of long-term debt . . . . . . . . . . . . | 6 | 266,676 | 236,709 |
| Accrued salaries, wages and commissions . . . . | | 369,009 | 194,910 |
| Accrued and withheld payroll taxes . . . . . . . . . . | | 69,267 | 144,111 |
| Income taxes payable . . . . . . . . . . . . . . . . . . . . . . | | 48,081 | 37,287 |
| Contributions to employee benefit plans . . . . . . . | 8 | 277,521 | 100,647 |
| Accrued rent . . . . . . . . . . . . . . . . . . . . . . . . . . . . . | | 67,500 | 270,000 |
| Total current liabilities . . . . . . . . . . . . . . . . . . . . . | | 3,022,861 | 2,864,316 |
| LONG-TERM DEBT . . . . . . . . . . . . . . . . . . . . . . | 6,7,9 | 1,028,682 | 1,295,358 |
| DEFERRED INCOME TAXES . . . . . . . . . . . . . . | | 56,091 | 44,877 |
| **SHAREHOLDERS' EQUITY:** | | | |
| Capital stock — authorized and outstanding, | | | |
| 172,000 shares of $3 par value . . . . . . . . . . . . | | 516,000 | 516,000 |
| Additional paid-in capital . . . . . . . . . . . . . . . . . . . | | 36,927 | 36,927 |
| Retained earnings . . . . . . . . . . . . . . . . . . . . . . . . | | 6,887,171 | 6,660,291 |
| Shareholders' equity . . . . . . . . . . . . . . . . . . . . . . | | 7,440,098 | 7,213,218 |
| TOTAL LIABILITIES AND SHAREHOLDERS' EQUITY . . . . . . . . . . . . . . . . . . . . . . . . . . . . . . . . | | $11,547,732 | $11,417,769 |

# CARTER MANUFACTURING COMPANY

## STATEMENTS OF INCOME AND RETAINED EARNINGS FOR THE YEARS ENDED DECEMBER 31, 1982 AND 1981

|  | NOTE | 1982 | 1981 |
|---|---|---|---|
| SALES (Less returns of $237,782 in 1982 and $345,762 in 1981) | | $23,555,271 | $23,401,635 |
| COST OF GOODS SOLD | | 17,130,648 | 17,767,857 |
| GROSS PROFIT | | 6,424,623 | 5,633,778 |
| SELLING AND GENERAL EXPENSES | | 6,136,161 | 5,406,762 |
| INCOME FROM OPERATIONS | | 288,462 | 227,016 |
| OTHER INCOME (EXPENSES): | | | |
| Interest | | 167,978 | 84,732 |
| Dividends | | 50,268 | 50,124 |
| Sale of waste materials, etc. | | 183,526 | 91,365 |
| Gain from sale of property and equipment | | 4,581 | 3,600 |
| Unrealized loss on marketable securities | 2 | (28,824) | (80,388) |
| Interest expense | | (233,385) | (112,641) |
| Cash discount lost | | (63,924) | (108,987) |
| Total | | 80,220 | (72,195) |
| INCOME BEFORE INCOME TAXES | | 368,682 | 154,821 |
| INCOME TAX EXPENSE: | | | |
| Federal: | | | |
| Current | | 112,336 | 31,410 |
| Deferred | | 9,303 | 18,036 |
| Total federal | | 121,639 | 49,446 |
| State: | | | |
| Current | | 18,252 | 11,955 |
| Deferred | | 1,911 | 3,021 |
| Total state | | 20,163 | 14,976 |
| Total | | 141,802 | 64,422 |
| NET INCOME | | 226,880 | 90,399 |
| RETAINED EARNINGS, BEGINNING OF YEAR | | 6,660,291 | 6,569,892 |
| RETAINED EARNINGS, END OF YEAR | | $ 6,887,171 | $ 6,660,291 |

See notes to financial statements.

# CARTER MANUFACTURING COMPANY

## STATEMENTS OF CHANGES IN FINANCIAL POSITION FOR THE YEARS ENDED DECEMBER 31, 1982 AND 1981

|  | 1982 | 1981 |
|---|---|---|
| **SOURCES OF WORKING CAPITAL:** | | |
| Net income | $ 226,880 | $ 90,399 |
| Add charges not requiring an outlay of working capital: | | |
| Depreciation and amortization | 173,145 | 181,638 |
| Deferred income taxes | 11,214 | 21,057 |
| Total from operations | 411,239 | 293,094 |
| Proceeds from sale of plant and equipment—net of gains | | |
| included in operations | 11,019 | 1,800 |
| Increase in long-term debt | | 1,295,358 |
| Total | 422,258 | 1,590,252 |
| **USES OF WORKING CAPITAL:** | | |
| Purchase of plant and equipment | 187,782 | 1,322,398 |
| Reduction of long-term debt | 266,676 | |
| Total | 454,458 | 1,322,398 |
| INCREASE (DECREASE) IN WORKING CAPITAL | $ (32,200) | $ 267,854 |
| **COMPONENTS OF CHANGE IN WORKING CAPITAL:** | | |
| Cash and savings certificates and account | $ 85,089 | $ 325,572 |
| Marketable securities | (29,604) | (80,388) |
| Receivables | 193,005 | 290,889 |
| Inventories | (105,495) | (3,918) |
| Prepaid expenses | (16,650) | 77,820 |
| Trade accounts payable | (104,155) | (1,177) |
| Due under line of credit | 60,000 | (60,000) |
| Current portion of long-term debt | (29,967) | (236,709) |
| Accrued salaries, wages and commissions | (174,099) | (28,560) |
| Accrued and withheld payroll taxes | 74,844 | (102,966) |
| Income taxes payable—net | (10,794) | (35,937) |
| Contributions to employee benefit plans | (176,874) | 123,228 |
| Accrued rent | 202,500 | |
| INCREASE (DECREASE) IN WORKING CAPITAL | $ (32,200) | $ 267,854 |

See notes to financial statements.

# CARTER MANUFACTURING COMPANY

## NOTES TO FINANCIAL STATEMENTS FOR
## THE YEARS ENDED DECEMBER 31, 1982 AND 1981

### 1. SIGNIFICANT ACCOUNTING POLICIES

**Nature of Business** — The Company is principally engaged in the manufacture and sale of metal products.

**Inventories**

For the year ended December 31, 1980, the Company changed its method of accounting for inventories to a last-in, first-out (lifo) method. During a time of rapid price increases, the lifo method provides a better matching of revenue and expense than does the fifo method. The total effect of the change was included in the 1980 financial statements, and no restatement was made of amounts reported in prior years. The effect of this change was to reduce net income for 1980 by $298,944.

**Plant and Equipment**

Plant and equipment are stated at cost less accumulated depreciation and amortization. Depreciation on plant and equipment acquired after 1978 is computed using the straight-line method for financial reporting and accelerated methods for income tax purposes. Depreciation on previously acquired plant and equipment is computed using accelerated methods for financial reporting and income tax purposes, except that the straight-line method is used for tax purposes at such time as it results in a greater deduction than would result from continued use of an accelerated method. Rates are based upon the following estimated useful lives:

| Classification | Useful Life |
|---|---|
| Machinery and equipment | 7-10 Years |
| Delivery equipment | 6-7  Years |
| Furniture and fixtures | 8-10 Years |
| Leasehold improvements | 5-6  Years |

**Revenue Recognition** — Revenue from merchandise sales is recognized when the merchandise is shipped to the customer.

**Deferred Income Taxes**

Deferred income taxes are provided for timing differences between reported financial income before income taxes and taxable income. The timing differences arise from depreciation deductions for income tax purposes in excess of depreciation expense for financial reporting purposes.

### 2. MARKETABLE SECURITIES

The Company's marketable securities are stated at the lower of cost or market. At December 31, 1982 and 1981, the Company's investments had a cost of $582,876 and

$583,656 respectively. To reduce the carrying amount of this investment to market, which was lower than cost at December 31, 1982 and 1981, valuation allowances of $250,638 and $221,814, respectively, were established. This resulted in a charge to earnings of $28,824 in 1982 and a charge to earnings of $80,388 in 1981.

## 3. RECEIVABLE DUE FROM A SINGLE CUSTOMER

At December 31, 1982, approximately $700,000 was due from a single distributor. Approximately $435,000 of the allowance for doubtful accounts at December 31, 1982, relates specifically to this receivable.

At December 31, 1981, approximately $350,000 was due from the distributor.

## 4. INVENTORIES

At December 31, 1982 and 1981, inventories (see Note 1) consisted of the following:

|  | 1982 | 1981 |
|---|---|---|
| Raw materials | $1,654,563 | $1,491,876 |
| Work in process | 2,427,513 | 2,255,574 |
| Finished goods | 2,684,409 | 2,839,278 |
| Total cost | 6,766,485 | 6,586,728 |
| Less lifo reserve | 838,854 | 553,602 |
| Total lifo | $5,927,631 | $6,033,126 |

## 5. LINE OF CREDIT

The Company has an agreement with a bank for a line of credit, of which $180,000 was unused at December 31, 1982. Borrowings under the line are at an interest rate (14% at December 31, 1982) of 2% above the bank's prime lending rate. The Company's marketable securities are pledged as collateral for borrowings under the line.

## 6. LONG-TERM DEBT

At December 31, 1982 and 1981, the Company had three installment notes, payable to a bank as follows:

|  | 1982 | 1981 |
|---|---|---|
| Note dated February 2, 1981, due in $60,000 semi-annual installments, with interest payable monthly at 12.625% | $ 120,000 | $ 240,000 |
| Note dated March 2, 1981, due in $10,000 semiannual installments, with interest payable monthly at 14.125% | 20,000 | 40,000 |
| Note dated December 12, 1981, due in 120 monthly payments of increasing amounts with interest at 14.00% | 1,155,358 | 1,252,067 |
| Total | 1,295,358 | 1,532,067 |
| Less amount due within one year | 266,676 | 236,709 |
| Total | $1,028,682 | $1,295,358 |

# CARTER MANUFACTURING COMPANY

## NOTES TO FINANCIAL STATEMENTS

### 7. LONG-TERM LIABILITIES

The long-term liabilities have the following aggregate minimum maturities during the next five years:

| | |
|---|---:|
| 1983 | $  266,676 |
| 1984 | 131,122 |
| 1985 | 135,103 |
| 1986 | 140,503 |
| 1987 | 146,299 |
| After 1987 | 475,655 |
| Total | $1,295,358 |

### 8. EMPLOYEE BENEFIT PLANS

The Company has a profit-sharing plan for its salaried employees and a defined benefit retirement plan for its hourly paid employees. Both plans are noncontributory, are funded annually, and have been amended to comply with the Employee Retirement Income Security Act of 1974.

The contributions to the profit-sharing plan are made at the discretion of the Board of Directors and were $138,261 for 1982 and $57,750 for 1981.

Annual contributions to the retirement plan were $139,260 for 1982 and $42,897 for 1981. The plan is being funded based upon actuarial computations of costs which include consideration of normal cost, interest on the unfunded prior service cost, and amortization of the prior service cost over a forty-year period.

At January 1, 1982 and 1981, net assets available for retirement plan benefits were $824,214 and $622,518 respectively; the actuarial present values of vested plan benefits were $984,666 and $885,435, respectively; and nonvested accumulated plan benefits were $87,522 and $90,788, respectively. The assumed rate of return used in determining the actuarial present values of accumulated plan benefits was 5%.

### 9. OPERATING LEASE

The Company leases land and buildings under a 5-year noncancelable operating lease which expires on December 31, 1985. Future minimum lease payments are as follows:

| | |
|---|---:|
| 1983 | $  300,000 |
| 1984 | 330,000 |
| 1985 | 360,000 |
| Total | $  990,000 |

## Consolidated Statements Of Income
(In thousands except per share data)

*The Coca-Cola Company and Subsidiaries*

| Year Ended December 31, | 1982 | 1981 | 1980 |
|---|---|---|---|
| Net operating revenues | $6,249,718 | $5,889,035 | $5,620,749 |
| Cost of goods and services | 3,453,493 | 3,307,574 | 3,197,733 |
| **Gross Profit** | 2,796,225 | 2,581,461 | 2,423,016 |
| Selling, administrative and general expenses | 1,901,962 | 1,782,875 | 1,681,861 |
| **Operating Income** | 894,263 | 798,586 | 741,155 |
| Interest income | 106,177 | 70,632 | 40,099 |
| Interest expense | 74,561 | 38,349 | 35,102 |
| Other income (deductions)—net | 6,112 | (23,615) | (9,425) |
| **Income From Continuing Operations** | | | |
| **Before Income Taxes** | 931,991 | 807,254 | 736,727 |
| Income taxes | 419,759 | 360,184 | 330,409 |
| **Income From Continuing Operations** | 512,232 | 447,070 | 406,318 |
| Discontinued operations: | | | |
| Income from discontinued operations | | | |
| (net of applicable income taxes of $7,271 in 1981, | | | |
| and $11,782 in 1980) | — | 5,641 | 15,790 |
| Gain on disposal of discontinued operations | | | |
| (net of applicable income taxes of $13,274) | — | 29,071 | — |
| **Net Income** | $ 512,232 | $ 481,782 | $ 422,108 |
| **Per Share:** | | | |
| Continuing operations | $ 3.95 | $ 3.62 | $ 3.29 |
| Discontinued operations | — | .28 | .13 |
| Net income | $ 3.95 | $ 3.90 | $ 3.42 |
| **Average Shares Outstanding** | 129,793 | 123,610 | 123,578 |

See Notes to Consolidated Financial Statements

**Consolidated Balance Sheets**
(In thousands except share data)

*The Coca-Cola Company and Subsidiaries*
December 31,

| Assets | 1982 | 1981 |
|---|---|---|
| **Current** | | |
| Cash | $ 177,530 | $ 120,908 |
| Marketable securities, at cost (approximates market) | 83,381 | 218,634 |
| Trade accounts receivable, less allowances of | | |
| $21,336 in 1982 and $8,579 in 1981 | 751,775 | 483,491 |
| Inventories and unamortized film costs | 808,799 | 750,719 |
| Prepaid expenses and other assets | 255,080 | 62,494 |
| **Total Current Assets** | 2,076,565 | 1,636,246 |
| **Investments, Film Costs and Other Assets** | | |
| Investments, at cost | 221,909 | 176,332 |
| Unamortized film costs | 211,460 | — |
| Other assets | 241,395 | 211,086 |
| | 674,764 | 387,418 |
| **Property, Plant and Equipment** | | |
| Land and improvements | 126,201 | 96,468 |
| Buildings | 602,475 | 570,356 |
| Machinery and equipment | 1,383,668 | 1,271,065 |
| Containers | 333,472 | 306,243 |
| | 2,445,816 | 2,244,132 |
| Less allowances for depreciation | 907,250 | 834,676 |
| | 1,538,566 | 1,409,456 |
| **Goodwill and Other Intangible Assets** | 633,415 | 131,661 |
| | $4,923,310 | $3,564,781 |

| Liabilities and Shareholders' Equity | 1982 | 1981 |
|---|---|---|
| **Current** | | |
| Loans and notes payable | $ 70,561 | $ 89,647 |
| Current maturities of long-term debt | 50,623 | 5,515 |
| Accounts payable and accrued expenses | 792,250 | 672,049 |
| Participations and other entertainment obligations | 154,803 | — |
| Accrued taxes—including income taxes | 258,574 | 239,114 |
| **Total Current Liabilities** | 1,326,811 | 1,006,325 |
| **Participations and Other Entertainment Obligations** | 190,408 | — |
| **Long-Term Debt** | 462,344 | 137,278 |
| **Deferred Income Taxes** | 165,093 | 150,406 |
| **Shareholders' Equity** | | |
| Common stock, no par value— | | |
| Authorized—140,000,000 shares; | | |
| Issued: 136,099,741 shares in 1982 | | |
| and 124,024,735 shares in 1981 | 68,427 | 62,389 |
| Capital surplus | 478,308 | 114,194 |
| Retained earnings | 2,300,217 | 2,109,542 |
| Foreign currency translation adjustment | (54,486) | — |
| | 2,792,466 | 2,286,125 |
| Less treasury stock, at cost (359,338 shares | | |
| in 1982; 401,338 shares in 1981) | 13,812 | 15,353 |
| | 2,778,654 | 2,270,772 |
| | $4,923,310 | $3,564,781 |

See Notes to Consolidated Financial Statements

**Consolidated Statements of Shareholders' Equity**       *The Coca-Cola Company and Subsidiaries*

(In thousands except per share data)

Three Years Ended December 31, 1982

| | Number of Shares | | Amount | | | | |
|---|---|---|---|---|---|---|---|
| | Common Stock | Treasury Stock | Common Stock | Capital Surplus | Retained Earnings | Foreign Currency Translation | Treasury Stock |
| Balance January 1, 1980 | 123,960 | 401 | $62,357 | $112,333 | $1,759,367 | $ — | $(15,353) |
| Sales to employees exercising stock options and appreciation rights | 30 | — | 15 | 711 | — | — | — |
| Tax benefit from sale of option shares by employees | — | — | — | 128 | — | — | — |
| Net income | — | — | — | — | 422,108 | — | — |
| Dividends (per share—$2.16) | — | — | — | — | (266,928) | — | — |
| Balance December 31, 1980 | 123,990 | 401 | 62,372 | 113,172 | 1,914,547 | — | (15,353) |
| Sales to employees exercising stock options and appreciation rights | 35 | — | 17 | 841 | — | — | — |
| Tax benefit from sale of option shares by employees | — | — | — | 181 | — | — | — |
| Net income | — | — | — | — | 481,782 | — | — |
| Dividends (per share—$2.32) | — | — | — | — | (286,787) | — | — |
| Balance December 31, 1981 | 124,025 | 401 | 62,389 | 114,194 | 2,109,542 | — | (15,353) |
| Effect of restating asset and liability balances as of January 1, 1982 for adoption of SFAS No. 52 (net of income taxes of $2,316) | — | — | — | — | — | (11,657) | — |
| Sales to employees exercising stock options and appreciation rights | 121 | — | 61 | 3,685 | — | — | — |
| Tax benefit from sale of option shares by employees | — | — | — | 814 | — | — | — |
| Purchase of Columbia Pictures Industries, Inc. | 11,954 | — | 5,977 | 359,579 | — | — | — |
| Translation adjustments (net of income taxes of $11,188) | — | — | — | — | — | (42,829) | — |
| Treasury stock issued to officers | — | (42) | — | 36 | — | — | 1,541 |
| Net income | — | — | — | — | 512,232 | — | — |
| Dividends (per share—$2.48) | — | — | — | — | (321,557) | — | — |
| Balance December 31, 1982 | 136,100 | 359 | $68,427 | $478,308 | $2,300,217 | $(54,486) | $(13,812) |

See Notes to Consolidated Financial Statements

**Consolidated Statements of**
**Changes In Financial Position** (In thousands)

*The Coca-Cola Company and Subsidiaries*

| Year Ended December 31, | 1982 | 1981 | 1980 |
|---|---|---|---|
| **Source Of Working Capital** | | | |
| From operations: | | | |
| Income from continuing operations | $ 512,232 | $447,070 | $ 406,318 |
| Add charges not requiring outlay of working capital during the year: | | | |
| Depreciation | 148,856 | 136,868 | 131,042 |
| Amortization of noncurrent film costs | 43,495 | — | — |
| Deferred income taxes | 50,807 | 23,692 | 31,500 |
| Other (principally amortization of goodwill and container adjustments) | 34,304 | 61,009 | 37,932 |
| **Total From Continuing Operations** | 789,694 | 668,639 | 606,792 |
| Discontinued operations (excludes provisions for depreciation, amortization and deferred income taxes of $2,429 in 1981, and $4,521 in 1980) | — | 37,141 | 20,311 |
| **Total From Operations** | 789,694 | 705,780 | 627,103 |
| Common stock issued | 370,152 | 1,090 | 854 |
| Increase in long-term debt | 249,392 | 4,057 | 99,415 |
| Transfer of noncurrent film costs to current | 93,909 | — | — |
| Disposals of property, plant and equipment | 44,467 | 71,788 | 77,053 |
| Decrease in investments and other assets | 21,836 | — | — |
| Other | 5,153 | — | — |
| | 1,574,603 | 782,715 | 804,425 |
| **Application Of Working Capital** | | | |
| Cash dividends | 321,557 | 286,787 | 266,928 |
| Acquisitions of purchased companies excluding net current assets: | | | |
| Property, plant and equipment—net | 56,739 | 9,814 | 5,885 |
| Other assets net of other liabilities | 89,693 | 103 | (2,862) |
| Goodwill | 516,115 | 10 | 10,455 |
| Additions to property, plant and equipment | 325,016 | 319,792 | 287,186 |
| Additions to noncurrent film costs | 95,804 | — | — |
| Increase in investments and other assets | — | 85,131 | 95,254 |
| Foreign currency translation | 21,693 | — | — |
| Other | 28,153 | 11,830 | 2,348 |
| | 1,454,770 | 713,467 | 665,194 |
| **Increase In Working Capital** | $ 119,833 | $ 69,248 | $ 139,231 |
| **Increase (Decrease) In Working Capital By Component** | | | |
| Cash | $ 56,622 | $ (8,777) | $ 22,799 |
| Marketable securities | (135,253) | 117,233 | 59,716 |
| Trade accounts receivable | 268,284 | (39,632) | 88,044 |
| Inventories and unamortized film costs | 58,080 | (59,516) | 140,621 |
| Prepaid expenses and other current assets | 192,586 | 4,685 | 5,470 |
| Loans and notes payable | 19,086 | (2,060) | 16,229 |
| Current maturities of long-term debt | (45,108) | 2,013 | (3,144) |
| Accounts payable and accrued expenses | (120,201) | 60,974 | (156,161) |
| Participations and other entertainment obligations | (154,803) | — | — |
| Accrued taxes—including income taxes | (19,460) | (5,672) | (34,343) |
| **Increase In Working Capital** | $ 119,833 | $ 69,248 | $ 139,231 |

See Notes to Consolidated Financial Statements

**Notes to Consolidated Financial Statements**                              *The Coca-Cola Company and Subsidiaries*

**1. Accounting Policies.** The major accounting policies and practices followed by the Company and its subsidiaries are as follows:

*Consolidation*

The consolidated financial statements include the accounts of the Company and its majority-owned subsidiaries. All significant inter-company accounts and transactions are eliminated in consolidation.

*Inventories and Unamortized Film Costs*

Inventories are valued at the lower of cost or market. The last-in, first-out (LIFO) method of inventory valuation is used for sugar and other sweeteners used in beverages in the United States, for certain major citrus concentrate and wine products, for substantially all inventories of United States bottling subsidiaries and for certain other operations. All other inventories are valued on the basis of average cost or first-in, first-out (FIFO) methods. The excess of current costs over LIFO stated values amounted to approximately $72 million and $76 million at December 31, 1982 and 1981, respectively.

Unamortized film costs include film production, print, pre-release and national advertising costs, and capitalized interest. The individual film forecast method is used to amortize these costs based on the revenues recognized in proportion to management's estimate of ultimate revenues to be received.

The costs of feature and television films are classified as current assets to the extent such costs are expected to be recovered through the respective primary markets. Other costs relating to film production are classified as noncurrent.

Revenues from theatrical exhibition of feature films are recognized on the dates of exhibition. Revenues from television licensing agreements are recognized when films are available for telecasting.

*Property, Plant and Equipment*

Property, plant and equipment is stated at cost, less allowance for depreciation, except that foreign subsidiaries carry bottles and shells in service at amounts (less than cost) which generally correspond with deposit prices obtained from customers. Approximately 89% of depreciation expense was determined by the straight-line method for 1982 and approximately 87% for both 1981 and 1980. Investment tax credits are accounted for by the flow-through method.

*Goodwill and Other Intangible Assets*

Goodwill and other intangible assets are stated on the basis of cost, if purchased subsequent to October 31, 1970, are being amortized, principally on a straight-line basis, over the estimated future periods to be benefited (not exceeding 40 years). Accumulated amortization amounted to $26 million and $16 million at December 31, 1982 and 1981, respectively.

*Capitalized Interest*

Interest capitalized as part of the cost of acquisition, construction or production of major assets (including film costs)

was $14 million, $8 million and $6 million in 1982, 1981, and 1980, respectively.

*Foreign Currency Translation*

In the second quarter of 1982, the Company adopted Statement of Financial Accounting Standards No. 52, "Foreign Currency Translation" (SFAS 52), effective as of January 1, 1982, and restated the results for the first quarter. Exchange gains (gains and losses on foreign currency transactions and translation of balance sheet accounts of operations in hyperinflationary economies) included in income were $27 million for 1982. Under the translation rules used in prior years, such gains would have been approximately $10 million. The impact on 1981 and 1980 operating results is not material and such financial statements have not been restated.

An equity adjustment ($11.7 million) was recorded as of January 1, 1982, for the cumulative effect of SFAS 52 on prior years.

**2. Inventories and Unamortized Film Costs.** Inventories and unamortized film costs are comprised of the following (in thousands):

|  | December 31, | |
|---|---|---|
|  | 1982 | 1981 |
| Finished goods | $219,000 | $259,391 |
| Work in process | 96,305 | 92,464 |
| Raw materials and supplies | 368,730 | 398,864 |
| Unamortized film costs (includes in process costs of $23,260) | 124,764 | — |
|  | $808,799 | $750,719 |
| Noncurrent—Unamortized film costs | | |
| Completed | $113,527 | $ — |
| In process | 97,933 | — |
|  | $211,460 | $ — |

**3. Short-Term Borrowings and Credit Arrangements.** Loans and notes payable include amounts payable to banks of $71 million and $61 million at December 31, 1982 and 1981, respectively.

Under line of credit arrangements for short-term debt with various financial institutions, the Company and its subsidiaries may borrow up to $768 million. These lines of credit are subject to normal banking terms and conditions. At December 31, 1982, the unused portion of the credit lines was $674 million. Some of the financial arrangements require compensating balances which are not material.

**Notes to Consolidated Financial Statements** (continued)

**4. Accounts Payable and Accrued Expenses** are composed of the following amounts (in thousands):

| | December 31, | |
| --- | --- | --- |
| | 1982 | 1981 |
| Trade accounts payable | $647,061 | $565,697 |
| Deposits on bottles and shells | 67,725 | 67,489 |
| Other | 77,464 | 38,863 |
| | $792,250 | $672,049 |

**5. Accrued Taxes** are composed of the following amounts (in thousands):

| | December 31, | |
| --- | --- | --- |
| | 1982 | 1981 |
| Income taxes | $190,790 | $175,753 |
| Sales, payroll and miscellaneous taxes | 67,784 | 63,361 |
| | $258,574 | $239,114 |

**6. Long-Term Debt** consists of the following amounts (in thousands):

| | December 31, | |
| --- | --- | --- |
| | 1982 | 1981 |
| $9^7/8$% notes due June 1, 1985 | $ 99,928 | $ 99,898 |
| $11^3/4$% notes due October 1, 1989 | 97,548 | — |
| $10^3/8$% notes due June 1, 1988 | 23,200 | — |
| Short-term borrowings to be refinanced with long-term debt | 173,000 | — |
| Other | 119,291 | 42,895 |
| | 512,967 | 142,793 |
| Less current portion | 50,623 | 5,515 |
| | $462,344 | $137,278 |

The $9^7/8$% notes may not be redeemed before June 1, 1983. After that date, the notes may be redeemed at the option of the Company in whole or in part at 100% of their principal amount, plus accrued interest.

The $11^3/4$% notes were issued in international markets and may not be redeemed prior to October 1, 1986, except under certain limited conditions. After that date, the notes may also be redeemed at the option of the Company in whole or in part at 101% of the principal amount during the succeeding twelve month period, and thereafter at 100% of the principal amount, together in each case with accrued interest.

The principal amount of the $10^3/8$% notes is $100 million. The notes were issued in the international markets on a partly paid basis, whereby 25% of the issue price was received on December 1, 1982, and the remaining 75% will be received on June 1, 1983. These notes may not be redeemed prior to maturity, except under certain limited conditions.

At December 31, 1982, $173 million of short-term borrowings have been classified as long-term debt as management intends to repay such borrowings with proceeds from the remaining installment of the $10^3/8$% notes, and from the proceeds of an additional $100 million of partly paid notes issued on February 2, 1983 (these notes have an annual coupon rate of $9^7/8$%, require payment in installments of 30% on February 2, 1983, and 70% on August 1, 1983, and mature on August 1, 1992).

Other long-term debt consists of various mortgages and notes with maturity dates ranging from 1983 to 2010. Interest on a portion of this debt varies with the changes in the prime rate, and the weighted average interest rate applicable to the remainder is approximately 11.3%.

The above notes and other long-term debt instruments include various restrictions, none of which are presently significant to the Company.

Maturities of long-term debt for the five years succeeding December 31, 1982, are as follows (in thousands):

| | |
| --- | --- |
| 1983 | $ 50,623 |
| 1984 | 12,822 |
| 1985 | 110,357 |
| 1986 | 8,856 |
| 1987 | 10,990 |

The Company is contingently liable for guarantees of indebtedness by its independent bottling companies and others in the approximate amount of $70 million at December 31, 1982.

**7. Foreign Operations.** The Company's identifiable assets and liabilities outside the United States and Puerto Rico are shown below (in thousands):

| | December 31, | |
| --- | --- | --- |
| | 1982 | 1981 |
| Current assets | $ 776,095 | $ 751,835 |
| Property, plant and equipment—net | 585,320 | 567,179 |
| Other assets | 77,003 | 121,903 |
| | 1,438,418 | 1,440,917 |
| Liabilities | 626,888 | 637,015 |
| Net assets | $ 811,530 | $ 803,902 |

Appropriate United States and foreign income taxes have been provided for on earnings of subsidiary companies which are expected to be remitted to the parent company in the near future. Accumulated unremitted earnings of foreign subsidiaries which are expected to be required for use in the foreign operations amounted to approximately $63 million at December 31, 1982, exclusive of amounts which if remitted would result in little or no tax.

## Notes to Consolidated Financial Statements (continued)

**8. Stock Options.** The Company's 1979 stock option plan provides for the granting of stock appreciation rights and stock options to certain officers and employees. Stock appreciation rights permit the holder, upon surrendering all or part of the related stock option, to receive cash, common stock, or a combination thereof, in an amount up to 100% of the difference between the market price and the option price. Included in options outstanding at December 31, 1982, are various options granted under a previous plan and other options granted not as a part of an option plan.

Further information relating to options is as follows:

| | 1982 | 1981 | 1980 |
|---|---|---|---|
| Options outstanding at January 1 | 1,406,360 | 1,392,457 | 1,259,886 |
| Options granted in the year | 288,300 | 244,975 | 362,350 |
| Options exercised in the year | (120,791) | (35,651) | (29,559) |
| Options cancelled in the year | (66,707) | (195,421) | (200,220) |
| Options outstanding at December 31 | 1,507,162 | 1,406,360 | 1,392,457 |
| Options exercisable at December 31 | 781,906 | 755,598 | 728,067 |
| Shares available at December 31 for options which may be granted | 25,261 | 278,121 | 400,408 |
| Option prices per share | | | |
| Exercised in the year | $22-$44 | $22-$34 | $19-$25 |
| Unexercised at year-end | $25-$68 | $22-$68 | $19-$68 |

Not included above are options assumed in connection with the purchase of Columbia Pictures Industries, Inc. covering 504,997 shares of the Company's common stock. The value of these options in excess of the option price has been included in the acquisition cost. At December 31, 1982, options for 263,281 such shares were outstanding at an average option price of $31.

**9. Pension Plans.** The Company and its subsidiaries sponsor and/or contribute to various pension plans covering substantially all domestic employees and certain employees in foreign countries. Pension expense for continuing operations determined under various actuarial cost methods, principally the aggregate level cost method, amounted to approximately $37 million in 1982, $35 million in 1981, and $32 million in 1980. Amendments which resulted in improved benefits for retired employees increased 1982 pension expense by $1.2 million and increased the value of vested benefits by $12 million at January 1, 1982.

The actuarial present value of accumulated benefits, as estimated by consulting actuaries, and net assets available for benefits of Company and subsidiary-sponsored domestic plans are presented below (in thousands):

| | January 1, | |
|---|---|---|
| | 1982 | 1981 |
| Actuarial present value of accumulated plan benefits: | | |
| Vested | $178,343 | $146,884 |
| Nonvested | 14,284 | 12,669 |
| | $192,627 | $159,553 |
| Net assets available for benefits | $234,836 | $193,268 |

The weighted average assumed rates of return used in determining the actuarial present value of accumulated plan benefits were approximately 10% for 1982 and 9% for 1981. Changes in the assumed rates of return reduced the actuarial present value of accumulated plan benefits by approximately $18 million and $19 million at January 1, 1982 and 1981, respectively.

The Company has various foreign pension plans which are not required to report to certain governmental agencies pursuant to the Employee Retirement Income Security Act (ERISA) and do not otherwise determine the actuarial present value of accumulated plan benefits or net assets available for benefits as calculated and disclosed above. For such plans, the value of the pension funds and balance sheet accruals exceeded the actuarially computed value of vested benefits as of January 1, 1982 and 1981, as estimated by consulting actuaries.

**Notes to Consolidated Financial Statements** (continued)

**10. Income Taxes.** The components of income before income taxes for both continuing and discontinued operations consisted of the following (in thousands):

|  | Year Ended December 31, | | |
|---|---|---|---|
|  | 1982 | 1981 | 1980 |
| United States | $357,063 | $309,654 | $251,807 |
| Foreign | 574,928 | 552,857 | 512,492 |
|  | $931,991 | $862,511 | $764,299 |

Income taxes for continuing and discontinued operations consisted of the following amounts (in thousands):

|  | Year Ended December 31, | | | |
|---|---|---|---|---|
|  | United States | State & Local | Foreign | Total |
| **1982** | | | | |
| Current | $79,605 | $22,638 | $266,709 | $368,952 |
| Deferred | 33,281 | 1,363 | 16,163 | 50,807 |
| **1981** | | | | |
| Current | $86,589 | $22,461 | $248,292 | $357,342 |
| Deferred | 15,574 | 1,646 | 6,167 | 23,387 |
| **1980** | | | | |
| Current | $63,636 | $17,438 | $228,013 | $309,087 |
| Deferred | 25,518 | 2,390 | 5,196 | 33,104 |

Total tax expense differed from the amount computed by applying the statutory federal income tax rate to income before income taxes principally because of investment tax credits which had the effect of reducing the tax provision by approximately $24 million in 1982, $14 million in 1981 and $11 million in 1980.

Deferred taxes are provided principally for depreciation and film costs which are recognized in different years for financial statement and income tax purposes.

**11. Acquisitions.** On June 21, 1982, the Company acquired all of the outstanding capital stock of Columbia Pictures Industries, Inc. ("Columbia") in a purchase transaction. The purchase price, consisting of cash and common stock of the Company, is valued at approximately $692 million. The values assigned to assets acquired and liabilities assumed are based on studies conducted to determine their fair values. The excess cost over net fair value is being amortized over forty years using the straight-line method; amortization amounted to $6 million in 1982.

The pro forma consolidated results of operations of the Company, as if Columbia had been acquired as of January 1, 1981, are as follows (in thousands, except per share data):

|  | Year Ended December 31, | |
|---|---|---|
|  | 1982 | 1981 |
| Net operating revenues | $6,602,571 | $6,623,775 |
| Income from continuing operations | 498,692 | 456,452 |
| Income from continuing operations per share | 3.67 | 3.36 |

The pro forma results include adjustments to reflect interest expense on $333 million of the purchase price assumed to be financed with debt bearing interest at an annual rate of 11%, the amortization of the unallocated excess cost over net assets of Columbia, the income tax effects of pro forma adjustments and the issuance of 12.2 million shares of the Company's common stock.

The pro forma results for the twelve months ended December 31, 1981, have been further adjusted to reflect Columbia's repurchase in February, 1981, of 2.4 million shares of Columbia common stock from certain shareholders as if such repurchase had been consummated as of January 1, 1981. Accordingly, interest expense has been increased for amounts necessary to fund the cash portion of the purchase price, legal expenses incurred in litigation with such shareholders have been eliminated and income taxes have been adjusted.

In June 1982, the Company purchased Associated Coca-Cola Bottling Co., Inc. ("Associated") at a cost of approximately $419 million. Associated was acquired with the intent of selling its properties to other purchasers as part of the Company's strategy to assist in restructuring the bottler system. Accordingly, the acquisition has been accounted for as a temporary investment under the cost method of accounting. At December 31, 1982, approximately 70% of Associated's operating assets had been sold for cash equal to the allocated costs of such assets. A substantial portion of such assets were sold for $245 million to a corporation principally owned by a former director of the Company.

The remaining investment in Associated of $120 million at December 31, 1982 is included in other current assets.

In September 1982, the Company purchased Ronco Foods Company, a manufacturer and distributor of pasta products, for cash. This transaction had no significant effect on the Company's operating results.

**12. Discontinued Operations.** In 1981, the Company sold Aqua-Chem, Inc., a wholly-owned subsidiary which produced steam generators, industrial boilers and water treatment equipment. In February 1982, the Company sold its Tenco Division for approximately book value. Tenco was an operating unit which manufactured and distributed private label instant coffees and teas.

Net sales of discontinued operations were $240 million and $292 million in 1981 and 1980, respectively.

**Notes to Consolidated Financial Statements** (continued)

**13. Industry Segments.** The Company operates principally in the soft drink industry. Carbonated and noncarbonated beverages and Hi-C fruit drinks are classified as soft drinks. In June 1982, the Company acquired Columbia Pictures Industries, Inc., which operates in the entertainment industry. Citrus, coffee, wine and plastic products are included in other industries. Inter-segment transfers are not material. Information concerning operations in different industries is as follows (in thousands):

| Year Ended December 31, | 1982 | 1981 | 1980 |
|---|---|---|---|
| Net operating revenues:* | | | |
| Soft drinks | $4,515,813 | $4,683,467 | $4,522,048 |
| Entertainment | 457,305 | — | — |
| Other industries | 1,276,600 | 1,205,568 | 1,098,701 |
| Total | $6,249,718 | $5,889,035 | $5,620,749 |
| Income from industry segments:* | | | |
| Soft drinks | $ 893,221 | $ 803,748 | $ 731,783 |
| Entertainment | 35,535 | — | — |
| Other industries | 127,196 | 113,759 | 101,138 |
| Total | 1,055,952 | 917,507 | 832,921 |
| Other income, net of other deductions | (50,089) | (37,671) | (37,893) |
| General expenses | (73,872) | (72,582) | (58,301) |
| Income from continuing operations before income taxes | $ 931,991 | $ 807,254 | $ 736,727 |
| Identifiable assets at year-end:* | | | |
| Soft drinks | $2,521,410 | $2,472,533 | $2,436,192 |
| Entertainment | 1,309,837 | — | — |
| Other industries | 615,872 | 578,588 | 529,184 |
| Total | 4,447,119 | 3,051,121 | 2,965,376 |
| Corporate assets (principally marketable securities, investments and fixed assets) | 476,191 | 452,693 | 289,202 |
| Discontinued operations | — | 60,967 | 151,380 |
| Total | $4,923,310 | $3,564,781 | $3,405,958 |
| Capital expenditures by industry segment including fixed assets of purchased companies: | | | |
| Soft drinks | $ 249,529 | $ 251,539 | $ 224,152 |
| Entertainment | 53,913 | — | — |
| Other industries | 53,686 | 58,422 | 40,924 |
| Depreciation of fixed assets and amortization of intangible assets by industry segment:* | | | |
| Soft drinks | $ 118,404 | $ 112,476 | $ 108,126 |
| Entertainment | 8,296 | — | — |
| Other industries | 26,455 | 22,817 | 20,731 |

*Amounts for 1980 have been restated to reflect the sale of the Company's Aqua-Chem, Inc., subsidiary and Tenco Division.

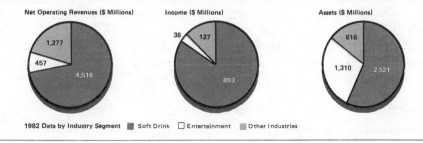

Net Operating Revenues ($ Millions)   Income ($ Millions)   Assets ($ Millions)

1982 Data by Industry Segment   ■ Soft Drink   □ Entertainment   ▨ Other Industries

**Notes to Consolidated Financial Statements** (continued)

**14. Operations in Geographic Areas.** Information about the Company's operations in different geographic areas is presented below (in thousands). Africa, which is not a significant geographic area as defined by SFAS 14, has been grouped with Europe in accordance with the Company's management organizational structure. Other insignificant geographic areas are combined as Canada and Pacific. Inter-company transfers between geographic areas are not material.

| Year Ended December 31, | 1982 | 1981 | 1980 |
|---|---|---|---|
| **Net operating revenues:*** | | | |
| United States and Puerto Rico | $3,580,140 | $3,238,673 | $3,059,953 |
| Latin America | 516,336 | 608,110 | 560,164 |
| Europe and Africa | 1,155,564 | 1,096,257 | 1,170,294 |
| Canada and Pacific | 997,678 | 945,995 | 830,338 |
| Total | $6,249,718 | $5,889,035 | $5,620,749 |
| **Income from geographic areas:*** | | | |
| United States and Puerto Rico | $ 417,542 | $ 337,522 | $ 279,315 |
| Latin America | 174,742 | 179,739 | 148,055 |
| Europe and Africa | 276,279 | 248,802 | 278,707 |
| Canada and Pacific | 187,389 | 151,444 | 126,844 |
| Total | 1,055,952 | 917,507 | 832,921 |
| Other income, net of other deductions | (50,089) | (37,671) | (37,893) |
| General expenses | (73,872) | (72,582) | (58,301) |
| Income from continuing operations before income taxes | $ 931,991 | $ 807,254 | $ 736,727 |
| **Identifiable assets at year-end:*** | | | |
| United States and Puerto Rico | $3,008,701 | $1,631,123 | $1,604,490 |
| Latin America | 435,879 | 436,215 | 420,197 |
| Europe and Africa | 582,037 | 583,017 | 579,851 |
| Canada and Pacific | 420,502 | 400,766 | 360,838 |
| Total | 4,447,119 | 3,051,121 | 2,965,376 |
| Corporate assets (principally marketable securities, investments and fixed assets) | 476,191 | 452,693 | 289,202 |
| Discontinued operations | — | 60,967 | 151,380 |
| Total | $4,923,310 | $3,564,781 | $3,405,958 |

*Amounts for 1980 have been restated to reflect the sale of the Company's Aqua-Chem, Inc., subsidiary and Tenco Division.

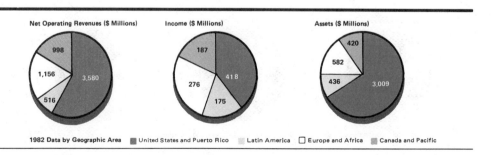

1982 Data by Geographic Area  ■ United States and Puerto Rico   ▨ Latin America   ☐ Europe and Africa   ▨ Canada and Pacific

**Report of Independent Accountants**                    *The Coca-Cola Company and Subsidiaries*

Board of Directors and Shareholders
The Coca-Cola Company
Atlanta, Georgia

We have examined the consolidated balance sheets of The Coca-Cola Company and subsidiaries as of December 31, 1982 and 1981, and the related consolidated statements of income,
shareholders' equity and changes in financial position for each of the three years in the period
ended December 31, 1982. Our examinations were made in accordance with generally accepted
auditing standards and, accordingly, included such tests of the accounting records and such
other auditing procedures as we considered necessary in the circumstances.

In our opinion, the financial statements referred to above present fairly the consolidated
financial position of The Coca-Cola Company and subsidiaries at December 31, 1982 and 1981,
and the consolidated results of their operations and the changes in their financial position for
each of the three years in the period ended December 31, 1982, in conformity with generally
accepted accounting principles consistently applied during the period except for the change in
1982, with which we concur, in the method of accounting for foreign currency translation as
described in Note 1 to the consolidated financial statements.

Atlanta, Georgia
February 14, 1983                              *Ernst & Whinney*

**Report of Management**

Management is responsible for the preparation and integrity of the consolidated financial
statements appearing in this Annual Report. The financial statements were prepared in conformity with generally accepted accounting principles appropriate in the circumstances and, accordingly, include some amounts based on management's best judgments and estimates. Other
financial information in this Annual Report is consistent with that in the financial statements.

Management is responsible for maintaining a system of internal accounting controls and procedures to provide reasonable assurance, at an appropriate cost/benefit relationship, that assets
are safeguarded and that transactions are authorized, recorded and reported properly. The
internal accounting control system is augmented by a program of internal audits and appropriate reviews by management, written policies and guidelines, careful selection and training of
qualified personnel and a written Code of Business Conduct adopted by the Board of Directors,
applicable to all employees of the Company and its subsidiaries. Management believes that the
Company's internal accounting controls provide reasonable assurance that assets are safeguarded against material loss from unauthorized use or disposition and that the financial
records are reliable for preparing financial statements and other data and maintaining accountability for assets.

The Audit Committee of the Board of Directors, composed solely of Directors who are not
officers of the Company, meets with the independent accountants, management and internal
auditors periodically to discuss internal accounting controls, auditing and financial reporting
matters. The Committee reviews with the independent accountants the scope and results of the
audit effort. The Committee also meets with the independent accountants without management present to ensure that the independent accountants have free access to the Committee.

The independent accountants, Ernst & Whinney, are recommended by the Audit Committee
of the Board of Directors, selected by the Board of Directors and ratified by the shareholders.
Ernst & Whinney are engaged to examine the financial statements of The Coca-Cola Company
and subsidiaries and conduct such tests and related procedures as they deem necessary in conformity with generally accepted auditing standards. The opinion of the independent accountants, based upon their examination of the consolidated financial statements, is contained in this
Annual Report.

Roberto C. Goizueta
Chairman, Board of Directors,
and Chief Executive Officer

Sam Ayoub
Senior Executive Vice President
and Chief Financial Officer

February 14, 1983

**Unaudited Quarterly Data**
(For the years ended December 31, 1982 and 1981)

*The Coca-Cola Company and Subsidiaries*

**Quarterly Results of Operations**
(In thousands except per share data)

| | Net Operating Revenues | | Gross Profit | |
|---|---|---|---|---|
| | 1982 | 1981 | 1982 | 1981 |
| First quarter | $1,271,289 | $1,346,462 | $ 589,071 | $ 584,925 |
| Second quarter | 1,567,851 | 1,600,247 | 727,885 | 701,879 |
| Third quarter | 1,745,157 | 1,529,810 | 747,365 | 661,166 |
| Fourth quarter | 1,665,421 | 1,412,516 | 731,904 | 633,491 |
| | $6,249,718 | $5,889,035 | $2,796,225 | $2,581,461 |

| | Income From Continuing Operations | | Net Income | |
|---|---|---|---|---|
| | 1982 | 1981 | 1982 | 1981 |
| First quarter | $ 107,616 | $ 97,633 | $ 107,616 | $ 100,097 |
| Second quarter | 139,821 | 126,992 | 139,821 | 128,876 |
| Third quarter | 143,463 | 116,219 | 143,463 | 146,581 |
| Fourth quarter | 121,332 | 106,226 | 121,332 | 106,228 |
| | $ 512,232 | $ 447,070 | $ 512,232 | $ 481,782 |

| | Income Per Share From Continuing Operations | | Net Income Per Share | |
|---|---|---|---|---|
| | 1982 | 1981 | 1982 | 1981 |
| First quarter | $ .87 | $ .79 | $ .87 | $ .81 |
| Second quarter | 1.13 | 1.03 | 1.13 | 1.04 |
| Third quarter | 1.06 | .94 | 1.06 | 1.19 |
| Fourth quarter | .89 | .86 | .89 | .86 |
| | $ 3.95 | $ 3.62 | $ 3.95 | $ 3.90 |

Net operating revenues and gross profit for the first three quarters of 1981 have been restated to reflect the sale of the Company's Aqua-Chem, Inc., subsidiary and Tenco Division.

**Supplemental Information on the Effects of Changing Prices (Unaudited)**

*The Coca-Cola Company and Subsidiaries*

*General.* The following unaudited disclosures were prepared in accordance with Statement Nos. 33 and 70 issued by the Financial Accounting Standards Board and are intended to quantify the impact of inflation on earnings and production facilities. The inflation-adjusted data is presented under the specific price changes method (current cost). Only those items most affected by inflation have been adjusted; i.e., inventories, property, plant and equipment, the related costs of goods and services sold and depreciation and amortization expense. Although the resulting measurements cannot be used as precise indicators of the effects of inflation, they do provide an indication of the effect of increases in specific prices of the Company's inventories and properties.

The adjustments for specific price changes involve a substantial number of judgments as well as the use of various estimating techniques employed to control the cost of accumulating the data. The data reported should not be thought of as precise measurements of the assets and expenses involved, or of the amount at which the assets could be sold. Rather, they represent reasonable approximations of the price changes that have occurred in the business environment in which the Company operates.

Inflation-adjusted data based on the constant dollar method is not presented because a significant part of the Company's operations is in foreign locations whose functional currency is not the U.S. dollar.

A brief explanation of the current cost method is presented below.

*Current Cost.* The current cost method attempts to measure the effect of increases in the specific prices of the Company's inventories and properties. It is intended to estimate what it would cost in 1982 dollars to replace the Company's inventories and existing properties.

Under this method, cost of goods sold valued on the average method is adjusted to reflect the current cost of inventories at the date of sale. That portion of cost of goods sold valued on the LIFO method approximates the current cost of inventory at the date of sale and generally remains unchanged from the amounts presented in the primary financial statements.

Current cost depreciation expense is based on the average current cost of properties in the year. The depreciation methods, salvage values and useful lives are the

### Statement of Income Adjusted for Changing Prices
(In millions except per share data)

| Year Ended December 31, 1982 | As Reported in the Primary Statements | Adjusted for Changes in Specific Prices (Current Costs) |
|---|---|---|
| Net operating revenues | $6,249.7 | $6,249.7 |
| Cost of goods and services (excluding depreciation) | 3,386.8 | 3,412.0 |
| Depreciation and amortization | 156.9 | 235.4 |
| Other operating expenses | 1,817.6 | 1,817.6 |
| Net of other (income) and deductions | (43.6) | (41.3) |
| Income from continuing operations before income taxes | 932.0 | 826.0 |
| Income taxes | 419.8 | 419.8 |
| Income from continuing operations | $ 512.2 | $ 406.2 |
| Income per share from continuing operations | $ 3.95 | $ 3.13 |
| Effective income tax rate | 45.0% | 50.8% |
| Purchasing power gain from holding net monetary liabilities in the year | | $ 17.7 |
| Increase in specific prices of inventories and property, plant and equipment held in the year | | $ 261.8 |
| Less effect of increase in general price level | | 147.2 |
| Increase in specific prices over increase in the general price level | | $ 114.6 |
| Estimated translation adjustment | | $ (300.0) |
| Inventory and film costs | $1,020.3 | $1,109.7 |
| Property, plant and equipment—net | $1,538.5 | $2,342.8 |

A significant part of the Company's operations are measured in functional currencies other than the U.S. dollar. Adjustments to reflect the effects of general inflation were determined on the translate-restate method using the U.S. CPI(U).

## Supplemental Information on the Effects of Changing Prices (Unaudited) (continued)

same as those used in the primary statements.

The current cost of finished products inventory was approximated by adjusting historical amounts to reflect current costs for material, labor and overhead expenses as well as current cost depreciation, where applicable. The current cost for inventories other than finished products was determined on the basis of price lists or appropriate supplier quotations and by other managerial estimates consistent with established purchasing and production procedures.

Since motion picture films are the result of a unique blending of the artistic talents of many individuals and are produced under widely varying circumstances, it is not feasible to develop the current cost of film inventories, particularly since the Company would rarely, if ever, attempt to duplicate an existing film property. As a result, film inventories have been valued based on studies conducted to determine their fair value in connection with the purchase price allocation process.

Direct supplier quotations, published price lists, engineering estimates, construction quotations, appraisals, published and internally developed indexes were the methods used to determine the current cost of property, plant and equipment.

Under current cost accounting, increases in specific prices (current cost) of inventories and properties held during the year are not included in income from continuing operations.

*Income Taxes.* Taxes on income included in the supplementary statement of income are the same as reported in the primary financial statements. In most countries, present tax laws do not allow deductions for the effects of inflation. Thus, taxes are levied on the Company at rates which, in real terms, exceed established statutory rates.

*Purchasing Power Gain.* During periods of inflation, monetary assets, such as cash, marketable securities and accounts receivable, lose purchasing power since they will buy fewer goods when the general price level increases. The holding of monetary liabilities, such as accounts payable, accruals and debt, results in a gain of purchasing power because cheaper dollars will be used to repay the obligations. The Company has benefited from a net monetary liability position in recent years, resulting in a net gain in purchasing power. This gain does not represent an increase in funds available for distribution to shareholders and does not necessarily imply that incurring more debt would be beneficial to the Company.

*Increase in Specific Prices.* Shown separately are the total changes in current costs for inventories and properties, that component of the total change due to general inflation and that component of the change attributable to fluctuations in exchange rates.

### Five-Year Comparison of Selected Supplemental Financial Data
### Adjusted for Effects of Changing Prices (In Average 1982 Dollars)
(In millions except per share data)

| Year Ended December 31, | 1982 | 1981 | 1980 | 1979 | 1978 |
|---|---|---|---|---|---|
| Net operating revenues | $6,249.7 | $6,258.6 | $6,595.5 | $6,245.9 | $6,069.6 |
| Current cost information: | | | | | |
|   Income from continuing operations | 406.2 | 372.7 | 310.7 | 369.0 | |
|   Income per share from continuing operations | 3.13 | 3.02 | 2.51 | 2.99 | |
|   Increase in specific prices over (under) increase in the general price level, including translation adjustments | (185.4) | (220.0) | 25.9 | 213.8 | |
|   Net assets at year-end | 3,622.8 | 3,334.2 | 3,733.3 | 3,768.4 | |
| Purchasing power gain on net monetary items | 17.7 | 26.0 | 50.6 | 27.6 | |
| Cash dividends declared per share: | | | | | |
|   As reported | 2.48 | 2.32 | 2.16 | 1.96 | 1.74 |
|   Adjusted for general inflation | 2.48 | 2.47 | 2.53 | 2.61 | 2.58 |
| Market price per common share at year-end: | | | | | |
|   Historical amount | 52.00 | 34.75 | 33.375 | 34.50 | 43.875 |
|   Adjusted for general inflation | 52.00 | 36.93 | 39.16 | 45.96 | 65.03 |
| Average Consumer Price Index—Urban | 289.6 | 272.5 | 246.8 | 217.4 | 195.4 |

## Statement of earnings

General Electric Company and consolidated affiliates

| For the years ended December 31 (In millions) (note 1) | 1982 | 1981 | 1980 |
|---|---|---|---|
| **Sales** Sales of products and services to customers | $26,500 | $27,240 | $24,959 |
| **Operating costs** Cost of goods sold | 18,605 | 19,476 | 18,171 |
| Selling, general and administrative expense | 4,506 | 4,435 | 3,838 |
| Depreciation, depletion and amortization | 984 | 882 | 707 |
| Operating costs (notes 2 and 3) | 24,095 | 24,793 | 22,716 |
| Operating margin | 2,405 | 2,447 | 2,243 |
| Other income (note 4) | 692 | 614 | 564 |
| Interest and other financial charges (note 5) | (344) | (401) | (314) |
| **Earnings** Earnings before income taxes and minority interest | 2,753 | 2,660 | 2,493 |
| Provision for income taxes (note 6) | (900) | (962) | (958) |
| Minority interest in earnings of consolidated affiliates | (36) | (46) | (21) |
| Net earnings applicable to common stock | $ 1,817 | $ 1,652 | $ 1,514 |
| Earnings per common share (in dollars) (note 7) | $8.00 | $7.26 | $6.65 |
| Dividends declared per common share (in dollars) | $3.35 | $3.15 | $2.95 |
| Operating margin as a percentage of sales | 9.1% | 9.0% | 9.0% |
| Net earnings as a percentage of sales | 6.9% | 6.1% | 6.1% |

## Statement of retained earnings

General Electric Company and consolidated affiliates

| For the years ended December 31 (In millions) (note 1) | 1982 | 1981 | 1980 |
|---|---|---|---|
| **Retained earnings** Balance January 1 | $8,088 | $7,151 | $6,307 |
| Net earnings | 1,817 | 1,652 | 1,514 |
| Dividends declared on common stock | (760) | (715) | (670) |
| Balance December 31 | $9,145 | $8,088 | $7,151 |

The information on pages 32 and 36-44 is an integral part of these statements.

# CONSOLIDATED BALANCE SHEETS

Hershey Foods Corporation

(in thousands of dollars)

| December 31 | 1982 | 1981 |
|---|---|---|
| **ASSETS** | | |
| **Current Assets:** | | |
| Cash and short-term investments | $ 17,820 | $ 53,879 |
| Accounts receivable—trade (less allowances for doubtful accounts of $3,040 and $2,792) | 65,129 | 56,241 |
| Inventories (Note 1) | 178,585 | 151,890 |
| Other current assets | 13,411 | 25,020 |
| Total current assets | 274,945 | 287,030 |
| **Property, Plant and Equipment, at cost:** (Notes 1 and 4) | | |
| Land | 51,050 | 46,592 |
| Buildings | 183,387 | 174,705 |
| Machinery and equipment | 474,918 | 358,446 |
| Capitalized leases | 19,920 | 18,238 |
| | 729,275 | 597,981 |
| Less—accumulated depreciation and amortization | 189,361 | 157,797 |
| | 539,914 | 440,184 |
| **Excess of Cost Over Net Assets of Businesses Acquired** (Note 1) | 52,609 | 53,911 |
| **Investments and Other Assets** | 20,603 | 25,675 |
| | $888,071 | $806,800 |

| December 31 | 1982 | 1981 |
|---|---|---|
| **LIABILITIES AND STOCKHOLDERS' EQUITY** | | |
| **Current Liabilities:** | | |
| Accounts payable | $ 45,288 | $ 48,085 |
| Accrued liabilities | | |
| Payroll and other compensation costs | 29,208 | 23,916 |
| Advertising and promotional expenses | 12,805 | 14,415 |
| Other | 23,281 | 18,702 |
| | 65,294 | 57,033 |
| Accrued income taxes | 11,399 | 10,006 |
| Current portion of long-term debt (Note 4) | 19,579 | 2,131 |
| Total current liabilities | 141,560 | 117,255 |
| **Long-Term Debt** (Notes 4 and 5) | 140,250 | 158,182 |
| **Deferred Income Taxes** (Note 2) | 73,766 | 61,699 |
| **Stockholders' Equity:** (Note 1) | | |
| Common stock without par value (stated value $1 per share)— authorized 20,000,000 shares; outstanding 15,668,556 shares | 15,669 | 15,669 |
| Additional paid-in capital | 54,006 | 54,006 |
| Retained earnings | 462,820 | 399,989 |
| Total stockholders' equity | 532,495 | 469,664 |
| | $888,071 | $806,800 |

The accompanying notes are an integral part of these balance sheets.

# CONSOLIDATED STATEMENTS OF INCOME AND RETAINED EARNINGS

(in thousands of dollars except per share amounts)

| For the years ended December 31 | 1982 | 1981 | 1980 |
|---|---|---|---|
| Net Sales | $1,565,736 | $1,451,151 | $1,335,289 |
| **Costs and Expenses:** | | | |
| Cost of sales | 1,084,748 | 1,015,767 | 971,714 |
| Selling, general and administrative | 301,586 | 267,930 | 224,615 |
| Total costs and expenses | 1,386,334 | 1,283,697 | 1,196,329 |
| Income from Operations | 179,402 | 167,454 | 138,960 |
| Interest expense, net (Note 1) | 7,859 | 12,512 | 14,100 |
| Income before Taxes | 171,543 | 154,942 | 124,860 |
| Provision for income taxes (Note 2) | 77,375 | 74,580 | 62,805 |
| Net Income | 94,168 | 80,362 | 62,055 |
| Retained Earnings at January 1 | 399,989 | 345,131 | 304,316 |
| Less—Cash Dividends | 31,337 | 25,504 | 21,240 |
| Retained Earnings at December 31 | $ 462,820 | $ 399,989 | $ 345,131 |
| Net Income per Common Share (Note 1) | $ 6.01 | $ 5.61 | $ 4.38 |
| Cash Dividends per Common Share | $ 2.00 | $ 1.75 | $ 1.50 |

The accompanying notes are an integral part of these statements

## SUPPLEMENTARY INFORMATION REGARDING THE EFFECTS OF INFLATION (Unaudited)

The Company's consolidated financial statements are prepared based upon the historical prices in effect when the transactions occurred. The following supplementary information reflects certain effects of inflation upon the Company's operations in accordance with the requirements of Statement of Financial Accounting Standards No. 33, "Financial Reporting and Changing Prices", issued by the Financial Accounting Standards Board.

The effects of inflation on income have been measured in two ways as described below and presented in the following statements. The first method, "constant dollar", measures the effect of general inflation determined by using the 1982 average Consumer Price Index for all Urban Consumers (CPI-U) to recompute results of operations. The second method, "current cost", is more specific to the Company in that it measures inflation by recomputing results of operations using the current cost of inventory and property, plant and equipment rather than the historical cost of such assets. Current costs of property, plant and equipment were developed from external price indices, quotations or similar measurements.

The inflation-adjusted information presented may not necessarily be comparable with other companies within the same industry because of differences in assumptions and judgments. However, of the two methods required, the Company believes the current cost method is more meaningful because it better measures the effects of inflation on Company operations.

Depreciation expense increased under both methods because of inflation. Current cost depreciation exceeds constant dollar depreciation because the cumulative increases in the Company's specific cost of property, plant and equipment have exceeded the general inflation rate. Both methods represent costs of property, plant and equipment currently used in operations. However, the Company generally takes advantage of the latest technological improvements when actual replacement occurs.

The adjustment to current cost of sales is not significant because substantial portions of inventories in the historical financial statements are stated at LIFO cost. Under LIFO cost, current costs are included in cost of sales in the historical financial statements. During 1982, the costs of non-LIFO components of cost of sales increased only slightly, resulting in a minor increase in current cost over historical cost of sales.

The statement shows that the historical effective income tax rate for 1982 of 45.1% increases under both methods since Federal Income Tax Regulations do not provide for a tax deduction for these inflation adjustments.

The gain from decline of purchasing power of net amounts owed set forth in the following schedule presents the Company's gain from holding more monetary liabilities (requiring fixed future cash settlements) than monetary assets (right to receive fixed amounts of future cash) during periods of inflation, thereby requiring less purchasing power to satisfy such future obligations. However, since this gain will not be realized until the obligations are repaid, it is excluded from inflation-adjusted net income.

### Five-Year Comparison

The five-year comparison on page 35 shows the effect of adjusting historical net sales, net income, dividends per common share, market price per common share, net assets and other information, to dollar amounts expressed in terms of average 1982 dollars, as measured by the average Consumer Price Index. After adjustment for inflation, net sales have increased 38% from 1978 through 1982.

Management recognizes the impact of inflation and has taken various steps to minimize its impact on the Company's businesses. The use of LIFO inventory accounting for the major portion of its inventories reduces reported earnings, thereby reducing taxes and improving cash flow, in periods of inflation by matching current costs with current revenues. The capital expenditure program, through investment in modern plant and equipment, not only improves productivity and manufacturing efficiencies, but also provides for future sales growth. Programs designed to identify cost reductions and productivity improvements which would result in improved margins are a continuing part of the Company's approach to inflation management. In 1982, the Company achieved approximately an 11% increase in current cost net income compared with a 17% increase in historical dollar net income.

The Company also recognizes that the purchasing power of the dollar significantly affects its stockholders and has attempted to maintain or improve the inflation-adjusted dividend. In 1982, the Company provided real growth of 7.5% in dividends paid per common share. Dividends paid in 1982 are approximately 41% of earnings per share when stated in both constant dollar and current cost amounts compared with a 33% historical dollar basis.

The increase in specific prices compared with general inflation increases has changed annually since costs for agricultural commodities often do not follow the trend of general inflation. Comparisons of other amounts for years prior to 1979 were neither readily available nor required by Statement No. 33. Historical cost data presented for 1979 includes results of Friendly Ice Cream Corporation subsequent to its acquisition in January 1979.

# FIVE–YEAR COMPARISON OF SELECTED SUPPLEMENTARY FINANCIAL DATA ADJUSTED FOR EFFECTS OF INFLATION (Unaudited)

(in thousands of average 1982 dollars except per share amounts)

| For the years ended December 31 | 1982 | 1981 | 1980 | 1979 | 1978 |
|---|---|---|---|---|---|
| **Net sales** | | | | | |
| As reported . . . . . . . . . . . . . . | $1,565,736 | 1,451,151 | 1,335,289 | 1,161,295 | 767,880 |
| In constant dollars . . . . . . . . | $1,565,736 | 1,540,117 | 1,564,149 | 1,544,298 | 1,136,101 |
| **Net Income** | | | | | |
| As reported . . . . . . . . . . . . . . | $ 94,168 | 80,362 | 62,055 | 53,504 | 41,456 |
| In constant dollars . . . . . . . . | $ 77,171 | 64,982 | 53,302 | 52,357 | |
| At current cost . . . . . . . . . . . | $ 76,536 | 69,148 | 50,564 | 56,837 | |
| **Net Income per share** | | | | | |
| As reported . . . . . . . . . . . . . . | $ 6.01 | 5.61 | 4.38 | 3.78 | 3.02 |
| In constant dollars . . . . . . . . | $ 4.93 | 4.54 | 3.76 | 3.70 | |
| At current cost . . . . . . . . . . . | $ 4.88 | 4.83 | 3.57 | 4.02 | |
| **Dividends per common share** | | | | | |
| As reported . . . . . . . . . . . . . . | $ 2.00 | 1.75 | 1.50 | 1.35 | 1.225 |
| In constant dollars . . . . . . . . | $ 2.00 | 1.86 | 1.76 | 1.80 | 1.81 |
| **Market price per common share at year-end** | | | | | |
| As reported . . . . . . . . . . . . . . | $ 56.38 | 36.00 | 23.50 | 24.63 | 20.63 |
| In constant dollars . . . . . . . . | $ 55.74 | 36.97 | 26.29 | 30.97 | 29.39 |
| **Net assets at year-end** | | | | | |
| As reported . . . . . . . . . . . . . . | $ 532,495 | 469,664 | 361,550 | 320,730 | 284,389 |
| In constant dollars . . . . . . . . | $ 797,098 | 752,957 | 631,159 | 590,342 | |
| At current cost . . . . . . . . . . . | $ 836,224 | 854,152 | 845,134 | 804,996 | |
| **Gain from decline in purchasing power of net amounts owed** . . . | $ 10,595 | 22,872 | 31,974 | 35,360 | |
| **Excess of increase in general price level over decrease in specific prices** . . . . . . . . . . . . . . | $ 62,011 | 90,376 | (210) | (28,712) | |
| **Average Consumer Price Index (1967 = 100)** . . . . . . . . . . . . . . | 289.1 | 272.4 | 246.8 | 217.4 | 195.4 |

# CONSOLIDATED STATEMENT OF INCOME ADJUSTED FOR EFFECTS OF INFLATION (Unaudited)

(in thousands of dollars)

| For the year ended December 31, 1982 | As Reported in the Primary Statement | Adjusted for General Inflation | Adjusted for Changes in Specific Prices |
|---|---|---|---|
| | (historical dollars) | (constant dollar) | (current cost) |
| Net sales . . . . . . . . . . . . . . . . . . . . . . . . . . . . | $1,565.736 | $1,565.736 | $1,565.736 |
| Cost of sales . . . . . . . . . . . . . . . . . . . . . . . . (excluding depreciation) | 1,057.761 | 1,061.054 | 1,059.505 |
| Selling, general and administrative expenses . . . . . . . . . . . . . . . . . . . . (excluding depreciation) | 297.892 | 297.892 | 297.892 |
| Depreciation expense . . . . . . . . . . . . . . . . . . | 30.681 | 44.385 | 46.569 |
| Interest expense—net . . . . . . . . . . . . . . . . . . | 7.859 | 7.859 | 7.859 |
| Income before taxes . . . . . . . . . . . . . . . . . . | 171.543 | 154.546 | 153.911 |
| Income taxes . . . . . . . . . . . . . . . . . . . . . . . . | 77.375 | 77.375 | 77.375 |
| Net income . . . . . . . . . . . . . . . . . . . . . . . . . | $ 94.168 | $ 77.171 | $ 76.536 |
| Effective tax rate . . . . . . . . . . . . . . . . . . . . . | 45.1% | 50.1% | 50.3% |
| Gain from decline of purchasing power of net amounts owed . . . . . . . . . . . . . | | $ 10.595 | $ 10.595 |
| Decrease in specific prices (current cost) of inventories and property, plant and equipment held during the year (see Note). . . . . . . . . . . . . . . . . | | | $ (24.924) |
| Effect of increase in general price level of inventories and property, plant and equipment . . . . . . . . . . . . . . . . . | | | 37.087 |
| Excess of increase in general price level over decrease in specific prices . . . . . . . . . . . . . . . . . . . . . . . | | | $ 62.011 |

Note: At December 31, 1982, current cost of inventory was $240.7 million and current cost of property, plant and equipment, net of accumulated depreciation was $778.6 million.

Hilton Hotels Corporation
and Subsidiaries

## Consolidated Statements of Income
*(In thousands of dollars
except share data)*

| Year Ended December 31, | | 1982 | 1981 | 1980 |
|---|---|---|---|---|
| Revenue | Rooms | $223,627 | 218,952 | 216,153 |
| | Food and beverage | 163,920 | 161,411 | 155,010 |
| | Casino | 163,302 | 145,054 | 141,095 |
| | Casino promotional allowances | (25,168) | (20,746) | (19,392) |
| | Management and franchise fees | 37,234 | 34,586 | 30,229 |
| | Interest and dividends | 20,965 | 27,481 | 21,266 |
| | Other | 36,604 | 45,966 | 31,232 |
| | | 620,484 | 612,704 | 575,593 |
| Expenses | Rooms | 67,541 | 63,557 | 59,523 |
| | Food and beverage | 126,041 | 118,330 | 112,581 |
| | Casino | 64,892 | 50,690 | 45,509 |
| | Other operating expenses | 123,888 | 112,777 | 102,606 |
| | Property operations | 59,008 | 51,003 | 44,971 |
| | Lease rentals | 6,491 | 6,591 | 5,923 |
| | Property taxes | 12,776 | 10,837 | 12,892 |
| | Interest (net of $3,813, $1,926 and $2,625 capitalized) | 8,962 | 10,955 | 8,572 |
| | Depreciation | 37,826 | 29,603 | 26,493 |
| | | 507,425 | 454,343 | 419,070 |
| Income from Operations | | 113,059 | 158,361 | 156,523 |
| | Earnings from unconsolidated affiliates | 25,645 | 38,222 | 38,785 |
| Income Before Property Transactions | | 138,704 | 196,583 | 195,308 |
| | Property transactions | 2,764 | — | — |
| Income Before Income Taxes | | 141,468 | 196,583 | 195,308 |
| | Federal and state income taxes | 58,095 | 83,960 | 89,176 |
| Net Income | | $ 83,373 | 112,623 | 106,132 |
| Net Income per Share | | $3.12 | 4.22 | 4.00 |

See notes to financial statements

International Business Machines Corporation
and Subsidiary Companies

## Consolidated Statement of Financial Position
at December 31:

| (Dollars in millions) | 1982 | | 1981* | |
|---|---:|---:|---:|---:|
| *Assets* | | | | |
| **Current Assets:** | | | | |
| Cash | $ 405 | | $ 454 | |
| Marketable securities, at lower of cost or market | 2,895 | | 1,575 | |
| Notes and accounts receivable–trade, less allowance: | | | | |
| 1982, $216; 1981, $187 | 4,976 | | 4,382 | |
| Other accounts receivable | 457 | | 410 | |
| Inventories | 3,492 | | 2,803 | |
| Prepaid expenses | 789 | | 685 | |
| | | $ 13,014 | | $ 10,309 |
| **Rental Machines and Parts** | 16,527 | | 16,599 | |
| Less: Accumulated depreciation | 7,410 | | 7,347 | |
| | | 9,117 | | 9,252 |
| **Plant and Other Property** | 14,240 | | 12,702 | |
| Less: Accumulated depreciation | 5,794 | | 5,157 | |
| | | 8,446 | | 7,545 |
| **Deferred Charges and Other Assets** | | 1,964 | | 2,001 |
| | | $ 32,541 | | $ 29,107 |
| *Liabilities and Stockholders' Equity* | | | | |
| **Current Liabilities:** | | | | |
| Taxes | $ 2,854 | | $ 2,412 | |
| Loans payable | 529 | | 773 | |
| Accounts payable | 983 | | 872 | |
| Compensation and benefits | 1,959 | | 1,556 | |
| Deferred income | 402 | | 390 | |
| Other accrued expenses and liabilities | 1,482 | | 1,323 | |
| | | $ 8,209 | | $ 7,326 |
| **Deferred Investment Tax Credits** | | 323 | | 252 |
| **Reserves for Employees' Indemnities and Retirement Plans** | | 1,198 | | 1,184 |
| **Long-Term Debt** | | 2,851 | | 2,669 |
| **Stockholders' Equity:** | | | | |
| Capital stock, par value $1.25 per share | 5,008 | | 4,389 | |
| Shares authorized: 750,000,000 | | | | |
| Issued: 1982–602,406,128; 1981–592,293,624 | | | | |
| Retained earnings | 16,259 | | 13,909 | |
| Translation adjustments | (1,307) | | (622) | |
| | | 19,960 | | 17,676 |
| | | $ 32,541 | | $ 29,107 |

\*Restated. See Accounting Change–
Foreign Currency Translation note on page 36.

The notes on pages 35 through 42 are an integral part of this statement.

Kidde, Inc. and Subsidiaries

## Consolidated Statements of Income for the years ended December 31:

|  | 1982 | 1981 | 1980 |
|---|---|---|---|
|  | *(dollars in thousands except per share amounts)* | | |
| **Net Sales** | $2,655,335 | $2,849,170 | $2,539,275 |
| **Costs, Expenses and Other:** | | | |
| Cost of sales | 1,949,846 | 2,118,365 | 1,885,193 |
| Selling, general and administrative expenses | 488,716 | 495,712 | 449,443 |
| Interest and debt expense, net | 70,996 | 64,174 | 55,037 |
| Other, net | 587 | (2,379) | (3,666) |
| Taxes on income | 60,980 | 74,085 | 65,881 |
|  | 2,571,125 | 2,749,957 | 2,451,888 |
| **Net Income** | $   84,210 | $   99,213 | $   87,387 |
| Per share—primary | $4.02 | $4.87 | $4.30 |
| Per share—fully diluted | $3.60 | $4.22 | $3.71 |

The accompanying notes are an integral part of these statements.

## SFN Companies, Inc. and Subsidiaries

### Consolidated Statements of Earnings

For the years ended April 30, 1982, 1981 and 1980 (in thousands except per share amounts)

| | 1982 | 1981 Restated | 1980 Restated |
|---|---|---|---|
| **Revenues:** | | | |
| Net sales | $251,102 | $270,813 | $254,151 |
| Royalties and miscellaneous | 999 | 4,905 | 5,054 |
| Total revenues | $252,101 | $275,718 | $259,205 |
| **Operating Costs:** | | | |
| Cost of goods sold (Note 3) | $ 63,147 | $ 74,107 | $ 70,126 |
| Selling and shipping expenses | 59,199 | 57,353 | 51,380 |
| Publishing and editorial expenses | 40,050 | 41,627 | 39,562 |
| Administrative and general expenses | 35,931 | 33,771 | 30,705 |
| Depreciation and amortization | 16,109 | 12,825 | 10,998 |
| **Operating Income** | $ 37,665 | $ 56,035 | $ 56,434 |
| Interest expense | (540) | (617) | (661) |
| Investment income | 9,832 | 4,491 | 4,929 |
| Gain on sale of subsidiary (Note 10) | — | 8,763 | — |
| **Earnings Before Taxes Based on Income** | $ 46,957 | $ 68,672 | $ 60,702 |
| **Taxes Based on Income** (Note 6) | 21,029 | 32,681 | 28,887 |
| **Earnings Before Cumulative Effect of a Change in Accounting Principle** | $ 25,928 | $ 35,991 | $ 31,815 |
| Cumulative effect as of May 1, 1981 of change in method of accounting for investment tax credit (Note 2) | 1,736 | — | — |
| **Net Earnings for the Year** | $ 27,664 | $ 35,991 | $ 31,815 |
| **Per Common Share:** | | | |
| Earnings before cumulative effect of a change in accounting principle | $2.27 | $3.08 | $2.73 |
| Cumulative effect as of May 1, 1981 of change in method of accounting for investment tax credit | .16 | — | — |
| Net earnings | $2.43 | $3.08 | $2.73 |
| **Pro Forma Data:** | | | |
| Pro forma amounts, assuming retroactive application of the 1982 change to the flow-through method of accounting for investment tax credit, are as follows: | | | |
| Net earnings | $ 25,928 | $ 36,391 | $ 31,942 |
| Net earnings per common share | $2.27 | $3.11 | $2.75 |

The accompanying notes are an integral part of these statements.

## SFN Companies, Inc. and Subsidiaries

### Consolidated Statements of Changes in Financial Position

For the years ended April 30, 1982, 1981 and 1980. (in thousands)

|  | 1982 | 1981 Restated | 1980 Restated |
|---|---|---|---|
| **Source of Funds:** | | | |
| Net earnings for the year | $ 27,664 | $ 35,991 | $ 31,815 |
| Depreciation and amortization | 16,109 | 12,825 | 10,998 |
| Provision for deferred income taxes | (1,922) | 2,963 | 498 |
| Writedown of long-term investment | — | 1,861 | — |
| Funds derived from operations | $ 41,851 | $ 53,640 | $ 43,311 |
| Long-term portion of note receivable becoming current | 3,429 | — | — |
| Property, non-current assets and liabilities, disposed of through sale of subsidiary | — | 6,886 | — |
| Common stock issued to retire preferred stock | 707 | 583 | 420 |
|  | $ 45,987 | $ 61,109 | $ 43,731 |
| **Application of Funds:** | | | |
| Acquisition of treasury shares | $ 26,558 | $ — | $ — |
| Net increase to property, plant, equipment, and book plates | 17,545 | 16,916 | 12,955 |
| Business acquisition, net of working capital acquired | 2,778 | — | — |
| Note receivable acquired through sale of subsidiary | — | 16,508 | — |
| Dividends | 12,035 | 10,792 | 9,361 |
| Prepayment of long-term debt | — | — | 250 |
| Long-term debt becoming current | 1,540 | 1,410 | 1,279 |
| Redemption and conversion of preferred stock | 801 | 679 | 927 |
| Other items—net | 655 | (2,152) | 1,045 |
|  | $ 61,912 | $ 44,153 | $ 25,817 |
| **Increase (Decrease) in Working Capital** | $(15,925) | $ 16,956 | $ 17,914 |
| **Increase (Decrease) in Working Capital:** | | | |
| Cash and temporary investments | $(10,468) | $ 9,895 | $ 11,192 |
| Accounts receivable | (5,712) | 6,626 | 1,009 |
| Note receivable | (3,540) | 7,041 | — |
| Inventories | 3,131 | 1,117 | 13,064 |
| Other current assets | 551 | 336 | 913 |
| Accounts payable | (1,733) | 3,747 | (5,403) |
| Accrued royalties | — | 129 | (296) |
| Income taxes | 3,483 | (2,221) | (1,579) |
| Other current liabilities | (1,637) | (1,814) | (986) |
| Working capital disposed of through sale of subsidiary | — | (7,900) | — |
| **Increase (Decrease) in Working Capital** | $(15,925) | $ 16,956 | $ 17,914 |

The accompanying notes are an integral part of these statements.

## TELEDYNE, INC. AND SUBSIDIARIES

### Consolidated Balance Sheets
*December 31, 1982 and 1981*
*(In millions)*

|  | 1982 | 1981 |
|---|---|---|
| **ASSETS** | | |
| **Current Assets:** | | |
| Cash and marketable securities | $ 723.3 | $ 448.4 |
| Receivables | 329.4 | 385.0 |
| Inventories | 128.0 | 164.4 |
| Prepaid expenses | 7.1 | 7.2 |
| Total current assets | 1,187.8 | 1,005.0 |
| **Investments in Unconsolidated Subsidiaries** | 1,624.2 | 1,463.8 |
| **Property and Equipment** | 395.7 | 364.9 |
| **Other Assets** | 34.4 | 34.5 |
|  | $3,242.1 | $2,868.2 |
| **LIABILITIES AND SHAREHOLDERS' EQUITY** | | |
| **Current Liabilities:** | | |
| Accounts payable | $ 105.8 | $ 122.1 |
| Accrued liabilities | 246.2 | 216.4 |
| Accrued income taxes | 12.0 | 15.2 |
| Current portion of long-term debt | 29.0 | 33.5 |
| Total current liabilities | 393.0 | 387.2 |
| **Long-Term Debt** | 570.6 | 595.9 |
| **Deferred Income Taxes** | 157.8 | 156.6 |
| **Other Long-Term Liabilities** | 34.3 | 22.0 |
| **Shareholders' Equity** | 2,086.4 | 1,706.5 |
|  | $3,242.1 | $2,868.2 |

*The accompanying notes are an integral part of these balance sheets.*

# Check Figures for Selected Problems

*Agreement between the following "check" figures and those obtained in solving the problems is an indication that a significant portion of the solution is basically correct, aside from matters of form and procedure.*

| | | |
|---|---|---|
| Problem | 2-1A | Finished goods, $14,674 |
| | 2-3A | Total assets, $429,435 |
| | 2-4A | Trial balance totals, $2,254,550 |
| | 2-1B | Finished goods, $13,356 |
| | 2-4B | Trial balance totals, $935,650 |
| Problem | 3-1A | Work in process, May 31, $32,160 |
| | 3-2A | Equivalent units of production, 7,850 units |
| | 3-3A | Total assets, $1,167,330 |
| | 3-4A | Work in process, Oct. 31, $124,200 |
| | 3-6A | Work in process, May 31, $8,625 |
| | 3-1B | Work in process, March 31, $51,730 |
| | 3-4B | Work in process, March 31, $44,160 |
| | 3-6B | Work in process, Sept. 30, $15,125 |
| Problem | 4-2A | Total production, Product P2, 40,400 units |
| | 4-3A | Total revenue from sales, $2,985,975 |
| | 4-4A | Deficiency, Sept., $30,500 |
| | 4-5A | Net income, $84,000; cash, $37,800 |
| | 4-3B | Total revenue from sales, $2,694,000 |
| | 4-4B | Deficiency, June, $13,500 |
| Problem | 5-1A | Total factory overhead cost variance — unfavorable, $3,000 |
| | 5-2A | Total factory overhead cost variance — unfavorable, $7,025 |
| | 5-3A | Total factory overhead cost variance — unfavorable $8,520 |
| | 5-4A | Income from operations, $39,375 |
| | 5-5A | Work in Process (debit), $2,225 |
| | 5-1B | Total factory overhead cost variance — unfavorable, $2,900 |
| | 5-3B | Total factory overhead cost variance — unfavorable, $3,920 |
| | 5-5B | Work in Process (debit), $2,570 |
| Problem | 6-1A | Decrease in gross profit, $45,000 |
| | 6-2A | Income from operations, variable costing, $60,000 |
| | 6-3A | Operating loss, $49,000 |
| | 6-4A | Contribution to company profit, F, $72,700 |
| | 6-5A | Total contribution margin, (1) $308,000; (3) $332,780 |
| | 6-1B | Decrease in gross profit, $25,000 |

| | | | | | |
|---|---|---|---|---|---|
| | 6-2B | Income from operations, variable costing, $50,000 | | 9-2B | Excess of present value over amount to be invested, Project Y, $14,750 |
| | 6-3B | Operating loss, $53,600 | | 9-3B | Present value index, Project A, 1.12 |
| Problem | 7-1A | Break-even point, $600,000 | | | |
| | 7-2A | Maximum operating profit: (2), $1,000,000; (4) $750,000 | | 9-4B | Discounted rate of return, Project B, 12% |
| | 7-3A | Maximum operating profit: (2), $200,000; (4) $150,000 | Problem | 10-1A | Corporation form less, A, $1,377 |
| | 7-4A | Break-even point, $900,000 | | 10-2A | Net income, cash method, $33,100 |
| | 7-5A | Break-even point, $1,650,000 | | 10-3A | Net income, lifo, $35,200 |
| | 7-6A | Present break-even point, $1,800,000 | | 10-4A | Income, percentage-of-completion method, 1984, $974,500 |
| | 7-1B | Break-even point, $400,000 | | | |
| | 7-2B | Maximum operating profit: (2), $1,000,000; (4) $800,000 | | 10-5A | Earnings per share on common stock, Plan 1, $2.90 |
| | 7-3B | Maximum operating profit: (2), $300,000; (4) $250,000 | | 10-3B | Net income, fifo, $24,225 |
| | 7-5B | Break-even point, $1,440,000 | | 10-4B | Income, percentage-of-completion method, 1985, $540,000 |
| Problem | 8-1A | Gain from operating warehouse, $202,500 | | | |
| | | | | 10-5B | Earnings per share on common stock, Plan 2, $2.73 |
| | 8-2A | Net cost reduction, $165,000 | | | |
| | 8-3A | Gain from promotion campaign, Product A, $348,000 | Problem | 11-2A | Net income, $22,340 |
| | | | | 11-3A | Departmental margin, Department 8, $5,400 |
| | 8-4A | Net disadvantage, $(200) | | | |
| | 8-5A | Net advantage, $3,136 | | 11-4A | Total departmental margin, $219,610 |
| | 8-6A | Selling price, $15.60 | | | |
| | 8-1B | Gain from operating warehouse, $250,000 | | 11-5A | Total departmental margin, $162,800 |
| | 8-2B | Net cost reduction, $164,000 | | 11-2B | Net income, $64,954 |
| | 8-5B | Net advantage, $6,590 | | 11-3B | Departmental margin, Department L, $4,000 |
| | 8-6B | Selling price, $14.40 | | | |
| | | | | 11-4B | Total departmental margin, $153,956 |
| Problem | 9-1A | Excess of present value over amount to be invested, Project A, $9,992 | | | |
| | | | Problem | 12-1A | Rate of return on investment, Division F, 13.2% |
| | 9-2A | Excess of present value over amount to be invested, Project P, $3,600 | | 12-2A | Rate of return on investment, Proposal 3, 17.4% |
| | 9-3A | Present value index, Proposal Y, 1.06 | | 12-3A | Division X is most profitable |
| | | | | 12-4A | Rate of return on investment, Division J, 18% |
| | 9-4A | Discounted rate of return, Proposal II, 15% | | | |
| | 9-5A | Excess of present value over amount to be invested, $17,058 | | 12-5A | Total operating income, $1,360,000 |
| | | | | 12-1B | Rate of return on investment, Division R, 16% |
| | 9-6A | Excess of present value over amount to be invested, (2) Project Z, $20,000 | | 12-3B | Division Q is most profitable |
| | | | | 12-4B | Rate of return on investment, Division M, 17% |
| | 9-1B | Excess of present value over amount to be invested, Project B, $11,260 | | | |

| | | | | |
|---|---|---|---|---|
| 12-5B | Total operating income, $2,500,000 | | 16-5A | Net income, $41,380 |
| | | | 16-1B | Constant dollar net income, $22,976 |
| Problem 13-1A | Economic order quantity, 1,200 units | | 16-2B | Net purchasing power loss, $4,410 |
| 13-2A | Economic order quantity, (2), 600 units | | 16-3B | Net purchasing power loss, $2,470 |
| 13-3A | Most economical purchase, 100 units from Supplier K for Pekin Branch; 60 units from Supplier L for Elgin Branch | | 16-4B | Current cost net income, $51,034 |
| | | | Problem 17-1A | Increase in working capital, $1,250 |
| 13-4A | Variable cost per unit, (1), $.75 | | 17-2A | Increase in working capital, $14,700 |
| 13-5A | Variable cost per unit, (2), $1.04 | | 17-3A | Cash provided by operations, $95,350 |
| 13-6A | Variable cost per unit, (2), $1.25 | | | |
| 13-1B | Economic order quantity, 800 units | | 17-4A | Working capital provided by operations, $45,850 |
| 13-3B | Most economical purchase, 200 units from Supplier X for Akron Branch; 300 units from Supplier Y for Tifton Branch | | 17-5A | Cash provided by operations, $11,800 |
| | | | 17-6A | Working capital provided by operations, $120,000; Cash provided by operations, $79,700 |
| 13-4B | Variable cost per unit, (1), $.62 | | | |
| 13-6B | Variable cost per unit, (2), $2.00 | | 17-1B | Decrease in working capital, $27,500 |
| Problem 14-1A | Expected value, Patent B, $8,400,000 | | 17-2B | Increase in working capital, $48,450 |
| 14-2A | Total expected value of purchase of 125 papers, $11.75 | | 17-3B | Cash provided by operations, $97,600 |
| 14-3A | Total expected value of Plat #1200, $24,100,000 | | 17-4B | Working capital provided by operations, $184,775 |
| 14-4A | Value of conducting an investigation, $3,500 | | 17-5B | Cash provided by operations, $138,500 |
| 14-6A | Expected value, lake front location, $15,000,000 | | Problem 18-1A | Total expenditures, crime prevention, $959,500 |
| 14-1B | Expected value, Autobiography F, $10,600,000 | | 18-2A | Fund balance, June 30, $654,700 |
| 14-2B | Total expected value of purchase of 60 magazines, $106 | | 18-3A | Trial balance totals, $1,165,000 |
| | | | 18-4A | Fund balance, June 30, $480,400 |
| 14-3B | Total expected value of Plat #2400, $14,600,000 | | 18-1B | Total expenditures, crime prevention, $1,216,500 |
| 14-4B | Value of conducting an investigation, $6,000 | | 18-2B | Fund balance, June 30, $170,750 |
| | | | 18-3B | Trial balance totals, $833,200 |
| Problem 15-4A | Working capital, Dec. 31, 1984, (4), $165,750 | | Problem D-1 | Cost of goods manufactured, $636,700 |
| Problem 16-1A | Constant dollar net income, $40,660 | | D-2 | Cost of goods manufactured, $661,050 |
| 16-2A | Net purchasing power loss, $6,330 | | D-3 | Cost of goods manufactured, $521,775 |
| 16-3A | Net purchasing power loss, $11,760 | | D-4 | Cost of goods manufactured, $472,900 |
| 16-4A | Current cost net income, $86,970 | | | |

# Index